OFFICIAL (ISC)²®
GUIDE TO THE
CSSLP®

OTHER BOOKS IN THE (ISC)²® PRESS SERIES

Official (ISC)²® Guide to the CSSLP®
Mano Paul
ISBN: 978-1-4398-2605-8

Official (ISC)²® Guide to the ISSMP® CBK®
Harold F. Tipton, Editor
ISBN: 978-1-4200-9443-5

Official (ISC)²® Guide to the SSCP® CBK®, Second Edition
Harold F. Tipton, Editor
ISBN: 978-1-4398-0483-4

Official (ISC)²® Guide to the ISSAP® CBK®
Harold F. Tipton, Editor
ISBN: 978-1-4398-0093-5

Official (ISC)²® Guide to the ISSMP® CBK®
Harold F. Tipton, Editor
ISBN: 978-1-4200-9443-5

Official (ISC)²® Guide to the CISSP® CBK®, Second Edition
Harold F. Tipton, Editor
ISBN: 978-1-4398-0959-3

CISO Leadership: Essential Principles for Success
Todd Fitzgerald and Micki Krause, Editors
ISBN: 978-0-8493-7943-X

Building and Implementing a Security Certification and Accreditation Program: Official (ISC)²® Guide to the CAP® CBK®
Patrick D. Howard
ISBN: 978-0-8493-2062-3

Official (ISC)²® Guide to the CISSP®-ISSEP® CBK®
Susan Hansche
ISBN: 978-0-8493-2341-X

OFFICIAL (ISC)²
GUIDE TO THE
CSSLP®

Mano Paul, CSSLP, CISSP

SECURITY TRANSCENDS TECHNOLOGY®

CRC Press
Taylor & Francis Group
Boca Raton London New York

CRC Press is an imprint of the
Taylor & Francis Group, an **informa** business
AN AUERBACH BOOK

CRC Press
Taylor & Francis Group
6000 Broken Sound Parkway NW, Suite 300
Boca Raton, FL 33487-2742

© 2011 by Taylor and Francis Group, LLC
CRC Press is an imprint of Taylor & Francis Group, an Informa business

No claim to original U.S. Government works

Printed in the United States of America on acid-free paper
10 9 8 7 6 5 4 3 2

International Standard Book Number: 978-1-4398-2605-8 (Hardback)

This book contains information obtained from authentic and highly regarded sources. Reasonable efforts have been made to publish reliable data and information, but the author and publisher cannot assume responsibility for the validity of all materials or the consequences of their use. The authors and publishers have attempted to trace the copyright holders of all material reproduced in this publication and apologize to copyright holders if permission to publish in this form has not been obtained. If any copyright material has not been acknowledged please write and let us know so we may rectify in any future reprint.

Library of Congress Cataloging-in-Publication Data

Paul, Mano.
    Official (ISC)2 guide to the CSSLP / by Mano Paul.
        p. cm.
    Includes bibliographical references and index.
    ISBN 978-1-4398-2605-8
    1. Computer software--Development. 2. Computer security. I. Title.

QA76.76.D47P3775 2011
005.8--dc22   2010053695

Visit the Taylor & Francis Web site at
http://www.taylorandfrancis.com

and the CRC Press Web site at
http://www.crcpress.com

Contents

Foreword

The software industry has, on aggregate, made a great deal of progress securing software against attacks over the last ten or so years. But for many, any improvement has been small because of the piecemeal nature of their security efforts. There is always more to be done as attackers become savvier and, in many cases, more determined to compromise systems for malevolent gain. This ongoing arms-race between attackers and defenders will only escalate as more devices are connected to the Internet. I say "devices" and not "computers" on purpose because we are seeing millions of smaller devices such as smartphones join the throngs of other systems that are already active Internet citizens. We're seeing the rate at which software is developed for these smaller devices increase; development times are shrinking; software designers and developers are rushing their code to market and often forget some of the fundamental security disciplines required to build code that is robust in the face of attack. I use the term "forget" simply to be polite; in many cases, software development shops simply do not understand basic security principles.

Clearly, all software is subject to attack, and the only way to help produce software that is not only resilient to attack but helps protect sensitive and private data is to update the current software development process with practices that infuse security and privacy discipline.

We *need* more people to understand how to secure their development processes and then apply those principles in practice.

And this is the book to help do that!

(ISC)² has published this very easy-to-read-and-understand book that can help anyone involved with software development, whether they design, build or test software; create more secure software by incorporating the principles of secure software development covered in this comprehensive book into their software development lifecycle.

But this book is not just teaching theory. This book can serve in a dual function—as an academic reference to those learning about software security, while at the same time as a very pragmatic reference to those hoping to improve their state of software security. The material that is covered in this book is proven and reflective of the author's in-depth experience in helping many companies improve their overall software development processes to produce secure software. As the software assurance advisor for (ISC)², the author of this book, Mano Paul, has been an instrumental resource in the development of the Certified Secure Software Lifecycle Professional (CSSLP) credential.

To reiterate and summarize:

- Most software is insecure.
- Most software development shops can improve their processes to improve security.
- This book covers what you need to know.
- This book is a must have for a prospective CSSLP candidate.

Michael Howard
Principal Security Program Manager, Microsoft
Author, Writing Secure Code

About the Author

 **Manoranjan (Mano) Paul** is the software assurance advisor for (ISC)², the global leader in information security education and certification, representing and advising the organization on software assurance strategy, training, education and certification. His information security and software assurance experience includes designing and developing security programs from compliance-to-coding, security in the SDLC, writing secure code, risk management, security strategy, and security awareness training and education. Mr. Paul started his career as a shark researcher in the Bimini Biological Field Station, Bahamas. His educational pursuit took him to the University of Oklahoma where he received his business administration degree in management information systems (MIS) with various accolades and the coveted 4.0 GPA. Following his entrepreneurial acumen, he founded and serves as the CEO & president of Express Certifications, a professional certification assessment and training company that developed studISCope, (ISC)²'s official self-assessment offering for their certifications. Express Certifications is also the self-assessment testing company behind the US Department of Defense certification education program as mandated by the 8570.1 directive. He also founded SecuRisk Solutions, a company that specializes in security product development and consulting. Before Express Certifications and SecuRisk Solutions, Mr. Paul played several roles, including software developer, quality assurance engineer, logistics manager, technical architect, IT strategist and security engineer/program manager/strategist at Dell Inc.

Mr, Paul is a contributing author for the *Information Security Management Handbook*, *Certification* magazine and has contributed to several security topics for the Microsoft Solutions Developer Network (MSDN). He has served as vice president, an industry representative and is an appointed faculty member of the Capitol of Texas Information System Security Association (ISSA) chapter. He has been featured in various domestic and international security conferences and is an invited speaker and panelist, delivering talks and keynotes at conferences such as the SANS, OWASP (Open Web Application Security Project), CSI (Computer Security Institute), Burton Group Catalyst, SC World Congress, and TRISC (Texas Regional Infrastructure Security Conference). Mr. Paul holds the following professional certifications: CSSLP, CISSP, AMBCI, MCSD, MCAD, CompTIA Network+ and the ECSA certification.

Mano is married to whom he calls the "most wonderful and sacrificial person in this world," Sangeetha Johnson, and their greatest fulfillment comes from spending time with their son, Reuben A. Paul.

Introduction

In a day and age when security breaches in software are costing companies large fines and regulatory burdens, developing software that is reliable in its functionality, resilient against attackers, and recoverable when the expected business operations are disrupted, is a must have. The assurance of confidentiality, integrity and availability is becoming an integral part of software development.

(ISC)² has a proven track record in educating and certifying information security professionals and is the global leader in information security. Its newest certification, the Certified Secure Software Lifecycle Professional (CSSLP®) is a testament to the organization's ongoing commitment to information security in general and specifically to software security. A decade from now, it is highly unlikely that anyone who is involved with software development would do so, without giving attention to the security aspects of software development. The CSSLP certification is therefore a must have for all the stakeholders, from the business analyst and builder of code to the executives in the boardroom, who either interface with or participate in a software development project.

The CSSLP takes a holistic approach to secure software development. It covers the various people, processes and technology elements of developing software securely throughout the entire lifecycle of a project. Starting with requirements analysis to final retirement, and proceeding through design, implementation, release and operations, the CSSLP covers all of the necessary aspects of secure software development. Since software is not developed and executed in a silo, the CSSLP not only focuses on the security aspects of software development, but it also takes into account the security aspects of the networks and hosts on which the software will run. Additionally, it takes a strategic long term view to improve the overall state of software security within an organization while providing tactical solutions. The CSSLP certification is vendor agnostic and language agnostic.

The following list represents the current seven domains of the CSSLP common body of knowledge (CBK®) and the high level topics covered in each domain.

A comprehensive list can be obtained by requesting the Candidate Information Bulletin from the (ISC)² website at www.isc2.org.

1. Secure Software Concepts

   Without a strong foundation, buildings have been known to collapse and the same is true when it comes to building software. For software to be secure and resilient against hackers, it must take into account certain foundational concepts of information security. These include confidentiality, integrity, availability, authentication, authorization, auditing, and management of sessions, exceptions/errors, and configuration. The candidate is expected to be familiar with these foundational concepts and how to apply them while developing software. They must be familiar with the principles of risk management and governance as it applies to software development. Regulatory, privacy and compliance requirements that impose the need for secure software and the repercussions of non-compliance must be understood. Security models and trusted computing concepts that can be applied in software that is built in-house or purchased are covered and it is imperative that the candidate is familiar with their applications.

2. Secure Software Requirements

   The lack of secure software requirements plagues many software development projects today. It is important to explicitly articulate and capture the security requirements that need to be designed and implemented in the software and in the requirements traceability matrix, for without it, software not only suffers from poor product quality, but extensive timelines, increased cost of re-architecture, end-user dissatisfaction and even security breaches. The internal and external sources of secure software requirements, along with the processes to elicit these requirements are covered. Protection needs elicitation using data classification, use and misuse case modeling, subject-object matrices and sequencing and timing aspects as it pertains to software development is to be thoroughly understood. The candidate is expected to be familiar with these sources and processes that can be used for determining secure software requirements.

3. Secure Software Design

   Addressing security early on the life cycle is not only less costly but resource- and schedule-efficient as well. Securely designing software takes into account the implementation of several secure design principles, such as least privilege, separation of duties, open design, complete mediation, etc. Threat modeling that is initiated in the design phase is an important activity that helps in identifying threats to software and the controls that should be implemented to address the risk. The candidate must be familiar with the principles of designing software securely, know how to threat model software and be aware of the inherent security benefits that are evident or are lacking in different architectures. Practical knowledge of how to conduct a design and architecture review with a security perspective is expected.

4. Secure Software Implementation/Coding

Writing secure code is one of the most important aspects of secure software development. There are several software development methodologies ranging from the traditional Waterfall model to the current agile development methodologies such as extreme programming and Scrum. The security benefits and drawbacks of each of these methodologies must be understood. Code that is written without the appropriate implementation of secure controls is prone to attack. Some of the most common attacks against software applications today include injection attacks against databases and directory stores, cross site scripting (XSS) attacks, cross-site request forgery (CSRF), and buffer overflows. It is important to be familiar with how a vulnerability can be exploited and what controls can be implemented to address the risk. The anatomy of the attacks that exploit the vulnerabilities published by the Open Web Application Security Project (OWASP) as the Top Ten application security risks and the CWE/SANS top 25 most dangerous software errors are to be known. Additionally one is expected to know defensive coding techniques and processes, including memory management, static and dynamic code analysis, code/peer review and build/compiler security.

5. Secure Software Testing

The importance of validating the presence of and verifying the effectiveness of security controls implemented in software cannot be overstated. The reliability, resiliency and recoverability aspect of software assurance can be accomplished using quality assurance and security testing. What to test, who is to test and how to test software for security issues, must be understood. The candidate must be familiar with the characteristics and differences between black box, white box and gray box testing and know about the different types of fuzz testing. One must be familiar with logic testing, penetration testing, fuzz testing, simulation testing, regression testing and user acceptance testing, which are covered in detail. Upon the successful completion of functional and security tests, the defects that are determined need to be tracked and addressed accordingly. The CSSLP candidate is not expected to know all the tools that are used for software testing, but one must be familiar with what tests need to be performed and how they can be performed, with or without tools.

6. Software Acceptance

Before software is released or deployed into production, it is imperative to ensure that the developed software meets the required compliance, quality, functional and assurance requirements. The software, which is either built or bought, needs to be validated and verified within the computing ecosystems, where it will be deployed against a set of defined acceptance criteria. Certification and accreditation exercises need to be undertaken to ensure that the residual risk is below the acceptable threshold. It is important for one to be familiar with legal protection mechanisms that need to exist when procuring commercially off the shelf (COTS) software. The importance of software escrowing and the security benefits it offers is covered in detail and the candidate must know the reasons for software escrowing.

7. Software Deployment, Operations, Maintenance and Disposal

Upon successful formal acceptance of the software by the customer/client, the installation of the software must be performed with security in mind. Failure to do so can potentially render all of the software security efforts that were previously undertaken to design and build the software futile. Once software is installed, it needs to be continuously monitored to guarantee that the software will continue to function in a reliable, resilient and recoverable manner as expected. Continuous monitoring, patch management, incident management, problem management, and configuration management are covered. The development and enforcement of End-of-Life (EOL) policies that define the criteria for disposal of data and software must be understood, because improper data and media sanitization can lead to serious security ramifications.

This guide is a valuable resource to anyone preparing for the CSSLP certification examination and can serve as a software security reference book to even those who are already part of the certified elite. The *Official (ISC)²® Guide to the CSSLP®* is a must have to anyone involved in software development!

Chapter 1

Secure Software Concepts

1.1 Introduction

Ask any architect and they are likely to agree with renowned author Thomas Hemerken on his famous quote, "the loftier the building, the deeper the foundation must be laid." For superstructures to withstand the adversarial onslaught of natural forces, they must stand on a very solid and strong foundation. Hack-resilient software is one that reduces the likelihood of a successful attack and mitigates the extent of damage if an attack occurs. In order for software to be secure and hack resilient, it must factor in secure software concepts. These concepts are foundational and should be considered for incorporation into the design, development, and deployment of secure software.

1.2 Objectives

As a Certified Secure Software Lifecycle Professional (CSSLP), you are expected to:

- Understand the concepts and elements of what constitutes secure software.
- Be familiar with the principles of risk management as it pertains to software development.
- Know how to apply information security concepts to software development.
- Know the various design aspects that need to be taken into consideration to architect hack-resilient software.
- Understand how policies, standards, methodologies, frameworks, and best practices interplay in the development of secure software.

- Be familiar with regulatory, privacy, and compliance requirements for software and the potential repercussions of noncompliance.
- Understand security models and how they can be used to architect hacker-proof software.
- Know what trusted computing is and be familiar with mechanisms and related concepts of trusted computing.
- Understand security issues that need to be considered when purchasing or acquiring software.

This chapter will cover each of these objectives in detail. It is imperative that you fully understand not just what these secure software concepts are but also how to apply them in the software that your organization builds or buys.

1.3 Holistic Security

A few years ago, security was about keeping the bad guys out of your network. Network security relied extensively on perimeter defenses such as firewalls, demilitarized zones (DMZ), and bastion hosts to protect applications and data that were within the organization's network. These perimeter defenses are absolutely necessary and critical, but with globalization and the changing landscape in the way we do business today, where there is a need to allow access to our internal systems and applications, the boundaries that demarcated our internal systems and applications from the external ones are slowly thinning and vanishing. This warrants that the hosts (systems) on which our software runs are even more closely guarded and secured. Having the need to open our networks and securely allow access now requires that our applications (software) are hardened, in addition to the network or perimeter security controls. The need is for secure applications running on secure hosts (systems) in secure networks. The need is for holistic security, which is the first and foremost software security concept that one must be familiar with. It is pivotal to recognize that software is only as secure as the weakest link. Today, software is rarely deployed as a stand-alone business application. It is often complex, running on host systems that are interconnected to several other systems on a network. A weakness (vulnerability) in any one of the layers may render all controls (safeguards and countermeasures) futile. The application, host, and network must all be secured adequately and appropriately. For example, a Structured Query Language (SQL) injection vulnerability in the application can allow an attacker to be able to compromise the database server (host) and from the host, launch exploits that can impact the entire network. Similarly, an open port on the network can lead to the discovery and exploitation of unpatched host systems and vulnerabilities in applications. Secure software is characterized by the securing of applications, hosts, and networks holistically, so there is no weak link, i.e., no Achilles' heel (Figure 1.1).

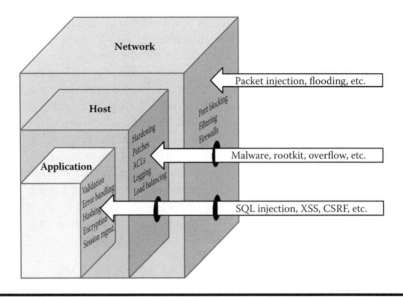

Figure 1.1 Securing the network, hosts, and application layer.

1.4 Implementation Challenges

Despite the recognition of the fact that the security of networks, systems, and software is critical for the operations and sustainability of an organization or business, the computing ecosystem today seems to be plagued with a plethora of insecure networks and systems and more particularly insecure software. In today's environment where software is rife with vulnerabilities, as is evident in full disclosure lists, bug tracking databases, and hacking incident reports, software security cannot be overlooked, but it is. Some of the primary reasons why there is a prevalence of insecure software may be attributed to the following:

- Iron triangle constraints
- Security as an afterthought
- Security versus usability

1.4.1 Iron Triangle Constraints

From the time an idea to solve a business problem using a software solution is born to the time that solution is designed, developed, and deployed, there is a need for time (schedule), resources (scope), and cost (budget). Resources (people) with appropriate skills and technical knowledge are not always readily available and are costly. The defender is expected to play vigilante 24/7, guarding against all attacks while being constrained to play by the rules of engagement, whereas the attacker has the upper hand because the attacker needs to be able to exploit just one weakness and can strike anytime without the need to have to play by the rules. Additionally, depending on your business model or type of organization, software development can involve many stakeholders. To say the least, software development in and of itself is a resource-, schedule- (time-), and budget-intensive process. Adding the need to incorporate security into the software is seen as having the need to do "more" with what is already deemed "less" or "insufficient". Constraints in schedule, scope, and budget (the components of the iron triangle as shown in Figure 1.2) are often the reasons why security requirements are left out of software. If the software development project's scope, schedule (time), and budget are very rigidly defined (as is often the case), it gives little to no room to incorporate even the basic, let alone additional, security requirements, and unfortunately what is typically overlooked are elements of software security.

1.4.2 Security as an Afterthought

Developers and management tend to think that security does not add any business value because it is not very easy to show a one-to-one return on security investment (ROSI). Iron triangle constraints often lead to add-on security, wherein secure features are bolted on and not built into the software. It is important that secure features are built into the software, instead of being added on at a later stage, because it has been proven that the cost to fix insecure software earlier in the software development life cycle (SDLC) is significantly lower when compared to having the same issue addressed at a later stage, as illustrated in Figure 1.3. Addressing vulnerabilities just before a product is released is very expensive.

1.4.3 Security versus Usability

Another reason why it is a challenge to incorporate secure features in software is that the incorporation of secure features is viewed as rendering the software to

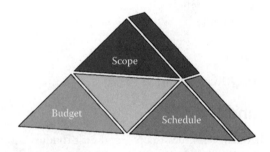

Figure 1.2   Iron triangle.

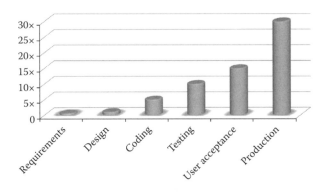

Figure 1.3   Relative cost of fixing code issues at different stages of the SDLC.

become very complex, restrictive, and unusable. For example, the human resources organization needs to be able to view payroll data of employees and the software development team has been asked to develop an intranet Web application that the human resources personnel can access. When the software development team consults with the security consultant, the security consultant recommends that such access should be granted to only those who are authenticated and authorized and that all access requests must be logged for review purposes. The security consultant also advises the software team to ensure that the authentication mechanism uses passwords that are at least 15 characters long, require upper- and lowercase characters, and have a mix of alphanumeric and special characters, which need to be reset every 30 days. Once designed and developed, this software is deployed for use by the human resources organization. It is quickly apparent that the human resources personnel are writing their complex passwords on sticky notes and leaving them in insecure locations such as their desk drawers or in some cases even on their system monitors. They are also complaining that the software is not usable because it takes a lot of time for each access request to be processed, because all access requests are not only checked for authorization but also audited (logged). There is absolutely no doubt that the incorporation of security comes at the cost of performance and usability. This is true if the software design does not factor in the concept known as psychological acceptability. Software security must be balanced with usability and performance. We will be covering "psychological acceptability" in detail along with many other design concepts in Chapter 3.

1.5 Quality and Security

In a world that is driven by the need for and assurance of quality products, it is important to recognize that there is a distinction between quality and security, particularly as they apply to software products. Almost all software products go through a quality assurance (or testing) phase before being released or deployed, wherein the functionality of the software, as required by the business client or customer, is validated and verified. Quality assurance checks are indicative of the fact that the software is reliable (functioning as designed) and that it is functional (meets the requirements as specified by the business owner). Following Total Quality Management (TQM) processes like the Six Sigma (6σ) or certifying software with International Organization for Standardization (ISO) quality standards are important in creating good quality software and achieving a competitive edge in the marketplace, but it is important to realize that such quality validation and certifications do not necessarily mean that the software product is secure. A software product that is secure will add to the quality of that software, but the inverse is not always necessarily true.

It is also important to recognize that the presence of security functionality in software may allow it to support quality certification standards, but it does not necessarily imply that the software is secure. Vendors often tout the presence of security functionality in their products in order to differentiate themselves from their competitors, and while this may be true, it must be understood that the mere presence of security functionality in the vendor's software does not make it secure. This is because security functionality may not be configured to work in your operating environment, or when it is, it may be implemented incorrectly. For example, software that has the functionality to turn on logging of all critical and administrative transactions may be certified as a quality secure product, but unless the option to log these transactions is turned on within your computing environment, it has added nothing to your security posture. It is therefore extremely important that you verify the claims of the vendors within your computing environment and address any concerns you may come across before purchase. In other words, trust, but always verify. This is vital when evaluating software whether you are purchasing it or building it in-house.

1.6 Security Profile: What Makes a Software Secure?

As mentioned, in order to develop hack-resilient software, it is important to incorporate security concepts in the requirements, design, code, release, and disposal phases of the SDLC.

The makeup of your software from a security perspective is the security profile of your software, and it includes the incorporation of these concepts in the SDLC. As Figure 1.4 illustrates, some of these concepts can be classified as core security concepts, whereas others are general or design security concepts. However, these security concepts are essential building blocks for secure software development. In other words, they are the bare necessities that need to be addressed and cannot be ignored.

This section will cover these security concepts at an introductory level. They will be expanded in subsequent sections within the scope of each domain.

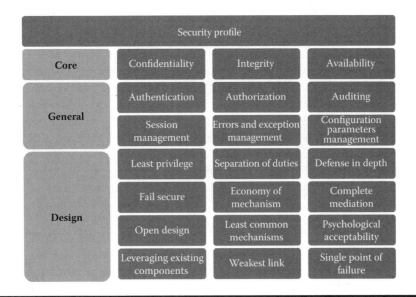

Figure 1.4   Security profile.

1.6.1 Core Security Concepts

1.6.1.1 Confidentiality

Prevalent in the industry today are serious incidents of identity theft and data breaches that can be directly tied to the lack or insufficiency of information disclosure protection mechanisms. When you log into your personal bank account, you expect to see only your information and not anyone else's. Similarly, you expect your personal information not to be available to anyone who requests it. Confidentiality is the security concept that has to do with protection against unauthorized information disclosure. It has to do with the viewing of data. Not only does confidentiality assure the secrecy of data, but it also can help in maintaining data privacy.

1.6.1.2 Integrity

In software that is reliable or, in other words, performs as intended, protecting against improper data alteration is also known as resilient software. Integrity is the measure of software resiliency, and it pertains to the alternation or modification of data and the reliable functioning of software.

When you use an online bill payment system to pay your utility bill, you expect that upon initiating a transfer of payment from your bank to the utility service provider, the amount that you have authorized to transfer is exactly the same amount that is debited from your account and credited into the service provider's account. Not only do you expect that the software that handles this transaction to work as it is intended, but you also expect that the amount you specified for the transaction is not altered by anyone or anything else. The software must debit from the account you specify (and not any other account) and credit into a valid account that is owned by the service provider (and not by anyone else). If you have authorized to pay $129.00, the amount debited from your account must be exactly $129.00 and the amount credited in the service provider's account must not be $12.90 or $1290.00, but $129.00 as well. From the time the data transaction commences until the time that data come to rest or are destroyed, it must not be altered by anyone or any process that is not authorized.

So integrity of software has two aspects to it. First, it must ensure that the data that are transmitted, processed, and stored are as accurate as the originator intended and second, it must ensure that the software performs reliably.

1.6.1.3 Availability

Availability is the security concept that is related to the access of the software or the data or information it handles. Although the overall purpose of a business continuity program (BCP) may be to ensure that downtime is minimized and that the impact upon business disruption is minimal, availability as a concept is not merely a business continuity concept but a software security concept as well. Access must take into account the "who" and "when" aspects of availability. First, the software or the data it processes must be accessible by only those who are authorized (who) and, second, it must be accessible only at the time (when) that it is required. Data must not be available to the wrong people or at the wrong time.

A service level agreement (SLA) is an example of an instrument that can be used to explicitly state and govern availability requirements for business partners and clients. Load balancing and replication are mechanisms that can be used to ensure availability. Software can also be developed with monitoring and alerting functionality that can detect disruptions and notify appropriate personnel to minimize downtime, once again ensuring availability.

1.6.2 General Security Concepts

In this section, we will cover general security concepts that aim at mitigating disclosure, alteration, and destruction threats thereby ensuring the core security concepts of confidentiality, integrity, and availability.

1.6.2.1 Authentication

Software is a conduit to an organization's internal databases, systems, and network, and so it is critically important that access to internal sensitive information is granted only to those entities that are valid. Authentication is a security concept that answers the question, "Are you who you claim to be?" It not only ensures that the identity of an entity (person or resource) is specified according to the format that the software is expecting it, but it also validates or verifies the identity information that has been supplied. In other words, it assures the claim of an entity by verifying identity information.

Authentication succeeds identification in the sense that the person or process must be identified before it can be validated or verified. The identifying information that is supplied is also known as credentials or claims. The most common form of credential is a combination of username (or user ID) and password, but authentication can be primarily achieved in any one or in combination of the following three factors:

1. Knowledge: The identifying information provided in this mechanism for validation is something that one knows. Examples of this type of authentication include username and password, pass phrases, or a personal identification number (PIN).
2. Ownership: The identifying information provided in this mechanism for validation is something that you own or have. Examples of this type of authentication include tokens and smart cards.
3. Characteristic: The identifying information provided in this mechanism for validation is something you are. The best known example for this type of authentication is biometrics. The identifying information that is supplied in characteristic-based authentication such as biometric authentication is digitized representations of physical traits or features. Blood vessel patterns of the retina, fingerprints, and iris patterns are some common physical features that are used but there are limitations with biometrics as physical characteristics can change with medically related maladies (Schneier, 2000). Physical actions such as signatures (pressure and slant) that can be digitized can also be used in characteristic-based authentication.

Multifactor authentication, which is the use of more than one factor to authenticate, is considered to be more secure than single-factor authentication where only one of the three factors (knowledge, ownership, or characteristic) is used for validating credentials. Multifactor authentication is recommended for validating access to systems containing sensitive or critical information. The Federal Financial Institutions Examination Council (FFIEC) guidance on authentication in an Internet banking environment highlights that the use of single-factor authentication as the only control mechanism in such an environment is inadequate and additional mitigation compensating controls, layered security including multifactor authentication is warranted.

1.6.2.2 Authorization

Just because an entity's credentials can be validated does not mean that the entity should be given access to all of the resources that it requests. For example, you may be able to log into the accounting software within your company, but you are still not able to access the human resources payroll data, because you do not have the rights or privileges to access the payroll data. Authorization is the security concept in which access to objects is controlled based on the rights and privileges that are granted to the requestor by the owner of the data or system or according to a policy. Authorization decisions are layered on top of authentication and must never precede authentication, i.e., you do not authorize before you authenticate unless your business requirements require you to give access to anonymous users (those who are not authenticated), in which case the authorization decision may be uniformly restrictive to all anonymous users.

The requestor is referred to as the subject and the requested resource is referred to as the object. The subject may be human or nonhuman such as a process or another object. The subject may also be categorized by privilege level such as an administrative user, manager, or anonymous user. Examples of an object include a table in the database, a file, or a view. A subject's actions such as creation, reading, update, or deletion (CRUD) on an object is dependent on the privilege level of the subject. An example of authorization based on the privilege level of the subject is that an administrative user may be able to create, read, update, and delete (CRUD) data, but an anonymous user may be allowed to only read (R) the data, whereas a manager may be allowed to create, read, and update (CRU) data.

1.6.2.3 Auditing/Logging

Consider the following scenario. You find out that the price of a product in the online store is different from the one in your brick and mortar store and you are unsure as to how this price discrepancy situation has come about. Upon preliminary research, it is determined that the screen used to update prices of products for the online store is not tightly controlled and any authenticated user within your company can make changes to the price. Unfortunately, there is no way to be able to tell who made the price changes because no information is logged for review upon the update of pricing information. Auditing is the security concept in which privileged and critical business transactions are logged. This logging can be used to build a history of events, which can be used for troubleshooting and forensic evidence. In the scenario above, if the authenticated credentials of the logged-on user who made the price changes is logged along with a timestamp of the change and the before and after price, the history of the changes can be built to track down the user who made the change. Auditing is a passive detective control mechanism.

At a bare minimum, audit fields that include who (user or process) did what (CRUD), where (file or table), and when (created or modified timestamp) along with a before and after snapshot of the information that was changed must be logged for all administrative (privilege) or critical transactions as defined by the business. Additionally, newer audit logs must always be appended to and never overwrite older logs. This could result in a capacity or space issue based on the retention period of these logs; this needs to be planned for. The retention period of these audit logs must be based on regulatory requirements or organizational policy, and in cases where the organizational policy for retention conflicts with regulatory requirements, the regulatory requirements must be followed and the organizational policy appropriately amended to prevent future conflicts.

Nonrepudiation addresses the deniability of actions taken by either a user or the software on behalf of the user. Accountability to ensure nonrepudiation can be accomplished by auditing when used in conjunction with identification. In the price change scenario, if the software had logged the price change action and the identity of the user who made that change, that individual can be held accountable for their action, giving the individual a limited opportunity to repudiate or deny their action, thereby assuring nonrepudiation.

Auditing is a *detective* control, and it can be a *deterrent* control as well. Because one can use the audit logs to determine the history of actions that are taken by a user or the software itself, auditing or logging is a passive detective control. The fore knowledge of being audited could potentially deter a user from taking unauthorized actions, but it does not necessarily prevent them from doing so.

It is understood that auditing is a very important security concept that is often not given the attention it deserves when building software. However, there are certain challenges with auditing as well that warrant attention and addressing. They are

1. Performance impact
2. Information overload
3. Capacity limitation
4. Configuration interfaces protection
5. Audit log protection

Auditing can have impact on the performance of the software. It was noted earlier that there is usually a trade-off decision that is necessary when it comes to security versus usability. If your software is configured to log every administrative and critical business transaction, then each time those operations are performed, the time to log those actions can have a bearing on the performance of the software.

Additionally, the amount of data logged may result in information overload, and without proper correlation and pattern discerning abilities, administrative and critical operations may be overlooked, thereby reducing the security that auditing provides. It is therefore imperative to log only the needed information at the right frequency. A best practice would be to classify the logs when being logged using a bucketing scheme so that you can easily sort through large volumes of logs when trying to determine historical actions. An example of a bucketing scheme can be "Informational Only," "Administrative," "Business Critical," "Error," "Security," "Miscellaneous," etc. The frequency for reviewing the logs need to be defined by the business, and this is usually dependent on the value of the software or the data it transmits, processes, and stores to the business.

In addition to information overload, logging all information can result in capacity and space issues for the systems that hold the logs. Proper capacity planning and archival requirements need to be predetermined to address this.

Furthermore, the configuration interfaces to turn on or off the audit logs and the types of logs to audit must also be designed, developed, and protected. Failure to protect the audit log configuration interfaces can result in an attack going undetected. For example, if the configuration interfaces to turn auditing on or off is left unprotected, an attacker may be able to turn logging off, perform their attack, and turn it back on once they have completed their malicious activities. In this case, nonrepudiation is not ensured. So it must be understood that the configuration interfaces for auditing can potentially increase the attack surface area and nonrepudiation abilities can be seriously hampered.

Finally, the audit logs themselves are to be deemed an asset to the business and can be susceptible to information disclosure attacks. One must be diligent as to what to log and the format of the log itself. For example, if the business requirement for your software is to log authentication failure attempts, it is recommended that you do not log the value supplied for the password that was used, as the failure may have resulted from an inadvertent and innocuous user error. Should you have the need to log the password value for troubleshooting reasons, it would be advisable to hash the password before recording it so that even if someone gets unauthorized access to the logs, sensitive information is still protected.

1.6.2.4 Session Management

Just because someone is authenticated and authorized to access system resources does not mean that security controls can be lax after an authenticated session is established, because a session can be hijacked. Session hijacking attacks happen when an attacker impersonates the identity of a valid user and interjects themselves into the middle of an existing session, routing information from the user to the system and from the system to the user through them. This can lead to information disclosure (confidentiality threat), alteration (integrity threat), or a denial of service (availability threat). It is also known as a man-in-the-middle (MITM) attack. Session management is a security concept that aims at mitigating session hijacking or MITM attacks. It requires that the session is unique by the issuance of unique session tokens, and it also requires that user activity is tracked so that someone who is attempting to hijack a valid session is prevented from doing so.

1.6.2.5 Errors and Exception Management

Errors and exceptions are inevitable when dealing with software. Whereas errors may be a result of user ignorance or software breakdown, exceptions are software issues that are not handled explicitly when the software behaves in an unintended or unreliable manner. An example of user error is that the user mistypes his user ID when trying to log in. Now if the software was expecting the user ID to be supplied in a numeric format and the user typed in alpha characters in that field, the software operations will result in a data type conversion exception. If this exception is not explicitly handled, it would result in informing the user of this exception and in many cases disclose the entire exception stack. This can result in information disclosure potentially revealing the software's internal architectural details and in some cases even the data value. It is recommended as a secure software best practice to ensure that the errors and exception messages be nonverbose and explicitly specified in the software. An example of a verbose error message would be displaying "User ID did not match" or "Password is incorrect," instead of using the nonverbose or laconic equivalent such as "Login invalid." Additionally, upon errors or exceptions, the software is to fail to a more secure state. Organizations are tolerant of user errors, which are inevitable, permitting a predetermined number of user errors before recording it as a security violation. This predetermined number is established as a baseline and is referred to in operations as *clipping level*. An example of this is, after three failed incorrect PIN entries, your account is locked out until an out-of-band process unlocks it or a certain period has elapsed. The software should never fail insecure, which would be characterized by the software allowing access after three failed incorrect PIN entries. Errors and exception management is the security concept that ensures that unintended and unreliable behavior of the software is explicitly handled, while maintaining a secure state and protection against confidentiality, integrity, and availability threats.

1.6.2.6 Configuration Parameters Management

Software is made up of code and parameters that need to be established for it to run. These parameters may include variables that need to be initialized in memory for the software to start, connection strings to databases in the backend, or cryptographic keys for secrecy to just name a few. These configuration parameters are part of the software makeup that needs to be not only configured but protected as well because they are to be deemed an asset that is valuable to the business. What good is it to lock the doors and windows in an attempt to secure your valuables within the house when you leave the key under the mat on the front porch? Configuration management in the context of software security is the security concept that ensures that the appropriate levels of protection are provided to secure the configurable parameters that are needed for the software to run. Note that we will also be covering configuration management as it pertains to IT services in Chapters 6 and 7.

1.6.3 Design Security Concepts

In this section we will discuss security concepts that need to be considered when designing and architecting software. These concepts are defined in the following. We will expand on each of these concepts in more concrete detail in Chapter 3.

- Least Privilege: A security principle in which a person or process is given only the minimum level of access rights (privileges) that is necessary for that person or process to complete an assigned operation. This right must be given only for a minimum amount of time that is necessary to complete the operation.

- Separation of Duties (or) Compartmentalization Principle: Also known as the compartmentalization principle, or separation of privilege, separation of duties is a security principle stating that the successful completion of a single task is dependent on two or more conditions that need to be met and just one of the conditions will be insufficient in completing the task by itself.

- Defense in Depth (or) Layered Defense: Also known as layered defense, defense in depth is a security principle where single points of complete compromise are eliminated or mitigated by the incorporation of a series or multiple layers of security safeguards and risk-mitigation countermeasures.

- Fail Secure: A security principle that aims to maintain confidentiality, integrity, and availability by defaulting to a secure state, rapid recovery of software resiliency upon design, or implementation failure. In the context of software security, fail secure can be used interchangeably with fail safe.

- Economy of Mechanisms: This, in layman terms, is the keep-it-simple principle because the likelihood of a greater number of vulnerabilities increases with the complexity of the software architectural design and code. By keeping the software design and implementation details simple, the attackability or attack surface of the software is reduced.

- Complete Mediation: A security principle that ensures that authority is not circumvented in subsequent requests of an object by a subject by checking for authorization (rights and privileges) upon every request for the object. In other words, the access requests by a subject for an object is completely mediated each time, every time.

- Open Design: The open design security principle states that the implementation details of the design should be independent of the design itself, which can remain open, unlike in the case of security by obscurity wherein the security of the software is dependent on the obscuring of the design itself. When software is architected using the open design concept, the review of the design itself will not result in the compromise of the safeguards in the software.

- Least Common Mechanisms: The security principle of least common mechanisms disallows the sharing of mechanisms that are common to more than one user or process if the users and processes are at different levels of privilege. For example, the use of the same function to retrieve the bonus amount of an exempt employee and a nonexempt employee will not be allowed. In this case the calculation of the bonus is the common mechanism.

- Psychological Acceptability: This security principle aims at maximizing the usage and adoption of the security functionality in the software by ensuring that the security functionality is easy to use and at the same time transparent to the user. Ease of use and transparency are essential requirements for this security principle to be effective.

■ Leveraging Existing Components: This is a security principle that focuses on ensuring that the attack surface is not increased and no new vulnerabilities are introduced by promoting the reuse of existing software components, code, and functionality.

■ Weakest Link: You have heard of the saying, a chain is only as strong as the weakest link. This security principle states that the hack resiliency of your software security will depend heavily on the protection of weakest components, be it code, service, or interface. A breakdown in the weakest link will result in a security breach.

■ Single Point of Failure: Single point of failure is the security principle that ensures that your software is designed to eliminate any single source of complete compromise. Although this is similar to the weakest link principle, the distinguishing difference between the two is that the weakest link need not necessarily be a single point of failure but could be as a result of various weak sources. Usually, in software security, the weakest link is a superset of several single points of failure.

1.7 Security Concepts in the SDLC

Security concepts span across the entire life cycle and will need to be addressed in each phase. Software security requirements, design, development, and deployment must take into account all of these security concepts. Lack or insufficiency of attention in any one phase may render the efforts taken in other phases completely futile. For example, capturing requirements to handle disclosure protection (confidentiality) in the requirements gathering phase of your SDLC but not designing confidentiality controls in the design phase of your SDLC can potentially result in information disclosure breaches.

Often, these concepts are used in conjunction with other concepts or they can be used independently, but it is important that none of these concepts are ignored, even if it is deemed as not applicable or in some cases contradictory to other concepts. For example, the economy of mechanism concept in implementing a single sign-on mechanism for simplified user authentication may directly conflict with the complete mediation design concept and necessary architectural decisions must be taken to address this without compromising the security of the software. In no situation can they be ignored.

1.8 Risk Management

One of the key aspects of managing security is risk management. It must be recognized that the goal of risk management spans more than the mere protection of information technology (IT) assets as it is intended to protect the entire organization so that there are minimal to no disruption in the organization's abilities to accomplish its mission. Risk management processes include the preliminary assessment for the need of security controls, the identification, development, testing, implementation, and verification (evaluation) of security controls so that the impact of any disruptive processes are at an acceptable or risk-appropriate level. Risk management, in the context of software security, is the balancing act between the protection of IT assets and the cost of implementing software security controls, so that the risk is handled appropriately. The second revision of the *Special Publication 800-64* by the National Institute of Standards and Technology (NIST), entitled "Security Considerations in the Systems Development Life Cycle (SDLC)," highlights that a prerequisite to a comprehensive strategy to manage risk to IT assets is to consider security during the SDLC. By addressing risk throughout the SDLC, one can avoid a lot of headaches upon release or deployment of the software.

1.8.1 Terminology and Definitions

Before we delve into the challenges with risk management as it pertains to software and software development, it is imperative that there is a strong fundamental understanding of terms and risk computation formulae used in the context of traditional risk management.

Some of the most common terms and formulae that a CSSLP must be familiar with are covered in this section. Some of the definitions used in this section are from *NIST Risk Management Guide to Information Technology Systems Special Publication 800-30.*

1.8.1.1 Asset

Assets are those items that are valuable to the organization, the loss of which can potentially cause disruptions in the organization's ability to accomplish its missions. These may be tangible or intangible in nature. Tangible assets, as opposed to intangible assets, are those that can be perceived by physical senses. They can be more easily evaluated than intangible assets. Examples of tangible IT assets include networking equipment, servers, software code, and also data that are transmitted and stored by your applications. In the realm of software security, data are the most important tangible asset, second only to people. Examples of intangible assets include intellectual property rights such as copyright, patents, trademarks, and brand reputation. The loss of brand reputation for an organization may be disastrous, and recovery from such a loss may be nearly impossible. Arguably, company brand reputation is the most valuable intangible asset, and the loss of intangible assets may have more dire consequences than the loss of tangible assets; however, regardless of whether the asset is tangible, the risk of loss must be assessed and appropriately managed. In threat modeling terminology, an asset is also referred to as an "Object." We will cover subject/object matrix in the context of threat modeling in Section 3.3.3.2.

1.8.1.2 Vulnerability

A weakness or flaw that could be accidently triggered or intentionally exploited by an attacker, resulting in the breach or breakdown of the security policy is known as vulnerability. Vulnerabilities can be evident in the process, design, or implementation of the system or software. Examples of process vulnerabilities include improper check-in and check-out procedures of software code or backup of production data to nonproduction systems and incomplete termination access control mechanisms. The use of obsolete cryptographic algorithms such as Data Encryption Standard (DES), not designing for handling resource deadlocks, unhandled exceptions, and hard-coding database connection information in clear text (humanly readable form) in line with code are examples of design vulnerabilities. In addition to process and design vulnerabilities, weaknesses in software are made possible because of the way in which software is implemented. Some examples of implementation vulnerabilities are: the software accepts any user supplied data and processes it without first validating it; the software reveals too much information in the event of an error and not explicitly closing open connections to backend databases.

Some well-known and useful vulnerability tracking systems and vulnerability repositories that can be leveraged include the following:

- U.S. Computer Emergency Readiness Team (US-CERT) Vulnerability Notes Database: The CERT vulnerability analysis project aims at reducing security risks due to software vulnerabilities in both developed and deployed software. In software that is being developed, they focus on vulnerability discovery and in software that is already deployed, they focus on vulnerability remediation. Newly discovered vulnerabilities are added to the Vulnerability Notes Database. Existing ones are updated as needed.
- Common Vulnerability Scoring System (CVSS): As the name suggests, the CVSS is a system designed to rate IT vulnerabilities and help organizations prioritize security vulnerabilities.
- Open Source Vulnerability Database: This database is independent and open source created by and for the security community, with the goal of providing accurate, detailed, current, and unbiased technical information on security vulnerabilities.
- Common Vulnerabilities and Exposures (CVE): CVE is a dictionary of publicly known information security vulnerabilities and exposures. It is free for use and international in scope.
- Common Weakness Enumeration (CWE™): This specification provides a common language for describing architectural, design, or coding software security weaknesses. It is international in scope, freely available for public

use, and intended to provide a standardized and definitive "formal" list of software weaknesses. Categorizations of software security weaknesses are derived from software security taxonomies.

1.8.1.3 Threat

Vulnerabilities pose threats to assets. A threat is merely the possibility of an unwanted, unintended, or harmful event occurring. When the event occurs upon manifestation of the threat, it results in an incident. These threats can be classified into threats of disclosure, alteration, or destruction. Without proper change control processes in place, a possibility of disclosure exists when sensitive code is disclosed to unauthorized individuals if they can check out the code without any authorization. The same threat of disclosure is possible when production data with actual and real significance is backed up to a developer or test machine, when sensitive database connection information is hard-coded in line with code in clear text, or if the error and exception messages are not handled properly. Lack of or insufficient input validation can pose the threat of data alteration, resulting in violation of software integrity. Insufficient load testing, stress testing, and code level testing pose the threat of destruction or unavailability.

1.8.1.4 Threat Source/Agent

Anyone or anything that has the potential to make a threat materialize is known as the threat source or threat agent. Threat agents may be human or nonhuman. Examples of nonhuman threat agents in addition to nature that are prevalent in this day and age are malicious software (malware), such as adware, spyware, viruses, and worms. We will cover the different types of threat agents when we discuss threat modeling in Chapter 3.

1.8.1.5 Attack

Threat agents may intentionally cause a threat to materialize or threats can occur as a result of plain user error or accidental discovery as well. When the threat agent actively and intentionally causes a threat to happen, it is referred to as an "attack" and the threat agents are commonly referred to as "attackers." In other words, an intentional action attempting to cause harm is the simplest definition of an attack. When an attack happens as a result of an attacker taking advantage of a known vulnerability, it is known as an "exploit." The attacker exploits a vulnerability causing the attacker (threat agent) to cause harm (materialize a threat).

1.8.1.6 Probability

Also known as "likelihood," probability is the chance that a particular threat can happen. Because the goal of risk management is to reduce the risk to an acceptable level, the measurement of the probability of an unintended, unwanted, or harmful event being triggered is important. Probability is usually expressed as a percentile, but because the accuracy of quantifying the likelihood of a threat is mostly done using best guesstimates or sometimes mere heuristic techniques, some organizations use qualitative categorizations or buckets, such as high, medium, or low to express the likelihood of a threat occurring. Regardless of whether a quantitative or qualitative expression, the chance of harm caused by a threat must be determined or at least understood as the bare minimum.

1.8.1.7 Impact

The outcome of a materialized threat can vary from very minor disruptions to inconveniences imposed by levied fines for lack of due diligence, breakdown in organization leadership as a result of incarceration, to bankruptcy and complete cessation of the organization. The extent of how serious the disruptions to the organization's ability to achieve its goal are referred to as the impact.

1.8.1.8 Exposure Factor

Exposure factor is defined as the opportunity for a threat to cause loss. Exposure factor plays an important role in the computation of risk. Although the probability of an attack may be high, and the corresponding impact severe, if the software is designed, developed, and deployed with security in mind, the exposure factor for attack may be low, thereby reducing the overall risk of exploitation.

1.8.1.9 Controls

Security controls are mechanisms by which threats to software and systems can be mitigated. These mechanisms may be technical, administrative, or physical in nature. Examples of some software security controls include input validation, clipping levels for failed password attempts, source control, software librarian, and restricted and supervised access control to data centers and filing cabinets that house sensitive information. Security controls can be broadly categorized into countermeasures and safeguards. As the name implies, countermeasures are security controls that are applied after a threat has been materialized, implying the reactive nature of these types of security controls. On the other hand, safeguards are security controls that are more proactive in nature. Security controls do not remove the threat itself but are built into the software or system to reduce the likelihood of a threat being materialized. Vulnerabilities are reduced by security controls.

However, it must be recognized that improper implementation of security controls themselves may pose a threat. For example, say that upon the failure of a login attempt, the software handles this exception and displays the message "Username is valid but the password did not match" to the end user. Although in the interest of user experience, this may be acceptable, an attacker can read that verbose error message and know that the username exists in the system that performs the validation of user accounts. The exception handling countermeasure in this case potentially becomes the vulnerability for disclosure, owing to improper implementation of the countermeasure. A more secure way to handle login failure would have been to use generic and nonverbose exception handling in which case the message displayed to the end user may just be "Login invalid."

1.8.1.10 Total Risk

Total risk is the likelihood of the occurrence of an unwanted, unintended, or harmful event. This is traditionally computed using factors such as the asset value, threat, and vulnerability. This is the overall risk of the system, before any security controls are applied. This may be expressed qualitatively (e.g., high, medium, or low) or quantitatively (using numbers or percentiles).

1.8.1.11 Residual Risk

Residual risk is the risk that remains after the implementation of mitigating security controls (countermeasures or safeguards).

1.8.2 Calculation of Risk

Risk is conventionally expressed as the product of the probability of a threat source/ agent taking advantage of a vulnerability and the corresponding impact. However, estimation of both probability and impact are usually subjective and so quantitative measurement of risk is not always accurate. Anyone who has been involved with risk management will be the first to acknowledge that the calculation of risk is not a black or white exercise, especially in the context of software security.

However, as a CSSLP, you are expected to be familiar with classical risk management terms such as single loss expectancy (SLE), annual rate of occurrence (ARO), and annual loss expectancy (ALE) and the formulae used to quantitatively compute risk.

■ *Single Loss Expectancy:* SLE is used to estimate potential loss. It is calculated as the product of the value of the asset (usually expressed monetarily) and the exposure factor, which is expressed as a percentage of asset loss when a threat is materialized. See Figure 1.5 for a calculation of SLE.

$$SLE = ASSET\ VALUE\ (\$) \times EXPOSURE\ FACTOR\ (\%)$$

Figure 1.5   Calculation of SLE.

ALE = SINGLE LOSS EXPECTANCY (SLE) × ANNUALIZED RATE OF OCCURRENCE (ARO)

Figure 1.6   Calculation of ALE.

■ *Annual Rate of Occurrence:* The ARO is an expression of the number of incidents from a particular threat that can be expected in a year. This is often just a guesstimate in the field of software security and thus should be carefully considered. Looking at historical incident data within your industry is a good start for determining what the ARO should be.

■ *Annual Loss Expectancy:* ALE is an indicator of the magnitude of risk in a year. ALE is a product of SLE × ARO (see Figure 1.6).

The identification and reduction of the total risk using controls so that the residual risk is within the acceptable range or threshold, wherein business operations are not disrupted, is the primary goal of risk management. To reduce total risk to acceptable levels, risk mitigation strategies in total instead of merely selecting a single control (safeguard) must be considered. For example, to address the risk of disclosure of sensitive information such as credit card numbers or personnel health information, mitigation strategies that include a layered defense approach using access control, encryption or hashing, and auditing of access requests may have to be considered, instead of merely selecting and implementing the Advanced Encryption Standard (AES). It is also important to understand that although the implementation of controls may be a decision made by the technical team, the acceptance of specific levels of residual risk is a management decision that factors in the recommendations from the technical team. The most effective way to ensure that software developed has taken into account security threats and addressed vulnerabilities, thereby reducing the overall risk of that software, is to incorporate risk management processes into the SDLC itself. From requirements definition to release, software should be developed with insight into the risk of it being compromised and necessary risk management decisions and steps must be taken to address it.

1.8.3 Risk Management for Software

It was aforementioned that risk management as it relates to software and software development has its challenges. Some of the reasons for these challenges are:

■ Software risk management is still maturing.
■ Determination of software asset values is often subjective.
■ Data on the exposure factor, impact, and probability of software security breaches is lacking or limited.
■ Technical security risk is only a portion of the overall state of secure software.

Risk management is still maturing in the context of software development, and there are challenges that one faces, because risk management is not yet an exact science when it comes to software development. Not only is this still an emerging field, but it is also difficult to quantify software assets accurately. Asset value is often determined as the value of the systems that the software runs on, instead of the value of the software itself. This is very subjective as well. The value of the data that the software processes is usually just an estimate of potential loss. Additionally, owing to the closed nature of the industry, wherein the exact terms of software security breaches are not necessarily fully disclosed, one is left to speculate on what it would cost an organization should a similar breach occur within their own organization. Although historical data such as the chronology of data breaches published by the Privacy Rights Clearing House are of some use to learn about the potential impact that can be imposed on an organization, they only date back a few years (since 2005) and there is really no way of determining the exposure factor or the probability of similar security breaches within your organization.

Software security is also more than merely writing secure code, and some of the current-day methodologies of computing risk using the number of threats and vulnerabilities that are found through source and object code scanning is only a small portion of the overall risk of that software. Process and people related risks must be factored in as well. For example, the lack of proper change control processes and inadequately trained and educated personnel can lead to insecure installation and operation of software that was deemed to be technically secure and had all of its code vulnerabilities addressed. A plethora of information breaches and data loss has been attributed to privileged third parties and employees who have access to internal systems and software. The risk of disclosure, alteration, and destruction of sensitive data imposed by internal employees and vendors who are allowed to have access within your organization is another very important aspect of software risk management that cannot be ignored.

Unless your organization has a legally valid document that transfers the liability to another party, your organization assumes all of the liability when it comes to software risk management. Your clients and customers will look for someone to be held accountable for a software security breach that affects them, and it will not be the perpetrators that they would go after but you, whom they have entrusted to keep them secure and serviced. The "real" risk belongs to your organization.

1.8.4 Handling Risk

Suppose your organization operates an e-commerce store selling products on the Internet. Today, it has to comply with data protection regulations such as the Payment Card Industry Data Security Standard (PCI DSS) to protect card holder data. Before the PCI DSS regulatory requirement was in effect, your organization has been transmitting and storing the credit card primary account number (PAN), card holder name, service code, expiration date of the card along with sensitive authentication data such as the full magnetic track data, the card verification code, and the PIN, all in clear text (humanly readable form). As depicted in Figure 1.7, PCI DSS version 1.2 disallows the storage of any sensitive authentication information even if it is encrypted or the storage of the PAN along with card holder name, service code, and expiration data is in clear text. Over open, public networks such as the Internet, Wireless, Global Systems for Mobile communications (GSM), or Global Packet Radio Service (GPRS), card holder data and sensitive authentication data cannot be transmitted in clear text.

Note that although the standard does not disallow transmission of these data in the clear over closed, private networks, it is still a best practice to comply with the standard and protect this information to avoid any potential disclosure, even to internal employees or privileged access users.

The following table illustrates commonly used elements of cardholder and sensitive authentication data, whether storage of data element is permitted or prohibited and whether each data element must be protected. This table is not exhaustive but is presented to illustrate the different types of requirements that apply to each data element. PCI DSS Requirement 3.4. is the requirement to render Primary Account Number (PAN), at minimum unreadable anywhere it is stored (including on portable digital media, backup media, in logs, etc.).

	Data Element	Storage Permitted	Protection Required	PCI DSS Req. 3.4.
Cardholder data	Primary account number (PAN)	Yes	Yes	Yes
	Cardholder name[1]	Yes	Yes[1]	No
	Service code[1]	Yes	Yes[1]	No
	Expiration date[1]	Yes	Yes[1]	No
Sensitive authentication data[2]	Full magnetic stripe data[3]	No	N/A	N/A
	CAV2/CVC2/CW2/CID	No	N/A	N/A
	PIN/PIN block	No	N/A	N/A

[1] These data elements must be protected if stored in conjunction with the PAN.
  This protection should be per PCI DSS requirements for general protection of the cardholder data environment. PCI DSS does not apply if PANs are not stored, processed, or transmitted.
[2] Sensitive authentication data must not be stored after authorization (even if encrypted).
[3] Full track data from the magnetic stripe, magnetic stripe image on the chip, or elsewhere.

Figure 1.7 Payment Card Industry Data Security Standard applicability information.

As a CSSLP, you advise the development team that the risk of disclosure is high and it needs to be addressed as soon as possible. The management team now has to decide on how to handle this risk, and they have five possible ways to address it.

1. Ignore the risk: They can choose to not handle the risk and do nothing, leaving the software as is. The risk is left unhandled. This is highly ill advised because the organization can find itself at the end of a class action lawsuit and regulatory oversight for not protecting the data that its customers have entrusted to it.
2. Avoid the risk: They can choose to discontinue the e-commerce store, which is not practical from a business perspective because the e-commerce store is the primary source of sales for your organization. In certain situations, discontinuing use of the existing software may be a viable option, especially when the software is being replaced by a newer product. Risk may be avoided, but it must never be ignored.
3. Mitigate the risk: The development team chooses to implement security controls (safeguards and countermeasures) to reduce the risk. They plan to use security protocols such as Secure Sockets Layer (SSL)/Transport Layer Security (TLS) or IPSec to safeguard sensitive card holder data over open, public networks. Although the risk of disclosure during transmission is reduced, the residual risk that remains is the risk of disclosure in storage. You advise the development team of this risk. They choose to encrypt the information before storing it. Although it may seem like the risk is mitigated completely, there still remains the risk of someone deciphering the original clear text from the encrypted text if the encryption solution is weakly implemented. Moreover, according to the PCI DSS standard, sensitive authentication data cannot be stored even if it is encrypted and so the risk of noncompliance still remains. So it is important that the decision makers who are responsible for addressing the risk are made aware of the compliance, regulatory, and other aspects of risk and not merely yield to choosing a technical solution to mitigate it.
4. Accept the risk: At this juncture, management can choose to accept the residual risk that remains and continue business operations or they can choose to continue to mitigate it by not storing disallowed card holder information. When the cost of implementing security controls outweighs the potential impact of the risk itself, one can accept the risk. However, it is imperative to realize that the risk acceptance process must be a formal process, and it must be well documented, preferably with a contingency plan to address the residual risk in subsequent releases of the software.
5. Transfer the risk: One additional method by which management can choose to address the risk is to simply transfer it. This is usually done by buying insurance and works best for the organization when the cost of implementing the security controls exceeds the cost of potential impact of the risk itself. It must be understood, however, that it is the liability that is transferred and not necessarily the risk itself. This is because your customers are still going to hold

you accountable for security breaches in your organization and the brand or reputational damage that can be realized may far outweigh the liability protection that your organization receives by way of transference of risk. Another way of transferring risk is to transfer the risk to independent third-party assessors who attest by way of vulnerability assessments and penetration testing that the software is secure for public release. However, when this is done, it must be contractually enforceable.

1.8.5 Risk Management Concepts: Summary

As you may know, a picture is worth a thousand words. The risk management concepts we have discussed so far are illustrated for easier understanding in Figure 1.8.

Owners value assets (software) and wish to minimize risk to assets. Threat agents wish to abuse and/or may damage assets. They may give rise to threats that increase the risk to assets. These threats may exploit vulnerabilities (weaknesses) leading to the risk to assets. Owners may or may not be aware of these vulnerabilities. When known, these vulnerabilities may be reduced by the implementation of controls that reduce the risk to assets. It is also noteworthy to understand that the controls themselves may pose vulnerabilities leading to risk to assets. For example, the implementation of fingerprint reader authentication in your software as a biometric control to mitigate access control issues may itself pose the threat of denial of

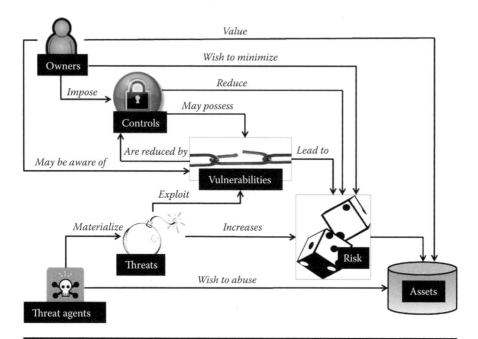

Figure 1.8   Risk management concept flow.

service to valid users, if the crossover error rate, which is the point at which the false rejection rate equals the false acceptance rate, for that biometric control is high.

1.9 Security Policies: The "What" and "Why" for Security

Contrary to what one may think it to be, a security policy is more than merely a written document. It is the instrument by which digital assets that require protection can be identified. It specifies at a high level "What" needs to be protected and the possible repercussions of noncompliance.

In addition to defining the assets that the organization deems as valuable, security policies identify the organization's goals and objectives and communicate management's goals and objectives for the organization.

Recently, legal and regulatory compliance has been evident as an important driver of information security spending and initiatives. Security policies help in ensuring an organization's compliance with legal and regulatory requirements, if they complement and not contradict these laws and regulations. With a clear-cut understanding of management's expectations, the likelihood of personal interpretations and claiming ignorance is curtailed, especially when auditors find gaps between organizational processes and compliance requirements. It protects the organization from any surprises by providing a consistent basis for interpreting or resolving issues that arise. The security policy provides the framework and point of reference that can be used to measure an organization's security posture. The gaps that are identified when being measured against a security policy, a consistent point of reference, can be used to determine effective executive strategy and decisions.

Additionally, security policies ensure nonrepudiation, because those who do not follow the security policy can be personally held accountable for their behavior or actions.

Security policies can also be used to provide guidance to architect secure software by addressing the confidentiality, integrity, and availability aspects of software.

Security policies can also define the functions and scope of the security team, document incident response and enforcement mechanisms, and provide for exception handling, rewards, and discipline.

1.9.1 Scope of the Security Policies

The scope of the information security policy may be *organizational* or *functional*. Organizational policy is universally applicable, and all who are part of the organization must comply with it, unlike a functional policy, which is limited to a specific functional unit or a specific issue. An example of organizational policy is the remote access policy that is applicable to all employees and nonemployees who require remote access into the organizational network. An example of a functional security policy is the data confidentiality policy, which specifies the functional units that are allowed to view sensitive or personal information. In some cases, these can even define the rights personnel have within these functional units. For example, not all members of the human resources team are allowed to view the payroll data of executives.

It may be a single comprehensive document or it may be comprised of many specific information security policy documents.

1.9.2 Prerequisites for Security Policy Development

It cannot be overstressed that security policies provide a framework for a comprehensive and effective information security program.

The success of an information security program and more specifically the software security initiatives within that program is directly related to the enforceability of the security controls that need to be determined and incorporated into the SDLC. A security policy is the instrument that can provide this needed enforceability. Without security policies, one can reasonably argue that there are no teeth in the secure software initiatives that a passionate CSSLP or security professional would like to have in place. Those who are or who have been responsible for incorporating security controls and activities within the SDLC know that a security program often initially faces resistance. You can probably empathize being challenged by those who are resistant, and who ask questions such as, "Why must I now take security more seriously as we have never done this before?" or "Can you show me where it mandates that I must do what you are asking me to do?" Security policies give authority to the security professional or security activity.

It is therefore imperative that security policies providing authority to enforce security controls in software are developed and implemented in case your organization does not already have them. However, the development of security policies is more than a mere act of jotting a few "Thou shall" or "Thou shall not" rules in paper. For security policies to be effectively developed and enforceable requires the support of executive management (top-level support). Without the support of executive management, even if security policies are successfully developed, their implementation will probably fail. The makeup of top-level support must include support from signature authorities from various teams and not just the security team. Including ancillary and related teams (such as legal, privacy, networking, development, etc.) in the development of the security policies has the added benefit of buy in and ease of adoption from the teams that need to comply with the security policy when implemented.

In addition to top-level support and inclusion of various teams in the development of a security policy, successful implementation of the security policy also requires marketing efforts that communicate the goals of management through the policy to end users. End users must be educated to determine security requirements (controls) that the security policy mandates, and those requirements must be factored into the software that is being designed and developed.

1.9.3 Security Policy Development Process

Security policy development is not a onetime activity. It must be an evergreen activity, i.e., security policies must be periodically evaluated so that they are contextually correct and relevant to address current-day threats. An example of a security policy that is not contextually correct is a regulatory imposed or adopted policy that mandates multifactor authentication in your software for all financial transactions, but your organization is not already set up to have the infrastructure such as token readers or biometric devices to support multifactor authentication. An example of a security policy that is not relevant is one in which the policy requires you to use obsolete and insecure cryptographic technology such as the DES for data protection. DES has been proven to be easily broken with modern technology, although it may have been the de facto standard when the policy was developed. With the standardization of the AES, DES is now deemed to be an obsolete technology. Policies that have explicitly mandated DES are no longer relevant, and so they must be reviewed and revised. Contextually incorrect, obsolete, and insecure requirements in policies are often flagged as noncompliant issues during an audit. This problem can be avoided by periodic review and revisions of the security policies in effect. Keeping the security policies high level and independent of technology alleviates the need for frequent revisions.

It is also important to monitor the effectiveness of security policies and address issues that are identified as part of the lessons learned.

1.10 Security Standards

High-level security policies are supported by more detailed security standards. Standards support policies in that adoption of security policies are made possible owing to more granular and specific standards. Like security policies, organizational standards are considered to be mandatory elements of a security program and must be followed throughout the enterprise unless a waiver is specifically granted for a particular function.

1.10.1 Types of Security Standards

As Figure 1.9 depicts, security standards can be broadly categorized into Internal or External standards.

Internal standards are usually specific. The coding standard is an example of an internal software security standard. External standards can be further classified based on the issuer and recognition. Depending on who has issued the standard, external security standards can be classified into industry standards or government standards. An example of an industry issued standard is the PCI DSS. Examples of government issued standards include those generated by the NIST. Not all standards are geographically recognized and enforceable in all regions uniformly. Depending

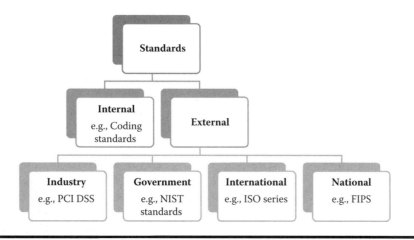

Figure 1.9   Categorization of security standards.

on the extent of recognition, external security standards (Weise, 2009) can be classified into national and international security standards. Although national security standards are often more focused and inclusive of local customs and practices, international standards are usually more comprehensive and generic in nature spanning various standards with the goal of interoperability. The most prevalent example of internationally recognized standards is ISO, whereas examples of nationally recognized standards are the Federal Information Processing Standards (FIPS) and those by the American National Standards Institute (ANSI), in the United States. It is also noteworthy to recognize that with globalization impacting the modicum of operations in the global landscape, most organizations lean more toward the adoption of international standards over national ones.

It is important to recognize that unlike standards that are mandatory, guidelines are not. External standards generally provide guidelines to organizations, but organizations tend to designate them as the organization's standard, which make them mandatory.

It must be understood that within the scope of this book, a complete and thorough exposition of each standard related to software security would not be possible. As a CSSLP, it is important that you are not only familiar with the standards covered here but also other standards that apply to your organization. In the next section, we will be covering the following internal and external standards pertinent to security professionals as it applies to software:

- Coding standards
- PCI DSS
- NIST standards
- ISO standards
- Federal Information Processing standards

1.10.1.1 Coding Standards

One of the most important internal standards that has a tremendous impact on the security of software is the coding standard. The coding standard specifies the requirements that are allowed and that need to be adopted by the development organization or team while writing code (building software). Coding standards need not be developed for each programming language or syntax but can include various languages into one. Organizations that do not have a coding standard must plan to have one created and adopted.

The coding standard not only brings with it many security advantages but provides for nonsecurity related benefits as well. Consistency in style, improved code readability, and maintainability are some of the nonsecurity related benefits one gets when they follow a coding standard. Consistency in style can be achieved by ensuring that all development team members follow the prescribed naming conventions, overloaded operations syntax, or instrumentation, etc., explicitly specified in the coding standard. Instrumentation is the inline commenting of code that is used to describe the operations undertaken by a code section. Instrumentation also considerably increases code readability. One of the biggest benefits of following a coding standard is maintainability of code, especially in a situation when there is a high rate of employee turnover. When the developer who has been working on your critical software products leaves the organization, the inheriting team or team member will have a reduced learning time, if the developer who left had followed the prescribed coding standard.

Following the coding standard has security advantages as well. Software designed and developed to the coding standard is less prone to error and exposure to threats, especially if the coding standard has taken into account and incorporated in it, security aspects when writing secure code. For example, if the coding standard specifies that all exceptions must be explicitly handled with a laconic error message, then the likelihood of information disclosure is considerably reduced. Also, if the coding standard specifics that each try-catch block must include a finally block as well, where objects instantiated are disposed, then upon following this requirement, the chances of dangling pointers and objects in memory are reduced, thereby addressing not only security concerns but performance as well.

1.10.1.2 Payment Card Industry Data Security Standards

With the prevalence of e-commerce and Web computing in this day and age, it is highly unlikely that those who are engaged with business that transmits and processes payment card information have not already been inundated with the PCI requirements, more particularly the PCI DSS. Originally developed by American Express, Discover Financial Services, JCB International, MasterCard Worldwide, and Visa, Inc. International, the PCI is a set of comprehensive requirements aimed at increasing payment account data security. It is regarded as a multifaceted security standard because it includes requirements not only for the technological elements of computing such as network architecture and software design but also for security management, policies, procedures, and other critical protective measures.

The goal of the PCI DSS is to facilitate organization's efforts to proactively protect card holder payment account data. It comprises 12 foundational requirements that are mapped into six sections or control objectives as Figure 1.10 illustrates.

If your organization has the need to transmit, process, or store the PAN, then PCI DSS requirements are applicable. Certain card holder data elements such as the sensitive authentication data comprised of the full magnetic strip, the security code, and the PIN block are disallowed from being stored after authorization even if it is cryptographically protected. Although all of the requirements have a bearing on software security, the requirement that is directly and explicitly related to software security is Requirement 6, which is the requirement to develop and maintain

Build and Maintain a Secure Network	
Requirement 1:	Install and maintain a firewall configuration to protect cardholder data
Requirement 2:	Do not use vendor-supplied defaults for system passwords and other security parameters
Protect Cardholder Data	
Requirement 3:	Protect stored cardholder data
Requirement 4:	Encrypt transmission of cardholder data across open, public networks
Maintain a Vulnerability Management Program	
Requirement 5:	Use and regularly update antivirus software
Requirement 6:	Develop and maintain secure systems and applications
Implement Strong Access Control Measures	
Requirement 7:	Restrict access to cardholder data by business need-to-know
Requirement 8:	Assign a unique ID to each person with computer access
Requirement 9:	Restrict physical access to cardholder data
Regularly Monitor and Test Networks	
Requirement 10:	Track and monitor all access to network resources and cardholder data
Requirement 11:	Regularly test security systems and processes
Maintain an Information Security Policy	
Requirement 12:	Maintain a policy that addresses information security

Figure 1.10   PCI DSS control objectives to requirements mapping.

secure systems and applications. Each of these requirements is further broken down into subrequirements, and it is recommended that you become familiar with each of the 12 foundational PCI DSS requirements if your organization is involved in the processing of credit card transactions. It is important to highlight Requirement 6 and its subrequirements (6.1 to 6.6) because they are directly related to software development. Table 1.1 tabulates PCI DSS Requirement 6 subrequirements one level deep.

1.10.1.3 NIST Standards

Founded in the start of the industrial revolution in 1901 by the Congress with a goal to prevent trade disputes and encourage standardization, the NIST develops technologies, measurement methods, and standards to aid U.S. companies in the

Table 1.1   PCI DSS Requirement 6 and Its Subrequirements

No.	Requirement
6	Develop and maintain secure systems and applications.
6.1	Ensure that all system components and software have the latest vendor-supplied security patches installed. Install critical security patches within 1 month of release.
6.2	Establish a process to identify newly discovered security vulnerabilities (e.g., alert subscriptions) and update configuration standards to address new vulnerability issues.
6.3	Develop software applications in accordance with industry best practices (e.g., input validation, secure error handling, secure authentication, secure cryptography, secure communications, logging, etc.), and incorporate information security throughout the software development life cycle.
6.4	Follow change control procedures for all changes to system components.
6.5	Develop all Web applications based on secure coding guidelines (such as OWASP) to cover common coding vulnerabilities in software development.
6.6	For public-facing Web applications, address new threats and vulnerabilities on an ongoing basis and ensure these applications are protected against known attacks by either reviewing these applications annually or upon change, using manual or automated security assessment tools or methods, or by installing a Web application firewall in front of the public-facing Web application.

global marketscape. Although NIST is specific to the United States, in outsourced situations, the company to which software development is outsourced may be required to comply with these standards. This is often contractually enforced.

NIST programs assist in improving the quality and capabilities of software used by business, research institutions, and consumers. They help secure electronic data and maintain availability of critical electronic services by identifying vulnerabilities and cost-effective security measures.

One of the core competencies of NIST is the development and use of standards. They have the statutory responsibility to set security standards and guidelines for sensitive federal systems, but these standards are selectively adopted and used by the private sector on a voluntary basis as well. The computer security division information technology laboratory (ITL) periodically publishes bulletins and the *Special Publications (SP) 500* and *800* series. While the SP 500 series are more generic IT-related publications, the SP 800 series was established in order to organize information technology security publications separately. NIST also includes computer security-related FIPS. Many of these publications are of interest to a security professional within the context of software security. One SP that is noteworthy is the *SP 800-64* publication, which discusses security considerations in the information systems development life cycle.

This section will introduce the various SP 800 series publications that have considerable implications for software security.

1.10.1.3.1 SP 800-12: An Introduction to Computer Security: The NIST Handbook

This handbook provides a broad overview of computer security, providing guidance to secure hardware, software, and information resources. It explains computer security-related concepts, cost considerations, and interrelationships of security controls. Security controls are categorized into management controls, operational controls, and technology controls. A section within the handbook is dedicated to security and planning in the computer systems life cycle. Figure 1.11 illustrates the breadth of security concepts and controls covered in the NIST *Special Publication 800-12* handbook. The handbook does not specify requirements explicitly but rather discusses the benefits of different security controls and the scenarios in which they would be appropriately applicable. It provides advice and guidance without stipulating any penalties for noncompliance.

1.10.1.3.2 SP 800-14: Generally Accepted Principles and Practices for Securing IT Systems

Similar to the SP 800-12 handbook in its organization, the SP 800-14 document provides a baseline that organizations can use to establish and review their IT security programs. Unlike SP 800-12, this document gives insight into the basic

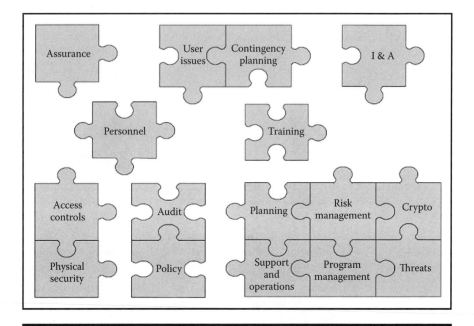

Figure 1.11 NIST SP 800-12 security concepts and controls.

security requirements that most IT systems should contain, to various stakeholders, including management, internal auditors, users, system developers, and security practitioners. It provides a foundation that can be used as a point of reference. The foundation starts with generally accepted system security principles and moves on to identify common practices that are used for securing IT systems.

1.10.1.3.3 SP 800-30: Risk Management Guide for IT

As mentioned earlier, one of the key aspects of security management is risk management, which plays a critical role in protecting an organization's information assets and its mission from IT-related risks. The SP 800-30 guide starts with an overview of risk management and covers items that are deemed critical success factors for an effective risk management program. The guide also covers how risk management can be integrated into the systems development life cycle along with the roles of individuals and their responsibilities in the process. It describes a comprehensive risk assessment methodology that includes nine primary steps for conducting a risk assessment of an IT system. It also covers control categories, cost–benefit analysis, residual risk evaluation, and the mitigation options and steps that need to be taken upon the completion of a risk assessment process. As an example, Figure 1.12 illustrates the risk mitigation action points that are part of the *NIST Special Publication 800-30* guide.

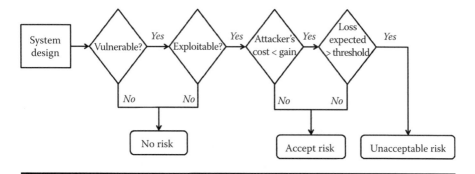

Figure 1.12 Risk management action points.

1.10.1.3.4 SP 800-64: Security Considerations in the Information Systems Development Life Cycle

Currently in second revision, the SP 800-64 is NIST's more directly related publication for a CSSLP because it provides guidance for building security into the IT systems (or software) development life cycle (SDLC) from the inception of the system or software. It serves a wide range of audiences of information systems and information security professionals ranging from system owners, information owners, developers, and program managers. Building security in as opposed to bolting it on at a later stage enables organizations to maximize their ROSI by:

■ Identifying and mitigating security vulnerabilities and misconfigurations early in the SDLC where the cost to implement security controls is considerably lower.
■ Bringing to light any engineering or design issues that may require redesign at a later stage of the SDLC, if security has not been considered early but is now required.
■ Identifying shared security services that can be leveraged, reducing development cost and time.
■ Comprehensively managing risk and facilitating executives to make informed risk related go/no-go and risk handling (accept, transfer, mitigate, or avoid) decisions.

In addition to describing security integration into a linear, sequential, and structured development methodology, such as the waterfall software development methodology, this document also provides insight into IT projects that are not as clearly defined. This includes SDLC-based development, such as supply chain, cross IT platforms (or in some cases, organization), virtualization, IT facility-oriented (data center, hot sites) developments, and the burgeoning service-oriented architectures (SOA). The core elements of integrating security into the SDLC for non-

SDLC–based development projects remain the same, but it must be recognized that key success factors for such projects are communications and documentation of stakeholder relationships apropos to securing the solution.

1.10.1.3.5 SP 800-100: Information Security Handbook: A Guide for Managers

While the SP 800-100 is a must read for management professionals who are responsible for establishing and implementing an information security program, it can also benefit nonmanagement personnel as it provides guidance from a management perspective for developers, architects, HR, operational, and acquisition personnel as well. It covers a wide range of information security program elements, providing guidance on information security governance, risk management, capital planning, and investment control, security planning, IT contingency planning, interconnecting systems, performance measures, incident response, configuration management, certification and accreditation, acquisitions, awareness and training, and even security in the SDLC. It is recommended that as a CSSLP, you are familiar with the contents of this guide.

1.10.1.4 ISO Standards

The ISO is the primary body that develops International Standards for all industry sectors except electrotechnology and telecommunications. Electrotechnology standards are developed by the International Electrotechnical Commission (IEC) and telecommunication standards are developed by the International Telecommunications Union (ITU), which is the same organization that establishes X.509 digital certificate versions. ISO in conjunction with IEC (prefixed as ISO/IEC) has developed several international standards that are directly related to information security. Unlike many other standards that are broad in their guidance, most ISO standards are highly specific. To ensure that the standards are aligned to changes in technology, periodic review of each standard after its publication (at least every 5 years) is part of the ISO standards development process.

The ISO standards related to information security and software engineering are covered in this section at a definitional and introductory level. It is highly recommended that as a CSSLP, you are not only familiar with these standards but also how they are applicable within your organization.

1.10.1.4.1 ISO/IEC 27000:2009—Information Security Management System (ISMS) Overview and Vocabulary

This standard aims to provide a common glossary of terms and definitions. It also provides an overview and introduction to the ISMS family of standards covering

- Requirements definition for an ISMS
- Detailed guidance to interpret the plan–do–check–act (PDCA) processes
- Sector-specific guidelines and conformity assessments for ISMS

1.10.1.4.2 ISO/IEC 27001:2005 — Information Security Management Systems

What the ISO 9001:2000 standards do for quality, the ISO 27001:2005 standard will do for information security. This standard is appropriate for all types of organizations ranging from commercial companies to not-for-profit organizations and the government.

ISO/IEC 27001:2005 specifies the requirements for establishing, implementing, operating, monitoring, reviewing, maintaining, and improving a documented ISMS. It can be used to aid in

- Formulating security requirements
- Ensuring compliance with external legal, regulatory, and compliance requirements and with internal policies, directives, and standards
- Managing security risks cost effectively
- Generating and selecting security controls requirements that will adequately address security risks
- Identifying existing ISMS processes and defining new ones
- Determining the status of the information security management program
- Communicating organizational information security policies, standards, and procedures to other partner organizations and relevant security information to their customers
- Enabling the business instead of impeding it

1.10.1.4.3 ISO/IEC 27002:2005/Cor1:2007 — Code of Practice for Information Security Management

This ISO/IEC 27002 is the replacement for the ISO 17799 standard, which was formerly known as BS 7799. Arguably, this is the most well-known security standard and is intended to provide a common basis and practical guidelines for developing organizational security standards and effective security management practices. This standard establishes guidelines and general principles for initiating, implementing, maintaining, and improving information security management in an organization. It outlines several best practices of control objectives and controls in diverse areas of information security management, ranging from security policy, information security organization, asset management, HR, physical and environmental security, access control, communications and operations management, business continuity management, incident management, compliance, and even information systems acquisition, development, and maintenance.

The control objectives and controls in this standard are intended to address the findings from the risk assessment. Cor. denotes a Technical corrigendum, which is a document issued to correct a technical error or ambiguity in a normative document or to correct information that has been outdated, provided the modification has no effect on the technical normative elements of the standard it corrects.

1.10.1.4.4 ISO/IEC FCD 27003—Information Security Management Systems Implementation Guidance

This standard is still under development and aims at providing guidance in implementing an ISMS focusing on the PDCA method, with respect to establishing, implementing, reviewing, and improving the ISMS itself.

1.10.1.4.5 ISO/IEC 27005:2008—Information Security Risk Management

It should be no surprise that a CSSLP must be familiar with the ISO/IEC 27005 standard as it is the International Standard for information security risk management. The basic principle of risk management is to ensure that organizational risk is reduced to acceptable thresholds and that the residual risk is at or preferably below that threshold. This standard provides the necessary guidance for information security risk management and is designed to assist the implementation of security control to a satisfactory level based on establishing the scope or context for risk assessment, assessing the risks, making risk-based decisions to treat the identified risks, and communicating and monitoring risk. The ISO/IEC 30001 standard is currently under development and is expected to be the likely replacement for or enhancement to the ISO/IEC 27005:2008 international information security risk management standard.

1.10.1.4.6 ISO/IEC 27006:2007—Requirements for Bodies Providing Audit and Certification of Information Security Management Systems

This primary goal of this standard is to support accreditation and certification bodies that audit and certify information security management systems. It includes the competency and reliability requirements that an auditing and certifying body must demonstrate and also provides guidance on how to interpret the requirements it contains to ensure reliable and consistent certification of Information Security Management Systems.

In addition to the several 27000 series of ISO/IEC standards that provide a blueprint for an ISMS, there are other ISO/IEC standards that have a noteworthy relationship to information security and software security, which are extremely important for a CSSLP to be familiar with. Two of these standards, the ISO/IEC 15408 and the ISO/IEC 9126, are covered in this section.

1.10.1.4.7 ISO/IEC 15408 — Evaluating Criteria for IT Security (Common Criteria)

The ISO/IEC 15408 is more commonly known as the Common Criteria and is a series of internationally recognized set of guidelines that define a common framework for evaluating security features and capabilities of IT security products. The Common Criteria allow vendors to have their products evaluated by an independent third party against the predefined evaluation assurance levels (EALs) clearly defined in the standard. It provides confidence to the owners that the security products they are developing or procuring meet and implement the minimum security functionality and assurance specifications and that the evaluation of the product itself has been conducted in a rigorous, neutral, objective, and standard manner. The Common Criteria can also be used by auditors to evaluate security functionality and assurance levels and to ensure that all organizational security policies are enforced, all threats are countered to acceptable levels, and that the security objectives are achieved.

It is a standard with multiple parts as listed here.

■ ISO/IEC 15408-1:2005 or Part 1 introduces the common criteria providing the evaluation criteria for IT security as it pertains to security functional requirements (SFRs) and security assurance requirements (SARs). It introduces the general model that covers the Protection Profile (PP), the Security Target (ST), and the Target of Evaluation (TOE), and the relationships between these elements of the Common Criteria evaluation process as depicted in Figure 1.13. The PP is used to create a set of generalized security requirements that are reusable. The ST expresses the security requirements and specifies the security functions for a particular product or system that is being evaluation. The ST is what is used by evaluators as the basis of their evaluations in conformance to the guidelines specified in the ISO/IEC 15408 standard. The product or system that is being evaluated is known as the TOE.
■ ISO/IEC 15408-2:2008 or Part 2 contains the comprehensive catalog of predefined SFRs that needs to be part of the security evaluation against the TOE. These requirements are hierarchically organized using a structure of classes, families, and components.
■ ISO/IEC 15408-3:2008 or Part 3 defines the SARs and includes the EALs for measuring assurance of a TOE. There are seven EAL ratings predefined in Part 3 of the ISO/IEC 15408 standards, and a security product with a higher EAL rating is indicative of a greater degree of security assurance for that product against comparable products with a lower EAL rating. Table 1.2 tabulates the seven EAL ratings and reflects what each EAL rating mean.

The predefined SFRs and SARs defined in the ISO/IEC 15408 standard can be used to address vulnerabilities that arise from failures in requirements, development, and/or in operations. Software that does not include security functional or

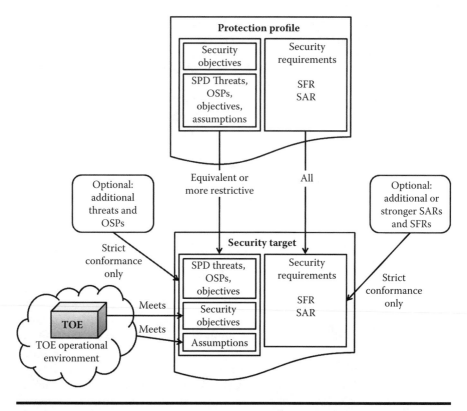

Figure 1.13   Relationships between common criteria elements.

assurance requirements can be rendered ineffective and insecure even if it meets all business functionality. Without security functional and assurance validation, poor development methodologies and incorrect design can also lead to vulnerabilities that can easily compromise not just the assurance of confidentiality, integrity, and availability of the software or the information it handles but also the business value it provides. Additionally, without an active evaluation of the security functionality and assurance, any software designed and developed to correct specifications may still be installed and deployed in a vulnerable state (e.g., admin privileges, unprotected audit logs, etc.) and thereby render operations insecure.

1.10.1.4.8 ISO/IEC 21827:2008—System Security Engineering Capability Maturity Model® (SSE-CMM)

The System Security Engineering Capability Maturity Model® (SSE-CMM) internationally recognized standard provides guidelines to ensure secure engineering of systems (and software) by augmenting existing project and organizational process

Table 1.2   ISO/IEC 15408 Evaluation Assurance Levels

Evaluation Assurance Level	TOE Assurance
EAL1	Functionally tested
EAL2	Structurally tested
EAL3	Methodically tested and checked
EAL4	Methodically designed, tested, and reviewed
EAL5	Semiformally designed and tested
EAL6	Semiformally verified design and tested
EAL7	Formally verified design and tested

areas and encompassing all phases in the SDLC in its scope from concepts definition, requirement analysis, design, development, testing, deployment, operations,
maintenance, and disposal. It also includes guidance on best practices for interactions with other organizations, acquisitions, and certification and accreditation
(C&A). This model is now the de facto standard metric for evaluating security
engineering practices for the organization or the customer and for establishing confidence in organizational processes to assure security. It has close affinity to other
CMMs that focus on other engineering disciplines and is often used in conjunction
with them.

1.10.1.4.9 ISO/IEC 9216—Software Engineering Product Quality

In addition to the ISO 9000 series of standards for quality, the ISO/IEC also publishes the ISO/IEC 9126 standard that provides the guidelines for quality of software products. Like the ISO/IEC 15408, this is a multipart standard. It currently
has four parts to it that cover the quality model, external and internal metrics, and
the quality in use metric, which are used to measure the quality of the software
product that is engineered. Internal metrics are those that measure the quality of
the software itself while external metrics measure software quality as part of measuring the overall behavior of the computer-based system that includes the software.
This standard provides the definition and associated quality evaluation process to
be used when specifying the requirements for software products throughout the
SDLC. It provides guidance on six external quality characteristics that can be used
to measure the quality of software. These six characteristics are functionality, reliability, usability, efficiency, maintainability, and portability. Quality of use metrics
are those that measure the quality of software when it is being used in a specific
context. Uniquely, this standard also takes into consideration the measurement
of software quality from the perspective of managers, developers, end users, and

evaluators. The guidance to evaluate software product quality that the ISO/IEC 9126 standard provides includes how to define the software quality requirements and how to prepare for and conduct the evaluation.

As a security professional, it is important to understand that not all quality software may be secure, and by leveraging the guidance established in this standard, which prescribes measuring software quality from different perspectives, one of which is an evaluator, a security professional can evaluate software quality from a security perspective.

1.10.1.5 Federal Information Processing Standards (FIPS)

In addition to the various Special Publications NIST produces, they also develop the FIPS. FIPS publications are developed to address federal requirements for

- Interoperability of disparate systems
- Portability of data and software
- Computer security

Some of the well-known FIPS publications closely related to software security are

- *FIPS 140-2: Security Requirement for Cryptographic Modules*
- *FIPS 197: Advanced Encryption Standard*
- *FIPS 201: Personal Identity Verification (PIV) of Federal Employees and Contractors*

This section covers these FIPS publications at an introductory level.

1.10.1.5.1 FIPS 140-2: Security Requirement for Cryptographic Modules

The FIPS 140-2 is the standard that specifies requirements that will need to be satisfied by a cryptographic module. It provides four increasing qualitative levels (Level 1 through Level 4) intended to cover a wide range of potential application and environments. The security requirements cover areas that are related to secure design and implementation of a cryptographic module, which include cryptographic module specification, ports and interfaces, roles, services, and authentication, finite state model, physical security, operational environment, cryptographic key management, electromagnetic interference/electromagnetic compatibility (EMI/EMC), self-tests, and design assurance. Additionally, this standard also specifies that cryptographic module developers and vendors are required to document implemented controls to mitigate other (noncryptographic) attacks (e.g., differential power analysis and TEMPEST).

1.10.1.5.2 FIPS 197: Advanced Encryption Standards (AES)

FIPS 197 specifies an approved cryptographic algorithm to ensure the confidentiality of electronic data. The AES algorithm is a symmetric block cipher that can be used to encrypt (convert humanly intelligible plaintext to unintelligible form called cipher text) and decrypt (convert cipher text to plaintext). This standard replaced the withdrawn FIPS 46-3 Data Encryption Standard that prescribed the need to use one of the two algorithms, DES or Triple Data Encryption Algorithm (TDEA), for data protection, because the AES algorithm was faster and stronger in its protection of data over the DES algorithm.

1.10.1.5.3 FIPS 201: Personal Identity Verification (PIV) of Federal Employees and Contractors

The FIPS 201 standard was developed in response to the need to ensure that the claimed identity of personnel (employees and contractors) who require physical or electronic access to secure and sensitive facilities and data are appropriately verified. This standard specifies the architecture and technical requirements for a common identification standard for federal employees and contractors.

1.10.2 Benefits of Security Standards

Security standards provide a common and consistent basis for building and maintaining secure software as they enable operational efficiency and organizational agility. For example, assume that all the software developed in your organization was developed using the then standard for cryptographic functionality DES and now your organization requires all of your software to use AES. In such a scenario, the effort to switch over can be consistently and efficiently addressed across various software teams in your organization, because there are no proprietary or nonstandard software that requires specialized attention. Security standards lower the total cost of ownership (TCO) by facilitating ease of adoption and maintenance and by increasing operational efficiency and organizational agility when changes to standards are needed.

Security standards are useful to provide interoperability as well. Today, we live in a world that is highly interconnected, despite the fact that not all players in the global marketscape use the same technology and communication protocols. Interoperability gives vendor independence and allows for these heterogeneous and disparate systems to communicate with each other using a common protocol. Such communication needs to be secure as well, and security standards such as WS-security, secure electronic transmission (SET) are good examples of standards that not only allow for interoperability but also security. WS-security is the secure communication protocol of Web services.

Security standards can also be leveraged to provide your company with a competitive advantage, in addition to providing some degree of liability protection.

It is not uncommon to observe that customers are more comfortable purchasing products and services from Web sites that publicize that they are compliant to the PCI DSS requirements than from those that do not. Organizations that choose to knowingly ignore such security standards can be held liable and accountable in a court of law.

Security standards provide a common baseline for assessments. Most standards complement best practices and adopt such a standard. Following this standard can facilitate formal evaluation and certification of the software product itself. The ISO 15408 standard provides common criteria (and hence this standard is also known as the Common Criteria) that can be used to evaluate a vendor product from not only a functionality perspective but also an assurance perspective. When evaluating software from several external third party vendors, it is therefore important to request the common criteria rating of their product, which will give an indication of the assurance (security) and reliability (functionality) of that product.

Security standards can be used to demonstrate indirect governance as well, because they contain security control objectives that when satisfied often address compliance and regulatory requirements. ISO/IEC 27001 certified ISMS demonstrates that your system is compliant with many of the information security requirements as mandated by state, national, and international regulations such as the California SB1386, Federal Information Security Management Act (FISMA), GLBA, HIPAA, EU Safe Harbor, and PIPEDA.

1.11 Best Practices

In addition to standards, there are several best practices for information security that are important for a security professional to be aware of. Some of these best practices have become de facto standards, and for all practical purposes, one can consider them to be standard in their implementation. Some of the popular best practices that have a direct bearing on software security are the Open Web Application Security Project (OWASP) and the Information Technology Infrastructure Library (ITIL).

1.11.1 Open Web Application Security Project (OWASP)

The OWASP is a worldwide free and open community that is focused on application security and predominantly Web application security. It can be considered the leading best practice for Web application security. All of OWASP undertakings are community focused and vendor neutral.

The projects undertaken aim at improving the current state of Web application security and the work and results are openly and freely available to anyone. OWASP projects can be broadly categorized as development or documentation projects. The development projects aim at providing the security community with free tools and the documentation projects help in generating practical guidance on various aspects of application security in the form of publications and guides.

One of the most popular publications within OWASP is the OWASP Top 10, which periodically publishes the Top 10 Web application security vulnerabilities as depicted in Figure 1.14 and their appropriate protection mechanisms. There have been two OWASP Top 10 publications so far, with the first one published in 2004 and superseded by the second one published in 2007. The current version of the PCI DSS (version 1.2.1) requires Web applications to be developed using secure coding guidelines to prevent common coding vulnerabilities in the SDLC and refers to the OWASP as a Web application secure coding guideline. Vulnerabilities that are part of the Top 10 and their remediation measures will be covered in depth in Chapters 4 and 5.

Some of the most popular guides developed in the OWASP are the

- Development Guide
- Code Review Guide
- Testing Guide

1.11.1.1 OWASP Development Guide

This is a comprehensive manual for designing, developing, and deploying secure Web applications and Web services. The target audiences for this guide are architects, developers, consultants, and auditors. This guide covers the various security controls that software developers should build into the software they design and develop.

Figure 1.14   OWASP Top 10.

1.11.1.2 OWASP Code Review Guide

This is a comprehensive manual for understanding how to detect Web application vulnerabilities in the code and what safeguards can be taken to address them. The guide calls out that for a successful code review process, the reviewer must be familiar with the following:

■ Programming language (code)
■ Working knowledge of the software (context)
■ End users (audience)
■ Impact of the availability of the software to the business or its lack thereof (importance)

Conducting code reviews to verify application security is much more cost-effective than having to test the software for security vulnerabilities.

1.11.1.3 OWASP Testing Guide

The Testing Guide is a comprehensive manual that covers the necessary procedures and tools to validate software assurance. This Testing Guide can also be used as part of a comprehensive application security verification. The target audiences for this guide are software developers, software testers, and security specialists.

1.11.1.4 Other OWASP Projects

OWASP is currently actively working on several other useful Web application security projects, some of which are worth mentioning here: the Application Security Desk Reference (ASDR), the Enterprise Security Application Programming Interface (ESAPI), and the Software Assurance Maturity Model (SAMM). More information about each of these projects can be obtained from the OWASP Web site.

It is highly recommended that you are familiar with these guides to be an effective secure software professional.

1.12 Information Technology Infrastructure Library (ITIL)

Although the ITIL has been around for nearly two decades, it is now gaining acceptance and popularity and is considered to be the de facto standard for service management. It was developed by the Central Computer and Telecommunication Agency in the United Kingdom. For an IT organization to be effective, it must be able to deliver to the business the expected level of service, even when operating within the constraints of scope, schedule, and budget. Delivering business value by meeting the business SLA is enhanced when the IT organization adopts a framework that includes best practices and standards on service management. The ITIL is a cohesive best practice framework that was originally developed in alignment with the then UK standard for IT Service Management (BS 15000), which is now ISO/IEC 20000, the first international standard for IT Service Management. ITIL today is in its third version (commonly known as ITIL V3) and considers the life cycle of a service from initial planning, alignment to business need to final retirement, unlike its previous versions, which were process focused. ITIL V3 was revised to be aligned with industry best practices and standards and aptly covers existing information security standards, such as those in the ISO 27000 series. Although security management is no longer a separate publication in the current version, it must still be recognized that the security framework guidance in ITIL aligns very closely to information security standards, and this can be leveraged to provide information security services to the business. As a CSSLP, it is recommended that you are familiar with ITIL and its relationship to security, especially security in the SDLC.

1.13 Security Methodologies

There are several security methodologies that aid in the design, development, testing, and deployment of secure software. These range from simple methodologies to those more robust and comprehensive that can be used at different stages of the SDLC. In this section we will discuss the most popular security methodologies and how they can be leveraged to build secure software.

1.13.1 Socratic Methodology

The Socratic methodology is a useful technique for addressing issues that arise from individuals who have opposing views on the need for security in the software they build. It is a form of cross-examination and is also known as the Method of Elenchus (Elenchus in ancient Greek means cross-examination) whose goal is to instigate ideas and stimulate rational thought. The way it works is that the one with the opposing viewpoint is questioned on their rationale for their position, often with a negative form of their question itself. The Socratic methodology in layman's terms can be referred to as the "Questioning the Questioner" methodology wherein the questioner is questioned on their viewpoint, often using their own question. For example, if someone were to challenge the need for encryption as a disclosure protection mechanism and asks you, "Why is it that I must ensure that data is protected against disclosure threats?", instead of giving them reasons such as "the security policy mandates it" or "the consequence of disclosure can be disastrous" or even that "it is the right thing to do for our customers," the Socratic method suggests that you revert the question back to the questioner in a negative form, which means, you question in return "Why is it that you must *not* ensure that data are protected against disclosure threats?" In addition to curtailing opposition to the incorporation of security in software, the Socratic methodology can also be used to analyze complex concepts and determine security requirements by asking questions that instigate ideas and stimulate rational thought.

1.13.2 Operationally Critical Threat, Asset, and Vulnerability Evaluation (OCTAVE®)

The Carnegie Mellon Software Engineering Institute (SEI) in conjunction with the US-CERT codeveloped OCTAVE, which is a risk-based information security strategic assessment methodology. OCTAVE is an acronym for Operationally Critical Threat, Asset, and Vulnerability Evaluation, and it includes a suite of tools, techniques, and methods.

OCTAVE provides insight into the organizational risk and the state of security and resiliency within the organization. It can be self-directed and supports cross-functional teams to assess organizational and technical risk and is available in three flavors: the original OCTAVE for any organization, OCTAVE-S for smaller organizations, and OCTAVE-Allegro, which is a streamlined approached for information security assessment and assurance.

OCTAVE is performed in three phases as depicted in Figure 1.15 and described in the following:

- Phase 1: Build asset-based threat profiles — In this phase, the risk analysis team determines information related items that are of value (*assets*) and important to the organization for continued business *operations*. The team then prioritizes those assets into *critical* assets and describes security requirements for each critical asset. In the next step, the team identifies potential *threats* that can be orchestrated against each critical asset, creating a threat profile for each asset. This evaluation is conducted to determine the risk at the organizational level.
- Phase 2: Identify infrastructure vulnerabilities — In this phase, the risk analysis team examines infrastructural components (such as network paths, ports, protocols) and their level of resistance against attacks with the intent to identify weaknesses (*vulnerabilities*). This evaluation is conducted to determine the technical risks.
- Phase 3: Develop security strategy and plans — In this phase, the risk analysis team makes plans to address threats to and mitigate vulnerabilities in critical assets that were identified in the first two phases.

A complete and in-depth description of OCTAVE is beyond the scope of this book. As a CSSLP, it is advisable to be familiar with this robust and comprehensive risk analysis and management methodology.

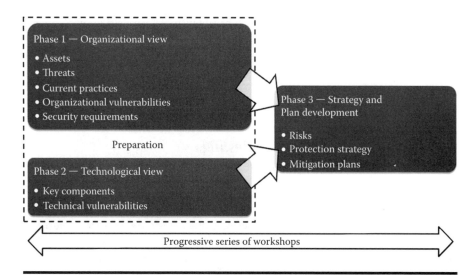

Figure 1.15 Operationally critical threats, assets, and vulnerability evaluation phases.

1.13.3 STRIDE and DREAD

STRIDE is a threat modeling methodology (Howard & LeBlanc, 2003) that is performed in the design phase of software development in which threats are grouped into the following six broad categories:

1. Spoofing: impersonating another user or process
2. Tampering: unauthorized alterations that impact integrity
3. Repudiation: cannot prove the action; deniability of claim
4. Information disclosure: exposure of information to unauthorized user or process that impacts confidentiality
5. Denial of service: service interruption that impacts availability
6. Elevation of privilege: unauthorized increase of user or process rights

DREAD is a risk calculation or rating methodology (Howard and LeBlanc, 2003) that is often used in conjunction with STRIDE but does not need to be. To overcome inconsistencies and qualitative risk ratings (such as high, medium, and low), the DREAD methodology aims to arrive at rating the identified (and categorized) threats by applying the following five dimensions:

1. Damage potential: What will be the impact upon exploitability?
2. Reproducibility: What is the ease of recreating the attack/exploit?
3. Exploitability: What minimum skill level is necessary to launch the attack/exploit?

4. Affected users: How many users will be potentially impacted upon a successful attack/exploit?
5. Discoverability: What is the ease of finding the vulnerability that yields the threat?

STRIDE and DREAD are covered in depth in Chapter 3.

1.13.4 Open Source Security Testing Methodology Manual (OSSTMM)

The Institute for Security and Open Methodologies (ISECOM) developed the *Open Source Security Testing Methodology Manual* (OSSTMM), which is a peer-reviewed testing methodology for conducting security tests and how to measure the results using applicable metrics. It is technically focused and broad in its evaluation covering three channels and five major sections as tabulated in Table 1.3.

The primary purpose of this manual is to provide a scientific methodology for the accurate characterization of security through examination and correlation of test results in a consistent and reliable way. Secondarily, it provides guidelines to auditors to perform an assurance audit to show that the tests themselves were thorough, complete, and compliant and the results of the test are quantifiable, reliable, consistent, and accurately representative of the tests. The output from an OSSTMM security audit is a report known as the Security Test Audit Report (STAR), which

Table 1.3 OSSTMM Channels and Sections

Channels	Sections	Tests
Communications	Data networks	Information and data controls
	Telecommunications	Computers and telecommunications networks
Physical	Human	Personnel security awareness levels
		Fraud and social engineering control levels
		Security processes
	Physical	Access controls
		Building and perimeter locations
Spectrum	Wireless	Wireless devices
		Mobile devices

includes the specific actions conducted in tests, the corresponding metrics, and the state of the strength of controls.

1.13.5 Flaw Hypothesis Method (FHM)

The Flaw Hypothesis Method (FHM) is as the name suggests a vulnerability prediction and analysis method that uses comprehensive penetration testing to test the strength of the security of the software. FHM is very useful in the area of software certification. By simulating attacks (penetration testing), weaknesses in design (flaws) and coding (bugs) can be uncovered in the current version of the software, but this can be used to determine security requirements for future versions of the software as well. There are four primary phases (stages) in the FHM as described in the following:

- Phase 1: Hypothesizing potential flaws in the software from documentation. This documentation can be internal documentation that describes the software context and working knowledge (behavior) of the software or it can be externally published vulnerability reports or lists. One major technique used in this phase of the FHM is the deviational method, in which deviations from known software behavior (misuse cases) is used to generate or hypothesize flaws.
- Phase 2: Confirmation of flaws by conducting actual simulation penetration tests and desk checking tests. Desk checking attests program logic by executing program statements using sample data. The flaws that are exploitable are marked as "confirmed" and those that are not are marked as "refuted."
- Phase 3: Generalization of confirmed flaws to uncover other possibilities of weaknesses in the software.
- Phase 4: Addressing the discovered flaws in the software to mitigate risk by either adding countermeasures in the current version or designing in safeguards for future versions.

One of the major drawbacks of the FHM is that it can help identify only known threats; nonetheless, this is a very powerful methodology to attest to the security strength of software that has already been deployed or is being developed.

1.13.6 Six Sigma (6σ)

Sigma in statistics is used to represent deviation from the norm. Although Six Sigma is a business management strategy for quality, it can be closely related to security because it is used for process improvement by measuring if a product (software) or service is near perfect in quality by eliminating defects. Defects are defined as deviations from specifications (requirements). Near perfect implies that the process is as close as possible to having zero defects.

For a process to be certified as having Six Sigma quality, it must have at the maximum 3.4 defects per million opportunities (DPMO) where an opportunity is defined as a chance for deviation (or nonconformance) to specifications. The key submethodologies by which Six Sigma quality can be achieved are:

- DMAIC (define, measure, analyze, improve, and control), which is used for incremental improvement of *existing* processes that are below Six Sigma quality.
- DMADV (define, measure, analyze, design, and verify), which is used to develop *new* processes for Six Sigma products and services. It can also be used for new versions of the product or service when the extent of changes is substantially greater than what incremental improvements can address.

The Six Sigma processes are usually executed by trained professionals who are certified as Six Sigma green belts or black belts.

It is important to note that although a software product may be of Six Sigma quality, it may still be insecure if the specifications do not include security requirements. This further accentuates the importance of ensuring that security requirements are determined and included in addition to functional specifications.

1.13.7 Capability Maturity Model Integration (CMMI)

Developed by the SEI and based on TQM, like Six Sigma, the Capability Maturity Model Integration (CMMI) is a process improvement methodology as well, which provides guidance for quality improvement and point of reference for appraising existing processes. Simply put, CMMI is a 1 to 5 rating scale that can be used to rate the maturity of the software development processes within one's organization.

Three areas in which CMMI can be used are development (products), delivery (services), and acquisition (products and services).

CMMI includes a collection of best practices that one can use to compare their organizational processes against. When this is done formally, it is referred to as an appraisal and the Standard CMMI Appraisal Method for Process Improvement (SCAMPI) incorporates some of the industry best practices for process improvements. The formal appraisals yield one of the five CMMI maturity levels that can be indicative of processes ranging from chaotic and ad hoc to highly optimized within your organization. The five CMMI maturity levels are:

- Initial (Level 1): Processes are ad hoc, poorly controlled, reactive, and highly unpredictable.
- Repeatable (Level 2): Also reactive in nature, the processes are grouped at the project level and are characterized as being repeatable and managed by basic project management tracking of cost and schedule.

- Defined (Level 3): Level 2 maturity level deals with processes at the project level, but in this level, the maturity of the organizational processes is established and improved continuously. Processes are characterized, well understood, and proactive in nature.
- Managed Quantitatively (Level 4): In this level, the premise for maturity is that what cannot be measured cannot be managed and so the processes are measured against appropriate metrics and controlled.
- Optimizing (Level 5): In this level, the focus is on continuous process improvements through innovative technologies and incremental improvements. Organizations with this level of software development process maturity have the ability to quickly and effectively adapt to changing business objectives, thereby allowing the organization to scale.

Incorporation of security into the SDLC is easier and more efficient if the organizations already have a higher level of process maturity.

1.14 Security Frameworks

Some of the most prominent security frameworks that are related with software security or associated areas are described in this section.

1.14.1 Zachman Framework

Although it is nearly three decades since the Zachman Framework was formulated by John Zachman, it is still regarded as a robust enterprise architecture framework. The goal of the framework is to align IT to the business. It is often depicted as a 6 × 6 matrix that factors in six reification transformations (strategist, owner, designer, builder, implementer, and workers) along the rows and six communication interrogatives (what, how, where, who, when, and why) as columns. The intersection of the six transformations and the six interrogatives yield the architectural elements. Using the same interrogative technique against the reification transformations from a security standpoint view can be useful in determining the security architecture that needs to be designed.

1.14.2 Control Objectives for Information and Related Technology (COBIT®)

Published by the IT Governance Institute (ITGI), the Control Objectives for Information and related Technology (COBIT®) is an IT governance framework with supporting tools that can be used to close gaps between control requirements, technical issues, and business risks. It defines the reasons for IT governance, the stakeholders, and what it needs to accomplish. It enables policy development and adds emphasis on regulatory compliance. The complete COBIT package includes the following six publications:

1. Executive Summary
2. Framework
3. Control Objectives
4. Audit Guidelines
5. Implementation Toolset
6. Management Guidelines

1.14.3 Committee of Sponsoring Organizations (COSO)

The Committee of Sponsoring Organizations (COSO) is a conglomeration of world-wide recognized frameworks that provides guidance on organizational governance, business ethics, internal controls, enterprise risk management, fraud, and financial reporting. COSO describes a unified approach for evaluation of internal control systems that have been designed to provide reasonable assurance. The Enterprise Risk Management (ERM) COSO framework that emphasizes the importance of identifying and managing risks across the enterprise is widely adopted and used.

1.14.4 Sherwood Applied Business Security Architecture (SABSA)

The Sherwood Applied Business Security Architecture (SABSA) is a framework for developing risk-based enterprise security architectures and for delivering security solutions that support business initiatives. It is based on the premise that security requirements are determined from the analysis of the business requirements. It is a layered model that covers the different phases of the IT life cycle from strategy, design, and implementation to operations. Each layer represents a view of a role played in the SDLC and the associated security architecture that can be derived from it as tabulated in Table 1.4. It is compliant with other acclaimed frameworks, standards, and methodologies such as COBIT, ISO 27000 series, and ITIL.

1.15 Regulations, Privacy, and Compliance

Until a few years ago, organizations that were under regulatory oversight for software security (more particularly data) breaches were an exception. This seems to be no longer the case as is evident from the chronology of data breaches report, published by the Privacy Rights Clearinghouse, which enlists to date 260 million or more records that have been breached as a result of software insecurity. Financial levies and cost of recovery have been so exorbitant in many cases that it caused disruptions up to total bankruptcy of organizations, not to mention the loss in

Table 1.4 SABSA Layers

View	Security Architecture Level
Business	Contextual
Architect	Conceptual
Designer	Logical
Builder	Physical
Tradesman	Component
Facilities manager	Operational

stakeholder trust. This has led to the plethora of regulations and privacy mandates that organizations need to comply with. The cost of noncompliance combined with the need to regain (in cases where it is lost) or retain (in cases where it is not yet lost) stakeholder trust have become driving factors for the organizations to include regulatory and privacy requirements as part of their governance programs that includes the need to incorporate security in the SDLC as an integral part of the process.

Regulations and privacy mandates exist primarily to provide a check-and-balance mechanism to earn stakeholder trust and prevent the disclosure of personal identifiable, health, or financial information (PII, PHI, and PFI). Regulatory and privacy requirements need to be determined during the requirements phase of the SDLC and control mechanisms to ensure that they are complied with must be factored into the software design, architecture, development, and deployment. It is imperative that software development team members work closely with the legal and/or privacy teams in your organization to obtain the list of applicable regulations for your organization.

Covering in detail each and every regulation and privacy requirement that is necessary to comply with is beyond the scope of this book. In this section, some of the significant regulations, acts, and privacy mandates are introduced. This is followed by the challenges they invoke and a brief description of how to ensure that privacy requirements are not ignored and privacy-related guidelines and concerns are addressed when dealing with building secure software. It is highly advisable that as a CSSLP, you are familiar with each of these significant regulations and acts as well as any other regulatory, privacy, and compliance requirements that your organization needs to be compliant with.

1.15.1 Significant Regulations and Acts

1.15.1.1 Sarbanes–Oxley (SOX) Act

The Sarbanes–Oxley Act, commonly referred to as SOX, is arguably the most significant of regulations that has a direct impact on security. Also known as the Public

Company Accounting Reform and Investor Protection Act, SOX was enacted in 2002 to improve quality and transparency in financial reporting and independent audits and accounting services for public companies. This came on the heels of major corporate and accounting frauds perpetrated by companies like Enron, Tyco International, and WorldCom and intended to increase corporate responsibility to its investors.

The SOX Act has 11 titles that mandate specific requirements for financial reporting and address:

1. Public Company Accounting Oversight Board
2. Auditor Independence
3. Corporate Responsibility
4. Enhanced Financial Disclosures
5. Analyst Conflicts of Interest
6. Commission Resources and Authority
7. Studies and Reports
8. Corporate and Criminal Fraud Accountability
9. White-Collar Crime Penalty Enhancements
10. Corporate Tax Returns
11. Corporate Fraud and Accountability

Two sections under the SOX Act that became prominent and in some cases contentious in the context of security controls and the Security Exchange Commission (SEC) directives that adopted rules to conform with the SOX Act were Section 302, which covers corporate responsibility for financial controls, and Section 404, which deals with management's assessment of internal controls. The strength of the controls is assessed, and an internal control report is generated that describes the adequacy and effectiveness of the disclosed controls.

1.15.1.2 BASEL II

BASEL II is the European Financial Regulatory Act that was originally developed to protect against financial operations risks and fraud. It was developed initially to be an international standard for banking regulators and provide recommendations on banking regulations and laws.

1.15.1.3 Gramm–Leach–Bliley Act (GLBA)

The Gramm–Leach–Bliley Act (GLB Act) is a financial privacy act that aims to protect consumers' personal financial information (PFI) contained in financial institutions. It is also known as the Financial Modernization Act of 1999, the GLB Act has the following three main parts to the privacy requirements:

1. Financial Privacy Rule governs the collection and disclosure of PFI. Inclusive in its scope are companies that are nonfinancial in nature as well.
2. Safeguards Rule applies only to financial institutions (banks, credit unions, securities firms, insurance companies, etc.) and mandates that these institutions design, implement, and maintain safeguards to protect customer information.
3. Pretexting Provisions of this Act provide protection to consumers from individuals and companies who falsely pretend (pretext) a need to obtain PFI.

All three rules are related to software that deals with the collection, processing, retention, and disposal of PFI.

1.15.1.4 Health Insurance Portability and Accountability Act (HIPAA)

This is another privacy rule but unlike the GLB Act that deals with PFI, the Health Insurance Portability and Accountability Act (HIPAA) deals with personal health information (PHI). Instituted by the Office of Civil Rights (OCR) in 1996, HIPAA protects the privacy of individual identifiable health information. It was developed to assure patient information confidentiality and safety.

1.15.1.5 Data Protection Act

The Data Protection Act of 1998 was enacted to regulate the collection, processing, holding, using, and disclosure of an individual's private or personal information. The European Union Personal Data Protection Directive (EUDPD), in fact, declares that personal data protection is a fundamental human right and requires that personal data that are no longer necessary for the purposes they were collected in the first place must either be deleted or modified so that they no longer can identify the individual that the data were originally collected from. Software that collects, processes, stores, and archives personal data must therefore be designed and developed with deletion or de-identification mechanisms. The Personal Information Protection and Electronics Document Act (PIPEDA) is in Canada what the EUDPD is in the European Union.

1.15.1.6 Computer Misuse Act

This act makes provisions for securing computer material against unauthorized access and/or modification. Computer misuse such as hacking, unauthorized access, unauthorized modification of contents, and disruptive activities like the introduction of viruses are designated as criminal offenses.

1.15.1.7 State Security Breach Laws

The majority of states in the United States of America now have some form of regulation or bill to deal with security breaches associated with the compromise of personal information. The one that needs special mention is the California State Bill 1386 (SB 1386), which was the harbinger of its kind. SB 1386 requires that personal information be destroyed when it is no longer needed by the collecting entity. It also requires that entities doing business in the state of California notify the owners of personal information that their information protection has been breached or reasonably believed to have been accessed or acquired by someone unauthorized.

1.15.2 Challenges with Regulations and Privacy Mandates

While it is necessary for organizations to comply with regulatory and privacy requirements, it has been observed that such compliance does come with some challenges. Some of the challenges that organizations face when they need to comply with regulations and privacy mandates are open interpretations, auditor's subjectivity, localized jurisdiction, regional variations, and inconsistent enforcement.

Most regulations are not very specific but are general and broad in their description. They do not call out specific security requirements that need to be incorporated into the software. This leaves room for different organizations to interpret the requirements as they see fit for their organization.

Additionally, an auditor's experience and knowledge has a lot to do with the interpretation of the regulatory and/or privacy requirements, because the requirements are usually generic and broad in nature.

Augmenting the open interpretations issue is the fact that when these regulations need to be enforced because of noncompliance, the applicability of these regulations is not universal, internationally or domestically. Jurisdiction is localized. For example, the European data protection act is much more stringent and different from that of the United States or Asia. Such regional variations can hamper the flow of business operations and application of security in software development because one region may have to comply with the regulations while the other region may not find it needful.

Open interpretation, auditor's subjectivity, localized jurisdiction, and regional variations make it difficult to enforce these regulations uniformly and consistently.

1.15.3 Privacy and Software Development

Privacy requirements must be taken into account and deemed as important as security or reliability requirements when developing secure and compliant software. Some standards and best practices such as the PCI DSS disallow the collection of certain private and sensitive information.

Privacy initiatives must consider data privacy and the support from the business as well. Data classification can help in identifying data that will need to have privacy protection requirements applied. Categorizing the data into tiers based on privacy impact (e.g., high, medium, or low) assists in ensuring that appropriate levels of privacy controls are in place. In order for the privacy program to be effective, some proven strategies have been gaining the support of executive and top-level management as sponsors or champions of enforcement using a policy or standard.

Best practice guidelines for data privacy that need to be included in software requirements analysis, design, and architecture can be addressed if one complies with the following rules:

- If you do not need it, do not collect it.
- If you need to collect it for processing only, collect it only after you have informed the user that you are collecting their information and they have consented, but do not store it.
- If you have the need to collect it for processing and storage, then collect it, with user consent, and store it only for an explicit retention period that is compliant with organizational policy and/or regulatory requirements.
- If you have the need to collect it and store it, then do not archive it if the data have outlived their usefulness and there is no retention requirement.

The Acceptably Use Policy (AUP) and log-in banners are two mechanisms that are commonly used to solicit user consent by informing users that their personal information is harvested and possibly retained or that they are being monitored when using company resources. The AUP protects the employer against violators of policy and is a deterrent to individuals who may be engaged in malicious or nefarious activities that put their employment at risk.

Additionally, AUPs must be complementary and not contradictory to information security policies, explicitly stating what users are allowed to do and what they are not allowed to do. Some examples of acceptable user behavior include the use of company resources diligently, limiting software to execute within an IP range, and restriction of trial version software components to development server instances only. Some examples of unacceptable user behavior include reverse engineering the software, prohibited resale of Original Equipment Manufacturer (OEM) individual licenses, surfing porn or hate sites, and sharing illegal software.

1.16 Security Models

Just as an architectural model is an abstraction of the real building, security models are a formal abstraction of the security policy that is comprised of the set of security requirements that needs to be part of the system or software, so that it is resistant to attack, can tolerate the attacks that cannot be resisted, and can recover quickly from the undesirable state, if compromised. In other words, it is a formal presentation of the security policy. Security models include the sequence of steps that are required to develop secure software or systems and provide the "blueprint" for the implementation of security policies.

Security models can be broadly categorized into confidentiality models, integrity models, and access control models.

In this section we will be covering the popular security models, with special attention given to how they apply to software security.

- Confidentiality Models
  - Bell–LaPadula (BLP)
- Integrity Models
  - Biba
  - Clark and Wilson
- Access Control Models
  - Brewer and Nash

1.16.1 BLP Confidentiality Model

If disclosure protection is the primary concern, one must consider the BLP confidentiality model in their software design. BLP is a confidentiality model that defines the notion of a secure state, i.e., access (read only, write only, or read and write) to information is permitted based on rules and the classification of the information itself (Tipton & Krause, 2007).

BLP rules can be specified using properties. The three properties are simple security property that has to do with read access, the star (*) security property that has to do with write access, and the strong star security property that has to do with both read and write access capabilities.

The *simple security property* states that if you have "read" capability, you can read data at your level of secrecy or at a lower level of secrecy, but you must not be allowed to read data at a higher level of secrecy. This is commonly known as the "No Read Up" rule of BLP.

The *star (*) security property* states that if you have "write" capability, you can write data at your level of secrecy or at a higher level of secrecy without compromising its value, but you must not be allowed to write data at a lower level of secrecy. Writing to a level you cannot read creates a type of covert channel because you cannot read what you write.

The *strong star security property* states that if you have both "read" and "write" capabilities, you can read and write data only at your level of secrecy and that you must not be allowed to read and write to levels of higher or lower secrecy.

Assume that the completion of your data classification exercise has yielded the following classification in decreasing order of protection needs, namely, Confidential > Restricted > Public.

BLP confidential model will mandate that someone who is allowed to view only Restricted information is not permitted to read information classified as Confidential ("no read up") and at the same time, they are not allowed to write at the Public level ("no write down") as depicted in Figure 1.16. BLP is often simplified in its description as the security model that enforces the "no read up" and "no write down" security policy.

BLP has a strong impact on software design. When a thread executing at a lower priority level is prevented from accessing (reading) a thread executing at a higher priority level or modifying (writing to) a thread executing at a lower priority level, it is operating in accordance with the rules of the BLP confidentiality model.

1.16.2 Biba Integrity Model

While the BLP model deals primarily with confidentiality assurance, the Biba Integrity model was the first to address modification or alteration protection. The BLP model has to do more with "read" capability and the Biba model has to do more with "write" capability. Like the BLP model, the Biba model also has the simple security property and the star (*) security property, and so it can be deemed to be the integrity equivalent of the BLP model (Tipton & Krause, 2007).

The *simple security property* states that if you have read capability, you can read data at your level of accuracy or from a higher level of accuracy, but you must not be allowed to read data from a lower level of accuracy. Allowing a read down operation can result in the risk of contaminating the accuracy of your data.

The *star (*) security policy* states that if you have write capability, you can write data at your own level of accuracy or to a lower level of accuracy, but you must not

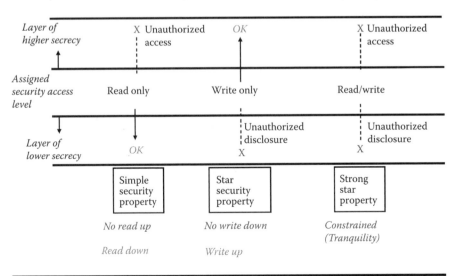

Figure 1.16   Bell–LaPadula confidentiality model.

be allowed to write data at a higher level of accuracy. Allowing a write up operation can result in the risk of possibly contaminating the data that exist at the higher level.

Assume that the completion of your data classification exercise has yielded the following classification in decreasing order of protection needs: Top Secret > Secret > Unclassified.

The Biba Integrity model will mandate that someone who is allowed to view only Secret information is not permitted to read information classified as Unclassified ("no read down"), and at the same time, they are not allowed to write at the Top Secret level ("no write up") as depicted in Figure 1.17. Biba is often simplified in its description as the security model that enforces the "no read down" and "no write up" security policy.

In addition to the simple security and the star (*) security property, Biba adds a third property, unique to the Biba security model, that is known as the *invocation property*. The invocation property states that subjects cannot send messages (invoke services) to objects with higher integrity.

1.16.3 Clark and Wilson Model (Access Triple Model)

Like the Biba Integrity model, the Clark and Wilson model is an integrity model as well. It not only focuses on unauthorized subjects making modifications to objects, but also addresses integrity aspects of authorized personnel making unauthorized changes. For example, an authenticated employee on your network (authorized personnel) should not be able to make changes to his own salary information and give himself a bonus (unauthorized changes) without being challenged. The Clark and

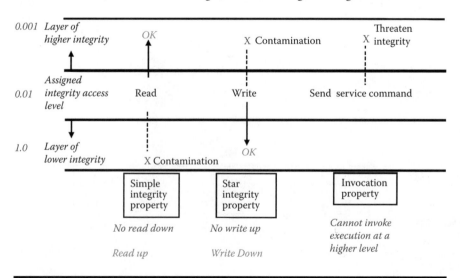

Figure 1.17   Biba Integrity model.

Wilson model is even more exhaustive in the sense that in addition to addressing integrity goals, it also aims at addressing consistency goals by maintaining internal and external consistency by defining well-formed transactions.

Let us take for example that customers are allowed place orders for your company's products over the Web using the company online e-commerce store. After the customer confirms their order submission, the software is designed to first add the customer to the database and then generate an order tied to the customer that is recorded in the customer order table. Order details (the products your customer selected) are then subsequently added to the order detail table in the database and are referenced to the customer order table using the order ID. Assume that while the order details are being added to the database, the database connection pools are maxed out and the transaction fails. If your software is designed and developed in accordance with the Clark and Wilson security model, then you can expect the software to rollback the order entry when the order details fails to ensure that data consistency is ensured. The Clark and Wilson model is also known as an access triple model. The access triple model ensures that access of a subject to an object is restricted and allowed only through a trusted program (which can be your software) as depicted in Figure 1.18. For example, all database operations are allowed only through a software program or application (which preferably is audited) and no direct database access is allowed. The user subject-to-program and program-to-object (data) binding creates a form of separation of duties that ensures integrity.

1.16.4 Brewer and Nash Model (Chinese Wall Model)

The Brewer and Nash model is an access control security model that was developed to ensure that the Chinese Wall security policy is met. The Chinese Wall security policy is a set of rules that allow individuals to access proprietary data as long as there is *no conflict of interest*, i.e., no subjects can access objects on the other side of a wall that is defined with two subjects as depicted in Figure 1.19. The motivation

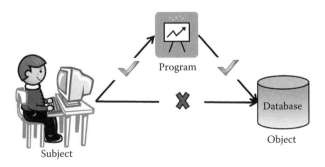

Figure 1.18   Clark and Wilson access triple model.

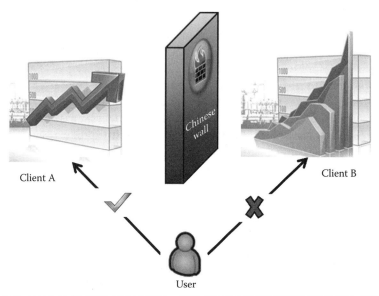

Client B data is off limits to user due to conflict of interest between Client A and Client B.

Figure 1.19 Chinese wall security model.

for this model came from the need to avoid exposing sensitive information about a company to its competitor, especially in settings where the same financial consultant is providing services to both competing organizations. In such a situation, the access rights of the individual must be dynamically established based on the data that the individual has previously accessed.

The Brewer and Nash Chinese Wall security model is very applicable in today's software landscape. With an increase in Software as a Service (SaaS) solution, the need for a definitive wall to exist between your organization's data and your competitor's data is a mandatory requirement. For example, if you use a Customer Relationship Management (CRM) SaaS solution, such as salesforce.com to manage your customer and prospective client list, and your sensitive data are hosted in a shared environment, then there needs to be a wall that is defined to prevent your competitor who is also using the same SaaS CRM solution from accessing your sensitive information and vice versa. If access to competitor information is allowed, then a conflict of interest situation is created and this is what the Brewer and Nash model aims to avoid. The Brewer and Nash model is not only an access control model but is also considered to be an information flow model.

The security models covered so far are by no means an exhaustive list of all information security models that exist today. There are other security models such as the noninterference model, state machine models, the Graham–Denning model, and the Harrison–Ruzzo–Ullman Result model that as a security professional, it is advisable for you to be familiar with, so that your role as a CSSLP is most effective.

1.17 Trusted Computing

The State-of-the-Art Report (SOAR) on Software Security Assurance starts by accurately stating that the objective of software assurance is to establish a basis for gaining justifiable confidence that software will consistently demonstrate desirable properties. These desirable properties can range from quality (error free), reliability (functioning as designed), dependability (predictable outputs), usability (nonrestrictive in performing what the user expects), interoperability (function in disparate heterogeneous environments), safely (without harm to user), fault-tolerant, and, of course, security (resistant to attack, tolerant upon breach, and quick to recover from an insecure state). Consistently demonstrate implies that these properties are evident each time every time. Justifiable confidence in other words is "Trust." So a simple layman's definition of software assurance is that it is the concept that aims to answer the question, "Can the software be trusted?"

Microsoft is known for its Trustworthy Computing initiative, but trusted computing is not a new concept nor is it a vendor proprietary concept, specific to Microsoft. Microsoft's Trustworthy Computing initiative aims at covering four tenets, one of which is security, the other three being privacy (individual rights of the user), reliability (predictable, resilient, and recoverable), and business integrity (social responsibility of the organization to its consumers). It was initiated to address security vulnerabilities in Microsoft's software, and its success has been demonstrated to be directly related to the incorporation of security into the software product development life cycle with the goal to address and avoid design flaws and implementation (coding) bugs before the product is released.

The key thing to note is that software assurance is about trust and not security, which is what software security assurance is about. Security is one of the various desirable properties, expected of the software under the superset of trust. Trusted computing, in other words, is ensuring software assurance, and in the context of the CSSLP, we focus primarily on software security assurance.

There are certain concepts that a CSSLP must be familiar with in regards to trusted computing. These include the Ring Protection, Trust Boundary (or Security Perimeter), Trusted Computing Base (TCB), and Reference Monitor.

1.17.1 Ring Protection

Current-day operating systems (OSs) employ a security mechanism known as ring protection. On the basis of the Honeywell Multics Operating System architecture, ring protection mechanism can be portrayed as a set of concentric numbered rings as depicted in Figure 1.20.

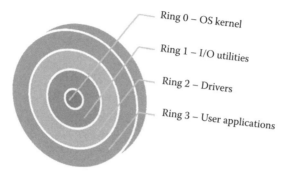

Ring 0 – OS kernel

Ring 1 – I/O utilities

Ring 2 – Drivers

Ring 3 – User applications

Figure 1.20   Ring protection.

It is the ring number that determines the level of access that is allowed. The ring number has an inverse relationship with the level of access, i.e., the lower the ring level, the higher the level of access and vice versa. Operations performed at ring 0 level are highly privileged, and this includes OS kernel functionality and access. Ring 3 level is where software applications run. Hackers use the terms root, owned, or pwned when they successfully exploit vulnerabilities and gain the highest level privilege (such as privileges at ring 0) in the system. Rootkits (covered later) operate by gaining ring 0 level privileges as well.

1.17.2 Trust Boundary (or Security Perimeter)

Trust boundary is the abstract concept that determines the point at which trust levels change. It is also referred to as the security perimeter. There is a very clear-cut trust boundary at each ring level starting with the outermost user-land ring level with low trust to the innermost kernel-land ring level that is highly privileged. The concept of a trust boundary is not just limited to ring protection mechanisms. Trust boundaries must be taken into account in software design and architecture. For example, in architecting software that will be deployed in an Internet environment, trust at different zones must be factored into the design and architecture. Security controls in the Internet zone where there is lower trust must be much more restrictive than what one can expect in the DMZ or the Intranet zone. We will revisit this concept under the context of Threat Modeling in Chapter 3.

1.17.3 Trusted Computing Base (TCB)

Even though the etymology of the term Trusted Computing Base (TCB) is from the Trusted Computer System Evaluation Criteria (TCSEC) more commonly known as the Orange Book, which is considered by some to be dated, its application in the software security world today is not vestigial by any account.

As described earlier, the security policy is the set of security requirements that needs to be part of the system or software that makes it resistant to most attacks, tolerable to attacks that cannot be resisted, and quickly recoverable from an undesirable state, if compromised. The TCB is the abstract concept that ensures that the security policy is enforced at all times. The TCB includes all of the components (hardware, software, and firmware) and mechanisms (process and interprocess communications) and human factors that provide security, which if failed would result in a security breach or violation. It is an abstract concept in the sense that software architects and designers must take into account all the hardware, software, and firmware components and their mechanisms to design secure software. The hardware, firmware, and software elements of a TCB are also referred to as the *security kernel.*

Two important characteristics for the TCB to be effective and efficient are that it must be simple and testable. The testability of the TCB means the TCB can be verified as being functionally complete and correct.

The TCB can ensure that the security policy is enforced by monitoring four basic functions. These are:

1. Process activation
2. Execution domain switching
3. Memory protection
4. Input/output operations

1.17.3.1 Process Activation

In-depth discussion of the process activation within a computer is beyond the scope of this book, and in this section, process activation is covered at a more generic and basic level. Most of us are probably familiar with an online e-commerce transaction. You add a product to your shopping cart, specify any discount code if available, verify the total amount, and place the order. What happens behind the scenes is that the software in such a scenario is designed for calculating the total price of the order using a few functions, such as function A, which is used to compute the subtotal amount (unit price times quantity before discounts), function B is used to compute the discount amount (discount percentage times sub total amount) if a discount is available, function C is used to calculate the tax amount (tax percentage times the subtotal price), and function D is used to determine the total price (subtotal price minus discount amount plus tax). At the bits and bytes level, these functions are translated into an executing process (say, A, B, C, and D) that can be made up of one or many threads (say A.1 to get unit price, A.2 to get quantity, A.3 to get the product of unit price and quantity, etc.), respectively. A thread is a single set of instructions and its associated data. The associated data values (such as unit price, quantity, discount code, tax percentage) are loaded into memory when the instructions call for them. Each of these process threads are controlled by the computers' central processing unit (CPU) that fills its own registers (holding spaces) with the instructions to execute for the processes to complete. In this case, in order for the total price (process D) to be determined, the process must be interrupted by the computation of the tax process (process C), which, in turn, is dependent on the computation of the subtotal price (process A). In other words, the instructions for process D in the CPU is to be interrupted by process C, which, in turn, will need to be interrupted by process A, so that this total operation can complete. A process is said to be activated when it is allowed to interact with the CPU or, in other words, when its own interrupt is called for by the CPU. When a process no longer needs to interact with the CPU upon the completion of all of the instructions within that process, that process is said to be deactivated.

In the context of software security, it is extremely important for the TCB to ensure that the activation of processes is not circumvented and sabotaged by a malicious process that can result in a compromise with undesirable effects.

1.17.3.2 Execution Domain Switching

Software applications are expected to operate at the outermost ring level with the highest ring number (ring 3 or user-land) and calls for native operating system kernel access at the lowest ring number (ring 0 or kernel-land) must not be directly allowed. There needs to be a strict dichotomy between kernel-land and user-land, and processes executing in one domain must not be allowed access to execute in the other domain. Benefits of such an isolation are not only for reasons of confidentiality and integrity, wherein the OS kernel execution is independent and contained, protecting against disclosure of sensitive information (such as cryptographic keys) or alteration of instruction sequences but also for availability as applications that crash in the user-land will not affect the stability of the entire system.

Each process and its set of data values must be isolated from other processes and the TCB must ensure that one process executing at a particular domain cannot switch to another domain that requires a different level of trust for operations to continue and complete, i.e., switching from low trust user-land to highly privileged kernel-land and back is not allowed.

1.17.3.3 Memory Protection

Because each execution domain includes instruction sets in CPU registers and data stored in memory, the TCB monitors memory references to ensure that disclosure, alteration (contamination), and destruction of memory contents is disallowed.

1.17.3.4 Input/Output Operations

Input/output (I/O) utilities execute at ring 1, the ring level closest to the kernel-land. This allows for the OS to control the access to input devices (e.g., keyboard and mouse) and output devices (e.g., monitor, printer, and disks). When your software needs to write to the database stored on a disk, the instruction for this operation will have to be passed from ring 3 where your software is executing to ring 1 to request access to the disk via ring 2, which is where the OS utilities and disk device drivers (programs) operate. The TCB ensures that the sequence of cross-domain communications for access to I/O devices does not violate the security policy.

1.17.4 Reference Monitor

Subjects are active entities that request a resource. Subjects can be human or non-human such as another program or a batch process. The resources that are requested are also referred to as objects. Objects are passive entities and examples of this include a file, a program, data, or hardware. A subject's access to an object must be mediated and allowed based on the subject's privilege level. This access is mediated by what is commonly known to as the reference monitor. The reference monitor is an abstract concept that enforces or mediates access relationships between subjects and objects.

Trusted Computing is only possible when the reference monitor itself is

- Tamper-proof (disallowing unauthorized modifications)
- Always invoked (so that other processes cannot circumvent the access checks)
- Verifiable (correct and complete in its access mediation functionality)

1.17.5 Rootkits

Authors Hoglund and Butler in their book, *Rootkits*, define a rootkit as "a set (kit) of programs and code that allows an attacker to maintain a permanent or consistent undetectable access to 'root,' the most powerful user on a computer." Because rootkits are programs and code that execute at the highest privilege levels and are undetectable, intent to maliciously use rootkits can have a dire and serious impact on trusted computing and security policy enforcement. Malicious users and programs usually use rootkits to modify the operating system (OS) and masquerade as legitimate programs such as kernel-loadable modules (*nix OS) or device drivers (Windows OS). Because they masquerade as legitimate programs, they are undetectable. These rootkits can be used to install keyloggers, alter log files, install covert channels, and evade detection and removal.

Rootkits are primarily used for remote control or for software eavesdropping. Hackers and malicious software (malware) such as spyware attempt to exploit vulnerabilities in software in order to install rootkits in unpatched and unhardened systems. It is therefore imperative that the security of the software we build or buy does not allow for the compromise of trusted computing by becoming victims to the malicious use of rootkits.

It must, however, be recognized that intrinsically, rootkits are not a security threat and there are several valid and legitimate reasons for developing this type of technology. These include using the rootkits for remote troubleshooting purposes, sanctioned and consented law enforcement, espionage situations, and also monitoring user behavior.

1.18 Trusted Platform Module (TPM)

Like the TCB, another concept and mechanism that helps ensure trusted computing is the Trusted Platform Module (TPM). Developed by the Trusted Computing Group (TCG), whose mission is to develop and support open industry specifications for trusted computing across multiple platform types, the TPM is a specification used in personal computers and other systems to ensure protection against disclosure of sensitive or private information as well as the implementation of the specification itself. The implementation of the specification, currently in version 1.2, is a microcontroller commonly referred to as the TPM chip usually affixed to the motherboard (hardware) itself.

Although the TPM itself does not control what software runs, the TPM provides generation and tamperproof storage of cryptographic keys that can be used to create and store identity (user or platform) credentials for authentication purposes. A TPM chip can be used to uniquely identify a hardware device and provide hardware-based device authentication. It can be complementary to smartcards and biometrics and in that sense facilitates strong multifactor authentication and enables true machine and user authentication by requiring the presentation of authorization data before disclosing sensitive or private information.

TPM systems offer enhanced and added security and protection against external software attack or physical theft because they take into account hardware-based security aspects in addition to the security capabilities provided by software. It must, however, be understood that keys and sensitive information stored in the TPM chip are still vulnerable to disclosure if the software that is requesting this information for processing is not architected securely, as has been demonstrated in the cold boot side channel attack. This further accentuates the fact that software security is critical to ensure trusted computing. The TPM can also be leveraged by software developers to increase security in the software they write by using the TCG's Trusted Software Stack (TSS) interface specification. The TCG also publishes the Trusted Server specification (for server security), the Trusted Network Connect architecture (for network security), and the Mobile Trusted Module (for mobile computing security).

Side channel attacks including the cold boot attack will be covered in Chapter 7.

1.19 Acquisitions

Security considerations in software acquisitions will be covered in-depth in Chapter 6. In this section, we will be introduced to the reasons for software acquisitions, acquisition mechanisms, and the security aspects to consider when acquiring software.

It is not surprising that not all software is built in-house. In fact, a substantial amount of software within one's organization is probably developed by a third party and purchased as commercial off-the-shelf (COTS) software. A buy versus build decision is usually dependent on the time (schedule), resource (scope), and cost (budget) elements of the iron triangle. Generally, when the time to market is short, the resources available with the appropriate skills are low and the cost for development is tight, management leans more toward a software acquisition (buy) decision. Table 1.5 illustrates some of the questions to ask when evaluating a buy versus build decision.

In addition to the iron triangle elements impacting a buy versus build decision, two other trends also demonstrate a direct effect on software acquisition over building it in-house. These are outsourcing and SaaS. With the abundance of qualified resources at a low cost in lower cost software development companies around the world, many organizations jumped on to the outsourcing bandwagon and had their software developed by someone on the other side of the globe, without factoring in the security aspects that need to be part of outsourcing. When software development is outsourced, it is critical that the organization is aware of who is writing the software for them and if the software can be trusted. Code developed outside the control of your organization will need to be thoroughly inspected and reviewed for back doors, Trojans, logic bombs, etc., before accepting that software and deploying it within your organization. Also, with the change in the way that software is sold as a service, instead of buying it as a product and hosting it within

Table 1.5 Buy versus Build Decision Evaluation

Build Considerations	Buy Considerations
Is it part of the overall strategy?	What is already available to buy?
Is it within the organization's capabilities?	Does it meet the organization's requirements?
Do we have the people resources to be successful?	What are the associated costs?
What are the associated risks?	Does the vendor have established secure software development practices?
What are the associated advantages?	Are the vendor employees trained?
What is already available to buy?	What other customers have purchased and are using the software?
	What is the maintenance and support model?

your organization, the software is often hosted as a service externally in a shared environment that you have little to no control over.

Software can be acquired using one or more of the following mechanisms:

■ Direct purchase
■ Original equipment manufacturer licenses
■ System integration (outsourced buy)
■ Partnering (alliance) with the software vendor

While the buy decision has the benefits of readily available software and appropriately skilled resources who work for the software vendor, it does come with some costs of customization that is invariably required, vendor dependence, and legal protection mechanisms such as contracts, SLAs, and intellectual property (IP) protection mechanisms such as copyright, trademarks, and patents. Legal and IP protection mechanisms are covered in-depth in Chapter 6.

Additionally, if security requirements are not explicitly stated before purchase, there is a high degree of likelihood that the software product you buy to deploy in-house does not meet the security requirements. When was the last time you saw a request for proposal with security requirements explicitly stated? Not only must security requirements be explicitly communicated to the software vendor in advance, but it must be verified as well. Unfortunately, in most cases, when software is acquired, evaluation of the COTS software is on the functionality, performance, and integration abilities of the software and not necessarily on security. And even in cases where the vendor claims security in their software as a differentiating factor, the claimed security is seldom verified within the organization's computing ecosystem, prior to its purchase. It is important that COTS software vendors are trusted, but it is even more imperative for secure software assurance that their claims are verified.

Software assurance in acquisitions is emerging and expected to become integral to the software security assurance initiatives. The U.S. Department of Defense (in conjunction with the Department of Homeland Security) is currently working on a reference guide for security-enhanced software acquisition and outsourcing entitled "Software Assurance in Acquisition: Mitigating Risks to the Enterprise," which is a document worth being familiar with for any CSSLP or security professional who is engaged in the software procurement or purchasing decision and/or process.

In essence, regardless of whether you buy or you build the software, SARs must be part of the process and in no situation can these requirements be ignored.

1.20 Summary

In conclusion, we have established that software security can no longer be on the sidelines and that it is important for security and secure design tenets to be factored into the SDLC. The interplay between software security and risk management was demonstrated with special attention given to challenges in software risk management. Governance instruments such as policies and standards were covered along with common methodologies, best practices, and framework. We looked at how abstract security models and trusted computing concepts (TCB and TPM) impact software security. Finally, we discussed the reasons for software acquisition, acquisition mechanisms, and the security aspects that need to be part of the SDLC.

1.21 Review Questions

1. The primary reason for incorporating security into the software development life cycle is to protect
   A. Unauthorized disclosure of information
   B. Corporate brand and reputation
   C. Against hackers who intend to misuse the software
   D. Developers from releasing software with security defects
2. The resiliency of software to withstand attacks that attempt to modify or alter data in an unauthorized manner is referred to as
   A. Confidentiality
   B. Integrity
   C. Availability
   D. Authorization
3. The main reason as to why the availability aspects of software must be part of the organization's software security initiatives is:
   A. Software issues can cause downtime to the business.
   B. Developers need to be trained in the business continuity procedures.
   C. Testing for availability of the software and data is often ignored.
   D. Hackers like to conduct denial of service attacks against the organization.
4. Developing the software to monitor its functionality and report when the software is down and unable to provide the expected service to the business is a protection to assure which of the following?
   A. Confidentiality
   B. Integrity
   C. Availability
   D. Authentication
5. When a customer attempts to log into his bank account, he is required to enter a number that is used only once (nonce) from the token device that was issued to the customer by the bank. This type of authentication is also known as which of the following?
   A. Ownership-based authentication
   B. Two factor authentication
   C. Characteristic-based authentication
   D. Knowledge-based authentication

6. Multifactor authentication is most closely related to which of the following security design principles?
   A. Separation of duties
   B. Defense in-depth
   C. Complete mediation
   D. Open design

7. Audit logs can be used for all of the following except
   A. Providing evidentiary information
   B. Assuring that the user cannot deny their actions
   C. Detecting the actions that were undertaken
   D. Preventing a user from performing some unauthorized operations

8. Impersonation attacks such as man-in-the-middle (MITM) attacks in an Internet application can be best mitigated using proper
   A. Configuration management
   B. Session management
   C. Patch management
   D. Exception management

9. Organizations often predetermine the acceptable number of user errors before recording them as security violations. This number is otherwise known as
   A. Clipping level
   B. Known error
   C. Minimum security baseline
   D. Maximum tolerable downtime

10. A security principle that maintains the confidentiality, integrity, and availability of the software and data, besides allowing for rapid recovery to the state of normal operations, when unexpected events occur is the security design principle of
    A. Defense in-depth
    B. Economy of mechanisms
    C. Fail safe
    D. Psychological acceptability

11. Requiring the end user to accept an "as-is" disclaimer clause before installation of your software is an example of risk
    A. Avoidance
    B. Mitigation
    C. Transference
    D. Acceptance

12. An instrument that is used to communicate and mandate organizational and management goals and objectives at a high level is a
    A. Standard
    B. Policy
    C. Baseline
    D. Guideline

13. The Systems Security Engineering Capability Maturity Model is an internationally recognized standard that publishes guidelines to
    A. Provide metrics for measuring the software and its behavior and using the software in a specific context of use
    B. Evaluate security engineering practices and organizational management processes
    C. Support accreditation and certification bodies that audit and certify information security management systems
    D. Ensure that the claimed identity of personnel are appropriately verified
14. Which of the following is a framework that can be used to develop a risk-based enterprise security architecture by determining security requirements after analyzing the business initiatives?
    A. Capability Maturity Model Integration (CMMI)
    B. Sherwood Applied Business Security Architecture (SABSA)
    C. Control Objectives for Information and related Technology (COBIT®)
    D. Zachman Framework
15. The property of this Biba security model prevents the contamination of data assuring its integrity by
    A. Not allowing the process to write above its security level
    B. Not allowing the process to write below its security level
    C. Not allowing the process to read above its security level
    D. Not allowing the process to read below its security level
16. Which of the following is known to circumvent the ring protection mechanisms in operating systems?
    A. Cross Site Request Forgery (CSRF)
    B. Coolboot
    C. SQL injection
    D. Rootkit
17. Which of the following is a primary consideration for the software publisher when selling commercial off-the-shelf (COTS) software?
    A. Service level agreements
    B. Intellectual property protection
    C. Cost of customization
    D. Review of the code for backdoors and Trojan horses
18. The single loss expectancy can be determined using which of the following formulae?
    A. Annualized rate of occurrence (ARO) × exposure factor
    B. Probability × impact
    C. Asset value × exposure factor
    D. Annualized rate of occurrence (ARO) × asset value
19. Implementing IPSec to assure the confidentiality of data when it is transmitted is an example of which type of risk?

A. Avoidance
B. Transference
C. Mitigation
D. Acceptance

20. The Federal Information Processing Standard (FIPS) that prescribe guidelines for biometric authentication is
    A. FIPS 46-3
    B. FIPS 140-2
    C. FIPS 197
    D. FIPS 201

21. Which of the following is a multifaceted security standard that is used to regulate organizations that collects, processes, and/or stores cardholder data as part of their business operations?
    A. FIPS 201
    B. ISO/IEC 15408
    C. NIST SP 800-64
    D. PCI DSS

22. Which of the following is the current Federal Information Processing Standard (FIPS) that specifies an approved cryptographic algorithm to ensure the confidentiality of electronic data?
    A. Security Requirements for Cryptographic Modules (FIPS 140-2)
    B. Data Encryption Standard (FIPS 46-3)
    C. Advanced Encryption Standard (FIPS 197)
    D. Digital Signature Standard (FIPS 186-3)

23. The organization that publishes the 10 most critical Web application security risks (Top Ten) is the
    A. U.S. Computer Emergency Readiness Team (US-CERT)
    B. Web Application Security Consortium (WASC)
    C. Open Web Application Security Project (OWASP)
    D. Forums for Incident Response and Security Teams (FIRST)

References

Common Criteria. n.d. Common Criteria recognition agreement. http://www.common criteriaportal.org/ccra/ (accessed Mar. 3, 2011).

Federal Financial Institutions Examination Council. 2010. Authentication in an Internet banking environment. http://www.ffiec.gov (accessed Mar. 10, 2010).

Howard, M., and D. LeBlanc. 2003. *Writing Secure Code*. Redmond, WA: Microsoft.

International Organization for Standardization. 2010. ISO standards. 10 Feb. 2010. http://www.iso.org/iso/iso_catalogue.htm (accessed Feb. 10, 2010).

National Institute of Standards and Technology (NIST). 1996. *Federal Information Processing Standards Publications*. http://www.itl.nist.gov/fipspubs (accessed May 15, 2010).

NIST. 2002. Federal Information Security Management Act (FISMA) implementation project. Computer Security Division, Computer Security Resource Center. http://csrc.nist.gov/groups/SMA/fisma/index.html (accessed June 15, 2010).

NIST. 2007. Special publications (800 Series). http://csrc.nist.gov/publications/PubsSPs.html (accessed June 15, 2010).

PCI Security Standards Council. n.d., a. Payment Application Data Security Standard (PA-DSS). https://www.pcisecuritystandards.org/ (accessed Feb. 10, 2010).

PCI Security Standards Council. n.d., b. Payment Card Industry Data Security Standard (PCI DSS). https://www.pcisecuritystandards.org/ (accessed Feb. 10, 2010).

Schneier, B. 2000. *Secrets and Lies: Digital Security in a Networked World.* New York, NY: John Wiley.

Tipton, H. F., and M. Krause. 2007. *Information Security Management Handbook.* Boca Raton, FL: Auerbach.

Trusted Computing Group. 2010. Trusted Platform Module. http://www.trustedcomputinggroup.org/ (accessed June 15, 2010).

Weise, J. 2009. Why security standards? *ISSA Journal* August: 29–32.

Chapter 2

Secure Software Requirements

2.1 Introduction

As a preface, it is important to establish the fact that "Without software requirements, software will fail and without secure software requirements, organizations will." Without properly understood, well-documented, and tracked software requirements, one cannot expect the software to function without failure or to meet expectations. It is vital to define and explicitly articulate the requirements of software that is to be built or acquired. Software development projects that lack software requirements suffer from a plethora of issues. These issues include and are not limited to poor product quality, extensive timelines, scope creep, increased cost to re-architect missed requirements or fix errors, and even customer or end user dissatisfaction. Software development projects that lack security requirements additionally suffer from the threats to confidentiality, integrity, and availability, which include unauthorized disclosure, alteration, and destruction. It is really not a question of "if" but "when," because it is only a matter of time before software built without security considerations will get hacked, provided the software is of some value to the attacker.

It would be extremely difficult to find a building architect who would engage in building a skyscraper without a blueprint or a chef who will indulge in baking world-famous pastries and cakes without a recipe that lists the ingredients. However, we often observe that when software is built, security requirements are not explicitly stated. The reasons for such a modus operandi are many. Security is first and foremost viewed as a nonfunctional requirement and in an organization that has to deal with functional requirements owing to the constraints posed by budget, scope, and schedule (iron triangle constraints), security requirements are considered to be an additional expense (impacting budget), increased nonvalue added functionality (impacting scope), and were time-consuming to implement (impacting schedule). Such an attitude is what leaves secure software requirements on the sidelines. Second, incorporating security in software is often misconstrued as an impediment to business agility and not necessarily as an enabler for the business to produce quality and secure software. Secure software is characterized by the following quality attributes:

- *Reliability*: The software functions as it is expected to.
- *Resiliency*: The software does not violate any security policy and is able to withstand the actions of threat agents that are posed intentionally (attacks and exploits) or accidentally (user errors).
- *Recoverability*: The software is able to restore operations to what the business expects by containing and limiting the damage caused by threats that materialize.

Third, depending on the security knowledge of business analysts who translate business requirements to functional specifications, security may or may not make it into the software that is developed. In certain situations, security in software is not even considered, leave alone being ignored! And in such situations, when an abuse of the software is reported, security is retrofitted and bolted on, instead of having been built in from the very beginning.

The importance of incorporating security requirements in the software requirements gathering and design phases is absolutely critical for the reliability, resiliency, and recoverability of software. When was the last time you noticed security requirements in the software requirement specifications documents? Explicit software security requirement such as "The user password will need to be protected against disclosure by masking it while it is input and hashed when it is stored" or "The change in pricing information of a product needs to be tracked and audited, recording the timestamp and the individual who performed that operation" are usually not found within the software requirements specifications document. What are usually observed are merely high-level nontestable implementation mechanisms and listing of security features such as passwords need to be protected, Secure Sockets Layer (SSL) needs to be in place or a Web application firewall needs to be installed in front of our public facing Web sites. It is extremely important to explicitly articulate security requirements for the software in the software requirements specifications documents.

2.2 Objectives

Leveraging the wisdom from the famous Chinese adage that "a journey of a thousand miles begins with the first step," we can draw the parallel that the first step in the journey to design, develop, and deploy secure software is the determination of security requirements in software.

As a CSSLP, you are expected to:

- Be familiar with various internal and external sources from which software security requirements can be determined.
- Know how to glean software security requirements from various stakeholders and sources.
- Be thorough in the understanding on the different types of security requirements for software.
- Understand and be familiar with data classification as a mechanism to elicit software security requirements from functional business requirements.
- Know how to develop misuse cases from use case scenarios as a means to determine security requirements.
- Know how to generate a subject–object matrix (SOM) and understand how it can be used for generating security requirements.
- Be familiar with timing and sequencing aspects of software as it pertains to software security.
- Be familiar with how the requirements traceability matrix (RTM) can be used for software security considerations.

This chapter will cover each of these objectives in detail. It is imperative that you fully understand the objectives and be familiar with how to apply them in the software that your organization builds or buys.

2.3 Sources for Security Requirements

There are several sources from which security requirements can be gleaned. They can be broadly classified into internal and external sources. Internal sources can be further divided into organizational sources that the organization needs to comply with. These include policies, standards, guidelines, and patterns and practices. The end user business functionality of the software itself is another internal source from which security requirements can be gleaned. Just as a business analyst translates business requirements into functionality specifications for the software development team, a CSSLP must be able to assist the software teams to translate functional specifications into security requirements. In the following section, we will cover the various types of security requirements and discuss requirements elicitation from software functionality in more detail. External sources for security requirements can be broadly classified into regulations, compliance initiatives, and geographical requirements. Equal weight should be given to security requirements regardless of whether the source of that requirement is internal or external.

Business owners, end users, and customers play an important role when determining software security requirements, and they must be actively involved in the requirements elicitation process. Business owners are responsible for the determination of the *acceptable risk threshold*, which is the level of residual risk that is acceptable. Business owners also own the risk, and they are ultimately accountable, should there be a security breach in their software. They should assist the CSSLP and software development teams in prioritizing the risk and be active in "what is important?" trade-off decisions. Business owners need to be educated on the importance and concepts of software security. Such education will ensure that they do not assign a low priority to security requirements or deem them as unimportant. Furthermore, supporting groups such as the operations group and the information security group are also vital stakeholders and are responsible for ensuring that the software being built for deployment or release is reliable, resilient, and recoverable.

2.4 Types of Security Requirements

Before we delve into mechanisms and methodologies by which we can determine security requirements, we must first be familiar with the different types of security requirements. These security requirements need to be explicitly defined and must address the security objectives or goals of the company. Properly and adequately defining and documenting security requirements makes the measurement of security objectives or goals once the software is ready for release or accepted for deployment possible and easy. A comprehensive list of security requirements for software is as tied as hand to glove to the software security profile, which is depicted in Figure 2.1.

For each characteristic of the software security profile, security requirements need to be determined. In addition, other requirements that are pertinent to software must be determined as well. The different types of software security requirements that need to be defined as illustrated in Figure 2.2 include the following:

Figure 2.1   Software security profile.

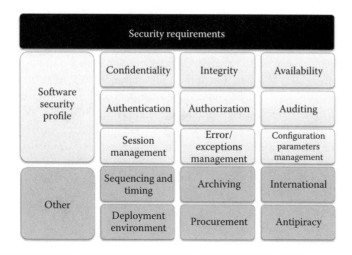

Figure 2.2 Types of software security requirements.

- Confidentiality requirements
- Integrity requirements
- Availability requirements
- Authentication requirements
- Authorization requirements
- Auditing requirements
- Session management requirements
- Errors and exceptions management requirements
- Configuration parameters management requirements
- Sequencing and timing requirements
- Archiving requirements
- International requirements
- Deployment environment requirements
- Procurement requirements
- Antipiracy requirements

In the requirements gathering phase of the software development life cycle (SDLC), we are only required to identify which requirements are applicable to the business context and the software functionality serving that context. Details on how these requirements will be implemented are to be decided when the software is designed and developed. In this chapter, a similar approach with respect to the extent of coverage of the different types of security requirements for software is taken. In Chapter 3, we will cover in-depth the translation of the identified requirements from the requirements gathering phase into software functionality and architecture, and in Chapter 4, we will learn about how the security requirements are built into the code to ensure software assurance.

2.4.1 Confidentiality Requirements

Confidentiality requirements are those that address protection against the disclosure of data or information that are either personal or sensitive in nature to unauthorized individuals. The classification of data (covered later in this chapter) into sensitivity levels is often used to determine confidentiality requirements. Data can be broadly classified into public and nonpublic data or information. Public data are also referred to as *directory* information. Any nonpublic data warrant protection against unauthorized disclosure, and software security requirements that afford such protection need to be defined in advance. The two common forms of confidentiality protection mechanisms as depicted in Figure 2.3 include secret writing and masking.

Secret writing is a protection mechanism in which the goal is to prevent the disclosure of the information deemed secret. This includes overt cryptographic mechanisms such as encryption and hashing or covert mechanisms such as steganography and digital watermarking (Bauer, 2000). The distinction between the overt and covert forms of secret writing lies in their objective to accomplish disclosure protection. The goal of overt secret writing is to make the information humanly indecipherable or unintelligible even if disclosed, whereas the goal of covert secret writing is to hide information within itself or in some other media or form.

Overt secret writing, also commonly referred to as cryptography, includes encryption and hashing. *Encryption* uses a bidirectional algorithm in which humanly readable information (referred to as clear text) is converted into humanly unintelligible information (referred to as cipher text). The inverse of encryption is *decryption*, the process by which cipher text is converted into plain text. *Hashing*, on the other hand, is a one-way function where the original data or information

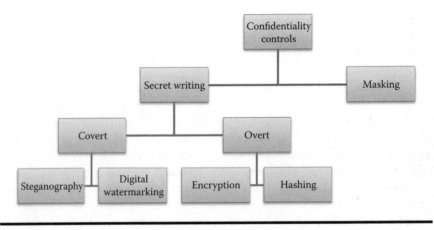

Figure 2.3 Confidentiality protection mechanisms.

that needs protection is computed into a fixed length output that is indecipherable. The computed value is referred to as a hash value, digest, or hash sum. The main distinction between encryption and hashing is that, unlike in encryption, the hashed value or hashed sum cannot be converted back to the original data and hence the one-way computation. So hashing is primarily used for integrity (nonalteration) protection, although it can be used as a confidentiality control, especially in situations when the information is stored and the viewers of that information should not be allowed to resynthesize the original value by passing it through the same hashing function. A good example of this is when there is a need to store passwords in databases. Only the creator of the password should be aware of what it is. When the password is stored in the backend database, its hashed value should be the one that is stored. This way hashing provides disclosure protection against insider threat agents who may very well be the database administration within the company. When the password is used by the software for authentication verification, the user can supply their password, which is hashed using the same hashing function and then the hash values of the supplied password and the hash value of the one that is stored can be compared and authentication decisions can be accordingly undertaken.

The most common forms of covert secret writing are steganography and digital watermarking (Johnson, Duric, and Jajodia, 2000). Steganography is more commonly referred to as *invisible ink* writing and is the art of camouflaging or hidden writing, where the information is hidden and the existence of the message itself is concealed. Steganography is primarily useful for covert communications and is useful and prevalent in military espionage communications. Digital watermarking is the process of embedding information into a digital signal. These signals can be audio, video, or pictures. Digital watermarking can be accomplished in two ways: visible and invisible. In visible watermarking, there is no special mechanism to conceal the information, and it is visible to plain sight. This is of little consequence to us from a security standpoint. However, in invisible watermarking, the information is concealed within other media and the watermark is used to uniquely identify the originator of the signal, thereby making it possible for authentication purposes as well, besides confidentiality protection. Invisible watermarking is, however, mostly used for copyright protection, deterring and preventing unauthorized copying of digital media. Digital watermarking can be accomplished using steganographic techniques as well.

Masking is a weaker form of confidentiality protection mechanism in which the original information is either asterisked or X'ed out. You may have noticed this in input fields that take passwords. This is primarily used to protect against shoulder surfing attacks, which are characterized by someone looking over another's shoulder and observing sensitive information. The masking of credit card numbers or social security numbers (SSN), except for the last four digits, when printed on receipts or displayed on a screen is an example of masking providing confidentiality protection.

Confidentiality requirements need to be defined throughout the information life cycle from the origin of the data in question to its retirement. It is necessary to explicitly state confidentiality requirements for nonpublic data:

- In transit: When the data are transmitted over unprotected networks
- In processing: When the data are held in computer memory or media for processing
- In storage: When the data are at rest, within transactional systems as well as nontransactional systems including archives

Confidentiality requirements may also be *time bound*, i.e., some information may require protection only for a certain period. An example of this is news about a merger or acquisition. The date when the merger will occur is deemed sensitive and if stored or processed within internal information technology (IT) systems, it requires protection until this sensitive information is made public. Upon public press release of the merger having been completed, information deemed sensitive may no longer require protection as it becomes directory or public information. The general rule of thumb is that confidentiality requirements need to be identified based on the classification data given, and when that classification changes (say from sensitive to public), then appropriate control requirements need to be redefined.

Some good examples of confidentiality security requirements that should be part of the software requirements specifications documentation are given in the following:

- "Personal health information must be protected against disclosure using approved encryption mechanisms."
- "Password and other sensitive input fields need to be masked."
- "Passwords must not be stored in the clear in backend systems and when stored must be hashed with at least an equivalent to the SHA-256 hash function."
- "Transport layer security (TLS) such as Secure Socket Layer must be in place to protect against insider man-in-the-middle (MITM) threats for all credit card information that is transmitted."
- "The use of nonsecure transport protocols such as File Transfer Protocol (FTP) to transmit account credentials in the clear to third parties outside your organization should not be allowed."
- "Log files must not store any sensitive information as defined by the business in humanly readable or easily decipherable form."

As we determine requirements for ensuring confidentiality in the software we build or acquire, we must take into account the timeliness and extent of the protection required.

2.4.2 *Integrity Requirements*

Integrity requirements for software are those security requirements that address two primary areas of software security, namely, reliability assurance and protection or prevention against unauthorized modifications. Integrity refers not only to the system or software modification protection (system integrity) but also the data that the system or software handles (data integrity). When integrity protection assures *reliability*, it essentially refers to ensuring that the system or software is functioning as it is designed and expected to. In addition to reliability assurance, integrity requirements are also meant to provide security controls that will ensure that the *accuracy* of the system and data is maintained. This means that data integrity requires that information and programs be changed only in a specified and authorized manner by authorized personnel. Although integrity assurance primarily addresses the reliability and accuracy aspects of the system or data, it must be recognized that integrity protection also takes into consideration the *completeness* and *consistency* of the system or data that the system handles.

Within the context of software security, we have to deal with both system and data integrity. Injection attacks such as SQL injection that makes the software act or respond in a manner not originally designed to is a classic example of system integrity violation. Integrity controls for data in transit or data at rest need to provide assurance against deliberate or inadvertent unauthorized manipulations. The requirement to provide assurance of integrity needs to be defined explicitly in the software requirements specifications. Security controls that provide such assurance include input validation, parity bit checking and cyclic redundancy checking (CRC), and hashing.

Input validation provides a high degree of protection against injection flaws and provides both system and data integrity. Allowing only valid forms of input to be accepted by the software for processing mitigates several security threats against software (covered in the secure software implementation chapter). In Chapters 3 and 4, we will cover input validation in depth and the protections it provides. *Parity bit checking* is useful in the detection of errors or changes made to data when they are transmitted. Mathematically, parity refers to the evenness or oddness of an integer. A parity bit (0 or 1) is an extra bit that is appended to a group of bits (byte, word, or character) so that the group of bits will either have an even or odd number of 1's. The parity bit is 0 (even) if the number of 1's in the input bit stream is even and 1 (odd) if the number of 1's in the input bit stream is odd. Data integrity checking is performed at the receiving end of the transmission by computing and comparing the original bit stream parity with the parity information of the received data. A common usage of parity bit checking is to do a *cyclic redundancy check* (*CRC*) for data integrity as well, especially for messages longer than 1 byte (8 bits) long. Upon data transmission, each block of data is given a computed CRC value, commonly referred to as a *checksum*. If there is an alteration between the origin of data and its destination, the checksum sent at the origin will not match with the one that is computed at the destination. Corrupted media (CDs and DVDs) and incomplete downloads of software yield CRC errors. The checksum is the end product of a nonsecure hash function. *Hashing* provides the strongest forms of data integrity. Although hashing is mainly used for integrity assurance, it can also provide confidentiality assurance as we covered earlier in this chapter.

Some good examples of integrity security requirements that should be part of the software requirements specifications documentation are given in the following:

- "All input forms and query string inputs need to be validated against a set of allowable inputs before the software accepts it for processing."
- "Software that is published should provide the recipient with a computed checksum and the hash function used to compute the checksum, so that the recipient can validate its accuracy and completeness."
- "All nonhuman actors such as system and batch processes need to be identified, monitored, and prevented from altering data as it passes on systems that they run on, unless explicitly authorized to."

As we determine requirements for ensuring integrity in the software we build or acquire, we must take into account the reliability, accuracy, completeness, and consistency aspects of systems and data.

2.4.3 Availability Requirements

Although the concept of availability may seem to be more closely related to business continuity or disaster recovery disciplines than it is to security, it must be recognized that improper software design and development can lead to destruction of the system/data or even cause denial of service (DoS). It is therefore imperative that availability requirements are explicitly determined to ensure that there is no disruption to business operations. Availability requirements are those software requirements that ensure the protection against destruction of the software system and/or data, thereby assisting in the prevention against DoS to authorized users. When determining availability requirements, the maximum tolerable downtime (MTD) and recovery time objective (RTO) must both be determined. MTD is the measure of the maximum amount of time that the software can be in a state of not providing expected service. In other words, it is the measure of the minimum level of availability that is required of the software for business operations to continue without unplanned disruptions as per expectations. However, because all software fails or will fail eventually, in addition to determining the MTD, the RTO must also be determined. RTO is the amount of time by which the system or software needs to be restored back to the expected state of business operations for authorized business users when it goes down. Both MTD and RTO should be explicitly stated in the service level agreements (SLAs). There are several ways to determine availability requirements for software. These methods include determining the adverse effects of software downtime through business impact analysis (BIA) or stress and performance testing.

BIA must be conducted to determine the adverse impact that the unavailability of software will have on business operations. This may be measured quantitatively such as loss of revenue for each minute the software is down, cost to fix and restore the software back to normal operations, or fines that are levied on the business upon software security breach. It may also be qualitatively determined, including loss of credibility, confidence, or loss of brand reputation. In either case, it is imperative to include the business owners and end users to accurately determine MTD and RTO as a result of the BIA exercise. BIA can be conducted for both new and existing versions of software. In situations when there is an existing version of the software, then stress and performance test results from the previous version of the software can be used to ensure high-availability requirements are included for the upcoming versions as well. Table 2.1 tabulates the downtime that will be allowed for a percentage of availability that is usually measured in units of nines. Such availability requirements and planned downtime amounts must be determined and explicitly stated in the SLA and incorporated into the software requirements documents.

In determining availability requirements, understanding the impact of failure due to a breach of security is vitally important. Insecure coding constructions such as dangling pointers, improper memory deallocations, and infinite loop constructs can all impact availability, and when requirements are solicited, these repercussions of insecure development must be identified and factored in. End-to-end configuration requirements ensure that there is no single point of failure and should be part of the software requirements documentation. A single point of failure is characterized by having no redundancy capabilities, and this can undesirably affect end users when a failure occurs. In addition to end-to-end configuration requirements, load balancing requirements need to be identified and captured as well. By replicating data, databases, and software across multiple computer systems, a degree of redundancy is made possible. This redundancy also helps to provide a means for

Table 2.1 High-Availability Requirements as Measures of Nines

Measurement	Availability (%)	Downtime per year	Downtime per month (30 days)	Downtime per week
Three nines	99.9	8.76 hours	43.2 min	10.1 min
Four nines	99.99	52.6 min	4.32 min	1.01 min
Five nines	99.999	5.26 min	25.9 s	6.05 s
Six nines	99.9999	31.5 s	2.59 s	0.605 s

reducing the workload on any one particular system. Replication usually follows a master–slave or primary–secondary backup scheme in which there is one master or primary node and updates are propagated to the slaves or secondary node either actively or passively. Active/active replication implies that updates are made to both the master and slave systems at the same time. In the case of active/passive replication, the updates are made to the master node first and then the replicas are pushed the changes subsequently. When replication of data is concerned, special considerations need to be given to address the integrity of data as well, especially in active/passive replication schemes.

Some good examples of availability requirements that have a bearing on software security are given in the following and should be part of the software requirements specifications documentation.

- "The software shall ensure high availability of five nines (99.999%) as defined in the SLA."
- "The number of users at any one given point of time who should be able to use the software can be up to 300 users."
- "Software and data should be replicated across data centers to provide load balancing and redundancy."
- "Mission critical functionality in the software should be restored to normal operations within 1 hour of disruption; mission essential functionality in the software should be restored to normal operations within 4 hours of disruption; and mission support functionality in software should be restored to normal operations within 24 hours of disruption."

2.4.4 Authentication Requirements

The process of validating an entity's claim is authentication. The entity may be a person, a process, or a hardware device. The common means by which authentication occurs is that the entity provides identity claims and/or credentials that are validated and verified against a trusted source holding those credentials. Authentication requirements are those that verify and assure the legitimacy and validity of the identity that is presenting entity claims for verification.

In the secure software concepts domain, we learned that authentication credentials could be provided by different factors or a combination of factors that include knowledge, ownership, or characteristics. When two factors are used to validate an entity's claim and/or credentials, it is referred to as *two-factor* authentication, and when more than two factors are used for authentication purposes, it is referred to as *multifactor* authentication. It is important to determine, first, if there exists a need for two- or multifactor authentication. It is also advisable to leverage existing and proven authentication mechanisms, and requirements that call for custom authentication processes should be closely reviewed and scrutinized from a security standpoint so that no new risks are introduced in implementing custom and newly developed authentication validation routines.

There are several means by which authentication can be implemented in software. Each has its own pros and cons as it pertains to security. In this section, we cover some of the most common forms of authentication. However, depending on the business context and needs, authentication requirements need to be explicitly stated in the software requirements document so that when the software is being designed and built, security implications of those authentication requirements can be determined and addressed accordingly. The most common forms of authentication are:

- Anonymous
- Basic
- Digest
- Integrated
- Client certificates
- Forms
- Token
- Smart cards
- Biometrics

2.4.4.1 Anonymous Authentication

Anonymous authentication is the means of access to public areas of your system without prompting for credentials such as username and password. As the name suggests, anyone—even anonymous users—are allowed access and there is no real authentication check for validating the entity. Although this may be required from a privacy standpoint, the security repercussions are serious because with anonymous authentication there is no way to link a user or system to the actions they undertake. This is referred to as *unlinkability*, and if there is no business need for anonymous authentication to be implemented, it is best advised to avoid it.

2.4.4.2 Basic Authentication

One of the Hypertext Transport Protocol (HTTP) 1.0 specifications is basic authentication that is characterized by the client browser prompting the user to supply their credentials. These credentials are transmitted in Base-64 encoded form. Although this provides a little more security than anonymous authentication, basic authentication must be avoided as well, because the encoded credentials can be easily decoded.

2.4.4.3 Digest Authentication

Digest authentication is a challenge/response mechanism, which unlike basic authentication, does not send the credentials over the network in clear text or encoded form but instead sends a message digest (hash value) of the original credential. Authentication is performed by comparing the hash values of what was previously established and what is currently supplied as an entity claim. Using a unique hardware property, that cannot be easily spoofed, as an input (salt) to calculate the digest provides heightened security when implementing digest authentication.

2.4.4.4 Integrated Authentication

Commonly known as NTLM authentication or NT challenge/response authentication, like Digest authentication, the credentials are sent as a digest. This can be implemented as a stand-alone authentication mechanism or in conjunction with Kerberos v5 authentication when delegation and impersonation is necessary in a trusted subsystem infrastructure. Wherever possible, especially in intranet settings, it is best to use integrated authentication since the credentials are not transmitted in clear text and it is efficient in handling authentication needs.

2.4.4.5 Client Certificate-Based Authentication

Client certificate-based authentication works by validating the identity of the certificate holder. These certificates are issued to organizations or users by a certification authority (CA) that vouches for the validity of the holder. These certificates are usually in the form of digital certificates, and the current standard for digital certificates is ITU X.509 v3. If you trust the CA and you validate that the certificate presented for authentication has been signed by the trusted CA, then you can accept the certificate and process access requests. These are particularly useful in an Internet/e-commerce setting, when you cannot implement integrated authentication across your user base. Figure 2.4 illustrates an example of a digital SSL server certificate that provides information about the CA, its validity, and fingerprint information.

2.4.4.6 Forms Authentication

Predominantly observed in Web applications, forms authentication requires the user to supply a username and password for authentication purposes, and these credentials are validated against a directory store that can be the active directory, a database, or configuration file. Because the credentials collected are supplied in clear text form, it is advisable to first cryptographically protect the data being transmitted in addition to implementation TLS such as SSL or network layer security

This certificate has been verified for the following uses:	
SSL Server Certificate	
Issued To	
Common Name(CN)	www.expresscertifications.com
Organization (O)	www.expresscertifications.com
Organizational Unit (OU)	GT26673911
Serial Number	0B:61:E7
Issued By	
Common Name(CN)	Equifax Secure Global eBusiness CA-1
Organization (O)	Equifax Secure Inc.
Organizational Unit (OU)	<Not Part Of Certificate>
Validity	
Issued On	4/21/2009
Expires On	6/21/2010
Fingerprints	
SHA1 Fingerprint	32:93:13:C5:1C:42:8C:1F:87:95:F2:7F:0F:C5:7E:EF:C3:77:C5:69
MD5 Fingerprint	5A:6A:21:31:A7:08:F2:C:06:FC:FE:FC:B9:AE:C1:9B

Figure 2.4   Certificate.

such as IPSec. Figure 2.5 illustrates an example of a username and password login box used in Forms authentication.

2.4.4.7 Token-Based Authentication

The concept behind token-based authentication is pretty straightforward. It is usually used in conjunction with forms authentication where a username and password is supplied for verification. Upon verification, a token is issued to the user who supplied the credentials. The token is then used to grant access to resources that are requested. This way, the username and password need not be passed on each call. This is particularly useful in single sign-on (SSO) situations. While Kerberos tokens are restricted to the domain they are issued, Security Assertion Markup Language

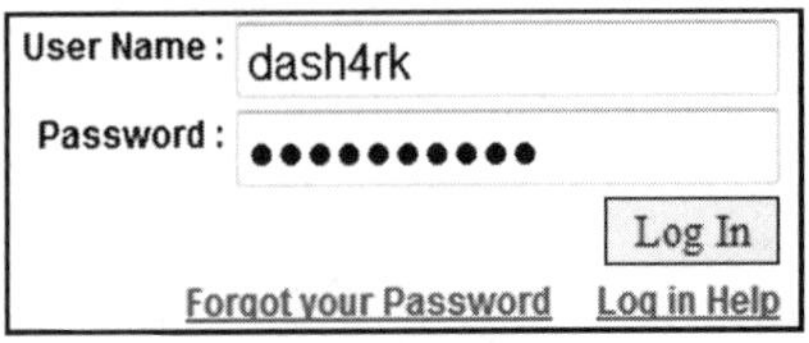

| User Name : | dash4rk |
| Password : | ●●●●●●●●● |

Log In

Forgot your Password   Log in Help

Figure 2.5   Forms authentication.

(SAML) tokens, which are XML representations of claims an entity makes about another entity, are considered the de facto tokens in cross-domain federated SSO architectures. We will cover SSO in more detail in Chapter 3.

2.4.4.8 Smart Cards–Based Authentication

Smart cards provide ownership-based (something you have) authentication. They contain a programmable embedded microchip that is used to store authentication credentials of the owner. The security advantage that smart cards provide is that they can thwart the threat of hackers stealing authentication credentials from a computer, because the authentication processing occurs on the smart card itself. However, a major disadvantage of smart cards is that the amount of information that can be stored is limited to the size of the microchip's storage area and cryptographic protection of stored credentials on the smart card is limited as well.

One-time (dynamic) passwords (OTP) provide the maximum strength of authentication security and OTP tokens (also known as key fobs) require two factors: knowledge (something you know) and ownership (something you have). These tokens dynamically provide a new password at periodic intervals. Like token-based authentication, the user enters the credential information they know and is issued a personal identification number (PIN) that is displayed on the token device such as an Radio Frequency Identification (RFID) device they own. Because the PIN is not static and dynamically changed every few seconds, it makes it virtually impossible for a malicious attacker to steal authentication credentials.

2.4.4.9 Biometric Authentication

This form of authentication uses biological characteristics (something you are) for providing the identity's credentials. Biological features such as retinal blood vessel patterns, facial features, and fingerprints are used for identity verification purposes. Because biological traits can potentially change over time owing to aging or pathological conditions, one of the major drawbacks of biometric-based authentication implementation is that the original enrollment may no longer be valid, and this can yield to DoS to legitimate users. This means that authentication workarounds need to be identified, defined, and implemented in conjunction to biometrics, and these need to be captured in the software requirements. The FIPS 201 Personal Identity Verification standard provides guidance that the enrollment data in systems implementing biometric-based authentication needs to be changed periodically.

Additionally, biometric authentication requires physical access that limits its usage in remote access settings.

Errors observed in biometric-based authentication systems are of two types: type I error and type II error. Type I error is otherwise known as false rejection error where a valid and legitimate enrollee is denied (rejected) access. It is usually computed as a rate and is referred to as false rejection rate (FRR). Type II error is otherwise known as false acceptance error where an imposter is granted (accepted) access. This is also computed as a rate and is referred to as false acceptance rate (FAR). The point at which the FRR equals the FAR is referred to as the crossover error rate (CER) as depicted in Figure 2.6. CER is primarily used in evaluating different biometric devices and technologies. Devices that assure more accurate identity verification are characterized by having a low CER.

Some good examples of authentication requirements that should be part of the software requirements documentation are given in the following:

- ■ "The software will be deployed only in the Intranet environment, and the authenticated user should not have the need to provide username and password once they have logged on to the network."
- ■ "The software will need to support single sign on with third party vendors and suppliers that are defined in the stakeholder list."
- ■ "Both Intranet and Internet users should be able to access the software."
- ■ "The authentication policy warrants the need for two- or multifactor authentication for all financially processing software."

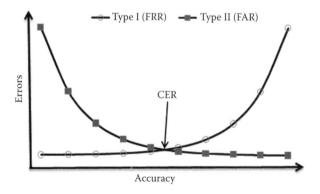

Figure 2.6   Crossover error rate.

Identifying the proper authentication requirements during the early part of the SDLC helps to mitigate many serious security risks at a later stage. These need to be captured in the software specifications so that they are not overlooked when designing and developing the software.

2.4.5 Authorization Requirements

Layered upon authentication, authorization requirements confirm that an authenticated entity has the needed rights and privileges to access and perform actions on a requested resource. These requirements answer the question of what one is allowed or not allowed to do. To determine authorization requirements, it is important to first identify the *subjects* and *objects*. Subjects are the entities that are requesting access, and objects are the items that subject will act upon. A subject can be a human user or a system process. Actions on the objects also need to be explicitly captured. Actions as they pertain to data or information that the user of the software can undertake are commonly referred to as CRUD (create, read, update, or delete data) operations. Later in this chapter, we shall cover subject–object modeling in more detail as one of the mechanisms to capture authorization requirements.

Access control models are primarily of three types:

1. Discretionary access control (DAC)
2. Nondiscretionary access control (NDAC)
3. Mandatory access control (MAC)
4. Role based Access Control (RBAC)
5. Resource Based Access Control

2.4.5.1 Discretionary Access Control (DAC)

DAC restricts access to objects based on the identity of the subject (Solomon and Chapple, 2005) and is distinctly characterized by the owner of the resource deciding who has access and their level of privileges or rights.

DAC is implemented by using either identities or roles. Identity-based access control means that the access to the object is granted based on the subject's identity. Because each identity will have to be assigned the appropriate access rights, the administration of identity-based access control implementations is an operational challenge. An often more preferred alternative in cases of a large user base is to use roles. Role-based access control (RBAC) uses the subject's role to determine whether access should be allowed or not. Users or groups of users are defined by roles and the owner (or a delegate) decides which role is granted access rights to objects and the levels of rights. RBAC is prominently implemented in software and is explained in more detail later in this section.

Another means by which DAC is often observed to be implemented is by using access control lists (ACLs). The relationship between the individuals (subjects) and

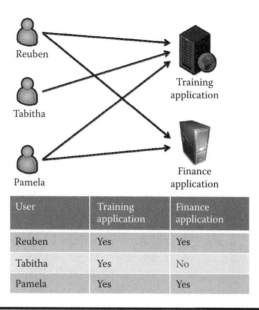

Figure 2.7   Discretionary access control (DAC) and a corresponding access control list (ACL).

the resources (objects) is direct, and the mapping of individuals to resources by the owner is what constitutes the ACLs as illustrated in Figure 2.7.

2.4.5.2 Nondiscretionary Access Control (NDAC)

NDAC is characterized by the system enforcing the security policies. It does not rely on the subject's compliance with security policies. The nondiscretionary aspect is that it is unavoidably imposed on all subjects. It is useful to make sure that the system security policies and mechanisms configured by the systems or security administrators are enforced and tamper-proof. NDACs can be installed on many operating systems. Because NDAC does not depend on a subject's compliance with the security policy as in the case of DAC but is universally applied, it offers a higher degree of protection. Without NDAC, even if a user attempts to comply with well-defined file protection mechanisms, a Trojan horse program could change the protection controls to allow uncontrolled access.

2.4.5.3 Mandatory Access Control (MAC)

In MAC, access to objects is restricted to subjects based on the sensitivity of the information contained in the objects. The sensitivity is represented by a label. Only subjects that have the appropriate privilege and formal authorization (i.e., clearance) are granted access to the objects. MAC requires sensitivity labels for all the objects, and clearance levels for all subjects and access is determined based on matching a subject's clearance level with the object's sensitivity level. Examples of government labels include top secret, secret, confidential, etc., and examples of private sector labels include high confidential, confidential-restricted, for your eyes only, etc.

MAC provides multilevel security because there are multiple levels of sensitivity requirements that can be addressed using this form of access control.

MAC systems are more structured in approach and more rigid in their implementation because they do not leave the access control decision to the owner alone as in the case of DAC, but both the system and the owner are used to determine whether access should be allowed or not. A common implementation of MAC is *rule-based access control*. In rule-based access control, the access decision is based on a list of rules that are created or authorized by system owners who specify the privileges (i.e., read, write, execute) that the subjects (users) have on the objects (resources). These rules are used to provide the need-to-know level of the subject. Rule-based MAC implementation requires the subject to possess the need-to-know property that is provided by the owner; however, in addition to the owner deciding who possesses need to know, in MAC, the system determines access decisions based on clearance and sensitivity.

2.4.5.4 Role-Based Access Control (RBAC)

Because the mapping of each subject to a resource (as in the case of DAC) or the assignment of subjects to clearance levels and objects to sensitivity levels (as in the case of MAC) can be an arduous task, for purposes of ease of user management, a more agile and efficient access control model is RBAC. Roles are defined by job functions that can be used for authorization decisions. Roles define the trust levels of entities to perform desired operations. These roles may be user roles or service roles. In RBAC, individuals (subjects) have access to a resource (object) based on their assigned role. Permissions to operate on objects such as create, read, update, or delete are also defined and determined based on responsibilities and authority (permissions) within the job function.

Access that is granted to subjects is based on roles. What this mainly provides is that the resource is not directly mapped to the individual but only to the role. Because individuals can change over time, whereas roles generally do not, individuals can be easily assigned to or revoked from roles, thereby allowing ease of user management. Roles are then allowed operations against the resource as depicted in Figure 2.8.

RBAC can be used to implement all three types of access control models, i.e., DAC, NDAC, and MAC. The discretionary aspect is that the owners need to determine which subjects need to be granted what role. The nondiscretionary aspect is that the security policy is universally enforced on the role regardless of the subject. It is also a form of MAC where the role is loosely analogous to the process

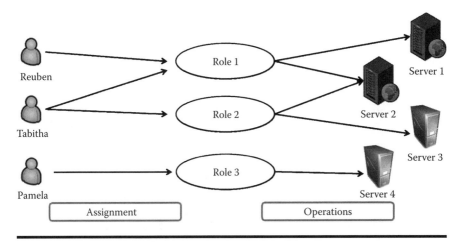

Figure 2.8   Role-based access control (RBAC).

of clearance levels (granting memberships) and the objects requested are labeled (associated operational sensitivities), but RBAC is not based on multilevel security requirements.

2.4.5.4.1 RBAC in Relation to Least Privilege and Separation of Duties

Roles support the principle of least privilege, because roles are given just the needed privileges to undertake an operation against a resource. When RBAC is used for authorization decisions, it is imperative to ensure that the principle of separation of duties (SoD) is maintained. This means that no individual can be assigned to two roles that are mutually exclusive in their permissions to perform operations. For example, a user should not be in a datareader role as well as a more privileged database owner role at the same time. When users are prevented from being assigned to conflicting roles, then it is referred to as static SoD. Another example that demonstrates SoD in RBAC is that a user who is in the auditor role cannot also be in the teller role at the same time. When users are prevented from operating on resources with conflicting roles, then it is referred to as dynamic SoD.

RBAC implementations require explicit "role engineering" to determine roles, authorizations, role hierarchies, and constraints. The real benefit of RBAC over other access control methods includes the following:

- Simplified subjects and objects access rights administration
- Ability to represent the organizational structure
- Force enterprise compliance with control policies more easily and effectively

2.4.5.4.2 Role Hierarchies

Roles can be hierarchically organized and when such a parent–child tree structure is in place, it is commonly referred to as a *role hierarchy.* Role hierarchies define the inherent relationships between roles. For example, an admin user may have read, write, and execute privileges, whereas a general user may have just read and write privileges and a guest user may only have read privilege. In such a situation, the guest user role is a subset of the general user role, which, in turn, is a subset of the admin user role as illustrated in Figure 2.9.

In generating role hierarchies, we start with the most common permissions for all users (e.g., read) and then iterate permissions to be more restrictive (read, write, execute), assigning them to roles (guest, general, admin) that are then assigned to users. It is also important to recognize that when determining role hierarchy it is also important to identify contextual and content-based constraints and grant access rights based on "only if" or "if and only if" relationships. Just basing the access decisions on an *if* relationship does not provide real separation of duties. For example, a doctor should be allowed to view the records of a patient, *only if* or *if and only if* that patient whose records are requested for is assigned to the doctor, not just *if* the requestor is a doctor.

2.4.5.4.3 Roles and Groups

Although it may seem like there is a high degree of similarity between roles and groups, there is a distinction that make RBAC more preferable for security than groups. A group is a collection of users and not a collection of permissions. In a group, permissions can be assigned to both users and groups to which users are part

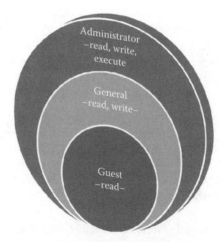

Figure 2.9 Role hierarchy.

of. The ability to associate a user directly with permissions in group-based access control can be the Achilles' heel for circumventing access control checks, besides making it more difficult to manage users and permissions. RBAC mandates that all access is done only through roles and permissions are never directly assigned to the users but to the roles; this addresses the challenges that one can have with group-based access control mechanisms.

2.4.5.5 Resource-Based Access Control

When the list of all users of your software are not known in advance, as in the case of a distributed Internet application, then DAC and MAC implementation using subject (user) mapping to objects (resources) may not always be possible. In such situations, access can also be granted based on the resources. Resource-based access control models are useful in architectures that are distributed and multitiered including service-oriented architectures. Resource-based access control models can be broadly divided into

- Impersonation and Delegation Model
- Trusted Subsystem Model

2.4.5.5.1 Impersonation and Delegation Model

Allowing a secondary entity to act on one's behalf is the principle of delegation. All of the privileges necessary for completing an operation are granted to the secondary entity. The secondary entity is considered to impersonate the identity of the primary entity when the complete sets of permissions of the primary entity are assigned to it. The identity of the primary entity is propagated to downstream systems. Kerberos uses the delegation and impersonation model where the user upon successful authentication is granted a Kerberos ticket, and the ticket is delegated the privileges and rights (sets of permission) to invoke services downstream. The ticket is the secondary entity that acts as if it is the primary entity by impersonating the user identity.

2.4.5.5.2 Trusted Subsystem Model

In a trusted subsystem model, access request decisions are granted based on the identity of a resource that is trusted instead of user identities. Trusted subsystem models are predominantly observed in Web applications. For example, a user logs into their bank account using a Web browser to transfer funds from one account to another. The Web application identity calls the database to first authenticate the user-supplied credentials. It is not the user identity that is checked but the Web application identity that is trusted and that can invoke the call to the database. Although this simplifies access management, it needs to be designed with security in mind, and such architectures need to be layered with additional defense in depth measures such as transport or network layer security controls.

Regardless of whether it is user- or resource-based access control models that need to be implemented, authorization requirements need to be explicitly identified and captured in the software specifications documentation. Some good examples of authorization requirements that should be part of the software requirements documentation are given in the following:

■ "Access to highly sensitive secret files will be restricted to users with secret or top secret clearance levels only."
■ "User should not be required to send their credentials each and every time once they have authenticated themselves successfully."
■ "All unauthenticated users will inherit read-only permissions that are part of guest user role while authenticated users will default to having read and write permissions as part of the general user role. Only members of the administrator role will have all rights as a general user in addition to having permissions to execute operations."

2.4.6 Auditing/Logging Requirements

Auditing requirements are those that assist in building a historical record of user actions. Audit trails can help detect when an unauthorized user makes a change or an authorized user makes an unauthorized change, both of which are cases of integrity violations. Auditing requirements not only help with forensic investigations as a detective control but can also be used for troubleshooting errors and exceptions, if the actions of the software are tracked appropriately.

Auditing requirements at the bare minimum must include the following elements:

■ Identity of the subject (user or process) performing an action (who)
■ Action (what)
■ Object on which the action was performed (where)
■ Timestamp of the action (when)

What is to be logged (audit trail) and what is not is a decision that is to be made in discussions with the business managers. As a best practice for security, all critical business transactions and administrative functions need to be identified and audited. Some examples of critical business transactions include the changing of the price of a product, discounts by sales agents, or changing customer banking information. The business owner should be asked for audit trail information to be incorporated into the software requirements specification. Some examples of administrative functionality include authentication attempts such as log-on and log-off actions, adding a user to an administrator role, and changing software configuration.

Some good examples of auditing requirements that should be part of the software requirements documentation are given below.

- "All failed logon attempts will be logged along with the timestamp and the Internet Protocol address where the request originated."
- "A before and an after snapshot of the pricing data that changed when a user updates the pricing of a product must be tracked with the following auditable fields—identity, action, object and timestamp."
- "Audit logs should always append and never be overwritten."
- "The audit logs must be securely retained for a period of 3 years."

2.4.7 Session Management Requirements

Sessions are useful for maintaining state but also have an impact on the secure design principles of complete mediation and psychological acceptability. Upon successful authentication, a session identifier (ID) is issued to the user and that session ID is used to track user behavior and maintain the authenticated state for that user until that session is abandoned or the state changes from authenticated to not authenticated. Without session management, the user/process would be required to reauthenticate upon each access request (complete mediation), and this can be burdensome and psychologically unacceptable to the user. Because valid sessions can be potentially hijacked where an attacker takes control over an established session, it is necessary to plan for secure session management.

In stateless protocols, such as the HTTP, session state needs to be explicitly maintained and carefully protected from brute force or predictable session ID attacks. In Chapter 4, we will be covering attacks on session management in more detail.

Session management requirements are those that ensure that once a session is established, it remains in a state that will not compromise the security of the software. In other words, the established session is not susceptible to any threats to the security policy as it applies to confidentiality, integrity, and availability. Session management requirements assure that sessions are not vulnerable to brute force attacks, predictability, or MITM hijacking attempts.

Some good examples of session management secure software requirements that should be part of the requirements documentation are given in the following:

- "Each user activity will need to be uniquely tracked."
- "The user should not be required to provide user credential once authenticated within the Internet banking application."
- "Sessions must be explicitly abandoned when the user logs off or closes the browser window."
- "Session identifiers used to identify user sessions must not be passed in clear text or be easily guessable."

2.4.8 Errors and Exception Management Requirements

Errors and exceptions are potential sources of information disclosure. Verbose error messages and unhandled exception reports can result in divulging internal application architecture, design, and configuration information. Using laconic error messages and structured exception handling are examples of good security design features that can thwart security threats posed by improper error or exception management. Software requirements that explicitly address errors and exceptions need to be defined in the software requirements documentation to avoid disclosure threats.

Some good examples of error and exception management secure software requirements that should be part of the requirements documentation are given in the following:

- "All exceptions are to be explicitly handled using try, catch, and finally blocks."
- "Error messages that are displayed to the end user will reveal only the needed information without disclosing any internal system error details."
- "Security exception details are to be audited and monitored periodically."

2.4.9 Configuration Parameters Management Requirements

Software configuration parameters and code that make up the software need protection against hackers. These parameters and code usually need to be initialized before the software can run. Identifying and capturing configuration settings is vital to ensure that an appropriate level of protection is considered when the software is designed, developed, and, more importantly, deployed.

Some good examples of configuration parameters management secure software requirements that should be part of the requirements documentation are given in the following:

- "The Web application configuration file must encrypt sensitive database connections settings and other sensitive application settings."
- "Passwords must not be hard coded in line code."
- "Initialization and disposal of global variables need to be carefully and explicitly monitored."
- "Application and/or session OnStart and OnEnd events must include protection of configuration information as a safeguard against disclosure threats."

2.4.10 Sequencing and Timing Requirements

Sequencing and timing design flaws in software can lead to what is commonly known as race conditions or time of check/time of use (TOC/TOU) attacks. Race conditions are, in fact, one of the most common flaws observed in software design. It is also referred to sometimes as race hazard. Some of the common sources of race conditions include, but are not limited to, the following:

- Undesirable sequence of events, where one event that is to follow in the program execution order attempts to supersede its preceding event in its operations.
- Multiple unsynchronized threads executing simultaneously for a process that needs to be completed atomically.
- Infinite loops that prevent a program from returning control to the normal flow of logic.

2.4.10.1 Race Condition Properties

In order for race conditions to occur, the following three properties need to be fulfilled:

1. Concurrency property
2. Shared object property
3. Change state property

Concurrency property means that there must be at least two threads or control flows executing concurrently. *Shared object property* means that the threads executing concurrently are both accessing the same object, i.e., the object is shared between the two concurrent flows. *Change state property* means that at least one of the control flows must alter the state of the shared object.

Only when all of these conditions are fulfilled does a race condition occur.

2.4.10.2 Race Conditions Protection

It is not only important to understand how race conditions occur but also to know about the protection mechanisms that are available to avoid them. Some of the prevalent protection measures against race conditions or TOC/TOU attacks are:

- Avoid race windows
- Atomic operations
- Mutual exclusion (Mutex)

A *race window* is defined as the window of opportunity when two concurrent threads race against one another trying to alter the same object. The first step in avoiding race conditions is to identify race windows. Improperly coded segments of code that access objects without proper control flow can result in race windows.

Upon identification of race windows, it is important to fix them in code or logic design to mitigate race conditions. In addition to addressing race windows, atomic operations can also help prevent race condition attacks.

Atomic operations means that the entire process is completed using a single flow of control and that concurrent threads or control flow against the same object is disallowed. Single threaded operations are a means to ensure that operations are performed sequentially and not concurrently. However, such design comes with a cost on performance, and it must be carefully considered by weighing the benefits of security over performance.

Race conditions can also be eliminated by making two conflicting processes or race windows, mutually exclusive of each other. Race windows are referred to as critical sections because it is critical that two race windows do not overlap one another. *Mutual exclusions* or Mutex can be accomplished by resource locking, wherein the object being accessed is locked and does not allow any alteration until the first process or threat releases it. Resource locking provides integrity assurance. Assume, for example, in the case of an online auction, Jack bids on a particular item and Jill, who is also interested in that same item, places a bid as well. Both Jack and Jill's bids should be mutually exclusive of one another, and until Jack's bid is processed entirely and committed to the backend database, Jill bid's operation should not be allowed. The backend record that holds the item information must be locked from any operations until Jack's transaction commits successfully or is rolled back in the case of an error.

If software requirements do not explicitly specify protection mechanisms for race conditions, there is a high degree of likelihood that sequencing and timing attack flaws will result when designing it. Race windows and Mutex requirements must be identified as part of security requirements.

2.4.11 Archiving Requirements

If the business requires that archives be maintained either as a means for business continuity or as a need to comply with a regulatory requirement or organizational policy, the archiving requirement must be explicitly identified and captured. It is also important to recognize that organizational retention policies, especially if the information will be considered sensitive or private, do not contradict but complement regulatory requirements. In situations when there is a conflict between the organizational policy and a regulatory requirement, it is best advice to follow and comply with the regulatory requirement. Data or information may be stored and archived until it has outlived its usefulness or there is no regulatory or organizational policy requirement to comply with.

During the requirements gathering phase, the *location*, *duration*, and *format* of archiving information must be determined. Some important questions that need to be answered as part of this exercise are:

- Where will the data or information be stored?
- Will it be in a transactional system that is remote and online or will it be in offline storage media?
- How much space do we need in the archival system?
- How do we ensure that the media is not rewritable? For example, it is better to store archives in read-only media instead of read–write media.
- How fast will we need to be able to retrieve from archives when needed? This will not only help in answering the online or offline storage location question but also help with determining the type of media to use. For example, for a situation when fast retrieval of archived data is necessary, archives in tape media is not advisable because retrieval is sequential and time consuming in tape media.
- How long will we need to store the archives for?
- Is there a regulatory requirement to store the data for a set period of time?
- Is our archival retention policy contradictory to any compliance or regulatory requirements?
- In what format will the data or information be stored? Clear text or cipher text?
- If the data or information are stored in cipher text, how is this accomplished and are there management processes in place that will ensure proper retrieval?
- How will these archives themselves be protected?

It is absolutely essential to ensure that archiving requirements are part of the required documentation and that they are not overlooked when designing and developing the software.

2.4.12 International Requirements

In a world that is no longer merely tied to geographical topographies, software has become a necessary means for global economies to be strong or weak. When developing software, international requirements need to be factored in. International requirements can be of two types: *legal* and *technological*.

Legal requirements are those requirements that we need to pay attention to so that we are not in violation of any regulations. For example, a time accounting system must allow the employees in France to submit their timesheets with a 30-hour workweek (which is a legal requirement according to the French employment laws) and not be restrictive by disallowing the French employee to submit if his total time per week is less than 40 hours, as is usually the case in the United States. This requirement by country must be identified and included in the software specifications document for the time accounting system.

International requirements are also technological in nature, especially if the software needs to support multilingual, multicultural, and multiregional needs.

Character encoding and display direction are two important international software requirements that need to be determined. Character encoding standards not only define the identity of each character and its numeric value (also known as code point) but also how the value is represented in bits. The first standard character encoding system was ASCII, which was a 7-bit coding system that supported up to 128 characters. ASCII supported the English languages, but fell short of coding all alphabets of European languages. This limitation led to the development of the Latin-1 international coding standard, ISO/IEC 646, that was an 8-bit coding system that could code up to 256 characters and was inclusive of European alphabets. But even the ISO/IEC 646 encoding standard fell short of accommodating logographic and morphosyllabic writing systems such as Chinese and Japanese. To support these languages, the 16-bit Unicode standard was developed that could support 65,536 characters, which was swiftly amended to include 32 bits supporting more than 4 billion characters. The Unicode standard is the universal character encoding standard that is fully compatible and synchronized with the versions of the ISO/IEC 10646 standard. The Unicode standard supports three encoding forms that make it possible for the same data to be transmitted as a byte (UTF-8), a word (UTF-16), or double word (UTF-32) format. UTF-8 is popular for the Hypertext Markup Language (HTML) where all Unicode characters are transformed into a variable length encoding of bytes. Its main benefit is that the Unicode characters that correspond to the familiar ASCII set have the same byte values as ASCII, which makes conversion of legacy software to support UTF-8, not require extensive software rewrites. UTF-16 is popular in environments where there is a need to balance efficient character access with economical use of storage. UTF-32 is popular in environments where memory space is not an issue but fixed width single code unit access to characters is essential. In UTF-32, each character is encoded in a single 32-bit code unit. All three encoding forms at most require 4 bytes (32 bits) of data for each character. It is important to understand that the appropriate and correct character encoding is identified and set in the software to prevent Unicode security issues such as spoofing, overflows, and canonicalization. Canonicalization is the process of converting data that has more than one possible representation into a standard canonical form. We will cover canonicalization and related security considerations in more detail in Chapter 4.

In addition to character encoding, it is also important to determine display direction requirements. A majority of the western languages that have their roots in Latin or Greek, such as English and French, are written and read left to right. Other languages such as Chinese are written and read top to bottom and then there are some languages, such as Hebrew and Arabic, that are bidirectional, i.e., text is written and read right to left, whereas numbers are written and read left to right. Software that needs to support languages in which the script is not written and read from left to right must take into account the directionality of their written and reading form. This must be explicitly identified and included in the software user interface (UI) or display requirements.

2.4.13 Deployment Environment Requirements

While eliciting software requirements, it is important to also identify and capture pertinent requirements about the environment in which the software will be deployed. Some important questions to have answered include:

- Will the software be deployed in an Internet, Extranet, or Intranet environment?
- Will the software be hosted in a demilitarized zone (DMZ)?
- What ports and protocols are available for use?
- What privileges will be allowed in the production environment?
- Will the software be transmitting sensitive or confidential information?
- Will the software be load balanced and how is clustering architected?
- Will the software be deployed in a Web farm environment?
- Will the software need to support SSO authentication?
- Can we leverage existing operating system event logging for auditing purposes?

Usually, production environments are far more restrictive and configured differently than development/test environments. Some of these restrictions include ports and protocols restrictions, network segmentation, disabled services, and components. Infrastructure, platform, and host security restrictions that can affect software operations must be elicited. Implementation of clustering and load balancing mechanisms can also have a potential impact on how the software is to be designed and these architectural considerations must be identified. Special attention needs to be given to implementing cryptographic protection in Web farm environments to avoid data corruption issues, and these need to be explicitly identified. Additionally, compliance initiatives may require certain environmental protection controls such as secure communications to exist. As an example, the Payment Card Industry Data Security Standard (PCI DSS) mandates that sensitive card holder data needs to be protected when it is transmitted in public open networks. Identifying and capturing constraints, restrictions, and requirements of the environment in which the software is expected to operate, in advance during the requirements gathering phase, will alleviate deployment challenges later besides assuring that the software will be deployed and function as designed.

2.4.14 Procurement Requirements

The identification of software security requirements is no less important when a decision is made to procure the software instead of building it in-house. Sometimes the requirement definition process itself leads to a buy decision. As part of the procurement methodology and process, in addition to the functional software requirements, secure software requirements must also be communicated and appropriately evaluated. Additionally, it is important to include software security requirements in legal protection mechanisms such as contracts and SLAs. The need for software escrow is an important requirement when procuring software. Chapter 6 will cover these concepts in more detail.

2.4.15 Antipiracy Requirements

Particularly important for shrink-wrap commercial off-the-shelf (COTS) software as opposed to business applications developed in-house, antipiracy protection requirements should be identified. Code obfuscation, code signing, antitampering, licensing, and IP protection mechanisms should be included as part of the requirements documentation especially if you are in the business of building and selling commercial software. Each of these considerations will be covered in more detail in Chapter 4, but for now, in the requirements gathering phase, antipiracy requirements should not be overlooked.

2.5 Protection Needs Elicitation

In addition to knowing the sources for security requirements and the various types of secure software requirements that need to be determined, it is also important to know the process of eliciting security requirements. The determination of security requirements is also known as protection needs elicitation (PNE). PNE is one of the most crucial processes in information systems security engineering. For PNE activities to be effective and accurate, strong communication and collaboration with stakeholders is required, especially if the stakeholders are nontechnical business folks and end users. With varying degrees of importance placed on security requirements, combined with individual perceptions and perspectives on the software development project, PNE activities have been observed to be a challenge.

PNE begins with the discovery of assets that need to be protected from unauthorized access and users. The Information Assurance Technical Framework (IATF) issued by the U.S. National Security Agency (NSA) is a set of security guidelines that covers Information Systems Security Engineering (ISSE). It defines a methodology for incorporation assurance/security requirements for both the hardware and software components of the system. The first step in the IATF process is PNE, which is suggested to be conducted in the following order:

- Engage the customer
- Information management modeling
- Identify least privilege applications
- Conduct threat modeling and analysis
- Prioritize based on customer needs
- Develop information protection policy
- Seek customer acceptance

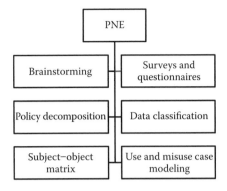

Figure 2.10   Protection needs elicitation methodologies.

PNE activities may be conducted in several ways as Figure 2.10 illustrates.

Some of the most common mechanisms to elicit security requirements include:

- Brainstorming
- Surveys (questionnaires and interviews)
- Policy decomposition
- Data classification
- Subject–object matrix
- Use and misuse case modeling

2.5.1 Brainstorming

Brainstorming is the quickest and most unstructured method to glean security requirements. In this process, none of the expressed ideas on security requirements are challenged, but instead they are recorded. Although this may allow for a quick-and-dirty way to determine protection needs, especially in rapid application development situations, it is not advised for PNE because it has several shortcomings. First, there is a high degree of likelihood that the brainstormed ideas do not directly relate to the business, technical, and security context of the software. This can either lead to ignoring certain critical security considerations or going overboard on a nontrivial security aspect of the software. Additionally, brainstorming solutions are usually not comprehensive and consistent because it is very subjective. Brainstorming may be acceptable to determine preliminary security requirements, but it is imperative to have a more structured and systematic methodology for consistency and comprehensiveness of security requirements.

2.5.2 Surveys (Questionnaires and Interviews)

Surveys are effective means to collect functional and assurance requirements. The effectiveness of the survey is dependent on how applicable the questions in the surveys are to the audience that is being surveyed. This means that the questionnaires are not a one size fits all type of survey. This also means that both explicitly specified questions as well as open-ended questions should be part of the questionnaire. The benefit of including open-ended questions is that the responses to such questions can yield security-related information that may be missed if the questions are very specific. Questionnaires developed should take into account *business* risks, *process* (or *project*) risks, and *technology* (or *product*) risks. It is advisable to have the questions developed so that they cover elements of the software security profile and secure design principles. This way, the answers to these questions can be directly used to generate the security requirements. Some examples of questions that be asked are:

- What kind of data will be processed, transmitted, or stored by the software?
- Is the data highly sensitive or confidential in nature?
- Will the software handle personally identifiable information or privacy-related information?
- Who are all the users who will be allowed to make alterations and will they need to be audited and monitored?
- What is the MTD for the software?
- How quickly should the software be able to recover and restore to normal operations when disrupted?
- Is there a need for SSO authentication?
- What are the roles of users that need to be established and what privileges and rights (such as create, read, update, or delete) will each role have?
- What are the set of error messages and conditions that you would need the software to handle when an error occurs?

These questions can be either delivered in advance using electronic means or asked as part of an interview with the stakeholders. As a CSSLP, it is expected that one will be able to facilitate this interview process. It is also a recommended practice to include and specify a scribe who records the responses provided by the interviewee. Like questionnaires, the interview should also be conducted in an independent and objective manner with different types of personnel. Additional PNE activities may be necessary, especially if the responses from the interview have led to new questions that warrant answers. Collaboration and communications between the responders and the interviewers are both extremely important when conducting a survey-based security requirements exercise.

2.5.3 Policy Decomposition

One of the sources for security requirements is internal organizational policies that the organization needs to comply with. Because these policies contain in them high-level mandates, they need to be broken down (or, in other words, decomposed) into detailed security requirements. However, this process of breaking high-level mandates into concrete security requirements is not limited only to organizational policies. External regulations, privacy, and compliance mandates can also be broken down to glean detailed security requirements. To avoid any confusion, for the remainder of this chapter, we will refer all these high-level sources of security requirements as *policy documents*, regardless of whether they are internal or external in their origin.

Although superficially it may seem as though the policy decomposition process may be pretty simple and straightforward, because policies are high level and open to interpretation, careful attention is paid to the scope of the policy. This is to ensure that the decomposition process is objective and compliant with the security policy, and not merely someone's opinion. The policy decomposition process is a sequential and structured process as illustrated in Figure 2.11.

It starts by breaking the high-level requirements in the policy documents into high-level objectives, which are, in turn, decomposed to generate security requirements, the precursors for software security requirement. As an illustration, consider the following PCI DSS requirement 6.3 example, which mandates the following:

> *Develop software applications in accordance with PCI DSS and based on industry best practices, and incorporate information security throughout the SDLC.*

This requirement is pretty high level and can be subject to various interpretations. What is the meaning of incorporating information security through the SDLC? Additionally, what may be considered as an industry best practice for someone may not even be applicable to another. This is why the high-level policy document requirement must be broken down into high-level objectives such as:

- CFG: Configuration management
- SEG: Segregated environments
- SOD: Separation of duties

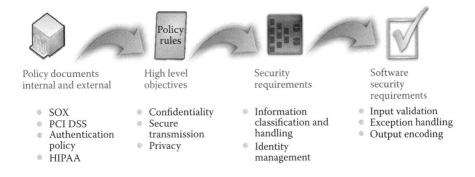

Policy documents internal and external	High level objectives	Security requirements	Software security requirements
● SOX ● PCI DSS ● Authentication policy ● HIPAA	● Confidentiality ● Secure transmission ● Privacy	● Information classification and handling ● Identity management	● Input validation ● Exception handling ● Output encoding

Figure 2.11   Policy decomposition process.

- DAT: Data protection
- PRC: Production readiness checking
- CRV: Code review

These high-level objectives can be used to glean security requirements as shown:

- CFG1: Test all security patches and system and software configuration changes before deployment.
- SEG1: Separate development/test and production environment.
- SOD1: Separation of duties between development/test and production environments.
- DAT1: Production data (live sensitive cardholder data) are not used for testing or development.
- PRC1: Removal of test data and accounts before production systems become active.
- PRC2: Removal of custom application accounts, user IDs, and passwords before applications become active or are released to customers.
- CRV1: Review of custom code before release to production or customers in order to identify any potential coding vulnerability.

From each security requirement, one or more software security requirements can be determined. For example, the CFG1 high-level objective can be broken down into several security requirements as shown below.

- CFG1.1: Validate all input on both server and client end.
- CFG1.2: Handle all errors using try, catch, and finally blocks.
- CFG1.3: Cryptographically protect data using 128-bit encryption of SHA-256 hashing when storing it.
- CFG1.4: Implement secure communications using Transport (TLS) or Network (IPSec) secure communications.
- CFG1.5: Implement proper RBAC control mechanisms.

Decomposition of policy documents is a crucial step in the process of gathering requirements, and an appropriate level of attention must be given to this process.

2.5.4 Data Classification

Within the context of software assurance, data or information can be considered to be the most valuable asset that a company has, second only to its people. Like any asset that warrants protection, data as a digital asset need to be protected as well. But not all data need the same level of protection, and some data that make up public data or directory information require minimal to no protection against disclosure. Data classification is the conscious effort to assign a level of sensitivity to data assets, based on potential impact upon disclosure, alteration, or destruction. The results of the classification exercise can then be used to categorize the data elements into appropriate buckets as depicted in Figure 2.12. *NIST Special Publication 800-18* provides a framework for classifying information assets based on impact to the three core security objectives, i.e., confidentiality, integrity, and availability. This is highly qualitative in nature, and the buckets used to classify are tied to impact as high, medium, and low. This categorization is then used to determine security requirements and the appropriate levels of security protection by category.

The main objective of data classification is to lower the cost of data protection and maximize the return on investment when data are protected. This can be accomplished by implementing only the needed levels of security controls on data assets based on their categorization. In other words, security controls must commensurate with the classification level. For example, there is no point to encrypt data or information that is to be publicly disclosed or implementing full-fledged load balancing and redundancy control for data that have a very limited adverse effect on organizational operations, assets, or individuals. In addition to lowering the cost of data protections and maximizing return on investment (ROI) data classification can also assist in increasing the quality of risk-based decisions. Because the data quality and characteristics are known upon classification, decisions that are made to protect them can also be made appropriately.

Decisions to classify data (e.g., who has access and what level of access) are decisions that are made by the business owner. It is also imperative to understand that it is the business that owns the data and not IT. The business owner or data owner has the responsibility for the following:

■ Ensure that information assets are appropriately classified.
■ Validate that security controls are implemented as needed by reviewing the classification periodically.
■ Define authorized list of users and access criteria based on information classification. This supports the separation of duties principle of secure design.
■ Ensure appropriate backup and recovery mechanisms are in place
■ Delegate as needed the classification responsibility, access approval authority, backup, and recovery duties to a data custodian.

The data custodian is delegated by the data owner and is the individual who is responsible for the following:

■ Perform the information classification exercise.
■ Perform backups and recovery as specified by the data owner.
■ Ensure records retention is in place according to regulatory requirements or organizational retention policy.

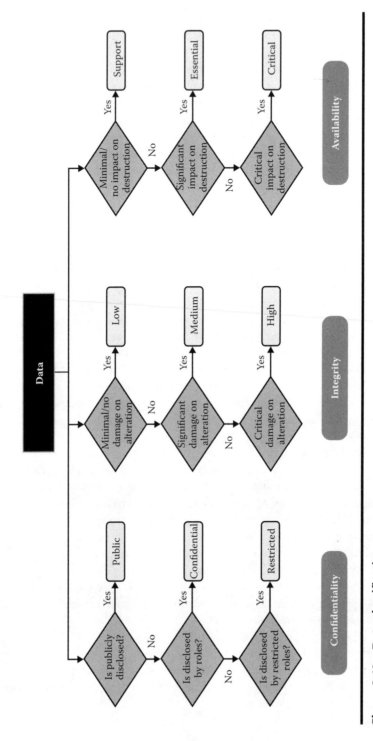

Figure 2.12 Data classification.

It is also important to recognize that data need to be protected throughout the information life cycle, i.e., from the time they are created to the time they are disposed or deleted. Information life cycle management (ILM) includes the creation, use, archival, and removal of data. When data are created and used (processed, transmitted, or stored), appropriate protection mechanisms need to exist. Security requirements when archiving data, covered earlier in this chapter, must be considered when data are archived. However, when data have outlived their usefulness and there is no regulatory or compliance requirement to retain them, the data must be deleted. The rules for data retention are determined by the corporate data retention period, which must complement local legal and legislative procedures.

Proper implementation of data classification can be effective in determining security requirements because a one-size-fits-all security protection mechanism is not effective in today's complex heterogeneous computing ecosystems. Data classification can ensure that confidentiality, integrity, and availability security requirements are adequately identified and captured in the software specifications documentation.

2.5.5 Use and Misuse Case Modeling

2.5.5.1 Use Cases

Like data classification, use case modeling is another mechanism by which software functional and security requirements can be determined. A use case models the intended behavior of the software or system. In other words, the use case describes behavior that the system owner intended. This behavior describes the sequence of actions and events that are to be taken to address a business need. Use case modeling and diagramming is very useful for specifying requirements. It can be effective in reducing ambiguous and incompletely articulated business requirements by explicitly specifying exactly when and under what conditions certain behavior occurs. Use case modeling is meant to model only the most significant system behavior and not all of it and so should not be considered a substitute for requirements specification documentation.

Use case modeling includes identifying actors, intended system behavior (use cases), and sequences and relationships between the actors and the use cases. Actors may be an individual, a role, or nonhuman in nature. As an example, the individual John, an administrator, or a backend batch process can all be actors in a use case. Actors are represented by stick people and use case scenarios by ellipses when the use case is diagrammatically represented. Arrows that represent the interactions or relationships connect the use cases and the actors. These relationships may be an includes or extends type of relationship. Figure 2.13 depicts a use case for an online auction. There are two types of actors, namely, an authenticated user and an anonymous user depicted in this use case. The user must first sign in and be authenticated before an item can be added to their watch list or a bid for an item can be placed in

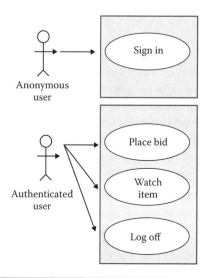

Figure 2.13   Use case diagram example.

the system. This sequence of actions is not represented within the use case itself, but this is where a sequence diagram comes handy. Sequence diagrams usually go hand in hand with use case diagrams. Preconditions such as a user must be authenticated before placing a bid and postconditions such as when the user logs off the system, should be required to re-log-in before performing authenticated user actions, can be used to clarify the scope of the use case and document any assumptions the use case author has made about the system.

2.5.5.2 Misuse Cases

From use cases, misuse cases can be developed. Misuse cases, also known as abuse cases, help identify security requirements by modeling negative scenarios (McGraw, 2006). A negative scenario is an unintended behavior of the system, one that the system owner does not want to occur within the context of the use case. Misuse cases provide insight into the threats that can occur against the system or software. It provides the hostile users point of view and is an inverse of the use case. Misuse case modeling is similar to the use case modeling, except that in misuse case modeling, mis-actors and unintended scenarios or behaviors are modeled. Misuse cases may be intentional or accidental. One of the most distinctive traits of misuse cases is that they can be used to elicit security requirements unlike other requirements determination methods that focus on end user functional requirements.

Misuse cases can be created through brainstorming negative scenarios like an attacker. A misuse case can also be generated by thwarting the sequence of actions that is part of the use case scenario. In our online auction example, if an anonymous user is able to place a bid on an item before first signing it, a misuse of intended behavior has occurred. Misuse cases must not only take into account adversaries that are external to the company but also the insider. A database administrator who has direct access to unprotected sensitive data in the databases is a potential insider mis-actor and a misuse case to represent this scenario must be specified. Auditing can assist in determining insider threats, and this must be a security control that is taken into account when generating misuse cases for mis-actors that are internal to the company. Additionally, a Subject–Object Matrix can also be very useful in determining misuse cases.

2.5.6 Subject–Object Matrix

When there are multiple subjects (roles) that require access to functionality within the software, it is critical to understand what each subject is allowed to do. Objects (components) are those items that a subject can act upon. They are the building blocks of software. Higher-level objects must be broken down into more granular objects for better accuracy of subject–object relationship representations. For example, the "database" object can be broken down into finer objects such as "data table," "data view," and "stored procedures," and each of these objects can now be mapped to subjects or roles. It is also important to capture third party components as objects in the software requirements specification documents.

A Subject–Object Matrix is used to identify allowable actions between subjects and objects based on use cases. Once use cases are enumerated with subjects (roles) and the objects (components) are defined, a Subject–Object Matrix can be developed. A Subject–Object Matrix is a two-dimensional representation of roles and components. The subjects or roles are listed across the columns and the objects or components are listed down the rows. A Subject–Object Matrix is a very effective tool to generate misuse cases. Once a Subject–Object Matrix is generated, by inversing the allowable actions captured in the Subject–Object Matrix, one can determine threats, which, in turn, can be used to determine security requirements. In a Subject–Object Matrix, when the subjects are roles, it is also referred to as a role matrix.

2.5.7 Templates and Tools

Some of the common templates that can be used for use and misuse case modeling are templates by Kulak and Guiney and by Cockburn. The Security Quality Requirements Engineering (SQUARE) methodology consists of nine steps that generate a final deliverable of categorized and prioritized security requirements (Allen et al. 2008). The SQUARE process model tool has been developed by the U.S. Computer Emergency Readiness Team (US-CERT). Objectiver is software that uses a goal-oriented methodology to build requirements specifications. The Microsoft Threat Analysis and Modeling (TAM) tools enable nonsecurity subject matter experts to enter business information and intended software design features that are used to generate use cases, misuse cases, SOM, and threat models.

2.6 Requirements Traceability Matrix (RTM)

The output from the data classification exercise, use and misuse case modeling, SOM, and other requirement elicitation processes can be tabulated into the RTM. A generic RTM is a table of information that lists the business requirements in the leftmost column, the functional requirements that address the business requirements are in the next column. Next to the functional requirements are the testing requirements. From a software assurance perspective, a generic RTM can be modified to include security requirements as well.

RTMs provide the following benefits to software development:

- Ensures that no scope creep occurs, i.e., the software development team has not inadvertently or intentional added additional features that were not requested by the user.
- Assures that the design satisfies the specified security requirements.
- Ensures that implementation does not deviate from secure design.
- Provides a firm basis for defining test cases.

By incorporating security requirements in the RTM, the chances of security functionality being missed out in design are reduced considerably. Specifying security requirements next to functional requirements also provides the business with insight into how security functionality maps to the end user business requirements. Additionally, requirements documentation also allows for appropriate resource allocation as needed.

2.7 Summary

In this chapter, we have covered the need for and the importance of eliciting security requirements early in the SDLC. Sources for security requirement include both internal organizational policy documents as well as external regulatory and compliance requirements. It is also extremely important to engage the appropriate stakeholders from the business, end user, IT, legal, privacy, networking, and software development teams. There are several types of security requirements that address the various tenets of software security, and the applicability of each of these types of requirements within the business context of the software being designed and developed must be determined. Protection needs can be elicited using several methods including brainstorming, surveys, policy decomposition, data classification, and use and misuse case modeling. The policy decomposition process is made up of breaking down high-level requirements into granular finer level software security requirements. Data classification can help with assuring that appropriate levels of security controls are assigned to data based on their sensitivity levels. Use and misuse case modeling, sequence diagrams, and subject–object models can be used to glean software security requirements. Software security requirements help ensure that the software that will be designed, developed, and deployed include secure features that make it reliable, resilient, and recoverable.

2.8 Review Questions

1. Which of the following must be addressed by software security requirements? Choose the best answer.
   A. Technology used in building the application
   B. Goals and objectives of the organization
   C. Software quality requirements
   D. External auditor requirements
2. Which of the following types of information is exempt from confidentiality requirements?
   A. Directory information
   B. Personally identifiable information (PII)
   C. User's card holder data
   D. Software architecture and network diagram
3. Requirements that are identified to protect against the destruction of information or the software itself are commonly referred to as
   A. Confidentiality requirements
   B. Integrity requirements
   C. Availability requirements
   D. Authentication requirements
4. The amount of time by which business operations need to be restored to service levels as expected by the business when there is a security breach or disaster is known as
   A. Maximum tolerable downtime (MTD)
   B. Mean time before failure (MTBF)
   C. Minimum security baseline (MSB)
   D. Recovery time objective (RTO)
5. The use of an individual's physical characteristics such as retinal blood patterns and fingerprints for validating and verifying the user's identity is referred to as
   A. Biometric authentication
   B. Forms authentication
   C. Digest authentication
   D. Integrated authentication

6. Which of the following policies is most likely to include the following requirement? "All software processing financial transactions need to use more than one factor to verify the identity of the entity requesting access."
   A. Authorization
   B. Authentication
   C. Auditing
   D. Availability

7. A means of restricting access to objects based on the identity of subjects and/or groups to which they belong is the definition of
   A. Nondiscretionary access control (NDAC)
   B. Discretionary access control (DAC)
   C. Mandatory access control (MAC)
   D. Rule-based access control

8. Requirements that when implemented can help to build a history of events that occurred in the software are known as
   A. Authentication requirements
   B. Archiving requirements
   C. Auditing requirements
   D. Authorization requirements

9. Which of the following is the primary reason for an application to be susceptible to a man-in-the-middle (MITM) attack?
   A. Improper session management
   B. Lack of auditing
   C. Improper archiving
   D. Lack of encryption

10. The process of eliciting concrete software security requirements from high-level regulatory and organizational directives and mandates in the requirements phase of the SDLC is also known as
    A. Threat modeling
    B. Policy decomposition
    C. Subject–object modeling
    D. Misuse case generation

11. The first step in the protection needs elicitation (PNE) process is to
    A. Engage the customer
    B. Model information management
    C. Identify least privilege applications
    D. Conduct threat modeling and analysis

12. A requirements traceability matrix (RTM) that includes security requirements can be used for all of the following except
    A. Ensuring scope creep does not occur
    B. Validating and communicating user requirements
    C. Determining resource allocations
    D. Identifying privileged code sections

13. Parity bit checking mechanisms can be used for all of the following except
    A. Error detection
    B. Message corruption
    C. Integrity assurance
    D. Input validation

14. Which of the following is an activity that can be performed to clarify requirements with the business users using diagrams that model the expected behavior of the software?
    A. Threat modeling
    B. Use case modeling
    C. Misuse case modeling
    D. Data modeling

15. Which of the following is least likely to be identified by misuse case modeling?
    A. Race conditions
    B. Mis-actors
    C. Attacker's perspective
    D. Negative requirements

16. Data classification is a core activity that is conducted as part of which of the following?
    A. Key Management Life Cycle
    B. Information Life Cycle Management
    C. Configuration management
    D. Problem management

17. Web farm data corruption issues and card holder data encryption requirements need to be captured as part of which of the following requirements?
    A. Integrity
    B. Environment
    C. International
    D. Procurement

18. When software is purchased from a third party instead of being built in-house, it is imperative to have contractual protection in place and have the software requirements explicitly specified in which of the following?
    A. Service level agreements (SLAs)
    B. Nondisclosure agreements (NDA)
    C. Noncompete agreements
    D. Project plan

19. When software is able to withstand attacks from a threat agent and not violate the security policy it is said to be exhibiting which of the following attributes of software assurance?
    A. Reliability
    B. Resiliency

    C. Recoverability

    D. Redundancy

20. Infinite loops and improper memory calls are often known to cause threats to which of the following?

    A. Availability

    B. Authentication

    C. Authorization

    D. Auditing

21. Which of the following is used to communicate and enforce availability requirements of the business or client?

    A. Nondisclosure agreement (NDA)

    B. Corporate contract

    C. Service level agreements

    D. Threat model

22. Software security requirements that are identified to protect against disclosure of data to unauthorized users is otherwise known as

    A. Integrity requirements

    B. Authorization requirements

    C. Confidentiality requirements

    D. Nonrepudiation requirements

23. The requirements that assure reliability and prevent alterations are to be identified in which section of the software requirements specifications (SRS) documentation?

    A. Confidentiality

    B. Integrity

    C. Availability

    D. Auditing

24. Which of the following is a covert mechanism that assures confidentiality?

    A. Encryption

    B. Steganography

    C. Hashing

    D. Masking

25. As a means to assure confidentiality of copyright information, the security analyst identifies the requirement to embed information insider another digital audio, video, or image signal. This is commonly referred to as

    A. Encryption

    B. Hashing

    C. Licensing

    D. Watermarking

26. Checksum validation can be used to satisfy which of the following requirements?

    A. Confidentiality

    B. Integrity

    C. Availability

    D. Authentication

27. A requirements traceability matrix (RTM) that includes security requirements can be used for all of the following except

    A. Ensure scope creep does not occur

    B. Validate and communicate user requirements

    C. Determine resource allocations

    D. Identifying privileged code sections

References

Allen, J. H., S. Barnum, R. J. Ellison, G. McGraw, and N. R. Mead. 2008. *Software Security Engineering: A Guide for Project Managers*. Boston, MA: Addison-Wesley.

Bauer, F. L. 2000. *Decrypted Secrets: Methods and Maxims of Cryptology*. New York, NY: Springer.

Ferraiolo, D., and P. Mell. 2006. Operating system security: Adding to the arsenal of security techniques. NIST, Computer Security Division, Information Technology Laboratory. http://csrc.nist.gov/publications/nistbul/itl99-12.txt (accessed Mar 3, 2011).

Guidance Share. 2007. .Net 2.0 security guidelines—Exception management. http://www.guidanceshare.com/wiki/.NET_2.0_Security_Guidelines_-_Exception_Management.

Johnson, N. F., Z. Duric, and S. Jajodia. 2000. *Information Hiding: Steganography and Watermarking*. New York, NY: Springer.

Lindell, A. 2007. Anonymous authentication. Security token and smart card authentication Whitepaper. Blackhat. http://searchsecurity.techtarget.com/tip/0,289483,sid14_gci1338503,00.html (accessed Mar 3, 2011).

McGraw, G. 2006. *Software Security: Building Security*. Boston, MA: Addison-Wesley.

NIST. 2007. Role-based access control—Frequently asked questions. Computer Security Division, Computer Security Resource Center. http://csrc.nist.gov/groups/SNS/rbac/faq.html.

Seacord, R. C. 2006. CERT: File I/O secure programming. Carnegie Mellon University. https://www.securecoding.cert.org/confluence/download/attachments/3524/07+Race+Conditions.pdf (accessed Mar 3, 2011).

Solomon, M., and M. Chapple. 2005. *Information Security Illuminated*. Sudbury, MA: Jones & Bartlett Learning.

Tsai, C.-H. 2004. On unicode and the Chinese writing system. http://technology.chtsai.org/unicode/ (accessed Mar 3, 2011).

Chapter 3

Secure Software Design

3.1 Introduction

One of the most important phases in the software development life cycle (SDLC) is the design phase. During this phase, software specifications are translated into architectural blueprints that can be coded during the implementation (or coding) phase that follows. When this happens, it is necessary for the translation to be inclusive of secure design principles. It is also important to ensure that the requirements that assure software security are designed into the software in the design phase. Although writing secure code is important for software assurance, the majority of software security issues has been attributed to insecure or incomplete design. Entire classes of vulnerabilities that are not syntactic or code related such as semantic or business logic flaws are related to design issues. Attack surface evaluation using threat models and misuse case modeling (covered in Chapter 2), control identification, and prioritization based on risk to the business are all essential software assurance processes that need to be conducted during the design phase of software development. In this chapter, we will cover secure design principles and processes and learn about different architectures and technologies, which can be leveraged for increasing security in software. We will end this chapter by understanding the need for and the importance of conducting architectural reviews of the software design from a security perspective.

3.2 Objectives

As a CSSLP, you are expected to

- Understand the need for and importance of designing security into the software.
- Be familiar with secure design principles and how they can be incorporated into software design.
- Have a thorough understanding of how to threat model software.
- Be familiar with the different software architectures that exist and the security benefits and drawbacks of each.
- Understand the need to take into account data (type, format), database, interface, and interconnectivity security considerations when designing software.
- Know how the computing environment and chosen technologies can have an impact on design decisions regarding security.
- Know how to conduct design and architecture reviews with a security perspective.

This chapter will cover each of these objectives in detail. It is imperative that you fully understand the objectives and be familiar with how to apply them to the software that your organization builds or procures.

3.3 The Need for Secure Design

Software that is designed correctly improves software quality. In addition to quality aspects of software, there are other requirements that need to be factored into its design. Some are privacy requirements as well as globalization and localization requirements, including security requirements. We learned in earlier chapters that software can meet all quality requirements and still be insecure, warranting the need for explicitly designing the software with security in mind.

IBM Systems Sciences Institute, in its research work on implementing software inspections, determined that it was 100 times more expensive to fix software bugs after the software is in production than when it is being designed. The time that is necessary to fix identified issues is shorter when the software is still in the design phase. The cost savings are substantial because there is minimal to no disruption to business operations. Besides the aforementioned time and cost-saving benefits, there are several other benefits of designing security early in the SDLC. Some of these include the following:

- Resilient and recoverable software: Security designed into software decreases the likelihood of attack or errors, which assures resiliency and recoverability of the software.

- Quality, maintainable software that is less prone to errors: Secure design not only increases the resiliency and recoverability of software, but such software is also less prone to errors (accidental or intentional), and that is directly related to the reliability of the software. This makes the software easily maintainable while improving the quality of the software considerably.
- Minimal redesign and consistency: When software is designed with security in mind, there is a minimal need for redesign. Using standards for architectural design of software also makes the software consistent, regardless of who is developing it.
- Business logic flaws addressed: Business logic flaws are those which are characterized by the software's functioning as designed, but the design itself makes circumventing the security policy possible. Business logic flaws have been commonly observed in the way password-recovery mechanisms are designed. In the early days, when people needed to recover their passwords, they were asked to answer a predefined set of questions for which they had earlier provided answers that were saved to their profiles on the system. These questions were either guessable or often had a finite set of answers. It is not difficult to guess the favorite color of a person or provide an answer from the finite set of primary colors that exists. The software responds to the user input as designed, and so there is really no issue of reliability. However, because careful thought was not given to the architecture by which password recovery was designed, there existed a possibility of an attacker's brute-forcing or intelligently bypassing security mechanisms. By designing software with security in mind, business logic flaws and other architectural design issues can be uncovered, which is a main benefit of securely designing software.

Investing the time up front in the SDLC to design security into the software supports the "build-in" virtue of security, as opposed to trying to bolt it on at a later stage. The bolt-on method of implementing security can become very costly, time-consuming, and generate software of low quality characterized by being unreliable, inconsistent, and unmaintainable, as well as by being error prone and hacker prone.

3.4 Flaws versus Bugs

Although it may seem like many security errors are related to insecure programming, the majority of security errors are also architecture based. The line of demarcation between when a software security error is due to improper architecture and when it is due to insecure implementation is not always very distinct, as the error itself may be a result of both architecture and implementation failure. In the design stage, because no code is written, we are primarily concerned with design issues related to software assurance. For the rest of this chapter and book, we will refer to design and architectural defects that can result in errors as "flaws" and to coding/ implementation constructs that can cause a breach in security as "bugs."

It is not quite as important to know which security errors constitute a flaw and which ones a bug, but it is important to understand that both flaws and bugs need to be identified and addressed appropriately. Threat modeling and secure architecture design reviews, which will we cover later in this chapter, are useful in the detection of architecture (flaws) and implementation issues (bugs), although the latter are mostly determined by code reviews and penetration testing exercises after implementation. Business logic flaws that were mentioned earlier are primarily a design issue. They are not easily detectable when reviewing code. Scanners and intrusion detection systems (IDSs) cannot detect them, and application-layer firewalls are futile in their protection against them. The discovery of nonsyntactic design flaws in the logical operations of the software is made possible by security architecture and design reviews. Security architecture and design reviews using outputs from attack surface evaluation, threat modeling, and misuse cases modeling are very useful in ensuring that the software not only functions as it is expected to but that it does not violate any security policy while doing so. Logic flaws are also known as *semantic* issues. Flaws are broad classes of vulnerabilities that at times can also include *syntactic* coding bugs. Insufficient input validation and improper error and session management are predominantly architectural defects that manifest themselves as coding bugs.

3.5 Design Considerations

In addition to designing for functionality of software, design for security tenets and principles also must be conducted. In Chapter 2, we learned about various types of security requirements. In the design phase, we will consider how these requirements can be incorporated into the software architecture and makeup. In this section, we will cover how the identified security requirements can be designed and what design decisions are to be made based on the business need. We will start with how to design the software to address the core security elements of confidentiality, integrity, availability, authentication, authorization, and auditing, and then we will look at examples of how to architect the secure design principles covered Chapter 1.

3.5.1 Core Software Security Design Considerations

3.5.1.1 Confidentiality Design

Disclosure protection can be achieved in several ways using cryptographic and masking techniques. Masking, covered in Chapter 2, is useful for disclosure protection when data are displayed on the screen or on printed forms; however, for assurance of confidentiality when the data are transmitted or stored in transactional data stores or offline archives, cryptographic techniques are primarily used. The most predominant cryptographic techniques include overt techniques such as hashing and encryption and covert techniques such as steganography and digital water-marking as depicted in Figure 3.1. These techniques were introduced in Chapter 2 and are covered here in a little more detail with a design perspective.

Cryptanalysis is the science of finding vulnerabilities in cryptographic protection mechanisms. When cryptographic protection techniques are implemented, the primary goal is to ensure that an attacker with resources must make such a large effort to subvert or evade the protection mechanisms that the required effort, itself, serves as a deterrent or makes the subversion or evasion impossible. This effort is referred to as *work factor*. It is critical to consider the work factor when choosing a technique while designing the software. The work factor against cryptographic protection is exponentially dependent on the key size. A *key* is a sequence of symbols that controls the encryption and decryption operations of a cryptographic algorithm, according to ISO/IEC 11016:2006. Practically, this is usually a string of bits that is supplied as a parameter into the algorithm for encrypting plaintext to cipher text or for decrypting cipher text to plaintext. It is vital that this key is kept a secret.

The *key size,* also known as *key length,* is the length of the key, measured usually in bits or bytes that are used in the algorithm. Given time and computational power, almost all cryptographic algorithms can be broken, except for the *one-time pad,* which is the only algorithm that is provably unbreakable by exhaustive brute-force attacks. This is, however, only true if the key used in the algorithm is truly random and discarded permanently after use. The key size in a one-time pad is equal to the size of the message itself, and each key bit is used only once and discarded.

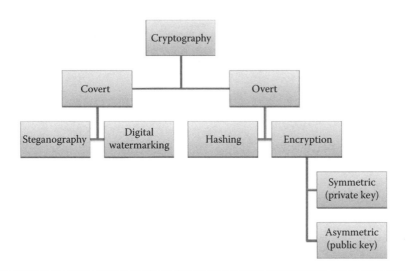

Figure 3.1   Types of cryptography.

In addition to protecting the secrecy of the key, key management is extremely critical. The key management life cycle includes the generation, exchange, storage, rotation, archiving, and destruction of the key as illustrated in Figure 3.2. From the time that the key is generated to the time that it is completely disposed of (or destroyed), it needs to be protected. The exchange mechanism itself needs to be secure so that the key is not disclosed when the key is shared. When the key is stored in configuration files or in a hardware security module (HSM) such as the Trusted Platform Modules (TPMs) chip for increased security, it needs to be protected using access control mechanisms, TPM security, encryption, and secure startup mechanisms, which we will cover in Chapter 7.

Rotation (swapping) of keys involves the expiration of the current key and the generation, exchange, and storage of a new key. Cryptographic keys need to be swapped periodically to thwart insider threats and immediately upon key disclosure. When the key is rotated as part of a routine security protocol, if the data that are backed up or archived are in an encrypted format, then the key that was used for encrypting the data must also be archived. If the key is destroyed without being archived, the corresponding key to decrypt the data will be unavailable, leading to a denial of service (DoS) should there be a need to retrieve the data for forensics or disaster recovery purposes.

Encryption algorithms are primarily of two types: symmetric and asymmetric.

3.5.1.1.1 Symmetric Algorithms

Symmetric algorithms are characterized by using a single key for encryption and decryption operations that is shared between the sender and the receiver. This is

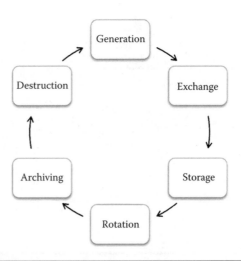

Figure 3.2   Key management framework.

also referred to by other names: private key cryptography, shared key cryptography, or secret key algorithm. The sender and receiver need not be human all the time. In today's computing business world, the senders and receivers can be applications or software within or external to the organization.

The major benefit of symmetric key cryptography is that it is very fast and efficient in encrypting large volumes of data in a short period. However, this advantage comes with significant challenges that have a direct impact on the design of the software. Some of the challenges with symmetric key cryptography include the following:

- *Key exchange and management:* Both the originator and the receiver must have a mechanism in place to share the key without compromising its secrecy. This often requires an out-of-band secure mechanism to exchange the key information, which requires more effort and time, besides potentially increasing the attack surface area. The delivery of the key and the data must be mutually exclusive as well.
- *Scalability:* Because a unique key needs to be used between each sender and recipient, the number of keys required for symmetric key cryptographic operations is exponentially dependent on the number of users or parties involved in that secure transaction. For example, if Jack wants to send a message to Jill, then they both must share one key. If Jill wants to send a message to John, then there needs to be a different key that is used for Jill to communicate with John. Now, between Jack and John, there is a need for another key, if they need to communicate. If we add Jessie to the mix, then there is a need to have six keys, one for Jessie to communicate with Jack, one for Jessie to communicate with Jill, and one for Jessie to communicate with John, in addition to the three keys that are necessary as mentioned earlier and depicted in Figure 3.3. The computation of the number of keys can be mathematically represented as

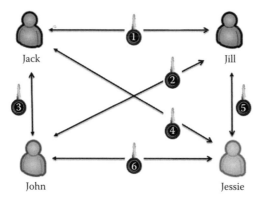

Figure 3.3   Example showing number of keys in a symmetric key cryptography system.

$$\frac{n(n-1)}{2}$$

So if there are 10 users/parties involved, then the number of keys required is 45 and if there are 100 users/parties involved, then we need to generate, distribute, and manage 4,950 keys, making symmetric key cryptography not very scalable.

■ *Nonrepudiation not addressed:* Symmetric key simply provides confidentiality protection by encrypting and decrypting the data. It does not provide proof of origin or nonrepudiation.

Some examples of common symmetric key cryptography algorithms along with their strength and supported key size are tabulated in Table 3.1. RC2, RC4, and RC5 are other examples of symmetric algorithms that have varying degrees of strength based on the multiple key sizes they support. For example, the RC2-40 algorithm is considered to be a weak algorithm, whereas the RC2-128 is deemed to be a strong algorithm.

3.5.1.1.2 Asymmetric Algorithms

In asymmetric key cryptography, instead of using a single key for encryption and decryption operations, two keys that are mathematically related to each other are used. One of the two keys is to be held secret and is referred to as the *private* key, whereas the other key is disclosed to anyone with whom secure communications and transactions need to occur. The key that is publicly displayed to everyone is known as the *public* key. It is also important that it should be computationally

Table 3.1 **Symmetric Algorithms**

Algorithm Name	Strength	Key Size
DES	Weak	56
Skipjack	Medium	80
IDEA	Strong	128
Blowfish	Strong	128
3DES	Strong	168
Twofish	Very strong	256
RC6	Very strong	256
AES / Rijndael	Very strong	256

infeasible to derive the private key from the public key. Though there is a private key and a public key in asymmetric key cryptography, it is commonly known as *public key* cryptography.

Both the private and the public keys can be used for encryption and decryption. However, if a message is encrypted with a public key, it is only the corresponding private key that can decrypt that message. The same is true when a message is encrypted using a private key. That message can be decrypted only by the corresponding public key. This makes it possible for asymmetric key cryptographic to provide both confidentiality and nonrepudiation assurance.

Confidentiality is provided when the sender uses the receiver's public key to encrypt the message and the receiver uses the corresponding private key to decrypt the message, as illustrated in Figure 3.4. For example, if Jack wants to communicate with Jill, he can encrypt the plaintext message with her public key and send the resulting cipher text to her. Jill can user her private key that is paired with her public key and decrypt the message. Because Jill's private key should not be known to anyone other than Jill, the message is protected from disclosure to anyone other than Jill, assuring confidentiality. Now, if Jill wants to respond to Jack, she can encrypt the plaintext message she plans to send him with his public key and send the resulting cipher text to him. The cipher text message can then be decrypted to plaintext by Jack using his private key, which again, only he should know.

In addition to confidentiality protection, asymmetric key cryptography also can provide nonrepudiation assurance. Nonrepudiation protection is known also as *proof-of-origin* assurance. When the sender's private key is used to encrypt the message and the corresponding key is used by the receiver to decrypt it, as illustrated in Figure 3.5, proof-of-origin assurance is provided. Because the message can be decrypted only by the public key of the sender, the receiver is assured that the message originated from the sender and was encrypted by the corresponding private key of the sender. To demonstrate nonrepudiation or proof of origin, let us consider the following example. Jill has the public key of Jack and receives an encrypted message from Jack. She is able to decrypt that message using Jack's public key. This assures her that the message was encrypted using the private key of Jack and

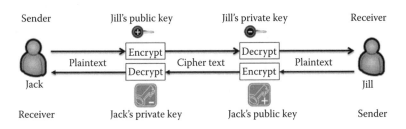

Figure 3.4   Confidentiality assurance in asymmetric key cryptography.

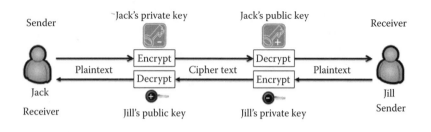

Figure 3.5 Proof of origin assurance in asymmetric key cryptography.

provides her the confidence that Jack cannot deny sending her the message, because he is the only one who should have knowledge of his private key.

If Jill wants to send Jack a message and he needs to be assured that no one but Jill sent him the message, Jill can encrypt the message with her private key and Jack will use her corresponding public key to decrypt the message. A compromise in the private key of the parties involved can lead to confidentiality and nonrepudiation threats. It is thus critically important to protect the secrecy of the private key.

In addition to confidentiality and nonrepudiation assurance, asymmetric key cryptography also provides *access control, authentication,* and *integrity assurance.* Access control is provided because the private key is limited to one person. By virtue of nonrepudiation, the identity of the sender is validated, which supports authentication. Unless the private–public key pair is compromised, the data cannot be decrypted and modified, thereby providing data integrity assurance.

Asymmetric key cryptography has several advantages over symmetric key cryptography. These include the following:

- *Key exchange and management:* In asymmetric key cryptography, the overhead costs of having to securely exchange and store the key are alleviated. Cryptographic operations using asymmetric keys require a *public key infrastructure* (PKI) key identification, exchange, and management. PKI uses digital certificates to make key exchange and management automation possible. Digital certificates is covered in the next section.
- *Scalability:* Unlike symmetric key cryptography, where there is a need to generate and securely distribute one key between each party, in asymmetric key cryptography, there are only two keys needed per user: one that is private and held by the sender and the other that is public and distributed to anyone who wishes to engage in a transaction with the sender. One hundred users will require 200 keys, which is much easier to manage than the 4,950 keys needed for symmetric key cryptography.
- *Addresses nonrepudiation:* It also addresses nonrepudiation by providing the receiver assurance of proof of origin. The sender cannot deny sending the message when the message has been encrypted using the private key of the sender.

Although asymmetric key cryptography provides many benefits over symmetric key cryptography, there are certain challenges that are prevalent, as well. Public key cryptography is computationally intensive and much slower than symmetric encryption. This is, however, a preferable design choice for Internet environments.

Some common examples of asymmetric key algorithms include Rivest, Shamir, Adelman (RSA), El Gamal, Diffie–Hellman (used only for key exchange and not data encryption), and Elliptic Curve Cryptosystem (ECC), which is ideal for small, hardware devices such as smart cards and mobile devices.

3.5.1.1.3 Digital Certificates

Digital certificates carry in them the public keys, algorithm information, owner and subject data, the digital signature of the certification authority (CA) that issued and verified the subject data, and a validity period (date range) for that certificate. Because a digital certificate contains the digital signature of the CA, it can be used by anyone to verify the authenticity of the certificate itself.

The different types of digital certificates that are predominantly used in Internet settings include the following:

- *Personal certificates* are used to identify individuals and authenticate them with the server. Secure e-mail using S-Mime uses personal certificates.
- *Server certificates* are used to identify servers. These are primarily used for verifying server identity with the client and for secure communications and transport layer security (TLS). The Secure Sockets Layer (SSL) protocol uses server certificates for assuring confidentiality when data are transmitted. Figure 3.6 shows an example of a server certificate.
- *Software publisher certificates* are used to sign software that will be distributed on the Internet. It is important to note that these certificates do not necessarily assure that the signed code is safe for execution but are merely informative in role, informing the software user that the certificate is signed by a trusted, software publisher's CA.

3.5.1.1.4 Digital Signatures

Certificates hold in them the digital signatures of the CAs that verified and issued the digital certificates. A digital signature is distinct from a digital certificate. It is similar to an individual's signature in its function, which is to authenticate the identity of the message sender, but in its format it is electronic. Digital signatures not only provide identity verification but also ensure that the data or message have not been tampered with, because the digital signature that is used to sign the message cannot be easily imitated by someone unless it is compromised. It also provides nonrepudiation.

There are several design considerations that need to be taken into account when choosing cryptographic techniques. It is therefore imperative to first understand

This certificate has been verified for the following uses:

SSL Server Certificate	
Issued To	
Common Name (CN)	www.expresscertifications.com
Organization (O)	www.expresscertifications.com
Organizational Unit (OU)	GT26673911
Serial Number	0B:61:E7
Issued By	
Common Name (CN)	Equifax Secure Global eBusiness CA-1
Organization (O)	Equifax Secure Inc.
Organizational Unit (OU)	<Not Part Of Certificated>
Validity	
Issued On	4/21/2009
Expires On	6/21/2010
Fingerprints	
SHA1 Fingerprint	32:93:13:C5:1C:42:8C:1F:87:95:F2:7F:0F:C5:7E:EF:C3:77:C5:69
MD5 Fingerprint	5A:6A:21:31:A7:08:F2:6C:06:FC:FE:FC:B9:AE:C1:9B

Figure 3.6   Server certificate.

business requirements pertaining to the protection of sensitive or private information. When these requirements are understood, one can choose an appropriate design that will be used to securely implement the software. If there is a need for secure communications in which no one but the sender and receiver should know of a hidden message, steganography can be considered in the design. If there is a need for copyright and IP protection, then digital watermarking techniques are useful. If data confidentiality in processing, transit, storage, and archives need to be assured, hashing or encryption techniques can be used.

3.5.2 Integrity Design

Integrity in the design assures that there is no unauthorized modification of the software or data. Integrity of software and data can be accomplished by using any one of the following techniques or a combination of the techniques, such as hashing (or hash functions), referential integrity design, resource locking, and code signing. Digital signatures, covered earlier, also provide data or message alteration protection.

3.5.2.1 Hashing (Hash Functions)

Here is a recap of what was introduced about hashing in Chapter 2: Hash functions are used to condense variable length inputs into an irreversible, fixed-sized output known as a message digest or hash value. When designing software, we must ensure that all integrity requirements that warrant irreversible protection, which is provided by hashing, are factored in. Figure 3.7 describes the steps taken in verifying integrity with hashing. John wants to send a private message to Jessie. He passes the message through a hash function, which generates a hash value, H1. He sends the message digest (original data plus hash value H1) to Jessie. When Jessie receives the message digest, she computes a hash value, H2, using the same hash function that John used to generate H1. At this point, the original hash value (H1) is compared with the new hash value (H2). If the hash values are equal, then the message has not been altered when it was transmitted.

In addition to assuring data integrity, it is also important to ensure that hashing design is *collision free*. "Collision free" implies that it is computationally infeasible

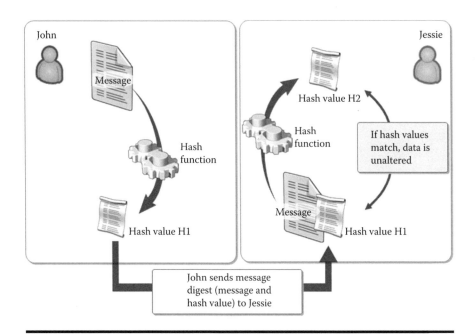

Figure 3.7   Data integrity using hash function.

to compute the same hash value on two different inputs. Birthday attacks are often used to find collisions in hash functions. A *birthday attack* is a type of brute-force attack that gets its name from the probability that two or more people randomly chosen can have the same birthday. Secure hash designs ensure that birthday attacks are not possible, which means that an attacker will not be able to input two messages and generate the same hash value. Salting the hash is a mechanism that assures collision-free hash values. Salting the hash also protects against *dictionary attacks,* which are another type of brute-force attack. A "dictionary attack" is an attempt to thwart security protection mechanisms by using an exhaustive list (like a list of words from a dictionary).

Salt values are random bytes that can be used with the hash function to prevent prebuilt dictionary attacks. Let us consider the following: There is a likelihood that two users within a large organization have the same password. Both John and Jessie have the same password, "tiger123" for logging into their bank account. When the password is hashed using the same hash function, it should produce the same hashed value as depicted in Figure 3.8. The password "tiger123" is hashed using the MD5 hash function to generate a fixed-sized hash value "9E107D9D372BB6826BD81D3542A419D6."

Even though the user names are different, when the password is hashed, because it generates the same output, it can lead to impersonation attacks, where John can login as Jessie or vice versa. By adding random bytes (salt) to the original plaintext before passing it through the hash function, the output that is generated for the same input is made different. This mitigates the security issues discussed earlier. It is recommended to use a salt value that is unique and random for each user. When the salt value is "1234ABC" for John and is "9876XYZ" for Jessie, the same password, "tiger123" results in different hashed values as depicted in Figure 3.9.

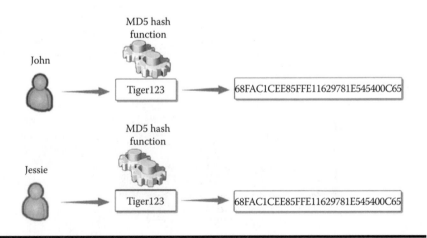

Figure 3.8   Unsalted hash.

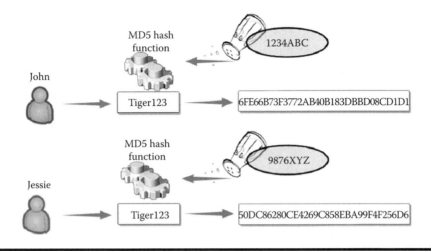

Figure 3.9   Salted hash.

Design considerations should take into account the security aspects related to the generation of the salt, which should be unique to each user and random.

Some of the most common hash functions are the MD2, MD4, and MD5, which were all designed by Ronald Rivest; the Secure Hash Algorithms family (SHA-0, SHA-1, SHA-, and SHA-2) designed by NSA and published by NIST to complement digital signatures and HAVAL. The Ronald Rivest MD series of algorithms generate a fixed, 128-bit size output and has been proven to be not completely collision free. The SHA-0 and SHA-1 family of hash functions generated a fixed, 160-bit sized output. The SHA-2 family of hash functions includes SHA-224 and SHA-256, which generate a 256-bit sized output and SHA-384 and SHA-512 which generate a 512-bit sized output. HAVAL is distinct in being a hash function that can produce hashes in variable lengths (128–256 bits). HAVAL is also flexible to let users indicate the number of rounds (3–5) to be used to generate the hash for increased security. As a general rule of thumb, the greater the bit length of the hash value that is supported, the greater the protection that is provided, making cryptanalysis work factor significantly greater. So when designing the software, it is important to consider the bit length of the hash value that is supported. Table 3.2 tabulates the different hash value lengths that are supported by some common hash functions.

Table 3.2   Hash Functions and Supported Hash Value Lengths

Hash Function	Hash Value Length (in bits)
MD2, MD4, MD5	128
SHA	160
HAVAL	Variable lengths (128, 160, 192, 224, 256)

Another important aspect when choosing the hash function for use within the software is to find out if the hash function has already been broken and deemed unsuitable for use. The MD5 hash function is one such example that the U.S. Computer Emergency Response Team (CERT) of the Department of Homeland Security (DHS) considers as cryptographically broken. DHS promotes moving to the SHA family of hash functions.

3.5.2.2 Referential Integrity

Integrity assurance of the data, especially in a relational database management system (RDBMS) is made possible by referential integrity, which ensures that data are not left in an orphaned state. Referential integrity protection uses primary keys and related foreign keys in the database to assure data integrity. Primary keys are those columns or combination of columns in a database table, which uniquely identify each row in a table. When the column or columns that are defined as the primary key of a table are linked (referenced) in another table, these column or columns are referred to as foreign keys in the second table. For example, as depicted in Figure 3.10, Customer_ID column in the CUSTOMER table is the primary key because it uniquely identifies a row in the table. Although there are two users with the same first name and last name, "John Smith," the Customer_ID is unique and can identify the correct row in the database. Customers are also linked to their orders

Customer

Customer_ID	First_Name	Last_Name	User_Name	Password
1	John	Smith	Jsmith1	9E107D9D372BB682
2	John	Smith	Jsmith2	6A207E9F154CC753
3	Mary	Johnson	MJohson	8A219E7E135AA717

Order

Order_ID	Customer_ID	Order_Amount	Order_Date
101	1	129.00	January 20, 2009
102	3	289.00	March 06, 2009
103	1	129.00	August 15, 2009

Order_Detail

Order_Detail_ID	Order_ID	Product_Code	Product_Desc
1001	101	CSSLPEX1	CSSLP Self Assessment Exam 1
1002	102	CSSLPEX1	CSSLP Self Assessment Exam 1
1003	102	CSSLPEX2	CSSLP Self Assessment Exam 2
1004	102	CSSLPEX3	CSSLP Self Assessment Exam 3
1005	103	CSSLPEX1	CSSLP Self Assessment Exam 1

Figure 3.10   Referential integrity.

using their Customer_Id, which is the foreign key in the ORDER table. This way, all of the customer information need not be duplicated in the ORDER table. The removal of duplicates in the tables is done by a process called *normalization,* which is covered later in this chapter. When one needs to query the database to retrieve all orders for customer John Smith whose Customer_ID is 1, then two orders (Order_ID 101 and 103) are returned. In this case, the parent table is the CUSTOMER table and the child table is the ORDER table. The Order_ID is the primary key in the ORDER table, which, in turn, is established as the foreign key in the ORDER_DETAIL table. In order to find out the details of the order placed by customer Mary Johnson whose Customer_ID is 3, we can retrieve the three products that she ordered by referencing the primary key and foreign key relationships. In this case, in addition to the CUSTOMER table being the parent of the ORDER table, the ORDER table, itself, is parent to the ORDER_DETAIL child table.

Referential integrity ensures that data are not left in an orphaned state. This means that if the customer Mary Johnson is deleted from the CUSTOMER table in the database, all of her corresponding order and order details are deleted, as well, from the ORDER and ORDER_DETAIL tables, respectively. This is referred to as *cascading deletes.* Failure to do so will result in records being present in ORDER and ORDER_DETAILS tables as orphans with a reference to a customer who no longer exists in the parent CUSTOMER table. When referential integrity is designed, it can be set up to either delete all child records when the parent record is deleted or to disallow the delete operation of a customer (parent record) who has orders (child records), unless all of the child order records are deleted first. The same is true in the case of updates. If for some business need, Mary Johnson's Customer_ID in the parent table (CUSTOMER) is changed, then all subsequent records in the child table (ORDER) should also be updated to reflect the change, as well. This is referred to as *cascading updates.*

Decisions to normalize data into atomic (nonduplicate) values and establish primary keys and foreign keys and their relationships, cascading updates and deletes, in order to assure referential integrity are important design considerations that ensure the integrity of data or information.

3.5.2.3 Resource Locking

In addition to hashing and referential integrity, resource locking can be used to assure data or information integrity. When two concurrent operations are not allowed on the same object (say a record in the database), because one of the operations locks that record from allowing any changes to it, until it completes its operation, it is referred to as *resource locking.* Although this provides integrity assurance, it is critical to understand that if resource locking protection is not properly designed, it can lead to potential deadlocks and subsequent DoS. *Deadlock* is a condition that exists when two operations are racing against each other to change the state of a shared object and each is waiting for the other to release the shared object that is locked.

When designing software, there is a need to consider the protection mechanisms that assure that data or information has not been altered in an unauthorized manner or by an unauthorized person or process, and the mechanisms need to be incorporated into the overall makeup of the software.

3.5.2.4 Code Signing

Code signing is the process of digitally signing the code (executables, scripts, etc.) with the digital signature of the code author. In most cases, code signing is implemented using private and public key systems and digital signatures. Each time code is built, it can be signed or code can be signed just before deployment. Developers can generate their own key or use a key that is issued by a trusted CA for signing their code. When developers do not have access to the key for signing their code, they can sign it at a later phase of the development life cycle, just before deployment, and this is referred to as *delayed signing*. Delayed signing allows development to continue. When code is signed using the code author's digital signature, a cryptographic hash of that code is generated. This hash is published along with the software when it is distributed. Any alteration of the code will result in a hash value that will no longer match the hash value that was published. This is how code signing assures integrity and antitampering.

Code signing is particularly important when it comes to *mobile code*. Mobile code is code that is downloaded from a remote location. Examples of mobile code include Java applets, ActiveX components, browser scripts, Adobe Flash, and other Web controls. The source of the mobile code may not be obvious. In such situations, code signing can be used to assure the proof of origin or its authenticity. Signing mobile code also gives the runtime (not the code itself) permission to access system resources and ensures the safety of the code by sandboxing. Additionally, code signing can be used to ensure that there are no namespace conflicts and to provide versioning information when the software is deployed.

3.5.3 Availability Design

When software requirements mandate the need for continued business operations, the software should be carefully designed. The output from the business impact analysis can be used to determine how to design the software. Special considerations need to be given to software and data replication so that the MTD and the RTO are both within acceptable levels. Destruction and DoS protection can be achieved by proper coding/implementation of the software. Although no code is written in the design phase, in the software design, coding and configuration requirements such as connection pooling, memory management, database cursors, and loop constructions can be looked at. *Connection pooling* is a database access efficiency mechanism. A connection pool is the number of connections that are cached by the database for reuse. When your software needs to support a large number of users, the appropriate number of connection pools should be configured. If the number of connection pools is low in a highly transactional environment, then the database will be under heavy workload, experiencing performance issues that can possibly lead to DoS. Once a connection is opened, it can be placed in the pool so that other users can reuse that connection, instead of opening and closing a connection for each user. This will increase performance, but security considerations should be taken into account and this is why designing the software from a security (availability) perspective is necessary. Memory leaks can occur if the default query processing, thread limits are not optimized, or because of bad programming; so pertinent considerations of how memory will be managed need to be accounted for in design. Once the processes are terminated, allocated memory resources must be released. This is known as *garbage collection* and is another important design consideration. Coding constructs that use incorrect cursors and infinite loops can lead to deadlocks and DoS. When these constructs are properly designed, availability assurance is increased.

3.5.4 Authentication Design

When designing for authentication, it is important to consider multifactor authentication and single sign-on (SSO), in addition to determining the type of authentication required as specified in the requirements documentation. Multifactor or the use of more than one factor to authenticate a principal (user or resource) provides heightened security and is recommended. For example, validating and verifying one's fingerprint (something you are) in conjunction with a token (something you have) and pin code (something you know) before granting access provides more defense in depth than merely using a username and password (something you know). Additionally, if there is a need to implement SSO, wherein the principal's asserted identity is verified once and the verified credentials are passed on to other systems or applications, usually using tokens, then it is crucial to factor into the design of the software both the performance impact and its security. Although SSO simplifies credential management and improves user experience and performance because the principal's credential is verified only once, improper design of SSO can result in security breaches that have colossal consequences. A breach at any point in the application flow can lead to total compromise, akin to losing the keys to the kingdom. SSO is covered in more detail in the technology section of this chapter.

3.5.5 Authorization Design

When designing for authorization, give special attention to the impact on performance and to the principles of separation of duties and least privilege. The type of authorization to be implemented as per the requirements must be determined as well. Are you going to use roles or will we need to use a resource-based authorization, such as a trusted subsystem with impersonation and delegation model, to manage the granting of access rights? Checking for access rights each and every time, as per the principle of complete mediation, can lead to performance degradation and decreased user experience. On the contrary, a design that calls for caching of verified credentials that are used for access decisions can become the Achilles' heel from a security perspective. When dealing with performance versus security trade-off decisions, it is recommended to err on the side of caution, allowing for security over performance. However, this decision is one that needs to be discussed and approved by the business.

When roles are used for authorization, design should ensure that there are no conflicting roles that circumvent the separation of duties principle. For example, a user cannot be in a teller role and also in an auditor role for a financial transaction. Additionally, design decisions are to ensure that only the minimum set of rights is granted explicitly to the user or resource, thereby supporting least privilege. For example, users in the "Guest" or "Everyone" group account should be allowed only read rights and any other operation should be disallowed.

3.5.6 Auditing/Logging Design

Although it is often overlooked, design for auditing has been proven to be extremely important in the event of a breach, primarily for forensic purposes, and so it should be factored into the software design from the very beginning. Log data should include the who, what, where, and when aspects of software operations. As part of the "who," it is important not to forget the nonhuman actors such as batch processes and services or daemons.

It is advisable to log by default and to leverage the existing logging functionality within the software, especially if it is commercial off-the-shelf (COTS) software. Because it is a best practice to append to logs and not overwrite them, capacity constraints and requirements are important design considerations. Design decisions to retain, archive, and dispose logs should not contradict external regulatory or internal retention requirements.

Sensitive data should never be logged in plaintext form. Say that the requirements call for logging failed authentication attempts. Then it is important to verify with the business if there is a need to log the password that is supplied when authentication fails. If requirements explicitly call for logging the password upon failed authentication, then it is important to design the software so that the password is not logged in plaintext. Users often mistype their passwords and logging this information can lead to potential confidentiality violation and account compromise. For example, if the software is designed to log the password in plaintext and user Scott whose password is "tiger" mistypes it as "tigwr," someone who has access to the logs can easily guess the password of the user.

Design should also factor in protection mechanisms of the log itself; and maintaining the chain of custody of the logs will ensure that the logs are admissible in court. Validating the integrity of the logs can be accomplished by hashing the before and after images of the logs and checking their hash values. Auditing in conjunction with other security controls such as authentication can provide nonrepudiation. It is preferable to design the software to automatically log the authenticated principal and system timestamp and not let it be user-defined to avoid potential integrity issues. For example, using the Request.ServerVariables[LOGON_USER] in an IIS Web application or the T-SQL in-built getDate() system function in SQL Server is preferred over passing a user-defined principal name or timestamp.

We have learned about how to design software incorporating core security elements of confidentiality, integrity, availability, authentication, authorization, and auditing.

3.6 Information Technology Security Principles and Secure Design

Special Publication 800-27 of the NIST, which is entitled, "Engineering principles for information technology security (a baseline for achieving security)," provides various IT security principles as listed below. Some of these principles are people oriented, whereas others are tied to the process for designing security in IT systems.

1. Establish a sound security policy as the "foundation" for design.
2. Treat security as an integral part of the overall system design.
3. Clearly delineate the physical and logical security boundaries governed by associated security policies.
4. Reduce risk to an acceptable level.
5. Assume that external systems are insecure.
6. Identify potential trade-offs between reducing risk and increased costs and decreases in other aspects of operational effectiveness.
7. Implement layered security. (Ensure no single point of vulnerability.)
8. Implement tailored, system security measures to meet organizational security goals.
9. Strive for simplicity.
10. Design and operate an IT system to limit vulnerability and to be resilient in response.
11. Minimize the system elements to be trusted.
12. Implement security through a combination of measures distributed physically and logically.
13. Provide assurance that the system is, and continues to be, resilient in the face of expected threats.
14. Limit or contain vulnerabilities.

15. Formulate security measures to address multiple, overlapping, information domains.
16. Isolate public access systems from mission critical resources (e.g., data, processes, etc.).
17. Use boundary mechanisms to separate computing systems and network infrastructures.
18. Where possible, base security on open standards for portability and interoperability.
19. Use common language in developing security requirements.
20. Design and implement audit mechanisms to detect unauthorized use and to support incident investigations.
21. Design security to allow for regular adoption of new technology, including a secure and logical technology upgrade process.
22. Authenticate users and processes to ensure appropriate, access control decisions both within and across domains.
23. Use unique identities to ensure accountability.
24. Implement least privilege.
25. Do not implement unnecessary security mechanisms.
26. Protect information while it is processed, in transit, and in storage.
27. Strive for operational ease of use.
28. Develop and exercise contingency or disaster recovery procedures to ensure appropriate availability.
29. Consider custom products to achieve adequate security.
30. Ensure proper security in the shutdown or disposal of a system.
31. Protect against all likely classes of attacks.
32. Identify and prevent common errors and vulnerabilities.
33. Ensure that developers are trained in how to develop secure software.

Some of the common, insecure design issues observed in software are the following:

- Not following coding standards
- Improper implementation of least privilege
- Software fails insecurely
- Authentication mechanisms easily bypassed
- Security through obscurity
- Improper error handling
- Weak input validation

3.7 Designing Secure Design Principles

In the following section we will look at some of the IT engineering security principles that are pertinent to software design. The following principles were introduced and defined in Chapter 1. It is revisited here as a refresher and discussed in more depth with examples.

3.7.1 Least Privilege

Although the principle of least privilege is more applicable to administering a system where the number of users with access to critical functionality and controls is restricted, least privilege can be implemented within software design. When software is said to be operating with least privilege, it means that only the necessary and minimum level of access rights (privileges) has been given explicitly to it for a minimum amount of time in order for it to complete its operation. The main objective of least privilege is containment of the damage that can result from a security breach that occurs accidentally or intentionally. Some of the examples of least privilege include the military security rule of "need-to-know" clearance level classification, modular programming, and nonadministrative accounts.

The military security rule of need-to-know limits the disclosure of sensitive information to only those who have been authorized to receive such information, thereby aiding in confidentiality assurance. Those who have been authorized can be determined from the clearance level classifications they hold, such as Top Secret, Secret, Sensitive but Unclassified, etc. Best practice also suggests that it is preferable to have many administrators with limited access to security resources instead of one user with "super user" rights.

Modular programming is a software design technique in which the entire program is broken down into smaller subunits or modules. Each module is discrete with unitary functionality and is said to be therefore *cohesive,* meaning each module is designed to perform one and only one logical operation. The degree of how cohesive a module is indicates the strength at which various responsibilities of a software module are related. The discreetness of the module increases its maintainability and the ease of determining and fixing software defects. Because each unit of code (class, method, etc.) has a single purpose and the operations that can be performed by the code is limited to only that which it is designed to do, modular programming is also referred to as the Single Responsibility Principle of software engineering. For example, the function CalcDiscount() should have the single responsibility to calculate the discount for a product, while the CalcSH() function should be exclusively used to calculate shipping and handling rates. When code is not designed modularly, not only does it increase the attack surface, but it also makes the code difficult to read and troubleshoot. If there is a requirement to restrict the calculation of discounts to a sales manager, not separating this functionality into its own function, such as CalcDiscount(), can lead potentially to a nonsales manager's running code that is privileged to a sales manager. An aspect related to cohesion is *coupling.* Coupling is a reflection of the degree of dependencies between modules, i.e., how dependent one module is to another. The more dependent one module is to another, the higher its degree of coupling, and "loosely coupled modules" is the condition where the interconnections among modules are not rigid or hardcoded.

Good software engineering practices ensure that the software modules are *highly cohesive* and *loosely coupled* at the same time. This means that the dependencies between modules will be weak (loosely coupled) and each module will be responsible to perform a discrete function (highly cohesive).

Modular programming thereby helps to implement least privilege, in addition to making the code more readable, reusable, maintainable, and easy to troubleshoot.

The use of accounts with nonadministrative abilities also helps implement least privilege. Instead of using the "sa" or "sysadmin" account to access and execute database commands, using a "datareader" or "datawriter" account is an example of least privilege implementation.

3.7.2 Separation of Duties

When design compartmentalizes software functionality into two or more conditions, all of which need to be satisfied before an operation can be completed, it is referred to as *separation of duties*. The use of split keys for cryptographic functionality is an example of separation of duties in software. Keys are needed for encryption and decryption operations. Instead of storing a key in a single location, splitting a key and storing the parts in different locations, with one part in the system's registry and the other in a configuration file, provides more security. Software design should factor in the locations to store keys, as well as the mechanisms to protect them.

Another example of separation of duties in software development is related to the roles that people play during its development and the environment in which the software is deployed. The programmer should not be allowed to review his own code nor should a programmer have access to deploy code to the production environment. We will cover in more detail the separation of duties based on the environment in the configuration section of Chapter 7.

When architected correctly, separation of duties reduces the extent of damage that can be caused by one person or resource. When implemented in conjunction with auditing, it can also discourage insider fraud, as it will require collusion between parties to conduct fraud.

3.7.3 Defense in Depth

Layering security controls and risk mitigation safeguards into software design incorporates the principle of *defense in depth*. This is also referred to as *layered defense*. The reasons behind this principle are twofold, the first of which is that the breach of a single vulnerability in the software does not result in complete or total compromise. In other words, defense in depth is akin to not putting all the eggs in one basket. Second, incorporating the defense of depth in software can be used as a deterrent for the curious and nondetermined attackers when they are confronted with one defensive measure over another.

Some examples of defense in depth measures are

- Use of input validation along with prepared statements or stored procedures, disallowing dynamic query constructions using user input to defend against injection attacks
- Disallowing Cross-Site Scripting active scripting in conjunction with output encoding and input or request validation to defend against (XSS)
- The use of security zones, which separates the different levels of access according to the zone that the software or person is authorized to access

3.7.4 Fail Secure

Fail secure is the security principle that ensures that the software *reliably* functions when attacked and is rapidly *recoverable* into a normal business and secure state in the event of design or implementation failure. It aims at maintaining the *resiliency* (confidentiality, integrity, and availability) of software by defaulting to a secure state. Fail secure is primarily an availability design consideration, although it provides confidentiality and integrity protection as well. It supports the design and default aspects of the SD3 initiative, which implies that the software or system is secure by design, secure by default, and secure by deployment. In the context of software security, "fail secure" can be used interchangeably with "fail safe," which is commonly observed in physical security.

Some examples of fail secure design in software include the following:

- The user is denied access by default and the account is locked out after the maximum number (clipping level) of access attempts is tried.
- Not designing the software to ignore the error and resume next operation. The On Error Resume Next functionality in scripting languages such as VBScript as depicted in Figure 3.11.
- Errors and exceptions are explicitly handled and the error messages are non-verbose in nature. This ensures that system exception information, along with the stack trace, is not bubbled up to the client in raw form, which an attacker can use to determine the internal makeup of the software and launch attacks accordingly to circumvent the security protection mechanisms or take advantage of vulnerabilities in the software. Secure software design will take into account the logging of the error content into a support database and the bubbling up of only a reference value (such as error ID) to the user with instructions to contact the support team for additional support.

```
Option Explicit
Dim objNetwork, strDrive, strRemotePath

strDrive = "J:"
strRemotePath = "\\FinServer\Software"

On Error Resume Next

Set objNetwork = CreateObject("WScript.Network")
objNetwork.MapNetworkDrive strDrive, strRemotePath

Wscript.Quit
```

Figure 3.11   On error resume next.

3.7.5 Economy of Mechanisms

In Chapter 1, we noted that one of the challenges to the implementation of security is the trade-off that happens between the usability of the software and the security features that need to be designed and built in. With the noble intention of increasing the usability of software, developers often design and code in more functionality than is necessary. This additional functionality is commonly referred to as "bells-and-whistles." A good indicator of which features in the software are unneeded bells-and-whistles is reviewing the requirements traceability matrix (RTM) that is generated during the requirements gathering phase of the software development project. Bells-and-whistles features will never be part of the RTM. While such added functionality may increase user experience and usability of the software, it increases the attack surface and is contrary to the *economy of mechanisms,* secure design principle, which states that the more complex the design of the software, the more likely there are vulnerabilities. Simpler design implies easy-to-understand programs, decreased attack surface, and fewer weak links. With a decreased attack surface, there is less opportunity for failure and when failures do occur, the time needed to understand and fix the issues is less, as well. Additional benefits of economy of mechanisms include ease of understanding program logic and data flows and fewer inconsistencies. Economy of mechanism in layman's terms is also referred to as the KISS (Keep It Simple Stupid) principle and in some instances as the principle of *unnecessary complexity.* Modular programming not only supports the principle of least privilege but also supports the principle of economy of mechanisms.

Taken into account, the following considerations support the designing of software with the economies of mechanisms principle in mind:

■ *Unnecessary functionality or unneeded security mechanisms should be avoided.* Because patching and configuration of newer software versions has been known to security features that were disabled in previous versions, it is advisable to not even design unnecessary features, instead of designing them and leaving the features in a disabled state.

■ *Strive for simplicity.* Keeping the security mechanisms simple ensures that the implementation is not partial, which could result in compatibility issues. It is also important to model the data to be simple so that the data validation code and routines are not overly complex or incomplete. Supporting complex, regular expressions for data validation can result in algorithmic complexity weaknesses as stated in the Common Weakness Enumeration publication 407 (CWE-407).

■ *Strive for operational ease of use.* SSO is a good example that illustrates the simplification of user authentication so that the software is operationally easy to use.

3.7.6 Complete Mediation

In the early days of Web application programming, it was observed that a change in the value of a QueryString parameter would display the result that was tied to the new value without any additional validation. For example, if Pamela is logged in, and the Uniform Resource Locator (URL) in the browser address bar shows the name value pair, user=pamela, changing the value "pamela" to "reuben" would display Reuben's information without validating that the logged-on user is indeed Reuben. If Pamela changes the parameter value to user=reuben, she can view Reuben's information, potentially leading to attacks on confidentiality, wherein Reuben's sensitive and personal information is disclosed to Pamela.

While this is not as prevalent today as it used to be, similar design issues are still evident in software. Not checking access rights each time a subject requests access to objects violates the principle of complete mediation. *Complete mediation* is a security principle that states that access requests need to be mediated each time, every time, so that authority is not circumvented in subsequent requests. It enforces a system-wide view of access control. Remembering the results of the authority check, as is done when the authentication credentials are cached, can increase performance; however, the principle of complete mediation requires that results of an authority check be examined skeptically and systematically updated upon change. Caching can therefore lead to an increased security risk of authentication bypass, session hijacking and replay attacks, and man-in-the-middle (MITM) attacks. Therefore, designing the software to rely solely on client-side, cookie-based caching of authentication credentials for access should be avoided, if possible.

Complete mediation not only protects against authentication threats and confidentiality threats but is also useful in addressing the integrity aspects of software, as well. Not allowing browser postbacks without validation of access rights, or checking that a transaction is currently in a state of processing, can protect against the duplication of data, avoiding data integrity issues. Merely informing the user to not click more than once, as depicted in Figure 3.12, is not foolproof and so design

Figure 3.12   Weak design of complete mediation.

should include the disabling of user controls once a transaction is initiated until the transaction is completed.

The complete mediation design principle also addresses the failure to protect alternate path vulnerability. To properly implement complete mediation in software, it is advisable during the design phase of the SDLC to identify all possible code paths that access privileged and sensitive resources. Once these privileged code paths are identified, then the design must force these code paths to use a single interface that performs access control checks before performing the requested operation. Centralizing input validation by using a single input validation layer with a single, input filtration checklist for all externally controlled inputs is an example of such design. Alternatively, using an external input validation framework that validates all inputs before they are processed by the code may be considered when designing the software.

Complete mediation also augments the protection against the *weakest link.* Software is only as strong as its weakest component (code, service, interface, or user). It is also important to recognize that any protection that technical safeguards provide can be rendered futile if people fall prey to social engineering attacks or are not aware of how to use the software. The catch 22 is that *people* who are the first line of defense in software security can also become the weakest link, if they are not made aware, trained, and educated in software security.

3.7.7 Open Design

Dr. Auguste Kerckhoff, who is attributed with giving us the cryptographic *Kerckhoff's principle,* states that all information about the crypto system is public knowledge except the key, and the security of the crypto system against cryptanalysis attacks is dependent on the secrecy of the key. An outcome of Kerckhoff's principle is the open design principle, which states that the implementation of security safeguards should be independent of the design, itself, so that review of the design does not compromise the protection the safeguards offer. This is particularly applicable in cryptography where the protection mechanisms are decoupled from the keys that are used for cryptographic operations and algorithms used for encryption and decryption are open and available to anyone for review.

The inverse of the open design principle is *security through obscurity,* which means that the software employs protection mechanisms whose strength is dependent on the obscurity of the design, so much so that the understanding of the inner workings of the protection mechanisms is all that is necessary to defeat the protection mechanisms. A classic example of security through obscurity, which must be avoided if possible, is the hard coding and storing of sensitive information, such as cryptographic keys, or connection strings information with username and passwords inline code, or executables. Reverse engineering, binary analysis of executables, and runtime analysis of protocols can reveal these secrets. Review of the Diebold voting machines code revealed that passwords were embedded in the source code, cryptographic implementation was incorrect, the design allowed voters to vote an unlimited number of times without being detected, privileges could be escalated, and insiders could change a voter's ballot choice, all of which could have been avoided if the design was open for review by others. Another example of security through obscurity is the use of hidden form fields in Web applications, which affords little, if any protection against disclosure, as they can be processed using a modified client.

Software design should therefore take into account the need to leave the design open but keep the implementation of the protection mechanisms independent of the design. Additionally, while security through obscurity may increase the work factor needed by an attacker and provide some degree of defense in-depth, it should not be the sole and primary security mechanism in the software. Leveraging publicly vetted, proven, tested industry standards, instead of custom developing one's own protection mechanism, is recommended. For example, encryption algorithms, such as the Advanced Encryption Standard (AES) and Triple Data Encryption Standard (3DES), are publicly vetted and have undergone elaborate security analysis, testing, and review by the information security community. The inner workings of these algorithms are open to any reviewer, and public review can throw light on any potential weaknesses. The key that is used in the implementation of these proven algorithms is what should be kept secret.

Some of the fundamental aspects of the open design principle are as follows:

■ The security of your software should not be dependent on the *secrecy of the design*.
■ Security through obscurity should be avoided.

■ The design of protection mechanisms should be open for scrutiny by members of the community, as it is better for an ally to find a security vulnerability or flaw than it is for an attacker.

3.7.8 Least Common Mechanisms

Least common mechanisms is the security principle by which mechanisms common to more than one user or process are designed not to be shared. Because shared mechanisms, especially those involving shared variables, represent a potential information path, mechanisms that are common to more than one user and depended on by all users are to be minimized. Design should compartmentalize or isolate the code (functions) by user roles, because this increases the security of the software by limiting the exposure. For example, instead of having one function or library that is shared between members with supervisor and nonsupervisor roles, it is recommended to have two distinct functions, each serving its respective role.

3.7.9 Psychological Acceptability

One of the primary challenges in getting users to adopt security is that they feel that security is usually very complex. With a rise in attacks on passwords, many organizations resolved to implement strong password rules, such as the need to have mixed-case, alphanumeric passwords that are to be of a particular length. Additionally, these complex passwords are often required to be periodically changed. While this reduced the likelihood of brute-forcing or guessing passwords, it was observed that the users had difficulty remembering complex passwords. Therefore they nullified the effect that the strong password rules brought by jotting down their passwords and sticking them under their desks and, in some cases, even on their computer screens. This is an example of security protection mechanisms that were not psychologically acceptable and hence not effective.

Psychological acceptability is the security principle that states that security mechanisms should be designed to maximize usage, adoption, and automatic application.

A fundamental aspect of designing software with the psychological acceptability principle is that the security protection mechanisms

■ Are easy to use
■ Do not affect accessibility
■ Are transparent to the user

Users should not be additionally burdened as a result of security, and the protection mechanisms must not make the resource more difficult to access than if the security mechanisms were not present. Accessibility and usability should not be impeded by security mechanisms because users will elect to turn off or circumvent the mechanisms, thereby neutralizing or nullifying any protection that is designed.

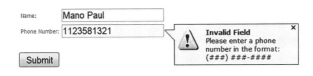

Figure 3.13   Callouts.

Examples of incorporating the psychological acceptability principle in software include designing the software to notify the user through explicit error messages and callouts as depicted in Figure 3.13, message box displays and help dialogs, and intuitive user interfaces.

3.7.10 Leveraging Existing Components

Service-oriented architecture (SOA) is prevalent in today's computing environment, and one of the primary aspects for its popularity is the ability it provides for communication between heterogeneous environments and platforms. Such communication is possible because the SOA protocols are understandable by disparate platforms, and business functionality is abstracted and exposed for consumption as contract-based, application programming interfaces (APIs). For example, instead of each financial institution writing its own currency conversion routine, it can invoke a common, currency conversion, service contract. This is the fundamental premise of the leveraging existing components design principle. Leveraging existing components is the security principle that promotes the reusability of existing components.

A common observance in security code reviews is that developers try to write their own cryptographic algorithms instead of using validated and proven cryptographic standards such as AES. These custom implementations of cryptographic functionality are also determined often to be the weakest link. Leveraging proven and validated cryptographic algorithms and functions is recommended.

Designing the software to scale using tier architecture is advisable from a security standpoint, because the software functionality can be broken down into presentation, business, and data access tiers. The use of a single data access layer (DAL) to mediate all access to the backend data stores not only supports the principle of leveraging existing components but also allows for scaling to support various clients or if the database technology changes. Enterprise application blocks are recommended over custom developing shared libraries and controls that attempt to provide the same functionality as the enterprise application blocks.

Reusing tested and proven, existing libraries and common components has the following security benefits. First, the attack surface is not increased, and second, no newer vulnerabilities are introduced. An ancillary benefit of leveraging existing components is increased productivity because leveraging existing components can significantly reduce development time.

3.8 Balancing Secure Design Principles

It is important to recognize that it may not be possible to design for each of these security principles in totality within your software, and trade-off decisions about the extent to which these principles can be designed may be necessary. For example, although SSO can heighten user experience and increase psychological acceptability, it contradicts the principle of complete mediation and so a business decision is necessary to determine the extent to which SSO is designed into the software or to determine that it is not even an option to consider. SSO design considerations should also take into account the need to ensure that there is no single point of failure and that appropriate, defense in-depth mitigation measures are undertaken. Additionally, implementing complete mediation by checking access rights and privileges, each and every time, can have a serious impact on the performance of the software. So this design aspect needs to be carefully considered and factored in, along with other defense in depth strategies, to mitigate vulnerability while not decreasing user experience or psychological acceptability. The principle of least common mechanism may seem contradictory to the principle of leveraging existing components and so careful design considerations need to be given to balance the two, based on the business needs and requirements, without reducing the security of the software. While psychological acceptability would require that the users be notified of user error, careful design considerations need to be given to ensure that the errors and exceptions are explicitly handled and nonverbose in nature so that internal, system configuration information is not revealed. The principle of least common mechanisms may seem to be diametrically opposed to the principle of leveraging existing components, and one may argue that centralizing functionality in business components that can be reused is analogous to putting all the eggs in one basket, which is true. However, proper defense in depth strategies should be factored into the design when choosing to leverage existing components.

3.9 Other Design Considerations

In addition to the core software security design considerations covered earlier, there are other design considerations that need to be taken into account when building software. These include the following:

- Programming language
- Data type, format, range, and length
- Database security
- Interface
- Interconnectivity

We will cover each of these considerations.

3.9.1 Programming Language

Before writing a single line of code, it is pivotal to determine the programming language that will be used to implement the design, because a programming language can bring with it inherent risks or security benefits. In organizations with an initial level of capability maturity, developers tend to choose the programming language that they are most familiar with or one that is popular and new. It is best advised to ensure that the programming language chosen is one that is part of the organization's technology or coding standard, so that the software that is produced can be universally supported and maintained.

The two main types of programming languages in today's world can be classified into *unmanaged* or *managed* code languages. Common examples of unmanaged code are C/C++ while Java and all .NET programming languages, which include C# and VB.Net, are examples of managed code programming languages.

Unmanaged code programming languages are those that have the following characteristics:

- The execution of the code is not managed by any runtime execution environment but is directly executed by the operating system. This makes execution relatively faster.
- Is compiled to native code that will execute only on the processor architecture (X86 or X64) against which it is compiled.
- Memory allocation is not managed and pointers in memory addresses can be directly controlled, which makes these programming languages more susceptible to buffer overflows and format string vulnerabilities that can lead to arbitrary code execution by overriding memory pointers.
- Requires developers to write routines to handle memory allocation, check array bounds, handle data type conversions explicitly, force garbage collection, etc., which makes it necessary for the developers to have more programming skills and technical capabilities.

Managed code programming languages, on the other hand, have the following characteristics:

- Execution of the code is not by the operating system directly, but instead, it is by a managed runtime environment. Because the execution is managed by the runtime environment, security and nonsecurity services such as memory management, exception handling, bounds checking, garbage collection, and type safety checking can be leveraged from the runtime environment and security checks can be asserted before the code executes. These additional services can cause the code to execute considerably slower than the same code written in an unmanaged code programming language. The managed runtime environment in the .NET Framework is the Common Language Runtime (CLR).

- Is not directly compiled into native code but is compiled into an Intermediate Language (IL) and an executable is created. When the executable is run, the Just-in-Time (JIT) compiler of the CLR compiles the IL into native code that the computer will understand. This allows for platform independence, as the JIT compiler handles the compilation of the IL into native code that is processor architecture specific. The Common Language Infrastructure (CLI) Standard provides encoding information and description on how the programming languages emit the appropriate encoding when compiled.
- Because memory allocation is managed by the runtime environment, buffer overflows and format string vulnerabilities are mitigated considerably.
- Time to develop software is relatively shorter because most memory management, exception handling, bounds checking, garbage collection, and type safety checking are automatically handled by the runtime environment. *Type safety* means that the code is not allowed to access memory locations outside its bounds if it is not authorized to do so. This also means that implicit casting of one data type to another, which can lead to errors and exceptions, is not allowed. Type safety plays a critical role in isolating assemblies and security enforcement. It is provided by default to managed code programming languages, making it an important consideration when choosing between an unmanaged or managed code programming language.

Choosing the appropriate programming language is an important design consideration. An unmanaged code programming language may be necessary when execution needs to be fast and memory allocation needs to be explicitly controlled. However, it is important to recognize that such degrees of total control can also lead to total compromise when a security breach occurs, and so careful attention should be paid when choosing an unmanaged code programming language over a managed code one. One strategy to get the benefits of both unmanaged and managed code programming languages is to code the software in a managed code language and call unmanaged code using wrappers only when needed, with defense in-depth protection mechanisms implemented alongside. It also must be understood that while managed code programming languages are less prone to errors caused by the ignorance of developers and or to security issues, it is no panacea to security threats and vulnerabilities. Regardless of whether one chooses an unmanaged or managed code programming language, security protection mechanisms must be carefully and explicitly designed.

3.9.2 Data Type, Format, Range, and Length

While protection mechanisms such as encryption, hashing, and masking help with confidentiality assurance, data type, format, range, and length are important design considerations, the lack of which can potentially lead to integrity violations.

Programming languages have what is known as built-in or *primitive* data types. Some common examples of primitive data types are Character (character, char), Integer (integer, int, short, long, byte), Floating-point numbers (double, float, real), and Boolean (true or false). Some programming languages also allow programmers to define their own data types; this is not recommended from a security standpoint because it potentially increases the attack surface. Conversely, strongly typed programming languages do not allow the programmer to define their own data types to model real objects, and this is preferred from a security standpoint as it does not allow the programmer to increase the attack surface.

The set of values and the permissible operations on that value set are defined by the data type. For example, a variable that is defined as an integer data type can be assigned a whole number but never a fraction. Integers may be signed or unsigned. Unsigned integers are those that allow only positive values, while signed integers allow both positive and negative values. Table 3.3 depicts the size and ranges of values dependent on the integer data type.

The reason why the data type is an important design consideration is because it is not only important to understand the limits that can be stored in memory for a variable defined as a particular data type, but it is also vital to know of the permissible operations on a data type. Failing to understand data type permissible operations can lead to conversion mismatches and casting or conversion errors that could prove detrimental to the secure state of the software.

When a numeric data type is converted from one data type to another, it can either be a *widening* conversion (also known as expansion) or a *narrowing* conversion (also known as truncation). Widening conversions are those where the data type is converted from a type that is of a smaller size and range to one that is of a larger size and range. An example of a widening conversion would be converting

Table 3.3 Integer Data Type Size and Ranges

Name	Size (in bits)	Range	
		Unsigned	*Signed*
Byte	8	0 to 255	−128 to +127
int, short, Int16, Word	16	0 to 65,535	−32,768 to +32,767
long int, Int32, Double Word	32	0 to 4,294,967,295	−2,147,483,648 to +2,147,483,647
long long	64	0 to 18,446,744,073,709,551,615	−9,223,372,036,854,775,808 to +9,223,372,036,854,775,807

Table 3.4 Conversions of Data Types without Loss of Data

Type	Can be Converted without Loss of Data to
Byte	UInt16, Int16, UInt32, Int32, UInt64, Int64, Single, Double, Decimal
SByte	Int16, Int32, Int64, Single, Double, Decimal
Int16	Int32, Int64, Single, Double, Decimal
UInt16	UInt32, Int32, UInt64, Int64, Single, Double, Decimal
Char	UInt16, UInt32, Int32, UInt64, Int64, Single, Double, Decimal
Int32 and UInt32	Int64, Double, Decimal
Int64 and UInt64	Decimal
Single	Double

an "int" to a "long." Table 3.4 illustrates widening conversions without the loss the data.

Not all widening conversions happen without the potential loss of data. In some cases, not only is data loss evident, but there is a loss of precision, as well. For example, converting from an Int64 or a single data type to a double data type can lead to loss of precision.

A narrowing conversion, on the other hand, can lead to loss of information. An example of a narrowing conversion is converting a Decimal data type to an Integer data type. This can potentially cause data loss truncation if the value being stored in the Integer data type is greater than its allowed range. For example, changing the data type of the variable "UnitPrice" that holds the value $19.99 from a Decimal data type to an Integer data type will result in storing $19 alone, ignoring the values after the decimal and causing data integrity issues. Improper casting or conversion can result in overflow exceptions or data loss. Input length and range validation using regular expression (RegEx) and maximum length (maxlength) restrictions, in conjunction with exception management protection controls, need to be designed to alleviate these issues.

3.9.3 Database Security

Just as important as data design is for security is the design of the database for the reliability, resiliency, and recoverability of software that depends on the data stored in the database. Not only is protection essential when data are in transit, but also when data are at rest, in storage, and in archives. Using a biological analogy, one can call the database that is connected to the network the heart of the organization, and a breach at this layer could prove disastrous to the life and continuity of the business. Regulations such as HIPAA and GLBA impose requirements to protect personally identifiable information (PII) when it is stored, and willful neglect can lead to fines being levied, incarceration of officers of the corporation, and regulatory oversight. The application layer is seen to be the conduit of attacks against the data stored in databases or data stores, as is evident with many injection attacks, such as SQL injection and Lightweight Directory Access Protocol (LDAP) injection attacks. Using such attacks, an attacker can steal, manipulate, or destroy data.

Database security design considerations are critically important because they have an impact on the confidentiality, integrity, and availability of data. One kind of attack against the confidentiality of data is the *inference* attack. An inference attack is one that is characterized by an attacker gleaning sensitive information about the database from presumably hidden and trivial pieces of information using data mining techniques without directly accessing the database. It is difficult to protect against an inference attack because the trivial piece of information may be legitimately obtained by the attacker. Inference attacks often go hand in hand with *aggregation* attacks. An aggregation attack is one where information at different, security classification levels, which are primarily nonsensitive in isolation, end up becoming sensitive information when pieced together as a whole. A well-known example of aggregation is the combining of longitudinal and latitudinal coordinates along with supply and delivery information to piece together and glean possible army locations. Individually, the longitudinal and latitudinal coordinates are generally not sensitive. Neither is the supply and delivery information. But when these two pieces of information are aggregated, the aggregation can reveal sensitive information through inference. Therefore, database queries that request trivial and nonsensitive information from various tables within the database must be carefully designed to be scrutinized, monitored, and audited.

Polyinstantiation, database encryption, normalization, and triggers and views are important protection design considerations concerning the organization's database assets.

3.9.3.1 Polyinstantiation

A well-known, database security approach to deal with the problems of inference and aggregation is *polyinstantiation*. Polyinstantiation means that there exist several instances (or versions) of the database information, so that what is viewed by a user is dependent on the security clearance or classification level attributes of the requesting user. For example, many instances of the president's phone number are maintained at different classification levels and only users with top secret clearance will be allowed to see the phone number of the president of the country, while those with no clearance are given a generic phone number to view. Polyinstantiation addresses inference attacks by allowing a means to hide information by using classification labels. It addresses aggregation by allowing the means to label different aggregations of data separately.

3.9.3.2 Database Encryption

Perimeter defenses such as firewalls offer little to no protection to stored, sensitive data from internal threat agents who have the means and opportunity to access and exploit data stored in databases. The threat to databases comes not only from external hackers but also from insiders who wish to compromise the data, i.e., data that are essentially the crown jewels of an organization. In fact, while external attacks may be seen on the news, many internal attacks often go unpublicized, even though they are equally, if not more, devastating to an organization. Insider threats to databases warrant close attention, especially those from disgruntled employees in a layoff economy. Without proper, database security controls, we leave an organization unguarded and solely reliant on the motive of an insider, who already has the means and the opportunity.

Data-at-rest encryption is a preventive, control mechanism that can provide strong protection against disclosure and alteration of data, but it is important to ensure that along with database encryption, proper authentication and access control protection mechanisms exist to secure the key that is used for the encryption. Having one without the other is equivalent to locking the door and leaving the key under the doormat, and this really provides little protection. Therefore, a proper database encryption strategy is necessary to implement database security adequately. This strategy should include encryption, access control, auditing for security and logging of privilege database operations and events, and capacity planning.

Encryption not only has an impact on performance but also on data size. If fields in the database that are indexed are encrypted, then lookup queries and searches will take significantly longer, therefore degrading performance. Additionally, most encryption algorithms output fixed, block sizes and pad the input data to match the output size. This means that smaller-sized input data will be padded and stored with an increased size and the database design must take this into account to avoid padding and truncation issues. To transform binary cipher text to character-type data where encoding is used with encryption, the data size is increased by approximately one-third its original size, and this should be factored into design, as well.

Some of the important factors that must be taken into account when determining the database encryption strategy are listed below. These include, but are not limited to, the following:

- Where the data should be encrypted: at its point of origin in the application or in the database where they reside?
- What should be the minimum level of data classification before it warrants protection by encryption?
- Is the database designed to handle data sizes upon encryption?

- Is the business aware of the performance impact of implementing encryption and is the trade-off between performance and security within acceptable thresholds for the business?
- Where will the keys used for cryptography operations be stored?
- What authentication and access control measures will be implemented to protect the key that will be used for encryption and decryption?
- Are the individuals who have access to the database controlled and monitored?
- Are there security policies in effect to implement security auditing and event logging at the database layer in order to detect insider threats and fraudulent activities?
- Should there be a breach of the database, is there an incident management plan to contain the damage and respond to the incident?

Database encryption can be accomplished in one of two ways:

1. Using native Database Management System (DBMS) encryption
2. Leveraging cryptographic resources external to the database

In native DBMS encryption, the cryptographic operations including key storage and management are handled within the database itself. Cryptographic operations are transparent to the application layer, and this type of encryption is commonly referred to as Transparent Database Encryption (TDE). The primary benefit of this approach is that the impact on the application is minimal, but there can be a substantial performance impact. When native DBMS encryption capabilities are used, the performance and strength of the algorithm along with the flexibility to choose what data can be encrypted must be taken into account. From a security standpoint, the primary drawback to using native DBMS encryption is the inherent weakness that exists in the storage of the encryption key within the DBMS itself. The protection of this key will be primarily dependent on the strength of the DBMS access control protection mechanisms, but users who have access to the encrypted data will probably have access rights to the encryption key storage as well. When cryptographic resources external to the database are leveraged, cryptographic operations and key storage and management are off-loaded to external cryptographic infrastructure and servers. From a security standpoint, database architectures that separate encryption processing and key management are recommended and preferred as such architecture increases the work factor necessary for the attacker. The separation of the encrypted data from the encryption keys brings a significant security benefit. When these keys are stored in HSMs, they increase the security protection substantially and make it necessary for the attacker to have physical access in order to compromise the keys. Additionally, leveraging external infrastructure and servers for cryptographic operations moves the computational overhead away from the DBMS, significantly increasing performance. The primary

Table 3.5   Unnormalized Form

Customer_ID	First_ Name	Last_Name	Sales_ Rep_ID	Product_1	Product_2
1	Paul	Schmidt	S101	CSSLPEX1	CSSLPEX2
2	David	Thompson	S201	SSCPEX1	SSCPEX2

drawbacks of this approach are the need to modify or change applications, monitor and administer other servers, and communications overhead.

Each approach has its own advantages and disadvantages and when choosing the database encryption approach, it is important to do so only after fully understanding the pros and cons of each approach, the business need, regulatory requirements, and database security strategy.

3.9.3.3 Normalization

The maintainability and security of a database are directly proportional to its organization of data. Redundant data in databases not only waste storage but also imply the need for redundant maintenance as well as the potential for inconsistencies in database records. For example, if data are held in multiple locations (tables) in the database, then changes to data must be performed in all locations holding the same data. The change in the price of a product is much easier to implement if the product price is maintained only within the product table. Maintaining product information in more than one table in the database will require implementing changes to product-related information in each table. This cannot only be a maintenance issue, but also, if the updates are not uniformly applied across all tables that hold product information, inconsistencies can occur leading to loss of data integrity.

Normalization is a formal technique that can be used to organize data so that *redundancy* and *inconsistency* are eliminated. The organization of data is based on certain rules, and each rule is referred to as a "normal form." There are primarily three data organization or *normalization* rules. The database design is said to be in

Table 3.6   First Normal Form (1NF)

Customer_ID	First_Name	Last_Name	Sales_Rep_ID	Product_Code
1	Paul	Schmidt	S101	CSSLPEX1
1	Paul	Schmidt	S101	CSSLPEX2
2	David	Thompson	S201	SSCPEX1
2	David	Thompson	S201	SSCPEX2

Table 3.7 Customer Table in Second Normal Form (2NF)

Customer_ID	First_Name	Last_Name	Sales_Rep_ID
1	Paul	Schmidt	S101
2	David	Thompson	S201

the normal form that corresponds to the number of rules the design complies with. A database design that complies with one rule is known to be in first normal form, notated as 1NF. A design with two rules is known to be in second normal form, notated as 2NF, and one with compliance to all three rules is known to be in third normal form, notated as 3NF. Fourth (4NF) and Fifth (5NF) Normal Form of database design exist, as well, but they are seldom implemented practically. Table 3.5 is an example of a table that is in unnormalized form.

First Normal Form (1NF) mandates that there are no repeating fields or groups of fields within a table. This means that related data are stored separately. This is also informally referred to as the "No Repeating Groups" rule. When product information is maintained for each customer record separately instead of being repeated within one table, it is said to be compliant with 1NF. Table 3.6 is an example of a table that in is 1NF.

Second Normal Form (2NF) mandates that duplicate data are removed. A table in 2NF must first be in 1NF. This is also informally referred to as the "Eliminate Redundant Data" rule. The elimination of duplicate records in each table addresses data inconsistency and, subsequently, data integrity issues. 2NF means that sets of values that apply to multiple records are stored in separate tables and related using a primary key (PK) and foreign key (FK) relationship. In the previous table, Product_Code is not dependent on the Customer_ID PK, and so, in order to comply with 2NF, they must be stored separately and associated using a table. Tables 3.7 and 3.8 are examples of tables that are in 2NF. Third Normal Form (3NF) is a logical extension of the 2NF, and for a table to be in 3NF, it must first be in

Table 3.8 Customer Order Table in Second Normal Form (2NF)

Customer_ID	Product_Code
1	CSSLPEX1
1	CSSLPEX2
2	SSCPEX1
2	SSCPEX2

Table 3.9   Customer Table in Third Normal Form (3NF)

Customer_ID	First_Name	Last_Name
1	Paul	Schmidt
2	David	Thompson

2NF. 3NF mandates that data that are not dependent on the uniquely identifying PK of that table are eliminated and maintained in tables of their own. This is also referred to informally as the "Eliminate Non-Key-Dependent Duplicate Data" rule. Because the Sales_Rep_ID is not dependent on the Customer_ID in the CUSTOMER table, for the table to be in 3NF, data about the sales representatives must be maintained in their own table. Tables 3.9 and 3.10 are examples of tables that are in 3NF.

Benefits of normalization include elimination of redundancy and reduction of inconsistency issues. Normalization yields security benefits as well. Data integrity, which assures that the data are not only consistent but also accurate, can be achieved through normalization. Additionally, permissions for database operations can be granted at a more granular level per table and limited to users, when the data are organized using normal form. Data integrity in the context of normalization is the assurance of consistent and accurate data within a database.

It must also be recognized that although the security and database maintainability benefits of normalization are noteworthy, there is one primary drawback to normalization, which is degraded performance. When data that are not organized in a normalized form are requested, the performance impact is mainly dependent on the time it takes to read the data from a single table, but when the database records are normalized, there is a need to join multiple tables in order to serve the requested data. In order to increase the performance, a conscious decision may be required to denormalize a normalized database. *Denormalization* is the process of decreasing the normal form of a database table by modifying its structure to allow redundant data in a controlled manner. A denormalized database is not the same as a database that has never been normalized. However, when data are denormalized, it is critically important to have extraneous control and protection mechanisms

Table 3.10   Sales Representative Table in Third Normal Form (3NF)

Sales_Rep_ID	Sales_Rep_Name	Sales_Rep_Phone
S101	Marc Thompson	(202) 529-8901
S201	Sally Smith	(417) 972-1019

that will assure data consistency, accuracy, and integrity. A preferred alternate to denormalizing data at rest is to implement database views.

3.9.3.4 Triggers and Views

A database trigger is a special type of procedure that is automatically executed upon the occurrence of certain conditions within the database. It differs from a regular procedure in its manner of invocation. Regular, stored procedures and prepared statements are explicitly fired to run by either a user, an application, or, in some cases, even a trigger itself. A trigger, on the other hand, is fired to run implicitly by the database when the triggering event occurs. Events that fire triggers may be one or more of the following types:

- Data Manipulation Language (DML) statements that modify data, such as INSERT, UPDATE, and DELETE.
- Data Definition Language (DDL) statements that can be used for performing administrative tasks in the database, such as auditing and regulating database operations.
- Error events (OnError).
- System events, such as Start, Shutdown, and Restart.
- User events, such as Logon and Logoff.

Triggers are useful not only for supplementing existing database capabilities, but they can also be very useful for automating and improving security protection mechanisms. Triggers can be used to

- Enforce complex business rules such as restricting alterations to the database during nonbusiness hours or automatically computing the international shipping rates when the currency conversion rate changes.
- Prevent invalid transactions.
- Ensure referential integrity operations.
- Provide automated, transparent auditing and event-logging capabilities. If a critical business transaction that requires auditing is performed, one can use DML triggers to log the transaction along with pertinent audit fields in the database.
- Enforce complex security privileges and rights.
- Synchronize data across replicated tables and databases, ensuring the accuracy and integrity of the data.

Although the functional and security benefits of using triggers are many, triggers must be designed with caution. Excessive implementation of triggers can cause overly complex application logic, which makes the software difficult to maintain besides increasing the potential attack surface. Also, because triggers are responsive to triggering events, they cannot perform commit or rollback operations, and poorly constructed triggers can cause table and data mutations, impacting accuracy and integrity. Furthermore, when *cascading triggers,* which are characterized when triggers invoke other triggers, are used, interdependencies are increased, making troubleshooting and maintenance difficult.

A database view is a customized presentation of data that may be held in one or more physical tables (base tables) or another view itself. A view is the output of a query and is akin to a virtual table or stored query. A view is said to be virtual because unlike the base tables that supply the view with data, the view itself is not allocated any storage space in the physical database. The only space that is allocated is the space necessary to hold the stored query. Because the data in a view are not physically stored, a view is dynamically constructed when the query to generate the view is executed. Just like on a base table, DML CRUD (create, read, update, and delete) operations to insert, view, modify, or remove data, with some restrictions, can be performed on views. However, it must be understood that operations performed on the view affect the base tables serving the data, and so the same data integrity constraints should be taken into account when dealing with views.

Because views are dynamically constructed, data that are presented can be custom-made for users based on their rights and privileges. This makes it possible for protection against disclosure so that only those who have the authorization to view certain types of data are allowed to see those types of data and that they are not allowed to see any other data. Not only do views provide confidentiality assurance, they also support the principle of "need to know." Restricting access to predetermined sets of rows or columns of a table increases the level of database security. Figure 3.14 is an example of a view that results by joining the CATEGORY, PRODUCT, and ORDER tables.

	Category ID	Category Name	Product Name	Product Sales
1	1	Beverages	Outback Lager	5463 40
2	5	Grains/Cereals	Gnocchi di nonna Alice	32604.00
3	4	Dairy Products	Gudbrandsdalsost	13062.60
4	6	Meat/Poultry	Tourtière	3184.29
5	6	Meat/Poultry	Thüringer Rostbratwuret	34755.92
6	8	Seafood	Boston Crab Meat	9814.73
7	6	Meat/Poultry	Alice Mutton	17604.60

Figure 3.14   Database view.

Views can also be used to abstract internal database structure, hiding the source of data and the complexity of joins. A join view is defined as one that synthesizes the presentation of data by joining several base tables or views. The internal table structures, relationships, and constraints are protected and hidden from the end user. Even an end user who has no knowledge of how to perform joins can use a view to select information from various database objects. Additionally, the resulting columns of a view can be renamed to hide the actual database naming convention that an attacker can use to his or her advantage when performing reconnaissance. Views can also be used to save complicated queries. Queries that perform extensive computations are good candidates to be saved as views so that they can be repeatedly performed without having to reconstruct the query each and every time.

3.9.4 Interface

3.9.4.1 User Interface

The Clark and Wilson security model, more commonly referred to as the access triple security model, states that a subject's access to an object should always be mediated via a program and no direct subject–object access should be allowed. A user interface (UI) between a user and a resource can act as the mediating program to support this security model. User interfaces design should assure disclosure protection. Masking of sensitive information, such as a password or credit card number by displaying asterisks on the screen, is an example of a secure user interface that assures confidentiality. A database view can also be said as an example of a restricted user interface. Without giving an internal user direct access to the data objects, be they on the file system or the database, and requiring the user to access the resources using a UI protects against inference attacks and direct database attacks. Abstractions using user interfaces are also a good defense against insider threats. The UI provides a layer where auditing of business-critical and privileged actions can be performed, thereby increasing the possibility of uncovering insider threats and fraudulent activities that could compromise the security of the software.

3.9.4.2 Security Management Interfaces (SMI)

SMIs are interfaces used to configure and manage the security of the software itself. These are administrative interfaces with high levels of privilege. A SMI can be used for user-provisioning tasks such as adding users, deleting users, enabling or disabling user accounts, as well as granting rights and privileges to roles, changing security settings, configuring audit log settings and trails, exception logging, etc. An example of an SMI is the setup screens that are used to manage the security settings of a home router. Figure 3.15 depicts the SMI for a D-Link home router.

From a security standpoint, it is critical that these SMIs are threat modeled, as well, and appropriate protection designed, because these interfaces are usually not

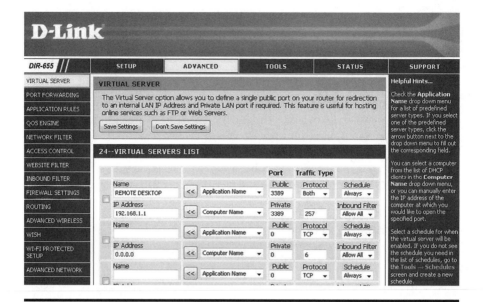

Figure 3.15 **Router security management interface (SMI).**

captured in the requirements explicitly. They are often observed to be the weakest link, as they are overlooked when threats to the software are modeled. The consequences of breaching an administrative interface are usually severe because the attacker ends up running with elevated privileges. A compromise of an SMI can lead to total compromise, disclosure, and alteration and destruction threats, besides allowing attackers to use these as backdoors for installing malware (Trojans, rootkits, spyware, adware, etc.). Not only should strong protection controls be implemented to protect SMIs, but these must be explicitly captured in the requirements, be part of the threat modeling exercise, and designed precisely and securely. Some of the recommended protection controls for these highly privileged and sensitive interfaces are as follows:

Avoid remote connectivity and administration, requiring administrators to log on locally

Employ data protection in transit, using channel security protection measures at the transport (e.g., SSL) or network (e.g., IPSec) layer.

Use least privilege accounts and RBAC to control access to and functionality of the interfaces

3.9.5 Interconnectivity

In the world we live in today, rarely is software deployed in a silo. Most business applications and software are highly interconnected, creating potential backdoors for attackers if they are designed without security in mind. Software design should factor in design consideration to ensure that the software is reliable, resilient, and recoverable. Upstream and downstream compatibility of software should be explicitly designed. This is particularly important when it comes to delegation of trust, SSO, token-based authentication, and cryptographic key sharing between applications. If an upstream application has encrypted data using a particular key, there must be a secure means to transfer the key to the downstream applications that will need to decrypt the data. When data or information are aggregated from various sources, as is the case with mashups, software design should take into account the trust that exists or that needs to be established between the interconnected entities. Modular programming with the characteristics of high cohesion and loose coupling help with interconnectivity design as it reduces complex dependencies between the connected components, keeping each entity as discreet and unitary as possible.

3.10 Design Processes

When you are designing software with security in mind, certain security processes need to be established and completed. These processes are to be conducted during the initial stages of the software development project. These include attack surface evaluation, threat modeling, control identification and prioritization, and documentation. In this section, we shall look at each of these processes and learn how they can be used to develop reliable, recoverable, and hack-resilient, secure software.

3.10.1 Attack Surface Evaluation

A software or application's attack surface is the measure of its exposure of being exploited by a threat agent, i.e., weaknesses in its entry and exit points that a malicious attacker can exploit to his or her advantage. Because each accessible feature of the software is a potential attack vector that an intruder can leverage, attack surface evaluation aims at determining the entry and exit points in the software that can lead to the exploitation of weaknesses and manifestation of threats. Often, attack surface evaluation is done as part of the threat modeling exercise during the design phase of the SDLC. We will cover threat modeling in a subsequent section. The determination of the software's "attackability" or the exposure to attack can commence in the requirements phase of the SDLC, when security requirements are determined by generating misuse cases and subject–object matrices. During the design phase, each misuse case or subject–object matrix can be used as an input to determine the entry and exit points of the software that can be attacked.

The attack surface evaluation attempts to enumerate the list of features that an attacker will try to exploit. These potential attack points are then assigned a weight or bias based on their assumed severity so that controls may be identified and prioritized. In the Windows operating system, open ports, open Remote Procedural Call (RPC) end points and sockets, open named pipes, Windows default and SYSTEM services, active Web handler files (active server pages, Hierarchical Translation Rotation (HTR) files, etc.), Internet Server Application Programming Interface (ISAPI) filters, dynamic Web pages, weak access control lists (ACLs) for files and shares, etc., are attackable entry and exit points. In the Linux and *nix operating systems, setuid root applications and symbolic links are examples of features that can be attacked.

3.10.1.1 Relative Attack Surface Quotient

The term *relative attack surface quotient* (RASQ) was introduced by renowned author and Microsoft security program manager Michael Howard to describe the relative attackability or likely opportunities for attack against software in comparison to a baseline. The baseline is a fixed set of dimensions. The notion of the RASQ metric is that, instead of focusing on the number of code level bugs or system level vulnerabilities, we are to focus on the likely opportunities for attack against the software and aim at decreasing the attack surface by improving the security of software products. This is particularly important to compute for shrink-wrap products, such as Windows OS, to show security improvements in newer versions, but the same can be determined for version releases of business applications as well. With each attack point assigned a value, referred to as the *attack bias,* based on its severity, the RASQ of a product can be computed by adding together the effective attack surface for all root vectors. A *root vector* is a particular feature of the OS or software that can positively or negatively affect the security of the product. The effective *attack surface value* is defined as the product of the number of attack surfaces within a root attack vector and the *attack bias*. For example, a service that runs by default under the SYSTEM account and opens a socket to the world is a prime attack candidate, even if the software is implemented using secure code, when compared to a scenario wherein the ACLS to the registry are weak. Each is assigned a bias, such as 0.1 for a low threat and 1.0 for a severe threat.

Researchers Howard, Pincus, and Wing, in their paper entitled "Measuring relative attack surfaces," break down the attack surface into three formal dimensions: targets and enablers, channels and protocols, and access rights. A brief introduction of these dimensions is given here.

- *Targets and enablers* are resources that an attacker can leverage to construct an attack against the software. An attacker first determines if a resource is a target or an enabler, and, in some cases, a target in a particular attack may be an enabler to another kind of attack and vice versa. The two kinds of targets and enablers are *processes* and *data*. Browsers, mailers, and servers are examples of process targets and enablers, while files, directories, and registries are examples of data targets and enablers. One aspect of determining the attack surface is determining the number of potential process and data targets and enablers and the likely opportunities to attack each of these.

■ *Channels and protocols* are mechanisms that allow for communication between two parties. The means by which a sender (or an attacker) can communicate with a receiver (a target) is referred to as a *channel* and the rule by which information is exchanged is referred to as a *protocol*. The endpoints of the channel are processes. There are two kinds of channels: message-passing channels and shared-memory channels. Examples of message-passing channels include sockets, RPC connections, and named pipes that use protocols such as ftp, http, RPC, and streaming to exchange information. Examples of shared-memory channels include files, directories, and registries that use open-before-read file protocols, concurrency access control checks for shared objects, and resource locking integrity rules. In addition to determining the number and "attackability" of targets and enablers, determining the attack surface includes the determination of channel types, instances of each channel type and related protocols, processes, and access rights.

■ *Access rights* are the privileges associated with each resource, regardless of whether it is a target or enabler. These include read, write, and execute rights

Table 3.11   Mapping RASQ Attack Vectors into Dimensions

Dimensions	Attack Vector
Targets (process)	Services
	Active Web handlers
	Active ISAPI filters
	Dynamic Web pages
Targets (process), constrained by access rights	Services running by default
	Services running as SYSTEM
Targets (data)	Executable virtual directories
	Enabled accounts
Targets (data), constrained by access rights	Enabled accounts in admin group
	Enabled guest account
	Weak ACLS in file system
	Weak ACLs in registry
	Weak ACLs on shares
Enablers (process)	VBScript enabled
	JScript enabled
	ActiveX enabled
Channels	Null sessions to pipes and shares

that can be assigned not only to data and process targets such as files, direc-tories, and servers but also to channels (which are essentially data resources) and endpoints (process resources). Table 3.11 is a tabulation of various root attack vectors to formal dimensions.

A complete explanation of computing RASQ is beyond the scope of this book, but a CSSLP must be aware of this concept and its benefits. Although the RASQ score may not be truly indicative of a software product's true exposure to attack or its security health, it can be used as a measurement to determine the improvement of code quality and security between versions of software. The main idea is to improve the security of the software by reducing the RASQ score in subsequent versions. This can also be extended within the SDLC, itself, wherein the RASQ score can be computed before and after software testing and/or before and after software deployment to reflect improvement in code quality and, subsequently, security. The paper by researchers Howard, Pincus, and Wing is recommended reading for addi-tional information on RASQ.

3.10.2 Threat Modeling

Threats to software are manifold. They range from disclosure threats against confi-dentiality to alteration threats against integrity to destruction threats against avail-ability, authentication bypass, privilege escalation, impersonation, deletion of log files, MITM attacks, session hijacking and replaying, injection, scripting, overflow, and cryptographic attacks. We will cover the prevalent attack types in more detail in Chapter 4.

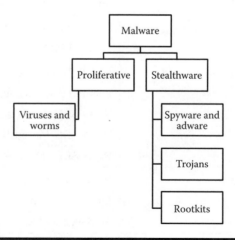

Figure 3.16   Types of malware.

3.10.2.1 Threat Sources/Agents

Like the various threats to software, several *threat sources/agents* also exist. These may be human or nonhuman. Nonhuman threat agents include malicious software (malware) such as viruses and worms, which are proliferative, and spyware, adware, Trojans, and rootkits that are primarily stealthy as depicted in Figure 3.16.

Human threat agents range from the ignorant user who causes plain, user error to the organized cybercriminals who can orchestrate infamous and disastrous threats to national and corporate security. Table 3.12 tabulates the various human threat agents to software based on their increasing degree of knowledge and the extent of damage they can cause.

Table 3.12 Human Threat Source/Agent

Threat Agent Type	Description
Ignorant user	The ignorant user is the one that is often the cause of unintentional and plain user error. Plain user error is also referred to sometimes as plain error or simply user error. To combat this threat source is simple but requires investment in time and effort. User education is the best defense against this type of threat agent. Mere documentation and help guides are insufficient measures, if they are not used appropriately.
Accidental discoverer	An ordinary user who stumbles upon a functional mistake in the software and who is able to gain privilege access to information or functionality. This user never sought to circumvent security protection mechanisms in the first place.
Curious attacker	An ordinary user who notices some anomaly in the functioning of the software and decides to pursue it further. Often, an accidental discoverer graduates into being a curious attacker.
Script kiddies	These types of threat agents are to be dealt with seriously, merely because of their prevalence in the industry. They are those ordinary users who execute hacker scripts against corporate assets without understanding the impact and consequences of their actions. Most elite hackers today were one-day script kiddies. A litmus test to the identification of a script kiddies work is that they do not often hide or know how to hide their footprint on the software or systems they have attacked.

Table 3.12   Human Threat Source/Agent (Continued)

Threat Agent Type	Description
Insider	One of the most powerful attackers in this day and age is the insider or the enemy inside the firewall. These are potentially disgruntled employees or staff members within the organization who have access to insider knowledge. The database administrator with unfettered and unaudited access to sensitive information directly is a potential threat source that should not be ignored. Proper identification, authentication, authorization, and auditing of user actions are important and necessary controls that need to be implemented to deter insider attacks. Auditing can also be used as a detective control in the cases where insider fraud and attack is speculated.
Organized cybercriminals	These are highly skilled malefactors that are paid professionally for using their skills to thwart security protection of software and systems, seeking high financial gain. They not only have a deep understanding of software development but also of reverse engineering and network and host security controls. They can be used for attacks against corporate assets as well as are a threat to national security as cyber terrorists. Malware developers fall into this category as well.

3.10.2.2 What Is Threat Modeling?

Threat modeling is a systematic, iterative, and structured security technique that should not be overlooked during the design phase of a software development project. Threat modeling is extremely crucial for developing hack-resilient software. It should be performed to identify security objectives and threats to and vulnerabilities in the software being developed. It provides the software development team an attacker's or hostile user's viewpoint, as the threat modeling exercise aims at identifying entry and exit points that an attacker can exploit. It also helps the team to make design and engineering trade-off decisions by providing insight into the areas where attention is to be prioritized and focused, from a security viewpoint. The rationale behind threat modeling is the premise that unless one is aware of the means by which software assets can be attacked and compromised, the appropriate levels of protection cannot be accurately determined and applied. Software assets include the software processes themselves and the data they marshal and process. With today's prevalence of attacks against software or at the application layer, no software should be considered ready for implementation or coding until after its relevant threat model is completed and the threats identified.

3.10.2.3 Benefits

The primary benefit of threat modeling during the design phase of the project is that design flaws can be addressed before a single line of code is written, thereby reducing the need to redesign and fix security issues in code at a later time. Once a threat model is generated, it should be iteratively visited and updated as the software development project progresses. In the design phase, threat models development commences as the software architecture teams identify threats to the software. The development team can use the threat model to implement controls and write secure code. Testers can use the threat models to not only generate security test cases but also to validate the controls that need to be present to mitigate the threats identified in the threat models. Finally, operations personnel can use threat models to configure the software securely so that all entry and exit points have the necessary protection controls in place. In fact, a holistic threat model is one that has taken inputs from representatives of the design, development, testing, and deployment and operations teams.

3.10.2.4 Challenges

Although the benefits of threat modeling are extensive, threat modeling does come with some challenges, the most common of which are given here. Threat modeling

- Can be a time-consuming process when done correctly.
- Requires a fairly mature SDLC.
- Requires the training of employees to correctly model threats and address vulnerabilities.
- Is not the most exciting exercise to be conducted. Developers prefer coding, and quality assurance personnel prefer testing over threat modeling.
- Is often not directly related to organizational business operations, and it is difficult to show demonstrable return on investment for threat models.

3.10.2.5 Prerequisites

Before we delve into the threat modeling process, let us first answer the question about what some of the *prerequisites* for threat modeling are. For threat models to be effective within an organization, it is essential to meet the following conditions:

- The organization must have clearly defined information security policies and standards. Without these instruments of governance, the adoption of threat modeling as an integral part of the SDLC within the organization will be a challenge. This is because, when the business and development teams push back and choose not to generate threat models because of the challenges imposed by the iron triangle, the information security organization will have no basis on which to enforce the need for threat modeling.

■ The organization must be aware of compliance and regulatory requirements. Just as organizational policies and standards function as internal governance instruments, arming the information security organization to enforce threat modeling as part of the SDLC, compliance and regulatory requirements function as external governance mandates that need to be factored into the software design addressing security.

■ The organization must have a clearly defined and mature SDLC process. Because the threat modeling activity is initiated during the design phase of a software development project, it is important that the organization employ a structured approach to software development. Ad hoc development will yield ad hoc, incomplete, and inconsistent threat models. Additionally, because threat modeling is an iterative process and the threat model needs to be revisited during the development and testing phase of the project, those phases need to be part of the SDLC.

■ The organization has a plan to act on the threat model. The underlying vulnerabilities that could make the threats (identified through the threat modeling exercise) materialize must also be identified and appropriately addressed. Merely completing a threat modeling exercise does no good in securing the software being designed. To generate a threat model and not act on it is akin to buying an exercise machine and not using it but expecting to get fit and in shape. The threat model needs to be acted upon. In this regard, it is imperative that the organization trains its employees to appropriately address the identified threats and vulnerabilities. Awareness, training, and education programs to teach employees how to threat model software and how to mitigate identified threats are necessary and critical for the effectiveness of the threat modeling exercise

3.10.2.6 What Can We Threat Model?

Because threat models require allocation of time and resources and have an impact on the project life cycle, threat modeling is to be performed selectively, based on the value of the software as an asset to the organization and on organizational needs.

We can threat model existing, upcoming versions, new, and legacy software. It is particularly important to threat model legacy software because the likelihood that software was originally developed with threat models and security in mind, and with consideration of present-day threats, is slim. When there is an organizational need to threat model legacy software, it is recommended to do so when the next version of the legacy software is being designed. We can also threat model interfaces (APIs, Web services, etc.) and third-party components. When third-party components are threat modeled, it is important to notify the software owner/publisher of the activity and gain their approval to avoid any intellectual property (IP) legal issues or violations of end user licensing agreements (EULAs). Threat modeling third-party software is often a behavioral or black box kind of testing, because performing structural analysis and inspections by reverse engineering COTS components, without proper authorization from the software publisher, can have serious IP violation repercussions.

3.10.2.7 Process

As a CSSLP, it is imperative for one to not only understand the benefits, key players, challenges, and prerequisites in developing a threat model, but one must also be familiar with the steps involved in threat modeling. The threat modeling process can be broken down into three, high-level phases, namely, define, model, and measure as depicted in Figure 3.17. Each phase is further broken into more specific activities, and through each activity, the threat modeling exercise takes inputs and generates outputs that are to be acted upon.

In the *definition* phase of the threat model, the following activities are conducted.

- ■ *Identify security objectives and assets:* Security objectives are those high-level objectives of the application that have an impact on the security tenets of the software. These include the requirements that have an impact on confidentiality, integrity, availability, authentication, authorization, auditing, session management, error and exception management, and configuration management. Some examples of security objectives include
  - – Prevention of data theft
  - – Protection of IP
  - – Provide high availability

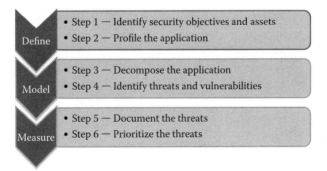

Figure 3.17 Threat modeling process.

Inputs that can be used to identify security objectives are
- Internal organizational policies and standards
- Regulations, compliance, and privacy requirements
- Business and functional requirements

Assets are those items that are of *value* to the business. Primarily assets need to be protected because their loss can cause a disruption to the business. Some of the other reasons that enforce the need to protect assets today are regulations, compliance, privacy, or the need to have a competitive advantage. Assets may be *tangible*, such as credit card data, PII, and the HR software, or *intangible*, such as customer loyalty or corporate brand and reputation.

■ *Profile the application:* The process of profiling the application includes creating an overview of the application by identifying the attributes of the application. This activity includes the following steps:
  - Identify the physical topology: The physical topology of the application gives insight into where and how the applications will be deployed. Will it be an internal-only application or will it be deployed in the demilitarized zone or will it be hosted in the cloud?
  - Identify the logical topology: This includes determining the logical tiers (presentation, business, service, and data) of the application.
  - Determine components, services, protocols, and ports that need to be defined, developed, and configured for the application.
  - Identify the identities that will be used in the application: Identify human and nonhuman actors of the system. Examples include customers, sales agents, system administrators, and database administrators.
  - Identify data elements: Examples include product information and customer information.
  - Generate a data access control matrix: This includes the determination of the rights and privileges that the actors will have on the identified data elements. Rights usually include CRUD privileges. For each actor the data access control matrix as depicted in Figure 3.18 must be generated.
  - Identify the technologies that will be used in building the application.
  - Identify external dependencies: The output of this activity is an architectural makeup of the application.

In the *modeling* phase of the threat modeling exercise, the following activities are conducted:

■ *Decompose the application:* With an understanding of the application makeup, it is important to break down (decompose) the application into finer components. A thorough understanding of how the application will work, also referred to as the "mechanics" of the application, will help uncover pertinent threats and vulnerabilities. The decomposition activity is made up of the following steps:
  - Identify trust boundaries: Boundaries help identify actions or behavior of the software that is allowed or not allowed. A trust boundary is the

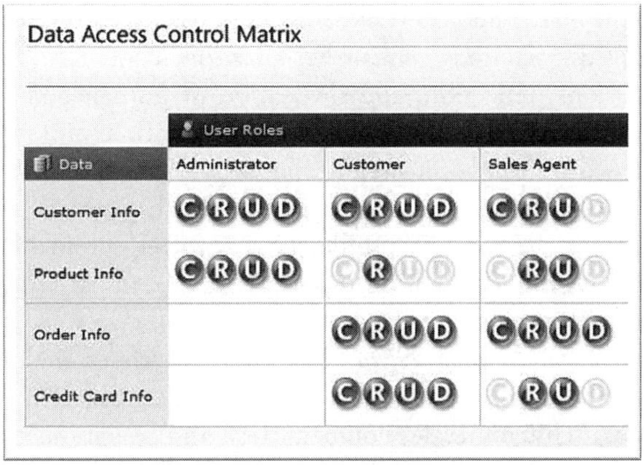

Figure 3.18 Data access control matrix.

point at which the trust level or privilege changes. Identification of trust boundaries is critical to ensure that the adequate levels of protection are designed within each boundary.

- Identify entry points: Entry points are those items that take in user input. Each entry point can be a potential threat source, and so all entry points must be explicitly identified and safeguarded. Entry points in a Web application could include any page that takes in user input. Some examples include the search page, logon page, registration page, checkout page, and account maintenance page.
- Identify exit points: It is just as important to identify exit points of the application as it is to identify entry points. Exit points are those items that display information from within the system. Exit points also include processes that take data out of the system. Exit points can be the source of information leakage and need to be equally protected. Exit points in a Web application include any page that displays data on the browser client. Some examples are the search results page, product page, and view cart page.
- Identify data flows: Data flow diagrams (DFDs) and sequence diagrams assist in the understanding of how the application will accept, process, and handle data as they are marshaled across different trust boundaries. It is important to recognize that a DFD is not a flow chart but a graphical representation of the flow of data, the backend data storage elements, and relationships between the data sources and destinations. Data flow diagramming uses a standard set of symbols.
- Identify privileged code: Code that attempts to perform privileged operations on resources that are deemed privileged is known as *privileged code*. Some of these privileged resources include environment variables, event logs, file systems, queuing infrastructures, registry, domain controllers,

Domain Name Servers (DNS), sockets, and Web services. Examples of privileged operations include serialization, code access security (CAS) permissions, reflection, and invocation of unmanaged code calls. It is extremely important to ensure that the operations and resources used by privileged code are protected from malicious mis-actors and so they need to be identified and captured as part of the threat model.

– Document the security profile: This involves the identification of the design and implementation mechanisms that impact the security tenets of the application.

■ *Identify threats and vulnerabilities:* During this activity, the intent is to identify relevant threats that can compromise the assets. It is important that members of architecture, development, test, and operations teams are part of this activity, in conjunction with security team members. The two primary ways in which threats and vulnerabilities can be identified are: (1) think like an attacker (brainstorming and using attack trees) and (2) use a categorized threat list.

1. Think like an attacker (brainstorming and using attack trees)

To think like an attacker is to subject the application to a hostile user's perspective. One can start by brainstorming possible attack vectors and threat scenarios using a whiteboard. Although brainstorming is a quick and simple methodology, it is not very scientific and has the potential of identifying nonrelevant threats and not identifying pertinent threats. So another approach is to use an attack tree.

An attack tree is a hierarchical treelike structure, which has either an attacker's objective (e.g., gain administrative level privilege, determine application makeup and configuration, and bypass authentication mechanisms) or a type of attack (e.g., buffer overflow and cross-site scripting) at its root node. Figure 3.19 is an illustration of an attack tree with the attacker's objective at its root node. Figure 3.20 depicts an attack tree with an attack vector at its root node. When the root node is an attack vector, the child node from the root nodes is the unmitigated or

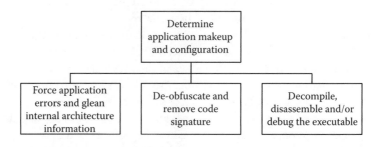

Figure 3.19   Attack tree: attacker's objective in the root node.

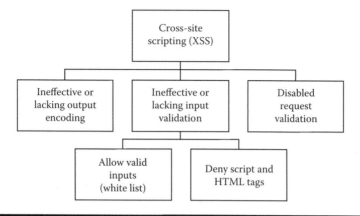

Figure 3.20   Attack tree: attack vector in the root node.

vulnerability condition. The next level node (child node of an unmitigated condition) is usually the mitigated condition or a safeguard control
to be implemented. One can also use the OWASP Top 10 or the CWE/
SANS Top 25 most dangerous programming errors as a starting point to
identify root vectors pertinent to their application. It is a method of collecting and identifying potential attacks in a structured and hierarchical
manner. It is a method used by security professionals because it allows
the threat modeling team to analyze threats in finer detail and greater
depth. The treelike structure provides a descriptive breakdown of various
attacks that the attacker could use to compromise the asset. The creation
of attack trees for your organization has the added benefit of creating a
reusable representation of security issues that can be used across multiple
projects to focus mitigation efforts. Developers are given insight into the
types of attacks that can be used against their software and then implement appropriate safeguard controls, while test teams can use the attack
trees to write test plans. The tests ensure that the controls are in place and
effective.

2. Use categorized threat lists

    In addition to thinking like an attacker, another methodology to iden-
tify threats is using a categorized list of threats. Some methodologies, such
as the NSA IAM methodology, OCTAVE risk modeling, and Microsoft
STRIDE, have as part of their methodology a list of threat types or categories that can be used to identify threats. STRIDE is an acronym for a
category of threats. Using the STRIDE category threat list is a goal-based
approach to threat modeling because the goals of the attacker are taken
into consideration. Table 3.13 depicts the Microsoft STRIDE category
of threats.

Table 3.13   STRIDE Category of Threats

Goal	Description
Spoofing	Can an attacker impersonate another user or identity?
Tampering	Can the data be tampered with while it is in transit or in storage or archives?
Repudiation	Can the attacker (user or process) deny the attack?
Information Disclosure	Can information be disclosed to unauthorized users?
Denial of service	Is denial of service a possibility?
Elevation of privilege	Can the attacker bypass least privilege implementation and execute the software at elevated or administrative privileges?

When a category of threats is used, there is a high degree of likelihood that a particular threat may have cross-correlation with other threats. For example, the elevation of privilege may be as a result of spoofing due to information disclosure or simply the result of the lack of repudiation controls. In such cases, it is recommended to use your best judgment when categorizing threats. One can select the most relevant category or document all of the applicable threat categories and rank them according to the likelihood of the threat being materialized.

In the *measurement* phase of the threat modeling exercise, the following activities are conducted:

■ *Document the threats:* The importance of documenting the threat model cannot be underestimated because threat modeling is iterative, and, through the life cycle of the project, the protection controls to address the identified threats in the threat model need to be appropriately implemented, validated, and the threat model itself updated. Threats can be documented diagrammatically or in textual format. Diagrammatic documentation provides a context for the threats. Textual documentation allows for more detail of each threat. It is best advised to do both. Document each threat diagrammatically and expand on the details of the threat using textual description.

When documenting the threats, it is recommended to use a template to maintain consistency of documenting and communicating the threats. Some of a threat's attributes that need to be documented include the type of threat with a unique identifier, the description, the threat target, attack techniques, security impact, the likelihood or risk of the threat's materializing, and, if available, the possible controls to implement. Figure 3.21 depicts the textual documentation of an injection attack.

■ *Prioritize the threats:* It was mentioned earlier that the threat modeling exercise is a systematic and structured methodology that is performed to assist teams in making security versus engineering design or business trade-off decisions. Merely cataloging a list of threats provides little assistance to a design team that needs to decide how to address the threat. Providing the design team with a ranking or rating of the identified and documented threats proves invaluable in prioritizing decisions that impact the allocation of resources to address the threats.

There are several ways to quantitatively or qualitatively determine the risk ranking for a threat. These range from the simple, nonscientific, Delphi heuristic methodology to more statistically sound risk ranking using the probability of impact and the business impact. The three common ways to rank threats are:

1. Delphi ranking
2. Average ranking
3. Probability × Impact ($P \times I$) ranking

1. Delphi Ranking — The Delphi technique of risk ranking is one in which each member of the threat modeling team makes his or her best guesstimate on the level of risk for a particular threat. During a Delphi risk ranking exercise, individual opinions on the level of risk for a particular threat are stated and the stated opinions are not questioned but accepted as stated. The individuals

Threat Identifier	T#0001
Threat description	Injection of SQL commands.
Threat targets	Data access component. Backend database.
Attack techniques	Attacker appends SQL commands to user name, which is used to form an SQL query.
Security impact	Information disclosure. Alteration. Destruction (drop table, procedures, delete data, etc.). Authentication bypass.
Risk	High.

Figure 3.21 Threat documentation.

who are identified for this exercise include both members with skills at an expert level and those who are not skilled, but the participating members only communicate their opinions to a facilitator. This is to avoid dominance by strong personalities who can potentially influence the risk rank of the threat. The facilitator must provide, in advance, predefined ranking criteria (1, Critical; 2, Severe; 3, Minimal) along with the list of identified threats, to ensure that the same ranking criteria are used by all members. The criteria are often based merely on the potential impact of the threat materializing, and the ranking process is performed until there is consensus or confidence in the way the threats are ranked. While this may be a quick method to determine the consensus of the risk potential of a threat, it may not provide a complete picture of the risk and should be used sparingly and only in conjunction with other risk ranking methodologies. Furthermore, ambiguous or undefined risk ranking criteria and differing viewpoints and backgrounds of the participants can lead to the results' being diverse and the process itself, inefficient.

2. Average Ranking — Another methodology to rank the risk of the threat is to calculate the average of numeric values assigned to risk ranking categories. One such risk ranking categorization framework is DREAD, which is an acronym for damage potential, reproducibility, exploitability, affected users, and discoverability. Each category is assigned a numerical range, and it is preferred to use a smaller range (such as 1 to 3 instead of 1 to 10) to make the ranking more defined, the vulnerabilities less ambiguous, and the categories more meaningful.

■ *Damage potential* ranks the damage that will be caused when a threat is materialized or vulnerability exploited.
  1 = Nothing
  2 = Individual user data are compromised or affected
  3 = Complete system or data destruction
■ *Reproducibility* ranks the ease of being able to re-create the threat and the frequency of the threat exploiting the underlying vulnerability successfully.
  1 = Very hard or impossible, even for administrators of the application
  2 = One or two steps required; may need to be an authorized user
  3 = Just the address bar in a Web browser is sufficient, without authentication
■ *Exploitability* ranks the effort that is necessary for the threat to be manifested and the preconditions, if any, that are needed to materialize the threat.
  1 = Advanced programming and networking knowledge, with custom or advanced attack tools
  2 = Malware exists on the Internet, or an exploit is easily performed using available attack tools
  3 = Just a Web browser
■ *Affected users* ranks the number of users or installed instances of the software that will be impacted if the threat materializes.

1 = None
2 = Some users or systems, but not all
3 = All users

▪ *Discoverability* ranks how easy it is for external researchers and attackers to discover the threat, if left unaddressed.
1 = Very hard to impossible; requires source code or administrative access
2 = Can figure it out by guessing or by monitoring network traces
3 = Information is visible in the Web browser address bar or in a form
Once values have been assigned to each category, then the average of those values is computed to give a risk ranking number. Mathematically, this can be expressed as

$$(D_{value} + R_{value} + E_{value} + A_{value} + DI_{value})/5$$

Figure 3.22 is an example illustrating the use of an average ranking to rank various Web application threats.

The average rank and categorization into buckets such as high, medium, or low can then be used to prioritize mitigation efforts.

3. Probability × Impact (P × I) Ranking — Conventional risk management calculation of the risk to a threat materializing or to exploiting a vulnerability is performed by using the product of the probability (likelihood) of occurrence and the impact the threat will have on business operations, if it materializes. Organizations that use risk management principles for their governance use the formula shown below to assign a risk ranking to the threats and vulnerabilities.

Threat	D	R	E	A	DI	Average Rank (D+R+E+A+DI)/ 5
SQL Injection	3	3	2	3	2	2.6 (High)
XSS	3	3	3	3.	3	3.0 (High)
Cookie Replay	3	2	2	1	2	2.0 (Med)
Session Hijacking	2	2	2	1	3	2.0 (Med)
CSRF	3	1	1	1	1	1.4 (Med)
Audit Log Deletion	1	0	0	1	3	1.0 (Low)
High: 2.1 to 3.0; medium: 1.1 to 2.0; low: 0.0 to 1.0						

Figure 3.22   Average ranking.

Risk = Probability of Occurrence × Business Impact

This methodology is relatively more scientific than the Delphi or the average ranking methodology. For the Probability × Impact ($P \times I$) ranking methodology, we will once again take into account the DREAD framework. The risk rank will be computed using the following formula:

$$\text{Risk} = \text{Probability of Occurrence} \times \text{Business Impact}$$
$$\text{Risk} = (R_{value} + E_{value} + DI_{value}) \times (D_{value} + A_{value})$$

Figure 3.23 is an example illustrating the use of the $P \times I$ ranking methodology to rank various Web application threats.

From this example, we can see that the cross-site scripting (XSS) threat and SQL injection threats are high risks, which need to be mitigated immediately, while the cookie replay and session hijacking threats are of medium risk. There should be a plan in place to mitigate those as soon as possible. CSRF and audit log deletion threats have a low risk rank and may be acceptable. To prioritize the efforts of these two, high risk items (SQL injection and XSS), we can use the computed risk rank ($P \times I$) or we can use either the probability of occurrence (P) or business impact (I) value. Because both SQL injection and XSS have the same business impact value of 6, we can use the probability of occurrence value to prioritize mitigation efforts, choosing to mitigate XSS first and then SQL injection, because the probability of occurrence value for XSS is 9, while the probability of occurrence value for SQL injection is 7.

Threat	Probability of Occurrence (P)			Business Impact (I)		P	I	Risk
	R	E	DI	D	A	$(R + E + DI)$	$(D + A)$	$P \times I$
SQL Injection	3	2	2	3	3	7	6	42
XSS	3	3	3	3	3	9	6	54
Cookie Replay	2	2	2	3	1	6	4	24
Session Hijacking	2	2	3	2	1	7	3	21
CSRF	1	1	1	3	1	3	4	12
Audit Log Deletion	0	0	3	1	1	3	2	6
High: 41 to 60; medium: 21 to 40; low: 0 to 20								

Figure 3.23   Probability × Impact (*P* × *I*) ranking.

3.10.2.8 Comparison of Risk Ranking Methodologies

While the Delphi methodology usually focuses on risk from a business impact vantage point, the average ranking methodology, when using the DREAD framework, takes into account both business impact (damage potential and affected users) and the probability of occurrence (reproducibility, exploitability, and discoverability); however, because of averaging the business impact and probability of occurrence values uniformly, the derived risk rank value does not give insight into the deviation (lower and upper limits) from the average. This can lead to uniform application of mitigation efforts to all threats, thereby potentially applying too much mitigation control effort on threats that are not really certain or too little mitigation control effort on threats that are serious. The $P \times I$ ranking methodology gives insight into risk as a measure of both probability of occurrence and the business impact independently, as well as when considered together. This allows the design team the flexibility to reduce the probability of occurrence or alleviate the business impact independently or together, once it has used the $P \times I$ risk rank to prioritize where to focus its mitigation efforts. Additionally, the $P \times I$ methodology gives a more accurate picture of the risk. Notice that in the average ranking methodology, both cookie replay and session hijacking threats had been assigned a medium risk of 2.0. This poses a challenge to the design team: which threat must one consider mitigating first? However, in the $P \times I$ ranking of the same threats, you notice that the cookie replay threat has a risk score of 24, whereas the session hijacking threat has a risk score of 21, based on probability of occurrence and business impact. This facilitates the design team's consideration of mitigating the cookie replay threat before addressing the session hijacking threat.

3.10.2.9 Control Identification and Prioritization

Threats to software are inevitable, and the threat modeling exercise helps us identify entry and exit points that can render the software vulnerable to attack. Knowledge of vulnerabilities is worthless unless appropriate controls are identified to mitigate the threats that can exploit the vulnerabilities. The identification of controls needs to be specific to each threat. A threat may be completely mitigated by a single control or a combination of controls may be necessary. In instances where more than one control is needed to mitigate a threat, the defense in depth measures should ensure that the controls complement rather than contradict one another. It is also important to recognize that the controls (safeguards and countermeasures) do not eliminate the threat but only reduce the overall risk that is associated with the threat. Figure 3.24 is an illustration of documenting identifying controls to address a threat.

Because addressing all the identified threats is unlikely to be economically feasible, it is important to address the threats that pose the greatest risk before addressing those that have minimal impact to business operations. The risk ranks derived

Threat Identifier	T#0001
Threat Description	Injection of SQL commands
Safeguard controls to implement	Use a regular expression to validate the user name. Disallow dynamic construction of queries using user-supplied input without validation. Use parameterized queries.

Figure 3.24   Control identification.

from the security risk assessment activity (SRA) of the threat modeling exercise are used to prioritize the controls that need to be implemented. Quantitative risk ranks are usually classified into qualitative bands such as high, medium, or low or, based on the severity of the threat, into severity 1, severity 2, and severity 3. These bands are also known as *bug bars* or *bug bands,* and they are not just limited to security issues. There are bug bars for privacy as well. Bug bars help with prioritizing the controls to be implemented post design.

3.11 Architectures

Because business objectives and technology change over time, it is important for software architectures to be strategic, holistic, and secure. Architecture must be strategic, meaning that the software design factors in a long-term perspective and addresses more than just the short-term, tactical goals. This reduces the need for redesigning the software when there are changes in business goals or technology. By devising the architecture of software to be highly cohesive and loosely coupled, software can be scaled with minimal redesign when changes are required. Architecture must also be holistic. This means that software design is not just IT-centric in nature but is also inclusive of the perspectives of the business and other stakeholders. In a global economy, locale considerations are an important, architectural consideration as well. Holistic software architecture also means that it factors not only the people, process, and technology aspects of design but also the network, host, and application aspects of software design. Implementation security across the different layers of the Open Systems Interconnect (OSI) reference model of ISO/IEC 7498-1:1994 is important so that there is no weak link from the physical layer to the application layer. Table 3.14 illustrates the different layers of the OSI reference model, the potential threats at each layer, and what protection control or technology can be leveraged at each layer. Using IPSec at the network layer (layer 3), SSL at the transport layer (layer 4), and Digital Rights Management (DRM) at the presentation layer (layer 6) augments the protection controls that are designed at the application layer (layer 7), and this demonstrates two, secure design principles: defense in depth and leveraging existing components.

Table 3.14   Open Systems Interconnect Layers

Layer	Layer Name	Layer Description	Threats	Protection Controls/ Technology
7	Application	Describes the structure, interpretation, and handling of information	Flaws, bugs, backdoors, malware	Application layer firewalls, secure design, coding, testing, deployment, maintenance, operations, and disposal
6	Presentation	Describes the presentation of information, doing syntax conversions such as ASCII/EBCDIC	Information leakage and disclosure of content	Masking and other cryptographic controls, RBAC and content dependent rights, liability protection controls such as "forwarding not allowed," DRM
5	Session	Describes the handshake between applications (authentication, sign on)	Authentication bypass, guessable and weak session identifiers, spoofing, MITM, credential theft, data disclosure, brute-force attacks	Strong authentication controls, unique and random session ID generation, encryption in transmission and storage, account lockout clipping levels
4	Transport	Describes data transfer between applications; provides flow control, error detection, and correction (e.g., TCP and UDP)	Loss of packets, fingerprinting, and host enumeration; open ports	Stateful inspection firewalls, SSL, port monitoring, flow control

Table 3.14 Open Systems Interconnect Layers (Continued)

Layer	Layer Name	Layer Description	Threats	Protection Controls/ Technology
3	Network	Describes data transfer between networks (e.g., Internet protocol)	Spoofing of routes and IP addresses; identity impersonation	Packet filtering firewalls, ARP/ broadcast monitoring, network edge filters, IPSec
2	Data Link	Describes data transfer between machines (e.g., RJ11-modem and RJ45-ethernet)	MAC address spoofing, VLAN circumvention, spanning tree errors, wireless attacks	MAC filtering, firewalls, and segmentation (isolation) of networks; wireless authentication and strong encryption
1	Physical	Describes the networking hardware such as network interfaces and physical cables, and the way to transmit bits and bytes of data (electrical pulses, radio waves, or light)	Physical theft, power loss, keyloggers and other interceptors of data	Locked perimeters and surveillance; PIN and password secured locks, biometric authentication, electromagnetic shielding, secure data transmission and storage

Finally, software architecture must be not only strategic and holistic but also secure. The benefits of enterprise security architecture are many. Some of these are listed here. Enterprise security architecture

- Provides protection against security-related issues that may be related to the architecture (flaws) or implementation (bugs) or both.
- Makes it possible to implement common security solutions across the enterprise.
- Promotes interoperability and makes it easy for integrating systems while effectively managing risk.

■ Allows for leveraging industry-leading best practices. The OWASP Enterprise Security Application Programming Interface (ESAPI) is an example of a toolkit that can be leveraged to uniformly manage risks by allowing software development team members to guard against flaws and bugs.

■ Facilitates decision makers to make better and quicker security-related decisions across the enterprise.

Changes in the hardware computing power have led to shifts in software architectures from the centralized mainframe architecture to the highly distributed computing architecture. Today, many distributed architectures, such as the client/server model, P2P networking, SOA, rich Internet applications (RIA), pervasive computing, Software as a Service (SaaS), cloud computing, and Virtualization, exist and are on the rise. In the following section, we will look into the different types of architectures that are prevalent today and how to design software to be secure when using these architectures.

3.11.1 Mainframe Architecture

Colloquially referred to as the Big Iron, mainframes are computers that are capable of bulk data processing with great computation speed and efficiency. The speed is usually measured in millions of instructions per second (MIPS). In the early days of mainframe, computing involved tightly coupled mainframe servers and dumb terminals that were merely interfaces to the functionality that existed on the high processing, backend servers. All processing, security, and data protection was the responsibility of the mainframe server, which usually operated in a closed network with a restricted number of users.

In addition to the increased computational speed, redundancy engineering for high availability, and connectivity over IP networks, today's mainframe computing brings remote connectivity, allowing scores of users access to mainframe data and functionality. This is possible because of the access interfaces, including Web interfaces that have been made available in mainframes. The mainframe provides one of the highest degrees of security inherently with an Evaluation Assurance Level of 5. It has its own networking infrastructure, which augments its inherent, core, security abilities.

However, with the increase in connectivity, the potential for attack increases and the security provided by the closed network and restricted access control mechanisms wanes. Furthermore, one of the challenges surfacing is that the number of people skilled in the operational procedures and security of mainframes is dwindling, with people's retiring or moving toward newer platforms. This is an important issue from a security standpoint because those who are leaving are the ones who have likely designed the security of these mainframes and this brain drain can leave the mainframe systems in an operationally insecure state.

To address security challenges in the evolving mainframe computing architecture, data encryption and end-to-end transit protection are important risk mitigation controls to implement. Additionally, it is important to design in the principle of psychological acceptability by making security transparent. This means that solutions that require rewriting applications, mainframe Job Control Language (JCL), and network infrastructure scripts, must be avoided. The skills shortage problem must be dealt with by employing user education and initiatives that make a future in mainframe lucrative, especially in relation to its crossover with new applications and newer, open platforms such as Linux.

3.11.2 Distributed Computing

Business trends have moved from the centralized world of the mainframe to the need for more remote access; so, a need for distributed computing arose. Distributed computing is primarily of the following types: client/server model and peer-to-peer (P2P).

■ *Client/Server model:* Unlike the case of a traditional monolithic mainframe architecture where the server does the heavy lifting and the clients were primarily dumb terminals, in client/server computing, the client is also capable of processing and is essentially a program that requests service from a server program which may in turn be a client requesting service from other backend server programs. This distinction is, however, thinning with the mainframe computing model becoming more interconnected. Within the context of software development, clients that perform minimal processing are referred to commonly as *thin clients,* while those which perform extensive processing are known as *fat clients.* With the rise in SaaS, the number of thin-client deployments is expected to increase. The client/server model is the main architecture in today's network computing. This model makes it possible to interconnect several programs that are distributed across various locations. The Internet is a primary example of client/server computing.

When designing applications for operating in a client/server architecture, it is important to design the software to be scalable, highly available, easily maintainable, and secure. Logically breaking down the software's functionality into chunks or tiers has an impact on the software's ease of adapting to changes. This type of client/server architecture is known as *N*-Tier architecture, where *N* stands for the number of tiers the software is logically broken into. 1-Tier means there is only one tier. All the necessary components of the software, which include the presentation (user interface), the business logic, and the data layer, are contained within the same tier, and, in most cases, within the same machine. When software architecture is 1-Tier, the implementation of the software is usually done by intermixing client and server code, with no distinct tiering. This type of programming is known as *spaghetti code* programming. Spaghetti code is complex, with unstructured go-to statements and arbitrary flow. 1-Tier architecture spaghetti code is highly coupled. This makes it very difficult to maintain the software. While 1-Tier architecture may be the simplest and easiest to design, it is not at all scalable, difficult to maintain, and must be avoided, unless the business has a valid reason for such a design. In a 2-Tier architecture, the software is functionally broken into a client program and a server program. The client usually has the presentation and business logic layer while the server is the backend data or resource store. A Web browser (client) requesting the Web server (server) to serve it Web pages is an example of 2-Tier architecture. While this provides a little more scalability than 1-Tier architecture, it still requires updating the entire software, so changes are all-or-nothing, making it difficult to maintain and scale. The most common *N*-Tier architecture is the 3-Tier architecture, which breaks the software functionality distinctly into three tiers; the presentation tier, the business logic tier, and the data tier. The benefits of the 3-Tier architecture are as follows:

- Changes in a tier are independent of the other tiers. So if you choose to change the database technology, the presentation and business logic tiers are not necessarily affected.
- It encapsulates the internal makeup of the software by abstracting the functionality into contract-based interfaces between the tiers.

However, this can also make the design complex and if error-reporting mechanisms are not designed properly, it can make troubleshooting very difficult. Further, it introduces multiple points of failure, which can be viewed as a detriment; however, this can be also viewed as a security benefit because it eliminates a single point of failure.

■ *Peer-to-Peer:* When one program controls other programs, as is usually the case with client/server architecture, it is said to have a master and slave configuration. However, in some distributed computing architecture, the client and the server programs each have the ability to initiate a transaction and act as peers. Such a configuration is known as a P2P architecture. Management of these resources in a P2P network is not centralized but spread among the resources on the P2P network uniformly, and each resource can function as a client or a server. File-sharing programs and instant messaging are well-known examples of this type of architecture. P2P file-sharing networks are a common ground for hackers to implant malware, so when P2P networks are designed, it is imperative to include strong access control protection to prevent the upload of malicious files from sources that are not trusted.

When you are designing software to operate in a distributed computing environment, security becomes even more important because the attack surface includes the client, the server, and the networking infrastructure. The following security design considerations are imperative to consider in distributed computing:

- Channel security: As data are passed from the client to the server and back or from one tier to another, it is necessary to protect the channel on which the data are transmitted. Transport level protocols such as SSL or network level protection using IPSec are means of implementing channel security.

– Data confidentiality and integrity: Protecting the data using crypto-graphic means such as encryption or hashing is important to protect against disclosure and alteration threats.

– Security in the call stack/flow: Distributed systems often rely on security protection mechanisms such as validation and authorization checks at various points of the call stack/flow. Design should factor in the entire call stack of software functionality so that security is not circumvented at any point of the call stack.

– Security zoning: Zoning using trust boundaries is an important security protection mechanism. There exists a security boundary between the client and the server in a client/server distributed computing architecture, and these trust levels should be determined and appropriately addressed. For example, performing client-side input validation may be useful for heightening user experience and performing, but trusting the client for input validation is a weak security protection mechanism, as it can be easily bypassed.

3.11.3 Service Oriented Architecture

SOA is a distributed computing architecture that has the following characteristics:

■ Abstracted business functionality: The actual program, business logic, pro-cesses, and the database are abstracted into logical views, defined in terms of the business operations and exposed as services. The internal implementation language, inner working of the business operation, or even the data structure is abstracted in the SOA.

■ Contract-based interfaces: Communication (messages) between the service providing unit (provider agent) and the consuming unit (requestor agent) is done using messages that are of a standardized format delivered through an interface. Developers do not need to understand the internal implementa-tion of the service, as long as they know how to invoke the service using the interface contract.

■ Platform neutrality: Messages in SOA are not only standardized, but they are also sent in a platform-neutral format. This maximizes cross-platform operability and makes it possible to operate with legacy systems. Most SOA implementations use the Extensible Markup Language (XML) as their choice of messaging because it is platform neutral.

■ Modularity and reusability: Services are defined as discreet, functional units (modular) that can be reused. Unlike applications that are tightly coupled in a traditional computing environment, SOA is implemented as loosely coupled network services that work together to form the application. The centralization of services that allows for reusability can be viewed on one hand as minimizing the attack surface but, on the other, as the single point of failure. Therefore, careful design of defense in depth protection is necessary in SOA implementations.

■ Discoverability: In order for the service to be available for use, it must be discoverable. The service's discoverability and interface information are published so that requestor agents are made aware of what the service contract is and how to invoke it. When SOA is implemented using Web services technology, this discoverable information is published using Universal Description, Discovery and Interface (UDDI). UDDI is a standard published by the Organization for the Advancement of Structured Information Standards (OASIS). It defines a universal method for enterprises to dynamically discover and invoke Web services. It is a registry of services and could be called the yellow pages of the interface definition of services that are available for consumption.

■ Interoperability: Because knowledge of the internal structure of the services is not necessary and the messaging between the provider and requestor agents is standardized and platform neutral, heterogeneous systems can interoperate, even in disparate processing environments, as long as the formal service definition is adhered to. This is one of the primary benefits of SOA.

Although SOA is often mistakenly used synonymously with Web services technologies, SOA can be implemented using several technologies. The most common technologies used to architect SOA solutions are Component Object Model (COM), Common Object Request Broker Architecture (CORBA), and Web services (WS). Web services provide platform and vendor neutrality, but it must be recognized that performance and implementation immaturity issues can be introduced. If platform and vendor neutrality are not business requirements, then using COM or CORBA implementations along with XML-based protocols for exchanging information such as Simple Object Access Protocol (SOAP) may be a better choice for performance. However, SOAP was not designed with security in mind and so can be intercepted and modified while in transit. Web services are appropriate for software in environments

■ Where reliability and speed are not assured (e.g., the Internet)
■ Where managing the requestor and provider agents need to be upgraded at once, when deployment cannot be managed centrally
■ Where the distributed computing components run on different platforms
■ When products from different vendors need to interoperate
■ When an existing software functionality or the entire application can be wrapped using a contract-based interface and needs to be exposed for consumption over a World Wide Web (WWW)

Although SOA brings with it many benefits, such as interoperability and platform/vendor neutrality, it also brings challenges when it comes to performance and security. SOA implementation design needs to factor in various considerations. These include the following:

- *Secure messaging:* Because SOA messages traverse on networks that are not necessarily within the same domain or processing environment, such as the Internet, they can be intercepted and modified by an attacker. This mandates the need for confidentiality, integrity, and transport level protection. Any one or a combination of the following methods can be used to provide secure messaging:
  - XML encryption and XML signature: When an XML protocol for exchanging information is used, an entire message or portions of a message can be encrypted and signed using XML security standards. WS-Security is the Web services security standard that can be used for securing SOAP messages by providing SOAP extensions that define mechanisms using XML encryption and XML signature. This assures confidentiality and integrity protection.
  - Implement TLS: Use SSL/TLS to secure messages in transit. Hypertext Transport Protocol (HTTP) over SSL/TLS (HTTPS) can be used to secure SOAP messages that are transmitted over HTTP.
- *Resource protection:* When business functionality is abstracted as services using interfaces that are discoverable and publicly accessible, it is mandatory to ensure that these service resources are protected appropriately. Identification, authentication, and access control protection are critical to assure that only those who are authorized to invoke these services are allowed to do so. Services need to be *identity aware,* meaning that the services need to identify and authenticate one another. Identification and authentication can be achieved using token-based authentication, the SOAP authentication header, or transport layer authentication.
- *Contract negotiation:* The Web Service Description Language (WSDL) is an XML format used to describe service contracts and allowed operations. This also includes the network service endpoints and their messages. Newer functionalities in a service can be used immediately upon electronic negotiation of the contract and invocation, but this can pose a legal liability challenge. It is therefore recommended that the contract-based interfaces of the services be predefined and agreed upon between organizations that plan to use the services in an SOA solution. However, in an Internet environment, establishing trust and service definitions between provider agents (service publisher) and requestor agents (service consumer) are not always just time-consuming processes, but in some cases are impossible. This is the reason why most SOA implementations depend on the WSDL interface, which provides the service contract information implicitly. This mandates the need to protect the WSDL interface against scanning and enumeration attacks.

▪ *Trust relationships:* Establishing the trust between the provider and the consumer in an SOA solution is not a trivial undertaking, and it must be carefully considered when designing the SOA. Although identification and authentication are necessary, mere identity verification of a service or the service provider does not necessarily mean that the service, itself, can be trusted. The primary SOA trust models that can be used to assure the trustworthiness of a service are described here.

- Pairwise trust model: In this model, during the time of service configuration, each service is provided with all of the other services that it can interact (paired) with. Although this is the simplest of trust models, it cannot scale very well, because the adding of each new service will require associating or pairing a trust relationship with every other service, which can be resource intensive and time-consuming.

- Brokered trust model: In this model, an independent third party acts as a middleman (broker) to provide the identity information of the services that can interact with one another. This facilitates the distribution of identity information because services need not be aware of the identity of other services they must interact with but simply need to verify the identity of the service broker.

- Federated trust model: In this model, the trust relationship is established (federated) between two separate organizations. Either a pairwise or brokered trust relationship can be used within this model, but a predefinition of allowed service contracts and invocation protocols and interfaces is necessary. The location where the federated trust relationship mapping is maintained must be protected as well.

- Proxy trust model: In this model, perimeter defense devices are placed between the providers and requestor. These devices act as a proxy for allowing access to and performing security assertions for the services. An XML gateway is an example of a proxy trust device. However, the proxy device can become the single point of failure if layered defensive protection and least privilege controls are not in place. An attacker who bypasses the proxy protection can potentially have access to all internal services, if they are not designed, developed, and deployed with security in mind.

3.11.4 Rich Internet Applications

With the ubiquitous nature of the Web and the hype in social networking, it is highly unlikely that one has not already come across RIAs. Some examples of RIAs in use today are Facebook and Twitter. RIAs bring the richness of the desktop environment and software onto the Web. A live connection (Internet Protocol) to the network and a client (browser, browser plug-in, or virtual machine) are often all that is necessary to run these applications. Some of the frameworks that are commonly used in RIA are AJAX, Abode Flash/Flex/AIR, Microsoft Silverlight, and JavaFX. With increased client (browser) side processing capabilities, the workload on the server side is reduced, which is a primary benefit of RIA. Increased user experience and user control are also benefits that are evident.

RIA has some inherent, security control mechanisms as well. These include Same Origin Policy (SOP) and sandboxing. The origin of a Web application can be determined using the protocol (http/https), host name, and port (80/443) information. If two Web sites have the same protocol, host name, and port information or if the *document.domain* properties of two Web resources are the same, it can be said that both have the same source or origin. The goal of SOP is to prevent a resource (document, script, applets, etc.) from one source from interacting and manipulating documents in another. Most modern-day browsers have SOP security built into them and RIA with browser clients intrinsically inherit this protection. RIAs also run within the security sandbox of the browser and are restricted from accessing system resources unless access is explicitly granted. However, Web application threats, such as injection attacks, scripting attacks, and malware, are all applicable to RIA. With RIA, the attack surface is increased, which includes the client that may be susceptible to security threats. If sandboxing protection is circumvented, host machines that are not patched properly can become victims of security threats. This necessitates the need to explicitly design Web security protection mechanisms for RIA. Ensure that authentication and access control decisions are not dependent on client-side verification checks. Data encryption and encoding are important protection mechanisms. To assure SOP protection, software design should factor in determining the actual (or true) origin of data and services and not just validate the last referrer as the point of origin.

3.11.5 Pervasive Computing

The dictionary definition of the word, "pervade" is "to go through" or "to become diffused throughout every part of" and, as the name indicates, pervasive computing is characterized by computing being diffused through every part of day-to-day living. It is a trend of everyday distributed computing that is brought about by converging technologies, primarily the wireless technologies, the Internet, and the increase in use of mobile devices such as smart phones, personal digital assistants (PDAs), laptops, etc. It is based on the premise that any device can connect to a network of other devices.

There are two elements of pervasive computing and these include *pervasive computation* and *pervasive communication*. *Pervasive computation* implies that any device, appliance, or equipment that can be embedded with a computer chip or sensor can be connected as part of a network and access services from and through that network, be it a home network, work network, or a network in a public place like an airport, a train station, etc. *Pervasive communication* implies that the devices on a pervasive network can communicate with each other over wired and wireless protocols, which can be found pretty much everywhere in this digital age.

One of the main objectives of pervasive computing is to create an environment where connectivity of devices is unobtrusive to everyday living, intuitive, seamlessly portable, and available anytime and anyplace. This is the reason why pervasive computing is also known as *ubiquitous computing* and in laymen terms, everyday–everywhere computing. Wireless protocols remove the limitations imposed by physically wired computing and make it possible for such an "everywhere" computing paradigm. Bluetooth and ZigBee are examples of two, common, wireless protocols in a pervasive computing environment. Smart phones, PDAs, smart cars, smart homes, and smart buildings are some examples of prevalent pervasive computing.

In pervasive computing, devices are capable of hopping on and hopping off a network anytime, anywhere, making this type of computing an ad hoc, plug-and-play kind of distributed computing. The network is highly heterogeneous in nature and can vary in the number of connected devices at any given time. For example, when you are at an airport, your laptop or smart phone can connect to the wireless network at the airport, becoming a node in that network, or your smart phone can connect via Bluetooth to your car, allowing access to your calendar, contacts, and music files on your smart phone via the car's network.

While the benefits of pervasive computing include the ability to be connected always from any place, from a security standpoint, it brings with it some challenges that require attention. The devices that are connected as part of a pervasive network are not only susceptible to attack themselves, but they can also be used to orchestrate attacks against the network where they are connected. This is why complete mediation, implemented using node-to-node authentication, must be part of the authentication design. Applications on the device must not be allowed to directly connect to the backend network but instead should authenticate to the device, and the device in turn should authenticate to the internal applications on the network. Using the TPM chip on the device is recommended over using the easily spoofable media access control (MAC) address for device identification and authentication. Designers of pervasive computing applications need to be familiar with lower level mobile device protection mechanisms and protocol.

System designers are now required to design protection mechanisms against physical security threats as well. Owing to the small size of most mobile computing devices, they are likely to be stolen or lost. This means that the data stored on the device itself is protected against disclosure threats using encryption or other cryptographic means. Because a device can be lost or stolen, applications on the device should be designed to have an "auto-erase" capability that can be triggered either on the device itself or remotely. This means that data on the device are completely erased when the device is stolen or a condition for erasing data (e.g., tampering and failed authentication) is met. The most common triggering activity is the incorrect entry of the personal identification number (PIN) more times than the configured number of allowed authentication attempts. Encryption and authentication are of paramount importance for protection of data in pervasive computing devices. Biometric authentication is recommended over PIN-based authentication, as this will require an attacker to spoof physical characteristics of the owner, significantly increasing his or her work factor.

Wireless networks configuration and protocols on which a significant portion of pervasive computing is dependent are susceptible to attack as well. Most wireless access points are turned on with default manufacturer settings, which can be easily guessed if not broadcast as the service set identifier (SSID). The SSID lets other 802.11× devices join the network. Although *SSID cloaking,* which means that the SSID is not broadcast, is not foolproof, it increases protection against unapproved rogue and not previously configured devices' discovering the wireless network automatically. For a device to connect to the network, it must know the shared secret, and in this shared secret, authentication mechanism affords significantly more protection than open network authentication.

Not only is the wireless network configuration an area of threat, but the protocols themselves can be susceptible to breaches in security. The Wired Equivalent Privacy (WEP) uses a 40-bit RC4 stream cipher for providing cryptographic protection. This has been proven to be weak and has been easily broken. Using Wi-Fi protected access (WPA and WPA2) is recommended over WEP in today's pervasive computing environments. Attacks against the Bluetooth protocol are also evident, which include Bluesnarfing, Bluejacking, and Bluebugging.

A layered approach to pervasive computing security is necessary. The following are some proven best practices that are recommended as protection measures in a pervasive computing environment:

- Ensure that physical security protections (locked doors, badged access, etc.) are in place, if applicable.
- Change wireless access point devices' default configurations and do not broadcast SSID information.
- Encrypt the data while in transit using SSL/TLS and on the device.
- Use a shared-secret authentication mechanism to keep rogue devices from hopping onto your network.
- Use device-based authentication for internal application on the network.
- Use biometric authentication for user access to the device, if feasible.
- Disable or remove primitive services such as Telnet and FTP.
- Have an auto-erase capability to prevent data disclosure should the device be stolen or lost.
- Regularly audit and monitor access logs to determine anomalies.

3.11.6 Software as a Service (SaaS)

Traditionally, software was designed and developed to be deployed on the client systems using packagers and installers. Upon installation, the software files would be hosted on the client system. Patches and updates would then have to be pushed to each individual client system on which the software was installed. There is also a time delay between the time that newer features of the software are developed and the time it is made available to all the users of the software. Not only is this model of software development time intensive, but it is also resource and cost intensive.

To address the challenges imposed by traditional software development and deployment, software is designed today to be available as a service to the end users or clients. In this model, the end users are not the owners of the software, but they pay a royalty or subscription for using the business functionality of software, in its entirety or in parts. SaaS is usually implemented using Web technologies and the software functionality is delivered over the Internet. This is why the SaaS model is also referred to as a Web-based software model, an On-demand model, or a hosted software model.

It can be likened to the client/server model wherein the processing is done on the server side with some distinctions. One distinction is that the software is owned and maintained by the software publisher and the software is hosted on the provider's infrastructure. End user or client data are also stored in the software publisher's hosting environment. Furthermore, more than one client (also referred to as a tenant) can take advantage of the software functionality and a single instance of software can serve multiple clients at the same time. This is referred to as the *multitenancy* of SaaS. This one-code-base-serving-all feature requires administration to be centralized for all clients, and it is the responsibility of the software publisher to ensure that its software is reliable, resilient, and recoverable. Some of the well-known examples of SaaS implementations are the customer relationship management Salesforce.com, Google Docs, and Microsoft's Hosted Exchange services.

The SaaS model is garnering a lot of acceptance today primarily for the benefits it provides. These include the following:

- *Reduced cost:* Instead of paying huge costs for licensing software, clients can now use the business applications on-demand and pay only for the services they use. There is no requirement for supporting infrastructure.
- *Time saving and speed of delivery:* With the software already available for use as a service, time and resource (personnel) investment to develop the same functionality in house is reduced. This—along with lower training requirements, no need to test the application, and no ongoing changes to the business processes—makes it possible for organizations to quickly market their existing products and services.
- *Integrity of versions:* With the software being centrally administered and managed by the software publisher, the client is not responsible for patching and version updates, thereby ensuring versions are not outdated.

As with any other architecture, along with the benefits come some challenges, and SaaS is no exception. We will focus primarily on the security concerns that come with choosing SaaS as the architecture. The primary security considerations concern data privacy and security, data separation, access control, and availability.

- *Data privacy and security:* Because the data will be stored in a shared hosting environment with the possibility of multiple tenants, it is imperative to ensure that data stored on the software publisher's environment is not susceptible to disclosure. This makes it necessary for the software designers to ensure that the sensitive, personal, and private data are protected before being stored in an environment that they have little to no control over. Encryption of data at rest is an important design consideration.
- *Data separation:* It is also important to ensure that the data of one client is stored separately from that of another client in the software publisher's data stores.
- *Access control:* Because the services and data are shared across multiple tenants, it is imperative to ensure that the SaaS provider follows and implements strong access control protections. With multiple tenants possibly authenticated and connected to the shared hosting infrastructure, authorization decisions must be user based, i.e., dependent on the user that is requesting service and data. The Brewer and Nash Chinese Wall security model must be implemented to avoid any conflicts of interest in an SaaS environment.
- *Availability:* In a shared hosting environment, the disruption of the business operations of a tenant, either deliberately or accidently, can potentially cause disruption to all tenants on that same host. "Will the data be readily available whenever necessary?" is a primary question to answer when considering the implementation of an SaaS solution. Redundancy and high availability designs are imperative. The disaster recovery strategy must be multilevel in nature, meaning that the data are backed up from disk to disk and then to tape, and the tape backups function only as secondary data sources upon disaster.

With the gain in SaaS computing and the prevalence of security threats, SaaS providers are starting to make security integral to their service offerings. Software as a Secure Service (SaSS) is the new acronym that is starting to gain ground as the differentiator between providers who assure protection mechanisms and those who do not.

3.11.7 Integration with Existing Architectures

We have discussed different kinds of software architectures and the pros and cons of each. Unless we are developing new software, we do not start designing the entire solution anew. We integrate with existing architecture when previous versions of software exist. This reduces rework significantly and supports the principle of leveraging existing components. Integration with legacy components may also be the only option available as a time-saving measure or when pertinent specifications, source code, and documentation about the existing system are not available. It is not unusual to wrap existing components with newer generation wrappers. Façade programming makes it possible for such integration. When newer architectures are integrated with existing ones, it is important to determine that backward compatibility and security are maintained. Components written to operate securely in an architecture may wane in its protection when integrated with another. For example, when the business logic tier that performs access control decisions in a 3-tier architecture is abstracted using services interfaces as part of an SOA implementation, authorization decisions that were restricted to the business logic tier can now be discovered and invoked. It is therefore critical to make sure that integration of existing and new architectures does not circumvent or reduce security protection controls or mechanisms and maintains backward compatibility, while reducing rework.

3.12 Technologies

Holistic security, as was aforementioned, includes a technology component, in addition to the people and process components. The secure design principle of leveraging existing components does not apply to software components alone but to technologies as well. If there is an existing technology that can be used to provide business functionality, it is recommended to use it. This not only reduces rework but has security benefits, too. Proven technologies have the benefit of greater scrutiny of security features than do custom implementations. Additionally, custom implementations potentially can increase the attack surface. In the following section, we will cover several technologies that can be leveraged, their security benefits, and issues to consider when designing software to be secure.

3.12.1 Authentication

The process of verifying the genuineness of an object or a user's identity is authentication. This can be done using authentication technologies. In Chapter 1, we covered the various techniques by which authentication can be achieved. These ranged from proving one's identity using something one knows (knowledge based), such as username and password/pass-phrase, to using something one has (ownership based), such as tokens, public key certificates, and smart cards, to using something one is (characteristic based), such as biometric fingerprints, retinal blood patterns, and iris contours. Needing more than one factor (knowledge, ownership, or characteristic) for identity verification increases work factor for an attacker significantly and technologies that can support multifactor authentication seamlessly must be considered in design.

The Security Support Provider Interface (SSPI) is an implementation of the IETF RFCs 2743 and 2744, commonly known as Generic Security Service API

(GSSAPI). SSPI abstracts calls to authenticate and developers can leverage this, without needing to understand the complexities of this authentication protocol or, even worse, trying to write their own. Custom authentication implementation on an application-to-application basis is proven not only to be inefficient, but it can also introduce security flaws and must be avoided. SSPI supports interoperability with other authentication technologies by providing a pluggable interface, but it also includes by default the protocols to negotiate the best security protocol (SPNEGO), delegate (Kerberos), securely transmit (SChannel), and protect credentials using hashes (Digest).

Before developers start to write code, it is important that the software designers take into account the different authentication types and the protocols and interfaces used in each type.

3.12.2 Identity Management

Authentication and identification go hand in hand. Without identification, not only is authentication not possible, but accountability is nearly impossible to implement. Identity management (IDM) is the combination of policies, processes, and technologies for managing information about digital identities. These digital identities may be those of a human (users) or a nonhuman (network, host, application, and services). User identities are primarily of two types: insiders (e.g., employees and contractors) and outsiders (e.g., partners, customers, and vendors). IDM answers the questions, "Who or what is requesting access?" "How are they or it authenticated?", and "What level of access can be granted based on the security policy?"

IDM life cycle is about the provisioning, management, and deprovisioning of identities as illustrated in Figure 3.25.

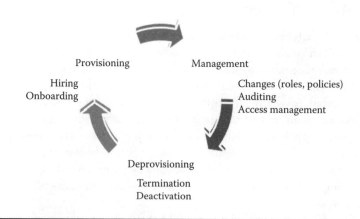

Figure 3.25   IDM life cycle.

Provisioning of identities includes the creation of digital identities. In an enterprise that has multiple systems, provisioning of an identity in each system can be a laborious, time-consuming, and inefficient process, if it is not automated. Automation of provisioning identities can be achieved by coding business processes, such as hiring and on-boarding, and this requires careful design. Roles in a user provisioning system are entitlement sets that span multiple systems and applications. Privileges that have some meaning in an application are known as entitlements. User provisioning extends role-based access control (RBAC) beyond single applications by consolidating individual system or application entitlements into fewer business roles, making it easier for a business to manage its users and their access rights.

The management of identities includes the renaming of identities, addition or removal of roles, the rights and privileges that are associated with those roles, the changes in regulatory requirements and policies, auditing of successful and unsuccessful access requests, and synchronization of multiple identities for access to multiple systems. When identities are renamed, it is imperative to document and record these changes. It is also important to maintain the histories of activity of the identities before they were renamed and map those histories to the new identity names to assure nonrepudiation capabilities.

Deprovisioning of identities includes termination access control (TAC) processes that are made up of the notification of termination and the deactivation or complete removal of identities. Organizations today are required to provide auditable evidence that access controls are in place and effective. The Sarbanes–Oxley (SOX) 404 section mandates that an annual review of the effectiveness of controls must be conducted and this applies to identity and access management (IAM) controls as well. Users are given rights and privileges (entitlements) over time but are rarely revoked of these entitlements when they are no longer needed. A business needs to be engaged in reviewing and approving access entitlements of identities, and the process is referred to as *access certification*. For legal and compliance reasons, it may be required to maintain a digital identity even after the identity is no longer active, and so deactivation may be the only viable option. If this is the case, software that handles termination access must be designed to allow "deactivate" only and not allow true "deletes" or "complete removal." Deactivation also makes it possible for the identity to remain as a backup just in case there is a need: however, this can pose a security threat as an attacker could reactivate a deactivated identity and gain access. The deactivated identities are best maintained in a backup or archived system that is offline with restricted and audited access.

Some of the common technologies that are used for IDM are as follows:

■ *Directories*
    A directory is the repository of identities. Its functionality is similar to that of yellow pages. A directory is used to find information about users and other

identities within a computing ecosystem. Identity information can be stored and maintained in network directories or backend application databases and data stores. When software is designed to use integrated authentication, it leverages network directories that are accessed using the Lightweight Directory Access Protocol (LDAP). LDAP replaced the more complex and outdated X.500 protocol.

Directories are a fundamental requirement for IDM and can be leveraged to eliminate silos of identity information maintained within each application. Some of the popular directory products are IBM (Tivoli) directory, Sun ONE directory, Oracle Internet Directory (OID), Microsoft Active Directory, Novell eDirectory, OpenLDAP, and Red Hat Directory Server.

■ *Metadirectories and virtual directories*

User roles and entitlements change with business changes and when the identity information and privileges tied to that identity change, those changes need to be propagated to systems that use that identity. Propagation and synchronization of identity changes from the system of record to managed systems are made possible by engines known as *metadirectories*. Human resources (HR), customer records management (CRM) systems, and corporate directory are examples of system of record. Metadirectories simplify identity administration. They reduce challenges imposed by manual updates and can be leveraged within software to automate change propagation and save time. Software design should include evaluating the security of the connectors and dependencies between identity source systems and downstream systems that use the identity. Microsoft Identity Lifecycle Management is an example of a metadirectory.

Metadirectories are like internal plumbing necessary for centralizing identity change and synchronization, but they usually do not have an interface that can be invoked. This shortfall gave rise to virtual directories. Within the context of an identity services-based architecture, virtual directories provide a service interface that can be invoked by an application to pull identity data and change it into claims that the application can understand. Virtual directories provide more assurance than metadirectories because they also function as gatekeepers and ensure that the data used are authorized and compliant to the security policy.

Designing to leverage IDM processes and technologies is important because it reduces risk by the following:

■ Consistently automating, applying, and enforcing identification, authentication, and authorization security policies.
■ Deprovisioning identities to avoid lingering identities past their allowed time. This protects against an attacker who can use an ex-employee's identity to gain access.

- Mitigating the possibility of a user or application gaining unauthorized access to privileged resources.
- Supporting regulatory compliance requirements by providing auditing and reporting capabilities.
- Leveraging common security architecture across all applications.

3.12.3 Credential Management

Chapter 1 covered different types of authentication, each requiring specific forms of credentials to verify and assure that entities that requested access to objects were truly whom they/it claimed to be. The identifying information that is provided by a user or system for validation and verification is known as credentials or claims. Although usernames and passwords are among the most common means of providing identifying information, authentication can be achieved by using other forms of credentials. Tokens, certificates, fingerprints, and retinal patterns are examples of other types of credentials.

Credentials need to be managed and credential management API can be used to obtain and manage credential information, such as user names and passwords. Managing credentials encompasses their generation, storage, synchronization, reset, and revocation. In this section, we will cover managing passwords, certificates, and SSO technology.

3.12.4 Password Management

When you use passwords for authentication, it is important to ensure that the passwords that are automatically generated, by the system, are random and not sequential or easily guessable. First and foremost, blank passwords should not be allowed. When users are allowed to create passwords, dictionary words should not be allowed as passwords because they can be discovered easily by using brute-force techniques and password-cracking tools. Requiring alphanumeric passwords with mixed cases and special characters increases the strength of the passwords.

Passwords must never be hardcoded in clear text and stored in-line with code or scripts. When they are stored in a database table or a configuration file, hashing them provides more protection than encryption because the original passwords cannot be determined. Although providing a means to remember passwords is good for user experience, from a security standpoint, it is not recommended.

Requiring the user to supply the old password before a password is changed, mitigates automated password changes and brute-force attacks. When passwords are changed, it is necessary to ensure that the change is replicated and synchronized within other applications that use the same password. Password synchronization fosters SSO authentication and addresses password management problems within an enterprise network.

When passwords need to be recovered or reset, special attention must be given to assure that the password recovery request is, first and foremost, a valid request, This assurance can be obtained by using some form of identification mechanism that cannot be easily circumvented. Most nonpassword-based authentication applications have a question and answer mechanism to identify a user when passwords need to be recovered. It is imperative for these questions and answers to be customizable by the user. Questions such as "What is your favorite color?" or "What is your mother's maiden name" do not provide as heightened a protection as do questions that can be defined and customized by the user.

Passwords must have expiration dates. Allowing the same password to be used once it has expired should be disallowed. One-time passwords (OTPs) provide maximum protection because the same password cannot be reused.

LDAP technology using directory servers can be used to implement and enforce password policies for managing passwords. One password policy for all users or a different policy for each user can be established. Directory servers can be used to notify users of upcoming password expirations, and they can also be used to manage expired passwords and account lockouts.

3.12.5 Certificate Management

Authentication can also be accomplished by using digital certificates. Today, asymmetric cryptography and authentication using digital certificates is made possible by using a PKI, as depicted in Figure 3.26.

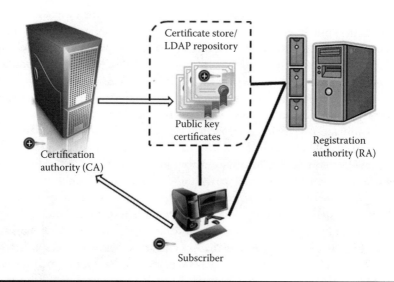

Figure 3.26 Public key infrastructure (PKI).

PKI makes secure communications, authentication, and cryptographic operations such as encryption and decryption possible. It is the security infrastructure that uses public key concepts and techniques to provide services for secure e-commerce transactions and communications. PKI manages the generation and distribution of public/private key pairs and publishes the public keys as certificates.

PKI consists of the following components:

- A certificate authority (CA), which is the trusted entity that issues the digital certificate that holds the public key and related information of the subject.
- A registration authority (RA), which functions as a verifier for the CA before a digital certificate is issued by the CA to the requestor.
- A certificate management system with directories in which the certificates can be held and with revocation abilities to revoke any certificates whose private keys have been compromised (disclosed). The CA publishes the certificate revocation lists (CRLs), which contain all certificates revoked by the CA. CRLs make it possible to withdraw a certificate whose private key has been disclosed. In order to verify the validity of a certificate, the public key of the CA is required and a check against the CA's CRL is made. The certification authority itself needs to have its own certificates. These are self-signed, which means that the subject data in the certificates are the same as the name of the authority who signs and issues the certificates.

PKI management includes the creation of public/private key pairs, public key certificate creation, private key revocation and listing in CRL when the private key is compromised, storage and archival of keys and certificates, and the destruction of these certificates at end of life. PKI is a means to achieve interorganizational trust and enforcement of restrictions on the usage of the issued certificates.

The current, internationally recognized, digital certificate standard is ITU X.509 version 3 (X.509 v3), which specifies formats for the public key, the serial number, the name of the pair owner, from when and for how long the certificate will be valid, the identifier of the asymmetric algorithm to be used, the name of the CA attesting ownership, the certification version numbers that the certificate conforms to, and an optional set of extensions, as depicted in Figure 3.27.

In addition to using PKI for authentication, X.509 certificates make possible strong authorization capabilities by providing Privilege Management Infrastructure (PMI) using X.509 *attribute* certificates, attribute authorities, target gateways, and authorization policies as depicted in Figure 3.28.

PMI makes it possible to define user access privileges in an environment that has to support multiple applications and vendors.

With the prevalence in online computing, the need for increased online identity assurance and browser representation of online identities gave rise to a special type of X.509 certificate. These are known as extended validation (EV) certificates. Unlike traditional certificates, which protected information only between a sender and a receiver,

X.509 v3 Certificate			
Required	Certificate	Version	
		Algorithm identifier	
		Serial number (unique identifier for each certificate of the CA issues)	
	Issuer	Distinguished CA name	
	Validity period	Period from and to which the certificate will be valid	
	Subject	Name (same as the issuer for a root certificate)	
		Public key	Algorithm identifier
			Value
Optional	Unique identifier	Issuer	
		Subject	
	Extensions	Additional certificate and policy information	
Digital signature of the CA			

Figure 3.27   ITU X.509 v3 digital certificate.

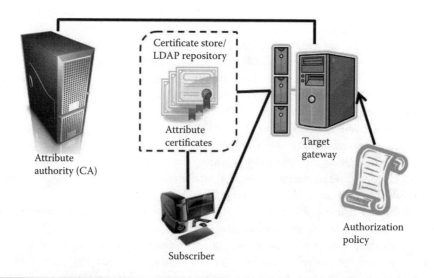

Figure 3.28   Privilege management infrastructure (PMI).

EV certificates also provide assurance that the sites or remote servers that users are connecting to are legitimate. EV certificates undergo more extensive validation of owner identity before they are issued, and they identify the owners of the sites that users connect to and thereby address MITM attacks. The main objectives of EV certificates are to improve user confidence and reduce Phishing attack threats.

3.12.6 Single Sign-On (SSO)

SSO makes it possible for users to log into one system and after being authenticated, launch other applications without having to provide their identifying information again. It is possible to store user credentials outside of an application and automatically reuse validated credentials in systems that prompt for them. However, SSO is usually implemented in conjunction with other technologies. The two common technologies that make sharing of authentication information possible are Kerberos and Secure Assertion Markup Language (SAML).

Credentials in a Kerberos authentication system are referred to as tickets. When you first log in to a system implemented with Kerberos and your password is verified, you are granted a master ticket, also known as a Ticket Granting Ticket (TGT), by the Ticket Granting Server (TGS). The TGT will act as proxy for your credentials. When you need to access another system, you present your master TGT to the Kerberos server and get a ticket that is specific to that other system. The second ticket is then presented to the system you are requesting access as a proof of who you are. When your identity is verified, access is granted to the system accordingly. All tickets are stored in what is called a ticket cache in the local system. Kerberos-based SSO can be used within the same domain in which the TGS functions and the TGT is issued. So Kerberos is primarily used in an intranet setting. Kerberos-based SSO is easier to implement in an intranet setting than SSO in an Internet environment.

To implement SSO in an Internet environment with multiple domains, SAML can be used. SAML allows users to authenticate themselves in a domain and use resources in a different domain without having to reauthenticate them. It is predominantly used in a Web-based environment for SSO purposes. The WS-Security specification recommends using SAML tokens for token-based authentication. SAML tokens can be used to exchange not just authentication information but also authorization data, user profiles, and preferences and so is a preferred choice. Although SAML tokens are a de facto standard for making authentication decisions in SOA implementations, authorization is often implemented as a custom solution. The OASIS eXtensible Access Control Markup Language (XACML) standard can be used for making authorization decisions and is recommended.

A concept related to SSO is federation. *Federation* extends SSO across enterprises. In a federated system, an individual can log into one site and access services at another, affiliated site without having to log in each time or reestablish an identity. For example, if you use an online travel site to book your flights, your same identity can be used in an affiliated, vacations and tours site to book your vacation package without having to create an account in the vacations site or login into it. Federation mainly fulfills a user need for convenience and when it is implemented, implementation must be done with legal protection agreements that can be enforced between the two affiliated companies. Until the SAML 2.0 standard specification was developed, organizations that engaged in federation had to work with three primary protocols, namely, OASIS SAML 1.0, Liberty Alliance ID-FF 1.1 and 1.2, and Shibboleth. OASIS SAML primarily dealt with business-to-business (B2B) federation, whereas Liberty focused on the B2B federation, and Shibboleth focused on educational institutions that required anonymity when engaging in federation. SAML 2.0 alleviates the challenges of multiprotocol complexity, making it possible to implement federation more easily. SAML 2.0 makes federation and interoperability possible with relative ease because the need to negotiate, map, and translate protocols are no longer necessary. It is also an open standard for Web-based, SSO service.

Although SSO is difficult to implement because trust needs to be established between the application that performs the authentication and the supported systems that will accept the authenticated credentials, it is preferred because it reduces the likelihood of human error. However, the benefits of simplified user authentication that SSO brings with it must be balanced with the following concerns about the SSO infrastructure:

- The ability to establish trust between entities participating in the SSO architecture.
- SSO implementation can be a single point of failure. If the SSO credentials are exposed, all systems in the SSO implementation are susceptible to breach. In layman's terms, the loss of SSO credentials is akin to losing the key to the entire kingdom.
- SSO implementation can be a source for DoS. If the SSO system fails, all users who depend on the SSO implementation will be unable to log into their systems, causing a DoS.
- SSO deployment and integration cost can be excessive.

3.12.7 Flow Control

In distributed computing, controlling the flow of information between processes on two systems that may or may not be trusted poses security challenges. Several security issues are related to information flow. Sensitive information (bank account information, health information, social security numbers, credit card statements, etc.) stored in a particular Web application should not be displayed on a client browser to those who are not authorized to view that information. Protection against malware such as spyware and Trojans means that network traffic that carries malicious payload is not allowed to enter the network. By controlling the flow of information or data, several threats to software can be mitigated and delivery of valid messages guaranteed. Enforcing security policies concerning how information can flow to and from an application, independent of code level security protection mechanisms, can be useful in implementing security protection when the code itself cannot be trusted. Firewalls, proxies, and middleware components such as queuing infrastructure and technologies can be used to control the rate of data transmission and allow or disallow the flow of information across trust boundaries.

3.12.7.1 Firewalls and Proxies

Firewalls, more specifically network layer firewalls, separate the internal network of an organization from that of the outside. They also are used to separate internal subnetworks from one another. The firewall is an enforcer of security policy at the perimeter and all traffic that flows through it is inspected. Whether network traffic is restricted or not is dependent on the predefined rules or security policy that is configured into the firewall.

The different types of firewalls that exist are packet filtering, proxy, stateful, and application layer firewall. Each type is covered in more detail in this section.

- *Packet filtering:* This type of firewall filters network traffic based on information that is contained in the packet header, such as source address, destination address, network ports, and protocol and state flags. Packet filtering firewalls are stateless, meaning they do not keep track of state information. These are commonly implemented using ACLs, which are primarily text-based lines of rules that define which packets are allowed to pass through the firewall and which ones should be restricted. They are also known as first generation firewalls. These are application independent, scalable, and faster in performance but provide little security because they look only at the header information of the packets. Because they do not inspect the contents (payload) of the packets, packet filtering firewalls are defenseless against malware threats. Packet filtering firewalls are also known as first-generation firewalls.
- *Proxy:* Proxy firewalls act as a middleman between internal trusted networks and the outside untrusted ones. When a packet arrives at a proxy firewall, the firewall terminates the connection from the source and acts as a proxy for the destination, inspects the packet to ascertain that it is safe before forwarding the packet to the destination. When the destination system responds, the packet is sent to the proxy firewall, which will repackage the packet with its own source address and abstract the address of the internal destination host system. Proxy firewalls also make decisions, as do packet filtering firewalls. However, proxy firewalls, by breaking the connection, do not allow direct connection between untrusted and trusted systems. Proxy firewalls are also known as second-generation firewalls.

- *Stateful:* Stateful firewalls or third-generation firewalls have the capability to track dialog by maintaining a state and data context in the packets within a state table. Unlike proxy firewalls, they are not as resource intensive and are usually transparent to the user.
- *Application layer:* Because stateless and stateful firewalls look only at a packet's header and not at the data content (payload) contained within a packet, application specific attacks will go undetected and pass through stateless and stateful firewalls. This is where application layer firewalls or layer 7 firewalls come in handy. Application layer firewalls provide flow control by intercepting data that originate from the client. The intercepted traffic is examined for potentially dangerous threats that can be executed as commands. When a threat is suspected, the application layer firewall can take appropriate action to contain and terminate the attack or redirect it to a honeypot for additional data gathering.

One of the two options in Requirement 6.6 of the PCI Data Security Standard is to have a (Web) application firewall positioned between the Web application and the client end point. The other option is to perform application code reviews. Application firewalls are starting to gain importance, and this trend is expected to continue because hackers are targeting the application layer.

3.12.7.2 Queuing Infrastructure and Technology

Queuing infrastructure and technology are useful to prevent network congestion when a sender sends data faster than a receiver can process it. Legacy applications are usually designed to be single threaded in their operations. With the increase in rich client functionality and without proper flow control, messages can be lost. Queuing infrastructure and technology can be used to backlog these messages in the right order for processing and guarantee delivery to the intended recipients. Some of the well-known queuing technologies include the Microsoft Message Queuing (MSMQ), Oracle Advance Queuing (AQ), and the IBM MQ Series.

3.12.8 Auditing/Logging

One of the most important design considerations is to design the software so it can provide historical evidence of user and system actions. Auditing or logging of user and system interactions within an application can be used as a detective means to find out who did what, where, when, and sometimes how. Regulation such as SOX, HIPAA, and Payment Card Industry Data Security Standard (PCI DSS) require companies to collect and analyze logs from various sources as means to demonstrate due diligence and comprehensive security. Information that is logged needs to be processed to deduce patterns and discover threats. However, before any processing takes place, it is best practice to consolidate the logs, after synchronizing the time clocks of the logs. Time clock synchronization makes it possible to correlate events recorded in the application log data to real-world events, such as badge readers, security cameras, and closed circuit television (CCTV) recordings. Log information needs to be protected when stored and in transit. System administrators and users of monitored applications should not have access to logs. This is to prevent anyone from being able to remove evidence from logs in the event of fraud or theft. The use of a log management service (LMS) can alleviate some of this concern. Also, IDSs and intrusion protection systems (IPSs) can be leveraged to record and retrieve activity. In this section, we will cover auditing technologies, specifically Syslog, IDS, and IPS.

3.12.8.1 Syslog

When logs need to be transferred over an IP network, syslog can be used. Syslog is used to describe the protocol, the application that receives and sends, as well as the logs. The protocol is a client/server protocol in which the client application transmits the logs to the syslog receiver server (commonly called a syslog daemon, denoted as syslogd). Although syslog uses the connectionless User Datagram Protocol (UDP) with no delivery confirmation as its underlying transport mechanism, syslog can use the connection-oriented Transmission Control Protocol (TCP) to assure or guarantee delivery. Reliable log delivery assures that not only are the logs received successfully by the receiver but that they are received in the correct order. It is a necessary part of a complete security solution and can be implemented using TCP. It can be augmented by using cache servers, but when this is done, the attack surface will include the cache servers and appropriate technical, administrative, and physical controls need to be in place to protect the cache servers.

Syslog can be used in multiple platforms and is supported by many devices, making it the de facto standard for logging and transmitting logs from several devices to a central repository where the logs can be consolidated, integrated, and normalized to deduce patterns. Syslog is quickly gaining importance in the Microsoft platforms and is the standard logging solution for Unix and Linux platforms. *NIST Special Publication 800-92* provides resourceful guidance on Computer Security Log Management and highlights how Syslog can be used for security auditing as well. However, Syslog has an inherent security weakness to which attention must be paid. Data that are transmitted using Syslog is in clear text, making it susceptible to disclosure attacks. Therefore, TLS measures using wrappers such as SSL wrappers or Secure Shell (SSH) tunnels must be used to provide encryption for confidentiality assurance. Additionally, integrity protection using SHA or MD5 hash functions is necessary to ensure that the logs are not tampered or tainted while they are in transit or stored.

3.12.8.2 Intrusion Detection System (IDS)

IDSs can be used to detect potential threats and suspicious activities. IDSs can be monitoring devices or applications at the network layer (NIDS) or host (HIDS) layer. They filter both inbound and outbound traffic and have alerting capabilities, which notify administrators of imminent threats. One of the significant challenges with NIDS is that malicious payload data that are encrypted, as is the case with encrypted viruses, cannot be inspected for threats and can bypass filtration or detection.

IDSs are not firewalls but can be used with one. Firewalls are your first line of network or perimeter defense, but they may be required to allow traffic to enter through certain ports such as port 80 (http), 443 (https), or 21 (ftp). This is where IDSs can come in handy, as they will provide protection against malicious traffic and threats that pass through firewalls. Additionally, IDSs are more useful than firewalls for detecting insider threats and fraudulent activities that originate from within the firewalls.

IDSs are implemented in one of the following ways:

- *Signature based:* Similar to how antivirus detects malware threats, signature-based IDSs detect threats by looking for specific signatures or patterns that match those of known threats. The weakness of this type of IDS is that new and unknown threats, whose signatures are not known yet, or polymorphic threats with changing signatures will not be detected and can evade intrusion detection. Snort is a very popular and widely used, freely available, open-source, signature-based IDS for both Linux and Window OSs.
- *Anomaly based:* An anomaly-based IDS operates by monitoring and comparing network traffic against an established baseline of what is deemed "normal" behavior. Any deviation from the normal behavioral pattern causes an alert as a potential threat. The advantage of this type of IDS is that it can be used to detect and discover newer threats. Anomaly-based IDSs are commonly known also as behavioral IDSs.
- *Rule based:* A rule-based IDS operates by detecting attacks based on programmed rules. These rules are often implemented as IF-THEN-ELSE statements.

When implemented with logging, an IDS can be used to provide auditing capabilities.

3.12.8.3 Intrusion Prevention Systems (IPS)

Most intrusion prevention systems (IDSs) are passive and simply monitor for and alert on imminent threats. Some current IDSs are reactive in operation as well and are capable of performing an action or actions in response to a detected threat. When these actions are preventive in nature, containing the threat first and preventing it from being manifested, these IDSs are referred to as intrusion prevention systems (IPSs). An IPS provides proactive protection and is essentially a firewall that combines network level and application level filtering. Some examples of proactive IPS actions include blocking further traffic from the source IP address and locking out the account when brute-force threats are detected.

When implemented with logging, an IPS can be used to provide auditing capabilities.

3.12.9 Data Loss Prevention

The most important asset of an organization, second only to its people assets, is data, and data protection is important to assure its confidentiality, integrity, and availability.

The chronology of data breaches, news reports, and regulatory requirements to protect data reflect the prevalence and continued growth of data theft that costs companies colossal remediation sums and loss of brand. Data encryption mitigates data disclosure in events of physical theft and perimeter devices such as firewalls can provide some degree of protection by filtering out threats that are aimed at stealing data and information from within the network. While this type of *ingress filtration* can be useful to protect data within the network, it does little to protect data that leaves the organizational network. This is where data loss prevention (DLP) comes in handy. DLP is the technology that provides *egress filtration,* meaning it prevents data from leaving the network. E-mails with attachments containing sensitive information are among the primary sources of data loss when data are in motion. By mistyping the recipient's e-mail address when sharing information with a client, vendor, or partner, one can unintentionally disclose information. A disgruntled employee can copy sensitive data onto an end-point device (such as portable hard drive or USB) and take it out of the network.

DLP prevents the loss of data by not allowing information that is classified and tagged as sensitive to be attached or copied. *Tagging* is the process of labeling information that is classified with its appropriate classification level. This can be an overwhelming endeavor to organizations that have a large amount of information that needs to be tagged, so tagging requires planning and strategy, along with management and business support. The business owner of the data is ultimately responsible and must be actively engaged either directly or by delegating a data custodian to work with the IT team, so that data are not only appropriately classified but also appropriately tagged. DLP brings both mandatory (labeling) and discretionary (based on discretion of the owner) security into effect.

Successful implementations of DLP bring not only technological protection but also the assurance that required human resource and process elements are in place. DLP technology works by monitoring the tagged data elements, detecting and preventing loss, and remediating should the data leave the network. Additionally, DLP technology protection includes protecting the gateway as well as the channel. DLP control is usually applied at the gateway, the point at which data can leave the network (escape point), at the next logical level from where data are stored. DLP also includes the protection of data when they are in transit and work in conjunction with TLS mechanisms by protecting the channel. It must be recognized that protecting against data loss by applying DLP technology can be thwarted if the users (people) are not aware of and educated about the mechanisms and the impact of sensitive data walking out of the door. DLP can also be implemented through a corporate security policy that mandates the shredding of sensitive documents, disallowing the printing of and storing of sensitive information in storage devices that can be taken out of the organization.

We have covered the ways by which DLP can protect the data that is on the inside from leaving the network, but in today's world, there is a push toward the SaaS model of computing. In such situations, organizational data are stored on the outside in the service provider's shared-hosted network. When this is the case, data protection includes preventing data leakage when data are at rest or stored, as well as when it is being marshaled to and from the SaaS provider. Cryptographic protection and access control protection mechanisms can be used to prevent data leakage in SaaS implementations. SaaS is a maturing trend, and it is recommended that when data are stored on the outside, proper Chinese Wall access control protection exist, based on the requestor's authorized privileges, to avoid any conflict of interest. TLS protection alleviates data loss while the data are in motion between the organization and the SaaS provider.

3.12.10 Virtualization

Virtualization is a software technology that divides a physical resource (such as a server) into multiple virtual resources called virtual machine (VM). It abstracts computer resources and reproduces the physical characteristics and behavior of the resources. Virtualization facilitates the consolidation of physical resources while simplifying deployment and administration. Not only can physical resources (servers) be virtualized, but data storage, networks, and applications can be virtualized as well. When virtualization technology leverages a single physical server to run multiple operating systems, or multiple sessions of a single OS, it is commonly referred to as *platform virtualization*. Storage area networks (SANs) are an example of data storage virtualization.

Virtualization is gaining a lot of ground today and its adoption is expected to continue to rise in the coming years. Some of the popular and prevalent virtualization products are VMware, Microsoft Hyper-V, and Xen.

Benefits of virtualization include the following:

- Consolidation of physical (server) resources and thereby reduced cost
- Green computing; reduced power and cooling
- Deployment and administration ease
- Isolation of application, data, and platforms
- Increased agility to scale IT environment and services to the business

Though virtualization aims at reducing cost and improving agility, without proper consideration of security, these goals may not be realized, and the security of the overall computing ecosystem can be weakened. It is therefore imperative to determine the security and securability of virtualization before selecting virtualization products. On one hand, it can be argued that virtualization increases security because virtual machines are isolated from one another and dependent on a single host server, making it possible to address physical security breaches relatively simply when compared to having to manage multiple stand-alone servers. On the other hand, virtualization can be said to increase the attack surface because virtualization software known as the hypervisor as depicted in Figure 3.29, which controls and manages virtual machines and their access to host resources, is a software that could potentially have coding bugs and it runs with privileged access rights, making it susceptible to attack.

Other security concerns of virtualization that require attention include the need to

- Implement all of the security controls such as antivirus, system scans, and firewalls as one would in a physical environment.
- Protect not only the VM but also the VM images from being altered.
- Patch and manage all of the VM appliances.
- Ensure protection against jail-breaking out of a VM. It is speculated that it is possible to attack the hypervisor that controls the VMs and circumvent the isolation protection that virtualization brings. Once the hypervisor is compromised, one can jump from (jail-break out of) one VM to another.
- Inspect inter-VM traffic by IDS and IPS, which themselves can be VM instances.
- Implement defense-in-depth safeguard controls.

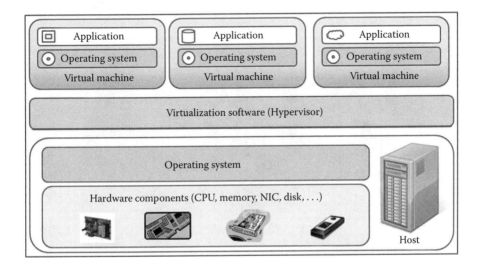

Figure 3.29   Virtualization.

■ Control VM sprawl. VM sprawl is the uncontrolled proliferation of multiple VM instances. It wastes resources and creates unmonitored servers that could contain sensitive data and makes troubleshooting and cleanup of unneeded servers extremely difficult.

Additionally, it is important to understand that technologies to manage VM security are still immature and currently in development. One such development is VM security API that makes it possible to help software development teams leverage security functionality and introspection ability within the virtualization products. However, performance considerations when using VM API need to be factored in.

3.12.11 Digital Rights Management

Have you ever experienced the situation when you chose to skip over the "FBI Antipiracy Warning" screen that appears when you load a Region 1 DVD movie and found out that you were not allowed to do so, as illustrated in Figure 3.30? This is referred to as *forward locking* and is a liability protection measure against violators who cannot claim ignorance of the consequences of their violating act. In this case, it is about copyright infringement and antipiracy protection. Forward locking is one example of a protection mechanism's using technology that is collectively known as DRM.

DRM refers to a broad range of technologies and standards that are aimed at protecting IP and content usage of digital works using technological controls. Copyright law (covered in detail in Chapter 6) is a deterrent control only against someone who wishes to make a copy of a protected file or resource (documents, music files, movies, etc.). It cannot prevent someone from making an illegal copy. This is why technology-based protection is necessary, and DRM helps in this

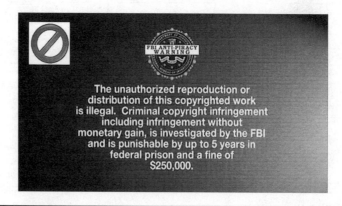

Figure 3.30 Forward locking.

endeavor. DRM is about protecting digital works, and it differs in its function from copyright law. Copyright law functions by permitting all that which is not forbidden. DRM conversely operates by forbidding all that which is not permitted.

DRM not only provides *copy protection* but can be configured granularly to provide *usage rights* and assure *authenticity* and *integrity* as well. This is particularly important when you have the need to share files with an external party over whom you have no control, such as a business partner or customer, but you still want to control the use of the files. DRM provides presentation layer (OSI layer 6) security not by preventing an unauthorized user from viewing the file but by preventing the receiving party from copying, printing, or sharing the file even though he may be allowed to open and view it. One of the most common ways in which file sharing is restricted is by tying the file to a unique hardware identifier or some hardware property that is not duplicated in other systems. This means that even though the file may be copied, it is still unusable in an unauthorized system or by a user who is not authorized. This type of protection mechanism is evident in music purchased from the iTunes store. Music purchased from the iTunes store is authorized to be used on one computer, and when it is copied over to another, it does not work unless proper authorization of the new computer is granted. DRM also assures content authenticity and integrity of a file, because it provides the ability to granularly control the use of a file.

The three core entities of a DRM architecture includes users, content, and rights. DRM implementation is made possible through the relationships that exist among these three core entities. Users can create and/or use content and are granted rights over the content. The user entity can be anyone: privileged or nonprivileged, employee or nonemployee, business partner, vendor, customer, etc. It need not be human, as a system can participate in a DRM implementation. The content entity refers to the protected resource, such as a music file, a document, or a movie. The rights entity expresses permissions, constraints, and obligations that the user entity has over the content entity. The expression of rights is made possible by formal language, known as Rights Expression Language (REL). Some examples of REL include the following:

- Open Digital Rights Language (ODRL): A generalized, open standard under development that expresses rights using XML.
- eXtensible rights Markup Language (XrML): Another generalized REL that is more abstract than ODRL. XrML is more of a metalanguage that can be used for developing other RELs.
- Publishing Requirements for Industry Standard Metadata (PRISM): Unlike ODRL and XrML, PRISM can be used to express rights specific to a task and is used for syndication of print media content such as newspapers and magazines. This is used primarily in a B2B setting where the business entities have a contractual relationship and the REL portion of PRISM is used to enforce copyright protection.

It must be recognized that an REL expresses rights, but it has no ability to enforce the rights. It is therefore critical for a software architect to design a protection mechanism, be it user-supplied data or hardware property, to restrict or grant usage rights. The entire DRM solution must be viewed from a security standpoint to ensure that there is no weak link that will circumvent the protection DRM provides.

Although DRM provides many benefits pertinent to IP protection, it does come with some challenges as well. Some of the common challenges are

- Using a hardware property as part of the expression of rights generally provides more security and is recommended. However, as the average life of hardware is not more than a couple of years, tying protection mechanisms to a hardware property can result in DoS when the hardware is replaced. Tying usage rights over content to a person alleviates this concern, but it is important to ensure that the individual's identity cannot be spoofed.
- Using personal data to uniquely identify an individual as part of the DRM solution could lead to some privacy concerns. The Sony rootkit music CD is an example of improper design that caused the company to lose customer trust, suffer several class action lawsuits, and recall its products.
- DRM not only forbids illegal copying, but it restricts and forbids legal copying (legitimate backups) as well, thereby affecting fair use.

When you design DRM solutions, you need to take into consideration both its benefits and challenges and security considerations should be in the forefront.

3.13 Secure Design and Architecture Review

Once software design is complete, before you exit the design phase and enter the development phase, it is important to conduct a review of the software's design and architecture. This is to ensure that the design meets the requirements. Not only should the application be reviewed for its functionality, but it should be reviewed for its security as well. This makes it possible to validate security design before code is written, thereby affording an opportunity to identify and fix any security vulnerabilities upfront, minimizing the need for reengineering at a later phase. The review should take into account the security policies and the target environment where the software will be deployed. Also, the review should be holistic in coverage, factoring in the network and host level protections that are to be in place so that safeguards do not contradict each other and minimize the protection they provide. Special attention should be given to the security design principles and security profile of the application to assure confidentiality, integrity, and availability of the data and of the software itself. Additionally, layer-by-layer analysis of the architecture should be performed so that defense in depth controls are in place.

3.14 Summary

The benefits of designing security into the software early are substantial and many. When you design software, security should be in forefront, and you should take into consideration secure design principles to assure confidentiality, integrity, and availability. Threat modeling is to be initiated and conducted during the design phase of the SDLC to determine entry and exit points that an attacker could use to compromise the software asset or the data it processes. Threat models are useful to identify and prioritize controls (safeguards) that can be designed, implemented (during the development phase), and deployed. Software architectures and technologies can be leveraged to augment security in software. Design reviews from a security perspective provide an opportunity to address security issues without its being too expensive. No software should enter the development phase of the SDLC until security aspects have been designed into it.

3.15 Review Questions

1. During which phase of the software development lifecycle (SDLC) is threat modeling initiated?
   A. Requirements analysis
   B. Design
   C. Implementation
   D. Deployment
2. Certificate authority, registration authority, and certificate revocation lists are all part of which of the following?
   A. Advanced Encryption Standard (AES)
   B. Steganography
   C. Public Key Infrastructure (PKI)
   D. Lightweight Directory Access Protocol (LDAP)
3. The use of digital signatures has the benefit of providing which of the following that is not provided by symmetric key cryptographic design?
   A. Speed of cryptographic operations
   B. Confidentiality assurance
   C. Key exchange
   D. Nonrepudiation
4. When passwords are stored in the database, the best defense against disclosure attacks can be accomplished using
   A. Encryption
   B. Masking
   C. Hashing
   D. Obfuscation

5. Nicole is part of the "author" role as well as she is included in the "approver" role, allowing her to approve her own articles before it is posted on the company blog site. This violates the principle of
   A. Least privilege
   B. Least common mechanisms
   C. Economy of mechanisms
   D. Separation of duties

6. The primary reason for designing single sign-on (SSO) capabilities is to
   A. Increase the security of authentication mechanisms
   B. Simplify user authentication
   C. Have the ability to check each access request
   D. Allow for interoperability between wireless and wired networks

7. Database triggers are primarily useful for providing which of the following detective software assurance capability?
   A. Availability
   B. Authorization
   C. Auditing
   D. Archiving

8. During a threat modeling exercise, the software architecture is reviewed to identify
   A. Attackers
   B. Business impact
   C. Critical assets
   D. Entry points

9. A man-in-the-middle (MITM) attack is primarily an expression of which type of the following threats?
   A. Spoofing
   B. Tampering
   C. Repudiation
   D. Information disclosure

10. IPSec technology, which helps in the secure transmission of information, operates in which layer of the Open Systems Interconnect (OSI) model?
    A. Transport
    B. Network
    C. Session
    D. Application

11. When internal business functionality is abstracted into service-oriented contract based interfaces, it is primarily used to provide for
    A. Interoperability
    B. Authentication
    C. Authorization
    D. Installation ease

12. At which layer of the OSI model must security controls be designed to effectively mitigate side channel attacks?
    A. Transport
    B. Network
    C. Data link
    D. Physical

13. Which of the following software architectures is effective in distributing the load between the client and the server but because it includes the client to be part of the threat vectors it increases the attack surface?
    A. Software as a Service (SaaS)
    B. Service-oriented architecture (SOA)
    C. Rich Internet application (RIA)
    D. Distributed network architecture (DNA)

14. When designing software to work in a mobile computing environment, the Trusted Platform Module (TPM) chip can be used to provide which of the following types of information?
    A. Authorization
    B. Identification
    C. Archiving
    D. Auditing

15. When two or more trivial pieces of information are brought together with the aim of gleaning sensitive information, it is referred to as what type of attack?
    A. Injection
    B. Inference
    C. Phishing
    D. Polyinstantiation

16. The inner workings and internal structure of backend databases can be protected from disclosure using
    A. Triggers
    B. Normalization
    C. Views
    D. Encryption

17. Choose the best answer. Configurable settings for logging exceptions, auditing and credential management must be part of
    A. Database views
    B. Security management interfaces
    C. Global files
    D. Exception handling

18. The token that is primarily used for authentication purposes in an SSO implementation between two different organizations is
    A. Kerberos
    B. Security Assert Markup Language (SAML)

  C. Liberty alliance ID-FF

  D. One time password (OTP)

19. Syslog implementations require which additional security protection mechanisms to mitigate disclosure attacks?

  A. Unique session identifier generation and exchange

  B. Transport layer security

  C. Digital Rights Management (DRM)

  D. Data loss prevention (DLP)

20. Rights and privileges for a file can be granularly granted to each client using which of the following technologies?

  A. Data loss prevention (DLP)

  B. Software as a Service

  C. Flow control

  D. Digital Rights Management

References

Adams, G. 2008. 21st Century mainframe data security: An exercise in balancing business priorities. http://www.mainframezone.com/mainframe-executive/september-october-2008 (accessed Sept. 30, 2010).

Booth, D., H. Haas, F. McCabe, E. Newcomer, M. Champion, C. Ferris, and D. Orchard. 2004. Service oriented architecture. http://www.w3.org/TR/ws-arch/#service_oriented_architecture (accessed Sept. 30, 2010).

Cochran, M. 2008. Writing better code—Keepin' it cohesive. http://www.c-sharpcorner.com/uploadfile/rmcochran/csharpcohesion02142008092055am/csharpcohesion.aspx (accessed Sept. 30, 2010).

Coyle, K. 2003. The technology of rights: Digital rights management. http://www.kcoyle.net/drm_basics.pdf (accessed Sept. 30, 2010).

Exforsys, Inc. 2007. NET type safety. http://www.exforsys.com/tutorials/csharp/.-net-type-safety.html (accessed Sept. 30, 2010).

Fei, F. 2007. Managed code vs. unmanaged code? http://social.msdn.microsoft.com/Forums/en-US/csharpgeneral/thread/a3e28547-4791-4394-b450-29c82cd70f70/ (accessed Sept. 30, 2010).

Fogarty Wed, K. 2009. Server virtualization: Top five security concerns. http://www.cio.com/article/492605/Server_Virtualization_Top_Five_Security_Concerns (accessed Sept. 30, 2010).

Grossman, J. 2007. Seven business logic flaws that put your Website at risk. Whitepaper. http://www.whitehatsec.com/home/resource/whitepapers/business_logic_flaws.html (accessed Sept. 30, 2010).

Hitachi ID Systems, Inc. Defining identity management. Whitepaper. http://identity-manager.hitachi-id.com/docs/identity-management-defined.html (accessed Sept. 30, 2010).

Housley, R., W. Polk, W. Ford, and D. Solo. 2002. Internet X.509 Public Key Infrastructure Certificate and Certificate Revocation List (CRL) Profile. Report IETF RFC 3280. http://www.ietf.org/rfc/rfc3280.txt (accessed Sept. 30, 2010).

International Telecommunication Union. 2006. Security in telecommunications and information technology. http://www.itu.int/publ/T-HDB-SEC.03-2006/en (accessed Sept. 30, 2010).

Kaushik, N. 2008. Virtual directories + provisioning = No more metadirectory. http://blog.talkingidentity.com/2008/03/virtual_directories_provisioni.html (accessed Sept. 30, 2010).

Kent, K., and M. Souppaya. 2006. Guide to computer security log management. *Special Publication 800-92* (SP 800-92), National Institute of Standards and Technology (NIST). http://csrc.nist.gov/publications/nistpubs/800-92/SP800-92.pdf (accessed Sept. 30, 2010).

Kohno, T., A. Stubblefield, A. D. Rubin, and D. S. Wallach. 2004. Analysis of an electronic voting system. *IEEE Symposium on Security and Privacy* 2004: 27–40.

LaPorte, P. 2009. Emerging market: Data loss prevention gets SaaS-y. *ECommerce Times*. http://www.ecommercetimes.com/rsstory/66562.html (accessed Sept. 30, 2010).

Microsoft, Inc. n.d. Extended validation certificates—FAQ. http://www.microsoft.com/windows/products/winfamily/ie/ev/faq.mspx (accessed Sept. 30, 2010).

Microsoft, Inc. 2003. Logon and authentication technologies. http://technet.microsoft.com/en-us/library/cc780455(WS.10).aspx (accessed Sept. 30, 2010).

Microsoft, Inc. 2007. Description of the database normalization basics. http://support.microsoft.com/kb/283878 (accessed Sept. 30, 2010).

Microsoft, Inc. 2009. A safer online experience. Whitepaper. http://download.microsoft.com/download/D/5/6/D562FBD1-B072-47F9-8522-AF2B8F786015/A%20Safer%20Online%20Experience%20FINAL.pdf (accessed Sept. 30, 2010).

Microsoft Solutions Developer Network (MSDN). n.d. Managing trigger security. http://msdn.microsoft.com/en-us/library/ms191134.aspx (accessed Sept. 30, 2010).

Messmer, E. 2009. Virtualization security remains a work in progress. http://www.networkworld.com/news/2009/122209-outlook-virtualization-security.html (accessed Sept. 30, 2010).

National Institute of Standards and Technology (NIST). n.d. Pervasive computing. http://www.itl.nist.gov/pervasivecomputing.html (accessed Sept. 30, 2010).

Newman, R C. 2010. *Computer Security: Protecting Digital Resources.* Sudbury, MA: Jones and Bartlett Learning.

O'Neill, D. 1980. The management of software engineering. Parts I–V. *IBM Systems Journal* 19(4): 414–77.

Oracle, Inc. n.d., a. Triggers. 11g Release 1 (11.1). http://download.oracle.com/docs/cd/B28359_01/server.111/b28318/triggers.htm#CNCPT118 (accessed Sept. 30, 2010).

Oracle, Inc. n.d., b. Views. 11g Release 1 (11.1). Schema Objects. http://download.oracle.com/docs/cd/B28359_01/server.111/b28318/schema.htm#CNCPT311>. (accessed Sept. 30, 2010).

Pettey, C. 2007. Organizations that rush to adopt virtualization can weaken security. http://www.gartner.com/it/page.jsp?id=503192 (accessed Sept. 30, 2010).

Phelps, J. R., and M. Chuba. 2005. IBM targets security issues with its new mainframe. *Gartner* 2005: 1–3.

Reed, D. 2003. Applying the OSI seven layer network model to information security. Whitepaper. *SANS Institute InfoSec Reading Room* 1–31. http://www.sans.org/reading_room/whitepapers/protocols/applying-osi-layer-network-model-information-security_1309 (accessed Nov. 29, 2010).

RSA Security, Inc. 2002. Securing data at rest: Developing a database encryption strategy. http://www.rsa.com/products/bsafe/whitepapers/DDES_WP_0702.pdf (accessed Sept. 30, 2010).

Singhal, A., T. Winograd, and K. Scarfone. 2007. Guide to secure Web services. *National Institute of Standards and Technology Special Publication* SP-800-95.

Stanford, V. 2002. Pervasive health care applications face tough security challenges. *IEEE Pervasive Computing* 1(2): 8–12.

Stephens, R. K., R. R. Plew, and A. Jones. 2008. The normalization process. In *Sams Teach Yourself SQL in 24 Hours*, 4th ed., 61–71. Indianapolis, IN: Sams.

Stoneburner, G., C. Hayden, and A. Feringa. 2004. Engineering principles for information technology security (A baseline for achieving security). *National Institute of Standards and Technology Special Publication* SP-800-27: sect. 3.3 (accessed September 30, 2010).

Sun Microsystems, Inc. 2004. Identity management: Technology cornerstone of the virtual enterprise. White Paper. http://www.sun.com/software/products/identity/wp_virtual_enterprise.pdf (accessed Sept. 30, 2010).

Sun Microsystems, Inc. 2007. Federation, SAML, and Web Services. *Sun Java System Access Manager 7.1 Technical Overview*, chap. 5. http://docs.sun.com/app/docs/doc/819-4669/ (accessed Sept. 30, 2010).

Syslog.org. n.d. Syslog. http://www.syslog.org/ (accessed Sept. 30, 2010).

Tomhave, B. 2008. Key management: The key to encryption. *EDPACS: The EDP Audit, Control, and Security Newsletter* 38(4): 12–19.

Williams, J. 2008. The trinity of RIA security explained of servers, data and policies. http://www.theregister.co.uk/2008/04/08/ria_security/ (accessed Sept. 30, 2010).

Zeldovich, N. 2007. Securing untrustworthy software using information flow control. Doctoral thesis. Stanford University, Stanford, CA. http://www.scs.stanford.edu/~nickolai/papers/zeldovich-thesis-phd.pdf (accessed Sept. 30, 2010).

Chapter 4

Secure Software Implementation/Coding

4.1 Introduction

Although software assurance is more than just writing secure code, writing secure code is an important and critical component to ensuring the resiliency of software security controls. Reports in full disclosure and security mailing lists are evidence that software written today is rife with vulnerabilities that can be exploited. A majority of these weaknesses can be attributed to insecure software design and/or implementation, and it is vitally important that software first and foremost be reliable, and second less prone to attack and more resilient when it is. Successful hackers today are identified as individuals who have a thorough understanding of programming. It is therefore imperative that software developers who write code must also have a thorough understanding of how their code can be exploited, so that they can effectively protect their software and data. Today's security landscape calls for software developers who additionally have a security mindset. This chapter will cover the basics of programming concepts, delve into topics that discuss common software coding vulnerabilities and defensive coding techniques and processes, cover code analysis and code protection techniques, and finally discuss building environment security considerations that are to be factored into the software.

4.2 Objectives

As a CSSLP, you are expected to

- Have a thorough understanding of the fundamentals of programming.
- Be familiar with the different types of software development methodologies.
- Be familiar with common software attacks and means by which software vulnerabilities can be exploited.
- Be familiar with defensive coding principles and code protection techniques.
- Know how to implement safeguards and countermeasures using defensive coding principles.
- Know the difference between static and dynamic analysis of code.
- Know how to conduct a code/peer review.
- Be familiar with how to build the software with security protection mechanisms in place.

This chapter will cover each of these objectives in detail. It is imperative that you fully understand the objectives and be familiar with how to apply them in the software that your organization builds.

4.3 Who Is to Be Blamed for Insecure Software?

Although it may seem that the responsibility for insecure software lies primarily on the software developers who write the code, opinions vary, and the debate on who is ultimately responsible for a software breach is ongoing. Holding the coder solely responsible would be unreasonable since software is not developed in a silo. Software has many stakeholders, as depicted in Figure 4.1, and eventually all play a crucial role in the development of secure software. Ultimately, it is the organization (or company) that will be blamed for software security issues, and this state cannot be ignored.

4.4 Fundamental Concepts of Programming

Who is a programmer? What is their most important skill? A programmer is essentially someone who uses his/her technical know-how and skills to solve problems that the business has. The most important skills a programmer (used synonymously with a coder) has is problem solving. Programmers use their skills to construct business problem-solving programs (software) to automate manual processes, improving the efficiency of the business. They use programming languages to write programs. In the following section, we will learn about computer architecture, types of programming languages and code, and program utilities, such as assembler, compilers, and interpreters.

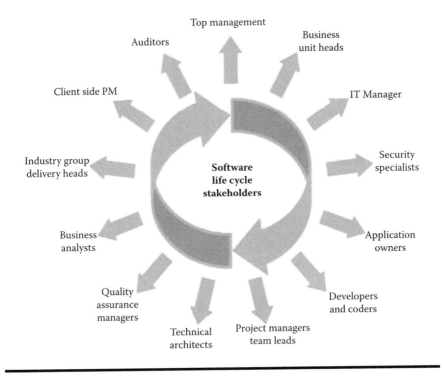

Figure 4.1   Software life cycle stakeholders.

4.4.1 Computer Architecture

Most modern-day computers are primarily composed of the computer processor, system memory, and input/output (I/O) devices. Figure 4.2 depicts a simplified illustration of modern-day computer architecture.

The computer processor is more commonly known as the central processing unit (CPU). The CPU is made up of the

- Arithmetic logic unit (ALU), which is a specialized circuit used to perform mathematical and logical operations on the data.
- Control unit, which acts as a mediator controlling processing instructions. The control unit itself does not execute any instructions, but instructs and directs other parts of the system, such as the registers, to do so.
- Registers, which are specialized internal memory holding spaces within the processor itself. These are temporary storage areas for instruction or data, and they provide the advantage of speed.

Because CPU registers have only limited memory space, memory is augmented by system memory and secondary storage devices, such as the hard disks, digital video

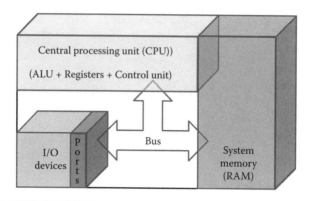

Figure 4.2 Computer architecture.

disks (DVDs), compact disks (CDs), and USB keys/fobs. The system memory is also commonly known as random access memory (RAM). The RAM is the main component with which the CPU communicates. I/O devices are used by the computer system to interact with external interfaces. Some common examples of input devices include a keyboard, mouse, etc., and some common examples of output devices include the monitor, printers, etc. The communication between each of these components occurs via a gateway channel that is called the *bus*.

The CPU, at its most basic level of operation, processes data based on binary codes that are internally defined by the processor chip manufacturer. These instruction codes are made up of several operational codes called opcodes. These opcodes tell the CPU what functions it can perform. For a software program to run, it reads instruction codes and data stored in the computer system memory and performs the intended operation on the data. The first thing that needs to happen is for the instruction and data to be loaded on to the system memory from an input device or a secondary storage device. Once this happens, the CPU does the following four functions for each instruction:

- Fetching: The control unit gets the instruction from system memory.
- The instruction pointer is used by the processor to keep track of which instruction codes have been processed and which ones are to be processed subsequently. The data pointer keeps track of where the data are stored in the computer memory, i.e., it points to the memory address.
- Decoding: The control unit deciphers the instruction and directs the needed data to be moved from system memory onto the ALU.
- Execution: Control moves from the control unit to the ALU, and the ALU performs the mathematical or logical operation on the data.
- Storing: The ALU stores the result of the operation in memory or in a register. The control unit finally directs the memory to release the result to an output device or a secondary storage device.

The fetch–decode–execute–store cycle is also known as the machine cycle. A basic understanding of this process is necessary for a CSSLP because they need to be aware of what happens to the code written by a programmer at the machine level.

When the software program executes, the program allocates storage space in memory so that the program code and data can be loaded and processed as the programmer has intended it. The CPU registers are used to store the most immediate data; the compilers use the registers to cache frequently used function values and local variables that are defined in the source code of the program. However, since there are only a limited number of registers, most programs, especially the large ones, place their data values on the system memory (RAM) and use these values by referencing their unique addresses. Internal memory layout has the following segments: program text, data, stack, and heap, as depicted in Figure 4.3. Physically the stack and the heap are allocated areas on the RAM. The allocation of storage space in memory (also known as a memory object) is called instantiation. Program code uses the variables defined in the source code to access memory objects.

The series of execution instructions (program code) is contained in the program *text* segment. The next segment is the read–write *data* segment, which is the area in memory that contains both initialized and uninitialized global data. Function variables, local data, and some special register values, such as the execution stack pointer (ESP), are placed on the *stack* part of the RAM. The ESP points to the memory address location of the currently executing program function. Variable sized objects and objects that are too large to be placed on the stack are dynamically allocated on the *heap* part of the RAM. The heap provides the ability to run more than one process at a time, but for the most part with software, memory attacks on the stack are most prevalent.

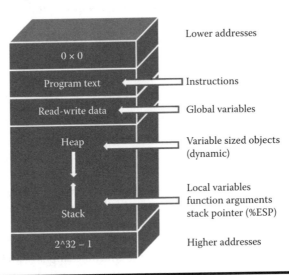

Figure 4.3 Memory layout.

The stack is an area of memory used to store function arguments and local variables, and it is allocated when a function in the source code is called to execute. When the function execution begins, space is allocated (pushed) on the stack, and when the function terminates, the allocated space is removed (popped off) the stack. This is known as the PUSH and POP operation. The stack is managed as a LIFO (last in, first out) data structure. This means that when a function is called, memory is first allocated in the higher addresses and used first. The PUSH direction is from higher memory addresses to lower memory addresses, and the POP direction is from lower memory addresses to higher memory addresses. This is important to understand because the ESP moves from higher memory to lower memory addresses, and, without proper management, serious security breaches can be evident.

Software hackers often have a thorough understanding of this machine cycle and how memory management happens, and without appropriate protection mechanisms in place, they can circumvent higher-level security controls by manipulating instruction and data pointers at the lowest level, as is the case with memory buffer overflow attacks and reverse engineering. These will be covered later in this chapter under the section about common software vulnerabilities and countermeasures.

4.4.2 Programming Languages

Knowledge of all the processor instruction codes can be extremely onerous on a programmer, if even humanly possible. Even an extremely simple program would require the programmer to write lines of code that manipulate data using opcodes, and in a fast-paced day and age where speed of delivery is critically important for the success of business, software programs, like any other product, cannot take an inordinate amount of time to create. To ease programmer's effort and shorten the time to delivery of software development, simpler programming languages that abstract the raw processor instruction codes have been developed. There are many programming languages that exist today.

Software developers use a programming language to create programs, and they can choose a low-level programming language. A low-level programming language is closely related to the hardware (CPU) instruction codes. It offers little to no abstraction from the language that the machine understands, which is binary codes (0s and 1s). When there is no abstraction and the programmer writes code in 0s and 1s to manipulate data and processor instructions, which is a rarity, they are coding in machine language. However, the most common low-level programming language today is the assembly language, which offers little abstraction from the machine language using opcodes. Appendix C has a listing of the common opcodes used in assembly language for abstracting processor instruction codes in an Intel 80186 or higher microprocessor (CPU) chip. Machine language and assembly language are both examples of low-level programming languages. An assembler converts assembly code into machine code.

In contrast, high-level programming languages (HLL) isolate program execution instruction details and computer architecture semantics from the program's functional specification itself. High-level programming languages abstract raw processor instruction codes into a notation that the programmer can easily understand. The specialized notation with which a programmer abstracts low-level instruction codes is called the syntax, and each programming language has its own syntax. This way, the programmer is focused on writing a code that addresses business requirements instead of being concerned with manipulating instruction and data pointers at the microprocessor level. This makes software development certainly simpler and the software program more easily understandable. It is, however, important to recognize that with the evolution of programming languages and integrated development environments (IDEs) and tools that facilitate the creation of software programs, even professionals lacking the internal knowledge of how their software program will execute at the machine level are now capable of developing software. This can be seriously damaging from a security standpoint because software creators may not necessarily understand or be aware of the protection mechanisms and controls that need to be developed and therefore inadvertently leave them out.

Today, the evolution of programming languages has given us goal-oriented programming languages that are also known as very high-level programming languages (VHLL). The level of abstraction in some of the VHLLs has been so increased that the syntax for programming in these VHLLs is like writing in English. Additionally, languages such as the natural language offer even greater abstraction and are based on solving problems using logic based on constraints given to the program instead of using the algorithms written in code by the software programmer. Natural languages are infrequently used in business settings and are also known as logic programming languages or constraint-based programming languages.

Figure 4.4 illustrates the evolution of programming languages from the low-level machine language to the VHLL natural language.

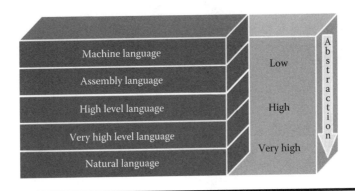

Figure 4.4   Programming languages.

The syntax in which a programmer writes their program code is the *source code*. Source code needs to be converted into a set of instruction codes that the computer can understand and process. The code that the machine understands is the *machine code*, which is also known as *native code*. In some cases, instead of converting the source code into machine code, the source code is simply interpreted and run by a separate program. Depending on how the program is executed on the computer, HLL can be categorized into compiled languages and interpreted languages.

4.4.2.1 Compiled Languages

The predominant form of programming languages are compiled languages. Examples include COBOL, FORTRAN, BASIC, Pascal, C, C++, and Visual Basic. The source code that the programmer writes is converted into machine code. The conversion itself is a two-step process, as depicted in Figure 4.5, that includes two subprocesses: compilation and linking.

- Compilation: The process of converting textual source code written by the programmer into raw processor specific instruction codes. The output of the compilation process is called the *object code,* which is created by the compiler program. In short, compiled source code is the object code. The object code itself cannot be executed by the machine unless it has all the necessary code files and dependencies provided to the machine.
- Linking: The process of combining the necessary functions, variables, and dependencies files and libraries required for the machine to run the program. The output that results from the linking process is the executable program or machine code/file that machine can understand and process. In short, linked object code is the executable. Link editors that combine object codes are known as linkers. Upon the completion of the compilation process, the compiler invokes the linker to perform its function.

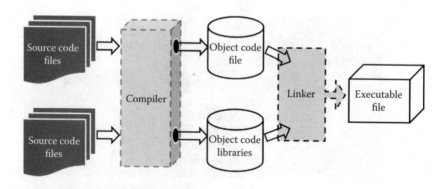

Figure 4.5   Compilation and linking.

There are two types of linking: static linking and dynamic linking. When the linker copies all functions, variables, and libraries needed for the program to run into the executable itself, it is referred to as static linking. Static linking offers the benefit of faster processing speed and ease of portability and distribution because the required dependencies are present within the executable itself. However, based on the size and number of other dependencies files, the final executable can be bloated, and appropriate space considerations needs to be taken. Unlike static linking, in dynamic linking only the names and respective locations of the needed object code files are placed in the final executable, and actual linking does not happen until runtime, when both the executable and the library files are placed in memory. Although this requires less space, dynamically linked executables can face issues that relate to dependencies if they cannot be found at run time. Dynamic linking should be chosen only after careful consideration to security is given, especially if the linked object files are supplied from a remote location and are open source in nature. A hacker can maliciously corrupt a dependent library, and when they are linked at runtime, they can compromise all programs dependent on that library.

4.4.2.2 Interpreted Languages

While programs written in compiled languages can be directly run on the processor, interpreted languages require an intermediary host program to read and execute each statement of instruction line by line. The source code is not compiled or converted into processor-specific instruction codes. Common examples of interpreted languages include REXX, PostScript, Perl, Ruby, and Python. Programs written in interpreted languages are slower in execution speed, but they provide the benefit of quicker changes because there is no need for recompilation and relinking, as is the case with those written in compiled languages.

4.4.2.3 Hybrid Languages

To leverage the benefits provided by compiled languages and interpreted languages, there is also a combination (hybrid) of both compiled and interpreted languages. Here, the source code is compiled into an intermediate stage that resembles object code. The intermediate stage code is then interpreted as required. Java is a common example of a hybrid language. In Java, the intermediate stage code that results upon compilation of source code is known as the byte code. The byte code resembles processor instruction codes, but it cannot be executed as such. It requires an independent host program that runs on the computer to interpret the byte code, and the Java Virtual Machine (JVM) provides this for Java. In .Net programming languages, the source code is compiled into what is known as the common intermediate language (CIL), formerly known as Microsoft Intermediate Language (MSIL). At run time, the common language runtime's (CLR) just in time compiler converts the CIL code into native code, which is then executed by the machine.

4.5 Software Development Methodologies

Software development is a structured and methodical process that requires the interplay of people expertise, processes, and technologies. The software development life cycle (SDLC) is often broken down into multiple phases that are either sequential or parallel. In this section, we will learn about the prevalent SDLC models that are used to develop software. These include:

- Waterfall model
- Iterative model
- Spiral model
- Agile development methodologies

4.5.1 Waterfall Model

The waterfall model is one of the most traditional software development models still in use today. It is a highly structured, linear, and sequentially phased process characterized by predefined phases, each of which must be completed before one can move on to the next phase. Just as water can flow in only one direction down a waterfall, once a phase in the waterfall model is completed, one cannot go back to that phase. Winston W. Royce's original waterfall model from 1970 has the following order of phases:

1. Requirements specification
2. Design
3. Construction (also known as implementation or coding)
4. Integration
5. Testing and debugging (also known as verification)
6. Installation
7. Maintenance

The waterfall model is useful for large-scale software projects because it brings structure by phases to the software development process. The National Institute of Standards and Technology (NIST) *Special Publication 800-64 REV 1d,* covering Security Considerations in the Information Systems Development Life Cycle, breaks the linear waterfall SDLC model into five generic phases: initiation, acquisition/development, implementation/assessment, operations/maintenance, and sunset (Figure 4.6). Today, there are several other modified versions of the original waterfall model that include different phases with slight or major variations, but the definitive characteristic of each is the unidirectional sequential phased approach to software development.

From a security standpoint, it is important to ensure that the security requirements are part of the requirements phase. Incorporating any missed security

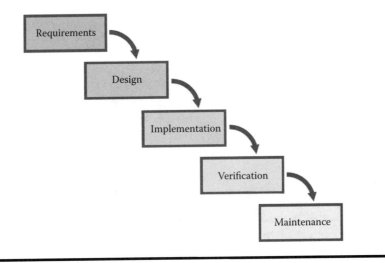

Figure 4.6   Waterfall model.

requirements at a later point in time will result in additional costs and delays to the project.

4.5.2 Iterative Model

In the iterative model of software development, the project is broken into smaller versions and developed incrementally, as illustrated in Figure 4.7. This allows the development effort to be aligned with the business requirements, uncovering any important issues early in the project and therefore avoiding disastrous faulty assumptions. It is also commonly referred to as the prototyping model in which

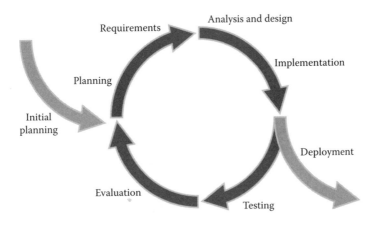

Figure 4.7   Iterative model.

each version is a prototype of the final release to manufacturing (RTM) version. Prototypes can be built to clarify requirements and then discarded, or they may evolve into the final RTM version. The primary advantage of this model is that it offers increased user input opportunity to the customer or business, which can prove useful to solidify the requirements as expected before investing a lot of time, effort, and resources. However, it must be recognized that if the planning cycles are too short, nonfunctional requirements, especially security requirements, can be missed. If it is too long, then the project can suffer from analysis paralysis and excessive implementation of the prototype.

4.5.3 Spiral Model

The spiral model, as shown in Figure 4.8, is a software development model with elements of both the waterfall model and the prototyping model, generally used for larger projects. The key characteristic of this model is that each phase has a risk

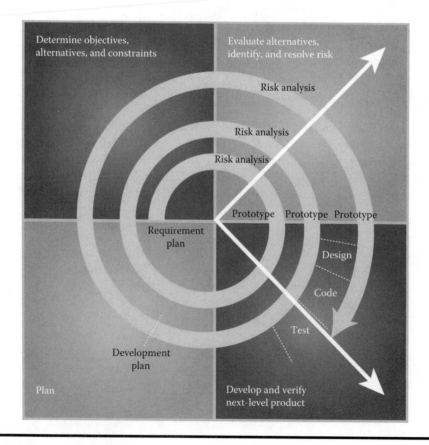

Figure 4.8 Spiral model.

assessment review activity. The risk of not completing the software development project within the constraints of cost and time is estimated, and the results of the risk assessment activity are used to find out if the project needs to be continued or not. This way, should the success of completing the project be determined as questionable, then the project team has the opportunity to cut the losses before investing more into the project.

4.5.4 Agile Development Methodologies

Agile development methodologies are gaining a lot of acceptance today, and most organizations are embracing them for their software development projects. Agile development methodologies are built on the foundation of iterative development with the goal of minimizing software development project failure rates by developing the software in multiple repetitions (iterations) and small timeframes (called timeboxes). Each iteration includes the full SDLC. The primary benefit of agile development methodologies is that changes can be made quickly. This approach uses feedback driven by regular tests and releases of the evolving software as its primary control mechanism, instead of planning in the case of the spiral model.

The two main agile development methodologies include:

- *Extreme Programming (XP) model:* The XP model is also referred to as the "people-centric" model of programming and is useful for smaller projects. It is a structured process, as depicted in Figure 4.9, that storyboards and architects user requirements in iterations and validates the requirements using acceptance testing. Upon acceptance and customer approval, the software is released. Success factors for the XP model are: (1) starting with the simplest solutions and (2) communication between team members. Some of the other distinguishing characteristics of XP are adaptability to change, incremental implementation of updates, feedback from both the system and the business user or customer, and respect and courage for all who are part of the project.
- *Scrum:* Another recent, very popular, and widely used agile development methodology is the Scrum programming approach. The Scrum approach calls for 30-day release cycles to allow the requirements to be changed on the fly, as necessary. In Scrum methodology, the software is kept in a constant state of readiness for release, as shown in Figure 4.10. The participants in Scrum have predefined roles of two types depending on their level of commitment: pig roles (those who are committed, whose bacon is on the line) and chicken roles (those who are part of the Scrum team participating in the project). Pig roles include the Scrum master who functions like a project manager in regular projects, the product owner who represents the stakeholders and is the voice of the customer, and the team of developers. The team size is usually between five and nine for effective communication. Chicken roles include the users who will use the software being developed, the stakeholders (the customer or

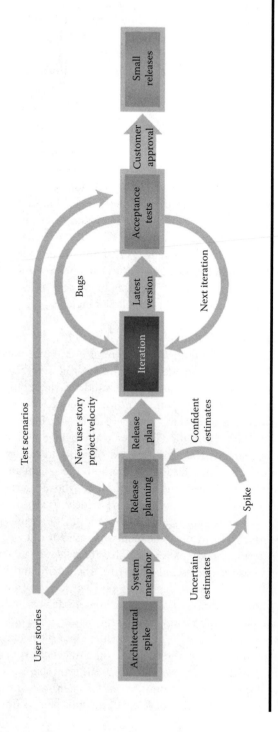

Figure 4.9 Extreme programming model.

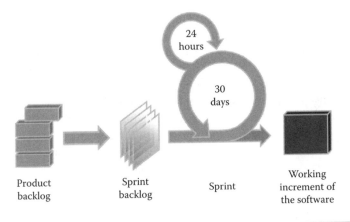

Product backlog   Sprint backlog   Sprint   Working increment of the software

Figure 4.10   Scrum.

vendor), and other managers. A prioritized list of high level requirements is first developed known as a product backlog. The time allowed for development of the product backlog, usually about 30 days, is called a sprint. The list of tasks to be completed during a sprint is called the sprint backlog. A daily progress for a sprint is recorded for review in the artifact known as the burn down chart.

4.5.5 Which Model Should We Choose?

In reality, the most conducive model for enterprise software development is usually a combination of two or more of these models. It is important, however, to realize that no model or combination of models can create inherently secure software. For software to be securely designed, developed, and deployed, a minimum set of security tasks needs to be effectively incorporated into the system development process, and the points of building security into the SDLC model should be identified.

4.6 Common Software Vulnerabilities and Controls

Although secure software is the result of a confluence between people, process, and technology, in this chapter, we will primarily focus on the technology and process aspects of writing secure code. We will learn about the most common vulnerabilities that result from insecure coding, how an attacker can exploit those vulnerabilities, and the anatomy of the attack itself. We will also discuss security controls that must be put in place (in the code) to resist and thwart actions of threat agents.

Nowadays, most of the reported incidents of security breaches seem to have one thing in common: they are attacks that exploited some weakness in the software layer. Analysis of the breaches invariably indicates one of the following to be the root cause of the breach: design flaws, coding (implementation) issues, and improper configuration and operations, with the prevalence of attacks exploiting software coding weaknesses. The Open Web Application Security Project (OWASP) Top 10 List and the Common Weakness Enumeration (CWE/SANS) Top 25 List of the most dangerous programming errors are testaments to the fact that software programming has a lot to do with its security. The 2010 OWASP Top 10 List, in addition to considering the most common application security issues from a weaknesses or vulnerabilities perspective (as did the 2004 and 2007 versions), views application security issues from an organizational risks (technical risk and business impact) perspective, as tabulated in Table 4.1. The 2009 CWE/SANS Top 25 List of the most dangerous programming errors is shown in Table 4.2.

The 2009 CWE/SANS Top 25 List of the most dangerous programming errors falls into the following three categories:

- Insecure interaction between components: includes weaknesses that relate to insecure ways in which data are sent and received between separate components, modules, programs, process, threads, or systems.
- Risky resource management: includes weaknesses that relate to ways in which software does not properly manage the creation, usage, transfer, or destruction of important system resources.
- Porous defenses: includes weaknesses that relate to defensive techniques that are often misused, abused, or just plain ignored.

The categorization of the 2009 CWE/SANS Top 25 List of most dangerous programming errors is shown in Table 4.3.

It is recommended that you visit the respective Web sites for the OWASP Top 10 List and the CWE/SANS Top 25 List, as a CSSLP is expected to be familiar with programming issues that can lead to security breaches and know how to address them. The most common software security vulnerabilities and risks are covered in the following section. Each vulnerability or risk is first described as to what it is and how it occurs and is followed by a discussion of security controls that can be implemented to mitigate it.

4.6.1 Injection Flaws

OWASP Top 10 Rank	1
CWE Top 25 Rank	2, 9

Considered one of the most prevalent software (or application) security weaknesses, injection flaws occur when the user-supplied data are not validated before being processed by an interpreter. The attacker supplies data that are accepted as they are and interpreted as a command or part of a command, thus allowing the attacker to execute commands using any injection vector. Almost any data accepting source are a potential injection vector if the data are not validated before they are processed. Common examples of injection vectors include QueryStrings, form input, and applets in Web applications. Injection flaws are easily discoverable using code review, and scanners, including fuzzing scans, can be used to detect them. There are several different types of injection attacks.

The most common injection flaws include SQL injection, OS command injection, LDAP injection, and XML injection.

■ *SQL Injection*

This is probably the most well-known form of injection attack, as the databases that store business data are becoming the prime target for attackers. In SQL (Structured Query Language) injection, attackers exploit the way in which database queries are constructed. They supply input that, if not sanitized or validated, becomes part of the query that the database processes as a command. Let us consider an example of a vulnerable code implementation in which the query command text (sSQLQuery) is dynamically built using data supplied from text input fields (txtUserID and txtPassword) from the Web form.

```
string sSQLQuery = " SELECT * FROM USERS WHERE user_id
= ' " + txtUserID.Text + " ' AND user_password = ' " +
txtPassword.Text + " '
```

If the attacker supplies ' OR 1=1 -- as the txtUserID value, then the SQL Query command text that is generated is as follows:

```
string sSQLQuery = " SELECT * FROM USERS WHERE user_id =
' " + ' OR 1=1 - - + " ' AND user_password = ' " +
txtPassword.Text + " '
```

This results in SQL syntax, as shown below, that the interpreter will evaluate and execute as a valid SQL command. Everything after the -- in T-SQL is ignored.

```
SELECT * FROM USERS WHERE user_id = ' ' OR 1=1 - -
```

The attack flow in SQL injection comprises the following steps:

1. Exploration by hypothesizing SQL queries to determine if the software is susceptible to SQL injection
2. Experimenting to enumerate internal database schema by forcing database errors

Table 4.1   OWASP Top 10

	Application Security Risks	Description
1	Injection flaws	Injection flaws, such as SQL, OS, and LDAP injection, occur when untrusted data are sent to an interpreter as part of a command or query. The attacker's hostile data can trick the interpreter into executing unintended commands or accessing unauthorized data.
2	Cross-site scripting (XSS)	XSS flaws occur whenever an application takes untrusted data and sends it to a Web browser without proper validation and escaping. XSS allows attackers to execute script in the victim's browser that can hijack user sessions, deface Web sites, or redirect the user to malicious sites.
3	Broken authentication and session management	Application functions related to authentication and session management are often not implemented correctly, allowing attackers to compromise passwords, keys, and session tokens, or to exploit implementation flaws to assume other users' identities.
4	Insecure direct object references	A direct object reference occurs when a developer exposes a reference to an internal implementation object, such as a file, directory, or database key. Without an access control check or other protection, attackers can manipulate these references to access unauthorized data.
5	Cross-site request forgery (CSRF)	A CSRF attack forces a logged-on victim's browser to send a forged HTTP request, including the victim's session cookie and any other authentication information, to a vulnerable Web application. This allows the attacker to force the victim's browser to generate requests that the vulnerable application thinks are legitimately coming from the victim.

6	Security misconfiguration	Security depends on having a secure configuration defined for the application, framework, Web server, application server, and platform. All these settings should be defined, implemented, and maintained, as many are not shipped with secure defaults.
7	Failure to restrict URL access	Many Web applications check URL access rights before rendering protected links and buttons. However, applications need to perform similar access control checks when these pages are accessed, or attackers will be able to forge URLs to access these hidden pages anyway.
8	Unvalidated redirects and forwards	Web applications frequently redirect and forward users to other pages and Web sites and use untrusted data to determine the destination pages. Without proper validation, attackers can redirect victims to phishing or malware sites or use forwards to access unauthorized pages.
9	Insecure cryptographic storage	Many Web applications do not properly protect sensitive data, such as credit cards, SSNs, and authentication credentials, with appropriate encryption or hashing. Attackers may use this weakly protected data to conduct identity theft, credit card fraud, or other crimes.
10	Insufficient transport layer protection	When transport layer protection is limited to certain operations such as authentication and end-to-end transport layer protection is absent, sensitive information can be intercepted and disclosed. Applications frequently fail to encrypt network traffic when it is necessary to protect sensitive communications.

Table 4.2   CWE/SANS Top 25 Most Dangerous Programming Errors

Rank	Programming Error	CWE ID
1	Failure to preserve Web page structure (XSS)	CWE-79
2	Improper sanitization of special elements used in a SQL command (SQL Injection)	CWE-89
3	Buffer copy without checking size of input (Classic Buffer Overflow)	CWE-120
4	Cross-site request forgery	CWE-352
5	Improper access control (Authorization)	CWE-285
6	Reliance on untrusted inputs in a security decision	CWE-807
7	Improper limitation of a pathname to a restricted directory (Path traversal)	CWE-22
8	Unrestricted upload of file with dangerous type	CWE-434
9	Improper sanitization of special elements used in an OS Command (OS Command Injection)	CWE-78
10	Missing encryption of sensitive data	CWE-311
11	Use of hard-coded credentials	CWE-798
12	Buffer access with incorrect length value	CWE-805
13	Improper check for unusual or exceptional conditions	CWE-754

14	Improper control of filename for include/require statement in PHP program (PHP File Inclusion)	CWE-98
15	Improper validation of array index	CWE-129
16	Integer overflow or wraparound	CWE-190
17	Improper exposure through error message	CWE-209
18	Incorrect calculation of buffer size	CWE-131
19	Missing authentication for critical function	CWE-306
20	Download of code without integrity checks	CWE-494
21	Incorrect permission assignment for critical resource	CWE-732
22	Allocation of resources without limits or throttling	CWE-770
23	URL redirection to untrusted site (Open Redirect)	CWE-601
24	Use of a broken or risky cryptographic algorithm	CWE-327
25	Race condition	CWE-362

Table 4.3 CWE/SANS Top 25 Most Dangerous Programming Errors Categorization

Category	Programming Error	Rank	CWE ID
Insecure interaction between components	Failure to preserve Web page structure (XSS)	1	CWE-79
	Improper sanitization of special elements used in a SQL command (SQL Injection)	2	CWE-89
	Cross-site request forgery	4	CWE-352
	Unrestricted upload of file with dangerous type	8	CWE-434
	Improper sanitization of special elements used in an OS Command (OS Command Injection)	9	CWE-78
	Improper exposure through an error message	17	CWE-209
	URL redirection to untrusted site (Open Redirect)	23	CWE-601
	Race condition	25	CWE-362

Category	Description	#	CWE-ID
Risky resource management	Buffer copy without checking size of input (Classic Buffer Overflow)	3	CWE-120
	Improper limitation of a pathname to a restricted directory (Path traversal)	7	CWE-22
	Buffer access with incorrect length value	12	CWE-805
	Improper check for unusual or exceptional conditions	13	CWE-754
	Improper control of filename for include/require statement in PHP program (PHP File Inclusion)	14	CWE-98
	Improper validation of array index	15	CWE-129
	Integer overflow or wraparound	16	CWE-190
	Incorrect calculation of buffer size	18	CWE-131
	Download of code without integrity check	20	CWE-494
	Allocation of resources without limits or throttling	22	CWE-770
Porous defenses	Improper access control (Authorization)	5	CWE-285
	Reliance on untrusted inputs in a security decision	6	CWE-807
	Missing encryption of sensitive data	10	CWE-311
	Use of hard-coded credentials	11	CWE-798
	Missing authentication for critical function	19	CWE-306
	Incorrect permission assignment for critical resource	21	CWE-732
	Use of a broken or risky cryptographic algorithm	24	CWE-327

3. Exploiting the SQL injection vulnerability to bypass checks or modify, add, retrieve, or delete data from the database

Upon determining that the application is susceptible to SQL injection, an attacker will attempt to force the database to respond with messages that potentially disclose internal database structure and values by passing in SQL commands that cause the database to error. Suppressing database error messages considerably thwarts SQL injection attacks, but it has been proven that this control measure is not sufficient to prevent SQL injection completely. Attackers have found a way to go around the use of error messages for constructing their SQL commands, as is evident in the variant of SQL injection known as *blind* SQL injection. In blind SQL injection, instead of using information from error messages to facilitate SQL injection, the attacker constructs simple Boolean SQL expressions (true/false questions) to probe the target database iteratively. Depending on whether the query was successfully executed, the attacker can determine the syntax and structure of the injection. The attacker can also note the response time to a query with a logically true condition and one with a false condition and use that information to determine if a query executes successfully or not.

■ *OS Command Injection*
This works in the same principle as the other injection attacks where the command string is generated dynamically using input supplied by the user. When the software allows the execution of operation system (OS) level commands using the supplied user input without sanitization or validation, it is said to be susceptible to OS Command injection. This could be seriously devastating to the business if the principle of least privilege is not designed into the environment that is being compromised. The two main types of OS Command injection are as follows:
  – The software accepts arguments from the user to execute a single fixed program command. In such cases, the injection is contained only to the command that is allowed to execute, and the attacker can change the input but not the command itself. Here, the programming error is that the programmer assumes that the input supplied by users to be part of the arguments in the command to be executed will be trustworthy as intended and not malicious.
  – The software accepts arguments from the user that specify what program command they would like the system to execute. This is a lot more serious than the previous case, because now the attacker can chain multiple commands and do some serious damage to the system by executing their own commands that the system supports. Here, the programming error is that the programmer assumes that the command itself will not be accessible to untrusted users.

An example of an OS Command injection that an attacker supplies as the value of a QueryString parameter to execute the bin/ls command to list all files in the "bin" directory is given below:

http://www.mycompany.com/sensitive/cgi-bin/userData.pl?doc=%20 %3B%20/bin/ls%20-l %20 decodes to a space and %3B decodes to a ; and the command that is executed will be /bin/ls -l listing the contents of the program's working directory.

■ *LDAP Injection*

LDAP is used to store information about users, hosts, and other objects. LDAP injection works on the same principle as SQL injection and OS command injection. Unsanitized and unvalidated input is used to construct or modify syntax, contents, and commands that are executed as an LDAP query. Compromise can lead to the disclosure of sensitive and private information as well as manipulation of content within the LDAP tree (hierarchical) structure. Say you have the ldap query (_sldapQuery) built dynamically using the user-supplied input (userName) without any validation, as shown in the example below.

```
String _sldapQuery = '' (cn='' + $userName + '') ' ';
```

If the attacker supplies the wildcard "*", information about all users listed in the directory will be disclosed. If the user supplies the value such as "'sjohnson) (|password=*))'", the execution of the LDAP query will yield the password for the user sjohnson.

■ *XML Injection*

XML injection occurs when the software does not properly filter or quote special characters or reserved words that are used in XML, allowing an attacker to modify the syntax, contents, or commands before execution. The two main types of XML injection are as follows:
- XPATH injection
- XQuery injection

In XPATH injection, the XPath expression used to retrieve data from the XML data store is not validated or sanitized before processing and built dynamically using user-supplied input. The structure of the query can thus be controlled by the user, and an attacker can take advantage of this weakness by injecting malformed XML expressions to perform malicious operations, such as modifying and controlling logic flow, retrieving unauthorized data, and circumventing authentication checks. XQuery injection works the same way as an XPath injection, except that the XQuery (not XPath) expression used to retrieve data from the XML data store is not validated or sanitized before processing and built dynamically using user-supplied input.

Consider the following XML document (accounts.xml) that stores the account information and pin numbers of customers and a snippet of Java code that uses XPath query to retrieve authentication information:

```
<customers>
      <customer>
            <user_name>andrew</user_name>
            <accountnum>1234987655551379</accountnum>
            <pin>2358</pin>
            <homepage>/home/astrout</homepage>
      </customer>
      <customer>
            <user_name>dave</user_name>
            <accountnum>9865124576149436</accountnum>
            <pin>7523</pin>
            <homepage>/home/dclarke</homepage>
      </customer>
</customers>
```

The Java code used to retrieve the home directory based on the provided credentials is:

```
XPath xpath = XPathFactory.newInstance().newXPath();
XPathExpression xPathExp = xpath.compile("//customers/
customer[user_name/text()='" + login.getUserName() + "' and
pin/text() = '" + login.getPIN() + "']/homepage/text()");
Document doc = DocumentBuilderFactory.newInstance()
.newDocumentBuilder().parse(new File("accounts.xml"));
String homepage = xPathExp.evaluate(doc);
```

By passing in the value "andrew" into the getUserName() method and the value "' or '='" into the getPIN() method call, the XPath expression becomes

```
//customers/customer[user_name/text()='andrew' or ''='' and
pin/text() = '' or ''='']/hompage/text()
```

This will allow the user logging in as andrew to bypass authentication without supplying a valid PIN.

Regardless of whether an injection flaw exploits a database, OS command, a directory protocol and structure, or a document, they are all characterized by one or more of the following traits:

■ User-supplied input is interpreted as a command or part of a command that is executed. In other words, data are misunderstood by the interpreter as code.

- Input from the user is not sanitized or validated before processing.
- The query that is constructed is generated using user-supplied input dynamically.

The consequences of injection flaws are varied and serious. The most common ones include:

- Disclosed, altered, or destroyed data
- Compromise of the operating system
- Discovery of the internal structure (or schema) of the database or data store
- Enumeration of user accounts from a directory store
- Circumvention of nested firewalls
- Execution of extended procedures and privileged commands
- Bypass of authentication

4.6.1.1 Injection Flaws Controls

Commonly used mitigation and prevention strategies and controls for injection flaws are as follows:

- Consider all input to be untrusted and validate all user input. Sanitize and filter input using a whitelist of allowable characters and their noncanonical forms. Although using a blacklist of disallowed characters can be useful in detecting potential attacks or determining malformed inputs, sole reliance on blacklists can prove to be insufficient, as the attacker can try variations and alternate representations of the blacklist form. Validation must be performed on both the client and server side, or at least on the server side, so that attackers cannot simply bypass client-side validation checks and still perform injection attacks. User input must be validated for data type, range, length, format, values, and canonical representations. SQL keywords such as union, select, insert, update, delete, and drop must be filtered in addition to characters such as single-quote (') or SQL comments (--) based on the context. Input validation should be one of the first lines of defense in an in-depth strategy for preventing or mitigating injection attacks, as it significantly reduces the attack surface.
- Encode output using the appropriate character set, escape special characters, and quote input, besides disallowing meta-characters. In some cases, when the input needs to be collected from various sources and is required to support free-form text, then the input cannot be constrained for business reasons, this may be the only effective solution to preventing injection attacks. Additionally, it provides protection even when some input sources are not covered with input validation checks.
- Use structured mechanisms to separate data from code.
- Avoid dynamic query (SQL, LDAP, XPATH Expression or XQuery) construction.

- Use a safe application programming interface (API) that avoids the use of the interpreter entirely or that provides escape syntax for the interpreter to escape special characters. A well-known example is the ESAPI published by OWASP.
- Just using parameterized queries (stored procedures or prepared statements) does not guarantee that the software is no longer susceptible to injection attacks. When using parameterized queries, make sure that the design of the parameterized queries truly accepts the user-supplied input as parameters and not the query itself as a parameter that will be executed without any further validation.
- Display generic error messages that yield minimal to no additional information.
- Implement failsafe by redirecting all errors to a generic error page and logging it for later review.
- Remove any unused, unnecessary functions or procedures from the database server. Remove all extended procedures that will allow a user to run system commands.
- Implement least privilege by using views, restricting tables, queries, and procedures to only the authorized set of users and/or accounts. The database users should be authorized to have only the minimum rights necessary to use their account. Using datareader, datawriter accounts as opposed to a database owner (dbo) account when accessing the database from the software is a recommended option.
- Audit and log the executed queries along with their response times to detect injection attacks, especially blind injection attacks.
- To mitigate OS command injection, run the code in a sandbox environment that enforces strict boundaries between the processes being executed and the operating system. Some examples include the Linux AppArmor and the Unix chroot jail. Managed code is also known to provide some degree of sandboxing protection.
- Use runtime policy enforcement to create the list of allowable commands (whitelist) and reject any command that does not match the whitelist.
- When having to implement defenses against LDAP injection attacks, the best method to handle user input properly is to filter or quote LDAP syntax from user-controlled input. This is dependent on whether the user input is used to create the distinguish name (DN) or used as part of the search filter text. When the input is used to create the DN, the backslash (\) escape method can be used, and when the input is used as part of the search filter, the ASCII equivalent of the character being escaped needs to be used. Table 4.4 lists the characters that need to be escaped and their respective escape method. It is important to ensure that the escaping method takes into consideration the alternate representations of the canonical form of user input.

In the event that the code cannot be fixed, using an application layer firewall to detect injection attacks can be a compensating control.

Table 4.4   LDAP Mitigation Character Escaping

User input used	Character(s)	Escape sequence substitute
To create DN	&, !, |, =, <, >, +,-,",' , ; , and comma (,)	\
As part of search filter	(	\28
	)	\29
	\	\5c
	/	\2f
	*	\2a
	NUL	\00

4.6.2 Cross-Site Scripting (XSS)

OWASP Top 10 Rank	2
CWE Top 25 Rank	1

Injection flaws and cross-site scripting (XSS) can arguably be considered as the two most frequently exploitable weaknesses prevalent in software today. Some experts refer to these two flaws as a "1-2 punch," as shown by the OWASP and CWE ranking.

XSS is the most prevalent Web application security attack today. A Web application is said to be susceptible to XSS vulnerability when the user-supplied input is sent back to the browser client without being properly validated and its content escaped. An attacker will provide a script (hence the scripting part) instead of a legitimate value, and that script, if not escaped before being sent to the client, gets executed. Any input source can be the attack vector, and the threat agents include anyone who has access to supplying input. Code review and testing can be used to detect XSS vulnerabilities in software.

The three main types of XSS are:

■ *Nonpersistent or reflected XSS*
  As the name indicates, nonpersistent or reflected XSS are attacks in which the user-supplied input script that is injected (also referred to as payload) is not stored, but merely included in the response from the Web server, either in the results of a search or as an error message. There are two primary ways in which the attacker can inject their malicious script. One is that they provide

the input script directly into your Web application. The other way is that they can send a link with the script embedded and hidden in it. When a user clicks the link, the injected script takes advantage of the vulnerable Web server, which reflects the script back to the user's browser, where it is executed.

■ *Persistent or stored XSS*

Persistent or stored XSS is characterized by the fact that the injected script is permanently stored on the target servers, in a database, a message forum, a visitor log, or an input field. Each time the victims visit the page that has the injected code stored in it or served to it from the Web server, the payload script executes in the user's browser. The infamous Samy Worm and the Flash worm are well-known examples of a persistent or stored XSS attack.

■ *DOM-based XSS*

DOM-based XSS is an XSS attack in which the payload is executed in the victim's browser as a result of DOM environment modifications on the client side. The HTTP response (or the Web page) itself is not modified, but weaknesses in the client side allow the code contained in the Web page client to be modified so that the payload can be executed. This is strikingly different from the nonpersistent (or reflected) and the persistent (or stored) XSS versions because, in these cases, the attack payload is placed in the response page due to weaknesses on the server side.

The consequences of a successful XSS attack are varied and serious. Attackers can execute script in the victim's browser and:

■ Steal authentication information using the Web application.
■ Hijack and compromise users' sessions and accounts.
■ Tamper or poison state management and authentication cookies.
■ Cause denial of service (DoS) by defacing the Web sites and redirecting users.
■ Insert hostile content.
■ Change user settings.
■ Phish and steal sensitive information using embedded links.
■ Impersonate a genuine user.
■ Hijack the user's browser using malware.

4.6.2.1 XSS Controls

Controls against XSS attacks include the following defensive strategies and implementations:

■ Handle the output to the client by either using escaping sequences or encoding. This can be considered as the best way to protect against XSS attacks in conjunction with input validation. Escaping all untrusted data based on the

HTML context (body, attribute, JavaScript, CSS, or URL) is the preferred option. Additionally, setting the appropriate character encoding and encoding user-supplied input renders the payload that the attacker injects as script into text-based output that the browser will merely read and not execute.

■ Validating user-supplied input with a whitelist also provides additional protection against XSS. All headers, cookies, URL querystring values, form fields, and hidden fields must be validated. This validation should decode any encoded input and then validate the length, characters, format, and any business rules on the data before accepting the input. Each of the requests made to the server should be validated as well. In .Net, when the *validateRequest* flag is configured at the application, Web, or page level, as depicted in Figure 4.11, any unencoded script tag sent to the server is flagged as a potentially dangerous request to the server and is not processed.

■ Disallow the upload of .htm or .html extensions.

■ Use the innerText properties of HTML controls instead of the innetHtml property when storing the input supplied, so that when this information is reflected back on the browser client, the data renders the output to be processed by the browser as literal and as nonexecutable content instead of executable scripts.

■ Use secure libraries and encoding frameworks that provide protection against XSS issues. The Microsoft Anti-Cross-Site Scripting, OWASP ESAPI Encoding module, Apache Wicket, and SAP Output Encoding framework are well-known examples.

■ The client can be secured by disabling the active scripting option in the browser so that scripts are not automatically executed on the browser. Figure 4.12 shows the configuration options for active scripting in the Internet Explorer browser. It is also advisable to install add-on plugins that will prevent the execution of scripts on the browser unless permissions are explicitly granted to run them. NoScript is a popular add-on for the Mozilla Firefox browser.

■ Use the HTTPOnly flag on the session or any custom cookie so that the cookie cannot be accessed by any client-side code or script (if the browser supports it), which mitigates XSS attacks. However, if the browser does not support HTTPOnly cookies, then even if you have set the HTTPOnly flag in the Set-Cookie HTTP response header, this flag is ignored, and the cookie may

```
<customErrors mode="RemoteOnly" defaultRedirect="~/errorPage.aspx"/>
<pages enableSessionState="true" validateRequest="true">
  <controls>
    <add tagPrefix="asp" namespace="System.Web.UI" assembly="System.Web
    <add tagPrefix="asp" namespace="System.Web.UI.WebControls" assembly
  </controls>
</pages>
```

Figure 4.11 *validateRequest* configuration.

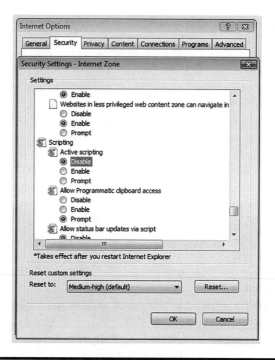

Figure 4.12 Active scripting disabled.

still be susceptible to malicious script modifications and theft. Additionally, with the prevalence in Web 2.0 technologies, primarily Asynchronous JavaScript and XML (AJAX), the XMLHTTPRequest offers read access to HTTP headers, including the Set-Cookie HTTP response header.

■ An application layer firewall can be useful against XSS attacks, but one must recognize that although this may not be preventive in nature, it is useful when the code cannot be fixed (as in the case of a third-party component).

4.6.3 Buffer Overflow

OWASP Top 10 Rank	N/A
CWE Top 25 Rank	3, 12, 14, 17, 18

Historically, one of the most dangerous and serious attacks against software has been buffer overflow attacks. To understand what constitutes a buffer overflow, it is first important that you understand how program execution and memory management work. This was covered earlier in Section 4.4.1.

A buffer overflow is the condition that occurs when data being copied into the buffer (contiguous allocated storage space in memory) are more than what the buffer can handle. This means that the length of the data being copied is equal to (in languages that need a byte for the NULL terminator) or is greater than the byte count of the buffer. The two types of buffer overflows are:

■ *Stack overflow*

A stack overflow occurs when the memory buffer has been overflowed in the stack space. When the software program runs, the executing instructions are placed on the program text segment of the RAM, global variables are placed on the read–write data section of the RAM, and the data (local variables, function arguments) and ESP register value that is necessary for the function to complete is pushed on to the stack (unless the datum is a variable sized object, in which case it is placed in the heap). As the program runs in memory, it calls each function sequentially and pushes that function's data on the stack from higher address space to lower address space, creating a chain of functions to be executed in the order the programmer intended. Upon completion of a function, that function and its associated data are popped off the stack, and the program continues to execute the next function in the chain.

But how does the program know which function it should execute and which function it should go to once the current function has completed its operation? The ESP register (introduced earlier) tells the program which function it should execute. Another special register within the CPU is the execution instruction counter (EIP), which is used to maintain the sequence order of functions and indicates the address of the next instruction to be executed. This is the return address (RET) of the function. The return address is also placed on the stack when a function is called, and the protection of the return address from being improperly overwritten is critical from a security standpoint. If a malicious user manages to overwrite the return address to point to an address space in memory, where an exploit code (also known as payload) has been injected, then upon the completion of a function, the overwritten (tainted) return address will be loaded into the EIP register, and program execution will be overflowed, potentially executing the malicious payload.

The use of unsafe functions such as strcpy() and strcat() can result in stack overflows, since they do not intrinsically perform length checks before copying data into the memory buffer.

■ *Heap overflow*

As opposed to a stack overflow, in which data flows from one buffer space into another, causing the return address instruction pointer to be overwritten, a heap overflow does not necessarily overflow, but corrupts the heap memory space (buffer), overwriting variables and function pointers on the heap. The corrupted heap memory may or may not be usable or exploitable. A heap overflow is not really an overflow, but rather a corruption of heap memory, and variable sized objects or objects too large to be pushed on the stack are dynamically allocated on the heap. Allocation of heap memory usually requires special function operators, such as malloc() (ANSI C), HeapAlloc() (Windows), and new() (C++), and deallocation of heap memory uses other special function operators, such as free(), HeapFree(), and delete(). Since no intrinsic controls on allocated memory boundaries exist, it is possible to over-write adjacent memory chunks if there is no validation of size coded by the programmer. Exploitation of the heap space requires many more requirements to be met than is the case with stack overflow. Nonetheless, heap corruption can cause serious side effects, including DoS and exploit code execution, and protection mechanisms must not be ignored.

Any one of the following reasons can be attributed to causing buffer overflows:

- Copying of data into the buffer without checking the size of input.
- Accessing the buffer with incorrect length values.
- Improper validation of array (simplest expression of a buffer) index: When proper out-of-bounds array index checks are not conducted, reference indices in array buffers that do not exist will throw an out-of-bounds exception and can potentially cause overflows.
- Integer overflows or wraparounds: When checks are not performed to ensure that numeric inputs are within the expected range (maximum and minimum values), then overflow of integers can occur, resulting in faulty calculations, infinite loops, and arbitrary code execution.
- Incorrect calculation of buffer size before its allocation: Overflows can result if the software program does not accurately calculate the size of the data that will be input into the buffer space that it is going to allocate. Without this size check, the buffer size allocated may be insufficient to handle the data being copied into it.

4.6.3.1 Buffer Overflow Controls

Regardless of what causes a buffer overflow or whether a buffer overflow is on the stack or on the heap memory buffer, the one thing common in software susceptible to overflow attacks is that the program does not perform appropriate size checks of the input data. Input size validation is the number one implementation (pro-gramming) defense against buffer overflow attacks. Double-checking buffer size to ensure that the buffer is sufficiently large enough to handle the input data copied into it, checking buffer boundaries to make sure that the functions in a loop do not attempt to write past the allocated space, and performing integer type (size, preci-sion, signed/unsigned) checks to make sure that they are within the expected range and values are other defensive implementations of controls in code.

Some programs are written to truncate the input string to a specified length before reading them into a buffer, but when this is done, careful attention must be given to ensure that the integrity of the data is not compromised.

In addition to implementation controls, there are other controls, such as requirements, architectural, build/compile, and operations controls, that can be put in place to defend against buffer overflow attacks:

- Choose a programming language that performs its own memory management and is type safe. Type safe languages are those that prevent undesirable type errors that result from operations (usually casting or conversion) on values that are not of the appropriate data type. Type safety (covered in more detail later in this chapter) is closely related to memory safety, as type unsafe languages will not prevent an arbitrary integer to be used as a pointer in memory. Ada, Perl, Java, and .Net programming languages are examples of languages that perform memory management and/or type safe. It is important, however, to recognize that the intrinsic overflow protection provided by some of these languages can be overwritten by the programmer. Also, although the language itself may be safe, the interfaces that they provide to native code can be vulnerable to various attacks. When invoking native functions from these languages, proper testing must be conducted to ensure that overflow attacks are not possible.

- Use a proven and tested library or framework that includes safer string manipulation functions, such as the Safe C String (SafeStr) library or the Safe Integer handling packages such as SafeInt (C++_ or IntegerLib (C or C++).

- Replace banned API functions that are susceptible to overflow issues with safer alternatives that perform size checks before performing their operations. It is recommended that you familiarize yourself with the banned API functions and their safer alternatives for the languages you use within your organization. When using functions that take in the number of bytes to copy as a parameter, such as the strncpy() or strncat(), one must be aware that if the destination buffer size is equal to the source buffer size, you may run into a condition where the string is not terminated because there is no place in the destination buffer to hold the NULL terminator.

- Design the software to use unsigned integers whenever possible, and when signed integers are used, make sure that checks are coded to validate both the maximum and minimum values of the range.

- Leverage compiler security if possible. Certain compilers and extensions provide overflow mitigation and protection by incorporating mechanisms to detect buffer overflows into the compiled (build) code. The Microsoft Visual Studio/ GS flag, Fedora/Red Hat FORTIFY_SOURCE GCC flag, and StackGuard (covered later in this chapter in more detail) are some examples of this.

- Leverage operating system features such as Address Space Layout Randomization (ASLR), which forces the attacker to have to guess the memory address since its layout is randomized upon each execution of the program. Another OS feature to leverage is data execution protection (DEP) or execution space protection (ESP), which perform additional checks on memory to prevent malicious code from running on a system. However, this protection can fall short when the malicious code has the ability to modify itself to seem like innocuous code. ASLR and DEP/ESP are covered in more detail later in this chapter under the memory management topic.

■ Use of memory checking tools and other tools that surround all dynamically allocated memory chunks with invalid pages so that memory cannot be over-flowed into that space is a means of defense against heap corruption. MemCheck, Memwatch, Memtest86, Valgrind, and ElectricFence are examples of such tools.

4.6.4 Broken Authentication and Session Management

OWASP Top 10 Rank	3
CWE Top 25 Rank	6, 11, 19, 21, 22

Weaknesses in authentication mechanisms and session management are not uncommon in software. Areas susceptible to these flaws are usually found in secondary functions that deal with logout, password management, time outs, remember me, secret questions, and account updates. Vulnerabilities in these areas can lead to the discovery and control of sessions. Once the attacker has control of a session (hijack) they can interject themselves in the middle, impersonating valid and legitimate users to both parties engaged in that session transaction. The man-in-the-middle (MITM) attack, as depicted in Figure 4.13, is a classic result of broken authentication and session management.

In addition to session hijacking, impersonation, and MITM attacks, these vulnerabilities can also allow an attacker to circumvent any authentication and authorization decisions that are in place. In cases when the account being hijacked is that of a privileged user, it can potentially lead to granting access to restricted resources and subsequently total system compromise.

Some of the common software programming failures that end up resulting in broken authentication and broken session management include, but are not limited to, the following:

■ Allowing more than one set of authentication or session management controls that allow access to critical resources via multiple communication channels or paths
■ Transmitting authentication credentials and session IDs over the network in cleartext

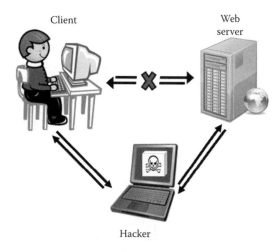

Client

Web
server

Hacker

Figure 4.13   Man-in-the-middle (MITM) attack.

- Storing authentication credentials without hashing or encrypting them
- Hard coding credentials or cryptographic keys in cleartext inline in code or in configuration files
- Not using a random or pseudo-random mechanism to generate system-generated passwords or session IDs
- Implementing weak account management functions that deal with account creation, changing passwords, or password recovery
- Exposing session IDs in the URL by rewriting the URL
- Insufficient or improper session timeouts and account logout implementation
- Not implementing transport protection or data encryption

4.6.4.1 Broken Authentication and Session Management Controls

Mitigation and prevention of authentication and session management flaws require careful planning and design. Some of the most important design considerations include:

- Built-in and proven authentication and session management mechanisms: These support the principle of leveraging existing components as well. When developers implement their custom authentication and session management mechanisms, the likelihood of programming errors are increased.
- A single and centralized authentication mechanism that supports multifactor authentication and role-based access control: Segmenting the software to provide functionality based on the privilege level (anonymous, guest, normal,

and administrator) is a preferred option. This not only eases administration and rights configuration, but it also reduces the attack surface considerably.

■ A unique, nonguessable, and random session identifier to manage state and session along with performing session integrity checks: For the credentials, do not use claims that can be easily spoofed and replayed. Some examples of these include IP address, MAC address, DNS or reverse-DNS lookups, and referrer headers. Tamper-proof, hardware-based tokens can also provide a high degree of protection.

■ When storing authentication credentials for outbound authentication, encrypt or hash the credentials before storing them in a configuration file or data store, which should also be protected from unauthorized users.

■ Do not hard code database connection strings, passwords, or cryptographic keys in cleartext in the code or configuration files. Figure 4.14 illustrates an example of insecure and secure ways of storing database connecting strings in a configuration file.

■ Identify and verify users at both the source as well as at the end of the communication channel to ensure that no malicious users have interjected themselves in between. Always authenticate users only from an encrypted source (Web page).

■ Do not expose session ID in URLs or accept preset or timed-out session identifiers from the URL or HTTP request. Accepting session IDs from the URL can lead to what are known as session fixation and session replay attacks.

■ Ensure that XSS protection mechanism are in place and working effectively, as XSS attacks can be used to steal authentication credentials and session IDs.

```
<connectionStrings>
    <add name="ContractFinConn"
    connectionString="Server=(local);uid=ContractFinUser;
    pwd=ContractFinPwd; Database=ContractFinance"
    providerName="System.Data.SqlClient" />
</connectionStrings>
```
Insecure — Cleartext

```
<connectionStrings configProtectionProvider="ConFinRSAProvider">
    <EncryptedData ...>
        <CipherData>
            <CipherValue>ZluePkgBjr8GR4DH0f9bsW7YeegeCe9MpFlpgCwHrtJukUre6sKmC6a8
            9efv00MWx0iKGhYd+/jQpvSMphy12+zvszEnBMmsR+6WNyb7xG/d6guF84VL+DKb+Z2jq
            5yFKqHpoLqjFAhAeLtv4JcOEiwFVjtkMh9Klk5GFEzGzuA=</CipherValue>
        </CipherData>
    ...
    </EncryptedData>
</connectionStrings>
```
Secure — Ciphertext

Figure 4.14   Insecure and secure ways of storing connection strings in a configuration file.

- Require the user to reauthenticate upon account update with such input as password changes, and, if feasible, generate a new session ID upon successful authentication or change in privilege level.
- Do not implement custom cookies in code to manage state. Use secure implementation of cookies by encrypting them to prevent tampering and cookie replay.
- Do not store, cache, or maintain state information on the client without appropriate integrity checking or encryption. If you are required to cache for user experience reasons, ensure that the cache is encrypted and valid only for an explicit period, after which it will expire. This is referred to as cache windowing.
- Ensure that all pages have a logout link. Do not assume that the closing of the browser window will abandon all sessions and client cookies. When the user closes the browser window, explicitly prompt the user to log off before closing the browser window. When you plan to implement user confirmation mechanisms, keep the design principle of psychological acceptability in mind: security mechanisms should not make the resource more difficult to access than if the security mechanisms were not present.
- Explicitly set a timeout, and design the software to log out of an inactive session automatically. The length of the timeout setting must be inversely proportional to the value of the data being protected. For example, if the software is marshalling and processing highly sensitive information, then the length of the timeout setting must be shorter.
- Implement the maximum number of authentication attempts allowed, and when that number has passed, deny by default and deactivate (lock) the account for a specific period or until the user follows an out-of-band process to reactivate (unlock) the account. Implementing throttle (clipping) levels prevents not only brute force attacks, but also DoS.
- Encrypt all client/server communications.
- Implement transport layer protection either at the transport layer (SSL/TLS) or at the network layer (IPSec), and encrypt data even if they are being sent over a protected network channel.

4.6.5 Insecure Direct Object References

OWASP Top 10 Rank	4
CWE Top 25 Rank	5

An insecure direct object reference flaw is one wherein an unauthorized user or process can invoke the internal functionality of the software by manipulating parameters and other object values that directly reference this functionality. Let us take

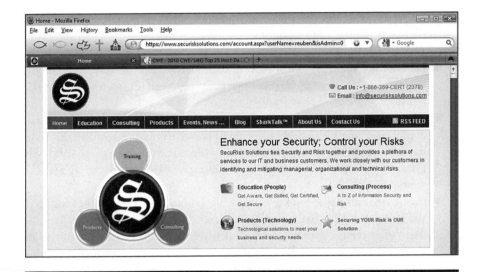

Figure 4.15   Insecure direct object reference.

a look at an example. A Web application is architected to pass the name of the logged-in user in cleartext as the value of the key "userName" and indicate whether the logged-in user is an administrator or not by passing the value to the key "isAdmin," in the querystring of the URL, as shown in Figure 4.15.

Upon load, this page reads the value of the userName key from the querystring and renders information about the user whose name was passed and displays it on the screen. It also exposes administrative menu options if the isAdmin value is 1. In our example, information about Reuben will be displayed on the screen. We also see that Reuben is not an administrator, as indicated by the value of the isAdmin key. Without proper authentication and authorization checks, an attacker can change the value of the userName key from "reuben" to "jessica" and view information about Jessica. Additionally, by manipulating the isAdmin key value from 0 to 1, a nonadministrator can get access to administrative functionality when the Web application is susceptible to an insecure direct object reference flaw.

Such flaws can be seriously detrimental to the business. Data disclosure, privilege escalation, authentication and authorization checks bypass, and restricted resource access are some of the most common impacts when this flaw is exploited. This can be exploited to conduct other types of attacks as well, including injection and scripting attacks.

4.6.5.1 Insecure Direct Object References Controls

The most effective control against insecure direct object reference attacks is to avoid exposing internal functionality of the software using a direct object reference that can be easily manipulated. The following are some defensive strategies that can be taken to accomplish this objective:

- Use indirect object reference by using an index of the value or a reference map so that direct parameter manipulation is rendered futile unless the attacker is also aware of how the parameter maps to the internal functionality.
- Do not expose internal objects directly via URLs or form parameters to the end user.
- Either mask or cryptographically protect (encrypt/hash) exposed parameters, especially querystring key value pairs.
- Validate the input (change in the object/parameter value) to ensure that the change is allowed as per the whitelist.
- Perform multiaccess control and authorization checks each and every time a parameter is changed, according to the principle of complete mediation. If a direct object reference must be used, first ensure that the user is authorized.
- Use RBAC to enforce roles at appropriate boundaries and reduce the attack surface by mapping roles with the data and functionality. This will protect against attackers who are trying to attack users with a different role (vertical authorization), but not against users who are at the same role (horizontal authorization).
- Ensure that both context- and content-based RBAC is in place.

Manual code reviews and parameter manipulation testing can be used to detect and address insecure direct object reference flaws. Automated tools often fall short of detecting insecure direct object reference because they are not aware of what object requires protection and what the safe or unsafe values are.

4.6.6 Cross-Site Request Forgery (CSRF)

OWASP Top 10 Rank	5
CWE Top 25 Rank	4

Although the cross-site request forgery (CSRF) attack is unique in the sense that it requires a user to be already authenticated to a site and possess the authentication token, its impact can be devastating and is rightfully classified within the top five application security attacks in both the OWASP Top 10 and the CWE/SANS Top 25. The most popular Web sites, such as ING Direct, NYTimes.com, and YouTube have been proven to be susceptible to this.

In CSRF, an attacker masquerades (forges) a malicious HTTP request as a legitimate one and tricks the victim into submitting that request. Because most browsers automatically include HTTP requests, that is, the credentials associated with the site (e.g., user session cookies, basic authentication information, source

IP addresses, windows domain credentials), if the user is already authenticated, the attack will succeed. These forged requests can be submitted using email links, zero-byte image tags (images whose height and width are both 0 pixel each so that the image is invisible to the human eye), tags stored in an iFrames (stored CSRF), URLs susceptible to clickjacking (where the URL is hijacked, and clicking on an URL that seems innocuous and legitimate actually results in clicking on the malicious URL that is hidden beneath), and XSS redirects. Forms that invoke state changing function are the prime targets for CSRF. CSRF is also known by a number of other names, including XSRF, Session riding attack, sea surf attack, hostile linking, and automation attack.

The attack flow in a CSRF attack is as follows:

1. User authenticates into a legitimate Web site and receives the authentication token associated with that site.
2. User is tricked into clicking a link that has a forged malicious HTTP request to be performed against the site to which the user is already authenticated.
3. Since the browser sends the malicious HTTP request, the authentication credentials, this request surfs or rides on top of the authenticated token and performs the action as if it were a legitimate action requested by the user (now the victim).

Although a preauthenticated token is necessary for this attack to succeed, the hostile actions and damage that can be caused from CSRF attacks can be extremely perilous, limited only to what the victim is already authorized to do. Authentication bypass, identity compromise, and phishing are just a few examples of impact from successful CSRF attacks. If the user is a privileged user, then total system compromise is a possibility. When CSRF is combined with XSS, the impact can be extensive. XSS worms that propagate and impact several Web sites within a short period usually have a CSRF attack fueling them. CSRF potency is further augmented by the fact that the forced hostile actions appear as legitimate actions (since they come with an authenticated token) and thereby may go totally undetected. The OWASP CSRF Tester tool can be used to generate test cases to demonstrate the dangers of CSRF flaws.

4.6.6.1 CSRF Controls

The best defense against CSRF is to implement the software so that it is not dependent on the authenticated credentials automatically submitted by the browser. Controls can be broadly classified into user controls and developer controls.

The following are some defensive strategies that can be employed by *users* to prevent and mitigate CSRF attacks:

- Do not save username/password in the browser.
- Do not check the "remember me" option in Web sites.

■ Do not use the same browser to surf the Internet and access sensitive Web sites at the same time, if you are accessing both from the same machine.

■ Read standard emails in plain text. Viewing emails in plain text format shows the user the actual link that the user is being tricked to click on by rendering the embedded malicious HTML links into the actual textual link. Figure 4.16 depicts how a phishing email is shown to a potential victim when the email client is configured to read email in HTML format and in plain text format.

■ Explicitly log off after using a Web application.

■ Use client-side browser extensions that mitigate CSRF attacks. An example of this is the CSRF Protector, which is a client-side add-on extension for the Mozilla Firefox browser.

The following are some defensive strategies that can be used by *developers* to prevent and mitigate CSRF attacks:

■ The most effective developer defensive control against CSRF is to implement the software to use a unique session-specific token (called a nonce) that is generated in a random, nonpredictable, nonguessable, and/or sequential manner. Such tokens need to be unique by function, page, or overall session.

■ CAPTCHAs (Completely Automated Public Turing Test to Tell Computers and Humans Apart) can be used to establish specific token identifiers per session. CAPTCHAs do not provide a foolproof defense, but they increase the work factor of an attacker and prevent automated execution of scripts that can exploit CSRF vulnerabilities.

■ The uniqueness of session tokens is to be validated on the server side and not be solely dependent on client-based validation.

■ Use POST methods instead of GET requests for sensitive data transactions and privileged and state change transactions, along with randomized session identifier generation and usage.

HTML enabled email

Plain text email

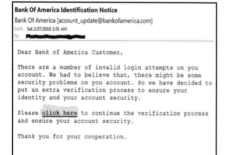

Figure 4.16 **Reading emails in plain text.**

- Use a double-submitted cookie. When a user visits a site, the site first generates a cryptographically strong pseudorandom value and sets it as a cookie on the user's machine. Any subsequent request from the site should include this pseudorandom value as a form value and also as a cookie value, and when the POST request is validated on the server side, it should consider the request valid if and only if the form value and the cookie value are the same. Since an attacker can modify form values but not cookie values as per the same-origin policy, an attacker will not be able to submit a form successfully unless she is able to guess the pseudorandom value.

- Check the URL referrer tag for the origin of request before processing the request. However, when this method is implemented, it is important to ensure that legitimate actions are not impacted. If the users or proxies have disabled sending the referrer information for privacy reasons, legitimate functionality can be denied. Also, it is possible to spoof referrer information using XSS, so this defense must be in conjunction with other developer controls as part of a defense in depth strategy.

- For sensitive transactions, reauthenticate each and every time (as per the principle of complete mediation).

- Use transaction signing to assure that the request is genuine.

- Build in automated logout functionality based on a period of inactivity, and log the user out when that timeframe elapses.

- Leverage industry tools that aid with CSRF defense. OWASP CSRF Guard and the OWASP ESAPI session management control provide anti-CSRF packages that can be used for generating, passing, and using a unique token per session. Code Igniter, a server-side plugin for the PHP MVC framework, is another well-known example of a tool that offers CSRF protection.

- Mitigate XSS vulnerabilities, as most CSRF defenses can be circumvented using attacker-controlled scripts.

4.6.7 Security Misconfiguration

OWASP Top 10 Rank	6
CWE Top 25 Rank	11, 20, 21

In addition to applying security updates and other updates to the operating system, it is critically important to harden the applications and software that run on top of these operating systems. Hardening software applications involves determining the necessary and correct configuration settings and architecting the software to be secure by default. We discuss software hardening in more detail in Chapter 7. In this chapter, we will primarily learn about the security misconfigurations that can render software susceptible to attack. These misconfigurations can occur at any level of the software stack and lead from data disclosure directly or, through an error message, to total system compromise.

Some of the common examples of security misconfigurations include:

- Hard coding credentials and cryptographic keys inline in code or in configuration files in cleartext.
- Not disabling the listing of directories and files in a Web server.
- Installation of software with default accounts and settings.
- Installation of the administrative console with default configuration settings.
- Installation or configuration of unneeded services, ports and protocols, unused pages, and unprotected files and directories.
- Missing software patches.
- Lack of perimeter and host defensive controls such as firewalls and filters.

4.6.7.1 Security Misconfiguration Controls

Effective controls against security misconfiguration issues include elements that design, develop, deploy, operate, maintain, and dispose of software in a reliable, resilient, and recoverable manner. The primary recommendations include:

- Installing software without the default configuration settings.
- Cryptographically protecting credentials and keys and not hard coding them inline in code.
- Removing any unneeded or unnecessary services and processes.
- Establishing and maintaining a configuration of the minimum level of acceptable security. This is referred to as the minimum security baseline (MSB).
- Establishing a process that hardens (locks down) the OS and the applications that run on top of it. Preferably, this should be an automated process using the established MSB to assure that there are no user errors.
- Handling errors explicitly using redirects and error messages so that a breach upon any misconfiguration does not result in the disclosure of more information than is necessary.
- Establishing a controlled patching process.
- Establishing a scanning process to detect and report automatically on software and systems that are not compliant to the established MSB.

4.6.8 Failure to Restrict URL Access

OWASP Top 10 Rank	7
CWE Top 25 Rank	5

One of the most easily exploitable weaknesses in Web applications is the failure to restrict URL access. In some cases, URL protection is provided and managed using configuration setting and code checks. In most cases, the only protection the software affords is not presenting the URL of the page to an unauthorized user. This kind of security by obscurity offers little to no protection against a determined and skilled attacker who can guess and/or forcefully browse to these URL locations and access unauthorized functionality. Furthermore, guessing of URLs is made easier if the URL naming pattern or scheme is predictable, defaulted, and/or left unchanged. Even if the URL is hidden and never displayed to an unauthorized user, without process authentication and access control checks, hidden URLs can be disclosed and their page functions invoked. Web pages that provide administrative functionality are the primary targets for this attack, but any page can be exploited if not protected properly. It is therefore imperative to verify the protection (authentication and authorization checks) of each and every URL, but this can be a daunting task when performed manually if the Web application has many pages.

4.6.8.1 Failure to Restrict URL Access Controls

RBAC of URLs that denies access by default, requiring explicit grants to users and roles, provides some degree of mitigation against the failure to restrict URL access attacks. In situations where the software is architected to accept a URL as a parameter before granting access (as in the case of checking the origin of referrer), the point at which the access control check is performed needs to be carefully implemented as well. Access control checks must be performed after the URL is decoded and canonicalized into the standard form. Obfuscation of URLs provides some defense against attackers who attempt forced browsing by guessing the URL. Additionally in cases where the Web page displays are based on a workflow, make sure that before the page is served to be displayed, proper checks for not just the authorization, but also state conditions are met. Whitelisting valid URLs and validating library files that are referenced from these URLs are other recommended prevention and mitigation controls. Do not cache Web pages containing sensitive information, and when these pages are requested, make sure to check that the authentication credentials and access rights of the user requesting access are checked and validated before serving the Web page. Authorization frameworks, such as the JAAS authorization framework and the OWASP ESAPI, can be leveraged.

4.6.9 Unvalidated Redirects and Forwards

OWASP Top 10 Rank	8
CWE Top 25 Rank	23

```
<html>
<head>
<script language="Javascript">
   document.location.href="http://www.isc2.org/csslp"
</script>
</head>
<body>
   Welcome ...
</body>
</html>
```

Figure 4.17 Changing document location using JavaScript.

Redirection and forwarding users from one location (page) to another either explicitly on the client or internally on the server side (also known as transfer) is not uncommon in applications. Redirecting usually targets external links while forwarding targets' internal pages. Scripts can also be used to redirect users from one document location to another, as depicted in Figure 4.17.

In situations where the target URL is supplied as an unvalidated parameter, an attacker can specify a malicious URL hosted in an external site and redirect users to that site. When an attacker redirects victims to an untrusted site, it is also referred to as open redirects. Once the victim lands on the malicious page, the attacker can phish for sensitive and personal information. They can also install malware automatically or by tricking users into clicking on masqueraded installation links. These unvalidated redirects and forwards can also be used by an attacker to bypass security controls and checks.

Detecting whether the application is susceptible to unvalidated redirects or forwards can be made possible by performing a code review and making sure that the target URL is a valid and legitimate one. A server responds to a client's request by sending an HTTP response message that includes in its status line the protocol version, a success or error code, and a reason (textual phrase), followed by header fields that contain server information, metadata information (resource, payload), and an empty line to indicate the end of the header section and the payload body (if present). Looking at the HTTP response codes by manually invoking the server to respond or by spidering the Web site, one can determine redirects and forwards. The 3XX series HTTP response codes (300-307) deal with redirection. Appendix D briefly introduces and lists the HTTP/1.1 status codes and reason phrases.

4.6.9.1 Unvalidated Redirects and Forwards Controls

Some of the common controls against unvalidated redirects and forwards include:

- Avoiding redirects and forwards (transfers) if possible.
- Using a whitelist target URLS that a user can be redirected to.
- Not allowing the user to specify the target (destination) URL as a parameter. If you are required to for business reasons, validate the target URL parameter before processing it.

- Using an index value to map to the target URL and using that mapped value as the parameter. This way the actual URL or portions of the URL are not disclosed to the attacker.
- Architecting the software to inform the user using an intermediate page, especially if the user is being redirected to an external site that is not in your control. This intermediate page should clearly inform and warn the user that they are leaving your site. It is preferable to prompt the user modally before redirecting them to the external site.
- Mitigating script attack vulnerabilities that can be used to change document location.

4.6.10 Insecure Cryptographic Storage

OWASP Top 10 Rank	9
CWE Top 25 Rank	10, 24

The impact of cryptographic vulnerabilities can be extremely serious and disastrous to the business, ranging from disclosure of data that brings with it fines and oversight (regulatory and compliance) to identity theft of customers, reputational damage, and, in some cases, complete bankruptcy. When it comes to protecting information cryptographically, the predominant flaw in software is the lack of encryption of sensitive data. Even when it is, there are often other design and implementation weaknesses that plague the software. Insecure cryptographic vulnerabilities are primarily comprised of the following:

- The use of a weak or custom-developed unvalidated cryptographic algorithm for encryption and decryption needs.
- The use of older cryptographic APIs.
- Insecure and improper key management comprised of unsafe key generation, unprotected key exchange, improper key rotation, unprotected key archival and key escrow, improper key destruction, and inadequate and improper protection measures to ensure the secrecy of the cryptographic key when it is stored. A common example is storing the cryptographic key along with the data in a backup tape.
- Inadequate and improper storage of the data (data at rest) that need to be cryptographically secure. Storing the sensitive data in plaintext or as unsalted ciphertext (which can be bruteforced) are examples of this.
- Insufficient access control that gives users direct access to unencrypted data or to cryptographic functions that can decrypt ciphertext and/or to the database where sensitive and private information is stored.

- Violation of least privilege, giving users elevated privileges allowing them to perform unauthorized operations and lack of auditing of cryptographic operations.

Not encrypting data that are being transmitted (*data in motion*) is a major issue, but securing stored data (*data at rest*) against cryptographic vulnerabilities is an equally daunting challenge. In many cases, the efforts to protect data in motion are negated when the data at rest protection mechanisms are inadequate or insecure. Attackers typically go after weaknesses that are the easiest to break. When data that need to be cryptographically secure are stored as plaintext, the work factor for an attacker to gain access to and view sensitive information is virtually nonexistent, as they do not have the need to break the cryptography algorithm or determine the key needed to decrypt. When cryptographic keys are not stored securely, the work factor for the attacker is a little more, but it is still considerably reduced, as they now do not have to break the cryptography algorithm itself, but can find and use the keys to decrypt ciphertext to cleartext leading to disclosure that impacts the confidentiality tenet of security.

4.6.10.1 Insecure Cryptographic Storage Controls

Prevention and mitigation techniques to address insecure cryptographic storage issues can be broadly classified into the following:

- Data at rest protection controls
- Appropriate algorithm usage
- Secure key management
- Adequate access control and auditing

Data at rest protection controls include the following:

- Encrypting and storing the sensitive data as ciphertext, at the onset.
- Storing salted ciphertext versions of the data to mitigate bruteforce cryptanalysis attacks.
- Not allowing data that are deemed sensitive to cross trust boundaries from safe zones into unsafe zones (as determined by the threat model).
- Separating sensitive from nonsensitive data (if feasible) by using naming conventions and strong types. This makes it easier to detect code segments where data used are unencrypted when they need to be.

Appropriate algorithm usage means that:

- The algorithm used for encryption and decryption purposes is not custom developed.

■ The algorithm used for encryption and decryption purposes is a standard (such as the AES) and not one historically proven weak (such as DES). AES is comprised of three block ciphers, each with a block size of 128 bits and key sizes of 128, 192, 256 bits (AES-128, AES-192, and AES-256), which are adopted from a larger collection originally published as Rijndael. A common implementation of AES in code is to use the RijndaelManaged class, but it must be understood that the use of the RijndaelManaged class does not necessarily make one compliant to the FIPS-197 specification for AES unless the block size and feedback size (when using the Cipher Feedback (CFB) mode) in both is 128 bits.

■ Older cryptography APIs (CryptoAPI) are not used and are replaced with the Cryptography API Next Generation (CNG). CNG is intended to be used by developers to provide secure data creation and exchange over nonsecure environments, such as the Internet, and is extremely extensible because of its cryptography agnostic nature. It is recommended that the CSSLP be familiar with CNG features and its implementation.

■ The design of the software takes into account the ability to swap cryptographic algorithms quickly as needed. Cryptographic algorithms that were considered to be strong in the past have been proven to be ineffective in today's computing world, and without the ability to swap these algorithms in code quickly, downtime impacting the availability tenet of security can be expected.

Secure key management means that the

■ Generation of the key uses a random or pseudo random number generator (RNG or PRNG) and is random or pseudo-random in nature.

■ Exchange of keys is done securely using out-of-band mechanisms or approved key infrastructure that is secure as well.

■ Storage of keys is protected, preferably in a system that is not the same as that of the data, whether it is the transactional system or the backup system.

■ Rotation of the key, where the old key is replaced by a new key, follows the appropriate process of first decrypting data with the old key and then encrypting data with the new key. Not following this process sequentially has been proven to cause a DoS, especially in archived data, because data that were encrypted with an older key cannot be decrypted by the new key.

■ Archival and escrowing of the key is protected with appropriate access control mechanisms and preferably not archived in the same system as the one that contains the encrypted data archives. When keys are escrowed, it is important to maintain the different versions of keys.

■ Destruction of keys ensures that once the key is destroyed, it will never again be used. It is critically important to ensure that all data that were encrypted using the key that is to be destroyed are decrypted before the key is permanently destroyed.

Adequate access control and auditing means that for both internal and external users, access to the cryptography keys and data is

- Granted explicitly.
- Controlled and monitored using auditing and periodic reviews.
- Not inadvertently thwarted by weaknesses, such as insecure permissions configurations.
- Contextually appropriate and protected, regardless of whether the encryption is one-way or two-way. One-way encryption context implies that only the user or recipient needs to have access to the key, as in the case of PKI. Two-way encryption context implies that the encryption can be automatically performed on behalf of the user, but the key must be available so that plaintext can be automatically recoverable by that user.

4.6.11 Insufficient Transport Layer Protection

OWASP Top 10 Rank	10
CWE Top 25 Rank	10

It was mentioned earlier that cryptographic protection of data in motion is important, but this is only one of the means of protecting transmitted information. Monitoring network traffic using a passive sniffer is a common means by which attackers steal information.

Leveraging transport layer (SSL/TLS) and/or network layer (IPSec) security technologies augments security protection of network traffic. It is insufficient merely to use SSL/TLS just during the authentication process, as is observed to be the case with most software/applications. When a user is authenticated to a Web site over an encrypted channel, e.g., https://www.mybank.com, and then either inadvertently or intentionally goes to its clear text link, e.g., http://www.mybank.com, with little effort, the session cookie can now be observed by an attacker who is monitoring the network. This is referred to as the surf jacking attack. Lack of or insufficient transport layer protection often results in a confidentiality breach's disclosing data. Phishing attacks are known to take advantage of this. It can result in session hijacking and replay attacks as well, once the authenticated victim's session cookie is determined by the attacker.

Transport layer protection, such as SSL, can mitigate disclosure of sensitive information when the data are being traversed on the wire, but this type of protection does not completely prevent MITM attacks unless the protection is end-to-end. In the case of 3-tier Web architecture, transport layer protection needs to be from the client to the Web server and from the Web server to the database server. Failure to have end-to-end transport layer protection, as shown in Figure 4.18, can lead to MITM and disclosure attacks.

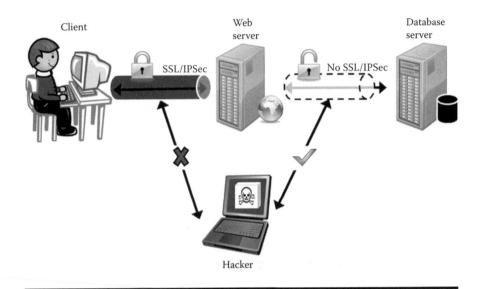

Figure 4.18   Importance of end-to-end transport layer protection.

Additionally, when digital certificates are used to assure confidentiality, integrity, authenticity, and nonrepudiation, they should be protected, properly configured, and not set to expire so that they are not spoofed. When certificates are spoofed, MITM and phishing attacks are common. It is noteworthy to discuss in this context that improper configuration of certificates or using expired certificates cause the browser to warn the end user, but with the user's familiarity with accepting browser warning prompts without really reading what they are accepting, this browser protection mechanism is rendered weak or futile. User education not to accept expired or lookalike certificates and browser warning prompts can come in handy to change this behavior and augment software security.

4.6.11.1 Insufficient Transport Layer Protection Controls

The following are some of the common preventative and mitigation recommendations against insufficient transport layer protection attacks:

■ Provide end-to-end channel security protecting the channel using SSL/TLS or IPSec.
■ Avoid using Mixed SSL when certain pages are protected using SSL while others are not because this can lead to the disclosure of session cookies from the unprotected pages. Redirect non-SSL pages to SSL ones.
■ Ensure that the session cookie's secure flag is set. This causes the browser cookie to be sent only over encrypted channels (HTTPS and not HTTP) mitigating surf jacking attacks.

- Provide cryptographic protection of data in motion and vetted and proven cryptographic algorithms or hashing functions compliant with FIPS 140-2 for cryptographic protection needs.
- Use unexpired and unrevoked digital certificates.
- Provide proper configuration of digital certificates. Educate users not to overlook warning prompts or accept lookalike certificates and phishing prompts.

It is important to note that, although it may seem that secure communications (using SSL/TLS or IPSec) is the most effective defense against insufficient transport layer protection attacks, a simple misconfiguration or partial implementation can render all other protection mechanisms ineffective. The best defense against these types of attacks is cryptographic protection of data (encryption or hashing) so that regardless of whether the data are being marshaled over secure communication channels or not, they are still protected.

4.6.12 *Information Leakage and Improper Error Handling*

OWASP Top 10 Rank (2007)	6
CWE Top 25 Rank	10, 11, 15, 16, 24

Without appropriate confidentiality controls in place, software can leak information about its configuration, state, and internal makeup that an attacker can use to steal information or launch further attacks. Because attackers usually have the benefit of time and can choose to attack at will, they usually spend a majority of their time in reconnaissance activities gleaning information about the software itself.

Phishing, a method of tricking users into submitting their personal information using electronic means such as deceptive emails and Web sites, is on the rise. The term "phishing" is believed to have its roots from the use of sophisticated electronic lures to fish out a victim's personal (e.g., financial, login, passwords) information. This form of electronic social engineering is so rampant in today's business computing that even large organizations have fallen prey to it. Although these sophisticated electronic lures usually target users *en masse,* they can also target a single individual, and when this is the case, it is commonly referred to as "spear phishing." With the sophistication of such deceptive attacks to disclose information, attackers have come up with a variant of phishing, called pharming, which is a scamming practice in which malicious code is installed on a system or server that misdirects users to fraudulent Web sites without the user's knowledge or consent. It is also referred to as "phishing without a lure." Unlike phishing, wherein individual users who receive the phishing lure (usually in the form of an email) are targets, in pharming a large number of users can be victimized as the attack does not require individual user actions, but rather systems that can be compromised. Pharming often works by modification of the local system host files that redirect users to a fraudulent Web site even if the user types in the correct Web address. Another popular way in which Pharming works, which is even more dangerous, is known as domain name system (DNS) poisoning. In the DNS poisoning pharming attack, the DNS table in the server is altered to point to fraudulent Web sites even when requests to legitimate ones are made. With DNS poisoning, there is no need to alter individual user's local system host files because the modification (exploit) is made on the server side, and all those who request resources from that server will now be potential victims without their knowledge or consent. Disclosure of personal information is often the result, and in some cases this escalates to identity theft. With Voice over IP (VoIP) telephony on the rise, phishing attacks have a new variant called vishing, which is made up of two words, "voice" and "phishing." This is the criminal fradulent activity in which an attacker steals sensitive information using deceptive social engineering techniques on VoIP networks.

The prime target for a phisher/pharmer is not a weakness in technology, but human trust. Secondarily exploitable weaknesses, such as no proper ACLs to host systems and servers, lack of spyware protection that can modify settings, and weaknesses in software code, can also result in significant information disclosure. Phishers and pharmers attempt to exploit these weaknesses to masquerade and execute their phishing/pharming scams.

Sources of information leakage include but are not limited to the following:

- Browser history
- Cache
- Backup and unreferenced files
- Log files
- Configuration files
- Comments in code
- Error messages

Browser history can be stolen using cascading style sheet (CSS) hacks with or without using JavaScript or by techniques called browser caching. Information about sites that a user has visited can be stolen from a user. Although caches can be used to improve performance and user experience significantly, sensitive information, if cached, can be disclosed, breaching confidentiality. Attackers usually look for backup and unreferenced files, log files, and configuration files that inadvertently get deployed or installed on the system. These files can potentially have sensitive information that comes in very handy for an attacker as they attempt to exploit the software. Developers usually do not like to document their code, and when instrumenting (inline commenting) of code is done without proper education and training, these comments in code can reveal more sensitive information than is

```
/// <summary>
/// Establishes the connection to the database
/// </summary>
/// <param name="p_sServerName">Name of the database server.
/// Use HAMMERHEAD for Test and GREATWHITE for Production.
/// </param>
/// <param name="p_sLoginAccount">Name of the database login account.
/// Use Sally for Test and McQueen for Production.
/// </param>
/// <param name="p_sPassword">The password for the database login account.
/// Use Doc for Test and Mater for Production.
/// </param>
/// <param name="p_sDatabaseName">Name of the database to connect to.
/// Use PIXAR for Test and DREAMWORKS for Production.
/// </param>
private void BuildConnection(string p_sServerName,
    string p_sLoginAccount,
    string p_sPassword,
    string p_sDatabaseName)
{
    StringBuilder _oSBConnection = new StringBuilder();
    _oSBConnection.Append("Server=" + p_sServerName + ";");
    _oSBConnection.Append("uid=" + p_sLoginAccount + ";");
    _oSBConnection.Append("pwd=" + p_sPassword + ";");
    _oSBConnection.Append("Database=" + p_sDatabaseName + ";");

    SqlConnection _oSqlConn = new SqlConnection(_oSBConnection.ToString());
    _oSqlConn.Open();
}
```

Figure 4.19   Sensitive information in comments.

necessary. Some examples of sensitive information in comments include database connection strings, validation routines, production and test data, production and test accounts, and business logic. Figure 4.19 depicts an example of code that has sensitive information in its comments.

Error messages are one of the first sources an attacker will look at to determine the information about the software. Without proper handling of input and the response generated from that input in the form of an exception or error message, sensitive information can be leaked. Input validation and output error handling can be regarded as two of the most basic and effective protection mechanisms that can be used to mitigate a lot of software attacks. Figure 4.20 discloses how an unhandled exception reveals a lot of sensitive information, including the internal makeup of the software.

4.6.12.1 Information Leakage and Improper Error Handling Controls

To mitigate and prevent information leakage and improper error handling issues, it is important that proper security controls are designed and implemented, such as those listed below.

■ Use private browsing mode in browsers and other plugins or extensions that do not cache the visited pages. Configure the browsers not to save history and clear all page visits upon closing the browser.

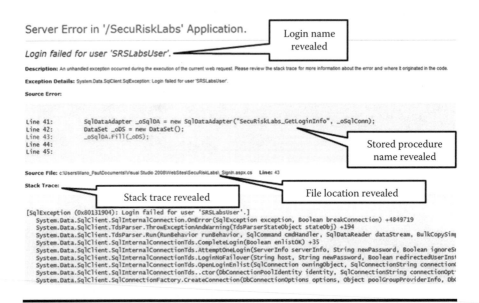

Figure 4.20 Improper error and exception handling.

- Encrypt the cache and/or explicitly set cache timeouts (sometimes referred to as cache windows).
- Do not deploy backup files to production systems. For disaster recovery purposes, sometimes the backup file is deployed by renaming the file extension to a .bak or a .old extension. Attackers can guess and forcefully browse these files, and without proper access controls in place, information in these files can be potentially disclosed.
- Harden servers so that their log files are protected.
- Remove installation scripts and change logs from production systems and store them in a nonproduction environment if they are not required for the software to function.
- Comment your code to explain what the code does, preferably for each function, but do not reveal any sensitive or specific information. Code review must not ignore the reviewing of comments in code.
- Validate all input to prevent an attacker from forcing an error by using an input (e.g., type, value, range, length) that the software is not expecting.
- Use concise error messages with just the needed information. System-generated errors with stack information and code paths must be abstracted into generic user friendly error messages that are laconic, with just the needed information.
- Handle all exceptions preferably with a common approach.
- Use an index of the value or reference map. An example of using indices would be to use an Error Globally Unique Identifier (GUID) that maps to

the internal error, but it is the GUID alone that is displayed to the user, informing the user to contact the support line for more assistance. This way, the internal error details are not directly revealed to the end user or to the attacker, who could be using them in their reconnaissance efforts as they plan to launch other attacks.

■ Redirect errors and exceptions to a custom and default error handling location, and, depending on the context of where the user has logged in (remote or local), appropriate message details can be displayed.

■ Leverage static code analysis tools to search for APIs that are known to leak information.

■ Remember that user awareness and education are the best defense against phishing and pharming electronic social engineering scams. Additionally, SPAM control, disabling of links in emails and instant messaging (IM) clients, viewing emails in non-HTML format, transport layer protection (SSL/TLS), phishing filter plugins, and offensive strategies, such as dilution and takedown, are other safeguards and countermeasures against phishing and pharming attacks. Dilution, also known as "spoofback," is sending bogus and faulty information to the phisher with the intent to dilute the real information that the attacker is soliciting. Takedown, on the other hand, involves actively bringing down the phishing/pharming Web site as a means to contain the exposure, but this must be down with proper legal guidance.

4.6.13 File Attacks

Attacks against software are also prevalent when data are exchanged in files. In this section, we will cover some of the most common attacks that involve files. These attacks include malicious file execution, path traversals, improper file includes, and download of code without integrity checks.

■ *Malicious File Execution*

OWASP Top 10 Rank (2007)	3
CWE Top 25 Rank	7, 8, 13, 20

When software is designed and implemented to accept files as input, unvalidated and unrestricted file uploads could lead to serious compromises of the security state of the software. Any feature in software that uses external object references (e.g., URLs and file system references) and which allow the upload of images (e.g., .gif, .jpg, .png), documents (e.g., .docx, .xlsx, .pdf) and other files are potential sources of attack vectors. Insufficient and improper validation can lead to arbitrary remote and hostile code upload, invocation and execution, rootkit installations, and complete system compromise. All

Web application frameworks are susceptible to malicious file execution if they accept filenames or files from users.

Malicious file execution attacks can occur in any of the following ways:

- Accepting user-supplied file names and files without validating them
- Not restricting files to nonexecutable types
- Uploading hostile data to the file system via image uploads
- Using compression or audio streams (e.g., zlib:// or ogg://) that allow the access of remote resources without the inspection of internal flags and settings
- Using input and data wrappers (e.g., php://input) that accept input from the request POST data instead of a file
- Using hostile document type definitions (DTDs) that force the XML parser to load a remote DTD and parse and process the results

■ *Path Traversals*

In situations where the software is architected to accept path names and directory locations from the end user without proper security controls, attackers can exploit weaknesses that allow them to traverse from the intended file paths to unintended directories and files in the system. Software susceptible to attacks using canonicalization of file paths such as using ".." or similar sequences are known to fall prey frequently to path traversal attacks.

■ Improper File Includes

Although file attacks are not limited to any one kind of programming language, programming languages such as PHP that allow remote file includes (RFI), where the file name can be built by concatenating user-supplied input using file or streams-based API, are particularly vulnerable. Breaking the software into smaller parts of a program (document) and then combining them into one big program (document) is a common way to build a program. When the location of the smaller parts of the program is user-defined and can be influenced by an end user, an attacker can point to locations with remote and dangerous files and exploit the software.

■ Download of Code without Integrity Checks

When you download code (or files) without checking if the code is altered, it can lead to very serious security breaches and repercussions. An attacker can modify code before you download it. Even locations (sites) that hold files that you trust and download can be attacked and impersonated using DNS spoofing or cache poisoning, redirecting users to attacker locations. This is particularly important when software updates are published using files from trusted locations. Downloading code and files without integrity checks can lead to the download of files that have been maliciously altered by an attacker.

4.6.13.1 File Attacks Controls

Automated scanning can be used to determine sections in code that accept file names and file paths, but are not very efficient in identifying the legitimacy of parameters that are used in file includes. Static analysis tools can be useful in determining banned APIs, but they cannot ensure that appropriate validation is in place. Manual code review is recommended to search for file attack vulnerabilities.

Controls that prevent and mitigate file attacks are necessary to ensure that software security is assured when dealing with files and their associated properties.

The following are recommended controls against malicious file execution attacks:

- Use a whitelist of allowable file extensions. Ensure that the check for the valid list of file names takes into account the case sensitivity of the file name.
- Allow only one extension to a file name. For example, "myfile.exe.png" should not be allowed.
- Use an indirect object reference map and/or an index for file names. Cryptographically protecting the internal file name by salting and hashing the file name can prevent bruteforce discovery of file names.
- Explicitly taint check. Taint checking is a feature in some programming languages, such as Perl and Ruby, which protects against malicious file execution attacks. Assuming that all values supplied by the user can be potentially modified and untrusted, each variable that holds values supplied by an external user is checked to see if the variable has been tainted by an attacker to execute dangerous commands.
- Automatically generate a filename instead of using the user-supplied one.
- Upload the files to a hardened staging environment and inspect the binaries before processing them. Inspection should cover more than just file type, size, MIME content type, or filename attribute, so also inspect the file contents as attackers can hide code in some file segments that will be executed.
- Isolate applications using virtualization or other sandboxing mechanisms, such as chroot jail in Unix.
- Avoid using file functions and streams-based APIs to construct filenames.
- Configure the application to demand appropriate file permissions. Using the Java Security Manager and the ASP.Net partial trust implementations can be leveraged to provide file permissions security.

The following are recommended controls against path traversal attacks:

- Use a whitelist to validate acceptable file paths and locations.
- Limit character sets before accepting files for processing. Examples include allowing a single "." character in the filename and disallowing directory separators such as "/" to mitigate path traversal attacks.

■ Harden the servers by configuring them not to allow directory browsing or contents.

■ Decode once and canonical file paths to internal representation so that dangerous inputs are not introduced after the checks are performed. Use built-in canonicalization functions that canonicalize pathname by removing ".." sequences and symbolic links. Examples include realpath() (C, Perl, PHP), getCanonicalPath (Java), GetFullPath() (ASP.Net), and abs_path() (Perl).

■ Use a mapping of generic values to represent known internal actual file names and reject any values not configured explicitly.

■ Run code using least privilege and isolated accounts with minimal rights in a sandbox (jail) that restricts access to other system resources. The Unix chroot jail, AppArmor, and SELinux are examples of OS-level sandboxing.

The following are recommended controls against improper file includes attacks:

■ Store library, include, and utility files outside of the root or system directories. Using a constant in a calling program and checking for its existence in the library or include file is a common practice to identify files that are approved or are not.

■ Restrict access to files within a specified directory.

■ Run code using least privilege and isolated accounts with minimal rights, in a sandbox (jail) that restricts access to other system resources. The Unix chroot jail, AppArmor, and SELinux are examples of OS-level sandboxing.

■ Limit the ability to include files from remote locations.

The following are recommended controls against download of code without integrity check attacks:

■ Use integrity checking on code downloaded from remote locations. Examples include hashing, code signing, and Authenticode technologies. These can be used cryptographically to validate the authenticity of the code publisher and the integrity of the code itself. Hashing the code before it is downloaded and validating the hash value before processing the code can be used to determine whether the code has been altered.

■ To detect DNS spoofing attacks, perform both forward and reverse DNS lookups. When this is used, be advised that this is only a partial solution as it will not prevent the tampering of code on the hosting site or when it is in transit.

■ When source code is not developed by you or not available, the use of monitoring tools to examine the software's interaction with the OS and the network can be used to detect code integrity issues. Some examples of common tools include process debuggers, system call tracing utilities, and system and process activity monitors (file monitors, registry monitors, system internals), sniffers, and protocol analyzers.

4.6.14 Race Condition

OWASP Top 10 Rank	Not specified
CWE Top 25 Rank	25

In Chapter 2, we learned about what a race condition is, its properties (concurrency, shared object, change state), how it occurs, and defensive controls (avoid race windows, atomic operations, and mutual exclusions) that need to be identified as part of the requirements.

Attackers deliberately look for race conditions because they are often missed in general testing and exploit them, resulting in sometimes very serious consequences that range from DoS (deadlocks) to data integrity issues and in some cases total compromise and control. Easy to introduce but difficult to debug and troubleshoot, race conditions can occur anywhere in the code (e.g., local or global state variables, security logic) and in any level of code (source code, assembly code, or object code). They can occur within multiple threads, processes, and systems as well.

4.6.14.1 Race Condition Controls

Design and implementation controls against race conditions include

- Identifying and eliminating race windows
- Performing atomic operations on shared resources
- Using Mutex operations
- Selectively using synchronization primitives around critical code sections to avoid performance issues
- Using multithreading and thread-safe capabilities and functions and abstractions on shared variables.
- Minimizing the usage of shared resources and critical sections that can be repeatedly triggered
- Disabling interrupts or signals over critical code sections
- Avoiding infinite loop constructs
- Implementing the principle of economy of mechanisms, keeping the design and implementation simple, so that there are no circular dependencies between components or code sections
- Implementing error and exception handling to avoid disclosure of critical code sections and their operations

■ Performing performance testing (load and stress testing) to ensure that software can reliably perform under heavy load and simultaneous resource requests conditions

4.6.15 Side Channel Attacks

OWASP Top 10 Rank	Not specified
CWE Top 25 Rank	Not specified

Although not listed as one of the top 10 or top 25 issues plaguing software, side channel attacks are an important class of attacks that can render the security protection effectiveness of a cryptosystem futile. They are of importance to us because attackers can use unconventional means to discover sensitive and secret information about our software, and even a full-fledged implementation of the controls determined from the threat model can fall short of providing total software assurance.

Although side channel attacks are predominantly observed in cryptographic systems, they are not limited to cryptography. In the context of cryptography, side channel attacks are those that use information that is neither plaintext nor ciphertext from a cryptographic device to discover secrets. Such information that is neither plaintext nor ciphertext is referred to as side channel information. A cryptographic device functions by converting plaintext to ciphertext (encryption) and from ciphertext to plaintext (decryption). Attackers of cryptosystems were required to know either the ciphertext (ciphertext-only attacks) or both the plaintext and the ciphertext (known plaintext attacks) or to be able to define what plaintext is to be encrypted and use the ciphertext output toward exploiting the cryptographic system (chosen plaintext attack). Nowadays, however, most cryptographic devices have or emit additional information that is neither plaintext nor ciphertext. Examples of some common side channel information include the time taken to complete an operation (timing information), power consumptions, radiations/emanations, and acoustic and fault information. These make it possible for an attacker to discover secrets, such as the key and memory contents, using all or some of the side channel information in conjunction with other known cryptanalysis techniques.

The most common classes of side channel attacks are the following:

Timing attacks
In timing attacks, the attacker measures how long each computational operation takes and uses that side channel information to discover other information about the internal makeup of the system. A subset of this timing attack is looking for delayed error messages, a technique used in blind SQL injection attacks.

Power analysis attacks

In power analysis attacks, the attacker measures the varying degrees of power consumption by the hardware during the computation of operations. For example, the RSA key can be decoded using the analysis of the power peaks, which represent times when the algorithms use or do not use multiplications.

TEMPEST attacks

These are also known as van Eck or radiation monitoring attacks. An attacker attempting TEMPEST attacks uses leaked electromagnetic radiation to discover plaintexts and other pertinent information that are based on the emanations.

Acoustic cryptanalysis attacks

Much like in the power analysis attacks, in acoustic cryptanalysis attacks, the attacker uses the sound produced during the computation of operations.

Differential fault analysis attacks

Differential fault analysis attacks aim at discovering secrets from the system by intentionally injecting faults into the computational operation and determining how the system responds to the faults. This is a form of fuzz testing (covered in Chapter 5) and can also be used to indicate the strength of the input validation controls in place.

Distant observation attacks

As the name suggests, distant observation attacks are shoulder surfing attacks, where the attacker observes and discovers information of a system indirectly from a distance. Observing through a telescope or using a reflected image off someone's eye, eyeglasses, monitor, or other reflective devices are some well-known examples of distant observation attacks.

Cold boot attacks

In a cold boot attack, an attacker can extract secret information by freezing the data contents of memory chips and the booting up to recover the contents in memory. Data remanence in the RAM was believed to be destroyed when the system shut down, but the cold boot attack proved traditional knowledge to be incorrect. This is of importance because not only is this an attack against confidentiality, but it also demonstrates the importance of secure startup.

4.6.15.1 Side Channel Attacks Controls

The following are recommended defensive strategies against side channel attacks:

- Leverage and use vetted, proven, and standardized cryptographic algorithms, which are less prone to side channel information leakage.
- Use a system where the time to compute an operation is independent of the input data or key size.
- Avoid the use of branching and conditional operational logic (IF-THEN-ELSE) in critical code sections to compute operations as they will have an

impact on the timing of each operation. Use simple and straightforward computational operations (AND, OR, XOR) to limit the amount of timing variances that can result and potentially be used for gleaning side channel timing and power consumption information.

■ The most effective protection against timing attacks is to standardize the time that each computation will take. This means that each and every operation takes the same amount of time to complete its operation. However, this could have an impact on performance. A fixed time implementation is not very efficient from a performance standpoint, but makes it difficult for the attacker to conduct timing attacks. Adding a random delay is also known to increase the work factor of an attacker. Also, standardizing on the time needed to compute a multiplication or an exponentiation can leave the attacker guessing as to what operation was undertaken.

■ Balancing power consumption independent of the type of operation along with reducing the signal size are useful controls to defend against power analysis attacks.

■ Adding noise is a proven control against acoustic analysis.

■ Physical shielding provides one of the best defenses against emanation or radiation security, such as TEMPEST attacks.

■ Double encryption, which is characterized by running the encryption algorithm twice and outputting the results only if both the operations match, is a recommended control against differential fault analysis. This works on the premise that the likelihood of a fault's occurring twice is statistically insignificant.

■ Physical protection of the memory chips, preventing memory dumping software from execution, not storing sensitive information in memory, scrubbing and overwriting memory contents that are no longer needed periodically or at boot time (using a destructive Power-On Self-Test), and using the Trusted Platform Module (TPM) chip are effective controls against cold boot attacks. It is important to know that the TPM chip can prevent a key from being loaded into memory, but it cannot prevent the key from being discovered once it is already loaded into memory.

4.7 Defensive Coding Practices— Concepts and Techniques

We started this chapter with the premise that secure software is more than just writing secure code. In the previous section, we learned about various security controls that can be implemented in code. In addition to those controls, there are other defensive coding practices that include concepts and techniques that assure the reliability, resiliency, and recoverability of software. In this section, we will learn about the most common defensive coding practices and techniques.

4.7.1 Attack Surface Evaluation and Reduction

Attack surface evaluation was covered extensively in the secure software design section, and it is important to understand that the moment a single line of code is written, the attack surface has increased. At this juncture of our software development project, as code is written, it is important to recognize that the attack surface of the software code is not only evaluated, but also reduced. Some examples of attack surface reduction are:

- Reducing the amount of code and services that execute by default
- Reducing the volume of code that can be accessed by untrusted users by default
- Limiting the damage when the code is exploited

Determining the RASQ before and after the implementation of code can be used to measure the effectiveness of the attack surface reduction activities.

4.7.2 Input Validation

Although it is important to trust, it is even more important to verify. This is the underlying premise behind input validation. When it comes to software, we must, in fact, consider all input as evil and validate all user input.

Input validation is the verification process that ensures the data that are supplied for processing

- Are of the correct data type and format.
- Fall within the expected and allowed range of values.
- Are not interpreted as code as is the case with injection attacks (covered later in this chapter).
- Do not masquerade in alternate forms that bypass security controls.

4.7.2.1 How to Validate?

Regular expressions (RegEx) can be used for validating input. A listing of common RegEx patterns is provided in Chapter 5. This process of verification can be achieved using one of two means: filtration or sanitization.

4.7.2.1.1 Filtration (Whitelists and Blacklists)

Filtering user input can be accomplished using either a whitelist or a blacklist. A whitelist is a list of allowable good and nonmalicious characters, commands, and/or data patterns. For example, the application might allow only "@" and ".com" in the email field. Items in a whitelist are known and usually deemed to be nonmalicious in nature. On the other hand, a blacklist is a list of disallowed characters, commands, and/or data patterns that are considered to be malicious. Examples include the single quote ('), SQL comment (- -), or a pattern such as (1=1).

4.7.2.1.2 Sanitization

Sanitization is the process of converting input that is considered to be dangerous into an innocuous form. For example, when the user supplies a character that is part of a blacklist, such as a single quote ('), data sanitization would include replacing that single quote with a double quote ("). This is also referred to as quoting input. Converting the input into its innerText form that cannot be executed, instead of processing, storing, and reflecting its innerHTML form that can be executed on the client, is another means of sanitization. However, when data sanitization is performed, it is critically important to make sure that the integrity of the data is not compromised. For example, if O'Shea is the value supplied as the last name of a user, by quoting the input before storing it, the value will change to O'Shea, which is not accurate.

4.7.2.2 Where to Validate?

The point at which the input is validated is also critically important. Input can be validated on the client or on the server or on both. It is best recommended that the input is validated both on the client (frontend) as well as on the server (backend), if the software is a client/server architected solution. Minimally, server-side validation must be performed. It is also insufficient to validate input solely on the client side, as this can be easily bypassed and afford minimal to no protection.

4.7.2.3 What to Validate?

One can validate pretty much for anything, from generic whitelist and blacklist items to specific business-defined patterns. When validating input, the supplied input must at a bare minimum be validated for:

- Data type
- Range
- Length
- Format
- Values
- Alternate representations of a standard (canonical) form

4.7.3 Canonicalization

Canonicalization is the process of converting data that has more than one possible representation to conform to a standard canonical form. Since "canonicalization"

Alternate Forms	http://crackzone.com
	http://www%2ecrackzone%2ecom
	http://208.87.33.151
Canonical Form	http://www.crackzone.com

Figure 4.21 Canonicalization of URL.

is a difficult word for some people to pronounce, it has been abbreviated as C14N. (There are 14 characters between the first letter C and the last letter N.) Although canonicalization is predominantly evident in Internet-related software, canonicalization can be used to convert any data into its standard forms and approved formats. In XML, canonicalization is used to ensure that the XML document adheres to the specified format. The canonical form is the most standard or simplest form.

URL encoding to IP address translations are well-known applications of canonicalization. Canonicalization also has international implications as it pertains to character sets or code pages, such as ASCII and Unicode (covered under the international requirements section of Chapter 2). It is therefore imperative that the appropriate character set and output locale are set in the software to avoid any canonicalization issues. From a security standpoint, canonicalization has an impact on input filtration. When filters (RegEx) are used to validate that the canonical or standard form of the input is part of a blacklist, they can be potentially bypassed when an alternate representation of the canonical form is passed in, if the validate check occurs before the canonicalization process is complete. It is recommended to decode once and canonicalize inputs into the internal representation before performing validation to ensure that validation is not circumvented. An example of canonicalization is depicted in Figure 4.21.

4.7.4 Code Access Security

Unlike in the case of an unmanaged code environment, in a managed code environment, when a software program is run, it is automatically evaluated to determine the set of permissions that needs to be given to the code during runtime. Based on what permissions are granted, the program will execute as expected or throw a security exception. The security settings of the host computer system on which the program is run decides the permissions sets that the code is granted. Code access security (CAS) prevents code from untrustworthy sources or unknown origins from having run time permissions to perform privileged operations. CAS also protects code from trusted sources from inadvertently or intentionally compromising security. Important CAS concepts include the following:

4.7.4.1 Security Actions

The permissions to be granted are evaluated by the runtime when code is loaded into memory. The three categories of security actions that can be performed are *request, demands,* and *overrides.* Requests are used to inform the runtime about the permissions that the code needs in order for it to run. It cannot be used to influence the runtime to grant the code more permissions than it should be granted. Demands are used in code to assert permissions and help protect resources from callers. Overrides are used in code to override default security behavior.

4.7.4.2 Type Safety

In order to implement CAS, the code must be generated by a programming language that can produce verifiable type-safe code. Type-safe code cannot access memory at arbitrary locations out of the range of memory address space that belongs to the object's publicly exposed fields. It cannot access memory locations it is not authorized to access. When the code is type safe, the runtime is given the ability to isolate assemblies from one another. Type-safe code accesses types only in explicitly defined (casted/converted) and allowed formats. Buffer overflow vulnerabilities are found to be prevalent in unmanaged non-type safe languages, such as C and C++. Type safety is an important consideration when choosing between a managed and unmanaged programming language. Parametric polymorphism or generics that allow a function or data type to be written generically so that it can handle values identically without depending on their type is a means to make a language more expressive while maintaining full type safety.

4.7.4.3 Syntax Security (Declarative and Imperative)

The two ways in which CAS can be implemented in the code syntax are by declarative or imperative security. We will cover later in this section the declarative vs. programmatic security concept as it pertains to container security. In the context of

```
[MyPermission(SecurityAction.Demand, Unrestricted = true)]
public class MyClass
{
    public MyClass()                 Security attributes
    {                                in metadata of code
        //The constructor is protected by the security call.
    }

    public void MyMethod()
    {
        //This method is protected by the security call.
    }
```

Figure 4.22   Declarative code access security.

```
public class MyClass {
  public MyClass(){

  }                              ┌─────────────────────┐
                                 │   Security calls    │
  public void MyMethod() {       │   inline with code  │
    //MyPermission is dem─────ued using imperative syntax.
    MyPermission Perm = new MyPermission();
    Perm.Demand();
    //This method is protected by the security call.
  }

  public void YourMethod() {
    //This method is not protected by the security call.
  }
}
```

Figure 4.23   Imperative code access security.

CAS, declarative security syntax means that the permissions are defined as security attributes in the metadata of the code, as shown in Figure 4.22. The scope of the security attributes that define the allowed security actions (requests, demands, and overrides) can be at the level of the entire assembly, a class, or the member level. Imperative security, on the other hand, is implemented using new instance of the permission object inline in code, as shown in Figure 4.23. The security action of demands and overrides are possible in imperative security, but imperative security cannot be used for requests. Imperative security is handy when the runtime permissions that are to be granted to the code are not known before it is run, in which case the permissions cannot be declaratively defined as security attributes of the code.

4.7.4.4 Secure Class Libraries

A secure class library is distinct in that it uses security demands to ascertain that the callers of the libraries have the permissions to access the functionality and resources it exposes. Code that does not have the necessary runtime permissions to access the secure class libraries will not be allowed to access the libraries resources. Additionally, even if code has the runtime permissions to call secure class libraries, if that code is in turn called by malicious code, then the malicious code (which is now the caller) will not be allowed to access the secure class libraries or its resources.

4.7.5 Container (Declarative) versus Component (Programmatic) Security

In addition to declarative syntax security to implement CAS, declarative security is also a container-managed approach to security. In this context, the main objective is to make the software portable, flexible, and less expensive to deploy, and the security rules are configured outside the software code as part of the deployment descriptor. Often this is server- (container-) based, and the server configuration settings for authentication and authorization are used to protect the resource from unauthorized access. It is usually an all-or-nothing kind of security. Since it is usually set up and maintained by the deployment personnel and not the developer, declarative security allows programmers to ignore the environment in which they write their software, and updates to the software do not require refactoring the security model.

Programmatic security, on the other hand, is a component-managed approach to security, and, much like the imperative CAS implementation, programmatic security works by defining the security rules in the component or code itself. This allows for a granular approach to implementing security, and it can be used to apply business rules when the all-or-nothing declarative container-based security cannot support the needed rules. Programmatic security is defined by the developer. If code reuse is a requirement, then programmatic component-based security that customizes code with business and security rules is not recommended. In such cases, declarative container-based security is preferred, which also leverages non-programmers and deployment personnel to enforce security policies.

4.7.6 Cryptographic Agility

One of the predominant flaws of cryptographic protection implementation in code is the use of unvalidated and custom-developed or weak cryptographic algorithms for encryption and decryption or noncollision free hashing functions for hashing purposes. The recommendation to address this concern was to use vetted, tested, and proven standardized algorithms. However, in the cryptanalysis cat-and-mouse game, cryptanalysts work equally hard to break secure algorithms that the cryptographers have been creating. It is no surprise that cryptographic algorithms that were once deemed secure are now proven to be broken, and some have even made into banned lists. Table 4.5 is a tabulation of some cryptographic algorithms and

Table 4.5   SDL Banned and Acceptable/Recommended Cryptographic Algorithms

Type of Algorithm	Banned Algorithm	Acceptable or Recommended Algorithm
Symmetric	DES, DESX, RC2, SKIPJACK, SEAL, CYLINK_MEK, RC4 (<128 bit)	3DES (2 or 3), RC4 (≥128 bit), AES
Asymmetric	RSA (<2048 bit), Diffie–Hellman (<2048 bit)	RSA (≥2048 bit), Diffie–Hellman (≥2048 bit), ECC (≥256 bit)
Hash (including HMAC usage)	SHA-0 (SHA), SHA-1, MD2, MD4, MD5	SHA-2 (includes: SHA-256, SHA-384, SHA-512)

hashing functions that are banned by the security development life cycle (SDL) at Microsoft and their recommended alternatives.

Code containing cryptographic algorithms that was once considered secure but is now determined to be insecure and found in a banned list needs to be reviewed and updated. This is not an easy task unless the code has been designed and implemented to be cryptographically agile or agnostic of the cryptographic algorithm. Cryptographic agility is the ability of the code to be able to switch from insecure algorithms to approved ones with ease, because the way in which the code is constructed is agnostic of the algorithm to provide cryptographic operations (encryption, decryption, and/or hashing). This means that a specific algorithm or the way it can be used is not hard-coded inline in code, and so replacing algorithms does not require code changes, rebuild, regression testing, updates (patches and service packs), and redeployment. Code that is cryptographically agile is characterized by maintaining the specification of the algorithm or hashing function outside the application code itself. Configuration files at the application or machine level are usually used to implement this. Additionally, even when the algorithm is specified in a configuration file, the implementation of the algorithm should be abstract within the code. Coding just the abstract type of the algorithm (e.g., SymmetricAlgorithm or AsymmetricAlgorithm) instead of a specific algorithm (e.g., RijndaelManaged or RSACryptoServiceProvider) provides greater agility. In addition to the benefit of quick and easy replacement of algorithms, cryptographic agility can be used to improve performance when newer and more efficient CNG implementations are leveraged.

CNG is the replacement to the CryptoAPI and is very extensible and cryptographically agnostic in nature. It was developed to give developers the ability to enable users to create and exchange documents and data in a secure manner over nonsecure environments, such as the Internet. The main features of CNG include:

- A new cryptographic configuration system that supports better cryptographic agility
- Abstraction for key storage and separation of the storage from the algorithm operations
- Process isolation for operations with long-term keys
- Replaceable random number generators
- Better export signing support
- Thread-safety throughout the stack
- Kernel-mode cryptographic API

Cryptographically agile code, however, poses some challenges. Cryptographic agility is observed to work better with nonpersisted transient data than persisted data. Persisted (stored) data that are encrypted with an algorithm that is being replaced may not be recoverable once the algorithm is replaced. This can also lead to a DoS to legitimate users when authentication relies on comparative matching of computed hashes and the account credentials are stored after being computed using a hashing function that has been replaced. It is recommended that, in such situations, the original hashing function be stored as metadata along with the actual hash value. Additionally, it is important to plan for the storage size of the outputs as the algorithm used to replace the insecure one can yield an output with a different size. For example, the MD5 hash is always 128 bits in length, bit the SHA-2 functions can yield a 256-bit (SHA-256), 384-bit (SHA-384), or 512-bit (SHA-512) length output, and if storage is not planned for allocated in advance, the upgrade may not even be a possibility.

4.7.7 Memory Management

We have covered the importance of memory management under the section on computer architecture and buffer overflow attacks. The following are other important memory management concepts that a CSSLP must be familiar with to assist appropriately in the implementation of security controls.

4.7.7.1 Locality of Reference

The locality of reference, also known as the principle of locality, is the principle that subsequent data locations referenced when a program is run are often predictable and in proximity to previous locations based on time or space. This is primarily to promote the reuse of recently used data and instructions. The main types of locality of reference are *temporal, spatial, branch,* and *equidistant* locality.

Temporal (or time-based) locality means that the same memory locations that have been recently accessed are more likely to be referenced again in the near future. *Spatial* (or space-based) locality means that memory locations near to recently accessed memory locations are more likely to be referenced in the near future. *Branch* locality means that, on the basis of the prediction of the memory manager, the processor uses branch predictors (such as conditional branching) to determine the location of the memory locations that will be accessed in the near future. *Equidistant* locality is halfway between spatial and branch locality and uses simple functions (usually linear) that look for equidistant locations of memory to predict which location will be accessed in the near future.

An understanding of the principle of locality is important since appropriate protection of memory can be implemented to avoid memory buffer overflow attacks.

4.7.7.2 Dangling Pointers

Dangling pointers are those pointers that do not point to a valid object of the appropriate type in memory. These occur when the object that the pointer was originally referencing was deleted or deallocated without the pointer value's being modified. Dangling pointers reference the memory location of the deallocated memory, and when that deallocated memory location is loaded with some other data, unpredictable results, including system instabilities, segmentation and general protection faults, can occur. Additionally, if an attacker can take advantage of the dangling pointer, serious overflow attacks can result. Dangling pointers differ from *wild pointers* in the sense that the wild pointers are used before being initialized, but they have been known to result in similar erratic, unpredictable, and dangerous results as do dangling pointers.

4.7.7.3 Address Space Layout Randomization (ASLR)

In order for most memory exploits and malware to be successful, the attacker must be able to identify and determine accurately the memory address where a specific process or function will be loaded. Due to the principle of locality (primarily temporal), processes and functions were observed to load in the same memory locations upon each run. This made it easy for the attackers to discover the memory location and exploit the process or function by telling their payload exploit code the memory address of the process or function they wished to exploit. ASLR is a memory management technique that can be used to protect against memory location discovery. It works by randomizing and moving the function entry points (addresses) in memory each time the program is run. An executable or dynamic link library (dll) can be loaded into any of the 256 memory locations, which means that, with ASLR turned on, the attacker has a 1 in 256 chance of discovering the exact memory address of the process or function they wish to exploit. ASLR protection is available in both Windows and Linux operating systems and is often used in conjunction with other memory protection techniques, such as data execution prevention (DEP) or executable space protection (ESP).

4.7.7.4 Data Execution Prevention (DEP)/ Executable Space Protection (ESP)

DEP, as the name implies, protects computers' systems by keeping software programs from accessing and manipulating memory in an unsafe manner. It is also known as no-execute (NX) protection because it marks the data segments (usually injected as part of a buffer overflow) that a vulnerable software will otherwise process as executable instructions as no-execute. If the software program attempts to execute the code from memory in an unapproved manner, DEP will terminate the process and close the program. Executable space protection (ESP) is the Unix or Linux equivalent of the Windows DEP. DEP can be implemented as a hardware-based technology or as a software-based technology.

Leveraging compiler switches and techniques can be useful to provide memory protection and pointer integrity checking. This limits the chances of buffer overflow attacks and increases the overall security of the software. The common compiler security switch (/GS flag) and technique (StackGuard) are discussed below.

4.7.7.5 /GS Flag

When the /GS flag is used in compilers that support it, the executable that is compiled is given the ability to detect and mitigate buffer overflows of the return address pointer stored on the stack memory. When the code compiled with the /GS flag turned on is run, before the execution of the functions that the compiler deems susceptible to buffer overflow attacks, space is allocated on the stack before the return address. On function entry, the allocated space is loaded with a security cookie that is the computed post load of the function. Upon exiting the function, a helper function is invoked that verifies that the security cookie value is not altered, which happens when the stack memory space is overwritten, indicating an overflow. If the security cookie value upon function exit is determined to be different from what it was when the function was entered, then the process will simply terminate to avoid any further consequences.

4.7.7.6 StackGuard

StackGuard is a compiler technique that provides code pointer integrity checking and protection of the return address in a function against being altered. It is implemented as a small patch of the GNU gcc compiler and works by detecting and defeating stack memory overflow attacks. StackGuard works by placing a known value (referred to as a *canary* or *canary word*) before the return address on the stack so that, should a buffer overflow occur, the first datum that will be corrupted is the canary. When the function exits, the code run to move the return address to its next instruction location (also known as the tear down code) checks to make sure that the canary word is not modified before jumping to the next return address. However, attackers have been known to forge a canary by embedding the canary word in their overflow exploit. StackGuard uses two methods to prevent forgery. These include using either a *terminator canary* or a *random canary*. A terminator canary is made up of common termination symbols for C standard string library functions, such as 0 (null), CR, LF (carriage return, line feed), and -1 (End of File or EOF), and when the attacker specifies these common symbols in their overflow string as part of their exploit code (shellcode or payload), the functions will terminate immediately. A random canary is a 32-bit random number that is set on function entry (on program start) and maintained only for the time frame of that function call or program execution. Each time the program starts, a new random canary word is set, and this makes the predictability and forging of the canary word by an attacker nearly impossible.

4.7.8 Exception Management

We covered error handling and exception management at length in previous sections. Additionally, an important exception management feature that can be leveraged during the compilation and linking process is to use the safe security exception handler (/SAFESEH) flag in systems that support it.

When the /SAFESEH flag is set, the linker will produce the executable's safe exception handlers table and write that information into the program executable (PE). This table in the PE is used to verify safe (or valid) exceptions by the OS. When an exception is thrown, the OS will check the exception handler against the safe exception handler list that is written in the PE, and if they do not match, the OS will terminate the process.

4.7.9 Anti-Tampering

The code (source or object) needs to be protected from unauthorized modifications to assure the reliable operations and integrity of the software. Source code anti-tampering assurance can be achieved using *obfuscation*. Obfuscation of the source code is the process of making the code obscure and confusing using a special program called the obfuscator so that, even if the source code is leaked to or stolen by an attacker, the source code is not easily readable and decipherable. This process usually involves complicating the code with generic variable names, convoluted loops, and conditional constructs and renaming text and symbols within the code to meaningless character sequences. Obfuscated code is also known as shrouded code. Obfuscation is not limited to source code; it can be used for object code as well. When object code is obfuscated, it acts as a deterrent to reverse engineering.

Reverse engineering or reversing is the process of gleaning information about the design and implementation details of the software from object code. It is analogous to going backward (reverse) in the SDLC. It can be used for legitimate purposes, such as understanding the blueprint of the software, especially in cases where the documentation is not available, but has legal ramifications if the software does not belong to the reverser. From a security standpoint, reverse engineering can be used for security research and to determine vulnerabilities in published software. However, skillful attackers are also known to reverse engineer and crack software, circumventing security protections, such as license restrictions, implemented in code. They can also tamper and repackage software with malicious intent. This is why anti-tampering protection of object code is necessary.

Besides using obfuscation as a deterrent control against reverse engineering, object code or executables can be also be protected from being reverse engineered using other anti-tampering protection mechanisms, such as removing symbolic information from the PE and embedding anti-debugger code. The removal of symbolic information involves the process of eliminating any symbolic information, such as class names, class member names, and names of global instantiated objects, and other textual information from the program executable by stripping them out before compilation or using obfuscation to rename symbols into meaningless sequences of characters. Embedding anti-debugger code means a user or kernel level debugger detector is included as part of the code, and it detects the presence of a debugger and terminates the process when one is found. The IsDebuggerPresent

API and SystemKernelDebuggerInformation API are examples of common APIs that can be leveraged to implement anti-debugger code.

Additionally, code signing (covered in Chapter 3) assures the authenticity of published code (especially mobile code) besides providing integrity and anti-tampering protection.

4.7.10 Secure Startup

It is important to recognize that software can be secure by default in design and implementation, but being without adequate levels of protection for the integrity of the software when it begins to execute can thwart the assurance of the software. It is therefore imperative to ensure that the software startup process itself is secure. Usually during the *bootstrapping* process of the startup phase, environment variables and configuration parameters are initialized. These variables and parameters need to be protected from disclosure, alteration, or destruction threats. Bootstrapping security is covered in more detail in Chapter 7. Secure startup prevents and mitigates side channel attacks, such as the cold boot attack.

4.7.11 Embedded Systems

A generic definition of an embedded system is a computer system that is a component of a larger machine or system. They are usually present as part of the whole system and are assigned to perform specific operations. The specificity of their operations often gives the embedded system increased reliability over a general multi-purpose system. Embedded systems can respond to and are governed by events in real time. They are usually standalone devices, but they need not be. The program instructions that are written for embedded systems are known as *firmware* and are usually stored in read-only chips or flash memory chips. If the firmware is stored in a read-only chip, then the embedded system microcontroller or digital signal processor (DSP) is not programmable by the end user. Another important aspect of many prominent embedded systems today is the open operating system that runs on the devices. The Microsoft Windows CE (to an extent) and the Apple iPhone applications are prime examples of open operating systems that allow third parties to develop software applications that can run on these devices.

Some common examples of embedded systems devices include home appliances, cars, traffic lights, mp3 players, watches, cellular telephones, and personal digital assistants (PDAs).

With the changes in technologies and the increase in the use of embedded systems for daily living, attackers are targeting embedded systems to compromise the security of the device or the host system of which the embedded system is a part. The threat agents of embedded systems are usually more sophisticated and skilled than the general software attacker, and this means that the defenders need to be equally qualified to address embedded system security threats.

Most attacks on embedded systems are primarily disclosure attacks, so it is essential that the embedded device that stores or displays sensitive and private information has product design and security controls in place to assure confidentiality. Nowadays, with embedded devices such as PDAs that handle personal and corporate data, it is critical to ensure that such devices support and implement a transport or network layer encryption and/or DRM scheme to protect sensitive and copyrighted information that is transmitted to, stored on, and displayed on these devices. A software technique that is used on devices today to ensure that private and sensitive information is not disclosed is to implement auto-erase functionality in the software. This way, when the necessary credentials to access the device data are not provided and the configured number of attempts has been superseded, the software will execute an auto-destruct function that erases all data on the device.

Memory management in embedded systems is critical because the memory in embedded systems usually holds both the data and the product's firmware as well. Leveraging a tamper-resistant sensor to detect and assure that memory remanence disclosure and alteration is mitigated is important.

In addition to disclosure threats, embedded systems also face a plethora of other attacks. The small size and portability often make them the target to side channel attacks (e.g., radiation and power analysis) and fault injection attacks. This mandates the need to protect the internal circuitry of the devices with physical deterrent controls, such as seals (epoxies), conformal coatings, and tapes that need to be broken before the device can be opened. The software running on these systems can then be used to signal physical breaches or tampering activities. Another technique that product designers use to deter reconnaissance and reverse engineering of the device itself is that they hide critical signals in the internal board layers.

When third-party applications and software are allowed to run on these embedded system devices, it is necessary to ensure that a safe execution environment is provided to the owner of the device. The third-party applications should be isolated from other applications running on the device and must be limited from accessing the owner's private and sensitive data stored on the device.

All of the security controls that are applicable in pervasive computing are also applicable to embedded systems. This means that before users are allowed to use the secure embedded system device, they must first verify their identity and be authenticated. Multifactor authentication is recommended to increase security. Additionally, the TPM chip on the device can be used for node-to-node authentication and provide for the tamper-resistant storage of keys and secrets.

The recognized ISO 15408 (common criteria) standard and the multiple independent levels of security (MILS) standard can be leveraged for embedded systems security. The MILS architecture makes it possible to create a verified, always invoked, and tamperproof application code with security features that thwart the attempts of an attacker. It is expected that future embedded systems development projects will focus their attention on increasing the security of the firmware and of the devices themselves.

4.7.12 Interface Coding

Software today is mostly developed using and leveraging APIs. APIs make the internal functionality of a software function accessible to external callers (other entities and code functions). They abstract the internal function details, and as long as the caller meets the interface requirements, they can invoke and benefit from the processing of the function. Interfaces are useful to implement the design principle of leveraging existing components. Threat modeling should identify APIs as potential entry points. Banned and deprecated APIs that are susceptible to security breaches should be avoided and replaced with secure counterparts.

When interfaces are used to access administrative features, Web services, or other third-party components, it is essential to ascertain that proper authentication is in place. It is also important to audit the access and user/system actions that are performed upon the invocation of privileged functions exposed by the interfaces. When confidentiality of sensitive information (e.g., usernames, passwords, connection string, keys) is required, CNG can be used. When an application's internal APIs are opened up to third-party developers, necessary protection mechanisms need to be in place.

4.8 Secure Software Processes

Software assurance is a confluence of secure processes and technologies implemented by trained and skilled people who understand how to design, develop, and deploy secure software. In addition to writing secure code, there are certain processes that must be conducted during the implementation phase that can assure the security of the software. These include:

- Versioning
- Code analysis
- Code/Peer review

4.8.1 Versioning

Configuration management has a direct impact on the state of software assurance and is applicable as part of development as well as deployment. Configuration management as it applies to deployment is covered in more detail in Chapter 7. In this chapter, we will cover the importance of configuration management as it pertains to code development and implementation, more particularly source code versioning or version control.

Versioning or version control of software not only ensures that the development team is working with the correct version of code, but also gives the ability to rollback to a previous version should there be a need. Additionally, software versioning provides the ability to track ownership and changes of code. If each version of the software is tracked and maintained, determining and analyzing the attack surface for each version can give insight into the RASQ and the overall trend of software security. Version control can reduce the incidences of a condition known as *regenerative bugs,* where previously fixed bugs reappear (are regenerated). This is known to occur when bug fixes are inadvertently overwritten when the correct version of code is not used.

From a security standpoint, it is important to ensure that the versioning uses *file locks* or *reserved checkouts.* This means that when the code is checked out by someone for changes, no one else can make changes to the code until it has been checked back in. Most current software development IDEs incorporate versioning. Well-known examples of version control software include Visual SourceSafe (VSS), Concurrent Versions System (CVS), StarTeam, and Team Foundation Server (TFS).

4.8.2 Code Analysis

Code analysis is the process of inspecting the code for exploitable weaknesses. It is primarily accomplished by two means: *static* and *dynamic.*

Static code analysis involves the inspection of the code without executing the code (or software program). This analysis can be performed manually by a code review (covered next in this section) or in an automated manner using tools. Any code, regardless of whether it is source code, bytecode, or object code, can be analyzed. Tools that are used to perform static source code analysis are commonly referred to as source code analyzers, and tools that are used to analyze intermediate bytecode are known as bytecode scanners. Tools used to analyze object code statically are referred to as binary analyzers or binary code scanners.

The benefits of performing static code analysis are that errors and vulnerabilities can be detected early and addressed before deployment of the software. Additionally, static code analysis does not need a simulated production environment and can be performed in the development or testing environment.

Dynamic code analysis is the inspection of the code when it is being executed (run as a program). Just because the code compiles without any errors that can be analyzed in static code analysis, it does not mean that it will run without any errors. Dynamic code analysis can be performed to ascertain that the code is reliably functioning as expected and is not prone to errors or exploitation. In order to perform dynamic analysis accurately, a simulated environment that mirrors the production environment where the code will be deployed is necessary. Tools used for dynamic code analysis are known as dynamic code analyzers, and they can be used to determine how the program will run as it interacts with other processes and the operating system itself.

4.8.3 Code/Peer Review

One way to inspect the code statically is to perform a code review. A code review is also referred to as a peer review when peers from the development team are part of the code review process. A code review can be performed manually or by using tools. It is a systematic evaluation of the source code with the goal of finding out syntax issues and weaknesses in the code that can impact the performance and security of the software. Semantic issues, such as business logic and design flaws, are usually not detected in a code review, but a code review can be used to validate the threat model generated in the design phase of the software development project. Tools can be used to automate and identify vulnerabilities quickly, but they must not be done in lieu of manual human review.

When a code review is conducted for security reasons, the code must at a bare minimum be inspected for the following:

- ◼ Insecure code
- ◼ Inefficient code: Code that has exploitable weaknesses in it

Common insecure code implementations include:

- ◼ Injection Flaws: Check for code that makes injection attacks possible. Examples include the lack of input validation or the dynamic construction of queries that accept user supplied data without proper validation or sanitization. Code review must check to ensure that proper input validation is in place.
- ◼ Nonrepudiation Mechanisms: Code review should ensure that auditing is properly implemented and that the authenticity of the code and the user or system actions are not disputable. If delayed signing is not the case, checks to make sure that the code is correctly signed should be undertaken as part of the review.
- ◼ Spoofing Attacks: Check for code that makes spoofing attacks possible. This check should ensure that session identifiers are not predictable, passwords are not hard-coded, credentials are not cached, and code that allows changes to the impersonation context is not implemented.
- ◼ Errors and Exception Handling: Code review must check to make sure that errors when reported do not reveal more information than is necessary and that the software fails securely when errors occur. Code should be implemented to handle exceptions. The check for the presence of try-catch-finally blocks must also check to make sure that objects created in code are destroyed in the finally blocks.
- ◼ Cryptographic Strength: Code that uses nonstandard or custom cryptographic algorithms are considered weak and must be avoided. Algorithms must not be hard-coded as they will impair the cryptographic agility of the software. The use of random number generators (RNG) and pseudo-random number generators (PRNG) must be validated. Keys must also not be hard-coded, and code review should ensure that cryptographic protections are strong enough to avoid any cryptanalytic attacks.

- Unsafe and Unused Functions and Routines in Code: The code must be reviewed to ascertain that deprecated and banned APIs are not used. Also, any unused functions in code should be removed. Explicit checks for Easter eggs and bells-and-whistles in code must be performed. A good way to determine if the code is required is to use the requirements traceability matrix.
- Reversible Code: Code that can be used to determine the internal architecture and design and implementation details of software functionality. Code must be reviewed to check for debugger detectors, and any symbolic and textual information that can aid a reverse engineer should be removed.
- Privileged Code: Code that violates the principle of least privilege. As part of the code review, checks must be performed to ensure that any code that requires administrative rights to execute is explicitly controlled and monitored.

Additionally, the code should also be reviewed for:

- Maintenance Hooks: Intentionally introduced, seemingly innocuous code that is implemented primarily to provide for maintenance needs. They are implanted to ease troubleshooting and better support. Maintenance hooks can be used to impersonate a user who is experiencing issues with the software to recreate the issue as a way to troubleshoot the issue. They can also function as a back door and allow developers access to privileged systems (usually in a production environment), even if they are not granted authorization rights to those systems. They are to be considered critical or privilege code because they usually provide administrative access with unrestricted rights. However, these maintenance hooks should not be deployed into the production environment because an attacker could easily take advantage of the maintenance hook and gain back door entry into the system, often circumventing all security protection mechanisms.
- Logic Bombs: Serious code security issues as they can be placed in the code and go undetected if a code review is not performed. Based on the logic (such as a condition or time), a logic bomb can be triggered to go off to perform some malicious and unintended operation when that logic is met. Logic bombs are implanted by an insider who has access to the source code. Disgruntled employees who feel wronged by their employers have been known to implant logic bombs in their code as a means of revenge. A logic bomb not only causes destruction of data, it can also disrupt or bring the business to a complete halt. They have been used for extortion scams as well where the publisher of the code threatens the subscriber that they will trigger the logic bomb in code unless the subscriber agrees to the terms of the publisher. When the software code is not directly developed and controlled by you, as in the case of an outsourcer or third party, code review to determine logic bombs becomes extremely critical. It is also important to note that to deactivate a trial piece of software after a certain period of time has elapsed (the condition), as it

was communicated in advance, is not regarded as a logic bomb because it is nonmalicious and functions as intended.

The review of the code must also identify code that is inefficient as it can have a direct impact on the security of the software. Making an improper system call and infinite loop constructs are some examples of inefficient code that can lead to system compromise, memory leaks, resource exhaustion, and DoS, impacting the core confidentiality, integrity, and availability tenets of software security. Specifically, code should be reviewed to eliminate the following inefficiencies:

- Timing and Synchronization Implementations: Race conditions in code that can result in covert channels and resource deadlocks can be identified using a code review. It is important to make sure that the code is constructed to be executed in a mutually exclusive (Mutex) manner so that timing and synchronization issues can be avoided. This is particularly important if the code is written to alter the state of a shared object simultaneously.

- Cyclomatic Complexity: A measure of the number of linearly independent paths in a program. This software metric used to find out the extent of decision logic within each module of the code. Highly cohesive and loosely coupled code will have little to no circular dependencies and will thus be less complex. The results of determining the cyclomatic complexity can be used as indicators of the software design as it pertains to the design principle of economy of mechanisms and least common mechanisms.

It is also important to recognize that the code review process is a structured and planned activity and must be conducted in a constructive manner. First and foremost, it is the code and not the coder that is being reviewed, and so mutual respect of all team members who are part of the code review is critically important. It is recommended that explicit roles and responsibilities are assigned to the participants of the code review. Moderators who facilitate the code review must be identified. A CSSLP is expected to function in this manner. It is also important to identify who the reviewers of the code will be and appoint a scribe who will be responsible to record the minutes of the code review meeting so that action items that arise from it are addressed. Informing the reviewer about the code that is going to be reviewed in the code review meeting in advance and securely giving them access to the code is advised, so that the reviewers come prepared to the meeting. As a means to demonstrate separation of duties, the programmer who wrote the code should not also be the moderator or the scribe. They are to participate in the code review with a mindset to accept action items that need to be addressed. The findings of the code review are to be communicated as constructive feedback rather than criticisms of the programmer's coding style or ability. Leveraging the coding standards and internal policies and external regulatory and compliance requirements to prioritize and handle code review findings is recommended.

4.9 Build Environment and Tools Security

Earlier in this chapter, we covered the different types of programming languages and code. Source code that is written by the programmer needs to be converted into a form that the machine can understand. This conversion process is generically referred to as the *build* process. The integrity of the build environment where the source code is converted into object code is important. The integrity of the build environment can be assured by:

- Physically securing access to the systems that build code
- Using access control lists (ACLs) that prevent access to unauthorized users
- Using version control software to assure that the code built is of the right version

It is also important to ensure that legacy source code can be built without errors. This mandates the need to maintain the legacy source code, the associated dependency files that need to be linked, and the build environment itself. Since most legacy code has not been designed and developed with security in mind, it is critical to ascertain that the secure state of the computing ecosystem is not reduced when legacy source code is rebuilt and redeployed.

During the build process, the security of the software can be augmented using features in the build tools. The main kinds of build tools are *packagers, compilers,* and *packers.*

Packagers are used to build software so that the software can be seamlessly installed without any errors. They make sure that all dependencies and resources necessary for the software to run are part of the software build. The Red Hat Package Manager (RPM) and the Microsoft Installer (MSI) are examples of packagers. When software is packaged, it is important to ensure that no new vulnerabilities are introduced.

Packers are used to compress executables primarily for the purpose of distribution and to reduce secondary storage requirements. Packed executables reduce the time and bandwidth required by users who download code and updates. Packed software executables need to be unpacked with the appropriate unpacker, and when proprietary and unpublished packers are used for packing the software executable, they provide some degree of protection against reverse engineering. Packed executables pose more challenges to a reverse engineer and are deterrent in nature, but they do not prevent reversing efforts. Packing software can also be used to obfuscate the contents of the executable. It is also important to recognize that attackers, especially malware writers, use packers to pack their malware programs because the packers transform the executables appearance to evade signature-based malware detection tools, but they do not affect its execution semantics in any way.

4.10 Summary

Although programmers primarily function as problem solvers for the business, the software that they write can potentially become the problem for the business, if it is written without a thorough understanding of how their programs run or without necessary security protection mechanisms. A fundamental understanding of programming utilities, such as the assembler, compiler, interpreters, and computer architecture, is essential so that code is first reliable and second resilient and recoverable when attacked. There are several different types of software development methodologies, and each has its benefits and disadvantages. Choosing a software development methodology must factor in the security advantages or lack thereof.

It is important to be familiar with common coding vulnerabilities that plague software and have a thorough understanding of how an attacker will try

---

Source code characteristics

- Validates input.
- Does not allow dynamic construction of queries using user-supplied data.
- Audits and logs business-critical functions.
- Is signed to verify the authenticity of its origin.
- Does not use predictable session identifiers.
- Does not hard-code secrets inline.
- Does not cache credentials.
- Is properly instrumented.
- Handles exceptions explicitly.
- Does not disclose too much information in its errors.
- Does not reinvent existing functionality, and uses proven cryptographic algorithms.
- Does not use weak cryptographic algorithms.
- Uses randomness in the derivation of cryptographic keys.
- Stores cryptographic keys securely.
- Does not use banned APIs and unsafe functions.
- Is obfuscated or shrouded.
- Is built to run with least privilege.

Figure 4.24   Secure code characteristics.

to exploit the software, so that the code has security protection controls implemented in it. Some of the basic characteristics of secure code are illustrated in Figure 4.24.

Secure software development processes include versioning, code analysis, and code review. Source code version control is necessary to track owners and changes to the code and to provide the ability to rollback to previous versions as needed. Code can be analyzed either statically or dynamically, and it is advisable that both static and dynamic analysis is conducted before code is deployed or released after it is tested. Statically reviewing the code involves checking the code for insecure and inefficient code issues, either manually as a code (or peer) review or using automatically by using tools.

Attack surface reduction, CAS, container (declarative) vs. component (programmatic) security, cryptographic agility, memory management, exception management, anti-tampering mechanisms, and interface coding security are other important security concepts that cannot be ignored while writing secure code. Maintaining the integrity of the build environment and process and knowing how to leverage the features of packagers, compilers (switches), and packers to augment the security protection in code is important.

4.11 Review Questions

1. Software developers write software programs primarily to
   A. create new products
   B. capture market share
   C. solve business problems
   D. mitigate hacker threats
2. The process of combining necessary functions, variables, and dependency files and libraries required for the machine to run the program is referred to as
   A. compilation
   B. interpretation
   C. linking
   D. instantiation
3. Which of the following is an important consideration to manage memory and mitigate overflow attacks when choosing a programming language?
   A. locality of reference
   B. type safety
   C. cyclomatic complexity
   D. Parametric polymorphism
4. Using multifactor authentication is effective in mitigating which of the following application security risks?
   A. injection flaws
   B. Cross-Site Scripting (XSS)

    C. buffer overflow

    D. Man-in-the-Middle (MITM)

5. Implementing Completely Automated Public Turing test to tell Computers and Humans Apart (CAPTCHA) protection is a means of defending against

    A. SQL injection

    B. Cross-Site Scripting (XSS)

    C. Cross-Site Request Forgery (CSRF)

    D. insecure cryptographic storage

6. The findings of a code review indicate that cryptographic operations in code use the Rijndael cipher, which is the original publication of which of the following algorithms?

    A. Skipjack

    B. Data Encryption Standard (DES)

    C. Triple Data Encryption Standard (3DES)

    D. Advanced Encryption Standard (AES)

7. Which of the following transport layer technologies can best mitigate session hijacking and replay attacks in a local area network (LAN)?

    A. Data Loss Prevention (DLP)

    B. Internet Protocol Security (IPSec)

    C. Secure Sockets Layer (SSL)

    D. Digital Rights Management (DRM)

8. Verbose error messages and unhandled exceptions can result in which of the following software security threats?

    A. spoofing

    B. tampering

    C. repudiation

    D. information disclosure

9. Code signing can provide all of the following except

    A. anti-tampering protection

    B. authenticity of code origin

    C. runtime permissions for code

    D. authentication of users

10. When an attacker uses delayed error messages between successful and unsuccessful query probes, he is using which of the following side channel techniques to detect injection vulnerabilities?

    A. distant observation

    B. cold boot

    C. power analysis

    D. timing

11. When the runtime permissions of the code are defined as security attributes in the metadata of the code, it is referred to as

    A. imperative syntax security

    B. declarative syntax security

    C. code signing

    D. code obfuscation

12. When an all-or-nothing approach to code access security is not possible and business rules and permissions need to be set and managed more granularly inline in code functions and modules, a programmer can leverage which of the following?

    A. cryptographic agility

    B. parametric polymorphism

    C. declarative security

    D. imperative security

13. An understanding of which of the following programming concepts is necessary to protect against memory manipulation buffer overflow attacks? Choose the best answer.

    A. error handling

    B. exception management

    C. locality of reference

    D. generics

14. Exploit code attempt to take control of dangling pointers that

    A. are references to memory locations of destroyed objects

    B. are the nonfunctional code left behind in the source

    C. are the payload code that the attacker uploads into memory to execute

    D. are references in memory locations that are used prior to being initialized

15. Which of the following is a feature of most recent operating systems (OS) that makes it difficult for an attacker to guess the memory address of the program as it makes the memory address different each time the program is executed?

    A. Data Execution Prevention (DEP)

    B. Executable Space Protection (ESP)

    C. Address Space Layout Randomization (ASLR)

    D. Safe Security Exception Handler (/SAFESEH)

16. When the source code is made obscure using special programs in order to make the readability of the code difficult when disclosed, the code is also known as

    A. object code

    B. obfuscated code

    C. encrypted code

    D. hashed code

17. The ability to track ownership, changes in code, and rollback abilities is possible because of which of the following configuration management processes?

    A. version control

    B. patching

    C. audit logging

    D. change control

18. The main benefit of statically analyzing code is that

    A. runtime behavior of code can be analyzed

    B. business logic flaws are more easily detectable

    C. the analysis is performed in a production or production-like environment

    D. errors and vulnerabilities can be detected earlier in the life cycle

19. Cryptographic protection includes all of the following except

    A. encryption of data when it is processed

    B. hashing of data when it is stored

    C. hiding of data within other media objects when it is transmitted

    D. masking of data when they are displayed

20. Assembly and machine language are examples of

    A. natural language

    B. Very High-Level Language (VHLL)

    C. High-Level Language (HLL)

    D. Low-Level Language

References

Aho, A., R. Sethi, and J. Ullman. 2007. *Compilers: Principles, Techniques, & Tools*. Boston, MA: Pearson/Addison Wesley.

Anley, C., and J. Koziol. 2007. *The Shellcoder's Handbook: Discovering and Exploiting Security Holes*. Indianapolis, IN: Wiley Pub.

Blum, R. 2005. *Professional Assembly Language*. Indianapolis, IN: Wrox.

Cannings, R., H. Dwivedi, and Z. Lackey. 2008. *Hacking Exposed Web 2.0: Web 2.0 Security Secrets and Solutions*. New York, NY: McGraw-Hill.

Cowan, C., P. Wagle, C. Pu, S. Beattle, and J. Walpole. 2003. Buffer overflows: Attacks and defenses for the vulnerability of the decade. *Foundations of Intrusion Tolerant Systems*: 227–237.

CWE. 2010. CWE/SANS top 25 most dangerous programming errors. http://cwe.mitre .org/top25 (accessed Apr. 5, 2010).

Eilam, E., and E. J. Chikofsky. 2005. *Reversing Secrets of Reverse Engineering*. Indianapolis, IN: Wiley.

Farley, J., and W. Crawford. 2006. *Java Enterprise in a Nutshell*. Sebastopol, CA: O'Reilly.

Fielding, R. et al. 1999. Hypertext Transfer Protocol—HTTP/1.1. Internet Engineering Task Force (IETF) RFC 2616. June 1999. http://www.ietf.org/rfc/rfc2616.txt (accessed May 1, 2010).

Foster, J. C. 2005. *Buffer Overflow Attacks: Detect, Exploit, Prevent*. Rockland, MA: Syngress.

Gauci, S. Surf jacking—HTTPS will not save you. EnableSecurity. 10 Aug. 2008. http:// enablesecurity.com/2008/08/11/surf-jack-https-will-not-save-you (accessed Apr. 30 2010).

Hagai Bar-El. Side channel attacks. http://www.hbarel.com/Misc/side_channel_attacks.html (accessed May 1, 2010).

Halderman, J., S. Schoen, N. Heninger, W. Clarkson, W. Paul, J. Calandrino, A. Feldmen, J. Applebaum, and E. Felten. 2008. Lest we remember: Cold boot attacks on encryption keys. Proc. 17th USENIX Security Symposium.

Herzog, P. 2008. *Hacking Exposed Linux Security Secrets and Solutions*. Berkeley, CA: McGraw-Hill Osborne Media.

Howard, M., and D. LeBlanc. 2003. *Writing Secure Code*. Redmond, WA: Microsoft.

Howard, M., and S. Lipner. 2006. *The Security Development Lifecycle: SDL, a Process for Developing Demonstrably More Secure Software*. Redmond, WA: Microsoft.

Jegerlehner, R. Intel Assembler CodeTable 80x86—Overview of Instructions (Cheat Sheet). http://www.jegerlehner.ch/intel (accessed May 1, 2010).

Litchfield, D. 2005. *The Database Hacker's Handbook: Defending Database Servers*. Indianapolis, IN: Wiley.

McClure, S., J. Scambray, and G. Kurtz. 2003. *Hacking Exposed: Network Security Secrets & Solutions*. Fourth ed. Berkeley, CA: McGraw-Hill Osborne Media.

Microsoft Developer Network. 2010. Security in the .NET framework. http://msdn.micro soft.com/en-us/library/fkytk30f%28VS.80%29.aspx (accessed May 1, 2010).

MITRE Corporation. 2011. Common attack pattern enumeration and classification. http:// capec.mitre.org (accessed May 1, 2010).

Morrison, J. 2009. Preventing race conditions in code that accesses global data. *It Goes To Eleven*. http://blogs.msdn.com/b/itgoestoeleven/archive/2009/11/11/preventing-race-conditions-in-code-that-accesses-global-data.aspx (accessed May 1, 2010).

Ogorkiewicz, M., and P. Frej. 2004. Analysis of buffer overflow attacks. http://www .windowsecurity.com/articles/Analysis_of_Buffer_Overflow_Attacks.html (accessed Apr. 30, 2010).

OWASP. 2010. Developer guide. http://www.owasp.org/index.php/Developer_Guide (accessed May 1, 2010).

OWASP. 2010. OWASP top 10 web application security risks. http://www.owasp.org/index. php/Top_Ten (accessed Apr. 19, 2010).

Paul, M. 2008a. Phishing: Electronic social engineering. *Certification Magazine*, Sept. 2008.

Paul, M. 2008b. TMI syndrome in Web applications. *Certification Magazine*, Apr. 2008.

Scambray, J., and S. McClure. 2008. *Hacking Exposed Windows: Windows Security Secrets & Solutions*. New York, NY: McGraw-Hill.

Scambray, J., M. Shema, and C. Sima. 2006. *Hacking Exposed: Web Applications*. New York, NY: McGraw-Hill.

Schneier, B. 1996. *Applied Cryptography: Protocols, Algorithms, and Source Code in C*. New York, NY: Wiley.

Schneier, B. 1998. Security pitfalls in cryptography. *Schneier on Security*. http://www .schneier.com/essay-028.html (accessed Apr. 30 2010).

Schneier, B., N. Ferguson, and T. Kohno. 2010. *Cryptography Engineering*. New York, NY: Wiley.

Shiel, S., and I. Bayley. 2005. A translation-facilitated comparison between the common language runtime and the Java Virtual Machine. *Electronic Notes in Theoretical Computer Science (ENTCS)* 141.1: 35–52.

Sullivan, B. 2009. Cryptographic agility. *MSDN: Microsoft Development, MSDN Subscriptions, Resources, and More*. http://msdn.microsoft.com/en-us/magazine/ee321570.aspx (accessed Aug. 2009).

Toll, D. C., S. Weber, P. A. Karger, E. R. Palmer, S. K. McIntosh. 2008. Tooling in support of common criteria evaluation of a high assurance operating system. *Build Security In*. https://buildsecurityin.us-cert.gov/bsi/961-BSI.html (accessed).

Web Application Security Consortium. Web Hacking Incident Database. http://projects. webappsec.org/w/page/13246995/Web-Hacking-Incident-Databasev (accessed May 1, 2010).

Webb, W. 2004. Hack this: Secure embedded systems. *EDN: Information, News, & Business Strategy for Electronics Design Engineers.* July 22, 2004. http://www.edn.com/article/479692-Hack_this_secure_embedded_systems.php (accessed May 1, 2010).

Zeller, W., and E. W. Felten. 2008. Cross-site request forgeries: Exploitation and prevention. Center for Information Technology Policy. Princeton, 15 Oct. 2008. http://from.bz/public/documents/publications/csrf.pdf (accessed Apr. 30, 2010).

Chapter 5

Secure Software Testing

5.1 Introduction

Just because software architects design software with a security mindset and developers implement security by writing secure code, it does not necessarily mean that the software is secure. It is imperative to validate and verify the functionality and security of software, and this can be accomplished by quality assurance (QA) testing, which should include testing for security functionality and security testing. Security testing is an integral process in the secure software development life cycle (SDLC). The results of security testing have a direct bearing on the quality of the software. Software that has undergone and passed validation of its security through testing is said to be of relatively higher quality than software that has not.

In this chapter, what to test, who is to test, and how to test for software security issues will be covered. The different types of functional and security testing that must be performed will be highlighted, and criteria that can be used to determine the type of security tests to be performed will be discussed. Security testing is necessary and must be performed in addition to functional testing. Testing standards such as the ISO 9126 and methodologies such as the *Open Source Security Testing Methodology Manual* (OSSTMM) and Systems Security Engineering Capability Maturity Model® (SSE-CMM) that were covered in chapter 1 can be leveraged when security testing is performed.

5.2 Objectives

As a CSSLP, you are expected to

- Understand the importance of security testing and how it impacts the quality of software.
- Have a thorough understanding of the different types of functional and security testing and the benefits and weaknesses of each.
- Be familiar with how common software security vulnerabilities (bugs and flaws) can be tested.
- Understand how to track defects and address test findings.

This chapter will cover each of these objectives in detail. It is imperative that you fully understand the objectives and be familiar with how to apply them in the software that your organization builds or procures. The CSSLP is not expected to know all the tools that are used for software testing, but must be familiar with what tests need to be performed and how they can be performed. In the last section of this chapter, we will cover some common tools for security testing, but this is primarily for informational purposes only. Appendix E describes several common tools that can be used for security testing, more particularly application security tests.

5.3 Quality Assurance

In many organizations, the software testing teams are rightfully referred to as QA teams. QA of software can be achieved by testing its reliability (functionality), recoverability, resiliency (security), interoperability, and privacy. Figure 5.1 illustrates the categorization of the different types of software QA testing.

Reliability implies that the software is functioning as is expected by the business or customer. Since software is generally complex, the likelihood that all functionality and code paths will be tested is less and this can lead to the software's being attacked. *Resiliency* is the measure of how strong the software is against attacks attempting to compromise it. Nonintentional and accidental user errors can cause downtime. Software attacks can also cause unavailability of the software. Software that is not highly resilient to attack will be susceptible to compromise, such as injection threats, denial of service (DoS), data theft, and memory corruption, and when this occurs, the ability of the software to be able to recover its operations should also be tested. *Recoverability* is the software's ability to restore itself to an operational state after downtime, which can be caused accidentally or intentionally. *Interoperability* testing validates the ability of the software to function in disparate environments. *Privacy* testing is conducted to check that personally identifying information (PII), personal health information (PHI), personal financial information (PFI), and any information that is exclusive to the owner of the information is assured confidentiality without intrusion.

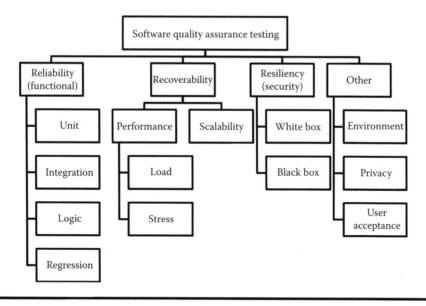

Figure 5.1 **Software quality assurance testing types.**

The results of these various types of testing can provide insight into the quality of software. However, as established in Chapter 1, software that is of high quality may not necessarily mean that it is secure. Software that performs efficiently to specifications may not have adequate levels of security controls in place. This is why security testing (covered later) is necessary, and since security is another attribute of quality, as is privacy and reliability, software that is secure can be considered as being of relatively higher quality. Testing can validate this.

5.4 Types of Software QA Testing

The following section will cover the different types of testing for software QA. It is important that you are familiar with the definition of these tests and what they are used for.

5.4.1 Reliability Testing (Functional Testing)

Software testing is performed primarily to attest to the functionality of the software as expected by the business or customer. Functional testing is also referred to as *reliability* testing. We test to check if the software is reliable (is functioning as it is supposed to) according to the requirements specified by the business owner.

5.4.1.1 Unit Testing

Although unit tests are not conducted by software testers but by the developers, it is the first process to ensure that the software is functioning properly, according to specifications. It is performed during the implementation phase (coding) of the SDLC by breaking the functionality of the software into smaller parts and testing each part in isolation for build and compilation errors as well as functional logic. If the software is architected with modular programming in mind, conducting unit tests are easier because each of the features is already isolated as discrete units (high cohesiveness) and has few dependencies (loose coupling) with other units.

In addition to functionality validation, unit testing can be used to find quality of code (QoC) issues as well. By stepping through the units of code methodically, one can uncover inefficiencies, cyclomatic complexities, and vulnerabilities in code. Some common examples of code that are inefficient include dangling code, code in which objects are instantiated but not destroyed, and infinite loop constructs that cause resource exhaustion and eventually DoS. Within each module, code that is complex in logic with circular dependencies on other code modules (not being linearly independent) is not only a violation of the least common mechanisms design principle, but is also considered to be cyclomatically complex (covered in Chapter 4). Unit testing is useful to find out the cyclomatic complexities in code. Unit testing can also help uncover common coding vulnerabilities, such as hard coding values, and sensitive information, such as passwords and cryptographic keys inline in code.

Unit testing can start as soon as the developer completes coding a feature. However, software development is not done in a silo, and there are usually many developers working together on a single project. This is especially true with current-day, agile programming methodologies such as extreme programming (XP) or Scrum. Additionally, a single feature that the business wants may be split into multiple modules and assigned to different developers. In such a situation, unit testing can be a challenge. For example, the feature to calculate the total price could be split into different modules: one to get the shipping rate (getShippingRate()), one to calculate the Tax (calcTax()), another to get the conversion rate for international orders (getCurrencyConversionRate()), and one to compute any discounts (calcDiscount) offered. Each of these modules can also be assigned to different developers, and some modules may be dependent on others. In our example, the getShippingRate() is dependent on the completion of the getCurrency ConversionRate(), and before its operation can complete, it will need to invoke the getCurrencyConversionRate() method and expect the output from the get CurrencyConversionRate() method as input into its own operation. In such situations, unit testing one module that is related to or dependent on other modules can be a challenge, particularly when the method that is being invoked has not yet been coded. The developer who is assigned to code the getShippingRate() method has to wait on the developer who is assigned the getCurrencyConversionRate() for the unit test of getShippingRate() to be completed. This is where *drivers and stubs* can come in handy. Implementing drivers and stubs is a very common approach to unit testing. Drivers simulate the calling unit whereas stubs simulate the called unit. In our case, the getShippingRate() method will be the driver because it calls the getCurrencyConversionRate() method, which will be the stub. Drivers and stubs are akin to mock objects that alleviate unit testing dependencies. Drivers and stubs also mitigate a very common coding problem, which is the hard coding of values inline code. By calling the stub, the developer of the driver does not have the need to hard code values within the implementation code of the driver method. This helps with the integrity (reliability) of the code. Additionally, drivers and stubs programming eases the development with third party components when the external dependencies are not completely understood or known ahead of time.

Unit testing also facilitates collective code ownership in agile development methodologies. With the accelerated development efforts and multiple software teams collectively responsible for the code that is released, unit testing can help identify any potential issues raised by a programmer on the shared code base before it is released.

Unit testing provides many benefits, including the ability to:

- Validate functional logic.
- Find out inefficiencies, complexities, and vulnerabilities in code, as the code is tested after being isolated into units, as opposed to being integrated and tested as a whole. It is easier to find that needle in a haystack when the code is isolated into manageable units and tested.
- Automate testing processes by integrating easily with automated build scripts and tools.
- Extend test coverage.
- Enable collective code ownership in agile development.

5.4.1.2 Integration Testing

Just because unit testing results indicate that the code tested is functional (reliable), resilient (secure), and recoverable, it does not necessarily mean that the system itself will be secure. The security of the *sum of all parts* should also be tested. When individual units of code are aggregated and tested, it is referred to as integration testing. Integration testing is the logical next step after unit testing to validate the software's functionality, performance, and security. It helps to identify problems that occur when units of code are combined. If individual code units have successfully passed unit testing, but fail when they are integrated, then it is a clear-cut indication of software problems upon integration. This is why integration testing is necessary.

5.4.1.3 Logic Testing

Logic testing validates the accuracy of the software processing logic. Most developers are very intelligent, and good ones tend to automate recurring tasks by leveraging and reusing existing code. In this effort, they tend to copy code from other libraries or code sets that they have written. When this is done, it is critically important to validate the implementation details of the copied code for functionality and logic. For example, if code that performs the addition of two numbers is copied to multiply two numbers, the copied code needs to be validated to be make sure that the sign within the code that multiples two numbers is changed from "+" to "×," as shown in Figure 5.2. Line-by-line manual validation of logic or step-by-step debugging (which is a means to unit test) ensures that the code is not only reliably functioning, but also provides the benefit of extended test coverage to uncover any potential issues with the code.

Logic testing also includes the testing of predicates. A predicate is something that is affirmed or denied of the subject in a proposition in logic. Software that has a high measure of cyclomatic complexity must undergo logic testing before being shipped or released, especially if the processing logic of the software is dependent on user input.

Boolean predicates return a true or false depending on whether the software logic is met. Logic testing is usually performed by negating or mutating (varying) the intended functionality. Variations in logic can be created by applying operators (e.g., AND, OR, NOT EQUAL TO, EQUAL TO) to Boolean predicates. The source of Boolean predicates can be one or more of the following:

- Functional requirements specifications, such as UML diagrams and RTM
- Assurance (security) requirements
- Looping constructs (for, foreach, do while, while)
- Preconditions (if-then)

Code was NOT unit tested	Code was unit tested

```public int Add(int p_iA, int p_iB)```
 ```{```
    ```return p_iA + p_iB;```
 ```}```
	```public int Add(int p_iA, int p_iB)```
	 ```{```
	    ```return p_iA + p_iB;```
	 ```}```

```public int Multiply(int p_iA, int p_iB)```
 ```{```
    //Code without logic validation
    //Functionally this is the same as the Add function
    //although the method name is 'Mulitply'
    ```return p_iA + p_iB;```
 ```}```
	```public int Multiply(int p_iA, int p_iB)```
	 ```{```
	    //Code with logic validation
	    //'+' is changed to 'x'
	    ```return p_iA x p_iB;```
	 ```}```

Figure 5.2   Unit testing for logic validation.

Testing for blind SQL Injection is an example of logic testing in addition to being a test for error and exception handling.

5.4.1.4 Regression Testing

Software is not static. Business requirements change, and newer functionality is added to the code as newer versions are developed. Whenever code or data are modified, there is a likelihood for those changes to break something that was previously functional. Regression testing is performed to validate that the software did not break previous functionality or security and regress to a nonfunctional or insecure state. It is also known as *verification* testing.

Regression testing is primarily focused on implementation issues over design flaws. A regression test must be written and conducted for each fixed bug or database modification. It is performed to ensure that:

■ It is not merely the symptoms of bugs that are fixed, but that the root cause of the bugs.
■ The fixing of bugs does not inadvertently introduce any new bugs or errors.
■ The fixing of bugs does not make old bugs that were once fixed recur.
■ Modifications are still compliant with specified requirements.
■ Unmodified code and data have not been impacted.

Not only functionality needs to be tested, but also the security of the software. Sometimes implementation of security itself can deny existing functionality to valid users. An example of this is that a menu option previously available to all users is no longer available upon the implementation of role-based access control of menu options. Without proper regression testing, legitimate users will be denied functionality. It is also important to recognize that data changes and database modifications can have side effects, reverting functionality or reducing the security of the software, and so these need to be tested for regression as well.

Adequate time needs to be allocated for regression testing. It is recommended that a library of tests be developed that includes a predefined set of tests to be conducted before the release of any new version. The challenge with this approach is determining what tests should be part of the predefined set. At a bare minimum, tests that involve boundary conditions and timing should be included. Determining the relative attack surface quotient (RASQ) for newer versions of software with the RASQ values of the software before it was modified can be used as a measure to determine the need for regression testing and the tests that need to be run.

Usually, software QA teams perform regression testing, but since the changes that need to be made are often code-related, changes that need to be made are costly and project timelines can be affected. It is therefore advisable that regression testing be performed by developers after integration testing for code-related changes and also in the testing phase before release.

5.4.2 Recoverability Testing

In addition to testing for reliability, software testing must be performed to assure the *recoverability* of software. Such tests check if the software will be available when required and that it has the appropriate replication, load balancing, and disaster recovery (DR) mechanisms functioning properly. Recoverability testing validates that the software meets the customer's maximum tolerable downtime (MTD) and recovery time objective (RTO) levels.

Performance testing (load testing, stress testing) and scalability testing are examples of common recoverability testing, which are covered in the following section.

5.4.2.1 Performance Testing

Testing should be conducted to ensure that the software is performing to the service level agreement (SLA) and expectations of the business. The implementation of secure features can have a significant impact on performance, and this must be taken into account. Having smaller cache windows, complete mediation, and data replication are examples of security design and implementation features that can adversely impact performance. However, performance testing is not performed with the intent of finding vulnerabilities (bugs or flaws), but with the goal of determining any bottlenecks in the software. It is used to find and establish a baseline for future regression tests (covered later in this chapter). The results of a performance test can be used to tune the software to organizational or established industry benchmarks. Bottlenecks can be reduced by tuning the software. Tuning is performed to optimize resource allocation. You can tune the software code and configuration, the operating system, or the hardware. Examples of configuration tuning include setting the connection pooling limits in a database server, setting the maximum number of users allowed in a Web server, and setting time limits for sliding cache windows.

The two common means to test for performance are load testing and stress testing the software.

- Load Testing: In the context of software QA, load testing is the process of subjecting the software to volumes of operating tasks or users until it cannot handle any more, with the goal of identifying the maximum operating capacity for the software. Load testing is also referred to as longevity, endurance, or volume testing. It is important to understand that load testing is an iterative process. The software is not subjected to maximum load the very first time a load test is performed. The software is subjected to incremental load (tasks or users). Generally, the normal load is known, and in some cases the peak (maximum) load is known as well. When the peak load is known, load testing can be used to validate it or determine areas of improvement. When the peak load is not already known, load testing can be used to find it by identifying the threshold limit at which the software no longer meets the business SLA.

■ Stress Testing: If load testing is to determine the zenith point at which the software can operate with maximum capacity, stress testing is taking that test one step further. It is mainly aimed to determine the breaking point of the software, i.e., the point at which the software can no longer function. In stress testing, the software is subjected to extreme conditions such as maximum concurrency, limited computing resources, or heavy loads.

It is performed to determine the ability of the software to handle loads beyond its maximum capabilities and is primarily performed with two objectives. The first is to find out if the software can recover gracefully upon failure after the software breaks. The second is to assure that the software operates according to the design principle of failing securely. For example, if the maximum number of allowed authentication attempts has been passed, then the user must be notified of invalid login attempts with a specific nonverbose error message, while at the same time, that user's account needs to be locked out, as opposed to granting the user access automatically, even if it is only low-privileged guest access. Stress testing can also be used to find timing and synchronization issues, race conditions, resource exhaustion triggers, and events and deadlocks.

5.4.2.2 Scalability Testing

Scalability testing augments performance testing. It is a logical next step from performance testing the software. Its main objectives are to identify the loads (obtained from load testing) and to mitigate any bottlenecks that will hinder the ability of the software to scale to handle more load or changes in business processes or technology. For example, if order_id, which is the unique identifier in the ORDER table, is set to be of an integer type (Int16), with the growth in the business, there is a high likelihood that the orders that are placed after the order_id has reached the maximum range (65535) supported by the Int16 datatype will fail. It may be wiser to set the datatype for order_id to be a long integer (Int32) so that the software can scale with ease and without failure. Performance test baseline results are usually used in testing for the effectiveness of scalability. Degraded performance upon scaling implies the presence of some bottleneck that needs to be addressed (tuned or eliminated).

5.4.3 Resiliency Testing (Security Testing)

While functional testing is done to make sure that the software does not fail during operations or under pressure, security testing is performed with the intent of trying to make the software fail. Security testing is a test for the *resiliency* of software. It is testing that is performed to see if the software can be broken. It differs from stress testing (covered earlier) in the sense that stress testing is primarily performed to determine the software's recoverability, whereas security testing is conducted to attest to the presence and effectiveness of the security controls that are designed and implemented in the software. It is to be performed with a hostile user (attacker or blackhat) mindset. Good security testers are focused on one thing and one thing only, which is to break the software by circumventing any protection mechanisms in the software. Typically, attackers think out of the box as a norm and are usually very creative, finding new ways to attack the software, while learning from and improving their knowledge and expertise from each experience. Security testing begins with creating a test strategy of high-risk items first, followed by low-risk items. The threat model from the design phase that was updated during the implementation phase can be used to determine critical sections of code and software features.

5.4.3.1 Motives, Opportunities, and Means

In the physical security world, for an attack to be successful there needs to be a confluence of three aspects: *motive, opportunity, and means*. The same is true in the information security space, as depicted in Figure 5.3. For cyber crime to be proven in a court of law, the same three aspects of crime must be determined. The motive of the attacker is usually tied to something that the attacker seeks to gain. This could range from just being recognized (fame) among peers, revenge from a disgruntled employee, or money. The opportunity for an attacker is directly related to the connectivity of the software and the vulnerabilities that exist in it. The expertise of and tools available to the hacker are the means by which they can exploit the

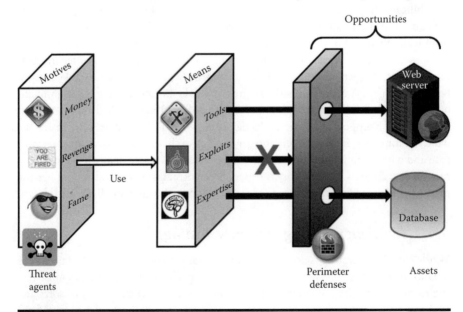

Figure 5.3   Motive, opportunity, and means.

software. Security testing can address two of the three aspects of crime. It can do little about the motive of an attacker, but the opportunities and means by which an attacker can exploit the software can be determined by security testing.

5.4.3.2 Testing of Security Functionality versus Security Testing

It is also important to distinguish between the testing of security functionality and security testing. Security testing is testing with an attacker perspective to validate the ability of the software to withstand attack (resiliency), while testing security functionality (e.g., authentication mechanisms, auditing capabilities, error handling) in software is meant to assure that the functionality of protection mechanisms is working properly. Testing security functionality is not necessarily the same as security testing.

Although security testing is aimed at validating software resiliency, it can also be performed to attest to the reliability and recoverability of software. Since integrity of data and systems is a measure of its reliability, security testing that validates data and system integrity issues attest to software reliability. Security testing can validate controls, such as fail secure mechanisms, and that proper error and exception handling are in place and are working properly to resume its functional operations as per the customer's MTD and RTO, which are measures of the software's recoverability. Security testing is also indicative of due diligence and due care measures that the organization takes to develop and release secure software for its customers.

5.4.3.3 The Need for Security Testing

Security testing should be part of the overall SDLC process, and engaging the testers to be part of the process early on is recommended. They should be allowed to assist in threat modeling exercises and be participants in the review of the threat model. This gives the software developer team an opportunity to discover and address prospective threats and gives the software testing team an advantage to start developing test scripts early on in the process. Architectural and design issues, weaknesses in logic, insecure coding, effectiveness of safeguards and countermeasures, and operational security issues can all be uncovered by security testing.

5.5 Security Testing Methodologies

Security testing can be accomplished using several different methodologies.

5.5.1 White Box Testing

Also known by other names such as glass box or clear box testing, white box testing is a security testing methodology based on the knowledge of how the software is designed and implemented. It is broadly known as *full knowledge* assessment because the tester has complete knowledge of the software. It can be used to test both the use case (intended behavior) as well as the misuse case (unintended behavior) of the software and can be conducted at any time after the development of code, although it is best advised to do so while conducting unit tests. In order to perform white box security testing, it is imperative first to understand the scope, context, and intended functionality of the software so that the inverse of that can be tested with an attacker's perspective.

Inputs to the white box testing method include architectural and design documents, source code, configuration information and files, use and misuse cases, test data, test environments, and security specifications. White box testing of code requires access to the source code. This makes it possible to detect embedded code issues, such as Trojans, logic bombs, impersonation code, spyware, and backdoors, implanted by insiders. These inputs are structurally analyzed to ensure that the implementation of code follows design specifications, and whether security protection mechanisms or vulnerabilities exist. White box testing is also known as structural analysis. Data/information flow, control flow, interfaces, trust boundaries (entry and exit points), configuration, and error handling are methodically and structurally analyzed for security. Source code analyzers can be used to automate some of the source code testing. The output of a white box test is the white box test report, which includes defects (or incidents), flaws and deviations from design specifications, change requests, and recommendations to address security issues. The white box security testing process is depicted in Figure 5.4.

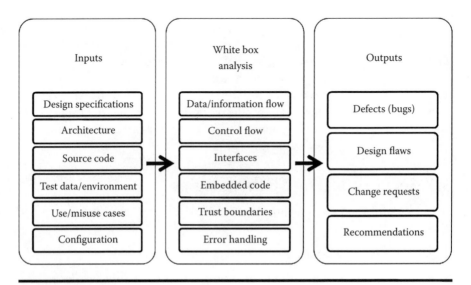

Figure 5.4   White box security testing.

5.5.2 Black Box Testing

If white box testing is full knowledge assessment, black box testing is its opposite. It is broadly known as *zero knowledge* assessment, because the tester has very limited to no knowledge of the internal workings of the software being tested. Architectural or design documents, configuration information or files, use and misuse cases, and the source code of the software is not available to or known by the testing team conducting black box testing. The software is essentially viewed as a "black box" that is tested for its resiliency by determining how it responds (outputs) to the tester's input, as illustrated in Figure 5.5. White box testing is structural analysis of the software's security, whereas black box testing is behavioral analysis of the software's security.

Black box testing can be performed before deployment (predeployment) or periodically once it is deployed (postdeployment). Depending on when black box testing is conducted, its objectives are different. Predeployment black box testing is used to identify and address security vulnerabilities proactively, so that the risk of the software's getting hacked is minimized. Postdeployment black box testing helps to find out vulnerabilities that exist in the deployed production (or actual runtime environment) and can also be used to attest to the presence and effectiveness of the software security controls and protection mechanisms. Because identifying and fixing security issues early in the life cycle is less expensive, it is advisable to conduct black box testing predeployment. But doing so will not give insight into actual runtime environment issues, so when predeployment black box tests are conducted, an environment that mirrors or simulates the deployed production environment should be used.

5.5.3 Fuzzing

Also known as fuzz testing or fault injection testing, fuzzing is a brute-force type of testing in which faults (random and pseudo-random input data) are injected into

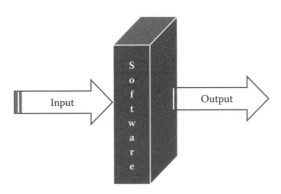

Figure 5.5   Black box testing.

the software and its behavior observed. It is a test whose results are indicative of the extent and effectiveness of input validation. Fuzzing can be used not only to test applications and their programming interfaces (application programming interfaces [APIs]), but also protocols and file formats. It is used to find coding defects and security bugs that can result in buffer overflows that cause remote code execution, unhandled exceptions, and hanging threads that cause DoS, state machine logic faults, and buffer boundary checking defects. The data that are used for fuzzing are commonly referred to as fuzz data or fuzzing oracles. Fuzz data can be either synthesized or mutated. Synthesized fuzz data are data that generated from scratch without being based on previous input, whereas mutated data are valid data that are corrupted so that their format (data structure) is not what the application expects.

Although fuzzing is a very common methodology of black box testing, not all fuzz tests are necessarily black box tests. Fuzzing can be performed as a white box test as well. Black box fuzzing is the sending of malformed data with any verification of the actual code paths that were covered and ones that were not. White box fuzzing is sending malformed data with verification of all code paths. When there is zero knowledge of the software and debugging the software to determine weaknesses is not an option, black box fuzzing is used, and when information about the makeup of the software (e.g., target code paths, configuration) is known, white box fuzzing is performed.

The two types of fuzzing prevalent today are *dumb fuzzing* and *smart fuzzing*. When truly random data without any consideration for the data structure is used, it is known as dumb fuzzing. This can be dangerous and lead to DoS, destruction, and complete disruption of the software's operations. Smart fuzzing is preferred because the data structure, such as encoding and relations (checksums, bit flags, and offsets), are known, and the input data are variations of these data structures.

Black box dumb fuzzing covers the least amount of code and finds the least number of bugs, whereas white box smart fuzzing has maximum code coverage and can detect all of the bugs or weaknesses in code.

5.5.4 Scanning

I once asked one of my students, "Why do we need to scan our networks and software for vulnerabilities?" and his response, although amusing, was profound. He said, "If we don't, someone else will." When there is very limited or no prior knowledge about the software makeup, its internal workings, or the computing ecosystem in which it operates, black box testing can start by scanning the network as well as the software for vulnerabilities. Network scans are performed with the goal of mapping out the computing ecosystem. Wireless access points and wireless infrastructure scans must also be performed. These scans help determine the devices, operating system software (applications), services (daemons), ports, protocols, application and infrastructural interfaces, and Web server versions that make up the environment in which the software will run. They can also be used to find out vulnerabilities that exist in the network or in the software that an attacker can exploit.

The process of determining an operating system version is known as *OS finger-printing*. OS fingerprinting is possible because each operating system has a unique way it responds to packets that hit the TCP/IP stack. An example of OS finger-printing using the Nmap (Network Mapper) scanner is illustrated in Figure 5.6.

There are two main means by which an OS can be fingerprinted: *active* and *passive*. Active OS fingerprinting involves the sending of crafted, abnormal packets to the remote host and analyzing the responses from the remote host. If the remote host network is monitored and protected using intrusion detection systems, active fingerprinting can be detected. The popular Nmap tool uses active fingerprint-ing to detect OS versions. Unlike active fingerprinting, passive OS fingerprinting does not contact the remote host. It captures traffic originating from a host on the network and analyzes the packets. In passive fingerprinting, the remote host is not aware that it is being fingerprinted. Tools such as Siphon, which was developed by the HoneyNet project, and P0f use passive fingerprinting to detect OS versions. Active fingerprinting is fast and useful when there are a large number of hosts to scan, but it can be detected by IDS and IPS. Passive fingerprinting is relatively slower and best used for single host systems, especially if there is historical data.

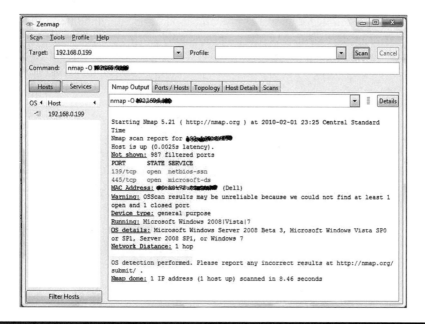

Figure 5.6   Fingerprinting operating system.

Passive fingerprinting can also go undetected since there is no active probe of the remote host being fingerprinted.

A scanning technique that can be used to enumerate and determine server versions is known as banner grabbing. Banner grabbing can be used for legitimate purposes, such as inventorying the systems and services on the network, but an attacker can use banner grabbing to identify network hosts that have vulnerable services running on them. The File Transfer Protocol (FTP) port 21, Simple Mail Transfer Protocol (SMTP) port 25, and Hypertext Transfer Protocol (HTTP) port 80 are examples of common ports used in banner grabbing. By looking at the server field in a HTTP response header, upon request, one can determine the Web server and its version. This is a very common Web server fingerprinting exercise when black box testing Web applications. Tools such as Netcat or Telnet are used in banner grabbing. Figure 5.7 depicts banner grabbing a Web server version using Telnet.

In addition to scanning the network (wired and wireless), software can be scanned. Software scanning can be either static or dynamic. Static scanning includes scanning the source code for vulnerabilities; dynamic scanning means that the software is scanned at runtime. Static scanning using source code analyzers is usually performed during the code review process in the development phase, whereas dynamic scanning is performed using crawlers and spidering tools during the testing phase of the SDLC.

Compliance with the Payment Card Industry Data Security Standard (PCI DSS) requires that organizations must periodically test their security systems and processes by scanning for network, host, and application vulnerabilities in the card holder data environment. The scan report should not only describe the type of vulnerability, but also provide risk ratings and recommendations on how to fix the vulnerabilities. Figure 5.8 is an illustration of a sample vulnerability scan report for PCI compliance.

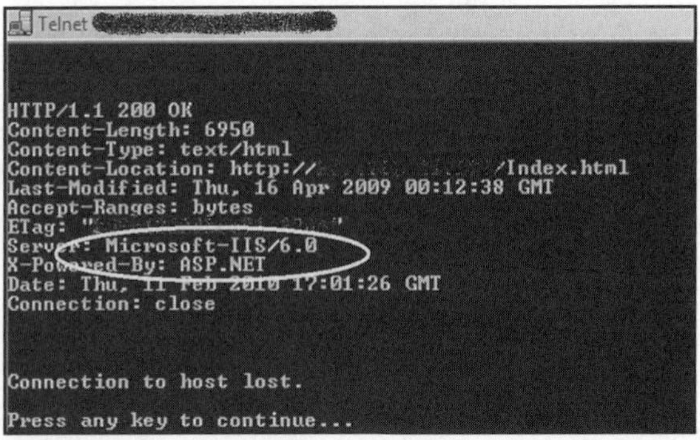

Figure 5.7   Banner grabbing Web server version.

Level	Severity	Description
5	**Urgent**	Trojan horses; file read and write exploit; remote command execution
4	**Critical**	Potential Trojan horses; file read exploit
3	**High**	Limited exploit of read; directory browsing; DoS
2	**Medium**	Sensitive configuration information can be obtained by hackers
1	**Low**	Information can be obtained by hackers on configuration

Figure 5.8   PCI scan report sample.

Scanning can therefore be used to

- Map the computing ecosystems, infrastructural, and application interfaces.
- Identify server versions, open ports, and running services.
- Inventory and validate asset management databases.
- Identify patch levels.
- Prove due diligence due care for compliance reasons.

5.5.5 Penetration Testing (Pen-Testing)

Vulnerability scanning is passive in nature, meaning we use it to detect the presence of weaknesses and loopholes that can be exploited by an attacker. On the other hand, penetration testing is active in nature, because it goes one step further than vulnerability scanning. The main objective of penetration testing is to see if the network and software assets can be compromised by exploiting the vulnerabilities that were determined by the scans. The subtle difference between vulnerability scans and penetration testing (commonly referred to as pen-testing) is that a vulnerability scan identifies issues that can be attacked, whereas penetration testing measures the resiliency of the network or software by evaluating real attacks against those vulnerabilities. In penetration testing, attempts to emulate the actions of a potential threat agent (e.g., hacker or malware) are performed. In most cases, pen-testing is done after the software has been deployed, but this need not be the case. It is advisable to perform black box assessments using penetration testing techniques before deployment for the presence of security controls and after deployment to ensure that they are working effectively to withstand attacks.

When penetration testing is performed after deployment, it is important to recognize that *rules of engagement* need to be followed, and the penetration test itself is methodically conducted. The rules of engagement should explicitly define the scope of the penetration test for the testing team, regardless of whether they are an internal team or an external security service provider. Definition of scope includes restricting IP addresses and the software interfaces that can be tested.

Most importantly, the environment, data, infrastructural, and application interfaces that are not within the scope must be identified before the test and communicated to the pen-testing team and, during the test monitoring, must be in place to assure that the pen-testing team does not go beyond the scope of the test. The technical guide to information security testing and assessment, published as *Special Publication (SP) 800-115* by the National Institute of Standards and Technology (NIST), provides guidance on conducting penetration testing. The *OSTMM* (covered in Chapter 1) is known for its prescriptive guidance on the activities that need to be performed before, during, and after a penetration test, including the measurement of results. When conducted postdeployment, penetration testing can be used as a mechanism to certify the software (or system) as part of the validation and verification (V&V) activity inside of certification and accreditation (C&A). V&V and C&A are covered in Chapter 7.

Generically, the pen-testing process includes the following steps:

1. *Reconnaissance (Enumeration and Discovery):* Enumeration techniques (covered under scanning), such as fingerprinting, banner grabbing, port and services scans, and vulnerability scanning, can be used to probe and discover the network layout and the internal workings of the software within that network. WHOIS, ARIN, and DNS lookups along with Web-based reconnaissance are common techniques for enumerating and discovering network infrastructure configurations.

2. *Resiliency Attestation (Attack and Exploitation):* Upon completion of reconnaissance activities, once potential vulnerabilities are discovered, the next step is to try to exploit those weaknesses. Attacks can include brute forcing of authentication credentials, escalation of privileges to administrator (root) level privileges, deletion of sensitive logs and audit records, disclosure of sensitive information, and alteration/destruction of data to causing DoS by crashing the software or system. Defensive coding tests for software threats and vulnerabilities are covered later in this chapter.

3. *Removal of Evidence (Cleanup Activities) and Restoration:* Penetration testers often establish back doors, turn on services, create accounts, elevate themselves to administrator privileges, load scripts, and install agents and tools in target systems. After attack and exploitation, it is important that any changes made in the target system or software for conducting the penetration test are removed and the original state of the system is restored. Not cleaning up and leaving behind accounts, services, and tools and not restoring the system leave it with an increased attack surface, and any subsequent attempts to exploit the software are made easy for the real attacker. It is therefore essential not to exit from the penetration testing exercise until all cleanup and restoration activities have been completed.

4. *Reporting and Recommendations:* The last phase of penetration testing is to report on the findings of the penetration test. This report should include

not only technical vulnerabilities covering the network and software, but also noncompliance with organization policy and weaknesses in organizational processes and people know-how. Merely identifying, categorizing, and reporting vulnerabilities are important, but value is added when the findings of the penetration test result in a plan of action and milestones (POA&M) and mitigation strategies. The POA&M is also referred to as a management action plan (MAP). Some examples of POA include updating policies and processes, redesigning the software architecture, patching and hardening, defensive coding, user awareness, and deployment of security technologies and tools. When choosing a mitigation strategy, it is recommended to compare the POA&M against the operational requirements of the business, balance the functionality expected with the security that needs to be in place, and use the computed residual risk to implement them.

The penetration test report has many uses as listed below. It can be used

- To provide insight into the state of security.
- As a reference for corrective action.
- To define security controls that will mitigate identified vulnerabilities.
- To demonstrate due diligence due care processes for compliance.
- To enhance SDLC activities such as security risk assessments, C&A, and process improvements.

5.5.6 *White Box Testing versus Black Box Testing*

As we have seen, security testing can be accomplished using either a white box approach or a black box approach. Each methodology has its merits and challenges. White box testing can be performed early in the SDLC processes, thereby making it possible to build security into the software. It can help developers to write hack-resilient code, as vulnerabilities that are detected can be identified precisely, in some cases to the exact line of code. However, white box testing may not cover code dependencies (e.g., services or libraries) or third party components. It provides little insight into the exploitability of the vulnerability itself and so may not present an accurate risk picture. Just because the vulnerability is present, it does not mean that it will be exploited, as compensating controls may be in place that white box testing may not uncover. On the other hand, black box testing can attest to the exploitability of weaknesses in both simulated and actual production systems. The other benefit of black box testing is that there is no need for source code, and the test can be conducted both before (pre-) and after (post-) deployment. The limitations of black box testing are that the exact cause of vulnerability may not be easily detectable, and the test coverage itself can be limited to the scope of the assessment.

The following section covers different criteria that can be used to determine the type of approach to take when validating software security. These include:

■ Root cause identification: When vulnerability is detected, the first and appropriate course of action that must be taken is to determine and address the root cause of the vulnerability. Root cause analysis (RCA) of software security is easier when the source code is available for review. Black box testing can provide information about the symptoms of vulnerabilities, but with white box testing, the exact line of code that causes the vulnerability can be determined and handled so that fixed bugs do not resurface in subsequent version releases.

■ Extent of code coverage: Because white box testing requires access to source code and each line of code can be analyzed for security issues, it provides greater code coverage than does black box testing. When complete code coverage is necessary, white box testing is recommended. Software that processes highly sensitive information and which is mission critical in nature must undergo complete code analysis for vulnerabilities.

■ Number of false positives and false negatives: When a vulnerability is reported and in reality it is not a true vulnerability, it is referred to as a false positive result of security testing. On the other hand, when a vulnerability that exists goes undetected in the results of security testing, it is said to be a false negative. The number of false positives and false negatives are relatively higher in black box testing than in white box testing because black box testing looks at the behavior of the software as opposed to its structure and normal or abnormal behavior may not be known.

■ Logical flaws detection: It is important to recognize that logical flaws are not really implementation bugs and syntactic in nature, but are design issues and semantic in nature. So white box testing using just source code analysis cannot help uncover these flaws. However, since, in white box testing, other contextual artifacts, such as the architectural and design documents and configuration information, are present, it is easier to find logical flaws using white box testing rather than black box testing.

■ Deployment issues determination: Since source code should not be available in the production environment, white box testing is done in the development or test environments, unlike black box testing, which can be done in a production or production-like environment. The attestation of deployment environment resilience and discovery of actual configuration issues in the environment where the software will be deployed is possible with black box testing. Both data and environment issues need to be covered as part of the attestation activity.

Table 5.1 tabulates the comparison between the white box and black box security testing methodologies.

Table 5.1 Comparison between White Box and Black Box Security Testing

	White Box	Black Box
Also known as	Full knowledge assessment	Zero knowledge assessment
Assesses the software's	Structure	Behavior
Root cause identification	Can identify the exact line of code or design issue causing the vulnerability	Can analyze only the symptoms of the problem and not necessarily the cause
Extent of code coverage possible	Greater; the source code is available for analysis	Limited; not all code paths may be analyzed
Number of false positives and false negatives	Low; contextual information is available	High; since normal behavior is unknown, expected behavior can also be falsely identified as anomalous
Logical flaws detection	High; design and architectural documents are available for review	Low; limited to no design and architectural documentation is available for review
Deployment issues identification	Limited; assessment is performed in predeployment environments	Greater; assessment can be performed in pre- as well as postdeployment production or production-like simulated environment

So then, what kind of testing is "best" to assure the reliability, resiliency and recoverability of software? The answer is, "It depends." For determining syntactic issues early on in the SDLC, white box testing is appropriate. If the source code is not available and testing needs to be performed with a truly hostile user perspective, then black box testing is the choice. In reality, however, usually a hybrid of the two approaches, also referred to as gray box or translucent box, is performed to validate security protection mechanisms in place. For a comprehensive security assurance assessment, the hybrid gray box approach is recommended, in which white box testing is conducted predeployment in development and test environments, and black box testing is performed pre- and postdeployment as well in production-like and actual production environments.

5.6 Software Security Testing

We have covered so far the various types of software testing for QA and the different methodologies for security testing. In the following section, security testing as it is pertinent to software security issues will be covered. We will learn about the different types of tests and how they can be performed to attest to the security of code that is developed in the development phase of the SDLC.

Before we start testing for software security issues in code, one of the first questions to ask is whether the software being tested is new or a version release. If it is a version release, we must check to ensure that the state of security has not regressed to a more insecure state than it had in its previous version. This can be accomplished by conducting regression tests (covered earlier) for security issues. We should specifically test for the introduction of any newer side effects that impact security and the use of banned or unsafe APIs in previous versions.

For software revisions, regression testing must be conducted, and for all versions, new or revisions, the following security tests must be performed, if applicable, to validate the strength of the security controls. Using a categorized list of threats as a template of security testing is effective in ensuring comprehensive coverage of the varied threats to software. The National Security Agency (NSA) identity and access management (IAM) threat list and STRIDE threat lists are examples of categorized threat lists that can be used in security testing. Ideally, the same threat list that was used when threat modeling the software will be used for conducting security tests. This way, security testing can be used to validate the threat model.

5.6.1 Testing for Input Validation

Most software security vulnerabilities can be mitigated by input validation. Such hostile actions as buffer overflows, injection flaws, and scripting attacks can be effectively reduced if the software performs validation of input before accepting it for processing.

In a client/server environment, input validation tests for both the client and the server should be performed. Client-side input validation tests are more a test for performance and user experience than for security. If you only have the time or resource to perform input validation tests on either the client or the server, choose to ensure that validation of input happens on the server side.

Attributes of the input, such as its range, format, data type, and values, must all be tested. When these attributes are known, input validation tests can be conducted using pattern matching expression and/or fuzzing techniques (covered earlier). Regular expression (RegEx) can be used for pattern matching input validation. Some common examples of RegEx patterns are tabulated in Table 5.2. Tests must be conducted to ensure that the whitelist (acceptable list) of input is allowed whereas the blacklist (dangerous or unacceptable) of input is denied. Not only must the test include the validation of the whitelists and blacklists, but it must also include the anti-tampering protection of these lists. Since canonicalization can be used to bypass input filters, both the normal and canonical representations of input should be tested. When the input format is known, smart fuzzing can be used, otherwise dumb fuzzing using random and pseudo-random inputs values can be used to attest the effective of input validation.

5.6.2 Injection Flaws Testing

Since injection attacks take the user-supplied input and treat it as a command or part of a command, input validation is an effective defensive safeguard against injection flaws. In order to perform input validation tests, it is first important to determine the sources of input and the events in which the software will connect to the backend store or command environment. These sources can include authentication forms, search input fields, hidden fields in Web pages, querystrings in the URL address bar, and more. Once these sources are determined, input validation tests can be used to ensure that the software will not be susceptible to injection attacks.

There are other tests that need to be performed as well. These include tests to ensure that

- Parameterized queries that are not themselves susceptible to injection are used.
- Dynamic query construction is disallowed.
- Error messages and exceptions are explicitly handled so that even Boolean queries (used in blind SQL injection attacks) are appropriately addressed.
- Nonessential procedures and statements are removed from the database.
- Database-generated errors do not disclose internal database structure.
- Parsers that prohibit external entities are used. External entities is a feature of XML that allows developers to define their own XML entities, and this can lead to XML injection attacks.
- Whitelisting that allows only alphanumeric characters is used when querying LDAP stores.
- Developers use escape routines for shell command instead of custom writing their own.

5.6.3 Testing for Nonrepudiation

The issue of nonrepudiation is enforceable by proper session management and auditing. Test cases should validate that audit trails can accurately determine the actor and their actions. It must also ensure that misuse cases generate auditable trails appropriately. If the code is written to perform auditing automatically, then tests to assure that an attacker cannot exploit this section of the code should be performed. Security testing should not fail to validate that user activity is unique, protected,

Table 5.2 Commonly Used Regular Expressions (RegEx)

Regular Expression	Validates	Description	Example
^[a-zA-Z"-'\s]{1,20}$	Name	Allows up to 20 uppercase and lowercase characters and some special characters that are common to some names	John Doe O' Hanley Johnson-Paul
^([0-9a-zA-Z]([-\.\w]*[0-9a-zA-Z])*@([0-9a-zA-Z][-\w]*[0-9a-zA-Z]\.)+[a-zA-Z]{2,9})$	Email	Validates an email address	mpaul@isc2.org user@ mycompany.com
^(ht|f)tp(s?)\:\/\/[0-9a-zA-Z]([-\.\w]*[0-9a-zA-Z])*(:(0-9)*)*(\/?)([a-zA-Z0-9\-\.\?\,\'\/\\\+&%\$#_]*)?$	URL	Validates a uniform resource locator (URL)	http://www.isc2 .org
(?!^[0-9]*$)(?!^[a-zA-Z]*$)^([a-zA-Z0-9]{8,15})$	Password	Validates a strong password; it must be between eight and 15 characters, contain at least one numeric value and one alphabetic character, and must not contain special characters	
^(-)?\d+(\.\d\d)?$	Currency	Validates currency format; if there is a decimal point, it requires two numeric characters after the decimal point	289.00

```
using System.Security.Principal;

//Code that will perform the impersonation of the authenticated user identity
WindowsImpersonationContext impersonationContext;
impersonationContext = ((WindowsIdentity)User.Identity).Impersonate();

//The code that runs below with the impersonation context of the authenticated user must also be tested
//Do some action here

//Reverting the impersonation identity to the original identity before it took the context of the authenticated user
impersonationContext.Undo();

//Test to make sure that the impersonation context was reverted successfully
```

Figure 5.9   Code that impersonates the authenticating user.

and traceable. Tests cases should also include verifying the protection and management of the audit trail and the integrity of audit logs. *NIST Special Publication 800-92* provides guidance on the protection of audit trails and the management of security logs. The confidentiality of the audited information and its retention for the required period of time should be checked as well.

5.6.4 Testing for Spoofing

Both network and software spoofing test cases need to be executed. Network spoofing attacks include address resolution protocol (ARP) poisoning, IP address spoofing, and media access control (MAC) address spoofing. On the software side, user and certificate spoofing tests, phishing tests, and verification of code that allows impersonation of other identities, as depicted in Figure 5.9, need to be performed. Testing the spoofability of the user and/or certificate along with verifying the presence of transport layer security can ensure secure communication and protection against man-in-the-middle (MITM) attacks. Cookie expiration testing must also be conducted, along with verifying that authentication cookies are encrypted.

The best way to check for defense against phishing attacks is to test users for awareness of social engineering techniques and attacks.

5.6.5 Failure Testing

Software is prone to failure due to accidental user error or intentional attack. Not only should software be tested for QA so that it does not fail in its functionality, but failure testing for security must be performed. Requirement gaps, omitted design, and coding errors can all result in defects that cause the software to fail. Testing to determine if the failure is a result of multiple defects or if a single defect yields multiple failures must be performed.

Software security failure testing includes the verification of the following security principles:

- Fail Secure (Fail Safe): Tests to verify if the confidentiality, integrity, and availability of the software or the data it handles when the software fails must be conducted. Special attention should be given to verifying any authentication processes. Test cases must be conducted to validate the proper functioning of account lockout mechanisms and denying access by default when the configured number of allowed authentication attempts has been exceeded.
- Error and Exception Handling: Errors and exception handling tests include testing the messaging and encapsulation of error details. Tests conducted should attempt to make the software fail, and when the software fails, error messages must be checked to make sure that they do not reveal any unnecessary details. Assurance tests to verify that exceptions are handled and the details are encapsulated using user-defined messages and redirects must be performed. If configuration settings allow displaying the error and exception details to a local user, but redirect a remote user to a default error handling page, then error handling tests must be conducted simulating the user to be local on the machine as well as coming from a remote location.

If the errors and exceptions are logged and only a reference identifier for that issue is displayed to the end user, as depicted in Figure 5.10, then tests to assure that the reference identifier mapping to the actual error or exception is protected need to be performed as well.

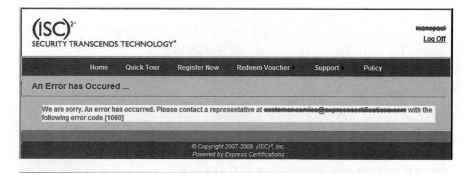

Figure 5.10   Reference identifier used to abstract actual error details.

5.6.6 Cryptographic Validation Testing

Cryptographic validation includes the following attestation:

■ Standards Conformance: Confirmation that cryptographic modules conform to prescribed standards, such as the Federal Information Processing Standards (FIPS) 140-2, and that cryptographic algorithms used are standard algorithms, such as AES, RSA, and DSA, is necessary. FIPS 140-2 testing is conducted against a defined cryptographic module and provides a suite of conformance tests to four security levels, from the lowest to the highest security. Knowledge of the details of each security level is beyond the scope of this book, but it is advisable that the CSSLP be familiar with the FIPS 140-2 requirements, specifications, and testing as published by NIST.

■ Environment Validation: The computing environment in which cryptographic operations occur must be tested as well. The ISO/IEC 15408 common criteria (CC) evaluation can be used for this attestation. CC evaluation assurance levels do not directly map to the FIPS 140-2 security levels, and a FIPS 140-2 certificate is usually not acceptable in place of a CC certificate for environment validation.

■ Data Validation: FIPS 140-2 testing considers data in unvalidated cryptographic systems and environments as data that are not protected at all, i.e., as unprotected cleartext. The protection of sensitive, private, and personal data using cryptographic protection should be validated for confidentiality assurance.

■ Cryptographic Implementation: Seed values needed for cryptographic algorithms should be checked to be random and not easily guessable. The uniqueness, randomness, and strength of identifiers, such as session ID, can be determined using phase space analysis, and resource and time permitting, these tests need to be conducted. White box tests to make sure that cryptographic keys are not hard code inline code in clear text should be conducted. Additionally, key generation, exchange, storage, retrieval, archival, and disposal processes must be validated as well. The ability to decrypt cipher text data when keys are cycled must be checked as well.

5.6.7 Testing for Buffer Overflow Defenses

Since the consequences of buffer overflow vulnerabilities are extremely serious, testing to ensure defense against buffer overflow weaknesses must be conducted. Buffer overflow defense tests can be both black box and white box in nature. Black box testing for overflow defense can be performed using fuzzing techniques. White box testing includes verifying

■ That the input is sanitized and its size validated.
■ Bounds checking of memory allocation is performed.

- Conversion of data types from one are explicitly performed.
- Banned and unsafe APIs are not used.
- Code is compiled with compiler switches that protect the stack and/or randomize address space layout.

5.6.8 Testing for Privilege Escalations Defenses

Testing for elevated privileges or privilege escalation is to be conducted to verify that the user or process cannot gain access to more resources or functionality than they are allowed. Privilege escalation can be either *vertical* or *horizontal* or both. Vertical escalation is the condition wherein the subject (user or process) with lower rights gets access to resources that are to be restricted to subjects with higher rights. An example of vertical escalation is a nonadministrator gaining access to administrator or super user functionality. Horizontal escalation is the condition wherein a subject gets access to resources that are to be restricted to other subjects at their same privilege level. An example of horizontal escalation is an online banking user's being able to view the bank accounts of other online banking users.

Insecure direct object reference design flaws and coding bugs with complete mediation can lead to privilege escalation, so parameter manipulation checks need to be conducted to verify that privileges cannot be escalated. In Web applications, both POST (form) and GET (querystring) parameters need to be checked.

5.6.9 Anti-Reversing Protection Testing

Testing for anti-reversing protection is particularly important for shrink wrap, commercial off-the-shelf (COTS) software, but even in business applications, tests to assure anti-reversing should be conducted. The following are some of the recommended tests.

- Testing to validate the presence of obfuscated code is important. Equally important is the testing of the processes to obfuscate and de-obfuscate code. The verification of the ability to de-obfuscate obfuscated code, especially if there is a change in the obfuscation software, is critically important.
- Binary analysis testing can be used to check if symbolic (e.g., class names, class member names, names of instantiated global objects) and textual information that will be useful to a reverse engineering is removed from the program executable.
- White box testing can be used to verify the presence of code that detects and prevents debuggers by terminating the executing program flow. User-level and kernel-level debugger APIs, such as the IsDebuggerPresent API and SystemKernelDebuggerInformation API, can be leveraged to protect against reversing debuggers, and testing should verify their presence and function.

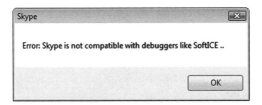

Figure 5.11   Program incompatibility with debugger warning.

Tests should attempt to attach debuggers to executing programs to see how the program responds. Figure 5.11 depicts how the Skype program is not compatible with debuggers such as SoftICE.

5.7 Other Testing

5.7.1 Environment Testing

Another important aspect of software security assurance testing includes the testing of the security of the environment itself in which the software will operate. Environment testing needs to verify the integrity not just of the configuration of the environment, but also that of the data. Trust boundaries demarcate one environment from another, and end-to-end scenarios need to be tested. With the adoption of Web 2.0 technologies, the line between the client and server is thinning, and in cases where content is aggregated from various sources (environments), as in the case of mashups, testing must be thorough to assure that the end user is not subject to risk. Interoperability testing, simulation testing, and DR testing are important verification exercises that must be performed to attest to the security aspects of software.

5.7.1.1 Interoperability Testing

When software operates in disparate environments, it is imperative to verify the resiliency of the interfaces that exist between the environments. This is particularly important if credentials are shared for authentication purposes between these environments, as is the case with single sign-on. The following is a list of interoperability testing that can be performed to verify that

- Security standards (such as WS-Security for Web services implementation) are used.
- Complete mediation is effectively working to ensure that authentication cannot be bypassed.

- Tokens used for transfer of credentials cannot be stolen, spoofed, or replayed.
- Authorization checks postauthentication are working properly.

It is also necessary to check the software's upstream and downstream dependency interfaces. For example, it is important to verify that there is secure access to the key by which a downstream application can decrypt data that were encrypted by an application upstream in the chain of dependent applications. Furthermore, tests to verify that the connections between dependent applications are secure need to be conducted.

5.7.1.2 Simulation Testing

The effectiveness of least privilege implementation and configuration mismatches can be uncovered using simulation testing. A common issue faced by software teams is that the software functions as desired in the development and test environments, but fails in the production environment. A familiar and dangerous response to this situation is that the software is configured to run with administrative or elevated privileges. The most probable root cause for such varied behavior is that the configuration settings in these environments differ. When production systems cannot be mirrored, assurance can still be achieved by simulation testing. By simulating the configuration settings between these environments, configuration mismatch issues can be determined. Additionally, the need to run the software in elevated privileges in the production environment can be determined and appropriate least privilege implementation measures can be taken.

It is crucially important to test data issues as well, but this can be a challenge. It may be necessary to test cascading relationships, but data to support that relationship may not be available in the test environment. Usually, production data are migrated to the testing environments, and this is a serious threat to confidentiality. It can also have compliance and legal ramifications. Production data must never be ported and processed in test environments. For example, payroll data of employees or credit card data of real customers should never be available in the test environments. It is advisable to use dummy data by creating them from scratch in the test or simulated environment. In cases where production data need to be migrated to maintain referential integrity between sets of data, then only nonconfidential information must be migrated, or the data must be obfuscated or masked. Testing must verify that data in test environments do not violate security and simulation testing for data issues must be controlled.

5.7.1.3 Disaster Recovery (DR) Testing

An important aspect of environment testing is the ability of the software to restore its operation after a disaster happens. DR testing verifies the recoverability of the software. It also uncovers data accuracy, integrity, and system availability issues. DR testing can be used to gauge the effectiveness of error handling and auditing in software as well. Important questions to answer using DR testing include: Does the software fail securely, and how does it report errors upon downtime? Is there proper logging of the failure in place? Failover testing is part of disaster testing, and the accuracy of the tests is dependent on how closely a real disaster can be simulated. Since this can be a costly proposition, proper planning, resource, and budget allocation is necessary, and testing by simulating disasters must be undertaken for availability assurance.

5.7.2 Privacy Testing

Software should be tested to assure privacy. For software that handles personal data, privacy testing must be part of the test plan. This should include the verification of organizational policy controls that impact privacy. It should also encompass the monitoring of network traffic and the communication between end points to assure that personal information is not disclosed. Tests for the appropriateness of notices and disclaimers when personal information is collected must also be conducted. This is critically important when collecting information from minors or children and privacy testing of protection data, such as the age of the child and parental controls, cannot be ignored in such situations. Both opt-in and opt-out mechanisms need to be verified. The privacy escalation response mechanisms upon a privacy breach must also be tested for accuracy of documentation and correctness of processes.

5.7.3 User Acceptance Testing

During the software acceptance phase before software release, the end user needs to be assured that the software meets their specified requirements. This can be accomplished using user acceptance testing (UAT), which is also known as end user testing or smoke testing. As the penultimate step before software is released, UAT is a gating mechanism used to determine whether the software is ready for release and can help with security because it gives the opportunity to prevent insecure software from being released into production or to the end user. Additionally, it brings the benefit of extending software testing to the end users, as they are the ones who perform the UAT before accepting it. The results of the UAT are used to provide the end user with confidence of the software's reliability. It can also be used to identify design flaws and implementation bugs that are related to the usability of the software.

Prerequisites of UAT include the following:

- The software must have exited the development (implementation) phase.
- Other QA and security tests, such as unit testing, integration testing, regression testing, and software security testing, must be completed.

- Functional and security bugs need to be addressed.
- Real world usage scenarios of the software are identified, and test cases to cover these scenarios are completed.

UAT is generally performed as a black box test that focuses primarily on the functionality and usability of the application. It is most useful if the UAT test is performed in an environment that most closely simulates the real world or production environment. Sometimes UAT is performed in a real production environment post-deployment to get a more accurate picture of the software's usability. However, when this is the case, the test should be conducted within an approved change window with the possibility of rolling back.

The final step in the successful completion of an UAT is a go/no-go decision, best implemented with a formal sign off. The decision is to be captured in writing and is the responsibility of the signature authority representing the end users.

5.8 Defect Reporting and Tracking

Coding bugs, design flaws, behavioral anomalies (logic flaws), errors, faults, and vulnerabilities all constitute software defects, as depicted in Figure 5.12, and once any defect is suspected and/or identified, it needs to be appropriately reported, tracked, and addressed before release. In this section, we will focus on how to report and track software defects. In the following section, we will learn about how these defects can be addressed based upon the potential impact they have and what corrective actions can be taken.

Software defects need first to be reported and then tracked. Reporting defects must be comprehensive and detailed enough to provide the software development teams the information that is necessary to determine the root cause of the issue so that they can address it.

5.8.1 Reporting Defects

The goal of reporting defects is to ensure that they get addressed. Information that must be included in a defect report is discussed in the following subsections.

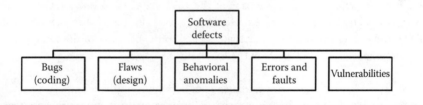

Figure 5.12   Software defects.

▪ Defect Identifier (ID)

A unique number or identifier must be given to each defect report so that each defect can be tracked appropriately. Do not clump multiple issues into one defect. Each issue should warrant its own defect report. Most defect tracking tools have an automated means to assign a defect ID when a new defect is reported.

▪ Title

Provide a concise yet descriptive title for the defect. For example, "Image upload fails."

▪ Description

Provide a summary of the defect to elaborate on the defect title you specified. For example, "When attempting to insert an image into a blog, the software does not allow the upload of the image and fails with an error message."

▪ Detailed Steps

If the defect is not reproducible, then the defect will not get fixed, so detailed steps are necessary as to how the defect can be reproduced by the software development team. For example, it is not sufficient to say that the "Upload feature does not work." Instead, it is important to list the steps taken by the tester, such as:

- Provided username and password and clicked on "Log in."
- Upon successful authentication, clicked on "New blog."
- Entered blog title as "A picture is worth a thousand words" in "Title" field.
- Entered description as "Please comment on the picture you see" in the "Description" field.
- Clicked on the "Upload image" icon.
- Clicked on the "Browse" button in the "Image Upload" popup screen.
- Browsed to the directory and selected the image to upload and clicked "Open" in the "Browse Directory" popup window.
- The "Browse Directory" windows closed and the "Image Upload" popup screen got focus.
- Clicked on the button "Upload" in the "Image Upload" popup screen.
- An error message was shown stating that the upload directory could not be created, and the upload failed.

▪ Expected Results

It is important to describe what the expected result of the operation is so that the development teams can understand the discrepancy from intended functionality. The best way to do this is to tie the defect ID with the requirement identifier in the requirements traceability matrix (RTM). This way any deviations from intended functionality as specified in the requirements can be reviewed and verified against.

▪ Screenshot

If possible and available, a screenshot of the error message should be attached. This proves very helpful to the software development team because:

Figure 5.13   Defect screenshot.

- It provides the development team members a means to visualize the defect symptoms that the tester reports.
- It assures the development team members that they have successfully reproduced the same defect that the tester reported.

An example of a screenshot is depicted in Figure 5.13.

Note that, if the screenshot image contains sensitive information, it is advisable to not capture the screenshot. If, however, a screenshot is necessary, then appropriate security controls, such as masking of the sensitive information in the defect screenshot or role-based access control, should be implemented to protect against disclosure threats.

■ Type

If possible, it is recommended to categorize the defect based on whether it is a functional issue or an assurance (security) one. You can also subcategorize the defect. Figure 5.14 is an example of categories and subcategories of software defects.

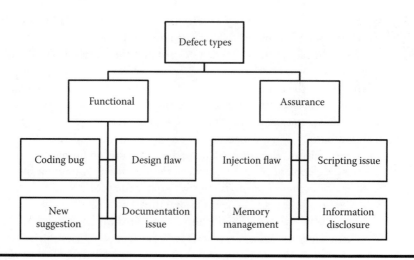

Figure 5.14   Defect types.

This way, pulling reports on the types of defects in the software is made easy. Furthermore, it makes it easy to find out the security defects that are to be addressed before release.

■ Environment

Capturing the environment in which the defect was evident is important. Some important considerations to report on include:

- Was it in the test environment, or was it in the production environment?
- Was the issue evident only in one environment?
- Was the issue determined in the intranet, extranet, or Internet environment?
- What is the operating system and the service pack on which the issue was experienced? Are systems with other service packs experiencing the same issue?
- Was this a Web application issue, and if so, what was the Web address?

■ Build Number

The version of the product in which the defect was determined is an important aspect in defect reporting. This makes it possible to compare versions to see if the defect is universal or specific to a particular version. From a security perspective, the build number can be used to determine the RASQ between versions, based on the number of security defects that are prevalent in each version release.

■ Tester Name

The individual who detected the defect must be specified so that the development team members know whom they need to contact for clarification or further information.

■ Reported On

The date and time (if possible) as to when the defect was reported needs to be specified. This is important in order to track the defect throughout its life cycle (covered later in this chapter) and determine the time it takes to resolve a defect, as a means to identify process improvement opportunities.

■ Severity

This is to indicate the tester's determination of the impact of the defect. This may or may not necessarily be the actual impact of the defect, but it provides the remediation team with additional information that is necessary to prioritize their efforts. This is often qualitative in nature, and some examples of severity types are:

- Critical: The impact of the defect will not allow the software to be functional as expected. All users will be affected.
- Major: Some of the expected business functionality has been affected, and operations cannot continue since there is no work-around available.
- Minor: Some of the expected business functionality has been affected, but operations can continue because a work-around is in place.

- Trivial: Business functionality is not affected, but can be enhanced with some changes that would be nice to have. UI enhancements usually fall into this category.

■ Priority

The priority indicator is directly related to the extent of impact (severity) of the defect and is assigned based on the amount of time within which the defect needs to be addressed. It is a measure of urgency and supports the availability tenet of software assurance. Some common examples of priority include mission critical (0 to 4 hours), high (>4 to 24 hours), medium (>24 to 48 hours), and low (>48 hours).

■ Status

Every defect that is reported automatically starts with the "new" status, and as it goes through its life cycle the status is changed from "new" to "confirmed", "assigned", "work-in-progress", "resolved/fixed", "fix verified", "closed", "reopened", "deferred", and so on.

■ Assigned To

When a software defect is assigned to a development team member so that it can be fixed, the name of the individual who is working the issue must be specified.

5.8.2 Tracking Defects

Upon the identification and verification of a defect, the defect needs to be tracked so that it can be addressed accordingly. It is advisable to track all defects related to the software in a centralized repository or defect tracking system. Centralization of defects makes it possible to have a comprehensive view of the software functionality and security risk. It also makes it possible to ensure that no two individuals are working on the same defect. A defect tracking system should have the ability to support the following requirements:

- Defect Documentation: All required fields from a defect report must be recorded. In situations where additional information needs to be recorded, the defect tracking system must allow for the definition of custom fields.
- Integration with Authentication Infrastructure: A defect tracking system that has the ability to fill the authenticated user information automatically by integrating with the authentication infrastructure is preferred to prevent user entry errors. It also makes it possible to track user activity as they work on a defect.
- Customizable Workflow: A software defect continues to be a defect until it has been fixed or addressed. Each defect goes through a life cycle, an example of which is depicted in Figure 5.15. As the software defect moves from one status to another, workflow information pertinent to that defect must be tracked and, if needed, customized.

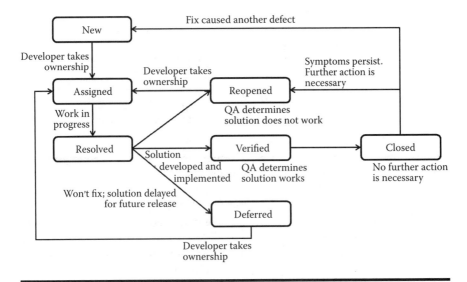

Figure 5.15   Defect life cycle.

- Notification: When a software defect state moves from one status to another, it is necessary to notify the appropriate personnel of the change so that processes in the SDLC are not delayed. Most defect tracking systems provide a notification interface that is configurable with whom and what to notify upon status change.
- Auditing Capability: For accountability reasons, all user actions within the software defect tracking system must be audited, and the software defect tracking system must allow for storing and reporting on the auditable information in a secure manner.

5.9 Impact Assessment and Corrective Action

Testing findings that are reported as defects need to be addressed. We can use the priority (urgency) and severity (impact) levels from the defect report to address software defects. High-impact, high-risk defects are to be addressed first. When agile or extreme programming methodologies are used, identified software defects need to be added to the backlog. Risk management principles (covered in Chapter 1) can be used to determine how the defect is going to be handled. Corrective actions have a direct bearing on the risk. These can include one or more of the following:

- Fixing the defect (mitigating the risk)
- Deferring the functionality (not the fix) to a latter version (transferring the risk)
- Replacing the software (avoiding the risk)

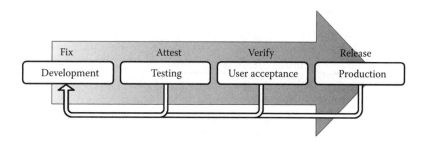

Figure 5.16 Fixing defects environment and process.

Knowledge of security defects in the software and ignoring the risk can have serious and detrimental effects when the software is breached. All security defects must be addressed and preferably mitigated.

Additionally, it is important to fix the defects in the development environment, attest the solution in the testing environment, verify functionality in the UAT environment, and only then release (promote) the fix to production environments, as illustrated in Figure 5.16.

5.10 Tools for Security Testing

It is not important for a CSSLP to have a thorough understanding of how each security tool can be used, but they must be familiar with what each tool can be used for and how it can impact the overall state of software security. Some of the common security tools include:

- Reconnaissance (information gathering) tools
- Vulnerability scanners
- Fingerprinting tools
- Sniffers/protocol analyzers
- Password crackers
- Web security tools (e.g., scanners, proxies, vulnerability management)
- Wireless security tools
- Reverse engineering tools (assembler and disassemblers, debuggers, and decompilers)
- Source code analyzers
- Vulnerability exploitation tools
- Security-oriented operating systems
- Privacy testing tools

It is recommended that you be familiar with some of the common tools that are described in Appendix E.

5.11 Summary

Security testing validates the resiliency, recoverability, and reliability of software, whereas functionality testing is primarily focused on the reliability and secondarily on the recoverability aspects of software. It is imperative to complement functionality testing with security testing of software. Security testing can be used to determine the means and opportunities by which software can be attacked. Both white box and black box security testing are used to determine the threats to software. Knowledge of how to test for common software vulnerabilities, such as failures in input validation, output encoding, improper error handling, least privilege implementation, and use of unsafe programming libraries and interfaces, is important. Various tools are used to conduct security testing. Both functional and security defects need to be reported, tracked through their life cycle, and addressed using risk management principles. Fixing defects must never be performed directly in the production environment, and proper change management principles must be used to promote fixes from development and test environments into the UAT and production environment.

5.12 Review Questions

1. The ability of the software to restore itself to expected functionality when the security protection that is built in is breached is also known as
   A. Redundancy
   B. Recoverability
   C. Resiliency
   D. Reliability
2. In which of the following software development methodologies does unit testing enable collective code ownership and is critical to assure software assurance?
   A. Waterfall
   B. Agile
   C. Spiral
   D. Prototyping
3. The use of if-then rules is characteristic of which of the following types of software testing?
   A. Logic
   B. Scalability
   C. Integration
   D. Unit
4. The implementation of secure features, such as complete mediation and data replication, needs to undergo which of the following types of test to ensure that the software meets the service level agreements (SLA)?
   A. Stress
   B. Unit

    C. Integration

    D. Regression

5. Tests that are conducted to determine the breaking point of the software after which the software will no longer be functional is characteristic of which of the following types of software testing?

    A. Regression

    B. Stress

    C. Integration

    D. Simulation

6. Which of the following tools or techniques can be used to facilitate the white box testing of software for insider threats?

    A. Source code analyzers

    B. Fuzzers

    C. Banner-grabbing software

    D. Scanners

7. When very limited or no knowledge of the software is made known to the software tester before she can test for its resiliency, it is characteristic of which of the following types of security tests?

    A. White box

    B. Black box

    C. Clear box

    D. Glass box

8. Penetration testing must be conducted with properly defined

    A. Rules of engagement

    B. Role-based access control mechanisms

    C. Threat models

    D. Use cases

9. Testing for the randomness of session identifiers and the presence of auditing capabilities provides the software team insight into which of the following security controls?

    A. Availability

    B. Authentication

    C. Nonrepudiation

    D. Authorization

10. Disassemblers, debuggers, and decompilers can be used by security testers primarily to determine which of the following types of coding vulnerabilities?

    A. Injection flaws

    B. Lack of reverse engineering protection

    C. Cross-site scripting

    D. Broken session management

11. When reporting a software security defect in the software, which of the following also needs to be reported so that variance from intended behavior of the software can be determined?

A. Defect identifier
B. Title
C. Expected results
D. Tester name

12. An attacker analyzes the response from the Web server that indicates that its version is the Microsoft Internet Information Server 6.0 (Microsoft-IIS/6.0), but none of the IIS exploits that the attacker attempts to execute on the Web server are successful. Which of the following is the most probable security control that is implemented?
    A. Hashing
    B. Cloaking
    C. Masking
    D. Watermarking

13. Smart fuzzing is characterized by injecting
    A. Truly random data without any consideration for the data structure
    B. Variations of data structures that are known
    C. Data that get interpreted as commands by a backend interpreter
    D. Scripts that are reflected and executed on the client browser

14. Which of the following is most important to ensure when the software is forced to fail as part of security testing? Choose the best answer.
    A. Normal operational functionality is not restored automatically
    B. Access to all functionality is denied
    C. Confidentiality, integrity, and availability are not adversely impacted
    D. End users are adequately trained and self-help is made available for the end user to fix the error on their own

15. Timing and synchronization issues such as race conditions and resource dead-locks can be most likely identified by which of the following tests? Choose the best answer.
    A. Integration
    B. Stress
    C. Unit
    D. Regression

16. The primary objective of resiliency testing of software is to determine
    A. The point at which the software will break
    B. If the software can restore itself to normal business operations
    C. The presence and effectiveness of risk mitigation controls
    D. How a blackhat would circumvent access control mechanisms

17. The ability of the software to withstand attempts of attackers who intend to breach the security protection that is built in is also known as
    A. Redundancy
    B. Recoverability
    C. Resiliency
    D. Reliability

18. Drivers and stub-based programming are useful to conduct which of the following tests?
   A. Integration
   B. Regression
   C. Unit
   D. Penetration
19. Assurance that the software meets the expectations of the business as defined in the SLAs can be demonstrated by which of the following types of tests?
   A. Unit
   B. Integration
   C. Performance
   D. Regression
20. Vulnerability scans are used to
   A. Measure the resiliency of the software by attempting to exploit weaknesses
   B. Detect the presence of loopholes and weaknesses in the software
   C. Detect the effectiveness of security controls that are implemented in the software
   D. Measure the skills and technical know-how of the security tester

References

Brown, J. 2009. Fuzzing for fun and profit. Krakow Labs Literature, 02 Nov.

Cannings, R., H. Dwivedi, and Z. Lackey. 2008. *Hacking Exposed Web 2.0: Web 2.0 Security Secrets and Solutions.* New York, NY: McGraw-Hill.

Cox, K., and C. Gerg. 2004. Anatomy of an attack: The five Ps. *Managing Security with Snort and IDS Tools.* Sebastopol, CA: O'Reilly.

Eilam, E., and E. J. Chikofsky. 2005. *Reversing Secrets of Reverse Engineering.* Indianapolis, IN: Wiley.

Gallagher, T., B. Jeffries, and L. Landauer. 2006. *Hunting Security Bugs.* Redmond, WA: Microsoft.

Herzog, P. 2010. *Open Source Security Testing Methodology Manual.* ISECOM. Apr. 23, 2010. http://www.isecom.org/osstmm (accessed March 6, 2011).

Howard, M., and D. LeBlanc. 2003. *Writing Secure Code.* Redmond, WA: Microsoft.

Kaminski, G. n.d. Software logic mutation testing. Lecture.

Kelley, D. 2009. Black box and white box testing: Which is best? SearchSecurity.com. Nov. 18, 2009. http://searchsecurity.techtarget.com/tip/0,289483,sid14_00,00.html (accessed March 6, 2011).

Microsoft. 2008. *Patterns & Practices: Performance Testing Guidance for Web Applications.* CodePlex. Aug. 28, 2008. http://perftestingguide.codeplex.com (accessed March 6, 2011).

Microsoft Developer Network. 2010. Unit testing. http://msdn.microsoft.com/en-us/library/aa292197(VS.71).aspx (accessed Apr. 30, 2010).

Neystadt, J. 2008. Automated penetration testing with white-box fuzzing. *MSDN: Microsoft Development, MSDN Subscriptions, Resources, and More.* Microsoft, Feb. 2008. http://msdn.microsoft.com/en-us/library/cc162782.aspx (accessed March 6, 2011).

OWASP. 208. *OWASP Testing Guide V3*. Sept. 15, 2008. Web. http://www.owasp.org/index .php/OWASP_Testing_Project (accessed March 6, 2011).

PCI Security Standards Council. Security scanning procedures. Sept. 2006. Web. https://www .pcisecuritystandards.org/pdfs/pci_scanning_procedures_v1-1.pdf (accessed March 6, 2011).

Petersen, B. 2010. Intrusion detection FAQ: What is P0f and what does it do? SANS.org. Apr. 30, 2010. http://www.sans.org/security-resources/idfaq/p0f.php (accessed March 6, 2011).

Piliptchouk, D. 2005. WS-security in the enterprise. ONJava.com. Sept. 2, 2005. http:// onjava.com/pub/a/onjava/2005/02/09/wssecurity.html (accessed March 6, 2011).

Rogers, L. 2000. Library | Cybersleuthing: Means, motive, and opportunity. *InfoSec Outlook* June. http://www.sei.cmu.edu/library/abstracts/news-at-sei/securitysum00.cfm.

Scarfone, K., M. Souppaya, A. Cody, and A. Orebaugh. 2008. *Technical Guide to Information Security Testing and Assessment*. National Institute of Standards and Technology. Sept. 2008. http://csrc.nist.gov/publications/nistpubs/800-115/SP800-115.pdf (accessed Apr. 30, 2010).

Sundmark, T., and D. Theertagiri. 2008. Phase space analysis of session cookies. Thesis, Linköpings Universitetet, Sweden. http://www.ida.liu.se/~TDDD17/oldprojects/2008/ projects/9.pdf (accessed March 6, 2011).

U.S. Department of Homeland Security. Security testing. Apr. 30, 2010. https://buildsecuri tyin.us-cert.gov/bsi/articles/best-practices/testing.html (accessed March 6, 2011).

Yarochki, F. V., O. Arkin, M. Kydyraliev, S. Dai, Y. Huang, and S. Kuo. Xprobe2++: Low volume remote network information gathering tool. Department of Electrical Engineering, National Taiwan University. http://xprobe.sourceforge.net/xprobe-ng .pdf (accessed Apr. 30, 2010).

Zalewski, M. 2005. *Silence on the Wire: A Field Guide to Passive Reconnaissance and Indirect Attacks*. San Francisco, CA: No Starch.

Chapter 6

Software Acceptance

6.1 Introduction

Have you ever been caught in a situation where you are not aware of what certain software does in your computing environment due to lack of pertinent documentation, or the need exists to configure the software to run with elevated or administrative privileges after its installation? These situations are far too familiar today, but they could be easily avoided if there were a formal software acceptance process in place.

Before accepting software for deployment into the production environment or release to the customers, it is important to ensure that the software that has been developed or acquired meets required compliance, quality, functional, and assurance (security) requirements. In today's security landscape, considerations when accepting software must go beyond mere functionality and take security into account as well. Validation and verification (V&V) of just the business functionality are insufficient to accept software for release. It is also critically important to understand the impact that the accepted software will have on the existing computing ecosystem, regardless of whether it has been developed (built) or procured (bought). Security requirements need to be validated and security controls (safeguards and countermeasures) verified by internal and/or independent third party security testing. Software must not be deployed/released until it has been certified and accredited that the residual risk is at the appropriate level. Additionally, in cases where software is procured from an external software publisher, certain nontechnical protection mechanisms need to be in place as acceptance criteria, and these must be validated and verified as well.

6.2 Objectives

As a CSSLP, you are expected to

- Understand the importance of pre- and postdeployment/release acceptance criteria and how it relates to software assurance.
- Be familiar with build considerations that need to be validated and verified before acceptance for deployment/release.
- Be familiar with procurement considerations that need to be validated and verified before acceptance for deployment/release.
- Know about software assurance in acquisitions and understand legal protection mechanisms that need to exist before procuring software.
- Know what software escrow constitutes and the protection it affords to the involved parties.
- Understand the need to measure the impact of the software that will be deployed into the existing computing ecosystem and existing processes.
- Know the difference between certification and accreditation (C&A) and understand how V&V can be used for C&A.

This chapter will cover each of these objectives in detail. It is imperative that you fully understand not just what software acceptance means, but also how it applies to the software that your organization builds or buys.

6.3 Guidelines for Software Acceptance

Software acceptance is the process of officially or formally accepting new or modified software components that, when integrated, form the information system. Objectives of software acceptance include

- Verification that the software meets specified functional and assurance requirements
- Verification that the software is operationally complete and secure as expected
- Obtaining the approvals from the system owner
- Transference of responsibility from the development team or company (vendor) to the system owner, support staff, and operations personnel if the software is deployed internally

It must, however, be highlighted that, just because software is engineered with security in mind, it does not necessarily assure that the software will be secure when it is released or deployed into what is most often a heterogeneous computing environment. Rarely is software deployed in a stand-alone setting.

Some of the guiding principles of software ready for release from a security viewpoint are given below. Software accepted for deployment or release must

- Be secure by design, default, and deployment (Howard and LeBlanc, 2003)
- Complement existing defense in depth protection
- Run with least privilege
- Be irreversible and tamper-proof
- Isolate and protect administrative functionality and security management interfaces (SMIs)
- Have nontechnical protection mechanisms in place

The mantra for defense in depth, commonly referred to as the SD3 initiatives for software security, ensures that the software is secure not only in design and by default, but also in deployment. Software that does not complement existing defense in depth principles must not be accepted for deployment. For example, if you have certain ports and protocols disabled for security reasons in your computing environment, the introduction of new software must not require the disabled ports and protocols to be enabled, unless when doing so proper security controls are designed to address the increased attack surface area. Software accepted should be able to run without having the need for elevated privileges. By default, the principle of least privilege must apply.

Reverse engineering protection mechanisms with contractual enforcement must be verified to ensure that competitors and hackers are deterred from figuring out the internal design and architectural details of the software itself, which will allow them to circumvent any protective mechanisms that are built in. Unfortunately, what is prevalent in the industry today to deter reversing are ineffective click-through end user licensing agreements (EULAs) with a "You shall not modify, translate, reverse engineer, decompile, or disassemble the software" clause, as depicted in Figure 6.1. The EULA is usually presented upon installation as a splash screen or upon login as a login banner. Software manufacturers deem the clicking of the EULA's "I agree" to be contractually binding, and the Digital Millennium Copyright Act (DMCA) considers some instances of reverse engineering as criminal offenses, but this is a deterrent control and is not preventative in nature. Reverse engineering protection is increased by code obfuscation and anti-tampering techniques (Eilam, 2005), which must be verified in the software before being accepted for release. Reverse engineering is also known as reversing or reverse code engineering (RCE).

Administrative functionality and SMIs need to be validated as being accessible only to those individuals who have the need for them, a small subset of users whose actions are also audited and reviewed periodically.

Additionally, software must not only first meet functional requirements, but also must include all applicable technical security protection mechanisms (architected using secure design principles and developed including elements of the security profile) and have nontechnical protection mechanisms, such as legal protections and escrow, in place before being considered ready for deployment or release.

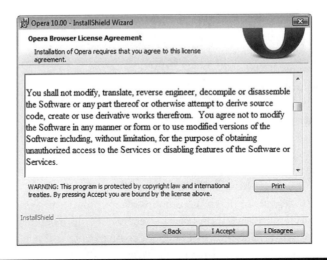

Figure 6.1 Example of a EULA (for Opera 10).

6.4 Benefits of Accepting Software Formally

The incorporation of a formal software acceptance process based on security is vital in the deployment or release of secure software. This is the final checkpoint for discovering the existence of missed and unforeseen security vulnerabilities and for validating the presence of security controls that will address known threats. Validating that security requirements are included in the design (for software built in-house) or in the request for proposals (RFPs) (for commercial off-the-shelf [COTS] software) and verifying that they have been addressed ensures that security does not need to be bolted on at a later stage after release. It not only ensures that software security issues are proactively addressed and that the software developed is operationally hack-resilient, but also that the software is compliant with applicable regulations. The software acceptance process helps to maintain the secure computing ecosystems by ensuring that new software products have achieved a formally defined level of quality and security. Software not meeting these requirements should not be approved for release into the secure computing ecosystem.

Legal and escrow mechanisms that are validated as part of the software acceptance process also ensure that the software publisher or acquirer is protected. In a nutshell, software acceptance can assure that the software is of high quality, reliable (functioning as expected), and secure from threats.

6.5 Software Acceptance Considerations

We have established the fact that a formal software acceptance must be in place, regardless of how insignificant one may feel this process to be. So what are some of the activities that need to be performed during the software acceptance phase? Software acceptance considerations to be taken into account vary depending on whether the software is built in-house or bought from an external software publisher. In this section, we will first learn about what one needs to consider when building software in-house before certifying the software as ready for deployment/release, and then cover assurance in the procurement methodology and protection mechanisms that need to be considered when buying software.

6.5.1 Considerations When Building Software

Some of the major items to consider before accepting software that is built in-house for deployment/release are illustrated in Figure 6.2. They are described in more detail in this section.

6.5.1.1 Completion Criteria

Functional and security requirements should have been captured in the requirements gathering phase of the software development life cycle (SDLC), and at this stage in the SDLC they need to be validated and verified as complete. Completion criteria for functionality and software security with explicit milestones must be defined well in advance. As a CSSLP, you are particularly interested in the milestones pertinent to security besides functionality. Some examples of security-related milestones include, but are not limited to, the following:

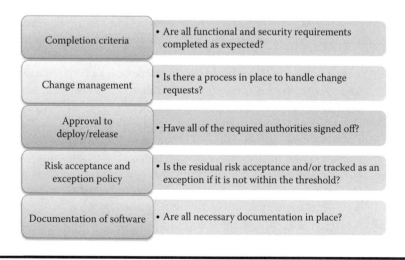

Figure 6.2   Software acceptance considerations when building software.

- Generation of the requirements traceability matrix (RTM) that includes security requirements besides functional requirements in the requirement phase (Stackpole, 2010)
- Completion of the threat model during the design phase
- Review and sign-off on the security architecture at the end of the design phase
- Review of code for security vulnerabilities after the development phase
- Completion of security testing at the end of the application testing phase
- Completion of documentation before the deployment phase commences

Each of these milestones must include the actual deliverable (e.g., RTM, threat model, security architecture design, code review report, security test report) that can be tracked. The existence and accuracy of these deliverables need to be verified. At the end of the requirements phase, the software requirements traceability matrix must include the security requirements as well. The threat model should be complete with documented threat lists and associated controls. The architecture review sign-off before code is written should include the various components of the security profile and principles of secure design. Verification of these components and principles must be conducted before acceptance. Code review for security issues must be conducted, and the issues that were identified in the review need to be fixed and tested in the testing phase. Achievement of these milestones is indicative of the state of security in software that is built. If any of these milestones is not completed, then serious thought needs to be given as to whether or not the software is ready for deployment/release, and appropriate risk-based actions need to be taken.

6.5.1.2 Change Management

Change management is a subset of configuration management. Changes to the computing environment and redesign of the security architecture may introduce new security vulnerabilities, thereby increasing risk. Necessary support queues and processes for the software that is to be deployed/released should be established.

Newer versions of software need to be approved, tracked, and validated to ensure that the current state and level of security in the software has not been reduced. If this is the first version of the software being deployed, then it must be recorded in the asset management database. If this a version release, then the asset management database must be updated before accepting the software for release.

Changes should not be allowed unless the appropriate authorities formally approve the change. Authorities should refrain from approving any change requests that have not communicated exactly what the residual risk is or if they do not completely understand the repercussions resulting from the change. Change requests should be approved based on risk and not on the grounds of schedule pressures, as is often observed to be the case.

All changes need to be formally requested by the software development organization, which is usually done through the Program Management Office (PMO). It must then be evaluated for approval or rejection by members of the Configuration/ Change Board (CCB).

As part of the software acceptance process, it must be verified that

- Change requests are evaluated for impact on the overall security of the software.
- The asset management database is updated with the new/updated software information.
- The change is requested formally, and evaluated and approved by appropriate signatory authorities.

6.5.1.3 Approval to Deploy/Release

It cannot be overstressed that, without approvals, no change should be allowed to the production computing environment. Before any new installation of software, a risk analysis needs to be conducted and the residual risk determined. The results of the risk analysis along with the steps taken to address it (mitigate or accept) must be communicated to the business owner. The authorizing official (AO) must be informed of the residual risk. The approval or rejection to deploy/release must include recommendations and support from the security team. Ultimately, it is the AO who is responsible for change approvals.

The software acceptance process should validate that approvals are not merely a "check in the checkbox" kind of activity, but that it includes review and oversight through an established governance process for maximum effectiveness. Approvals must be documented and retained.

6.5.1.4 Risk Acceptance and Exception Policy

Since the likelihood of "zero" or "no" risk is utopian, risk that remains after the implementation of security controls (residual risk) needs to be determined first. The best option to address total risk is to mitigate it so that the residual risk falls below the business-defined threshold, in which case the residual risk can be accepted. Risk must be accepted by the business owner and not by officials in the IT department.

For consistency, it is advisable to use the same template when accepting the risk. A risk acceptance template must include at least the following elements: risk, actions, issues, and decisions (RAID). The risk section is used to inform the business of the probability of an unfavorable security situation's occurring that can lead to disclosure, alteration, or destruction outcomes. Since it is the business owner that accepts the risk, the description in this section must be void of technical jargon. It must be explanatory in describing the risk to the business. The actions section in the risk acceptance document assists the IT and software development management teams by informing them of the steps that have been taken and the steps that are to be taken. The issues section provides the development teams with the technical details of how the threats to the software can be realized, and the decisions section

| Risk Acceptance Document #: | 12345 *[Specify a unique identifier]* |
| Risk Rating: | High/Medium/Low *[Specify one rating]* |

Risk: *[Describe the risk in nontechnical terms for the business owner to understand.]*

Actions: *[Describe the steps that software development management teams can take.]*

Issues: *[Describe in detail the threats in technical terms and how they can be materialized.]*

Decisions: *[Describe alternatives or options to handle the risk; include security controls and remediation mechanisms here.]*

Signatory Authorities

	Decision Taken	Justification
	Accept	
X	Transfer	
X	Mitigate	
	Avoid	

A. Business Owner Name and Title

Signature: _____Date:

Print name:

B. Security Officer Name and Title

Signature: _____Date:

Print name: Mano Paul. 112-358-1321 ext. 1337

Figure 6.3   Risk acceptance template example.

provides management and the AO the options to consider when accepting the risk. An example of a RAID risk acceptance template is illustrated in Figure 6.3.

How residual risk is handled depends on factors such as time and resources. In situations when you do not have the time or resource to mitigate the risk, it is best to transfer or avoid the risk. Risk transference can be achieved by transferring the risk to someone else, such as an insurance company. Risk avoidance can be achieved by discontinuing the use of the software (Kocher, 2004).

However, in certain situations, the risk that is observed is not as a result of security vulnerabilities in the software, but is attributable to noncompliance with a new policy instituted to address the changing security landscape. You also may not have the option to discontinue the use of the newly discovered noncompliant software, which means you cannot avoid the risk of noncompliance. For example, a legacy software very critical to the business cannot comply with the newly instituted 256-bit cipher strength advanced encryption standard (AES) for cryptographic functionality because it supports a maximum of 40 bit cipher strength. In such situations when you cannot mitigate, transfer, or avoid the risk, the best option is to accept the risk with a documented exception to policy. An exception to policy must, however, be allowed if and only if there exist contingency plans with explicit dates specified to address the risk. It is also advisable that the members of the exception review board include subject matter experts from different teams, such as the business (client or customer), software development team, networking team, legal team, privacy team, and the security team.

Accepting risk with an exception to policy has certain benefits. The first and foremost is that business operations are not disrupted. Second, the exception to policy and risk documentation can be used as an audit defense when external auditors determine that your organization is not compliant with policy.

The software acceptance process must ensure that risk management processes are thoroughly followed, that risk is within acceptable thresholds, and an exception to policy exists, if needed, before the software can be deployed or released.

6.5.1.5 Documentation of Software

Often overlooked or receiving little attention, documenting what the software is supposed to do, how it is architected, how it is to be installed, what configuration settings need to be preset, and how to use and administer it is extremely important for effective, secure, and continued use of the software. Some of the primary objectives for documentation are to make the software deployment process easy and repeatable, to ensure that operations are not disrupted, and to take care that the impact upon changes to the software is understood.

Although documentation is a key deliverable at the end of the SDLC predeployment process, it is best advised to commence and complete documentation at each phase. Unfortunately, this is often the most overlooked part of the SDLC, and without appropriate documentation, software must not be accepted for deployment or release.

A fundamental consideration for software acceptance is the existence and completeness of software-related documentation.

Table 6.1 tabulates some of the types of documents that need to be verified as complete.

What is documented should clearly articulate the functionality and security of the software code so that it allows for maintainability by the support team. It is advisable to include members from the support team to participate in observatory roles during the development and testing phases of the SDLC so that they are familiar with the operations of the software that they are expected to support.

Table 6.1   Types of Documents

Document type	Assurance aspect
RTM	Are functionality and security aspects traceable to customer requirements and specifications?
Threat Model	Is the threat model comprehensively representative of the security profile and addressing all applicable threats?
Risk Acceptance Document	Is the risk appropriately mitigated, transferred, or avoided? Is the residual risk below the acceptable level? Has the risk been accepted by the AO with signatory authority?
Exception Policy Document	Is there an exception to policy, and if so, is it documented? Is there a contingency plan in place to address risks that do not comply with the security policy?
Change Requests	Is there a process to formally request changes to the software and is this documented and tracked? Is there a control mechanism defined for the software so that only changes that are approved at the appropriate level can be deployed to production environments?
Approvals	Are approvals (risk, design and architecture review, change, exception to policy, etc.) documented and verifiable? Are appropriate approvals in place when existing documents like business continuity plan (BCP), disaster recovery plan (DRP), etc., need to be redrafted?
BCP or DRP	Is the software incorporated into the organizational BCP or DRP? Does the DRP include not only the software but also the hardware on which it runs? Is the BCP/DRP updated to include security procedures that need to be followed in the event of a disaster?
Incident Response Plan (IRP)	Is there a process and plan defined for responding to incidents (security violations) because of the software?
Installation Guide	Are steps and configuration settings predefined to ensure that the software can be installed without compromising the secure state of the computing ecosystem?
User Training Guide/Manual	Is there a manual to inform users how they will use the software?

It is important to document not just the first version of the software, but also subsequent version releases. This ensures that changes to the software are traceable back to requirements and customer requests.

To ensure that there are no disruptions to operations, critical software must be included in the Business Continuity Plan (BCP) or Disaster Recovery Plan (DRP). The incorporation of new software into the existing BCP/DRP is directly proportional to the importance of that software to the business.

It is also imperative to ensure that the Incident Response Plan (IRP) is available to the operations team. The IRP should include instructions on how to handle an unfavorable event resulting from a software breach. The effectiveness of an IRP is dependent on user awareness and training for how to respond in the event or suspicion of a security incident. Training takes documentation to the people. The dos and don'ts for incident response are covered in more detail in Chapter 7.

6.5.2 When Buying Software

If it has been determined that the benefits of purchasing software are more than the benefits of building the software in-house, a buy decision naturally is made. However, procurement of COTS software from an external software publisher is in and of itself a time-intensive and complex process. It requires a joint collaboration between several teams, such as business, IT software development, legal, and security, and also the vendor. It is crucial to make sure that the benefits gained from procuring software are not annulled by software that is not hack-resilient, thereby putting the organization at risk. Those involved with software procurement (acquisitions) must already be familiar with the fact that software that is not developed in-house requires customization to operate as expected within their environment. The return on investment (ROI) when purchasing software must also factor in the total cost of ownership (TCO), which includes the cost of support and maintenance and the investment of time and resources necessary to incorporate security when it is deployed within your organization's computing ecosystem. Before accepting software from the vendor, the acquisition phase or phases of the SDLC should include an assessment of security functionality in the software. Vendor claims for security in their software need to be verified. Overall systems assurance evaluation must include the evaluation of the software security as a part of software assurance throughout the acquisition process, as depicted in Figure 6.4.

It is advisable to have a separate software procurement policy, if your organization does not already have one. It must be recognized that the mere existence of a software procurement policy provides no software assurance, unless the policy is developed and followed consistently with best practices in security and compliance requirements. The vendor must be required to demonstrate that basic security tenets of confidentiality, integrity, and availability as well as other components of the security profile are factored into the design and development of the software

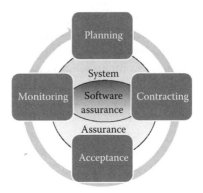

Figure 6.4 Software assurance in the acquisition life cycle.

they are selling, besides ensuring compliance to legal and international requirements. For example, if the software you are procuring will deal with processing and transmitting credit card information, the software must be able to assure confidentiality by protecting sensitive information using cryptographic functionality and also be compliant with Payment Card Industry Data Security Standard (PCI DSS) requirements.

International factors of the software that is being considered for purchase are also very important from a security vantage point. For example, if the software you are purchasing should provide support for international languages that are not of the western script type, then Unicode support and functionality need to be carefully scrutinized. Support of Unicode can arguably be said to double the attack surface since, unlike ASCII, which stores each character in a single byte, Unicode requires 2 bytes to store a character. Other international factors that require consideration include export regulations, cryptography strength standards, and outsourced development.

With a rise in globalization, outsourcing software development to companies and countries with access to cheap labor and intellectual capital has become a trend. Since the organization that outsources (outsourcee) has minimal to no control over the software development process of the outsourcer, extra attention needs to be given to software security in such situations. In outsourcing engagements, it is imperative to ensure the existence of protection mechanisms such as:

Contractual obligations: Contracts must first be established between the outsourcee and the outsourcer so that the outsourcee is provided coverage against liabilities arising from the outsourcing provider.
Secure SDLC: If possible, the outsourcee must require the vendor to integrate security into their SDLC.

Code verification: Before the implementation of software, it is vital that software (source code and object code) security controls are verified, and that it does not have vulnerabilities, such as backdoors, maintenance hooks, or logic bombs. The best way to detect such embedded code security issues is by code review.

Additionally, beware of evaluating software by checking a list of checkboxes that the vendor claims are security functionality in their software. Checklists do not secure. If your vendor claims that their software supports strong encryption, ask them to define "strong" instead of assuming what they mean. What they mean by "strong" may not, in fact, meet your organizational policy requirements, or it may be incompliant with industry regulations and standards. Verify that the cryptographic functionality in their software is indeed "strong," meeting your organizational requirements and being compliant with industry standards.

6.5.2.1 Procurement Methodology

Security of purchased software is closely tied to its procurement methodology. Specifying security requirements in the procurement methodology has a directly proportional relationship to the security of the software that is purchased. In other words, if the procurement methodology does not factor security into its requirements, the likelihood is high that the software you purchase will be insecure. So it is critical that, as part of the software acceptance process, the methodology employed in procuring software is carefully scrutinized and validated to ensure that security requirements are included and implemented appropriately.

The most common means by which organizations solicit software vendors is by initiating an RFP or a request for information (RFI) and, in some cases, a request for quote (RFQ). In other cases, the purchasing organization partners with the vendor and codevelops the software, but this practice is not as prevalent. Regardless of whether your organization is in the commercial, private, or government sector, when it comes to procuring software or software services from software publishers (vendors), the RFP methodology is the de facto standard in software acquisition. The software acquisition process is fairly direct and simple, as illustrated in Figure 6.5.

6.5.2.1.1 RFPs and Software Assurance

RFPs can be a valuable mechanism to ensure that solutions delivered by the vendor are useful and applicable to the business needs of your organization. It is only recently that the importance of the security in the software being purchased is reflected by the incorporation of security requirements in the RFPs.

Listed below in this section are some guidelines for effective issuance and evaluations of RFPs. These guidelines are:

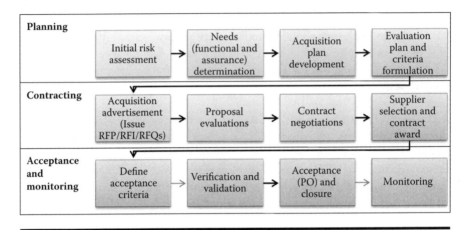

Figure 6.5   A general software acquisition process.

■ It is vital that, besides functional requirements that are specified in the RFP, which is usually the case, security requirements are explicitly stated as well. By clearly defining requirements, those participating in the RFP process will be clear on what your expectations are, leaving little room for guesswork.

■ RFPs responses must be time-bound. This means that the time that is allowed for responding to the RFPs must be adequate for vendors to make a solid proposal, but at the same time must not be inordinate. Provisions for late offers must be explicitly defined and stated, if allowed. This way, timely responses are tied directly to the specified requirements, and security vulnerabilities arising from changing requirements (scope creep) are reduced.

■ Evaluation criteria must be predefined and the evaluation process must be explicitly stated in the RFP. Some examples of evaluation criteria that are commonly observed in RFPs is how well the responses demonstrate:
  – An understanding of the requirements
  – A solution concept
  – Experiences of personnel
  – Valid references from past performance
  – Resources, cost, and schedule considerations

It is also important to evaluate the responses to the RFP based on how it addresses software assurance as part of the solution concept. It is important to use the same evaluation criteria and rank the responses using the same scoring mechanism so that the evaluation is fair, uniform, and consistent. Additionally, it is wise to include evaluators from various teams (e.g., software development, networking, operations, legal, privacy, security) so that adequate and appropriate subject matter expertise (SME) may be applied when evaluating the proposals.

6.5.2.1.2 Vendor Evaluations

Not only must the responses be evaluated, but the vendor who submitted the response must also be evaluated. Before accepting the software and issuing a purchase order, the vendor's SDLC and evidence of incorporating security in the vendor's SDLC, qualification of their personnel and their security know-how, support and maintenance model, and availability of independent references need to be evaluated.

■ Vendor SDLC: The software vendor's SDLC process must be investigated to ensure that they have a structured process that incorporates security into the software they build. Some questions to ask the vendor are: How is the software development process structured? What are some of the artifacts generated? Do you outsource your software development, and if so, what checks and balances exist that require validation? How current and accurate is the documentation that comes with the software?

■ Evidence of Security in the Software: Evidence of incorporating security in the vendor's SDLC needs to be verified. Some questions to ask the vendor are: Do you have a threat modeling process, and is there a threat model for the software you are proposing? What kind of reviews (design, architecture, code) do you conduct? How is the software tested against functional and security requirements? Has the software been attested and certified as secure by an independent third party? By understanding the vendor's SDLC process and how security is addressed through the different phases, one can get an insight into the secure state of the software one is purchasing.

Never take the vendor's claims for granted. Always verify their claims. Verification of assurance (security) starts with first determining if there are any known vulnerabilities in the vendor's software. Full disclosure lists and security bug tracking lists can help in this regard. Verifying claimed security features in the vendor software can also be achieved by black box penetration testing. This is usually the only way to attest third party software, since you do not have access to the source code, and reverse engineering the object code will be illegal. You must conduct black box tests against software that you have not yet purchased only after you have communicated to the vendor your intent to do so and legally received their approval. It is always advisable to have an independent third party perform this assurance check so that there is objectivity and neutrality. To avoid potential security issues after release, assurance checks are extremely critical steps that cannot be overlooked or taken lightly.

Table 6.2   Generic Software Acceptance Criteria

(a) The Supplier shall provide all operating system, middleware, and application software to the Acquirer security configured by Supplier in accordance with the FAR requirement based on 44 USC 3544 (b) (2) (D) (iii).
(b) The Supplier shall demonstrate that all application software is fully functional when residing on the operating system and on middleware platforms used by the Acquirer in its production environment, configured as noted above.
(c) The Supplier shall not change any configuration settings when providing software updates unless specifically authorized in writing by the Acquirer.
(d) The Supplier shall provide the Acquirer with software tools that the Acquirer can use to continually monitor software updates and the configuration status.
(e) At specified intervals by the Buyer, the Supplier shall provide the Acquirer with a comprehensive vulnerability test report for the suite of applications and associated operating system and middleware platforms used by the Acquirer in its production environment, configured as noted above.
(f) The Acquirer and Supplier agree to work together to establish appropriate measures to quantify and monitor the supplier's performance according to the contract requirements. Specific guidance should include types of measures to be used, measures reporting frequency, measures refresh and retirement, and thresholds of acceptable performance.
(g) The Supplier shall provide all operating system, middleware, and application software to the Acquirer free of common vulnerabilities as specified by the Common Vulnerabilities and Exposures (CVE®)—The Standard for Information Security Vulnerability Names that can be retrieved from http://cve.mitre.org/.
(h) The Supplier shall provide all operating system, middleware, and application software to the Acquirer free of common weaknesses as specified in the Common Weakness Enumeration, A Community-Developed Dictionary of Software Weakness Types that can be retrieved from http://cwe.mitre.org/.

- Personnel Qualifications: Close attention should be given to ensure that those who will be responsible for developing the software solution and incorporating security into the software are adequately qualified and familiar with new generation and current threats. Some questions to ask are: What is your training program and the frequency in which your employees (and nonemployee personnel) are trained in the latest security threats and controls to address those threats?
- Support and Maintenance Model: Vendor support and maintenance model must be reviewed to ensure that the vendor will be able to support, maintain, and release patches in time when security vulnerabilities are discovered in their software. One of the core software security concepts is the need to ensure that the software will be available when needed. An important consideration in this regard is to determine the service level agreement (SLA) to fix vulnerabilities.
- Independent References: The past performance of the vendor must be evaluated. You must request a list of references from customers of the vendor and make interview calls to verify the validity of vendor claims (Baschab and Piot, 2007). You can also determine if the vendor is willing to undergo an independent third party assessment.

RFP responses evaluation and vendor evaluation are both essential activities that need to be taken into account as part of the software acceptance process before buying the software. Acceptance criteria must be predefined, and only upon complete evaluation and validation that the software will satisfy the acceptance criteria should the purchase order be issued. Table 6.2 provides an example of generic acceptance criteria as listed in the *Software Assurance in Acquisitions: Mitigating Risks to the Enterprise* prepublication document.

6.6 Legal Protection Mechanisms

Besides an understanding of the procurement methodology and its impact on software security, a working knowledge of legal concepts related to information technology is required to understand fully the nontechnical threats and risks inherent with software. When these legal concepts are addressed, they protect not only the software purchaser, but also the software producers and related stakeholders engaged in the development and use of the software. In this section, we will discuss each of the legal protection mechanisms that are pertinent to software assurance. These include:

- Intellectual property (IP) protections
- Disclaimers
- Validity periods
- Contracts and agreements
- Software escrow

6.6.1 IP Protection

The software publisher, whether it is your organization or the organization from which you purchase the software, has the responsibility to protect the software it produces so that it does not lose its creation or competitive advantage to someone else. The World Intellectual Property Organization (WIPO) defines intellectual property as the creations of the mind. These include inventions, literary and artistic works, symbols, names, images, and designs that are used in commerce. IP is of two types, and the most common software-related IP categories are depicted in Figure 6.6.

Exhaustive coverage of IP protection topics is beyond the scope of this book, so in the following section, basic IP concepts and their intersect with software security will be covered. It is advisable for a CSSLP to work closely with the legal team when consulting on IP-related areas.

6.6.1.1 Patents (Inventions)

As the strongest form of IP protection, patents protect an invention by exclusively granting rights to the owner of a novel, useful, and nonobvious idea that offers a new way of doing something or solving a problem. Patents are given to the owner for a specified period of time, which is usually about 20 years, and after that time has elapsed, the patent is said to have expired and the item enters into the public domain, which means that that owner no longer has exclusive rights to the invention. The rights that are granted to the owner ensure that the invention cannot be commercially made, used, distributed, or sold without the owner's consent. Upon mutual agreement, the owner can grant permission to license to use or sell the invention to other parties. The invention may be a product or a process and is patentable as long as it meets the following conditions:

Figure 6.6 Software related intellectual property (IP) categories.

- It must be of practical use.
- It must be novel, with at least one new characteristic that is nonexistent in the domain of existing knowledge (technical field). In other words, there must be no prior-art.
- It must demonstrate an inventive step.
- It must be compliant with the law and deemed as acceptable in a court of law, usually in the country of origin and filing, since the jurisdiction for patents is not international, although they may be recognized worldwide.

Besides providing recognition of one's creativity and reward for inventions that are marketable, patents encourage innovation to determine better and newer ways of solving problems.

The debate on the patentability of software-related inventions is ongoing. In some countries, software is deemed patentable, whereas in others it is not. It is best advised to review the patentable guidelines for the country in which you file the software and to consult with an IP legal representative. However, computer programs may be protected under copyright.

6.6.1.2 Copyright

Copyright protects the expression of an idea and not the idea itself. It gives rights to the creator of literary and artistic works and architectural design. It includes the protection of technical drawings, such as software design and architecture specifications, that express the solution concept. While granting the creator with the exclusive rights to use, copyright also grants the creator rights to authorize or prohibit the use, reproduction, public performance, broadcasting, translation, or adaptation of their work to others. Creators can also sell their rights for payments referred to as royalties. Like patents, copyrights also have an expiration, which is nationally defined and usually extends even beyond the death of the creator, usually for about 50 years, as a means to protect the creator's heirs.

Unauthorized copying, illegal installations, and piracy of software are direct violations of the copyright laws against a creator. Peer-to-peer-based torrents' unauthorized sharing of copyrighted information also constitutes copyright violations. To protect against copyright infringement, it is advisable to design and develop your software so that it actively solicits acceptance of terms of use and licensing by presenting the EULA with "I accept" functionality. It must, however, be recognized that the EULA acceptance may only deter copyright infringement and not prevent it.

6.6.1.3 Trademark

Trademarks are distinctive signs that can be used to identify the maker uniquely from others who produce a similar product. UPS Brown, Intel's Pentium processor, and McDonald's golden arches are good examples of trademarks. When this is for a service, it is referred to as a service mark. The maker can be a specific person or an enterprise. The trademark can be a word, letter, phrase, numeral, drawing, three-dimensional sign, piece of music, vocal sound, fragrance, color, symbol of design, or combinations of these. Trademarks grant owners exclusive rights to use them to identify goods and services or to authorize others to use them in return for monetary remuneration for a period of time. The period of protection varies, but trademarks can be renewed indefinitely.

The protection of trademarks from infringement is based on the need to clarify the source of the goods or service exclusively to a particular supplier, but by definition, a trademark enjoys no protection from disclosure, because only when a trademark is disclosed can the consumers associate that trademark to the goods or services supplied by the company. On the other hand, before disclosure of a trademark, a company may need to protect the confidentiality of the trademark until it is made public, in which case it would be deemed a trade secret.

6.6.1.4 Trade Secret

A trade secret is not just limited to protection of a trademark, but is broadly inclusive of any confidential business information that provides a company with a competitive advantage. It can be a design, formula, instrument, method, pattern, practice, process, or strategy, as well as supplier or client lists that bear the following characteristics:

- The information must not be generally known, readily accessible, or reasonably ascertainable.
- It must have commercial value that is lost or reduced should the information be disclosed.
- It must be protected by the holder of the information (e.g., through confidentiality agreements).

Examples of well-known trade secrets include the formula for Coca-Cola, Colonel Sanders' fried chicken recipe, and Microsoft Windows operating system code. Even your software code may need to be protected as a trade secret if disclosure of the code will result in an unfair loss of your competitive advantage. The entire software code may need to be protected as a trade secret, or perhaps just portions of your code. Just because your software is deployed in object code form does not imply that trade secret protection is automatically present. Nondisclosure agreements (NDAs) are legally enforceable and must be in place with all developers who are writing such business-critical software. Additionally, protection against RCE should be architected and designed into the software because RCE can yield knowledge about the design and inner workings of the software and is, therefore, a potential threat to the confidentiality of trade secrets.

6.6.2 Disclaimers

IP protection mechanisms protect the company against known threats and scenarios. However, in the world of software, anything can go wrong at any time, and there are many unforeseen situations that can arise. For example, the installation of your software in a client system may require a certain configuration of the host operating system. Such configuration settings, however, have been known to put the client system in a state of compromise. Although it is not your software that is vulnerable, the state of security of the system has been reduced, and upon breach, you can be held liable for the breach. This is where disclaimers come in as a protective means. Disclaimers provide software companies legal protection from liability claims or lawsuits that are unforeseen. When selling or purchasing software, careful attention must be paid to disclaimers. Disclaimers protect the software publisher by informing the purchaser that the software is sold "as is." They shift the risks from the publisher to the acquirer, and for any unfortunate security incident that arises as a result of using the software, the publisher will not be held legally accountable.

A prevalent application of disclaimers today is in the context of Web applications, when a popup message appears informing the user that they are leaving the Web site they are on to another Web site to which they have linked. Figure 6.7 is an example of a disclaimer popup. When linking to an external Web site or listing contents from another Web site (as is the case with mashups), it is also imperative that appropriate permissions from the owner of the external Web site are explicitly obtained to avoid copyright and other liability concerns.

6.6.3 Validity Periods

You will have noticed that you can run some software, especially in the cases of "try before you buy" or "demo" software versions, only for a set period of time before

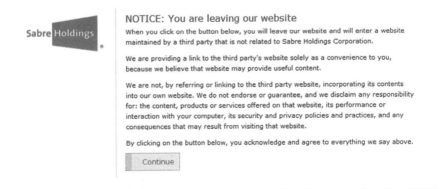

Figure 6.7   Example of a disclaimer.

the software is set to expire. Validity periods refer to the allowed length-of-use of the software or the outputs from the software. For example, if your software is used to print an invoice, then it is important that you explicitly state the number of days or hours that the invoice will be honored. This way, someone who prints an invoice with a discounted price does not hold you liable after the stated period has passed and take advantage of the offer when the product is not offered anymore at the discounted price.

Restrictions should be placed in the software to ensure that the software is not allowed continuance of use once the expiration has elapsed, unless the user purchases the software or agrees to your conditions. It is very important that the software is designed and deployed securely with regard to validity periods. It is advisable that, in the design of the trial and full version of the software, the extent of functionality is considered and addressed. The trial version of the software must not include the full functionality of the purchased version, which is merely protected by a license or expiration date check. This way, even if a software license or expiration data check is circumvented, full functionality of the software is not disclosed. RCE, byte patching (changing instruction sets of the program at the byte level), and repacking of the software program can be used to invalidate and bypass license and expiration date checks easily.

Licensing, either by establishing master agreements or EULAs, is a means to set out and communicate the conditions of use along with any restrictions for the software. Master agreements are broad and set out the general overall conditions of use along with any restrictions, and EULAs add granularity to these conditions and restrictions.

Another aspect of validity periods as they apply to software is with regard to logic bombs. This is especially important if you have outsourced your software development to an external third party. Logic bombs, which are embedded code that executes when certain conditions have been met, need to be discovered and addressed. One such condition may be the length-of-use term, and the trigger for the execution of the embedded code would be the time period. A programmer can embed in your software a piece of code that would render the software nonfunctional once the validity period has passed. Although this is needed to ensure discontinuance of use of the software post validity periods, it could also backfire and cause a denial of service (DoS) to valid customers if such protection mechanisms are not required in the first place. Careful thought and design need to be factored into the concept of validity periods in software.

6.6.4 Contracts and Agreements

Contracts protect an organization from liabilities that may arise against the organization. These are legally binding agreements, which means that the terms and conditions will hold up in a court of law, and violators can be penalized for violation of the terms and conditions. Unlike disclaimer-based protection, wherein there exists only a one-sided notification of terms, contracts require that both parties engaged in the transaction mutually agree to abide by any terms in the agreement. It is essential to have contracts in place when you outsource the development of your software or if you are developing the software exclusively for a particular customer.

In addition to contracts, there are other agreements that offer protection and software assurance. The ones covered in this section are:

■ Service level agreements
■ Nondisclosure agreements
■ Noncompete agreements

This section is not inclusive of all the types of agreements but it covers the main agreements that relate to software development. Data classification exercises are useful in defining and classifying the information and the elements of SLAs or NDAs in protecting that information.

6.6.4.1 Service Level Agreements (SLA)

SLAs are formal agreements between a service provider and a service recipient. They may include incentives and penalties, in which case they are deemed to be more in the nature of contracts.

SLAs are "requirements-dependent" and "requirements-based." Being requirements-dependent implies that the SLAs must include the requirements of the business. For example, a payroll system cannot suffer downtime, unlike a noncritical human resources training system. Being requirements-based means that, without clearly defined requirements, determination of actual service levels in the formulation of the SLA will be inaccurate. Data classification exercises can be useful in determining the requirements. For example, by classifying information based on criticality to the business, the maximum tolerable downtime (MTD) and recovery time objective (RTO) can be determined, which in turn can be used to determine and define the availability conditions of the SLA.

SLAs have a direct bearing on the TCO because they are the instrument that can be used to ensure support and maintenance by the software service provider. When accepting software for deployment, it is critical that all SLA terms and claims are verified. SLAs are usually observed to be more closely related to the availability tenet of security, but SLAs can address other elements of the security profile, including confidentiality and integrity. SLAs drafted with a time to respond provision, such as "severity 1 incidents will warrant a 1-4 hour workaround" and "severity 2 incidents will be serviced within 4-24 hours," are not uncommon.

Performance on the SLA is measured using metrics. Table 6.3 tabulates several common SLA metrics associated with what they cover.

Table 6.3   SLA Metrics Categories and Coverage

SLA metric category	Coverage
Performance	Reliability in the functionality of the software, i.e., is the software doing what it is supposed to do?
Issues Management	The number of issues (security) that have been addressed or deferred for future releases. How many bugs have been fixed? How many remain? How many are to be moved to the next version?
Disaster Recovery and Business Continuity	Speed of recovery of the software to a working state so that business disruptions are addressed.
Incident Response	Promptness in responding to security incidents. This is dependent on risk factors such as discoverability, reproducibility, elevated privileges, numbers of users affected, and damage potential.
Patch and Release Cycle	Frequency of patches that will be released and applied and the measurement as to whether the process is followed as expected.

6.6.4.2 Nondisclosure Agreements (NDA)

NDAs are basic legal protection mechanisms that ensure confidentiality of information. They protect individuals and organizations against inappropriate, unauthorized, and unlawful disclosure of their proprietary or confidential information that the other party is made aware of so that they may conduct business with each other. Most effective NDAs are mutual, implying that both the disclosing party and the receiving party are protected from their own information's being disclosed without appropriate permissions. Mutual NDAs promote equality in the protection of information.

If it is required for you to disclose your invention to a potential investor before a patent can be filed, it is advisable to protect it with an NDA. Additionally, sometimes when conducting business or acquiring software, you are required to disclose information that is classified as confidential or trade secrets and in such cases, it is essential that NDAs are established and in effect.

A typical NDA includes the following:

- Legal name and contact information of the entities (parties) entering into the agreement not to disclose each other's sensitive or proprietary information that they are privy to in the course of conducting business.
- A commencement date for the agreement to become effective. This is usually the date on which both parties sign the agreement.

■ The information that is to be protected. This must be clearly defined. It must not be limited to, but at least include information about the business practices, such as:
  – Business processes
  – Business affairs
  – Client lists and requirements
  – Development plans
  – Strategic alliances
  – Accounting and other financial information.

  It must also be inclusive of software development-related information, such as:
  – Logic and process flowcharts.
  – Functional specifications.
  – Screen layouts and mock-up.
  – Design and architecture documents (e.g., entity–relationship diagrams [ERD], network design, BCP and DRP logical and physical representations, threat models).
  – Diagrammatic representation of functionality (e.g., system context diagrams, use cases, misuse cases).
  – Pseudo-code documents.
  – Formal code (source) and executable (object/compiled) that is developed or deployed.
  – Web site uniform resource locators (URLs) and network Internet protocol (IP) addresses registered by the parties.
  – Ideas, functions, operations, and outcomes of products and services that are owned or currently developed; sometimes this section in the NDA also defines the forms of confidential information and includes oral, written, electronic or other machine readable forms for both the original and translated versions of information.

■ Permitted use of the information, such as disclosure only to parties that have a need to know and disclosure to third parties that have a binding equally or more restrictive contractual relationship with the disclosing party for the purposes of doing business.

■ Conditions and provisions to disclose information upon mutual written consent.

■ Exclusions or no obligation upon a recipient if the confidential information
  – Is or becomes publicly available through no fault of the recipient.
  – Was already in the recipient's possession before disclosure.
  – Is received rightfully by the recipient from a third party without the duty of confidentiality.
  – Is disclosed to a third party without a duty of confidentiality.
  – Is independently developed by the recipient.
  – Is required by a government body or a court of law; in situations when this is the case, advance notice must be given to the party whose information is being disclosed.

- A protection period that includes how long the agreement itself will be in effect and also how long the proprietary and sensitive information must remain protected or maintain confidentiality. The length of term to protect the information from disclosure usually extends beyond the life of the agreement itself. This may also require that after the effective term of the NDA, confidential information must be rightfully and securely returned to the owner and originals and copies (if any were made) must be destroyed.
■ Other pertinent information. Sometimes the NDA also includes sections on:
  - Export compliance
  - Ownership
  - Remedies
  - Governing law
  - Disclaimers

NDAs are useful instruments in ensuring confidentiality and must be established before any development work if the information is deemed as needing protection.

6.6.4.3 Noncompete Agreements

Noncompete agreements (also known as noncompete clauses) are legally enforceable contractual obligations between a company and an individual or another company that poses a threat to the competitive advantage of the company. This affords protection to the company in situations when a disgruntled employee is fired or when an employee with knowledge of the inner workings of the company leaves the company. It can also be extrapolated to prevent personnel with business and strategic know-how of your company who are solicited by your competitors to leave and work for your competitor, until the term specified in the noncompete agreement has elapsed.

If knowledge about your software is considered a trade secret, then in addition to NDAs, it is vital that noncompete agreements are established and enforced as well.

6.7 Software Escrow

When it comes to acceptance of third party software, consideration must be given to software escrow as well as the legal protection mechanisms that need to exist. Software escrow is the act of having a copy of the source code of the implemented software in the custody of a mutually agreed upon neutral third party known as the escrow agency or party. There are three parties involved in an escrow relationship: the acquirer (licensee or purchaser), the publisher (licensor or seller), and the escrow agency, as depicted in Figure 6.8.

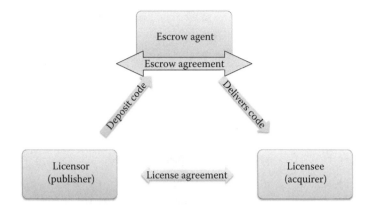

Figure 6.8   Software escrow parties.

This can be regarded as a form of risk transference by insurance, because it insures the licensee continued business operations, should the licensor be no longer alive (in case of a sole proprietorship), go out of business, or file for bankruptcy. Software escrow guards against loss of use of mission-critical software associated with vendor (publisher) failure. It is also important to understand that software escrow protects the licensor in guarding their IP rights as long as the publisher wishes to retain the rights. The licensee cannot purchase the software or reverse engineer the software to write their own. Determination of whether such a breach has occurred can be established by comparing the software to the copies and versions that are held in escrow.

What is escrowed is dependent on the escrow agreement. It is usually only the source code that is escrowed and so is commonly known as source code escrow. However, it is advisable that versions of both source and object code are escrowed along with appropriate documentation for each version.

One of the main failures in software escrow situations is not the fact that the code (source and/or object) is not escrowed properly, but in the verification and validation processes after the code has been escrowed.

Verification and validation should minimally include the following:

■ Retrieval Verification: Can the processes to retrieve the code from the escrow party be followed? Do you have the evidence to prove validity of your identity when requesting to retrieve the escrow versions, and can it be spoofed? Are there change and version control mechanisms in place that protect the integrity of the versions that are held in escrow, and is the check-out/check-in process audited?
■ Compilation Verification: Can the source code be compiled to executable (object) code without errors? Do you have a development and test environment in which to compile the source code that is retrieved from escrow?

■ Version Verification: Does the source code version that is escrowed match the version of the object code that is implemented in your environment?

Software escrow aids in software acceptance, and as a CSSLP it is important that you understand the processes and steps involved as well as the protection software escrowing affords your organization.

6.8 Verification and Validation (V&V)

The capability maturity model (CMM) for software version 1.1 defines verification and validation (V&V) as the process of evaluating software to determine whether the products of a given development phase satisfy the conditions imposed at the start of the phase. In other words, verification ensures that the software *performs* as it is required and designed to do. Validation is the process of evaluating software during and/or at the end of the development process to determine whether it satisfies specified requirements. In other words, validation ensures that the software meets required specifications.

Usually verification and validation go hand in hand, and the differences between the two are primarily definitional and matter more to a theorist than to a practitioner. Broadly speaking, V&V refer to all activities that are undertaken to ensure that the software is functioning and secured as required. V&V is a required step in the software acceptance process, regardless of whether the software is built in-house or procured (acquired).

V&V is not an ad hoc process. It is a very structured and systematic approach to evaluate the software technical functionality. It can be performed by the organization or by an independent third party. Regardless of who performs the V&V exercise, the evaluation is basically divided into two main activities: review, including inspection, and testing, as illustrated in Figure 6.9.

V&V should check for the presence of security protection mechanisms to ensure confidentiality, integrity of data and system, availability, authentication, authorization, auditing, secure session management, proper exception handling, and configuration management. In some cases, the software may be required to comply with certain external regulations and compliance initiatives (e.g., FIPS, PCI DSS, or Common Criteria), and proper V&V of these requirements is essential. The request for Common Criteria evaluation assurance levels (EAL) must be in place when procuring software, and the EAL claimed by the vendor must be verified. It is important to note that it is not sufficient simply to check for the existence of security features; the V&V process must verify the correct implementation of the security features that are present. It is superfluous to have a security feature in the software that is accepted, but which is or needs to be disabled when deployed in the production environment or released. V&V can be used for C&A of the software. The following section covers each of the V&V activities in more detail, followed by a discussion on C&A.

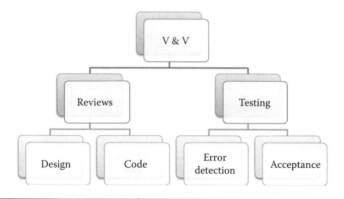

Figure 6.9   Verification and validation activities.

6.8.1 Reviews

At the end of each phase of the SDLC, reviews need to be conducted to ensure that the software performs as expected and meets business specifications. This can be done informally or formally.

Informal reviews usually do not involve a review panel or board and can be as simple as a developer's reviewing his/her own design and code. This is usually performed as needed, unlike a formal review, which is regarded to be a milestone in the SDLC.

The formal review process includes the presentation of the materials to a review panel or board for approval before proceeding to the next phase of the life cycle. Reviews must not be a mere check-the-box exercise wherein the panel simply checks an approval box to proceed to the next phase. The most effective reviews are observed when the personnel who are directly involved in the development of the software present the inner working design and instrumentation of the software to a review panel and answer any questions from the panel. The review panel is appointed by the acquirer of the software who has the authority to make a go/no-go decision and should include at least one member from the team responsible for software assurance.

Informal review may include review of the design and of the code, but formal reviews must include design and code review. One such formal inspection process is the Fagan inspection process, which is a highly structured process with several steps to determine defects in development results, such as specifications, design, and code. In addition to the review of the functionality design, a security design review (using threat models, misuse cases, and so on) must be performed. Design reviews are conducted at the end of the design phase with the goal of detecting any architectural flaw that would require redesign before code is created. Design reviews help in the validation of software. Code reviews happen at the end of the development phase and involve line-by-line review of the code and step-by-step inspection (sometimes also called a walkthrough) of software functionality and assurance capabilities. This is performed with the intent of detecting bugs and errors. Code reviews are usually conducted among peers from development and quality assurance teams and so are also referred to as peer reviews. Code reviews help in the verification of software. Automated code review scanners and data flow tracers can be used to augment more manual and structured inspection processes.

6.8.2 Testing

As a key activity in the V&V process, testing can help demonstrate that the software truly meets the requirements (validation) and determine any variances or deviations from what is expected (verification) using the actual results from the test. It also includes testing to determine the impact upon system integration. The different kinds of tests that are conducted as part of V&V are:

- Error detection tests
- Acceptance tests

Error detection tests include unit- and component-level testing. Errors may be flaws (design issues) or bugs (code issues). In addition to validation tests to ensure that the software satisfies the specified requirements, verification testing must be performed to ascertain the following at a minimum:

- Proper handling of input validation using fuzzing
- Proper output responses and filtration
- Proper error handling mechanisms
- Secure state transitions and management
- Proper handling of load and tests
- Resilience of interfaces
- Temporal (race conditions) assurance checks
- Spatial (locality of reference) assurance and memory management checks
- Secure software recovery upon failures

Acceptance testing is used to demonstrate whether the software is ready for its intended use. Software that is deemed ready should be validated not only for all functional requirements, but also to ensure that it meets assurance (security) requirements. This test cannot be overlooked or ignored and is a necessary milestone before acceptance of the software for deployment or release. Sometimes when software is released in increments, the acceptance test will include a regression test as part of the systems integration testing activity in addition to the incremental acceptance test.

The impact on integration of the different software components for the system can be determined by regression and/or simulation testing. Regression testing is performed to ensure that the software is backward-compatible and that the software does not introduce any new risks to the computing environment. Regression testing involves rerunning previously defined and run acceptance tests and verifying that the results are as expected. Simulation testing gives insight into configuration mismatches and data discrepancy issues and must be performed in an environment that mirrors the environment in which the accepted software will be deployed.

Once software is accepted, any changes to the software must be formally validated and verified. Impacts to existing processes, such as business continuity, disaster recovery, and incident response, must also be determined, and the maintenance and support model must be revisited and revalidated.

6.8.3 Independent (Third Party) Verification and Validation

Independent Verification and Validation (IV&V) or third party assessment of software functionality and assurance is the process in which the software is reviewed, verified, and validated by someone other than the developer of the software or the acquirer. This is mostly the case with software that is purchased. This is commonly also referred to as independent third party testing. The independent part of this type of testing is that the IV&V party can be neutral and objective in reporting their findings, as they have no stake in the success or failure of the software. All IV&V reviews and tests are formal by nature, and rules of engagement must be established in advance and formalized in the form of a contract or legally enforceable agreement.

IV&V is very helpful in validating vendor claims and assists with the compliance oversight process as it transfers the liability inherent from the software risks to the third party that conducts the reviews and tests, should a breach occur once the software has been accepted on grounds of the findings from the IV&V.

6.8.4 Checklists and Tools

It is important to recognize that merely completing checklists with proper verification of existence and validation of proper implementation are insufficient to ensure software assurance. Checklists may help with compliance, but they do not necessarily secure. All items in the checklist that address the functionality and assurance aspects of the software must be verified and validated.

The use of tools (e.g., code review scanners, vulnerability scanners) to evaluate software security is useful from a prioritization standpoint, but careful attention must be paid to false positives and false negatives. Solely relying on tools in lieu of manual V&V checks is not advised because tools cannot completely emulate human experience and decision-making capabilities. True indication of security maturity implies that the tool is part of a more holistic security program and not just the sole measure to secure software. If IV&V is undertaken, then it is important that you are aware of the checklists and tools they use and that you are fully aware of how the independent third party conducted their V&V process.

6.9 Certification and Accreditation

As aforementioned, V&V activities help with C&A. The ISO/IEC 27006:2007 standard specifies requirements and provides guidance for bodies providing audit and certification of an information security management system (ISMS) and is primarily intended to support software accreditation.

Certification is the technical verification of the software functional and assurance levels. Certification, in other words, is a set of procedures that assesses the suitability of software to operate in a computing environment by evaluating both the technical and nontechnical controls based on predefined criteria (e.g., Common Criteria). Security certification considers the software in the operational environment. At the minimum, it will include assurance evaluation of the following:

- User rights, privileges, and profile management
- Sensitivity of data and application and appropriate controls
- Configurations of system, facility, and locations
- Interconnectivity and dependencies
- Operational security mode

Accreditation is management's formal acceptance of the system after an understanding of the risks to that system rating in the computing environment. It is management's official decision to operate a system in the operational security mode for a stated period and the formal acceptance of the identified risk associated with operating the software.

Software must not be accepted as ready for release unless it is certified and accredited. At the completion of the V&V process, the evaluator can rate the software on functional and assurance requirements. Once software is rated by an evaluator, it is easier to make a determination as to whether the software is to be accepted or not.

6.10 Summary

In this chapter, we have learned that before built or bought software is labeled as ready for deployment or release, it needs to be formally accepted. Benefits of a formal software acceptance process include the validation of security requirements and the verification of security controls, ensuring that software is not only operationally hack-resilient, but also compliant with applicable regulations. Before the acceptance of software, there are many things that are to be taken into consideration.

When building software, some of these considerations include: the satisfaction of the predefined completion criteria, establishment of the change management process, approvals to deploy or release, risk acceptance and exceptions to policy, and the completeness of pertinent documentation. When buying software, the incorporation of software assurance requirements in the procurement methodology must be an important consideration. IP protection means using patents, copyrights, and trademarks. Legal protections using instruments such as contracts and agreements need to be factored in as well before accepting the software as ready for deployment/release. When purchasing software, another protection mechanism that needs to be validated is software escrowing, which protects both the licensor (software publisher) and the licensee (software purchaser). Additionally, software V&V activities must be undertaken for any software that is being accepted, regardless of whether it is built or bought. V&V activities can be performed by the organization or by an independent third party neutral and objective party. They are broadly categorized into reviews (design and code) and testing (error detection and acceptance) and also include regression, simulation, and integration testing, which ensure that the acceptance of the software will not reduce the existing state of operational security and help with evaluating the technical functional and assurance levels (certification). They also provide management with the residual risk levels, allowing them to accept (accreditation) or reject the software. The most important thing to remember is that without a formal software acceptance process, the likelihood that the software will be functionally reliable and at the same time operationally secure is bleak.

6.11 Review Questions

1. Your organization has the policy to attest the security of any software that will be deployed into the production environment. A third party vendor software is being evaluated for its readiness to be deployed. Which of the following verification and validation mechanism can be employed to attest the security of the vendor's software?
   A. Source code review
   B. Threat modeling the software
   C. Black box testing
   D. Structural analysis
2. When procuring commercial off-the-shelf (COTS) software for release within your global organization, special attention must be given to multilingual and multicultural capabilities of the software since they are more likely to have
   A. Compilation errors
   B. Canonicalization issues
   C. Cyclomatic complexity
   D. Coding errors

3. To meet the goals of software assurance, when accepting software from a vendor, the software acquisition phase must include processes to
   A. Verify that installation guides and training manuals are provided
   B. Assess the presence and effectiveness of protection mechanisms
   C. Validate vendor's software products
   D. Assist the vendor in responding to the request for proposals

4. Your organization's software is published as a trial version without any restricted functionality from the paid version. Which of the following must be designed and implemented to ensure that customers who have not purchased the software are limited in the availability of the software?
   A. Disclaimers
   B. Licensing
   C. Validity periods
   D. Encryption

5. Software escrowing is MORE closely related to which of the following risk handling strategy?
   A. Avoidance
   B. Mitigation
   C. Acceptance
   D. Transference

6. Which of the following legal instruments assures the confidentiality of software programs, processing logic, database schema, and internal organizational business processes and client lists?
   A. Noncompete agreements
   B. Nondisclosure agreements (NDA)
   C. Service level agreements (SLA)
   D. Trademarks

7. "As is" clauses and disclaimers transfer the risk of using the software from the software publisher to the
   A. Developers
   B. End users
   C. Testers
   D. Business owners

8. Improper implementation of validity periods using length-of-use checks in code can result in which of the following types of security issues for legitimate users?
   A. Tampering
   B. Denial of service
   C. Authentication bypass
   D. Spoofing

9. The process of evaluating software to determine whether the products of a given development phase satisfies the conditions imposed at the start of the phase is referred to as

    A. Verification
    B. Validation
    C. Authentication
    D. Authorization

10. When verification activities are used to determine if the software is functioning as it is expected to, it provides insight into which of the following aspects of software assurance?
    A. Redundancy
    B. Reliability
    C. Resiliency
    D. Recoverability

11. When procuring software the purchasing company can request the evaluation assurance levels (EALs) of the software product which is determined using which of the following evaluation methodologies?
    A. Operationally Critical Assets Threats and Vulnerability Evaluation® (OCTAVE^{SM})
    B. Security quality requirements engineering (SQUARE)
    C. Common criteria
    D. Comprehensive, lightweight application security process (CLASP)

12. The final activity in the software acceptance process is the go/no go decision that can be determined using
    A. Regression testing
    B. Integration testing
    C. Unit testing
    D. User acceptance testing

13. Management's formal acceptance of the system after an understanding of the residual risks to that system in the computing environment is also referred to as
    A. Patching
    B. Hardening
    C. Certification
    D. Accreditation

14. You determine that a legacy software running in your computing environment is susceptible to cross-site request forgery (CSRF) attacks because of the way it manages sessions. The business has the need to continue use of this software, but you do not have the source code available to implement security controls in code as a mitigation measure against CSRF attacks. What is the best course of action to undertake in such a situation?
    A. Avoid the risk by forcing the business to discontinue use of the software
    B. Accept the risk with a documented exception
    C. Transfer the risk by buying insurance
    D. Ignore the risk since it is legacy software

15. As part of the accreditation process, the residual risk of a software evaluated for deployment must be accepted formally by the
    A. Board members and executive management
    B. Business owner
    C. Information technology (IT) management
    D. Security organization
    E. Developers

References

Baschab, J., and Piot, J. 2007. Check vendor references. *The Executive's Guide to Information Technology*. Hoboken, NJ: John Wiley & Sons, 431–438.

Carnegie Mellon University Software Research Institute. 2011. CMMI models: What is the difference between verification and validation? Web. 4 Mar. 2011. http://www.sei.cmu.edu/cmmi/start/faq/models-faq.cfm (accessed 6 Mar. 2011).

Eilam, E. 2005. Obfuscation tools. *Reversing: Secrets of Reverse Engineering*. Indianapolis: Wiley, 345.

Howard, M., and LeBlanc, D. 2003. Security principles to live by. *Writing Secure Code*, 2nd ed. Redmond, WA: Microsoft, 51–53.

ISO/IEC 27006:2007. International Organization for Standardization, 19 Jan. 2011. Web. 04 Mar. 2011. http://www.iso.org/iso/catalogue_detail?csnumber=42505 (accessed 6 Mar. 2011).

Kocher, K. 2004. *Creating a Learning Culture: Strategy, Technology, and Practice*. ed. Marcia L. Conner and James G. Clawson. Cambridge, UK: Cambridge UP, 63.

Patton, C. 1987. Buyers turning toward software escrow plans. *InfoWorld Management* 9.43 (1987): 57–58.

SearchSecurity.com. 2004. What is non-disclosure agreement? Web. 4 Mar. 2011. http://searchsecurity.techtarget.com/sDefinition/0,,sid14_gci214435,00.html (accessed 6 Mar. 2011).

Shoemaker, D. 2007. Building security into the business acquisition process. *Build Security In*. Department of Homeland Security National Cyber Security Division. Web. 4 Mar. 2011. https://buildsecurityin.us-cert.gov/bsi/ (accessed 6 Mar. 2011).

Stackpole, Cynthia. 2010. Requirements traceability matrix. *A Project Manager's Book of Forms: A Companion to the PMBOK Guide*. Hoboken, NJ: Wiley, 29.

U.S. Department of Homeland Security. 2008. Software assurance (SwA) in acquisition: Mitigating risks to the enterprise. 2008. *Build Security In*. Web. 4 Mar. 2011. https://buildsecurityin.us-cert.gov/bsi/articles/best-practices/acquisition/896-BSI.html (accessed 6 Mar. 2011).

U.S. Department of Homeland Security. 2009. Software assurance in acquisition and contract language. 2009. *Acquisition & Outsourcing* 1.1.1 (2009): 1–27. *Build Security In*. Web. 4 Mar. 2011. https://buildsecurityin.us-cert.gov/swa/pocket_guide_series.html#acquisition (accessed 6 Mar. 2011).

World Intellectual Property Organization. 2011. What is intellectual property? Web. 4 Mar. 2011. http://www.wipo.int/about-ip/en/ (accessed 6 Mar. 2011).

Chapter 7

Software Deployment, Operations, Maintenance, and Disposal

7.1 Introduction

Once software has been formally accepted by the customer or client and is ready to be installed or released, the installation must be performed with security in mind. Just because software was designed and developed with security considerations, it does not necessarily mean that it will also be deployed with security controls in place. All of the software assurance efforts to design and build the software can be rendered useless if the deployment process does not take security into account. In fact, it has been observed that allowing the software to run with elevated privileges or turning off the monitoring and auditing functionality can adversely impact the overall security of the software.

Once software is deployed, it needs to be monitored to guarantee that the software will continue to function in a reliable, resilient, and recoverable manner as expected. Ongoing operations and maintenance include addressing incidents impacting the software and patching the software for malware threats.

Finally, there is a need to identify the software and conditions under which software needs to be disposed of or replaced, because insecure and improper disposal procedures can have serious security ramifications.

In this chapter, we will cover the security aspects that one needs to bear in mind when dealing with the last stage of the system/software development life cycle (SDLC), i.e., the deployment, operations, maintenance, and disposal of software.

7.2 Objectives

As a CSSLP, you are expected to

- Understand the importance of secure installation and deployment.
- Be familiar with secure startup or bootstrapping concepts.
- Know how to harden the software and hardware to assure trusted computing.
- Be familiar with configuration management concepts and how they can impact the security of the software.
- Understand the importance of continuous monitoring.
- Know how to manage security incidents.
- Understand the need to determine the root cause of problems that arise in software as part of problem management.
- Know what it means to patch software and how patching can impact the state of software security.
- Be aware of sunset criteria that must be used to determine and identify software to comply with end-of-life (EOL) policies.

This chapter will cover each of these objectives in detail. We will learn about security considerations that must be taken during installation and deployment, followed by a discussion of security processes, such as continuous monitoring, incident and problem management, and patching, to maintain operationally hack-resilient software. Finally we will learn about what it means to securely replace or remove old, unsupported, insecure software. It is imperative that you fully understand the objectives and be familiar with how to apply them to the software that your organization deploys or releases.

7.3 Installation and Deployment

When proper installation and deployment processes are not followed, there is a high likelihood that the software and the environment in which the software will operate can lack or have a reduced level of security. It is of prime importance to keep security in mind before and after software is installed. Without the necessary pre- and postinstallation software security considerations, expecting software to be operationally hack-resilient is a far-fetched objective.

Software needs to be configured so that security principles, such as least privilege, defense in depth, and separation of duties, are not violated or ignored during the installation or deployment phase. According to the Information Technology Infrastructure Library (ITIL), the goal of configuration management is to enable the control of the infrastructure by monitoring and maintaining information on all the resources that are necessary to deliver services.

Some of the necessary pre- and postinstallation configuration management security considerations include:

- Hardening (both software and hardware/minimum security baselines [MSBs])
- Enforcement of security principles
- Environment configuration
- Bootstrapping and secure startup

7.3.1 Hardening

Even before the software is installed into the production environment, the host hardware and operating system need to be hardened. Hardening includes the processes of locking down a system to the most restrictive level appropriate so that it is secure. These minimum (or most restrictive) security levels are usually published as a baseline with which all systems in the computing environment must comply. This baseline is commonly referred to as an MSB. An MSB is established to comply with the organizational security policies and help support the organization's risk management efforts. Hardening is effective in its defense against vulnerabilities that result from insecure, incorrect, or default system configurations.

Not only is it important to harden the host operating system by using an MSB, it is also critically important to harden the applications and software that run on top of these operating systems. Hardening of software involves implementing the necessary and correct configuration settings and architecting the software to be secure by default. In this section, we will primarily learn about the security misconfigurations that can render software susceptible to attack. These misconfigurations can occur at any level of the software stack and lead anywhere from data disclosure to total system compromise.

Some of the common examples of security errors and/or misconfigurations include:

- Hard coding credentials and cryptographic keys in inline code or in configuration files in clear text.
- Not disabling the listing of directories and files in a Web server.
- Installation of software with default accounts and settings.
- Installation of the administrative console with default configuration settings.
- Installation or configuration of unneeded services, ports and protocols, unused pages, or unprotected files and directories.
- Missing software patches.
- Lack of perimeter and host defensive controls, such as firewalls and filters.
- Enabling tracing and debugging, as these can lead to attacks on confidentiality assurance. Trace information can contain security-sensitive data about the

internal state of the server and workflow. When debugging is enabled, errors that occur on the server side can result in presenting all stack trace data to the client browser.

Although the hardening of host OS is usually accomplished by configuring the OS to an MSB and updating patches (patching is covered later in this chapter), hardening software is more code-centric and, in some cases, more complex, requiring additional effort. Examples of software hardening include:

■ Removal of maintenance hooks before deployment.
■ Removal of debugging code and flags in code.
■ Modifying the instrumentation of code not to contain any sensitive information. In other words, removing unneeded comments (dangling code) or sensitive information from comments in code.

Hardening is a very important process in the installation phase of software development and must receive proper attention.

7.3.2 Enforcement of Security Principles

Preinstallation checklists are useful to ensure that the needed parameters required for the software to run are appropriately configured, but since it is not always possible to identify issues proactively, checklists provide no guarantee that the software will function without violating the security principles with which it was designed and built.

A common error is granting inappropriate administrative rights to the software during the installation process. This is a violation of least privilege. Enabling disabled services, ports, and protocols so that the software can be installed to run is an example of defense in depth violations. When operations personnel allow developers access to production systems to install software, this violates the principle of separation of duties. If one is lax about the security principles with which the software was designed and built during the installation phase, then one must not be surprised when that software gets hacked.

7.3.3 Environment Configuration

When software that worked without issues in the development or test environment no longer functions as expected in the production environment, it is indicative of a configuration management issue with the environments. Often this problem is dealt with in an insecure manner. The software is granted administrative privileges to run in a production environment upon installation, and this could have serious security ramifications. It is therefore imperative to ensure that the development and test environment match the configuration makeup of the production environment, and simulation testing identically emulates the settings (including the restrictive settings) of the environment in which the software will be deployed postacceptance. Additional configuration considerations include:

■ Test and default accounts need to be turned off.
■ Unnecessary and unused services need to be removed in all environments.
■ Access rights need to be denied by default and granted explicitly even in development and test environments, just as they would be in the deployed production environment.

Configuration issues are also evident in disparate platforms or when platforms are changed. Software developed to run in one platform has been observed to face hiccups when the platform changes. The x86 to x64 processor architecture change has forced software development organizations to rethink the way they have been doing software development so that they can leverage the additional features in the newer platform. It has also mandated the need in these organizations to publish and support software in different versions so that it will function as expected in all supported platforms. Figure 7.1 shows an example of how the .Net Framework 4.0 software has to be published and supported for the x86, IA64, and x64 platforms.

Another environment consideration issue that is evident in software today is that bugs that were previously fixed reappear. In Chapter 4, we established that regenerative bugs can occur due to improper versioning or version management. It is also possible that regenerative bugs can result from improper configuration management. Say, for example, that during the user acceptance testing phase of the software development project, it was determined that there were some bugs that needed to be fixed. Proper configuration management would mandate that the fix happens in the development environment, which is then promoted to the test environment, where the fix is verified, and then promoted to the user acceptance testing environment, where the business can retest the functionality and ensure that the bug is fixed. But sometimes, the fix is made in the user acceptance testing environment and then deployed to the production environment upon acceptance. This is a configuration management issue as the correct process to address the fix is not followed or enforced. The fix is never back-ported to the development and test environments, and subsequent revisions of the software will yield in the reappearance of bugs that were previously fixed.

It is also important to ensure that the program database (pdb) file is not deployed into the production environment. The program database file holds debugging and

File Name:	File Size	
dotNetFx40_Full_x86.exe	35.3 MB	Download
dotNetFx40_Full_x86_ia64.exe	51.6 MB	Download
dotNetFx40_Full_x86_x64.exe	48.0 MB	Download

Figure 7.1 Software publication for different platforms.

project state information. It is used to link the debug configuration of the program incrementally, but an attacker can use it to discover the internal workings of the software using the debug information contained in the program database file.

To manage software configuration management properly, one of the first things is to document and maintain the configuration information in a formal and structured manner. Most organizations have what is called a configuration management database (CMDB) that records and consists of all the assets in the organization. The ISO/IEC 15408 (Common Criteria) requirements mandate that the implementation, documentation, tests, project-related documentation, and tools, including build tools, are maintained in a configuration management system (CMS). Changes to the security levels must be documented, and the MSB must be updated with the latest changes. Without proper software configuration management, managing software installations and releases/deployment is a very arduous undertaking and, more importantly, potentially insecure.

7.3.4 Bootstrapping and Secure Startup

Upon the installation of software, it is also important to make certain that the software startup processes do not in any way adversely impact the confidentiality, integrity, or availability of the software. When a host system is started, the sequences of events and processes that self-start the system to a preset state is referred to as booting or bootstrapping. Booting processes in general are also sometimes referred to as the initial program load (IPL). This includes the power-on self-test (POST), loading of the operating system, and turning on any of the needed services and settings for computing operations. The POST is the first step in an IPL and is an event that needs to be protected from tampering so that the trusted computing base (TCB) is maintained. The system's basic input/output system (BIOS) has the potential to overwrite portions of memory when the system undergoes the booting process. To ensure that there is no information disclosure from the memory, the BIOS can perform what is known as a destructive memory check during POST, but this is a setting that can be configured in the system and can be overridden or disabled. It is also important to recognize that protecting access to the BIOS using the password option provided by most chip manufacturers is only an access management control, and it provides no integrity check as the secure startup process does.

Secure startup refers to all the processes and mechanisms that assure the environment's TCB integrity when the system or software running on the system starts. It is usually implemented using the hardware's trusted platform module (TPM) chip, which provides heightened tamperproof data protection during startup. The TPM chip can be used for storing cryptographic keys and providing identification information on mobile devices for authentication and access management. Physically, the TPM chip is located on the motherboard and is commonly used to create a unique system fingerprint within the boot process. The unique fingerprint remains unchanged unless the system has been tampered with. Therefore, the

TPM fingerprint validation can be used to determine the integrity of the system's bootstrapping process. Once the fingerprint is verified, the TPM can also be used for disk cryptographic functions, specifically disk decryption of secure startup volumes, before handing over control to the operating system. This protection alleviates some of the concerns around data protection in the event of physical theft.

Interruptions in the host bootstrapping processes can lead to the unavailability of the systems and other security consequences. Side channel attacks, such as the cold boot attack (covered in Chapter 4), have demonstrated that the system shutdown and bootstrapping processes can be circumvented, and sensitive information can be disclosed. The same is true when it comes to software bootstrapping. Software is often architected to request a set of self-start parameters that need to be available and/or loaded into memory when the program starts. The parameter can be supplied as input from the system, a user, the code when coded inline, or from global configuration files. Application_Start events are used in Web applications to provide software bootstrapping. Malicious software (malware) threat agents, such as spyware and rootkits, are known to interrupt the bootstrapping process and interject themselves as the program loads.

7.4 Operations and Maintenance

Once the software is installed, it is operated to provide services to the business or end users. Released software needs to be monitored and maintained. Software operations and maintenance need to take into account the assurance aspects of reliable, resilient, and recoverable processing. Since total security (100% security), signified by no risk, is utopian and unachievable, all software that is deployed has a level of residual risk that is usually below the acceptable threshold as defined by the business stakeholders, unless the risk has been formally accepted. Despite best efforts, software deployed can still have unknown security and privacy issues. Even in software where software assurance is known at release time, due to changes such as those in the threat landscape and computing technologies, the ability of the software to withstand new threats (resiliency) and attacks may not be sufficient. Furthermore, many designs and technologies that have been previously deemed secure are no longer considered to be secure, as is evident with banned cryptographic algorithms and banned APIs. The resiliency of software must always be above the acceptable risk level/threshold, as depicted in Figure 7.2. The point at which the software's ability to withstand attacks falls below the acceptable threshold is the point when risk avoidance procedures, such as a version release, must be undertaken.

Continuing to operate without mitigating the risk in the current version and delaying the implementation of the next version defines the time when the software is most vulnerable to attack. This is where operations security comes into effect. Operations security is about staying secure or keeping the resiliency levels of the software above the acceptable risk levels. It is the assurance that the software will

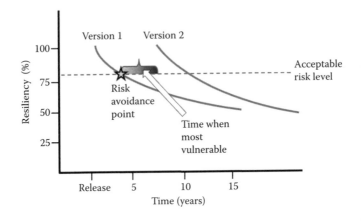

Figure 7.2 Software resiliency levels over time.

continue to function as expected, in a reliable fashion for the business, without compromising its state of security and includes monitoring, managing, and applying the needed controls to protect resources (assets).

These resources can be broadly grouped into hardware, software, media, and people. Examples of hardware resources include:

- Networking devices, such as switches, routers, and firewalls
- Communication devices, such as phones, fax, PDA, and VoIP devices
- Computing devices, such as servers, workstations, desktops, and laptops

Software resources are of the following type:

- In-house developed software
- External third party software
- Operating system software
- Data

All data need to be protected, whether they are transactional or stored in backups, archives, log files, and the like. Examples include an organization's proprietary information, customer information, and supplier or vendor information.

Examples of media resources are USB, tapes, hard drives, and optical CD/DVDs. People resources are comprised of employees and nonemployees (e.g., contractors, consultants). The types of operational security controls are broadly classified as follows:

- *Detective controls* are those that can be used to build historical evidence of user and system/process actions. They are directly related to the reliability aspect of software assurance. If the software is not reliable, i.e., not functioning as expected, those anomalous operations must be tracked and reviewed. These controls are usually passive in nature. Auditing (logging) and intrusion detection systems (IDS) are some examples of detective software operations controls.

■ *Preventive controls* are those that make the success of the attacker difficult, as their goal is to prevent the attack actively or proactively. They are directly related to the resiliency aspect of software assurance. They are useful to mitigate the impact of an attack while containing and limiting the consequences of a successful attack. Input validation, output encoding, bounds checking, patching, and intrusion prevention systems (IPS), are some examples of preventive software operations controls.

■ *Deterrent controls* are those that do not necessarily prevent an attack nor are merely passive in nature. Their aim is to dissuade an attacker from continuing their attack. For example, auditing can be a deterrent control when the users of the software are aware of being audited. In such situations, auditing can be used to deter an attacker while also serving as a detective control to determine what happened where, when, and by whom.

■ *Corrective controls* aim to provide the recoverability of software assurance. This means that when software fails, either due to accidental user error or due to being intentionally attacked, the software should have the necessary controls to bounce back into the normal operations state by use of corrective controls. Load balancing, clustering, and failover of data and systems are some examples of corrective software operations controls.

■ *Compensating controls* are those controls that must be implemented when the prescribed software controls, as mandated by a security policy or requirement, cannot be met due to legitimate technical or documented business constraints. Compensating controls must sufficiently mitigate the risk associated with the security requirement. The Payment Card Industry Data Security Standard (PCI DSS) standard is a set of requirements for enhancing payment account data security. It prescribes that compensating controls must satisfy all of the following criteria:
  - Meet the intent and rigor of the original requirement.
  - Provide a similar level of defense as the original requirement.
  - Be part of a defense in depth implementation so that other requirements are not adversely impacted.
  - Be commensurate with additional risk imposed by not adhering to the requirement.

When compensating controls are considered, the requirements that will be addressed by the controls need to be identified, and the controls need to be defined, documented, validated, maintained, and assessed periodically for their effectiveness. Figure 7.3 shows an example of how the PCI DSS expects the documentation of compensating controls.

Requirement Number and Definition:

		Information Required	Explanation
1.	**Constraints**	List constraints precluding compliance with the original requirement.	
2.	**Objective**	Define the objective of the original control; identify the objective met by the compensating control.	
3.	**Identified risk**	Identify any additional risk posed by the lack of the original control.	
4.	**Definition of compensating controls**	Define the compensating controls and explain how they address the objectives of the original control and the increased risk, if any.	
5.	**Validation of compensating controls**	Define how the compensating controls were validated and tested.	
6.	**Maintenance**	Define process and controls in place to maintain compensating controls.	

Figure 7.3 PCI DSS compensating controls worksheet.

In addition to understanding the types of controls, a CSSLP must also be familiar with some of the ongoing control activities that are useful to ensure that the software stays secure. These include:

- Monitoring
- Incident management
- Problem management
- Patching and vulnerability management

In the following section, we will learn about each of these operations security activities in more detail. As a CSSLP, you are expected not only to be familiar with the concepts covered in this section, but also be able to function in an advisory role to the operations personnel who may or may not have a background in software development or ancillary disciplines that are related to software development.

7.4.1 Monitoring

The premise behind monitoring is that what is not monitored cannot be measured and what is not measured cannot be managed. One of the defender's dilemmas is that the defender has the role of playing vigilante all the time whereas the attacker has the advantage of attacking at will, anytime. This is where continuous monitoring can be helpful. As part of security management activities pertinent to operations, continuous monitoring is critically important.

7.4.1.1 Why Monitor?

Monitoring can be used to:

- Validate compliance with regulations and other governance requirements.
- Demonstrate due diligence and due care on the part of the organization toward its stakeholders.
- Provide evidence for audit defense.
- Assist in forensics investigations by collecting and providing the requested evidence if tracked and audited.
- Determine that the security settings in the environment are not below the levels prescribed in the MSBs.
- Assure that the confidentiality, integrity, and availability aspects of software assurance are not impacted adversely.
- Detect insider and external threats that are orchestrated against the organization.
- Validate that the appropriate controls are in place and working effectively.
- Identify new threats, such as rogue devices and access points that are being introduced into the organization's computing environment.
- Validate the overall state of security.

7.4.1.2 What to Monitor?

Monitoring can be performed on any system, software, or their processes. It is important first to determine the monitoring requirements before implementing a monitoring solution. Monitoring requirements need to be solicited from the business early on in the SDLC. Besides using the business stakeholders to glean monitoring requirements, governance requirements, such as internal and external regulatory policies, can be used. Along with the requirements, associated metrics that measure actual performance and operations should be identified and documented. When the monitoring requirements are known, the software development team has the added benefit of assisting with operations security, because they can architect and design their software either to provide information useful for monitoring themselves or leverage APIs of third party monitoring devices, such as IDS and IPS.

Any operations that can have a negative impact on the brand and reputation of the organization, such as when it does not function as expected, must be monitored. This could include any operations that can cause a disruption to the business (business continuity operations) and/or operations that are administrative, critical, and privileged in nature. Additionally, systems and software that operate in environments that are of low trust, such as in a demilitarized zone (DMZ), must be monitored.

Even physical access must be monitored, although it may seem like there is little or no significant overlap with software assurance. This is because software assurance deals with data security issues, and if physical devices that handle, transport, or store these data are left unmonitored, they can be susceptible to disclosure, alteration, and destruction attacks, resulting in serious security breaches. The PCI DSS, as one of its requirements, mandates that any physical access to cardholder data or systems that house cardholder data must be appropriately restricted and the restrictions periodically verified. Physical access monitoring using surveillance devices such as video cameras is recommended. The surveillance data that are collected must also be reviewed and correlated with the entry and exit of personnel into these restricted areas. This data must be stored for a minimum of 3 months, unless regulatory requirements warrant a higher archival period. The PCI DSS also requires that access is monitored and tracked regularly.

7.4.1.3 Ways to Monitor

The primary ways in which monitoring is accomplished within organizations today is by

- Scanning
- Logging
- Intrusion detection

Scanning to determine the makeup of the computing ecosystem and to detect newer threats in the environment is important. It is advisable that you familiarize yourself with the concepts pertinent to scanning that were covered in Chapter 5. Logging and tracking user activities are critical in preventing, detecting, and mitigating data compromise impacts. The National Computer Security Center (NCSC), in their publication, *A Guide to Understanding Audits in Trusted Systems*, prescribes the following reasons as the five core security objectives of audit mechanisms, such as logging and tracking user activities. It states that the audit mechanism should:

1. Make it possible to review access patterns and histories and the presence and effectiveness of various protection mechanisms (security controls) supported by the system.
2. Make it possible to discover insider and external threat agents and their activities that attempt to circumvent the security control in the system or software.
3. Make it possible to discover the violations of the least privilege principle. When an elevation of privilege occurs (e.g., change from programmer to administrator role), the audit mechanisms in place should be able to detect and report on that change.

4. Be able to act as a deterrent against potential threat agents. This requires that the attacker is made aware of the audit mechanisms in place.
5. Be able to contain and mitigate the damage upon violation of the security policy, thereby providing additional user assurance.

IDS are used to monitor potential attacks and threats to which the organizational systems and software are subjected. As part of monitoring real threats that come into the network, it is not uncommon to see the deployment of *bastion hosts* in an IDS implementation. The name "bastion host" is said to be borrowed from medieval times when fortresses were built with bastions, or projections out of the wall, that allowed soldiers to congregate and shoot at the enemy. In computing, a bastion host is a fortified computer system completely exposed to external attack and illegal entry. It is deployed on the public side of the DMZ as depicted in Figure 7.4. It is not protected by a firewall or screened router. The deployment of bastion hosts must be carefully designed, as insecure design of these can lead to easy penetration by external threat agents into the internal network. The bastion hosts need to be hardened, and any unnecessary services, protocols, ports, programs, and services need to be disabled before deployment. Firewalls and routers themselves can be considered as bastion hosts, but other types of bastion hosts include DNS, Web servers, and mail servers.

Bastion hosts can be used in both a deterrent as well as in a detecting manner. They provide some degree of protection against script kiddies and curious, nonserious attackers. It is important that the bastion hosts are configured to record (log) all security-related events, and that the logs themselves are protected from tampering.

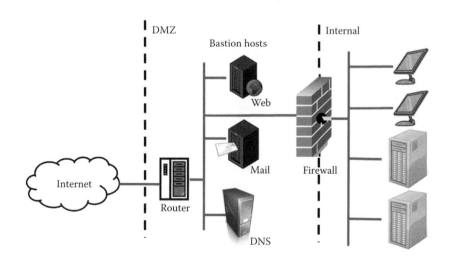

Figure 7.4   Bastion hosts.

When bastion hosts have logging enabled, they can be used to find out the threats that are coming into the network. In such situations, they assist in detective functions. A bastion host can also function as a honeypot. A honeypot is a monitored computer system that acts as a decoy and has no production value in it. When bastion hosts function as honeypots, they are useful for several reasons, including:

- Distracting attackers away from valuable resources within the network. In this case, the bastion host is also a deflective control, because it deflects the threat agent away from valuable resources.
- Acting as warning systems.
- Conducting research on newer threats and attacker techniques.

A honeypot functions as an *enticer* because it lures an attacker who is looking forward to breaking into your network or software. *Enticement* is not necessarily illegal, and the evidence collected from these honeypots may or may not be admissible in a court of law. *Entrapment,* on the other hand, which is characterized by encouraging someone to commit a crime when they originally had no intentions of committing it, is illegal, and the evidence is not admissible in a court of law. This means that while bastion hosts must undoubtedly be monitored, it must be performed without active solicitation of someone to come and test the security of your network and using the evidence collected against them, should they break in.

7.4.1.4 Metrics in Monitoring

Two other important operations security concepts related to monitoring are *metrics* and *audits*. Metrics are measurement information. These must be identified beforehand and clearly defined. Monitoring can then be used to determine if the software is operating optimally and securely at the levels as defined in the metrics definition. The service level agreement (SLA) often contains these metrics, but metrics are not just limited to SLAs. An example of an availability metric would be the uptime and downtime metric. The acceptable number of errors and security weaknesses in the released version of the software is another metric that indicates the quality of the software. Metrics are not only useful in measuring the actual state of security, but can also be useful in making information decisions that can potentially improve the overall state of security.

Not so long ago, when regulations and compliance initiatives did not mandate secure software development, making the case to have organizations adopt secure software processes as part of their software development efforts was always a challenge. The motivators that were used to champion security initiatives in software development were fear, uncertainty, and doubt (FUD), but these were not very effective. Telling management that something disastrous (fear) could happen that could cause the organization great damage (doubt) anytime (uncertainty) was not often well received, and security teams earned the reputation of being naysayers and traffic cops, impeding business. Organizations that were willing to accept high levels of risk often ignored security in the SDLC, and those that were more paranoid sometimes ended up with overly excessive implementations of security in their SDLC. Metrics takes the FUD out of decision making and provides insight into the real state of security. Metrics also give the decision makers a quantitative and objective view of what their state of security is. Key performance indicators (KPIs) are metrics used by organizations to measure their progress toward their goals, and security metrics must be part of the organization's KPI.

The quality of decisions made is directly proportional to the quality of metrics used in decision making. Good metrics help facilitate comprehensive secure decisions and bad metrics do not. So what makes a metric a good metric or a bad metric? Characteristics of good metrics include:

- Consistency: Consistency implies that, no matter how many times the metric is measured, each time the results from the same data sets must be the same or at least equivalent. There should be no significant deviation between each measurement.
- Quantitative: Good metrics are precise and expressed in terms of a cardinal number or as a percentage. A cardinal number is one that expresses the count of the items being measured, as opposed to an ordinal number, which expresses a thing's position. "The number of injection flaws in the payroll application is 6" is an example of a metric expressed in terms of a cardinal number. "65% of the 30 application security vulnerabilities that were measured can be protected by input validation" is an example of a metric expressed as a percentage. Expressing the value as a cardinal number or percentage is more specific to the subset than expressing it in terms of a term such as "high," "medium," or "low."
- Objectivity: Objectivity implies that, regardless of who is collecting the metric data, the results will be indicative of the real state of affairs. It should be that the numbers (metric information) tell the story, and not the other way around. Metrics that are not objective and depend on the subjective judgment of the person conducting the measurement are really not metrics at all, but a rating.
- Contextually Specific: Good metrics are usually expressed in more than one unit of measurement, and the different units provide the context of what is being measured. For example, it is better to measure "the number of injection flaws in the payroll application" or "the number of injection flaws per thousand lines of code (KLOC)," instead of simply measuring "the number of injection flaws in an application." Contextually specific metrics makes it not only possible to make informed and applicable decisions, but it also allows for determining trending information. Determining the number of security defects in different versions of a particular application gives insight into

Table 7.1 Characteristics of Metrics

Attribute	Good Metrics	Bad Metrics
Collection	Consistent	Inconsistent
Expressed	Quantitatively (cardinal or percentage)	Qualitatively (ratings)
Results	Objective	Subjective
Relevance	Contextually specific	Contextually irrelevant
Cost	Inexpensive (automated)	Expensive (manual)

whether the security of the application is increasing or decreasing and also provides the ability to compute the relative attack surface quotient (RASQ) between the versions.

■ Inexpensive: Good metrics are usually collected using automated means that are generally less expensive than using manual means to collect the same information.

In contrast, the characteristics of bad metrics are the opposite of those of good metrics, as tabulated comparatively in Table 7.1.

Although it is important to use good metrics, it is also important to recognize that not all bad metrics are useless. This is particularly true when qualitative and subjective measurements are used in conjunction with empirical measurements because comparative analysis may provide insight into conditions that may not be evident from just the cardinal numbers.

7.4.1.5 Audits for Monitoring

Audits are monitoring mechanisms by which an organization can ascertain the assurance aspects (reliability, resiliency, and recoverability) of the network, systems, and software that they have built or bought. It is an independent review and examination of system records and activities. An audit is conducted by an auditor, whose responsibilities include the selection of events to be audited on the system, setting up of the audit flags that enable the recording of those events, and analyzing the trail of audit events. Audits must be conducted periodically and can give insight into the presence and effectiveness of security and privacy controls. They are used to determine the organization's compliance with the regulatory and governance (policy) requirements and report on violations of the security policies. In and of itself, the audit does not prevent any noncompliance, but it is detective in nature. Audits can be used to discover insider attacks and fraudulent activities. They are effective in determining the implementation and effectiveness of security principles, such as separation of duties and least privilege. Audits have now become mandatory for most organizations. They are controlled by regulatory requirements, and a finding of noncompliance can have serious repercussions for the organization.

Some of the goals of periodic audits of software include:

- Determining that the security policy of the software is met.
- Assuring data confidentiality, integrity, and availability protections.
- Making sure that authentication cannot be bypassed.
- Ensuring that rights and privileges are working as expected.
- Checking for the proper function of auditing (logging).
- Determining whether the patches are up to date.
- Finding out if the unnecessary services, ports, protocols, and services are disabled or removed.
- Reconciling data records maintained by different people or teams.
- Checking the accuracy and completeness of transactions that are authorized.
- Determining that physical access to systems with sensitive data is restricted only to authorized personnel.

7.4.2 Incident Management

Whereas continuous monitoring activities are about tracking and monitoring attempts that could potentially breach the security of systems and software, incident management activities are about the proper protocols to follow and the steps to take when a security breach (or incident) occurs.

The first revision of the *NIST Special Publication on Computer Security Incident Handling Guide* (SP 800-61) prescribes guidance on how to manage computer security incidents effectively. Starting with the detection of the incident, which can be accomplished by monitoring, using incident detection and prevention systems (IDPS), and other mechanisms, the first step in incident response is to determine if the reported or suspected incident is truly an incident. If it is a valid incident, then the type of the incident must be determined. Upon the determination of valid incidents and their type, steps to minimize the loss and destruction and to correct, mitigate, remove, and remediate exploited weakness must be undertaken so that computing services can be restored as expected by the business. Clear procedures to assess the current and potential business impact and risk must be established along with the implementation of effective and efficient mechanisms to collect, analyze, and report incident data. Communication protocols and relationships to report on incidents both to internal teams and to external groups must also be established and followed. In the following section, we will learn about each of these activities in incident management in more detail. As a CSSLP, you are not only expected to know what constitutes an incident but also how to respond to one and advise your organization to do the same.

7.4.2.1 Events, Alerts, and Incidents

In order to determine if a security incident has truly occurred or not, it is first important to define what constitutes an incident. Failure to do so can lead to potential misclassification of events and alerts as real incidents, and this could be costly. It is therefore imperative to understand the differences and relationships between

- Events
- Alerts
- Incidents

Any action that is directed at an object that attempts to change the state of the object is an *event*. In other words, an event is any observable occurrence in a network, system, or software. When events are found, further analysis is conducted to see if these events match patterns or conditions that are being evaluated using signature-based pattern-matching or anomalous behavioral analysis.

When events match preset conditions or patterns, they generate alerts or red flags. Events that have negative or detrimental consequences are adverse events. Some examples of adverse events include flooded networks, rootkit installations, unauthorized data access, malicious code executions, and business disruptions. Alerts are flagged events that need to be scrutinized further to determine if the event occurrence is an incident. Alerts can be categorized into incidents, and adverse events and can be categorized into *security incidents* if they violate or threaten to violate the security policy of the network, system, or software applications. Events, alerts, and incidents have a pyramidal relationship; this means that there are more events than there are alerts and more alerts than there are incidents. It is on incidents, not events or alerts, that management decisions are made. It can be said that the events represent raw information and the system view of things happening. Alerts give a technical or operational view and incidents provide the management view. Events generate alerts that can be categorized into incidents. This relationship is depicted in Figure 7.5.

7.4.2.2 Types of Incidents

There are several types of inidents, and the main security incidents include the following:

- *Denial of Service (DoS):* Purportedly the most common type of security incident, DoS is an attack that prevents or impairs an authorized user from using the network, system, or software application by exhausting resources.
- *Malicious code:* This type of incident has to do with code-based malicious entities, such as viruses, worms, and Trojan horses, which can successfully infect a host.

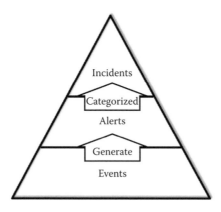

Figure 7.5   Relationship between events, alerts, and incidents.

- *Unauthorized access:* Access control-related incidents refer to those wherein a person gains logical or physical access to the network, system, or software application, data, or any other IT resource without being granted the explicit rights to do so.
- *Inappropriate usage:* Inappropriate usage incidents are those in which a person violates the acceptable use of system resources or company policies. In such situations, the security team (CSSLP) is expected to work closely with personnel from other teams, such as human resources (HR), legal, or, in some cases, even law enforcement.
- *Multiple component:* Multiple component incidents are those that encompass two or more incidents. For example, a SQL injection exploit at the application layer allowed the attacker to gain access and replace system files with malicious code files by exploiting weaknesses in the Web application that allowed invoking extended stored procedures in the insecurely deployed backend database. Another example of this is when a malware infection allows the attacker to have unauthorized access to the host systems.

The creation of what is known as a *diagnosis matrix* is also recommended. A diagnosis matrix is helpful to lesser-experienced staff and newly appointed operations personnel because it lists incident categories and the symptoms associated with each category. It can be used to provide advice on the type of incident and how to validate it.

7.4.2.3 Incident Response Process

There are several phases to the incident response process, ranging from initial preparation to postincident analysis. Each phase is important and must be thoroughly

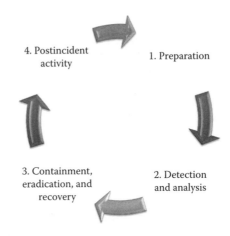

Figure 7.6   Incident response life cycle.

defined and followed within the organization as a means to assure operations security. The major phases of the incident response process are preparation, detection and analysis, containment, eradication and recovery, and postincident analysis, as depicted in Figure 7.6.

7.4.2.3.1 Preparation

During the preparation phase, the organization aims to limit the number of incidents by implementing controls that were deemed necessary from the initial risk assessments. Today regulations and standards such as FISMA and PCI DSS mandate that organizations must create, provision, and operate a formal incident response plan (IRP).

The following are recommendations of activities to perform during this phase:

- Establish incident response policies and procedures.
- Create and train an incident response team (IRT) that will be responsible for responding to and handling the incident.
- Perform periodic risk assessments, and reduce the identified risks to an acceptable level so that they are effective in reducing the number of incidents.
- Create an SLA that documents the appropriate actions and maximum response times.
- Identify additional personnel, both internal and external to the organization, who may have to be called upon to address the incident.
- Acquire tools and resources that the IRT personnel can use. The effectiveness of incident response is tied closely to the tools and resources they have readily available when responding to an incident. Some common examples include

contact lists, network diagrams, backup configurations, computer forensic software, port lists, security patches, encryption software, and monitoring tools.

■ Conduct awareness and training on the security policies and procedures and how they are related to actions that are prescribed in the IRP.

7.4.2.3.2 Detection and Analysis

Without the ability to detect security breaches, the organization will not be aware of incidents before or when they occur. If the incident is disruptive and goes undetected, appropriate actions that have to be taken will not be, and this could be very detrimental to the reputation of the organization.

One of the first activities performed in incident management is to look at the logs or audit trails that have been captured in the IDPS. The logs hold raw data. The log analysis process is made up of the following steps: collection, normalization, correlation and visualization. Automation of log analysis may be needed to select events of interest that can be further analyzed. Logging, reporting, and alerting are all parts of the information gathering activity and the first steps in incident analysis.

The different types of logs that should be collected for analysis include:

■ *Collection*
  - Network and host intrusion detection systems (NIDS and HIDS) logs
  - Network access control lists (ACL) logs
  - Host logs, such as OS system messages, logon success and failure information, and system errors, that are written locally on the host or as configured by administrators.
  - Application (software) logs that provide information about the activity and interactions between users/processes and the applications.
  - Database logs. These are difficult to collect and often require auditing configurations in the database so that database performance is not adversely impacted. They serve as an important source for security-related information and need to be protected with great care because databases can potentially house intellectual property and critical business data.
    It is critical to ensure that the logs themselves cannot be tampered with when the data are being collected or transmitted. Cryptographic computation of the hash value of the logs before and after being processed provides anti-tampering and integrity assurance.
■ *Normalization*
  The quality of the incident handling process is dependent on the quality of the incident data that are collected. Organizations must be able to identify data that are actionable and pertinent to the incident instead of working with

all available data that are logged. This is where normalization can be helpful. Normalization is also commonly referred to as parsing the logs to glean information from them. Regular expressions are handy in parsing the log data. The collected logs must be normalized so that redundant data are eliminated, especially if the logs are being aggregated from various sources. It is also very important to ascertain that the timestamps of the logs are appropriately synchronized so the log analysis provides the true sequence of actions that were conducted.

■ *Correlation*

Log analysis is performed to correlate the events to threats or threat agents. Some examples of log correlation are discussed here. The presence of "wait for delay" statements in your log must be correlated against SQL statements that were run in the database to determine if an attacker were attempting blind SQL injection attacks. If the logs indicate several "failed login" entries, then this must be correlated with authentication attempts that were either brute-forced (threat) or tried by a hacker (threat agent). The primary reason for the correlation of logs with threat or threat agent is to deduce patterns. Secondarily, it can be used to determine the incident type.

It is important to note that the frequency of the log analysis is directly related to the value of the asset whose logs are being analyzed. For example, the logs of the payroll application may have to be reviewed and analyzed daily, but the logs from the training application may not be.

■ *Visualization*

There is no point in analyzing the logs to detect malicious behavior or correlate occurrences to threats if that correlated information is not useful in addressing the incident. Visualization helps in depicting the incident information in a user-friendly and easy-to-understand format. The use of graphical constructs is common to communicate patterns and trends to technical, operations, management personnel, and decision makers.

The following are recommendations of activities to perform during this phase:

- Continuously monitor using monitoring software and IDPS that can generate alerts from events they record. Some examples of monitoring software include anti-virus, anti-spyware, and file integrity checkers.
- Provide mechanisms for both external parties and internal personnel to report incidents. Establishing a phone number and/or email address that assure anonymity is useful to accomplish this objective.
- Ensure that the appropriate level of logging is enabled. Activities on all systems must be logged to defined levels in the MSB, and crucial systems/software should have additional logging in place. For example, the verbosity of logs for all systems must be set to log at an "informational" level, whereas that for the sales or payroll application must log at a "full details" level.

- Since incident information can be recorded in several places to obtain a panoramic view of the attacks against your organization, it is a best practice to use centralized logging and create a log retention policy. When aggregating logs from multiple sources, it is important to synchronize the clocks of the source devices to prevent timing issues. The log retention policy is helpful because it can help detect repeat occurrences.
- Profile the network, systems, and software so that any deviations from the normal profile are alerted as behavioral anomalies that should warrant attention. Understanding the normal behavior also provides the team members the ability to recognize abnormal operations more easily.
- Maintain a diagnosis matrix, and use a knowledge base of information that is useful to incident handlers. They act as a quick reference source during critical times of containing, eradicating, and recovering activities.
- Document and timestamp all steps taken from the time of the incident's being detected to its final resolution. This could serve as evidence in a court of law if there is a need for legal prosecution of the threat agent. Documented procedures help in handling the incident correctly and systematically and, subsequently, more efficiently. Since the documentation can be used as evidence, it is also critical to make sure that the incident data themselves are safeguarded from disclosure, alteration, or destruction.
- Establish a mechanism to prioritize the incidents before they are handled. Incidents should not be on a first-come first-served basis. Incidents must be prioritized based on the impact the incident has on the business. It is advisable to establish written guidelines on how quickly the IRT must respond to an incident, but it is also important to establish an escalation process to handle situations when the team does not respond within the times prescribed in the SLA.

7.4.2.3.3 Containment, Eradication, and Recovery

Upon detection and validation of a security incident, the incident must first be contained to limit any further damage or additional risks. Examples of containment include shutting down the system, disconnecting the affected systems from the network, disabling ports and protocols, turning off services, and taking the application offline. Deciding how the incident is going to be contained is critical. Inappropriate ways of containing the security incident can not only prevent tracking the attacker, but can also contaminate the evidence being collected, which will render it inadmissible in a court of law should the attacker be taken to court for their malicious activities.

Containment strategies must be based on the type of incident since each type of incident may require a different strategy to limit its impact. It is a best practice for organizations to identify a containment strategy for each listed incident in the diagnosis matrix. Containment strategies can range from immediate shutdown to *delayed* containment. Delayed containment is useful in collecting more evidence by monitoring the attacker's activity, but this can be dangerous, as the attacker may have the opportunity to elevate privilege and compromise additional assets. Even when a highly experienced IRT capable of monitoring all attackers' activity and terminating attacker access instantaneously is available, the high risks posed by delayed containment may not make it an advisable strategy. Willingly allowing a known compromise to continue can have legal ramifications, and when delayed containment is chosen as the strategy to execute, it must first be communicated to and determined as feasible by the legal department.

Criteria to determine the right containment strategy include the following:

- Potential impact and theft of resources.
- The need to preserve evidence. The ways in which the collected evidence is and will be preserved must be clearly documented. Discussions on how to handle the evidence must be held with the organization's internal legal team and external law enforcement agencies, and their advice must be followed. What evidence to collect must also be discussed. Any data that are physically not persisted (volatile), when collected as evidence, need to be collected and preserved carefully. Subjects who have access to and custody of these data must be granted explicitly and monitored to prevent any unauthorized tampering or destruction. Maintaining the chain of custody is crucial in making the evidence admissible in a court of law. Some well-known examples of volatile data include:
  - List of network connections
  - Login sessions
  - Open files
  - Network interface configurations
  - Memory contents and processes

  In some cases, a snapshot of the original disk may need to be made since forensic analysis could potentially alter the original. It such situations, it is advisable that a forensic backup be performed instead of a full system backup, and that the disk image is made in sanitized write-once or write-protectable media for forensics and evidentiary purposes.
- The availability requirements of the software and its services.
- Time and resources needed to execute the strategy.
- The completeness (partial containment or full containment) and effectiveness of the strategy.
- The duration (temporary or permanent) and criticality (emergency or workaround) of the solution.
- The possibility of the attack to cause additional damage when the primary attack is contained. For example, disconnecting the infected system could trigger the malware to execute data destruction commands on the system to self-destruct, causing system compromise.

Incident data and information are privileged information and not "water cooler" conversation material. The information must be restricted to the authorized personnel only, and the principle of need-to-know must be strictly enforced.

Upon the containment of the incident, the steps necessary to remove and eliminate components of the incident must be undertaken. An eradication step can be performed as a standalone step in and of itself, or it may be performed during recovery. It is important to ensure that any fixes or steps to eradicate the incident are taken only after appropriate authorization is granted. When dealing with licensed or third party components or code, it is important to ensure that appropriate contractual requirements as to which party has the rights and obligations to make and redistribute security modifications is present and documented in the associated SLAs.

Recovery mechanisms aim to restore the resource (network, system, or software application) back to its normal working state. These are usually OS- or application-specific. Some examples include restoring systems from legitimate backups, rebuilding services, restoration of compromised accounts and files with correct ones, patch installations, password changes, and enhanced perimeter controls. A recovery process must also include putting a heightened degree of monitoring and logging in place to detect repeat offenders.

7.4.2.3.4 Postincident Analysis

One of the most important steps in the incident response process that can easily be ignored is the postmortem analysis of the incident. Lessons learned activities must produce a set of objective and subjective data regarding each incident. These action items must be completed within a certain number of days of the incident and can be used to achieve closure. For an incident that had minimal to low impact on the organization, the lessons learned meetings can be conducted periodically. This is important because a lesson learned activity can:

- Provide the data necessary to identify and address the problem at its root.
- Help identify security weaknesses in the network, system, or software.
- Help identify deficiencies in policies and procedures.
- Be used for evidentiary purposes.
- Be used as reference material in handling future incidents.
- Serve as training material for newer and lesser experienced IRT members.
- Help improve the security measures and the incident handling process itself so that future incidents are controlled.

Maintaining an incident database with detailed information about the incident that occurred and how it was handled is a very useful source of information for an incident handler.

Additionally, if the organization is required to communicate the findings of the incident externally either to those affected by the incident, law enforcement

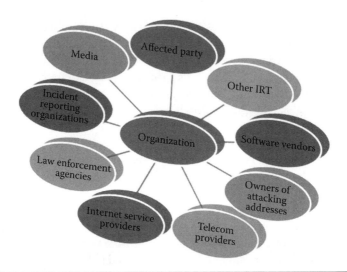

Figure 7.7 Incident response communication—outside parties.

agencies, vendors, or to the media, then it is imperative that the postincident analysis is conducted before that communication. Figure 7.7, taken from *The Computer Security Incident Handling Guide* special publication (SP 800-61), illustrates some of the outside parties that may have to be contacted and communicated with when security incidents occur within the organization.

In order to limit the disclosure of incident-related sensitive information to outside parties, which could potentially cause more damage than the incident itself, appropriate communication protocols need to be followed. This means that communication guidelines are established in advance, and a list of internal and external point of contacts (POCs) (along with backup for each) is identified and maintained. No communication to outside parties must be made without the IRT's discussing the issue with the need-to-know management personnel, legal department, and the organization's public affairs office POC. Only the authorized POC should then be authorized to communicate the incident to the associated parties. Additionally, only the pertinent information about the incident that is deemed applicable to the party receiving the information must be disclosed.

Not all incidents require a full-fledged postincident analysis, but at a bare minimum the following, which is referred to as the 5Ws, need to be determined and reported on:

- What happened?
- When did it happen?
- Where did it happen?
- Who was involved?
- Why did it happen?

It is the "Why" that we are particularly interested in, since it can provide us with insight into the vulnerabilities in our networks, systems, and software applications. Determining the reasons as to why the incident occurred in the first place is the first step in problem management (covered in the next section).

7.4.3 Problem Management

Incident management aims at *restoring* service and business operations as quickly as possible, whereas problem management is focused on *improving* the service and business operations. When the cause of an incident is unknown, it is said to be a *problem*. A *known error* is an identified root cause of a problem. The goal of problem management is to determine and eliminate the root cause and, in doing so, improve the service that IT provides to the business so the same issue may not be repeated again.

For example, it is observed that the software does not respond and hangs repeatedly after it has run for a certain period. This causes the software to be extremely slow or unavailable to the business. As part of addressing this issue, the incident management perspective would be to reboot the system repeatedly each time the software hangs so that the service can be restored to the business users within the shortest time possible. The problem management perspective would not be so simple. This problem of resource exhaustion and eventual DoS will need to be evaluated to determine what could be causing the problem. The root cause of the incident could be one of several things. The configuration settings of the system on which the software is run may be restricting the software to function, the code may be having extensive native API and memory operations calls, or the host system may have been infected by malicious software that is causing the resource exhaustion. Suppose it were determined that the calls to memory operations in the code were the reason why this incident was happening. Problem management would continue beyond simple identification of the root cause until the root cause was eliminated. Insecure memory calls would now be the known error, and it would need to be addressed. In this case, the code would need to be fixed with the appropriate coding constructs or throttling configuration, and the system might have to be upgraded with additional memory to handle the load.

The objective in problem management after fixing the identified root cause is to make sure that the same problem does not occur again. Avoidance of repeated incidents is one of the two main critical success factors (CSFs) of problem management. The other is to minimize the adverse impacts of incidents and problems on the business.

7.4.3.1 Problem Management Process

Problem management begins with notification and ends with reporting, as illustrated in Figure 7.8. Upon notification of the incident, root cause analysis (RCA) steps are taken to determine the reason for the problem.

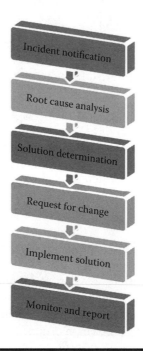

Figure 7.8 Problem management process flow.

RCA is performed to determine why the problem occurred in the first place. It is not just asking the question, "Why did the problem happen?" once, but repeatedly and systematically until there are no more reasons (or causes) that can be answered. A litmus test to classify an answer as the root cause is that, when the condition identified as the root cause is fixed, the problem no longer exists. Brainstorming using fishbone diagrams instead of ad hoc brainstorming and rapid problem resolution (RPR) problem diagnosis are common techniques that are used to identify root cause. Fishbone diagrams are also known as *cause and effect* diagrams. Fishbone diagrams help the team graphically to identify and organize possible causes of a problem (effect), and, using this technique, the team can identify the root cause of the problem. When brainstorming using fishbone diagrams, the RCA process can benefit if categories are used. These categories, when predefined, help the team to focus on the RCA activity appropriately. Some examples of categories that can be used are people (e.g., awareness, training, or education), process (e.g., nonexistent, ill-defined), technology, network, host, software (e.g., coding, third party component, API), and environment (e.g., production, development, test). Figure 7.9 shows an example of a fishbone diagram used for RCA. In the RPR problem diagnosis, a step-by-step approach to identifying the root cause is taken in three phases: discovery, investigation, and fixing. RPR is fully aligned with ITIL v3.

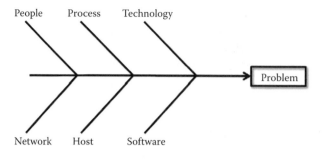

Figure 7.9   Root cause analysis using fishbone diagrams.

RCA can give us insight into such issues as systemic weaknesses, software coding errors, insecure implementation of security controls, improper configurations, and improper auditing and logging. When RCA is performed, it is important to identify and differentiate the symptoms of the incident from the underlying reason as to why the problem occurred in the first place. Incident management treats symptoms, whereas problem management addresses the core of the problem. In layman's terms, incident management is akin to spot control of lawn weeds, whereas problem management would be analogous to pulling out the weeds by the root. For security incidents, without activity logs, determining the root cause of an incident could be very difficult.

After the root cause is identified, workarounds (if needed), recovery, and resolution of the problem are then determined. A request for change is then initiated. It must also be recognized that problem management often results in changes to internal processes, procedures, or infrastructure. When change is determined to be a necessity upon undertaking problem management activities, the change management processes and protocols should be followed as published by the organization. At no time must the need to resolve the problem supersede or force the organization to circumvent the change management process. The appropriate request for change (RFC) must be made after the root cause is identified even if the solution to the problem is not a permanent fix, but just a workaround. Following the implementation of the change, it is important to monitor the problem resolution to ensure that it was effective and that the problem does not happen again and finally to report on the process improvement activities.

7.4.4 Patching and Vulnerability Management

Business applications and systems software are prone to exploitation, and as newer threats are discovered and orchestrated against software, there is a need to fix the vulnerabilities that make the attacks possible. In such situations, the software is not completely removed. Instead additional pieces of code that address the vulnerability or problems (also known as bugs) are developed and deployed. These additional pieces of code (used to update or fix existing software so that the software is not susceptible to the bugs), are known as patches, and patching is the process of applying these updates or fixes. Patches can be used to address security problems in software or simply provide additional functionality. Patching is a subset of hardening.

Patches are often made available from vendors in one of two ways. The most common mechanisms are:

- Hotfix or Quick Fix Engineering (QFE): A hotfix is a functional or security patch that is provided by the software vendor or developer. It usually includes no new functionality or features and makes no changes to the hardware or software. It is usually related to the operating system itself or to some related platform component (e.g., IIS, SQL Server) or product (e.g., MS Word, MS Outlook). Today the term QFE is being used in place of hotfix. The benefit of using a hotfix (or QFE) is that it allows the organization to apply the fix one at a time or selectively.
- Service Pack: Usually a roll up of multiple hotfixes (or QFEs), a service pack is an update to the software that fixes known problems and in some cases provides additional enhancements and functionality as well. Periodic software updates are often published as service packs, and newer product versions should incorporate all previously published service packs to ensure that there are no regression issues, particularly those related to security. The benefit of using a service pack is that multiple hotfixes (or QFEs) can be applied more efficiently because it eliminates the need to apply each fix one at a time.

Although the process of patching is viewed to be reactive, patch and vulnerability management is the security practice developed to prevent attacks and exploits against software and IT systems proactively. Applying a patch after a security incident has occurred is costly and time-consuming. With a well-defined patch and vulnerability management process in place, the likelihood of exploitation and the efforts to respond and remediate incidents will be reduced, thereby adding greater value and savings to the organization.

Although the benefits of patch and vulnerability management programs are many, there are some challenges that come with patching. The main challenge with patching is that the applied patch might cause a disruption of existing business processes and operations. If the application of the patch is not planned and properly tested, it could lead to business disruptions. In order to test the patch before it is deployed, an environment that simulates the production environment must be available. Lack of a simulated environment combined with lack of time, budget, and resources are patching challenges that must be addressed. Since making a change (such as installing a patch) has the potential of breaking something that is working, both upstream and downstream dependencies of the software being patched must be considered. Architecture, DFD, and threat model documentation that gives insight into the entry and exit points and dependencies can be leveraged to identify systems and software that could be affected by the installation of the patch. Additionally, the test for backward compatibility of software functionality must also be conducted postinstallation of patches. Furthermore, patches that are not tested for their security impact can potentially revert configuration settings from a secure to an insecure state. For example, ports that were disabled get enabled or unnecessary services that were removed are reinstalled along with the patch installation. This is why patches must be validated against the MSBs. The success of the patching process must be tested and postmortem analysis should be conducted. The MSB must be updated with successful security patches.

It is important to recognize that not all vulnerabilities have a patch associated with them. A more likely case is that a single patch addresses many software security vulnerabilities. This is important because, as part of the patch and vulnerability management process, the team responsible for patching must know what vulnerabilities are addressed by which patches. As part of the patch management process, not only must vulnerabilities alone be monitored, but remediations and threats as well. Vulnerabilities could be design flaws, coding bugs, or misconfigurations in software that weaken the security of the system. The three primary ways to remediate are the installation of the software patch, adjusting configuration settings, and removal of the affected software. Software threats usually take the form of malware (e.g., worms, viruses, rootkits, Trojan horses) and exploit scripts, but they can be human in nature. There is no software patch for human threats, but the best proactive defense in such situations is user awareness, training, and education.

Timely application of the patch is also an important consideration in the patch and vulnerability management process. If the time frame between the release of the patch and its installation is large, then it gives an attacker the advantage of time. Thus, they can reverse engineer how the patch will work, identify vulnerabilities that will or will not be addressed by the patch or those that will be introduced as a result of applying the patch, and write exploit code accordingly. Ironically, it has been observed that the systems and software are most vulnerable shortly after a patch is released.

It is best advised to follow a documented and structured patching process. Some of the necessary steps that need to be taken as part of the patching process include:

■ Notifying the users of the software or systems about the patch.
■ Testing the patch in a simulated environment so that there are no backward compatibility or dependency (upstream or downstream) issues.
■ Documenting the change along with the rollback plan. The estimated time to complete the installation of the patch, criteria to determine the success of the patch, and the rollback plan must be included as part of the documentation. This documentation needs to be provided along with a change request to be closely reviewed by the change advisory board (CAB) team members and their approvals obtained before the patch can be installed. This can also double as an audit defense as it demonstrates a structured and calculated approach to addressing changes within the organization.

■ Identifying *maintenance windows* or the time when the patch is to be installed. The best time to install the patch is when there is minimal disruption to the normal operations of the business. However, with most software operating in a global economy setting, identifying the best time for patch application is a challenge today.

■ Installing the patch.

■ Testing the patch postinstallation in the production environment is also necessary. Sometimes a reboot or restart of the system where the patch was installed is necessary to read or load newer configuration settings and fixes to be applied. Validation of backward compatibility and dependencies also needs to be conducted.

■ Validating that the patch did not regress the state of security and that it leaves the systems and software in compliance with the MSB.

■ Monitoring the patched systems so that there are no unexpected side effects upon the installation of the patch.

■ Conducting postmortem analysis in case the patch has to be rolled back and using the lessons learned to prevent future issues. If the patch is successful, the MSB needs to be updated accordingly.

The second revision of the special publication 800-40 published by NIST prescribes the following recommendations:

1. Establish a patch and vulnerability group (PVG).
2. Continuously monitor for vulnerabilities, remediations, and threats.
3. Prioritize patch applications and use phased deployments as appropriate.
4. Test patches before deployment.
5. Deploy enterprise-wide automated patching solutions.
6. Use automatically updating applications as appropriate.
7. Create an inventory of all information technology assets.
8. Use standardized configurations for IT resources as much as possible.
9. Verify that vulnerabilities have been remediated.
10. Consistently measure the effectiveness of the organization's patch and vulnerability management program, and apply corrective actions as necessary.
11. Train applicable staff on vulnerability monitoring and remediation techniques.
12. Periodically test the effectiveness of the organization's patch and vulnerability management program.

Patch and vulnerability management is an important maintenance activity, and careful attention must be given to the patching process to assure that software is not susceptible to exploitation and that security risks are addressed proactively for the business.

7.5 Disposal

As was covered earlier, the ability of the software to withstand attacks decreases over a period of time, due to either the discovery of newer threats and exploits or changes in technological advancements that provide a greater degree of security protection. It is therefore important not to forget about security once the software is deployed and running in an operations or maintenance mode. As long as the software is operational, there is always going to be an amount of residual risk to deal with, and all software is vulnerable until it is disposed of (or sunsetted) in a secure manner. In this section, we will learn about the criteria and processes that must be considered and undertaken to dispose of software securely.

7.5.1 End-of-Life Policies

The first requirement in secure disposal of software and its related data and documents is to establish an EOL policy. The *Risk Management Guide for Information Technology Systems*, published by the NIST as Special Publication 800-30 (SP 800-30), prescribes that risk management activities need to be performed for system components that will be disposed of or replaced to ensure that the hardware and software are properly disposed. Additionally, it is important to make sure that residual data are appropriately handled and that system migration is conducted in not just a systematic manner, but also in a secure manner. In order to manage risk during the disposal phase, it is essential that we have an EOL policy developed and followed. For commercial off-the-shelf (COTS) software, the EOL policy begins with the formal notification of end-of-sale (EOS) date; the goal is to provide customers with needed information to plan their migration confidently to replacement technologies. The EOL policy must provide the conditions in which systems and software must be securely disposed and provide guidance on how to accomplish this objective.

An EOL Policy must, in general, contain:

- Sunsetting criteria
- A notice of all the hardware and software that are being discontinued or replaced
- The duration of support for technical issues from the date of sale and how long that would be valid after the notice of disposal has been published
- Recommendations and alternatives for migration and transition along with the versions or products of software that will be supported in the future
- The duration of time when maintenance releases, workarounds, patches, and upgrades will be released and supported
- Contract renewal terms in cases of licensed or third party software

7.5.2 Sunsetting Criteria

Sunsetting criteria provide guidance as to when a particular product (software or the hardware on which the software runs) must be disposed of or replaced. There are several sunsetting criteria for software. We will focus primarily on sunsetting criteria for software alone as listed below in this section.

- Newer threats and attacks against software are discovered, and the risks they bring cannot be mitigated to the acceptable levels defined by the organization due to technical, operational, or management constraints.
- Contractual agreements to continue to use the software have come to an end, and the cost of maintaining and using the software is prohibitive for the business.
- The software has reached its end-of-warranty period.
- The software has reached its end of product support, especially COTS.
- The software has reached its end of vendor support.
- The software is no longer compatible with the architecture of the hardware. Platform/architecture changes, such as the move from x86 processor architecture to the x64 processor architecture, are examples of this.
- Software that can provide the same functionality in a more secure fashion is available as new products, upgrades, or versions release.

7.5.3 Sunsetting Processes

As a general rule, software or software-related technologies that are deemed insecure, but which have no means to mitigate the risk to the acceptable levels of the organization must be sunsetted as soon as possible. However, this may not be as easy a task as it may seem. In compliance with the organization's EOL policy, appropriate EOL processes must be established. EOL processes are the series of technical and business milestones and activities that when complete make the hardware or software obsolete and no longer produced, sold, improved, repaired, maintained, or supported. It also ensures that any related artifacts, such as data in media, code, and documents, are securely disposed.

Just as the deployment of software is governed by a plan, and necessary approvals from the change control or CAB are required, so also is disposal. The steps to follow as software is sunsetted are:

- Have a replacement if needed before disposing of software. The replacement software must already be built or bought, tested, and deployed in the operational environment before the previous software is retired, so that data and system migration and verification can be operationally viable.
- Obtain the necessary approvals from the authorized officials.

- Update the asset inventory database and CMDB with information related to the software being retired as well as the one replacing it (if that is the case).
- Shut down services and adjust or remove any monitoring that was in place for the software being sunsetted. When software that is monitored and configured to create trouble tickets automatically upon failure or unavailability of services is sunsetted, the failure to adjust or remove monitoring and ticket generation can lead to a lot of unnecessary trouble tickets generated and wasted time.
- Ensure that termination access control (TAC) processes are performed to de-provision digital identities and user accounts. If the software is being replaced with another, then it is important to set access control explicitly for the new software and not just copy and migrate the access control information and rights from the old to the new.
- Archive the software and associated data offline. This may be mandated as part of a regulatory or internal policy requirement. Archiving the software and data also allows for a reload of data if the migration process fails and the data are corrupted during the migration process.
- Do not just uninstall, but securely delete the software and data. Uninstalling software may not be sufficient to provide total removal of the software and software assurance. Sometimes the uninstall scripts do not remove all the directories and files or registry entries that were created when the software was installed. In some cases, the uninstall process and scripts generate an uninstall log file that is left behind on the system. This log file can have sensitive information, such as version information, location of configuration and code files, and default settings, which an attacker can find useful to profile your software and its operations. If you build software that use packagers for generating the installation packages, e.g., .msi, .rpm, or scripts, it is important to ensure that the uninstall scripts that come with the packagers do not leave any residue when executed. This is why the software must be securely deleted and not just uninstalled. Secure delete includes additional manual steps that are taken after the uninstall process to ensure that there is no software-related information about the software being retired left behind on the system. This can include manual cleanup and deletion of the registry entries, directories, and files. It also includes the secure disposal of residual or remnant data from storage media (covered in the next section).

7.5.4 Information Disposal and Media Sanitization

The importance of information disclosure protection cannot be overstressed when software that processes and stores that information in some media is being discontinued. Just as software disposal steps are taken to ensure that software assurance is maintained, an important part in that process is also to ensure that the media that stored the information are also sanitized or destroyed appropriately. Sanitization is the process of removing information from media such that data recovery and disclosure are not possible. It also includes the removal of classified labels, marking, and activity logs related to the information. It is not the media themselves, but the information recorded in them that needs protection. It is therefore important first to think in terms of information confidentiality assurance and then consider the type of media when selecting the best method to sanitize or destroy information and associated media.

Information is primarily stored in one of the following two types of media:

■ Hardcopy or physical representation of information. Examples include paper printouts (e.g., internal memoranda, software architecture and design documents, and printed software code), printer and facsimile ribbons, drums, and platens. Usually this type of media is uncontrolled, so without appropriate media protection methods, information can be susceptible to unauthorized individuals and dumpster divers.

■ Softcopy or electronic representation of information where the information is stored in the form of bits and bytes. Examples of this type of media include hard drives, RAM, read-only memory (ROM), disks, memory devices, mobile computing devices, and networking equipment.

Depending on the type of media and future plans for the media, different sanitization techniques can be used. The three most common means of media sanitization include:

■ Clearing
■ Purging
■ Destroying

Disposal is the act of discarding media without giving any considerations to sanitization. This is often done by recycling hardcopy media when no confidential information is present. Disposal is technically not a type of sanitization, but it is still a valid approach to handling media containing nonconfidential information.

Clearing is the process of sanitizing media by using software or hardware products that overwrite logical (e.g., file allocation tables) and addressable storage space on the media with nonsensitive random data. Clearing, however, does not guarantee that the data in the media have been successfully and securely erased. When data remain as residual information, the condition is referred to as *data remanence*. Clearing by overwriting cannot, however, be used for media that are either damaged or of the write-once read-many (WORM) type.

Purging is the process of sanitizing media by rendering the data into an unrecoverable state. Common methods to purge data in magnetic media are degaussing and executing the secure erase command in ATA drives. Degaussing is the process of reducing the magnetic flux of the media to virtual zero by applying a reverse magnetizing field. This will render the drive permanently unusable since the track location information stored in the drives between data sectors will be affected when subjected to a powerful reversed magnetic field.

Destroying or *destruction* is the process of ensuring that the media can no longer be reused as originally intended and the recovery of data from the media is virtually impossible or prohibitively costly. There are many ways in which media can be destroyed. Media containing classified information labeled as highly sensitive are best protected if they are completely destroyed. Upon the destruction of media with highly sensitive information, it is important to validate and verify that media are not susceptible to a laboratory attack. A *laboratory attack* is one where specially trained and skilled threat agents use nonstandard resources and systems to perform data recovery on media outside of their normal operating settings. The different techniques that can be used for physically destroying media for sanitization purposes are as follows:

■ *Disintegration* is the act of separating the media into component parts.
■ *Pulverization* is the act of grinding the media into a powder or dust.
■ *Melting* is the act of changing the state of the media from a solid into liquid by using an extreme application of heat.

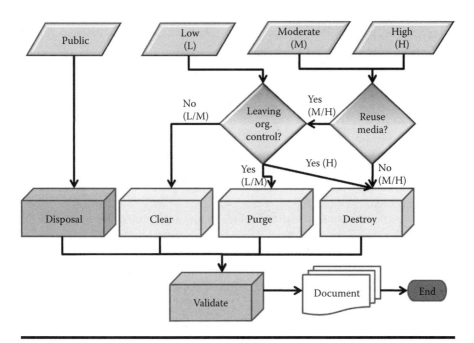

Figure 7.10   Data sanitization and decision flow.

- *Incineration or burning* is the act of completely burning the media into ashes.
- *Shredding* is the act of cutting or tearing the media into small particles. The shred size is an important consideration when choosing a shredder or a shredding service (if outsourced). The shred size should be small enough to provide a reasonable assurance that information cannot be reconstructed from the shredded output.

Knowing the type of sanitization method that should be used is important. If data are backed up on optical storage media such as compact disks (e.g., CD-ROM, CD-R), optical disks (DVD), and WORM types, then physical destruction using either pulverization, shredding, or burning is recommended. Figure 7.10 is an adaptation from the *Guidelines for Media Sanitization* special publication by NIST (SP 800-88), and it illustrates the data sanitization and decision flow. It is important to recognize that the last steps in the sanitization process are to validate that information reconstruction or recovery is not possible and to document the steps taken and the results from it.

7.6 Summary

In this chapter, we learned about the importance of security during the final stages of the SDLC. Security considerations during installation and deployment, operations, maintenance, and disposal are all important.

After software is accepted for deployment or release, the installation and deployment activity should not ignore the security aspects of software. Before deploying software, it is imperative that the host operating systems and the computing network in which the software will operate are locked down or hardened. After the hardening process, the installation of the software must not violate the principle of least privilege. When software starts, the booting process must also be resilient to common or side channel attacks. The startup variables and configuration parameters must be guarded to protect against attacks that impact the confidentiality or integrity of software. Without a proper and well defined configuration management process in place, the likelihood of regenerative bugs in software is high.

During the operations phase of SDLC, continuous monitoring of software is important to ensure the goal of operations security, which is to make certain that software remains secure. Knowing how to monitor software is just as important as why it should be monitored. Scanning, logging, and IDS are common ways to monitor, and monitoring can not only validate the state of security, but also provide insight on the state of compliance with security policies. Metrics can be used as a tool to provide management and operations team members with information about the real state of security affairs within the organization. Periodic audits are useful to validate compliance. Incident management is useful in restoring services and software functionality. The incident response process requires careful planning and is composed of the following phases: preparation, detection and analysis, containment, eradication and recovery, and postincident analysis. The analysis of software audit logs can provide valuable support and information to detect both insider and external threats attempted against the software. The goal of problem management is to improve the service. RCA is a very important means to answer why the problem occurred in the first place so that the core issue can be resolved once and for all. Patch and vulnerability management are necessary ongoing activities during the maintenance phase of the SDLC. Patching can adversely impact the state of software security if the patch is not tested in an environment that simulates the production environment. Patches can be delivered as a single hotfix or as components of a service pack. Patches must be tested for backward compatibility issues, upstream and downstream dependencies, impact, and regression of security features.

Software that is no longer required is not secure until it or its data and related components have been completely removed from the computing environment. Security cannot be ignored during the disposal stage of the software life cycle. EOL policies must be established and sunsetting criteria understood as part of the software disposal process. Along with the disposal or replacement of software, it is also important to address securely the information that was processed and stored by the software. Secure disposal of information is dependent on the type of media that contain it and the need for the media to be reused or not. Additionally, determining how the information and media containing it must be disposed of is dependent on whether the information will leave the organization's control. The primary protection methods against data remanence are clearing (overwriting), purging (degaussing), and destroying.

Software must be monitored, operated, maintained, and disposed of with security in mind so that the reliability, resiliency, and recoverability of software can be guaranteed, and the stakeholders can be assured of their trust in your organization.

7.7 Review Questions

1. When software that worked without any issues in the test environments fails to work in the production environment, it is indicative of
   A. Inadequate integration testing
   B. Incompatible environment configurations
   C. Incomplete threat modeling
   D. Ignored code review
2. Which of the following is not characteristic of good security metrics?
   A. Quantitatively expressed
   B. Objectively expressed

C. Contextually relevant

D. Collected manually

3. Removal of maintenance hooks, debugging code and flags, and unneeded documentation before deployment are all examples of software

A. Hardening

B. Patching

C. Reversing

D. Obfuscation

4. Which of the following has the goal of ensuring that the resiliency levels of software are always above the acceptable risk threshold as defined by the business post deployment?

A. Threat modeling

B. Code review

C. Continuous monitoring

D. Regression testing

5. Audit logging application events, such as failed login attempts, sales price updates, and user roles configuration, are examples of which of the following type of security control?

A. Preventive

B. Corrective

C. Compensating

D. Detective

6. When a compensating control is to be used, the Payment Card Industry Data Security Standard (PCI DSS) prescribes that the compensating control must meet all of the following guidelines except

A. Meet the intent and rigor of the original requirement

B. Provide a higher level of defense than the original requirement

C. Be implemented as part of a defense in depth measure

D. Be commensurate with additional risk imposed by not adhering to the requirement

7. Software that is deployed in a high trust environment such as the environment within the organizational firewall when not continuously monitored is most susceptible to which of the following types of security attacks? Choose the best answer.

A. Distributed denial of service (DDoS)

B. Malware

C. Logic bombs

D. DNS poisoning

8. Bastion host systems can be used continuously to monitor the security of the computing environment when it is used in conjunction with intrusion detection systems (IDS) and which other security control?

A. Authentication

B. Authorization

    C. Archiving

    D. Auditing

9. The first step in the incident response process of a reported breach is to

    A. Notify management of the security breach

    B. Research the validity of the alert or event further

    C. Inform potentially affected customers of a potential breach

    D. Conduct an independent third party evaluation to investigate the reported breach

10. Which of the following is the best recommendation to champion security objectives within the software development organization?

    A. Informing the developers that they could lose their jobs if their software is breached

    B. Informing management that the organizational software could be hacked

    C. Informing the project team about the recent breach of the competitor's software

    D. Informing the development team that there should be no injection flaws in the payroll application

11. Which of the following independent processes provides insight into the presence and effectiveness of security and privacy controls and is used to determine the organization's compliance with the regulatory and governance (policy) requirements?

    A. Penetration testing

    B. Audits

    C. Threat modeling

    D. Code review

12. The process of using regular expressions to parse audit logs into information that indicate security incidents is referred to as

    A. Correlation

    B. Normalization

    C. Collection

    D. Visualization

13. The final stage of the incident management process is

    A. Detection

    B. Containment

    C. Eradication

    D. Recovery

14. Problem management aims to improve the value of information technology to the business because it improves service by

    A. Restoring service to the expectation of the business user

    B. Determining the alerts and events that need to be continuously monitored

    C. Depicting incident information in easy-to-understand, user-friendly format

    D. Identifying and eliminating the root cause of the problem

15. The process of releasing software to fix a recently reported vulnerability without introducing any new features or changing hardware configuration is referred to as
    A. Versioning
    B. Hardening
    C. Patching
    D. Porting
16. Fishbone diagramming is a mechanism that is primarily used for which of the following processes?
    A. Threat modeling
    B. Requirements analysis
    C. Network deployment
    D. Root cause analysis
17. As a means to assure the availability of the existing software functionality after the application of a patch, the patch needs to be tested for
    A. The proper functioning of new features
    B. Cryptographic agility
    C. Backward compatibility
    D. The enabling of previously disabled services
18. Which of the following policies needs to be established to dispose of software and associated data and documents securely?
    A. End-of-life
    B. Vulnerability management
    C. Privacy
    D. Data classification
19. Discontinuance of a software with known vulnerabilities with a newer version is an example of risk called
    A. Mitigation
    B. Transference
    C. Acceptance
    D. Avoidance
20. Printer ribbons, facsimile transmissions, and printed information when not securely disposed of are susceptible to disclosure attacks by which of the following threat agents? Choose the best answer.
    A. Malware
    B. Dumpster divers
    C. Social engineers
    D. Script kiddies
21. System resources can be protected from malicious file execution attacks by uploading the user-supplied file and running it in which of the following environments?
    A. Honeypot
    B. Sandbox

    C. Simulated

    D. Production

22. As a means to demonstrate the improvement in the security of code that is developed, one must compute the relative attack surface quotient (RASQ)

    A. At the end of development phase of the project

    B. Before and after the code is implemented

    C. Before and after the software requirements are complete

    D. At the end of the deployment phase of the project

23. When the code is not allowed to access memory at arbitrary locations that are out of range of the memory address space that belong to the object's publically exposed fields, it is referred to as which of the following types of code?

    A. Object code

    B. Type safe code

    C. Obfuscated code

    D. Source code

24. Modifications to data directly in the database by developers must be prevented by

    A. Periodically patching database servers

    B. Implementing source code version control

    C. Logging all database access requests

    D. Proper change control management

25. Which of the following documents is the best source to contain damage, and which needs to be referred to and consulted upon the discovery of a security breach?

    A. Disaster Recovery Plan

    B. Project Management Plan

    C. Incident Response Plan

    D. Quality Assurance and Testing Plan

References

Cannon, J. C. 2009. *Privacy: What Developers and IT Professionals Should Know*. Reading: MA: Addison-Wesley Professional.

Colville, R. 2008. Recommendations for security patch management. Gartner Research. http://www.gartner.com/DisplayDocument?doc_cd=161535&ref=g_rss (accessed 6 March 2011).

Egan, M., and T. Mather. 2004. *The Executive Guide to Information Security: Threats, Challenges, and Solutions*. Reading: MA: Addison-Wesley Professional.

Fernandes, A. 2007. Operations security. March 23rd, 2007. Global Information Assurance Certification. http://www.giac.org/resources/whitepaper/operations/272.php (accessed 6 March 2011).

Fry, C., and M. Nystrom. 2009. *Security Monitoring: Proven Methods for Incident Detection on Enterprise Network*. Cambridge, MA: O'Reilly Media.

Grimes, R. 2006. *Professional Windows Desktop and Server Hardening (Programmer to Programmer)*. West Sussex, UK: Wrox Press.

Howard, M., and D. LeBlanc. 2002. *Writing Secure Code: Practical Strategies and Proven Techniques for Building Secure Applications in a Networked World*. 2nd ed. Cambridge, MA: Microsoft Press.

Howard, M. and D. LeBlanc. 2007. *Writing Secure Code for Windows Vista (Pro - Step By Step Developer)*. Cambridge, MA: Microsoft Press.

Howard, M., and S. Lipner. 2006. *The Security Development Lifecycle SDL: A Process for Developing Demonstrably More Secure Software*. Cambridge, MA: Microsoft Press.

Information Technology Infrastructure Library. 2010. *ITIL Open Guide*. http://www.itlibrary .org/index.php?page=ITIL (accessed March 23, 2010).

Jaquith, A. 2007. *Security Metrics: Replacing Fear, Uncertainty, and Doubt*. Reading: MA: Addison-Wesley Professional.

Kissel, R., M. Scholl, S. Skolochenko, and X. Li. 2006. *Guidelines for Media Sanitization*. NIST SP 800-88. http://csrc.nist.gov/publications/nistpubs/800-88/NISTSP800-88_ rev1.pdf (accessed 6 March 2011).

Litchfield, D., C. Anley, J. Heasman, B. Grindlay. 2005. *The Database Hacker's Handbook: Defending Database Servers*. New York, NY: John Wiley & Sons, Inc.

Mell, P., T. Bergeron, and D. Henning. 2005. *Creating a Patch and Vulnerability Management Program*. NIST SP 800-40. http://csrc.nist.gov/publications/nistpubs/800-40-Ver2/ SP800-40v2.pdf (accessed 6 March 2011).

NASA Process Control Focus Group. *Root Cause Analysis*. http://process.nasa.gov/documents/ RootCauseAnalysis.pdf (accessed 6 March 2011).

Nicolett, M., and R. J. Colville. 2006. Patch management best practices. Gartner Research. http://www.pixel.com.au/documentation//products/lumension/patchlink/ Gartner%20-%20Patch%20Management%20Best%20Pratices.pdf (accessed 6 March 2011).

Scarfone, K., T. Grance, and K. Masone. 2008. *Computer Security Incident Handling Guide*. NIST SP 800-61. http://csrc.nist.gov/publications/nistpubs/800-61-rev1/SP800-61rev1 .pdf (accessed 6 March 2011).

Scarfone, K., W. Jansen, and M. Tracy. 2008. *Guide to General Server Security*. NIST SP 800-123. http://csrc.nist.gov/publications/nistpubs/800-123/SP800-123.pdf (accessed 6 March 2011).

Swiderski, F., and W. Snyder. 2004. *Threat Modeling*. Cambridge, MA: Microsoft Press.

Venkatakrishnan, V. N., R. Sekar, T. Kamat, S. Tsipa, and Z. Liang. 2002. *An Approach for Secure Software Installation*. http://www.comp.nus.edu.sg/~liangzk/papers/lisa02.pdf (accessed 6 March 2011).

Williams, B. 2009. The art of the compensating control. *ISSA Journal* April 2009. https:// www.brandenwilliams.com/brwpubs/publishedversions/Williams-The%20Art%20 of%20the%20Compensating%20Control.pdf (accessed 6 March 2011).

Appendix A
Answers to Practice Questions

Chapter 1—Secure Software Concepts Questions

1. The primary reason for incorporating security into the software development life cycle is to protect
   A. The unauthorized disclosure of information
   B. The corporate brand and reputation
   C. Against hackers who intend to misuse the software
   D. The developers from releasing software with security defects
   Answer is B
   Rationale/Answer Explanation:
   When security is incorporated into the software development life cycle, confidentiality, integrity, and availability can be assured and external hacker and insider threat attempts thwarted. Developers will generate more hack-resilient software with fewer vulnerabilities, but protection of the organization's reputation and corporate brand is the primary reason for software assurance.

2. The resiliency of software to withstand attacks that attempt to modify or alter data in an unauthorized manner is referred to as
   A. Confidentiality
   B. Integrity
   C. Availability
   D. Authorization
   Answer is B
   Rationale/Answer Explanation:

When the software program operates as expected, it is said to be reliable or internally consistent. Reliability is an indicator of the integrity of software. Hack-resilient software are reliable (functioning as expected), resilient (able to withstand attacks), and recoverable (capable of being restored to normal operations when breached or upon error).

3. The main reason why the availability aspects of software must be part of the organization's software security initiatives is that
   A. Software issues can cause downtime to the business
   B. Developers need to be trained in the business' continuity procedures
   C. Testing for availability of the software and data is often ignored
   D. Hackers like to conduct denial of service (DoS) attacks against the organization

   Answer is A

   Rationale/Answer Explanation:

   One of the tenets of software assurance is "availability." Software issues can cause software unavailability and downtime to the business. This is often observed as a denial of service (DoS) attack.

4. Developing software to monitor its functionality and report when the software is down and unable to provide the expected service to the business is a protection to assure which of the following?
   A. Confidentiality
   B. Integrity
   C. Availability
   D. Authentication

   Answer is C

   Rationale/Answer Explanation:

   Confidentiality controls assure protection against unauthorized disclosure.

   Integrity controls assure protection against unauthorized modifications or alterations.

   Availability controls assure protection against downtime/denial of service and destruction of information.

   Authentication is the mechanism to validate the claims/credentials of an entity.

   Authorization covers the subject's rights and privileges upon requested objects.

5. When a customer attempts to log into his bank account, he is required to enter a nonce from the token device that was issued to the customer by the bank. This type of authentication is also known as which of the following?
   A. Ownership-based authentication
   B. Two-factor authentication
   C. Characteristic-based authentication
   D. Knowledge-based authentication

Answer is A

Rationale/Answer Explanation:

Authentication can be achieved in one or more of the following ways: using something one knows (knowledge-based), something one has (ownership-based), and something one is (characteristic-based). Using a token device is ownership-based authentication. When more than one way is used for authentication purposes, it is referred to as multifactor authentication, and this is recommended over single-factor authentication.

6. Multifactor authentication is most closely related to which of the following security design principles?

A. Separation of duties

B. Defense in depth

C. Complete mediation

D. Open design

Answer is B

Rationale/Answer Explanation:

Having more than one way of authentication provides for a layered defense, which is the premise of the defense in depth security design principle.

7. Audit logs can be used for all of the following except

A. Providing evidentiary information

B. Assuring that the user cannot deny their actions

C. Detecting the actions that were undertaken

D. Preventing a user from performing some unauthorized operations

Answer is D

Rationale/Answer Explanation:

Audit log information can be a detective control (providing evidentiary information) and a deterrent control when the users know that they are being audited, but it cannot prevent any unauthorized actions. When the software logs user actions, it also provides nonrepudiation capabilities because the user cannot deny their actions.

8. Impersonation attacks, such as man-in-the-middle (MITM) attacks, in an Internet application can be best mitigated using proper

A. Configuration management

B. Session management

C. Patch management

D. Exception management

Answer is B

Rationale/Answer Explanation:

An Internet application means that the ability to manage identities as would be possible in an Intranet application is not easy and, in some cases, infeasible. Internet applications also use stateless protocols, such as HTTP or HTTPS, and this requires the management of user sessions.

9. Organizations often predetermine the acceptable number of user errors before recording them as security violations. This number is otherwise known as the
   A. Clipping level
   B. Known error
   C. Minimum security baseline
   D. Maximum tolerable downtime

   Answer is A

   Rationale/Answer Explanation:

   The predetermined number of acceptable user errors before recording the error as a potential security incident is referred to as the clipping level. For example, if the number of allowed failed login attempts before the account is locked out is three, then the clipping level for authentication attempts is three.

10. A security principle that maintains the confidentiality, integrity, and availability of the software and data, besides allowing for rapid recovery to the state of normal operations, when unexpected events occur is the security design principle of
    A. Defense in depth
    B. Economy of mechanisms
    C. Failsafe
    D. Psychological acceptability

    Answer is C

    Rationale/Answer Explanation:

    The failsafe principle prescribes that access decisions must be based on permission rather than exclusion. This means that the default situation is lack of access, and the protection scheme identifies conditions under which access is permitted. The alternative, in which mechanisms attempt to identify conditions under which access should be refused, presents the wrong psychological base for secure system design. A design or implementation mistake in a mechanism that gives explicit permission tends to fail by refusing permission, which is a safe situation since it will be quickly detected. On the other hand, a design or implementation mistake in a mechanism that explicitly excludes access tends to fail by allowing access, a failure that may go unnoticed in normal use. This principle applies both to the outward appearance of the protection mechanism and to its underlying implementation.

11. Requiring the end user to accept an "as is" disclaimer clause before installation of your software is an example of risk
    A. Avoidance
    B. Mitigation
    C. Transference
    D. Acceptance

Answer is C

Rationale/Answer Explanation:

When an "as is" disclaimer clause is used, the risk is transferred from the publisher of the software to the user of the software.

12. An instrument that is used to communicate and mandate organizational and management goals and objectives at a high level is a

    A. Standard
    B. Policy
    C. Baseline
    D. Guideline

    Answer is B

    Rationale/Answer Explanation:

    Policies are high-level documents that communicate the mandatory goals and objectives of company management. Standards are also mandatory, but not quite at the same high level as policy. Guidelines provide recommendations on how to implement a standard. Procedures are usually step-by-step instructions of how to perform an operation. A baseline has the minimum levels of controls or configurations that need to be implemented.

13. The Systems Security Engineering Capability Maturity Model (SSE-CMM®) is an internationally recognized standard that publishes guidelines to

    A. Provide metrics for measuring the software and its behavior and using the software in a specific context of use
    B. Evaluate security engineering practices and organizational management processes
    C. Support accreditation and certification bodies that audit and certify information security management systems
    D. Ensure that the claimed identity of personnel are appropriately verified

    Answer is B

    Rationale/Answer Explanation:

    The evaluation of security engineering practices and organizational management processes are provided as guidelines and prescribed in the Systems Security Engineering Capability Maturity Model (SSE-CMM®). The SSE-CMM is an internationally recognized standard that is published as ISO 21827.

14. Which of the following is a framework that can be used to develop a risk-based enterprise security architecture by determining security requirements after analyzing the business initiatives?

    A. Capability Maturity Model Integration (CMMI)
    B. Sherwood Applied Business Security Architecture (SABSA)
    C. Control Objectives for Information and related Technology (COBIT®)
    D. Zachman Framework

    Answer is B

Rationale/Answer Explanation:

SABSA is a proven framework and methodology for Enterprise Security Architecture and Service Management. SABSA ensures that the needs of your enterprise are met completely and that security services are designed, delivered, and supported as an integral part of your business and IT management infrastructure.

15. The * property of this Biba security model prevents the contamination of data assuring its integrity by
    A. Not allowing the process to write above its security level
    B. Not allowing the process to write below its security level
    C. Not allowing the process to read above its security level
    D. Not allowing the process to read below its security level

    Answer is A

    Rationale/Answer Explanation:

    The Biba integrity model prevents unauthorized modification. It states that the maintenance of integrity requires that data not flow from a receptacle of a given integrity to a receptacle of higher integrity. If a process can write above its security level, trustworthy data could be contaminated by the addition of less trustworthy data.

16. Which of the following is known to circumvent the ring protection mechanisms in operating systems?
    A. Cross site request forgery (CSRF)
    B. Coolboot
    C. SQL injection
    D. Rootkit

    Answer is D

    Rationale/Answer Explanation:

    Rootkits are known to compromise the operating system ring protection mechanisms and masquerade as a legitimate operating system taking control of it.

17. Which of the following is a primary consideration for the software publisher when selling commercially off the shelf (COTS) software?
    A. Service level agreements (SLAs)
    B. Intellectual property protection
    C. Cost of customization
    D. Review of the code for backdoors and Trojan horses

    Answer is B

    Rationale/Answer Explanation:

    All of the other options are considerations for the software acquirer (purchaser).

18. The single loss expectancy can be determined using which of the following formulae?
    A. Annualized rate of occurrence (ARO) × exposure factor

B. Probability × impact

C. Asset value × exposure factor

D. Annualized rate of occurrence (ARO) × asset value

Answer is C

Rationale/Answer Explanation:

Single loss expectancy is the expected loss of a single disaster. It is computed as the product of asset value and the exposure factor. SLE = asset value × exposure factor.

19. Implementing IPSec to assure the confidentiality of data when they are transmitted is an example of risk

A. Avoidance

B. Transference

C. Mitigation

D. Acceptance

Answer is C

Rationale/Answer Explanation:

The implementation of IPSec at the network layer helps to mitigate threats to the confidentiality of transmitted data.

20. The Federal Information Processing Standard (FIPS) that prescribes guidelines for biometric authentication is

A. FIPS 46-3

B. FIPS 140-2

C. FIPS 197

D. FIPS 201

Answer is D

Rationale/Answer Explanation:

Personal identity verification (PIV) of federal employees and contractors is published as FIPS 201, and it prescribes some guidelines for biometric authentication.

21. Which of the following is a multifaceted security standard used to regulate organizations that collect, process, and/or store cardholder data as part of their business operations?

A. FIPS 201

B. ISO/IEC 15408

C. NIST SP 800-64

D. PCI DSS

Answer is D

Rationale/Answer Explanation:

The PCI DSS is a multifaceted security standard that includes requirements for security management, policies, procedures, network architecture, software design, and other critical protective measures. This comprehensive standard is intended to help organizations proactively protect customer account data.

22. Which of the following is the current Federal Information Processing Standard (FIPS) that specifies an approved cryptographic algorithm to ensure the confidentiality of electronic data?
    A. Security Requirements for Cryptographic Modules (FIPS 140-2)
    B. Data Encryption Standard (FIPS 46-3)
    C. Advanced Encryption Standard (FIPS 197)
    D. Digital Signature Standard (FIPS 186-3)
    Answer is C
    Rationale/Answer Explanation:
    The advanced encryption standard (AES) specifies a FIPS-approved cryptographic algorithm that can be used to protect electronic data. The AES algorithm is a symmetric block cipher that can encrypt (encipher) and decrypt (decipher) information. Encryption converts data to an unintelligible form called ciphertext; decrypting the ciphertext converts the data back into their original form, called plaintext. The AES algorithm is capable of using cryptographic keys of 128, 192, and 256 bits to encrypt and decrypt data in blocks of 128 bits.

23. The organization that publishes the ten most critical Web application security risks is the
    A. Computer Emergency Response Team (CERT)
    B. Web Application Security Consortium (WASC)
    C. Open Web Application Security Project (OWASP)
    D. Forums for Incident Response and Security Teams (FIRST)
    Answer is C
    Rationale/Answer Explanation:
    The Open Web Application Security Project (OWASP) Top Ten provides a powerful awareness document for Web application security. The OWASP Top Ten represents a broad consensus about what the most critical Web application security flaws are.

Chapter 2—Secure Software Requirements Questions

1. Which of the following must be addressed by software security requirements? Choose the best answer
    A. Technology used in building the application
    B. Goals and objectives of the organization
    C. Software quality requirements
    D. External auditor requirements
    Answer is B
    Rationale/Answer Explanation:
    When determining software security requirements, it is imperative to address the goals and objectives of the organization. Management's goals

and objectives need to be incorporated into the organizational security policies. While external auditor, internal quality requirements, and technology are factors that need consideration, compliance with organizational policies must be the foremost consideration.

2. Which of the following types of information is exempt from confidentiality requirements?
   A. Directory information
   B. Personally identifiable information (PII)
   C. User's card holder data
   D. Software architecture and network diagram

   Answer is A

   Rationale/Answer Explanation:

   Information that is public is also known as directory information. The name "directory" information comes from the fact that such information can be found in a public directory, such as a phone book. When information is classified as public information, confidentiality assurance protection mechanisms are not necessary.

3. Requirements that are identified to protect against the destruction of information or the software itself are commonly referred to as
   A. Confidentiality requirements
   B. Integrity requirements
   C. Availability requirements
   D. Authentication requirements

   Answer is C

   Rationale/Answer Explanation:

   Destruction is the threat against availability, as disclosure is the threat against confidentiality, and alteration is the threat against integrity.

4. The amount of time by which business operations need to be restored to service levels as expected by the business when there is a security breach or disaster is known as
   A. Maximum tolerable downtime (MTD)
   B. Mean time before failure (MTBF)
   C. Minimum security baseline (MSB)
   D. Recovery time objective (RTO)

   Answer is D

   Rationale/Answer Explanation:

   The maximum tolerable downtime (MTD) is the maximum length of time a business process can be interrupted or unavailable without causing the business itself to fail. The recovery time objective (RTO) is the time period in which the organization should have the interrupted process running again at or near the same capacity and conditions as before the disaster/downtime. MTD and RTO are part of availability requirements. It is advisable to set the RTO to be less than the MTD.

5. The use of an individual's physical characteristics, such as retinal blood patterns and fingerprints, for validating and verifying the user's identity if referred to as
   A. Biometric authentication
   B. Forms authentication
   C. Digest authentication
   D. Integrated authentication
   Answer is A
   Rationale/Answer Explanation:
   Forms authentication has to do with usernames and passwords that are input into a form (e.g., a Web page/form). Basic authentication transmits the credentials in Base64 encoded form, while digest authentication provides the credentials as a hash value (also known as a message digest). Token-based authentication uses credentials in the form of specialized tokens and is often used with a token device. Biometric authentication uses physical characteristics to provide the credential information.

6. Which of the following policies is most likely to include the following requirement? "All software processing financial transactions need to use more than one factor to verify the identity of the entity requesting access."
   A. Authorization
   B. Authentication
   C. Auditing
   D. Availability
   Answer is B
   Rationale/Answer Explanation:
   When two factors are used to validate an entity's claim and/or credentials, it is referred to as two-factor authentication, and when more than two factors are used for authentication purposes, it is referred to as multifactor authentication. It is important to determine first whether if there exists a need for two- or multifactor authentication.

7. A means of restricting access to objects based on the identity of subjects and/ or groups to which they belong is the definition of
   A. Nondiscretionary access control (NDAC)
   B. Discretionary access control (DAC)
   C. Mandatory access control (MAC)
   D. Rule-based access control
   Answer is B
   Rationale/Answer Explanation:
   Discretionary access control (DAC) is defined as "a means of restricting access to objects based on the identity of subjects and/or groups to which they belong." The controls are discretionary in the sense that a subject with a certain access permission is capable of passing that permission

(perhaps indirectly) on to any other subject. DAC restricts access to objects based on the identity of the subject and is distinctly characterized by the decision of the owner of the resource regarding who has access and their level of privileges or rights.

8. Requirements that when implemented can help to build a history of events that occurred in the software are known as
   A. Authentication requirements
   B. Archiving requirements
   C. Auditing requirements
   D. Authorization requirements
   Answer is C
   Rationale/Answer Explanation:
   Auditing requirements are those that assist in building a historical record of user actions. Audit trails can help detect when an unauthorized user makes a change or an authorized user makes an unauthorized change, both of which are cases of integrity violations. Auditing requirements not only help with forensic investigations as a detective control, but can also be used for troubleshooting errors and exceptions, if the actions of the software are tracked appropriately.

9. Which of the following is the primary reason for an application to be susceptible to a man-in-the-middle (MITM) attack?
   A. Improper session management
   B. Lack of auditing
   C. Improper archiving
   D. Lack of encryption
   Answer is A
   Rationale/Answer Explanation:
   Easily guessable and nonrandom session identifiers can be hijacked and replayed if not managed appropriately, and this can lead to MITM attacks.

10. The process of eliciting concrete software security requirements from high-level regulatory and organizational directives and mandates in the requirements phase of the SDLC is also known as
    A. Threat modeling
    B. Policy decomposition
    C. Subject–object modeling
    D. Misuse case generation
    Answer is B
    Rationale/Answer Explanation:
    The process of eliciting concrete software security requirements from high-level regulatory and organizational directives and mandates is referred to as policy decomposition. When the policy decomposition process completes, all the gleaned requirements must be measurable components.

11. The first step in the protection needs elicitation (PNE) process is to
    A. Engage the customer
    B. Model information management
    C. Identify least privilege applications
    D. Conduct threat modeling and analysis
    Answer is A
    Rationale/Answer Explanation:
    IT is there for the business and not the other way around. The first step when determining protection needs is to engage the customer, followed by modeling the information and identifying least privilege scenarios. Once an application profile is developed, we can undertake threat modeling and analysis to determine the risk levels, which can be communicated to the business to prioritize the risk.

12. A requirements traceability matrix (RTM) that includes security requirements can be used for all of the following except
    A. Ensuring scope creep does not occur
    B. Validating and communicating user requirements
    C. Determining resource allocations
    D. Identifying privileged code sections
    Answer is D
    Rationale/Answer Explanation:
    Identifying privileged code sections is part of threat modeling and not part of an RTM.

13. Parity bit checking mechanisms can be used for all of the following except
    A. Error detection
    B. Message corruption
    C. Integrity assurance
    D. Input validation
    Answer is D
    Rationale/Answer Explanation:
    Parity bit checking is primarily used for error detection, but it can be used for assuring the integrity of transferred files and messages.

14. Which of the following is an activity that can be performed to clarify requirements with the business users by using diagrams that model the expected behavior of the software?
    A. Threat modeling
    B. Use case modeling
    C. Misuse case modeling
    D. Data modeling
    Answer is B
    Rationale/Answer Explanation:
    A use case models the intended behavior of the software or system. In other words, the use case describes behavior that the system owner intended.

This behavior describes the sequence of actions and events that are to be taken to address a business need. Use case modeling and diagramming are very useful for specifying requirements. It can be effective in reducing ambiguous and incompletely articulated business requirements by explicitly specifying exactly when and under what conditions certain behaviors occur. Use case modeling is meant to model only the most significant system behavior, not all, and so it should not be considered a substitute for requirements specification documentation.

15. Which of the following is least likely to be identified by misuse case modeling?
    A. Race conditions
    B. Misactors
    C. Attacker's perspective
    D. Negative requirements
    Answer is A
    Rationale/Answer Explanation:
    Misuse cases, also known as abuse cases, help identify security requirements by modeling negative scenarios. A negative scenario is an unintended behavior of the system, one that the system owner does not want to have occur within the context of the use case. Misuse cases provide insight into the threats that can occur to the system or software. It provides the hostile users' point of view and is an inverse of the use case. Misuse case modeling is similar to the use case modeling, except that the former models misactors and unintended scenarios or behavior. Misuse cases may be intentional or accidental. One of the most distinctive traits of misuse cases is that they can be used to elicit security requirements, unlike other requirements determination methods that focus on end user functional requirements.

16. Data classification is a core activity that is conducted as part of which of the following?
    A. Key management life cycle
    B. Information life cycle management
    C. Configuration management
    D. Problem management
    Answer is B
    Rationale/Answer Explanation:
    Data classification is the conscious effort to assign a level of sensitivity to data assets based on potential impact upon disclosure, alteration, or destruction. The results of the classification exercise can then be used to categorize the data elements into appropriate buckets. Data classification is part of information life cycle management.

17. Web farm data corruption issues and card holder data encryption requirements need to be captured as part of which of the following requirements?

A. Integrity
B. Environment
C. International
D. Procurement
Answer is B
Rationale/Answer Explanation:
When determining requirements, it is important to elicit requirements that are tied to the environment in which the data will be marshaled or processed. Viewstate corruption issues in Web farm settings where all the servers were not configured identically or lack of card holder data encryption in public networks have been observed when the environmental requirements were not identified or taken into account.

18. When software is purchased from a third party instead of being built in-house, it is imperative to have contractual protection in place and have the software requirements explicitly specified in which of the following?
    A. Service level agreements (SLA)
    B. Nondisclosure agreements (NDA)
    C. Noncompete agreements
    D. Project plans
    Answer is A
    Rationale/Answer Explanation:
    SLAs should contain the levels of service expected for the software to provide, and this becomes crucial when the software is not developed in-house.

19. When software is able to withstand attacks from a threat agent and not violate the security policy, it is said to be exhibiting which of the following attributes of software assurance?
    A. Reliability
    B. Resiliency
    C. Recoverability
    D. Redundancy
    Answer is B
    Rationale/Answer Explanation:
    Software is said to be reliable when it is functioning as expected. Resiliency is the measure of the software's ability to withstand an attack. When the software is breached, its ability to restore itself back to normal operations is known as the recoverability of the software. Redundancy has to do with high availability.

20. Infinite loops and improper memory calls are often known to cause threats to which of the following?
    A. Availability
    B. Authentication
    C. Authorization

D. Auditing

Answer is A

Rationale/Answer Explanation:

Improper coding constructs such as infinite loops and improper memory management can lead to denial of service and resource exhaustion issues, which impact availability.

21. Which of the following is used to communicate and enforce availability requirements of the business or client?

A. Nondisclosure agreements (NDA)

B. Corporate contracts

C. Service level agreements (SLA)

D. Threat models

Answer is C

Rationale/Answer Explanation:

SLAs should contain the levels of service the software is expected to provide, and this becomes crucial when the software is not developed in-house.

22. Software security requirements that are identified to protect against disclosure of data to unauthorized users is otherwise known as

A. Integrity requirements

B. Authorization requirements

C. Confidentiality requirements

D. Nonrepudiation requirements

Answer is C

Rationale/Answer Explanation:

Destruction is the threat against availability, as disclosure is the threat against confidentiality, and alteration is the threat against integrity.

23. The requirements that assure reliability and prevent alterations are to be identified in which section of the software requirements specifications (SRS) documentation?

A. Confidentiality

B. Integrity

C. Availability

D. Auditing

Answer is B

Rationale/Answer Explanation:

Destruction is the threat against availability, as disclosure is the threat against confidentiality, and alteration is the threat against integrity.

24. Which of the following is a covert mechanism that assures confidentiality?

A. Encryption

B. Steganography

C. Hashing

D. Masking

Answer is B

Rationale/Answer Explanation:

Encryption and hashing are overt mechanisms to assure confidentiality. Masking is an obfuscating mechanism to assure confidentiality. Steganography is hiding information within other media as a cover mechanism to assure confidentiality. Steganography is more commonly referred to as *invisible ink* writing and is the art of camouflaging or hidden writing, where the information is hidden and the existence of the message itself is concealed. Steganography is primarily useful for covert communications and is prevalent in military espionage communications.

25. As a means to assure the confidentiality of copyright information, the security analyst identifies the requirement to embed information inside another digital audio, video, or image signal. This is commonly referred to as
   A. Encryption
   B. Hashing
   C. Licensing
   D. Watermarking
   Answer is D
   Rationale/Answer Explanation:
   Digital watermarking is the process of embedding information into a digital signal. These signals can be audio, video, or pictures.

26. Checksum validation can be used to satisfy which of the following requirements?
   A. Confidentiality
   B. Integrity
   C. Availability
   D. Authentication
   Answer is B
   Rationale/Answer Explanation:
   Parity bit checking is useful in the detection of errors or changes made to data when they are transmitted. A common use of parity bit checking is to do a cyclic redundancy check (CRC) for data integrity as well, especially for messages longer than one byte (8 bits) long. Upon data transmission, each block of data is given a computed CRC value, commonly referred to as a *checksum*. If there is an alteration between the origin of data and their destination, the checksum sent at the origin will not match the one computed at the destination. Corrupted media (CDs, DVDs) and incomplete downloads of software yield CRC errors.

27. A requirements traceability matrix (RTM) that includes security requirements can be used for all of the following except
   A. Ensuring against scope creep
   B. Validating and communicating user requirements
   C. Determining resource allocations
   D. Identifying privileged code sections
   Answer is D

Rationale/Answer Explanation:
Identifying privileged code sections is part of threat modeling and not part of an RTM.

Chapter 3—Secure Software Design Questions

1. During which phase of the software development life cycle (SDLC) is threat modeling initiated?
   A. Requirements analysis
   B. Design
   C. Implementation
   D. Deployment
      Answer is B
      Rationale/Answer Explanation:
      Although it is important to visit the threat model during the development, testing, and deployment phase of the software development life cycle (SDLC), the threat modeling exercise should commence in the design phase of the SDLC.

2. Certificate authority, registration authority, and certificate revocation lists are all part of which of the following?
   A. Advanced encryption standard (AES)
   B. Steganography
   C. Public key infrastructure (PKI)
   D. Lightweight directory access protocol (LDAP)
      Answer is C
      Rationale/Answer Explanation:
      PKI makes it possible to exchange data securely by hiding or keeping secret a private key on one system while distributing the public key to the other systems participating in the exchange.

3. The use of digital signatures has the benefit of providing which of the following not provided by symmetric key cryptographic design?
   A. Speed of cryptographic operations
   B. Confidentiality assurance
   C. Key exchange
   D. Nonrepudiation
      Answer is D
      Rationale/Answer Explanation:
      Nonrepudiation and proof of origin (authenticity) are provided by the certificate authority's (CA) attaching its digital signature, encrypted with the private key of the sender, to the communication that is to be authenticated, and this attests to the authenticity of both the document and the sender.

4. When passwords are stored in the database, the best defense against disclosure attacks can be accomplished using
   A. Encryption
   B. Masking
   C. Hashing
   D. Obfuscation
   Answer is C
   Rationale/Answer Explanation:
   An important use for hashes is storing passwords. The actual password should never be stored in the database. Using hashing functions, you can store the hash value of the user password and use that value to authenticate the user. Because hashes are one-way (not reversible), they offer a heightened level of confidentiality assurance.

5. Nicole is part of the "author" role as well as the "approver" role, allowing her to approve her own articles before they are posted on the company blog site. This violates the principle of
   A. Least privilege
   B. Least common mechanisms
   C. Economy of mechanisms
   D. Separation of duties
   Answer is D
   Rationale/Answer Explanation:
   Separation of duties, or separation of privilege, is the principle that it is better to assign tasks to several specific individuals so that no one user has total control over the task. It is closely related to the principle of least privilege, the idea that a minimum amount of privilege is granted to individuals with a need to know for the minimum (shortest) amount of time.

6. The primary reason for designing single sign on (SSO) capabilities is to
   A. Increase the security of authentication mechanisms
   B. Simplify user authentication
   C. Have the ability to check each access request
   D. Allow for interoperability between wireless and wired networks
   Answer is B
   Rationale/Answer Explanation:
   The design principle of economy of mechanism states that one must keep the design as simple and small as possible. This well known principle deserves emphasis for protection mechanisms because design and implementation errors that result in unwanted access paths will not be noticed during normal use. As a result, techniques that implement protection mechanisms, such as line-by-line inspection of software, are necessary. For such techniques to be successful, a small and simple design is essential. SSO supports this principle by simplifying the authentication process.

7. Database triggers are primarily useful for providing which of the following detective software assurance capabilities?

A. Availability

B. Authorization

C. Auditing

D. Archiving

Answer is C

Rationale/Answer Explanation:

All stored procedures could be updated to incorporate auditing logic, but a better solution is to use database triggers. You can use triggers to monitor actions performed on the database tables and automatically log auditing information.

8. During a threat modeling exercise, the software architecture is reviewed to identify

A. Attackers

B. Business impact

C. Critical assets

D. Entry points

Answer is D

Rationale/Answer Explanation:

During threat modeling, the application is dissected into its functional components. The development team analyzes the components at every entry point and traces data flow through all functionality to identify security weaknesses.

9. A man-in-the-middle (MITM) attack is primarily an expression of which type of the following threats?

A. Spoofing

B. Tampering

C. Repudiation

D. Information disclosure

Answer is A

Rationale/Answer Explanation:

Although it may seem that an MITM attack is an expression of the threat of repudiation, and it can be, it is primarily a spoofing threat. In a spoofing attack, an attacker impersonates a legitimate user of the system. A spoofing attack is mitigated through authentication so that adversaries cannot become any other user or assume the attributes of another user. When undertaking a threat modeling exercise, it is important to list all possible threats, regardless of whether they have been mitigated, so that you can later generate test cases where necessary. If the threat is not documented, there is a high likelihood that the software will not be tested for those threats. Using a categorized list of threats (such as spoofing, tampering, repudiation, information disclosure, denial of service, and elevation of privilege [STRIDE]) is useful to address all possible threats.

10. IPSec technology, which helps in the secure transmission of information, operates in which layer of the open systems interconnect (OSI) model?
    A. Transport
    B. Network
    C. Session
    D. Application
    Answer is B
    Rationale/Answer Explanation:
    Although software security has specific implications on layer seven, the application of the OSI stack, the security at other levels of the OSI stack is also important and should be leveraged to provide defense in depth. The seven layers of the OSI stack are physical (1), data link (2), network (3), transport (4), session (5), presentation (6), and application (7). SSL and IPSec can be used to assure confidentiality for data in motion. SSL operates at the transport layer (4), and IPSec operates at the network layer (3) of the OSI model.

11. When internal business functionality is abstracted into service-oriented contract-based interfaces, it is primarily used to provide for
    A. Interoperability
    B. Authentication
    C. Authorization
    D. Installation ease
    Answer is A
    Rationale/Answer Explanation:
    A distinctive characteristic of SOA is that the business logic is abstracted into discoverable and reusable contract-based interfaces to promote interoperability between heterogeneous computing ecosystems.

12. At which layer of the open systems interconnect (OSI) model must security controls be designed to mitigate side channel attacks effectively?
    A. Transport
    B. Network
    C. Data link
    D. Physical
    Answer is D
    Rationale/Answer Explanation:
    Side channel attacks use unconventional means to compromise the security of the system and, in most cases, require physical access to the device or system. Therefore, to mitigate side channel attacks, physical protection must be used.

13. Which of the following software architectures is effective in distributing the load between the client and the server, but increases the attack surface since it includes the client as part of the threat vectors?

A. Software as a service (SaaS)

B. Service-oriented architecture (SOA)

C. Rich Internet application (RIA)

D. Distributed network architecture (DNA)

Answer is C

Rationale/Answer Explanation:

RIAs require Internet protocol (IP) connectivity to the backend server. Browser sandboxing is recommended since the client is also susceptible to attack now, but it is not a requirement. The workload is shared between the client and the server, and the user's experience and control is increased in RIA architecture.

14. When designing software to work in a mobile computing environment, the trusted platform module (TPM) chip can be used to provide which of the following types of information?

A. Authorization

B. Identification

C. Archiving

D. Auditing

Answer is B

Rationale/Answer Explanation:

Trusted platform module (TPM) is the name assigned to a chip that can store cryptographic keys, passwords, and certificates. It can be used to protect mobile devices other than personal computers. It is also used to provide identity information for authentication purposes in mobile computing. It also assures secure startup and integrity. The TPM can be used to generate values used with whole-disk encryption, such as the Windows Vista's BitLocker. It is developed to specifications of the Trusted Computing Group.

15. When two or more trivial pieces of information are brought together with the aim of gleaning sensitive information, it is referred to as what type of attack?

A. Injection

B. Inference

C. Phishing

D. Polyinstantiation

Answer is B

Rationale/Answer Explanation:

An inference attack is one in which the attacker combines information available in the database with a suitable analysis to glean information that is presumably hidden or not as evident. This means that individual data elements when viewed collectively can reveal confidential information. It is therefore possible to have public elements in a database reveal private information by inference. The first things to ensure are that the database administrator does not have direct access to the data in the database and that the administrator's access to the database is mediated by a program (the application) and audited. In situations where direct database access is necessary, it is important to ensure that the database design is not susceptible to inference attacks. Inference attacks can be mitigated by polyinstantiation.

16. The inner workings and internal structure of backend databases can be protected from disclosure using
    A. Triggers
    B. Normalization
    C. Views
    D. Encryption
    Answer is C
    Rationale/Answer Explanation:
    Views provide a number of security benefits. They abstract the source of the data being presented, keeping the internal structure of the database hidden from the user. Furthermore, views can be created on a subset of columns in a table. This capability can allow users granular access to specific data elements. Views can also be used to limit access to specific rows of data.

17. Choose the best answer. Configurable settings for logging exceptions, auditing, and credential management must be part of
    A. Database views
    B. Security management interfaces
    C. Global files
    D. Exception handling
    Answer is B
    Rationale/Answer Explanation:
    Security management interfaces (SMIs) are administrative interfaces for your application that have the highest level of privileges on the system and can do tasks such as
    • User provisioning: adding/deleting/enabling user accounts
    • Granting rights to different user roles
    • System restarting
    • Changing system security settings
    • Accessing audit trails, user credentials, exception logs
    Although SMIs are often not explicitly stated in the requirements, and subsequently not threat modeled, strong controls, such as least privilege and access controls, must be designed and built in when developing

SMIs because the compromise of an SMI can be devastating, ranging from complete compromise and installing backdoors, to disclosure, alteration, and destruction (DAD) attacks on audit logs, user credentials, exception logs, etc. SMIs need not always be deployed with the default accounts set by the software publisher, although they are often observed to be.

18. The token that is primarily used for authentication purposes in a single sign on (SSO) implementation between two different organizations is
A. Kerberos
B. Security assert markup language (SAML)
C. Liberty alliance ID-FF
D. One-time password (OTP)
Answer is B
Rationale/Answer Explanation:
Federation technology is usually built on a centralized identity management architecture leveraging industry standard identity management protocols, such as SAML, WS Federation (WS-*), and Liberty Alliance. Of the three major protocol families associated with federation, SAML seems to be recognized as the de facto standard for enterprise-to-enterprise federation. SAML works in cross-domain settings, while Kerberos tokens are useful only within a single domain.

19. Syslog implementations require which additional security protection mechanisms to mitigate disclosure attacks?
A. Unique session identifier generation and exchange
B. Transport layer security
C. Digital rights management (DRM)
D. Data loss prevention
Answer is B
Rationale/Answer Explanation:
The syslog network protocol has become a de facto standard for logging programs and server information over the Internet. Many routers, switches, and remote access devices will transmit system messages, and there are syslog servers available for Windows and UNIX operating systems. TLS protection mechanisms such as SSL wrappers are needed to protect syslog data in transit as they are transmitted in the clear. SSL wrappers such as stunnel provide transparent SSL functionality.

20. Rights and privileges for a file can be granularly granted to each client using which of the following technologies?
A. Data loss prevention (DLP)
B. Software as a service (SaaS)
C. Flow control
D. Digital rights management (DRM)
Answer is D

Rationale/Answer Explanation:
Digital rights management (DRM) solutions give copyright owners control over access and use of copyright protected material. When users want to access or sue digital copyrighted material, they can do so on the terms of the copyright owner.

Chapter 4—Secure Software Implementation/Coding Questions

1. Software developers write software programs primarily to
   A. Create new products
   B. Capture market share
   C. Solve business problems
   D. Mitigate hacker threats
   Answer is C
   Rationale/Answer Explanation:
   IT and software development teams function to provide solutions to the business. Manual and inefficient business processes can be automated and made efficient using software programs.
2. The process of combining necessary functions, variables, and dependency files and libraries required for the machine to run the program is referred to as
   A. Compilation
   B. Interpretation
   C. Linking
   D. Instantiation
   Answer is C
   Rationale/Answer Explanation:
   Linking is the process of combining the necessary functions, variables, and dependencies files and libraries required for the machine to run the program. The output that results from the linking process is the executable program or machine code/file that the machine can understand and process. In short, linked object code is the executable. Link editors that combine object codes are known as linkers. Upon the completion of the compilation process, the compiler invokes the linker to perform its function. There are two types of linking: static linking and dynamic linking.
3. Which of the following is an important consideration to manage memory and mitigate overflow attacks when choosing a programming language?
   A. Locality of reference
   B. Type safety
   C. Cyclomatic complexity
   D. Parametric polymorphism

Answer is B

Rationale/Answer Explanation:

Code is said to be type safe if it only accesses memory resources that do not belong to the memory assigned to it. Type safety verification takes place during the just in time (JIT) compilation phase and prevents unsafe code from becoming active. Although you can disable type safety verification, it can lead to unpredictable results. The best example is that code can make unrestricted calls to unmanaged code, and if that code has malicious intent, the results can be severe. Therefore, the framework only allows fully trusted assemblies to bypass verification. Type safety is a form of "sandboxing." Type safety must be one of the most important considerations in regards to security when selecting a programming language.

4. Using multifactor authentication is effective in mitigating which of the following application security risks?

A. Injection flaws

B. Cross-site scripting (XSS)

C. Buffer overflow

D. Man-in-the-middle (MITM)

Answer is D

Rationale/Answer Explanation:

As a defense against man-in-the-middle (MITM) attacks, authentication and session management need to be in place. Multifactor authentication provides greater defense than single factor authentication and is recommended. Session identifiers that are generated should be unpredictable, random, and nonguessable.

5. Implementing completely automated public turing test to tell computers and humans apart (CAPTCHA) protection is a means of defending against

A. SQL injection

B. Cross-site scripting (XSS)

C. Cross-site request forgery (CSRF)

D. Insecure cryptographic storage

Answer is C

Rationale/Answer Explanation:

In addition to assuring that the requestor is a human, CAPTCHAs are useful in mitigating CSRF attacks. Since CSRF is dependent on a preauthenticated token's being in place, using CAPTCHA as the anti-CSRF token is an effective way of dealing with the inherent XSS problems regarding anti-CSRF tokens, as long as the CAPTCHA image itself is not guessable, predictable, or re-served to the attacker.

6. The findings of a code review indicate that cryptographic operations in code use the Rijndael cipher, which is the original publication of which of the following algorithms?

A. Skipjack
B. Data encryption standard (DES)
C. Triple data encryption standard (3DES)
D. Advanced encryption standard (AES)

Answer is D

Rationale/Answer Explanation:

Advanced encryption standard (FIPS 197) is published as the Rijndael cipher. Software should be designed so that you should be able to replace one cryptographic algorithm with a stronger one, when needed, without much rework or recoding. This is referred to as cryptographic agility.

7. Which of the following transport layer technologies can best mitigate session hijacking and replay attacks in a local area network (LAN)?

A. Data loss prevention (DLP)
B. Internet protocol security (IPSec)
C. Secure sockets layer (SSL)
D. Digital rights management (DRM)

Answer is C

Rationale/Answer Explanation:

SSL provides disclosure protection and protection against session hijacking and replay at the transport layer (layer 4), while IPSec provides confidentiality and integrity assurance operating in the network layer (layer 3). DRM provides some degree of disclosure (primarily IP) protection and operates in the presentation layer (layer 6), and data loss prevention (DLP) technologies prevent the inadvertent disclosure of data to unauthorized individuals, predominantly those external to the organization.

8. Verbose error messages and unhandled exceptions can result in which of the following software security threats?

A. Spoofing
B. Tampering
C. Repudiation
D. Information disclosure

Answer is D

Rationale/Answer Explanation:

Information disclosure is primarily a design issue and therefore is a language-independent problem, although with accidental leakage, many newer high-level languages can worsen the problem by providing verbose error messages that might be helpful to attack in their information gathering (reconnaissance) efforts. It must be recognized that there is a tricky balance between providing the user with helpful information about errors and preventing attackers from learning about the internal details and architecture of the software. From a security standpoint, it is advisable not to disclose verbose error messages and provide the users with a help-line to get additional support.

9. Code signing can provide all of the following except
   A. Anti-tampering protection
   B. Authenticity of code origin
   C. Runtime permissions for code
   D. Authentication of users

   Answer is D

   Rationale/Answer Explanation:

   Code signing can provide all of the following: anti-tampering protection assuring integrity of code, authenticity (not authentication) of code origin, and runtime permissions for the code to access system resources. The primary benefit of code signing is that it provides users with the identity of the software's creator, and this is particularly important for mobile code, which is code downloaded from a remote location over the Internet.

10. When an attacker uses delayed error messages between successful and unsuccessful query probes, he is using which of the following side channel techniques to detect injection vulnerabilities?
    A. Distant observation
    B. Cold boot
    C. Power analysis
    D. Timing

    Answer is D

    Rationale/Answer Explanation:

    Poorly designed and implemented systems are expected to be insecure, but even most well designed and implemented systems have subtle gaps between their abstract models and their physical realization due to the existence of side channels. A side channel is a potential source of information flow from a physical system to an adversary beyond what is available via the conventional (abstract) model. These include subtle observation of timing, electromagnetic radiations, power usage, analog signals, and acoustic emanations. The use of nonconventional and specialized techniques along with physical access to the target system to discover information is characteristic of side channel attacks. The analysis of delayed error messages between successful and unsuccessful queries is a form of timing side channel attacks.

11. When the runtime permissions of the code are defined as security attributes in the metadata of the code, it is referred to as
    A. Imperative syntax security
    B. Declarative syntax security
    C. Code signing
    D. Code obfuscation

    Answer is B

Rationale/Answer Explanation:

There are two types of security syntax: declarative security and imperative security. Declarative syntax addresses the "what" part of an action, whereas imperative syntax tries to deal with the "how" part. When security requests are made in the form of attributes (in the metadata of the code), it is referred to as declarative security. It does not precisely define the steps as to how the security will be realized. When security requests are made through programming logic within a function or method body, it is referred to as imperative security. Declarative security is an all-or-nothing kind of implementation, while imperative security offers greater levels of granularity and control because the security requests run as lines of code intermixed with the application code.

12. When an all-or-nothing approach to code access security is not possible and business rules and permissions need to be set and managed more granularly in inline code functions and modules, a programmer can leverage which of the following?

    A. Cryptographic agility
    B. Parametric polymorphism
    C. Declarative security
    D. Imperative security

    Answer is D

    Rationale/Answer Explanation:

    When security requests are made in the form of attributes, it is referred to as declarative security. It does not precisely define the steps as to how the security will be realized. Declarative syntax actions can be evaluated without running the code because attributes are stored as part of an assembly's metadata, while the imperative security actions are stored as intermediary language (IL). This means that imperative security actions can be evaluated only when the code is running. Declarative security actions are checks before a method is invoked and are placed at the class level, being applicable to all methods in that class, unlike imperative security. Declarative security is an all-or-nothing kind of implementation, while imperative security offers greater levels of granularity and control, because the security requests run as lines of code intermixed with the application code.

13. An understanding of which of the following programming concepts is necessary to protect against memory manipulation buffer overflow attacks? Choose the best answer.

    A. Error handling
    B. Exception management
    C. Locality of reference
    D. Generics

    Answer is C

Rationale/Answer Explanation:

Computer processors tend to access memory in a very patterned way. For example, in the absence of branching, if memory location X is accessed at time t, there is a high probability that memory location X+1 will also be accessed in the near future. This kind of clustering of memory references into groups is referred to as locality of reference. The basic forms of locality of reference are temporal (based on time), spatial (based on address space), (branch conditional), and equidistant (somewhere between spatial and branch using simple linear functions that look for equidistant locations of memory to predict which location will be accessed in the near future). While this is good from a performance vantage point, it can lead to an attacker's predicting memory address spaces and causing memory corruption and buffer overflow.

14. Exploit code attempts to take control of dangling pointers that are
    A. References to memory locations of destroyed objects
    B. Nonfunctional code left behind in the source
    C. Payload code that the attacker uploads into memory to execute
    D. References in memory locations used prior to being initialized

    Answer is A

    Rationale/Answer Explanation:

    A dangling pointer, also known as a stray pointer, occurs when a pointer points to an invalid memory address. This is often observed when memory management is left to the developer. Dangling pointers are usually created in one of two ways. An object is destroyed (freed), but the reference to the object is not reassigned and is later used. Or a local object is popped from the stack when the function returns, but a reference to the stack-allocated object is still maintained. Attackers write exploit code to take control of dangling pointers so that they can move the pointer to where their arbitrary shell code is injected.

15. Which of the following is a feature of the most recent operating systems (OS) that makes it difficult for an attacker to guess the memory address of the program by making the memory address different each time the program is executed?
    A. Data execution prevention (DEP)
    B. Executable space protection (ESP)
    C. Address space layout randomization (ASLR)
    D. Safe security exception handler (/SAFESEH)

    Answer is C

    Rationale/Answer Explanation:

    In the past, the memory manager would try to load binaries at the same location in the linear address space each time the program was run. This behavior made it easier for shell coders by ensuring that certain modules of code would always reside at a fixed address and could be referenced in exploit code using raw numeric literals. Address space layout randomization (ASLR) is a feature in newer operating systems (introduced in Windows Vista) that deals with this predictable and direct referencing issue. ASLR makes the binary load in a random address space each time the program is run.

16. When the source code is made obscure using special programs in order to make the readability of the code difficult when disclosed, the code is also known as

A. Object code
B. Obfuscated code
C. Encrypted code
D. Hashed code

Answer is B

Rationale/Answer Explanation:

Reverse engineering is used to infer how a program works by inspecting it. Code obfuscation, which makes the readability of code extremely difficult and confusing, can be used to deter (not prevent) reverse engineering attacks. Obfuscating code is not detective or corrective in its implementation.

17. The ability to track ownership, changes in code, and rollback abilities is possible because of which of the following configuration management processes?

A. Version control
B. Patching
C. Audit logging
D. Change control

Answer is A

Rationale/Answer Explanation:

The ability to track ownership, changes in code, and rollback abilities is possible because of versioning, which is a configuration management process. Release management of software should include proper source code control and versioning. A phenomenon known as "regenerative bugs" is often observed when it comes to improper release management processes. Regenerative bugs are fixed software defects that reappear in subsequent releases of the software. This happens when the software coding defect (bug) is detected in the testing environment (such as user acceptance testing), and the fix is made in that test environment and promoted to production without retrofitting it into the development environment. The latest version in the development environment does not have the fix, and the issue reappears in subsequent versions of the software.

18. The main benefit of statically analyzing code is that

A. Runtime behavior of code can be analyzed
B. Business logic flaws are more easily detectable
C. Analysis is performed in a production or production-like environment
D. Errors and vulnerabilities can be detected earlier in the life cycle

Answer is D

Rationale/Answer Explanation:

The one thing that is common in all software is source code, and this source code needs to be reviewed from a security perspective to ensure that security vulnerabilities are detected and addressed before the software is released into the production environment or to customers. Code review is the process of systematically analyzing the code for insecure and inefficient coding issues. In addition to static analysis, which reviews code before it goes live, there are also dynamic analysis tools, which conduct automated scans of applications in production to unearth vulnerabilities. In other words, dynamic tools test from the outside in, while static tools test from the inside out. Just because the code compiles without any errors, it does not necessarily mean that it will run without errors at runtime. Dynamic tests are useful to get a quick assessment of the security of the applications. This also comes in handy when source code is not available for review.

19. Cryptographic protection includes all of the following except
    A. Encryption of data when they are processed
    B. Hashing of data when they are stored
    C. Hiding of data within other media objects when they are transmitted
    D. Masking of data when they are displayed

    Answer is D

    Rationale/Answer Explanation:

    Masking does not use any overt cryptography operations, such as encryption, decryption, or hashing, or covert operations, such as data hiding, as in the case of steganography, to provide disclosure protection.

20. Assembly and machine language are examples of
    A. Natural language
    B. Very high-level language (VHLL)
    C. High-level language (HLL)
    D. Low-level language

    Answer is D

    Rationale/Answer Explanation:

    A programming language in which there is little to no abstraction from the native instruction codes that the computer can understand is also referred to as low-level language. There is no abstraction from native instruction codes in machine language. Assembly languages are the lowest level in the software chain, which makes them incredibly suitable for reversing. It is therefore important to have an understanding of low-level programming languages to understand how an attacker will attempt to circumvent the security of the application at its lowest level.

Chapter 5—Secure Software Testing Questions

1. The ability of the software to restore itself to expected functionality when the built-in security protection is breached is also known as
   A. Redundancy
   B. Recoverability
   C. Resiliency
   D. Reliability
   Answer is B
   Rationale/Answer Explanation:
   When the software performs as it is expected to, it is said to be reliable. When errors occur, the reliability of software is impacted, and the software needs to be able to restore itself to expected operations. The ability of the software to be restored to normal, expected operations is referred to as recoverability. The ability of the software to withstand attacks against its reliability is referred to as resiliency. Redundancy is about availability, and reconnaissance is related to information gathering, as in fingerprinting/footprinting.

2. In which of the following software development methodologies does unit testing enable collective code ownership and is critical to assure software assurance?
   A. Waterfall
   B. Agile
   C. Spiral
   D. Prototyping
   Answer is B
   Rationale/Answer Explanation:
   Unit testing enables collective code ownership. Collective code ownership encourages everyone to contribute new ideas to all segments of the project. Any developer can change any line of code to add functionality, fix bugs, or re-factor. No one person becomes a bottleneck for changes. The way this works is for each developer to work in concert (usually more in agile methodologies than the traditional model) to create unit tests for his code as it is developed. All code released into the source code repository includes unit tests. Code that is added, bugs as they are fixed, and old functionality as it is changed will be covered by automated testing.

3. The use of if-then rules is characteristic of which of the following types of software testing?
   A. Logic
   B. Scalability
   C. Integration
   D. Unit

Answer is A

Rationale/Answer Explanation:

If-then rules are constructs of logic, and when these constructs are used for software testing, it is generally referred to as logic testing.

4. The implementation of secure features, such as complete mediation and data replication, needs to undergo which of the following types of tests to ensure that the software meets the service level agreements (SLA)?
   A. Stress
   B. Unit
   C. Integration
   D. Regression

   Answer is A

   Rationale/Answer Explanation:

   Tests that assure that the service level requirements are met are characteristic of performance testing. Load and stress testing are types of performance tests. While stress testing is testing by starving the software, load testing is done by subjecting the software to extreme volumes or loads.

5. Tests conducted to determine the breaking point of the software after which the software will no longer be functional are characteristic of which of the following types of software testing?
   A. Regression
   B. Stress
   C. Integration
   D. Simulation

   Answer is B

   Rationale/Answer Explanation:

   The goal of stress testing is to determine if the software will continue to operate reliably under duress or extreme conditions. Often the resources that the software needs are taken away from the software, and the software's behavior is observed as part of the stress test.

6. Which of the following tools or techniques can be used to facilitate the white box testing of software for insider threats?
   A. Source code analyzers
   B. Fuzzers
   C. Banner grabbing software
   D. Scanners

   Answer is A

   Rationale/Answer Explanation:

   White box testing, or structural analysis, is about testing the software with prior knowledge of the code and configuration. Source code review is a type of white box testing. Embedded code issues that are implanted by insiders, such as Trojan horses and logic bombs, can be detected using source code analyzers.

7. When very limited or no knowledge of the software is made known to the software tester before she can test for its resiliency, it is characteristic of which of the following types of security tests?

   A. White box

   B. Black box

   C. Clear box

   D. Glass box

     Answer is B

     Rationale/Answer Explanation:

     In black box or behavioral testing, test conditions are developed on the basis of the program's or system's functionality; that is, the tester requires information about the input data and observed output, but does not know how the program or system works. The tester focuses on testing the program's behavior (or functionality) against the specification. With black box testing, the tester views the program as a black box and is completely unconcerned with the internal structure of the program or system. In white box or structural testing, the tester knows the internal program structure, such as paths, statement coverage, branching, and logic. White box testing is also referred to as clear box or glass box testing. Gray box testing is a software testing technique that uses a combination of black box and white box testing.

8. Penetration testing must be conducted with properly defined

   A. Rules of engagement

   B. Role-based access control mechanisms

   C. Threat models

   D. Use cases

     Answer is A

     Rationale/Answer Explanation:

     Penetration testing must be controlled, not ad hoc in nature, with properly defined rules of engagement.

9. Testing for the randomness of session identifiers and the presence of auditing capabilities provides the software team insight into which of the following security controls?

   A. Availability

   B. Authentication

   C. Nonrepudiation

   D. Authorization

     Answer is C

     Rationale/Answer Explanation:

     When session management is in place, it provides for authentication, and when authentication is combined with auditing capabilities, it provides nonrepudiation. In other words, the authenticated user cannot claim broken sessions or intercepted authentication and deny their user actions due to the audit logs' recording their actions.

10. Disassemblers, debuggers, and decompilers can be used by security testers primarily to determine which of the following types of coding vulnerabilities?
    A. Injection flaws
    B. Lack of reverse engineering protection
    C. Cross-site scripting
    D. Broken session management
    Answer is B
    Rationale/Answer Explanation:
    Disassemblers, debuggers, and decompilers are utilities that can be used for reverse engineering software, and software testers should have these utilities in their list of tools to validate protection against reversing.

11. When reporting a security defect in the software, which of the following also needs to be reported so that variance from the intended behavior of the software can be determined?
    A. Defect identifier
    B. Title
    C. Expected results
    D. Tester name
    Answer is C
    Rationale/Answer Explanation:
    Knowledge of the expected results along with the defect information can be used to determine the variance between what the results need to be and what is deficient.

12. An attacker analyzes the response from the Web server, which indicates that its version is Microsoft Internet Information Server 6.0 (Microsoft-IIS/6.0), but none of the IIS exploits that the attacker attempts to execute on the Web server is successful. Which of the following is the most probable security control that is implemented?
    A. Hashing
    B. Cloaking
    C. Masking
    D. Watermarking
    Answer is B
    Rationale/Answer Explanation:
    Detection of Web server versions is usually done by analyzing HTTP responses. This process is known as banner grabbing. But the administrator can change the information that gets reported, and this process is known as cloaking. Banner cloaking is a security through obscurity approach to protect against version enumeration.

13. Smart fuzzing is characterized by injecting
    A. Truly random data without any consideration for the data structure
    B. Variations of data structures that are known
    C. Data that get interpreted as commands by a backend interpreter

D. Scripts that are reflected and executed on the client browser

Answer is B

Rationale/Answer Explanation:

The process of sending random data to test security of an application is referred to as "fuzzing" or "fuzz testing." There are two levels of fuzzing: dumb fuzzing and smart fuzzing. Sending truly random data, known as dumb fuzzing, often does not yield great results and has the potential of bringing the software down, causing a denial of service (DoS). If the code being fuzzed requires data to be in a certain format but the fuzzer does not create data in that format, most of the fuzzed data will be rejected by the application. The more knowledge the fuzzer has of the data format, the more intelligent it can be at creating data. These more intelligent fuzzers are known as smart fuzzers.

14. Which of the following is the most important to ensure when the software is forced to fail as part of security testing? Choose the best answer.

A. Normal operational functionality is not restored automatically

B. Access to all functionality is denied

C. Confidentiality, integrity, and availability are not adversely impacted

D. End users are adequately trained and self-help is made available for the end user to fix the error on their own

Answer is C

Rationale/Answer Explanation:

As part of security testing, the principle of failsafe must be assured. This means that confidentiality, integrity, and availability are not adversely impacted when the software fails. As part of general software testing, the recoverability of the software, or restoration of the software to normal operational functionality, is an important consideration, but it need not always be an automated process.

15. Timing and synchronization issues, such as race conditions and resource deadlocks, can most likely be identified by which of the following tests? Choose the best answer.

A. Integration

B. Stress

C. Unit

D. Regression

Answer is B

Rationale/Answer Explanation:

Race conditions and resource exhaustion issues are more likely to be identified when the software is starved of the resources that it expects, as is done during stress testing.

16. The primary objective of resiliency testing of software is to determine

A. The point at which the software will break

B. If the software can restore itself to normal business operations

C. The presence and effectiveness of risk mitigation controls

D. How a blackhat would circumvent access control mechanisms

Answer is C

Rationale/Answer Explanation:

Security testing must include both external (blackhat) and insider threat analysis, and it should be more than just testing for the ability to circumvent access control mechanisms. The resiliency of software is the ability of the software to be able to withstand attacks. The presence and effectiveness of risk mitigation controls increase the resiliency of the software.

17. The ability of the software to withstand attempts of attackers who intend to breach the built-in security protection is also known as

A. Redundancy

B. Recoverability

C. Resiliency

D. Reliability

Answer is C

Rationale/Answer Explanation:

Resiliency of software is defined as the ability of the software to withstand attacker attempts.

18. Drivers and stub-based programming are useful to conduct which of the following tests?

A. Integration

B. Regression

C. Unit

D. Penetration

Answer is C

Rationale/Answer Explanation:

In order for unit testing to be thorough, the unit/module and the environment for the execution of the module need to be complete. The necessary environment includes the modules that either call or are called by the unit of code being tested. Stubs and drivers are designed to provide the complete environment for a module so that unit testing can be carried out. A stub procedure is a dummy procedure that has the same input/output (I/O) parameters as the given procedure. A driver module should have the code to call the different functions of the module being tested with appropriate parameter values for testing. In layman's terms, the driver module is akin to the caller, and the stub module can be seen as the callee.

19. Assurance that the software meets the expectations of the business as defined in the service level agreements (SLAs) can be demonstrated by which of the following types of tests?

A. Unit

B. Integration

C. Performance

D. Regression

Answer is C

Rationale/Answer Explanation:

Assurance that the software meets the expectations of the business as defined in the service level agreements (SLAs) can be demonstrated by performance testing. Once the importance of the performance of an application is known, it is necessary to understand how various factors affect the performance. Security features can have an impact on performance, and this must be checked to ensure that service level requirements can be met.

20. Vulnerability scans are used to

A. Measure the resiliency of the software by attempting to exploit weaknesses

B. Detect the presence of loopholes and weaknesses in the software

C. Detect the effectiveness of security controls that are implemented in the software

D. Measure the skills and technical know-how of the security tester

Answer is B

Rationale/Answer Explanation:

A vulnerability is a weakness (or loophole), and vulnerability scans are used to detect the presence of weaknesses in software.

Chapter 6—Software Acceptance Questions

1. Your organization has the policy to attest the security of any software that will be deployed into the production environment. A third party vendor software is being evaluated for its readiness to be deployed. Which of the following verification and validation mechanisms can be employed to attest the security of the vendor's software?

A. Source code review

B. Threat modeling the software

C. Black box testing

D. Structural analysis

Answer is C

Rationale/Answer Explanation:

Since third party vendor software is often received in object code form, access to source code is usually not provided, and structural analysis (white box) or source code analysis is not possible. Looking into the source code or source code look-alike by reverse engineering without explicit permission can have legal ramifications. Additionally, without documentation on the architecture and software makeup, a threat modeling exercise would most likely be incomplete. License validation is primarily used for curtailing piracy and is a component of verification and validation mechanisms. Black box testing or behavioral analysis would be the best option to attest the security of third party vendor software.

2. When procuring commercial off-the-shelf (COTS) software for release within your global organization, special attention must be given to multilingual and multicultural capabilities of the software since they are more likely to have
   A. Compilation errors
   B. Canonicalization issues
   C. Cyclomatic complexity
   D. Coding errors
   Answer is B
   Rationale/Answer Explanation:
   The process of canonicalization resolves multiple forms into standard canonical forms. In software that needs to support multilingual, multicultural capabilities such as Unicode, input filtration can be bypassed by a hacker who sends in data in an alternate form from the standard form. Input validation for alternate forms is therefore necessary.

3. To meet the goals of software assurance, when accepting software from a vendor, the software acquisition phase must include processes to
   A. Verify that installation guides and training manuals are provided
   B. Assess the presence and effectiveness of protection mechanisms
   C. Validate vendors' software products
   D. Assist the vendor in responding to the request for proposals
   Answer is B
   Rationale/Answer Explanation:
   To maintain the confidentiality, integrity, and availability of software and the data it processes, prior to the acceptance of software, vendor claims of security must be assessed not only for their presence, but also their effectiveness within your computing ecosystem.

4. Your organization's software is published as a trial version without any restricted functionality from the paid version. Which of the following must be designed and implemented to ensure that customers who have not purchased the software are limited in the availability of the software?
   A. Disclaimers
   B. Licensing
   C. Validity periods
   D. Encryption
   Answer is C
   Rationale/Answer Explanation:
   Software functionality can be restricted using a validity period as is often observed in the "try-before-you-buy" or "demo" versions of software. It is recommended to have a stripped down version of the software for the

demo version, and if feasible, it is advisable to include the legal team to determine the duration of the validity period (especially in the context of digital signatures and Public Key Infrastructure solutions).

5. Software escrowing is more closely related to which of the following risk-handling strategies?

A. Avoidance

B. Mitigation

C. Acceptance

D. Transference

Answer is D

Rationale/Answer Explanation:

Since there is an independent third party engaged in an escrow agreement, business continuity is assured for the acquirer when the escrow agency maintains a copy of the source/object code from the publisher. For the publisher, it protects the intellectual property since the source code is not handed to the acquirer directly, but to the independent third escrow party. For both the acquirer and the publishers, some risk is transferred to the escrow party, who is responsible for maintaining the terms of the escrow agreement.

6. Which of the following legal instruments assures the confidentiality of software programs, processing logic, database schema, and internal organizational business processes and client lists?

A. Noncompete agreements

B. Nondisclosure agreements (NDA)

C. Service level agreements (SLA)

D. Trademarks

Answer is B

Rationale/Answer Explanation:

Nondisclosure agreements assure confidentiality of sensitive information, such as software programs, processing logic, database schema, and internal organizational business processes and client lists.

7. "As is" clauses and disclaimers transfer the risk of using the software from the software publisher to the

A. Developers

B. End users

C. Testers

D. Business owners

Answer is B

Rationale/Answer Explanation:

Disclaimers, or "as is" clauses, transfer the risk from the software provider to the end user.

8. Improper implementation of validity periods using length-of-use checks in code can result in which of the following types of security issues for legitimate users?

A. Tampering

B. Denial of service

C. Authentication bypass

D. Spoofing

Answer is B

Rationale/Answer Explanation:

If the validity period set in the software is not properly implemented, then legitimate users can potentially be denied service. It is therefore imperative to ensure that the duration and checking mechanism of validity periods is properly implemented.

9. The process of evaluating software to determine whether the products of a given development phase satisfy the conditions imposed at the start of the phase is referred to as

A. Verification

B. Validation

C. Authentication

D. Authorization

Answer is A

Rationale/Answer Explanation:

Verification is defined as the process of evaluating software to determine whether the products of a given development phase satisfy the conditions imposed at the start of the phase. In other words, verification ensures that the software *performs* as it is required and designed to do. Validation is the process of evaluating software during or at the end of the development process to determine whether it satisfies specified requirements. In other words, validation ensures that the software *meets* required specifications.

10. When verification activities are used to determine if the software is functioning as expected, it provides insight into which of the following aspects of software assurance?

A. Redundancy

B. Reliability

C. Resiliency

D. Recoverability

Answer is B

Rationale/Answer Explanation:

Verification ensures that the software *performs* as it is required and designed to do, which is a measure of the software's reliability.

11. When procuring software, the purchasing company can request the evaluation assurance levels (EALs) of the software product, which are determined using which of the following evaluation methodologies?

A. Operationally Critical Assets Threats and Vulnerability Evaluation® (OCTAVE^SM)

B. Security quality requirements engineering (SQUARE)

C. Common criteria

D. Comprehensive, lightweight application security process (CLASP)

Answer is C

Rationale/Answer Explanation:

Common criteria (ISO 15408) are a security product evaluation methodology with clearly defined ratings, such as evaluation assurance levels (EALs). In addition to assurance validation, the common criteria also validate software functionality for the security target. EALs ratings assure the owner of the assurance capability of the software/system, so common criteria are also referred to as an owner assurance model.

12. The final activity in the software acceptance process is the go/no go decision that can be determined using

A. Regression testing

B. Integration testing

C. Unit testing

D. User acceptance testing

Answer is D

Rationale/Answer Explanation:

The end users of the business have the final say on whether the software can be deployed/released. User acceptance testing (UAT) determines the readiness of the software for deployment to the production environment or release to an external customer.

13. Management's formal acceptance of the system after an understanding of the residual risks to that system in the computing environment is also referred to as

A. Patching

B. Hardening

C. Certification

D. Accreditation

Answer is D

Rationale/Answer Explanation:

While certification is the assessment of the technical and nontechnical security controls of the software, accreditation is a management activity that assures that the software has adequate levels of software assurance protection mechanisms.

14. You determine that legacy software running in your computing environment is susceptible to cross site request forgery (CSRF) attacks because of the way it manages sessions. The business has the need to continue use of this software, but you do not have the source code available to implement security controls in code as a mitigation measure against CSRF attacks. What is the best course of action to undertake in such a situation?

A. Avoid the risk by forcing the business to discontinue use of the software

B. Accept the risk with a documented exception

C. Transfer the risk by buying insurance

D. Ignore the risk since it is legacy software

Answer is B

Rationale/Answer Explanation:

When there are known vulnerabilities in legacy software and there is not much you can do to mitigate the vulnerabilities, it is recommended that the business accept the risk with a documented exception to the security policy. When accepting this risk, the exception to policy process must ensure that there is a contingency plan in place to address the risk by either replacing the software with a new version or discontinuing its use (risk avoidance). Transferring the risk may not be a viable option for legacy software that is already in your production environment, and one must never ignore the risk or take the vulnerable software out of the scope of an external audit.

15. As part of the accreditation process, the residual risk of software evaluated for deployment must be accepted formally by the

A. Board members and executive management

B. Business owner

C. Information technology (IT) management

D. Security organization

E. Developers

Answer is B

Rationale/Answer Explanation:

Risk must always be accepted formally by the business owner.

Chapter 7—Software Deployment, Operations, Maintenance, and Disposal Questions

1. When software that worked without any issues in the test environments fails to work in the production environment, it is indicative of

A. Inadequate integration testing

B. Incompatible environment configurations

C. Incomplete threat modeling

D. Ignored code review

Answer is B

Rationale/Answer Explanation:

When the production environment does not mirror the development or test environments, software that works fine in nonproduction environments are observed to experience issues when deployed in the production environment. This underlines the need for simulation testing.

2. Good security metrics are characterized by all of the following except that they are

A. Quantitatively expressed

B. Objectively expressed

C. Contextually relevant

D. Collected manually

Answer is D

Rationale/Answer Explanation:

A good security metric is expressed quantitatively and is contextually accurate. Regardless of how many times the metrics are collected, the results are not significantly variant. Good metrics are usually collected in an automated manner so that the collector's subjectivity does not come into effect.

3. Removal of maintenance hooks, debugging code and flags, and unneeded documentation before deployment are all examples of software

A. Hardening

B. Patching

C. Reversing

D. Obfuscation

Answer is A

Rationale/Answer Explanation:

Locking down the software by removing unneeded code and documentation to reduce the attack surface of the software is referred to as software hardening. Before hardening the software, it is crucial to harden the operating system of the host on which the software program will be run.

4. Which of the following has the goal of ensuring that the resiliency levels of software are always above the acceptable risk threshold as defined by the business postdeployment?

A. Threat modeling

B. Code review

C. Continuous monitoring

D. Regression testing

Answer is C

Rationale/Answer Explanation:

Operations security is about staying secure or keeping the resiliency levels of the software above the acceptable risk levels. It is the assurance that the software will continue to function as expected in a reliable fashion for the business without compromising its state of security by monitoring, managing, and applying the needed controls to protect resources (assets).

5. Audit logging application events, such as failed login attempts, sales price updates, and user roles configuration, are examples of which of the following type of security control?

A. Preventive

B. Corrective

C. Compensating

D. Detective

Answer is D

Rationale/Answer Explanation:

Audit logging is a type of detective control. When the users are made aware that their activities are logged, audit logging could function as a deterrent control, but it is primarily used for detective purposes. Audit logs can be used to build the sequence of historical events and give insight into who (subject such as user/process) did what (action), where (object), and when (timestamp).

6. When a compensating control is to be used, the payment card industry data security standard (PCI DSS) prescribes that the compensating control must meet all of the following guidelines except

A. Meet the intent and rigor of the original requirement

B. Provide an increased level of defense over the original requirement

C. Be implemented as part of a defense in depth measure

D. Commensurate with additional risk imposed by not adhering to the requirement

Answer is B

Rationale/Answer Explanation:

PCI DSS prescribes that the compensating control must provide a similar level, not an increased level of defense over the original requirement.

7. Software deployed in a high-trust environment, such as the environment within the organizational firewall, when not continuously monitored is most susceptible to which of the following types of security attacks? Choose the best answer.

A. Distributed denial of service (DDoS)

B. Malware

C. Logic bombs

D. DNS poisoning

Answer is C

Rationale/Answer Explanation:

Logic bombs can be planted by an insider, and when the internal network is not monitored, the likelihood of this is much higher.

8. Bastion host systems can be used to monitor the security of the computing environment continuously when it is used in conjunction with intrusion detection systems (IDS) and which other security control?

A. Authentication

B. Authorization

C. Archiving

D. Auditing

Answer is D

Rationale/Answer Explanation:

IDS and auditing are both detective types of controls that can be used to monitor the security health of the computing environment continuously.

9. The first step in the incident response process of a reported breach is to
   A. Notify management of the security breach
   B. Research the validity of the alert or event further
   C. Inform potentially affected customers of a potential breach
   D. Conduct an independent third party evaluation to investigate the reported breach

   Answer is B

   Rationale/Answer Explanation:

   Upon the report of a breach, it is important to go into a triaging phase in which the validity and severity of the alert/event is investigated further. This reduces the number of false positives that are reported to management.

10. Which of the following is the best recommendation to champion security objectives within the software development organization?
    A. Informing the developers that they could lose their jobs if their software is breached
    B. Informing management that the organizational software could be hacked
    C. Informing the project team about the recent breach of the competitor's software
    D. Informing the development team that there should be no injection flaws in the payroll application

    Answer is D

    Rationale/Answer Explanation:

    Using security metrics over fear, uncertainty, and doubt (FUD) is the best recommendation to champion security objectives within the software development organization.

11. Which of the following independent processes provides insight into the presence and effectiveness of security and privacy controls and is used to determine the organization's compliance with the regulatory and governance (policy) requirements?
    A. Penetration testing
    B. Audits
    C. Threat modeling
    D. Code review

    Answer is B

    Rationale/Answer Explanation:

    Periodic audits (both internal and external) can be used to assess the overall state of the organization's security health.

12. The process of using regular expressions to parse audit logs into information that indicate security incidents is referred to as
    A. Correlation
    B. Normalization

C. Collection

D. Visualization

Answer is B

Rationale/Answer Explanation:

Normalizing logs means that duplicate and redundant information is removed from the logs after the time is synchronized for each log set, and the logs are parsed to deduce patterns that are identified in the correlation phase.

13. The final stage of the incident management process is

A. Detection

B. Containment

C. Eradication

D. Recovery

Answer is D

Rationale/Answer Explanation:

The incident response process involves preparation, detection, analysis, containment, eradication, and recovery. The goal of incident management is to restore (recover) service to normal business operations.

14. Problem management aims to improve the value of information technology to the business because it improves service by

A. Restoring service to the expectation of the business user

B. Determining the alerts and events that need to be continuously monitored

C. Depicting incident information in easy to understand user friendly format

D. Identifying and eliminating the root cause of the problem

Answer is D

Rationale/Answer Explanation:

The goal of problem management is to identify and eliminate the root cause of the problem. All of the other definitions are related to incident management. The goal of incident management is to restore service, while the goal of problem management is to improve service.

15. The process of releasing software to fix a recently reported vulnerability without introducing any new features or changing hardware configuration is referred to as

A. Versioning

B. Hardening

C. Patching

D. Porting

Answer is C

Rationale/Answer Explanation:

Patching is the process of applying updates and hot fixes. Porting is the process of adapting software so that an executable program can be created for a computing environment that is different from the one for which it was originally designed (e.g., different processor architecture, operating system, or third party software library).

16. Fishbone diagramming is a mechanism that is primarily used for which of the following processes?
    A. Threat modeling
    B. Requirements analysis
    C. Network deployment
    D. Root cause analysis
    Answer is D
    Rationale/Answer Explanation:
    Ishikawa diagrams or fishbone diagrams are used to identify the cause and effect of a problem and are commonly used to determine the root cause of the problem.

17. As a means to assure the availability of the existing software functionality after the application of a patch, the patch needs to be tested for
    A. Proper functioning of new features
    B. Cryptographic agility
    C. Backward compatibility
    D. Enabling of previously disabled services
    Answer is C
    Rationale/Answer Explanation:
    Regression testing of patches is crucial to ensure that there were no newer side effects and that all previous functionality as expected is still available.

18. Which of the following policies needs to be established to dispose of software and associated data and documents securely?
    A. End-of-life
    B. Vulnerability management
    C. Privacy
    D. Data classification
    Answer is A
    Rationale/Answer Explanation:
    End-of-life (EOL) policies are used for the disposal of code, configuration, and documents based on organizational and regulatory requirements.

19. Discontinuance of software with known vulnerabilities and replacement with a newer version is an example of risk
    A. Mitigation
    B. Transference
    C. Acceptance
    D. Avoidance
    Answer is D
    Rationale/Answer Explanation:

When software with known vulnerabilities is replaced with a secure version, it is an example of avoiding the risk. It is not transference because the new version may not have the same risks. It is not mitigation since no controls are implemented to address the risk of the old software. It is not acceptance since the risk of the old software is replaced with the risk of the newer version. It is not ignorance, because the risk is not left unhandled.

20. Printer ribbons, facsimile transmissions, and printed information not securely disposed of are susceptible to disclosure attacks by which of the following threat agents? Choose the best answer.

   A. Malware
   B. Dumpster divers
   C. Social engineers
   D. Script kiddies

   Answer is B

   Rationale/Answer Explanation:

   Dumpster divers are threat agents that can steal information from printed media (e.g., printer ribbons, facsimile transmission, printed paper).

21. System resources can be protected from malicious file execution attacks by uploading the user supplied file and running it in which of the following environments?

   A. Honeypot
   B. Sandbox
   C. Simulated
   D. Production

   Answer is B

   Rationale/Answer Explanation:

   Preventing malicious file execution attacks takes some careful planning from the architectural and design phases of the SDLC to thorough testing. In general, a well written application will not use user-supplied input in any filename for any server-based resource (such as images, XML and XSL transform documents, or script inclusions) and will have firewall rules in place preventing new outbound connections to the Internet or internally back to any other server. However, many legacy applications continue to have a need to accept user-supplied input and files without the adequate levels of validation built in. When this is the case, it is advisable to separate the production environment and upload the files to a sandbox environment before the files can be processed.

22. As a means to demonstrate the improvement in the security of code that is developed, one must compute the relative attack surface quotient (RASQ)

   A. At the end of development phase of the project
   B. Before and after the code is implemented
   C. Before and after the software requirements are complete

D. At the end of the deployment phase of the project

Answer is B

Rationale/Answer Explanation:

In order to understand if there is an improvement in the resiliency of the software code, the RASQ, which attempts to quantify the number and kinds of vectors available to an attacker, needs to be computed before and after code development is completed and the code is frozen.

23. When the code is not allowed to access memory at arbitrary locations that are out of range of the memory address space that belongs to the object's publicly exposed fields, it is referred to as which of the following types of code?

A. Object code

B. Type safe code

C. Obfuscated code

D. Source code

Answer is B

Rationale/Answer Explanation:

Code is said to be type safe if it only accesses memory resources that do not belong to the memory assigned to it. Type safety verification takes place during the just in time (JIT) compilation phase and prevents unsafe code from becoming active. Although you can disable type safety verification, it can lead to unpredictable results. The best example is that code can make unrestricted calls to unmanaged code, and if that code has malicious intent, the results can be severe. Therefore, the framework only allows fully trusted assemblies to bypass verification. Type safety is a form of "sandboxing." Type safety must be one of the most important considerations in regards to security when selecting a programming language and phasing out older generation programming languages.

24. Direct modifications to data in the database by developers must be prevented by

A. Periodically patching database servers

B. Implementing source code version control

C. Logging all database access requests

D. Proper change control management

Answer is D

Rationale/Answer Explanation:

Proper change control management is useful to provide separation of duties as it can prevent direct access to backend databases by developers.

25. Which of the following documents is the best source to contain damage, and which needs to be referred to and consulted with upon the discovery of a security breach?

A. Disaster Recovery Plan

B. Project Management Plan

C. Incident Response Plan

D. Quality Assurance and Testing Plan
   Answer is C
   Rationale/Answer Explanation:
   An Incident Response Plan (IRP) must be developed and tested for completeness as it is the document that one should refer to and follow in the event of a security breach. The effectiveness of an IRP is dependent on the awareness of users on how to respond to an incident, and increased awareness can be achieved by proper education and training.

Appendix B
Threat Modeling—
Zion, Inc.

In order to explain the threat modeling process, we will take a more practical approach of defining, modeling, and measuring the threats of a Web store for a fictitious company named Zion, Inc., that has the following requirements.

Zion, Inc. is in the business of selling and renting Zii game consoles, games, and accessories. Lately, it has been losing market share to online competitors who are providing a better customer experience than Zion's brick and mortar establishments. Zion, Inc. wants to secure its #1 market leader position for gaming products and services. The company plans to provide a secure, uninterrupted, and enhanced user experience to its existing and prospective customers. Zion, Inc. has contracted your organization to perform a threat modeling exercise for its online strategy. You are summoned to provide assistance and are given the following requirements:

- Customers should be able to search for products and place their orders using the Web store or by calling the sales office.
- Before a customer places an order, a customer account needs to be created.
- Customer must pay with a credit card or debit card.
- Customers must be logged in before they are allowed to personalize their preferences.
- Customers should be able to write reviews of only the products they purchase.
- Sales agents are allowed to give discounts to customers.
- Administrators can modify and delete customer and product information.

Your request for pertinent documentation yields the following statements and requirements:

- The Web store will need to be accessible from the Intranet as well as the Internet.
- The Web store will need to be designed with a distributed architecture for scalability reasons.
- User will need to authenticate to the Web store with the user account credentials, which, in turn, will authenticate to the backend database (deployed internally) via a Web services interface.
- User account information and product information will need to be maintained in a relational database for improved transactional processing.
- Credit card processing will be outsourced to a third-party processor.
- User interactions with the Web store will need to be tracked.
- The database will need to be backed up periodically to a third-party location for disaster recovery (DR) purposes.
- ASP.Net using C# and the backend database can be either Oracle or Microsoft SQL Server.

We will start threat modeling Zion, Inc.'s Web store by first defining the threat model. This includes identifying the assets and security objectives and creating an overview of the application.

In the *definition* phase of the threat modeling exercise, the following activities are conducted.

Step 1: Identify Security Objectives and Assets

For Zion, Inc.'s Web store, we start by identifying the security objectives. From the requirements, we can glean the following objectives:

- *Objective 1:* Secure #1 market leader position for gaming products and services.
- *Objective 2:* Provide secure service to existing and prospective customers.
- *Objective 3:* Provide uninterrupted service to existing and prospective customers.
- *Objective 4:* Provide an enhanced user experience to existing and prospective customers.

Objective 1 and Objective 4 are both more business objectives than they are security objectives, so while they are noted, we do not really address them as part of the threat model. However, Objective 2 and Objective 3 are directly related to security. To provide a secure service (Objective 2), the Web store must take into account the confidentiality, integrity, and availability of data, ensure that authentication, authorization, and auditing are in place and ensure that sessions, exceptions, and configurations are properly managed. To provide uninterrupted services (Objective 3), the Web store will have high availability requirements defined in the needs statement and SLA, which will be assured through monitoring, load balancing, replication, disaster recovery, and business continuity and recoverable backups.

Although the loss of customer data and downtime can cause detrimental and irrecoverable damage to the brand name of Zion, Inc. for this threat model, we will focus primarily on tangible assets, which include customer data, product data, and the application and database servers.

Step 2: Profile the Application

- Identify the physical topology: Zion, Inc.'s Web store will be deployed as an Internet-facing application in the DMZ with access for both internal and external users. Physically, the application will be entirely hosted on an application server hosted in the DMZ, with access to a database server that will be present internally as depicted in Figure B.1.
- Identify the logical topology: Zion, Inc.'s Web store will be logically designed as a distributed client/server application with distinct presentation, business, data, and service tiers as depicted in Figure B.2. Clients will access the application using their Web browsers on their desktops, laptops, and mobile devices.
- Determine components, services, protocols, and ports that need to be defined, developed, and configured for the application: Users will connect to the Web application over port 80 (using http) or over port 443 (using https). The Web application will connect to the SQL server database over port 1433 (using TCP/IP). When the users use a secure transport channel protocol such as

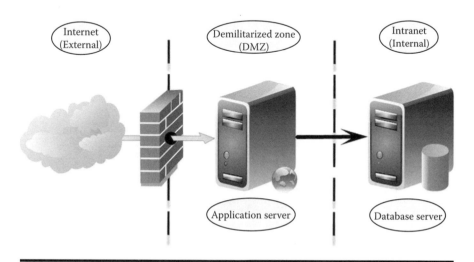

Figure B.1   Physical topology.

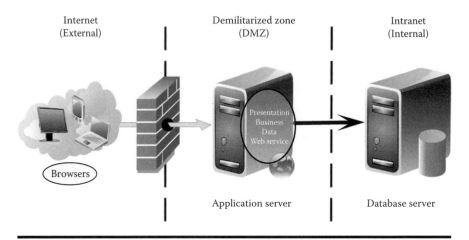

Figure B.2   Logical topology.

https over 443, the SSL certificate is also deemed a component and will need to be protected from spoofing threats. Figure B.3 illustrates the components, services, protocols, and ports for Zion, Inc.'s Web store.

■ Identify the identities that will be used in the application: User will authenticate to the Web application using forms authentication (user name and password), which, in turn, will authenticate to the SQL Server 2008 database (deployed internally) via a Web services application using a Web application identity as depicted in Figure B.4.

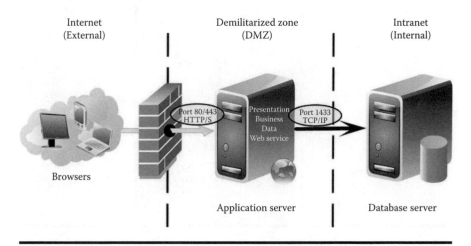

Figure B.3   Components, services, protocols, and ports.

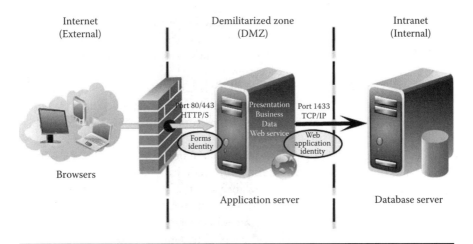

Figure B.4   Identities.

■ Identify human and nonhuman actors of the system: The requirements state
  that
  – Customers should be able to search for products and place their orders
    using the Web store or by calling the sales office.
  – Sales agents are allowed to give discounts to customers.
  – Administrators can modify and delete customer and product information.
  – The database will need to backed up periodically to a third-party location
    for disaster recovery (DR) purposes.

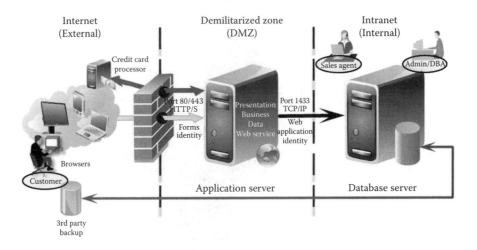

Figure B.5   Actors.

This helps us identify three human actors of the system: customers, sales agents, and administrators as depicted in Figure B.5. Nonhuman actors (not shown in the figure) can include batch processes that back up data periodically to the third-party DR location.

■ Identify data elements: Some of Zion, Inc.'s Web store data elements that need to be modeled for threats of disclosure, alteration, and destruction include customer information (account information, billing address, shipping address, etc.), product information (product data, catalog of items, product pricing, etc.), order information (data of order, bill of materials, shipping date, etc.), and credit card information (credit card number, verification code, expiration month and year, etc.). Because the Web store will be processing credit card information, customer card data information will need to be protected according to the PCI DSS requirements.

■ Generate a data access control matrix: The data access control matrix gives insight into the rights and privileges (create, read, update, or delete [CRUD]) that the actors will have on the identified data elements as depicted in Figure B.6. The same should be performed for any service roles in the application.

■ Identify the technologies that will be used in building the application:
  – Customer requirements stated that the Web application will need to be in ASP.Net using C#, while there was a choice of database technology between Oracle and Microsoft SQL Server. Figure B.7 depicts the choosing of the Internet Information Server as the Web server to support ASP.Net technology and the choosing of the SQL Server as the backend database. Whether ASP.Net will use the .Net 3.5 or .Net 4.0 framework and if the SQL server will be version 2005 or version 2008 are important

Data Access Control Matrix

Data	Administrator	Customer	Sales Agent
Customer Info	C R U D	C R U D	C R U
Product Info	C R U D	R	R U
Order Info		C R U D	C R U D
Credit Card Info		C R U D	R U

Figure B.6   Data access control matrix.

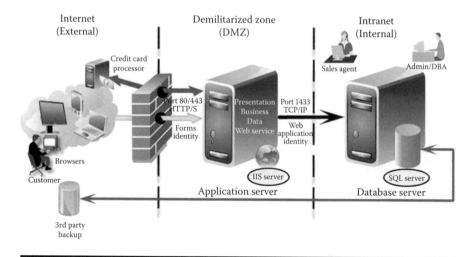

Figure B.7   Technologies.

determinations to make at this point to leverage security features within these frameworks or products.

■ Identify external dependencies: External dependencies include the credit card processor and the third-party backup service provider as depicted in Figure B.8.

■ The output of this activity is the architectural makeup of the application.

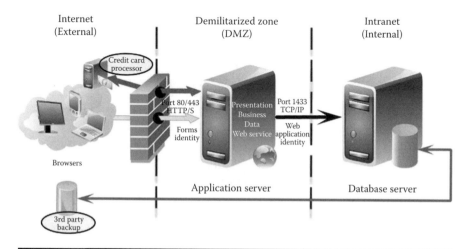

Figure B.8   Dependencies.

In the *modeling* phase of the threat modeling exercise, the following activities are conducted.

Step 3: Decompose the Application

- Identify trust boundaries: A trust boundary is the point at which the trust level or privilege changes. For the Zion, Inc.'s Web store, trust boundaries exist between the external (Internet) and the DMZ and between the DMZ and the internal (Intranet) zones.
- Identify entry points: Entry points are those items that take in user input. Each entry point can be a potential threat source and so each must be explicitly identified and safeguarded. Entry points in a Web application could include any page that takes in user input. Some of the entry points identified in the Zion, Inc.'s Web store include the following:
    - Port 80/443
    - Logon Page
    - User Preferences Page
    - Product Admin Page
- Identify exit points: Exit points are those items that display information from within the system. Exit points also include processes that take data out of the system. Exit points can be the source of information leakage and need to be equally protected. Some of the exit points identified in the Zion, Inc.'s Web store include the following:
    - Product Catalog Page
    - Search Results Page
    - Credit card verification processes
    - Backup processes
- Identify data flows: DFDs and sequence diagrams assist in understanding how the application will accept, process, and handle data as it is marshaled across different trust boundaries. Some of the data flows identified in Zion, Inc.'s Web store include the following:
    - Anonymous user browses product catalog page → Adds to Cart → Creates Account → Submits Order
    - User Logs In → Updates Preferences → User Logs Out
    - Administrator Logs In → Updates Product Information
- Identify privileged code: Code that allows elevation of privilege or the execution of privileged operations is identified. All administrator functions and critical business transactions are identified.
- Document the security profile: This involves identification of the design and implementation mechanisms that impact the security of the application as depicted in Table B.1.

Table B.1   Security Profile Documentation

Security Profile	Design/Implementation Requirement
Confidentiality	Customer information (PII) and credit card information should be protected in processing, transit, and storage.
Integrity	Only authorized users should be able to modify product information (pricing, shipping, etc.). Input parameters (search, etc.) should be validated.
Availability	Backup to third-party location must be in place to ensure fast recovery.
Authentication	Users will need to authenticate to the Web application and Web services will need to authenticate with the database using dedicated identities.
Authorization	Users are to be configured into roles such as sales agents and administrators and access must be controlled using RBAC mechanisms.
Auditing	User activity on the Web store is to be logged with the date, timestamp, and action taken.
Management	Session identifiers must be random to prevent session hijacking and replay attacks. Errors information must be predefined to security policy and be nonverbose. Exceptions need to be trapped and handled explicitly. Configuration information such as connection strings and application settings need to be protected using cryptographic protection and access control mechanisms.

Step 4: Identify Threats and Vulnerabilities

For Zion, Inc.'s threat model, although an attack-tree methodology could have been applied, it was determined that using a categorized threat list would be more comprehensive. The STRIDE threat list was used for this exercise and the results tabulated as shown in Table B.2.

In the *measurement* phase of the threat modeling exercise, the following activities are conducted.

Step 5: Document the Threats

Threats can be documented diagrammatically or in textual format. Zion, Inc.'s threats are documented diagrammatically as depicted in Figure B.9. An example of textually documenting the SQL injection threat is tabulated in Table B.3.

Table B.2   Threat Identification Using STRIDE Threat List

STRIDE List	Identified Threats
Spoofing	Cookie replay Session hijacking CSRF
Tampering	Cross-Site Scripting (XSS) SQL Injection
Repudiation	Audit log deletion Insecure backup
Information disclosure	Eavesdropping Verbose exception Output caching
Denial of service	Web site defacement
Elevation of privilege	Logic flaw

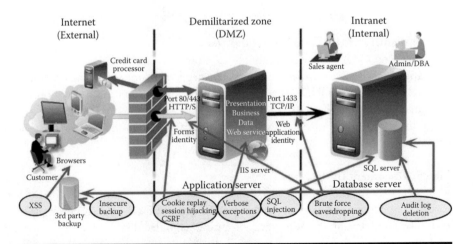

Figure B.9   Diagrammatically documents threats.

Table B.3   Textual Documentation of a SQL Injection Threat

Threat Description	*Injection of SQL Commands*
Threat targets	Data access component; backend database.
Attack techniques	Attacker appends SQL commands to user name, which is used to form an SQL query.
Security impact	Information disclosure; alteration; destruction (drop table, procedures, delete data, etc.); authentication bypass.
Safeguard controls to implement	Use a regular expression to validate the user name. Disallow dynamic construction of queries using user supplied input without validation; use parameterized queries.
Risk	High

Table B.4   Average Ranking

Threat	*Average Rank* $(D_{value} + R_{value} + E_{value} + A_{value} + DI_{value})/5$
SQL injection	2.6 (High)
XSS	3.0 (High)
Cookie replay	2.0 (Medium)
Session hijacking	2.0 (Medium)
CSRF	1.4 (Medium)
Verbose exception	1.8 (Medium)
Brute-forcing	1.8 (Medium)
Eavesdropping	2.0 (Medium)
Insecure backup	1.4 (Medium)
Audit log deletion	1.0 (Low)
Output caching	2.8 (High)
Web site defacement	2.2 (High)
Logic flaws	1.2 (Low)

Step 6: Prioritize the Threats

The three common ways to rank threats are

1. Delphi ranking
2. Average ranking
3. Probability × Impact ($P \times I$) ranking

Both average ranking and $P \times I$ ranking methodologies to rank threats were followed and the results tabulated for Zion, Inc.'s. The Delphi ranking exercise was conducted but because of its nonscientific approach to risk, the findings were not deemed useful. Table B.4 shows the threat ranks using the average ranking methodology. Table B.5 shows the risk rank based on $P \times I$ ranking methodology.

After the threats are prioritized, your findings and the threat model are submitted to the organization. On the basis of this threat model, appropriate controls are identified for implementation to bring the security risk of Zion, Inc.'s Web store within acceptable thresholds, as defined by the business. (See Table B.6.)

Table B.5 $P \times I$ Ranking[a]

Threat	Probability of Occurrence (P) $(R + E + DI)$	Business Impact (I) $(D + A)$	Risk $P \times I$
SQL injection	7	6	42
XSS	9	6	54
Cookie replay	6	4	24
Session hijacking	7	3	21
CSRF	3	4	12
Verbose exception	4	5	20
Brute-forcing	4	5	20
Eavesdropping	5	5	25
Insecure backup	5	2	10
Audit log deletion	3	2	06
Output caching	8	6	48
Web site defacement	5	6	30
Logic flaws	3	3	06

[a] High, 41 to 60; medium, 21 to 40; low, 0 to 20.

Table B.6   Control Identification

Threat (P × I rank)	Controls
XSS (54)	Encode output; validate request; validate input; disallow script tags; disable active scripting
Output caching (48)	Do not cache credentials; complete mediation
SQL injection (42)	Use parameterized queries; validate input; do not allow dynamic construction of SQL
Web site defacement (30)	Load balancing and DR; disallow URL redirection
Eavesdropping (25)	Data encryption; sniffers detection; disallow rogue systems
Cookie replay (24)	Cookie-less authentication; encrypt cookies to avoid tampering
Session hijacking (21)	Use random and nonsequential session identifiers; abandon sessions explicitly; auto log off/on browser shutdown
Verbose exception (20)	Use nonverbose error message; trap, record, and handle errors; fail secure
Brute-forcing (20)	Do not allow weak passwords; balance psychological acceptability with strong passwords
CSRF (12)	Use unique session token; use referrer origin checks; complete mediation
Insecure backup (10)	Data encryption; SSL (transport) or IPSec (network) in-transit protection; ACLs
Audit log deletion (06)	Do not allow direct access to the database; implement access triple security model; separation of privilege
Logic flaws (06)	Design reviews

Appendix C
Commonly Used
Opcodes in Assembly

TRANSFER Opcodes

Name	Description	Syntax
MOV	Move (copy)	MOV Dest,Source
XCHG	Exchange	XCHG Op1,Op2
STC	Set Carry	STC
CLC	Clear Carry	CLC
CMC	Complement Carry	CMC
STD	Set Direction	STD
CLD	Clear Direction	CLD
STI	Set Interrupt	STI
CLI	Clear Interrupt	CLI
PUSH	Push onto stack	PUSH Source
PUSHF	Push flags	PUSHF
PUSHA	Push all general registers	PUSHA
POP	Pop from stack	POP Dest
POPF	Pop flags	POPF

POPA	Pop all general registers	POPA
CBW	Convert byte to word	CBW
CWD	Convert word to double	CWD
CWDE	Convert word extended double	CWDE
IN	Input	IN Dest,Port
OUT	Output	OUT Port,Source

ARITHMETIC Opcodes

Name	Description	Syntax
ADD	Add	ADD Dest,Source
ADC	Add with carry	ADC Dest,Source
SUB	Subtract	SUB Dest,Source
SBB	Subtract with borrow	SBB Dest,Source
DIV	Divide (unsigned)	DIV Op
IDIV	Signed integer divide	IDIV Op
MUL	Multiply (unsigned)	MUL Op
IMUL	Signed integer multiply	IMUL Op
INC	Increment	INC Op
DEC	Decrement	DEC Op
CMP	Compare	CMP Op1,Op2
SAL	Shift arithmetic left	SAL Op,Quantity
SAR	Shift arithmetic right	SAR Op,Quantity
RCL	Rotate left through carry	RCL Op,Quantity
RCR	Rotate right through carry	RCR Op,Quantity
ROL	Rotate left	ROL Op,Quantity
ROR	Rotate right	ROR Op,Quantity

LOGIC Opcodes

Name	Description	Syntax
NEG	Negate (two-complement)	NEG Op
NOT	Invert each bit	NOT Op
AND	Logical and	AND Dest,Source
OR	Logical or	OR Dest,Source
XOR	Logical exclusive or	XOR Dest,Source
SHL	Shift logical left	SHL Op,Quantity
SHR	Shift logical right	SHR Op,Quantity

MISCELLANEOUS Opcodes

Name	Description	Syntax
NOP	No operation	NOP
LEA	Load effective address	LEA Dest,Source
INT	Interrupt	INT Nr

JUMPS (General) Opcodes

Name	Description	Syntax
CALL	Call subroutine	CALL Proc
JMP	Jump	JMP Dest
JE	Jump if equal	JE Dest
JZ	Jump if zero	JZ Dest
JCXZ	Jump if CX zero	JCXZ Dest
JP	Jump if parity (parity even)	JP Dest
JPE	Jump if parity even	JPE Dest
RET	Return from subroutine	RET
JNE	Jump if not equal	JNE Dest
JNZ	Jump if not zero	JNZ Dest
JECXZ	Jump if ECX zero	JECXZ Dest

JNP	Jump if no parity (parity odd)	JNP Dest
JPO	Jump if parity odd	JPO Dest

JUMPS Unsigned (Cardinal) Opcodes

JA	Jump if above	JA Dest
JAE	Jump if above or equal	JAE Dest
JB	Jump if below	JB Dest
JBE	Jump if below or equal	JBE Dest
JNA	Jump if not above	JNA Dest
JNAE	Jump if not above or equal	JNAE Dest
JNB	Jump if not below	JNB Dest
JNBE	Jump if not below or equal	JNBE Dest
JC	Jump if carry	JC Dest
JNC	Jump if no carry	JNC Dest

JUMPS Signed (Integer) Opcodes

JG	Jump if greater	JG Dest
JGE	Jump if greater or equal	JGE Dest
JL	Jump if less	JL Dest
JLE	Jump if less or equal	JLE Dest
JNG	Jump if not greater	JNG Dest
JNGE	Jump if not greater or equal	JNGE Dest
JNL	Jump if not less	JNL Dest
JNLE	Jump if not less or equal	JNLE Dest
JO	Jump if overflow	JO Dest
JNO	Jump if no overflow	JNO Dest
JS	Jump if sign (= negative)	JS Dest
JNS	Jump if no sign (= positive)	JNS Dest

Appendix D
HTTP/1.1 Status Codes and Reason Phrases (IETF RFC 2616)

The status code element is a three-digit integer result code of the attempt to understand and satisfy the request. The reason phrase exists for the sole purpose of providing a textual description associated with the numeric status code, done out of deference to earlier Internet application protocols that were more frequently used with interactive text clients. A client should ignore the content of the reason phrase. The reason phrases listed are only recommendations and may be replaced by local equivalents without affecting the protocol.

The first digit of the status code defines the class of response. The last two digits do not have any categorization role. There are five values for the first digit:

- 1xx: Informational: Request received, continuing process
- 2xx: Success: The action was successfully received, understood, and accepted
- 3xx: Redirection: Further action must be taken in order to complete the request
- 4xx: Client Error: The request contains bad syntax or cannot be fulfilled
- 5xx: Server Error: The server failed to fulfill an apparently valid request

Response Class	Status Code	Reason Phrase
1xx: Informational: Request received, continuing process	100	Continue
	101	Switching protocols
2xx: Success: The action was successfully received, understood, and accepted	200	OK
	201	Created
	202	Accepted
	203	Nonauthoritative
	204	No Content
	205	Reset Content
	206	Partial Content
3xx: Redirection: Further action must be taken in order to complete the request	300	Multiple Choices
	301	Moved Permanently
	302	Found
	303	See Other
	304	Not Modified
	305	Use Proxy
	307	Temporary Redirect
4xx: Client Error: The request contains bad syntax or cannot be fulfilled	400	Bad Request
	401	Unauthorized
	402	Payment Required
	403	Forbidden
	404	Not Found
	405	Method Not Allowed
	406	Not Acceptable
	407	Proxy Authentication Required
	408	Request Time-out
	409	Conflict
	410	Gone

4xx: Client Error:	411	Length Required
The request contains bad syntax or cannot be fulfilled	412	Precondition Failed
	413	Request Entity Too Large
	414	URI Too Long
	415	Unsupported Media Type
	416	Request range not satisfiable
	417	Expectation Failed
5xx: Server Error:	500	Internal Server Error
The server failed to fulfill an apparently valid request	501	Not Implemented
	502	Bad Gateway
	503	Service Unavailable
	504	Gateway Time-out
	505	HTTP Version not supported

HTTP status codes are extensible. HTTP applications are not required to understand the meaning of all registered status codes, although such understanding is obviously desirable. However, applications must understand the class of any status code, as indicated by the first digit, and treat any unrecognized response as being equivalent to the x00 status code of that class, with the exception that an unrecognized response must not be cached. For example, if an unrecognized status code of 431 is received by the client, it can safely assume that there was something wrong with its request and treat the response as if it had received a 400 status code.

For a complete understanding of the status codes and their response phases, it is recommended that you consult the IETF RFC 2616 publication.

Appendix E
Security Testing Tools

A list of common security testing tools is discussed in this section. This is by no means an all-inclusive list of security tools, and the tools that are applicable to your organizational requirements need to be identified and used accordingly.

E.1 Reconnaissance (Information Gathering) Tools

- Ping: By sending Internet control message protocol (ICMP) echo request packets to a target host and waiting for an ICMP response, the network administration utility Ping can be used to test whether a particular host is reachable across an Internet Protocol (IP) network. It can also be used to measure the round-trip time for packets sent from the local host to a destination computer, including the local host's own interfaces. More information can be obtained at http://ftp.arl.mil/~mike/ping.html.
- Traceroute (Tracert): Traceroute (or Tracert in Windows) can be used to determine the path (route) taken to a destination host by sending ICMP echo request messages to the destination with incrementally increasing time to live (TTL) field values. Traceroute utilizes the IP protocol TTL field and attempts to elicit an ICMP TIME_EXCEEDED response from each gateway along the path to the destination host. It can also be used to determine which hosts in the route are dropping the packets so that they can be addressed, if feasible. Visual traceroute programs that map the network path a packet takes when transmitted are now available.
- WHOIS: WHOIS is a query/response protocol widely used for querying databases in order to determine the registrant or assignee of Internet resources, such as a domain name, an IP address block, or an autonomous system number.

■ Domain Information Groper (dig): A Linux/Unix command, dig is a flexible tool for interrogating DNS name servers. It performs DNS lookups and displays the answers that are returned from the name server(s) that were queried. More information can be obtained at http://linux.about.com/od/commands/l/blcmdl1_dig.htm.

■ netstat: netstat (network statistics) is a command-line tool that displays network connections (both incoming and outgoing), routing tables, and a number of network interface statistics. It is available on Unix, Unix-like, and Windows NT-based operating systems. More information can be obtained at http://www.netstat.net.

■ Telnet: Telnet is a network protocol commonly used to refer to an application that uses that protocol. The application is used to connect to remote computers, usually via TCP port 23. Most often, you will be establishing a connection (telneting) to a UNIX-like server system or a simple network device, such as a switch. Once a connection is established, you can then log in with your account information and execute commands remotely on that computer. The commands you use are operating system commands, and not telnet commands. In most remote access situations, telnet has been replaced by SSH for improved security across untrusted networks. However, telnet continues to be used for remote access today and remains a solid network troubleshooting tool as well. Telnet is also used in banner grabbing. More information can be obtained at http://www.telnet.org.

E.2 Vulnerability Scanners

■ Network Mapper (Nmap): An extremely popular, free, and open source network exploration and security auditing tool. It uses raw IP packets to determine the hosts that are available on the network and can be used to fingerprint operating systems, determine application services (name and version) running on the hosts, and identify the types of packet filters and firewalls that are in use. It runs on all major operating systems, including Windows, Linux, and Mac OS X, and comes in both a command-line version as well as bundled with a GUI and result viewer called Zenmap. The Nmap suite additionally includes a Ncat, which is a flexible data transfer, redirection, and debugging tool, and Ndiff, a utility for comparing scan results. More information can be obtained at http://nmap.org.

■ Nessus: A very popular vulnerability scanner that is implemented with a client/server architecture. It has a graphical interface and more than 20,000 plugins that scan for several vulnerabilities. Both UNIX and Windows versions are available. Salient features include remote and local (authenticated) security checks and a proprietary scripting language called Nessus Attack Scripting Language (NASL) that allows security testers to write their own plugins. More information can be obtained at http://www.nessus.org.

■ Retina: Retina is a commercial vulnerability assessment scanner developed by eEye, a company known for security research. It functions like other vulnerability scanners and scans for systems aiming to detect and identify vulnerabilities. Both network and Web vulnerability scanners are available in eEye's product offering. By using signature pattern matching, intelligence inference engines, context-sensitive vulnerability checks, site analysis, application vulnerabilities, such as input validation, poor coding practices, weak configuration management, and threats in source code, it can evaluate and determine scripts, directory content, and more. More information can be obtained at http://www.eeye.com.

■ SAINT®: SAINT® scans the network to determine any weaknesses that will allow an attacker to gain unauthorized access, disclose sensitive information, or create a DoS in the network. Additionally, it gives the ability to remediate vulnerabilities. Other product offerings help with vulnerability management and penetration testing. More information can be obtained at http://www .saintcorporation.com.

■ GFI LANguard: A commercial network security scanner for Windows that scans IP address to determine active hosts (running machines) on the network. It can also fingerprint the operating system (OS), detect service pack versions, and identify missing patches, USB devices, open shares, open ports, running services, groups, users, and passwords that are incompliant with password policies. The built-in patch manager can be used for installing missing patches as well. More information can be obtained at http://www.gfi.com/lannetscan.

■ QualysGuard® Web Application Scanner (WAS): An on-demand scanner, the QualysGuard® WAS automates Web application security assessment, enabling organizations to assess, track, and remediate Web application vulnerabilities. It works by crawling Web applications and identifies Web application vulnerabilities, such as those in the OWASP Top 10 list and Web Application Security Consortium Threat Classification (WASC TC). It uses both pattern recognition and behavioral analysis to identify and verify vulnerabilities. It can also be used to detect sensitive content in HTML based on user setting and for conducting authenticated and nonauthenticated scanning tests. The QualysGuard WAS is one of the suite of security products that is offered by Qualys. The others include products for PCI compliance, policy compliance, and vulnerability management. More information can be obtained at http://www.qualys.com.

■ IBM Internet Scanner, formerly Internet Security Systems (ISS): The IBM Internet Scanner can identify more than 1,300 types of network devices, including desktops, servers, routers/switches, firewalls, security devices, and application routers. Upon identification of the devices, the scanner can also analyze device configurations, patch levels, OSes, and installed applications that are susceptible to threats and prioritize remediation tasks preemptively. It identifies critical assets and can be used to prevent the compromise of confidentiality, integrity, and availability of critical business information. More information can be obtained at http://www.ibm.com/iss.

■ Microsoft Baseline Security Analyzer (MBSA): MBSA can be used to detect common security misconfigurations and missing security updates on computer systems. Built on the Windows Update Agent and Microsoft Update infrastructure, MBSA ensures consistency with other Microsoft management products, including Microsoft Update (MU), Windows Server Update Services (WSUS), Systems Management Server (SMS), System Center Configuration Manager (SCCM) 2007, and Small Business Server (SBS). More information can be obtained at http://www.microsoft.com/mbsa.

E.3 Fingerprinting Tools

■ P0f v2: P0f version 2 (P0f v2) is a resourceful, passive, OS fingerprinting tool that identifies the OS of a target host by merely analyzing captured packets. It does not generate any additional traffic, direct or indirect, or perform any name lookups, ARIN queries, or probes. It can also be used to detect the presence of a firewall, the use of network address translation (NAT), or the existence of a load balancer. More information can be obtained at http://lcamtuf.coredump.cx/p0f.shtml.

■ XProbe-NG or XProbe2++: A low-volume, remote, network mapping and analysis tool that can be used for active OS fingerprinting. Using a signature engine and fuzzy signature matching process, a network traffic minimization algorithm, and module sequence optimization, this tool has been proven to fingerprint an OS successfully, even when the target host systems are behind protocol scrubbers. Additionally, XProbe2++ can be used to detect and identify HoneyNet systems that attempt to mimic actual network systems by responding to fingerprinting with packets that match certain OS signatures. More information can be obtained at http://xprobe.sourceforge.net.

E.4 Sniffers/Protocol Analyzers

■ Wireshark (formerly Ethereal): Wireshark is a very popular open source sniffer and network protocol analyzer for both wired and wireless networks. It sniffs detailed information about the packets transmitted on the network interfaces being configured for capture. Wireshark can be used to determine traffic generated by protocols used in your network or application, examine security problems, and learn about the internals of the protocol. More information can be obtained at http://www.wireshark.org.

■ Tcpdump and WinDump: Freely distributed under a BSD license, Tcpdump is another popular packet capture and analyzing tool. As the name suggests, it can be used to intercept and dump TCP/IP packets transmitted in the network. It works on almost all major Unix and Unix-like OSes (Linux, Solaris, BSD, Mac OS X, HP-UX, and AIX) as well as on a Windows version called WinDump. Tcpdump uses the libpcap library, and WinDump uses WinPcap for capturing packets. More information can be obtained at http://www.tcpdump.org and http://www.winpcap.org/windump.

■ Ettercap: A very popular tool for conducting MITM attacks on a LAN, Ettercap is a sniffer/interceptor and logging tool that supports active and passive analysis of protocols, including ones that implement encryption, such as SSH and HTTPS. It can be used for data injection, content filtering, and OS fingerprinting, and it supports plugins. More information can be obtained at http://ettercap.sourceforge.net.

■ DSniff: A very popular password sniffer, DSniff is not just one tool, but a collection of network auditing and penetration testing tools. These tools can be used for passively monitoring networks (dsniff, filesnarf, mailsnarf, msgsnarf, urlsnarf, and Webspy) for passwords, sensitive files, and emails, spoofing (arpspoof, dnsspoof, and macof), and actively conducting MITM attacks against redirected SSH and HTTPS sessions. More information can be obtained from http://monkey.org/~dugsong/dsniff.

E.5 Password Crackers

■ Cain & Abel: Although Cain & Abel is an extremely powerful and popular password sniffing and cracking tool that uses dictionary, brute force, and cryptanalysis to discover passwords, even encrypted ones, it is also much more. It can record VoIP conversations, recover wireless network keys, decode scrambled passwords, reveal password boxes, uncover cached passwords, and analyze routing protocols. Currently, it is solely available in a Windows version. It can also be used for ARP poison routing (APR), which makes it possible to sniff even on switched LANs and MITM attacks. The new version also ships routing protocols authentication monitors and routes extractors, dictionary, and brute-force crackers for all common hashing algorithms and for several specific authentications, password/hash calculators, cryptanalysis attacks, password decoders, and some not-so-common utilities related to network and system security. More information can be obtained at http://www.oxid.it.

■ John the Ripper: A free and open source software, John the Ripper is another powerful, flexible and fast multiplatform password hash cracker. Available in multiple flavors, it is primarily used to identify weak passwords, and a tester can use this to verify compliance with strong password policies. It can be used to determine various crypt(3) password hash types supported in Unix versions, Kerberos, and Windows LM hashes. With a wordlist, John the Ripper can be used for dictionary brute-force attacks. More information can be obtained at http://www.openwall.com/john.

- THC Hydra: A very fast network logon cracker that can be used to test the strength of a remote authentication service. Unlike many other password crackers that are restricted in the number of protocols they can support, THC supports multiprotocols. The current version supports 30+ protocols, including Telnet, FTP, HTTP, HTTPS, HTTP-Proxy, SMB, SMBNT, MS-SQL, MySQL, REXEC, RSH, RLOGIN, SNMP, SMTP-AUTH, SOCKS5, VNC, POP3, IMAP, ICQ, LDAP, Postgress, and Cisco. More information can be obtained at http://freeworld.thc.org/thc-hydra.
- L0phtcrack: One of the premier password cracking tools, L0phtcrack is a password audit and recovery tool for Windows and Unix passwords. It uses a scoring metric to assess the quality of passwords by measuring them against current industry best practices for password strength. It supports precomputed password hashes and can be used for password and network auditing from a remote interface. It also has the ability to schedule a password audit scan that is configurable based on the organization's auditing needs. More information can be obtained at http://www.L0phtcrack .com.
- RainbowCrack: Unlike brute-force crackers that generate and match hashes of plaintext on the fly to discover a password, RainbowCrack is a brute-force hash cracker that uses rainbow tables of precomputed hash values for discovering passwords. This works on the principle of time–memory tradeoff, which basically means that memory use can be reduced at the cost of slower program execution or vice versa. By precomputing hash values and storing them in a table (known as a rainbow table), this cracker can be used to look up values that match in determining the actual password. During the precomputation phase, all plaintext/hash pairs for a particular hash function, character set, and plaintext length are computed, and the results are stored in a rainbow table. This can be time-consuming initially, but once the hashes are precomputed, then cracking can be significantly faster as it primarily works by looking up and comparing values. More information can be obtained at http://project-rainbowcrack.com.

E.6 Web Security Tools: Scanners, Proxies, and Vulnerability Management

- Nikto2: An open source application and Web server scanner, Nikto2 performs comprehensive tests against Web servers for detecting dangerous files and common gateway interfaces (CGIs), determining outdated Web server versions, and finding potential vulnerabilities in them. It can also be used to identify installed Web servers and applications that run on them, besides having the ability to check for server configuration items, such as multiple index files and HTTP Server options settings. Although it is not a very stealthy tool and is often evident in IDS logs, Nikto2 is a powerful and fast Web security scanner that uses Libwhisker (a Perl module geared toward HTTP testing) and provides support for anti-IDS methods that can be used to test your IDS. It also supports plugins for other vulnerability scanners, such as Nessus. More information can be obtained at http://www.cirt.net/nikto2.

- Paros: Written in Java, Paros is a Web application vulnerability assessment proxy that intercepts and proxies HTTP and HTTPS data between the Web server and the browser client. This makes it possible to view and edit HTTP/HTTPS messages, cookie, and form fields on the fly. As Web application scanning for common Web application attacks like SQL injection and cross-site scripting (XSS), it can also be used for spidering Web sites and performing MITM attacks. It comes with a Web traffic recorder and hash calculator to assist vulnerability assessment testing. More information can be obtained at http://www.parosproxy.org.

- WebScarab-NG (New Generation): A Web application intercepting proxy tool supported as an OWASP Project. Similar in function to the Paros proxy, it can be used to analyze and modify requests from the browser or client to the Web server. It can be used by anyone who wishes to understand the internals of their HTTP/HTTPS application and by testing teams to debug and identify Web application issues, besides giving a security specialist a tool to help identify vulnerabilities in their implemented Web applications. The current version supports a floating tool bar that stays on top of the client window and the ability to annotate conversations, and it has the ability to provide feedback to the user. More information can be obtained at http://www.owasp.org/index.php/OWASP_WebScarab_NG_Project.

- Burp Suite: Written in Java, Burp Suite is an integrated platform that can be used to test the resiliency of Web applications. It provides the ability to combine manual and automated testing techniques to analyze, scan, attack, and exploit Web applications. All tools in the suite use the same robust framework as used for handling HTTP requests, scanning, spidering, persistence, authentication, proxying, sequencing, decoding, logging, alternating, comparisons, and extensibility. More information can be obtained at http://www.portswigger.net/suite.

- Wikto: Written in Microsoft .Net, Wikto is one of the power tools that check for flaws in Web servers. In its functioning, it is very similar to Nikto2, but it has some unique features, such as the back-end miner and integration with Google that can be used in the assessment of the Web servers. More information can be obtained at http://www.sensepost.com/research/wikto.

- HP WebInspect: A popular Web application security assessment tool, HP WebInspect is built on Web 2.0 technologies that provide fast scanning capabilities and broad coverage for common and emerging Web application threats. It uses innovative assessment techniques, such as simultaneous crawl and audit (SCA), and concurrent application scanning for faster scans with accurate results. More information can be obtained at http://www.hp.com/go/securitysoftware.

- IBM Rational AppScan: This product suite has a list of products that makes it easy to integrate security testing throughout the application development life cycle, thereby providing security assurance early on in the development phase. Using multiple testing techniques, AppScan offers both static and dynamic security testing and can scan for many common vulnerabilities, such as XSS, HTTP response splitting, parameter tampering, hidden field manipulation, backdoors/debug options, and buffer overflow. There is a developer edition that automates security scanning for nonsecurity professionals and a tester edition that integrates Web application security testing into the QA process. More information can be obtained from http://www-01.ibm.com/software/awdtools/appscan.

- WhiteHat Sentinel: A software-as-a-service (SaaS) scalable Web site vulnerability management platform offered as a subscription-based service. It leverages technology with its advanced scanning technologies and complements that with human testing. It has the ability to integrate with some Web application firewalls (WAFs) and can be used to protect Web applications from attackers. More information can be obtained at http://www.whitehatsec.com.

E.7 Wireless Security Tools

- Kismet: A versatile and powerful 802.11 Layer 2 wireless network detector, sniffer, and IDS that works with any wireless card that supports raw monitoring (rfmon) mode. With the appropriate hardware, it can sniff 802.11 a/b/g and n network traffic as well. It is a passive sniffer that collects packets and detects standard named networks. It is commonly used for finding wireless access points (wardriving). It can also be used to discover WEP keys, decloak hidden networks and SSIDs, and infer the presence of nonbeaconing networks via data traffic that it sniffs. More information can be obtained at http://www.kismetwireless.net.

- NetStumbler: NetStumbler is a Windows-only tool used to detect wireless local area networks (WLANs) and sniff 802.11 a/b and g network traffic. It can be used to test correct configuration of your wireless network and find areas where the wireless signals are attenuated. It can also be used to detect interfering wireless networks and rogue access points installed within or in proximity to your network. Like Kismet, it is also used for wardriving. More information can be obtained at http://www.netstumbler.com.

- Aircrack-ng: A 802.11 suite of tools as listed below that can be used to test the strength of a wireless defense or its lack thereof. It is used primarily for cracking WEP and WPA-PSK keys by recovering the keys once enough data packets have been captured. The set of tools within the Aircrack-ng suite for auditing wireless networks includes a multipurpose tool aimed at attacking clients, as opposed to the access point (AP) itself (airbase-ng), a WEP/WPA/WPA2 captured files decryptor (airdecap-ng), a WEP Cloaking remover (airdecloak-ng), a script that allows installation of wireless drivers (airdriver-ng), a tool to inject and replay wireless frames (aireplay-ng), a wireless interface monitoring mode enabler and disabler (airmon-ng), a tool to dump and capture raw 802.11 frames (airodump-ng), a tool to precompute WPA/WPA2 passphrases in a database to use later with aircrack-ng (airolib-ng), a wireless card TCP/IP server that allows multiple applications to use a wireless card (airserv-ng), a virtual tunnel interface creator (airtun-ng), a packet forger that can be used in injection attacks (packetforge-ng), and more. More information can be obtained at http://www.aircrack-ng.org/.

■ KisMAC-ng: A popular free and open source wireless stumbling and security tool for the Mac OS X. Originally developed in Germany, but with the introduction of the StGB §202c law in Germany that distribution of security software was a punishable offense, it had to find a place outside Germany for continued development. Its advantage over other wireless stumblers is that it uses monitor mode and passive scanning for detecting and sniffing wireless packets. Most major wireless cards and chipsets are supported. It also offers packet capture (Pcap) format import and logging and decryption and can be used for some deauthentication attacks. More information can be obtained at http://kismac-ng.org.

E.8 Reverse Engineering Tools (Assembler and Disassemblers, Debuggers, and Decompilers)

■ ILDASM and ILASM: The Microsoft Intermediate Language Disassembler (ILDASM) takes a portable executable (PE) file that contains Microsoft Intermediate Language (MSIL) code and outputs a text file that can be used as an input into its companion tool, the Microsoft Intermediate Assembler (ILASM). Metadata attribute information of the MSIL code can be determined, and running a PE through ILDASM can help identify missing run-time metadata attributes. The text file output from ILDASM can then be edited to include any missing metadata attributes, and this can be input into the ILASM tool to generate a final executable. The ILDASM and ILASM tools can be used by a reverse engineer to understand the internal workings of a PE for which the source code is not available. More information can be obtained by searching for ILDASM and/or ILASM at http://msdn.microsoft.com.

■ OllyDbg: A 32-bit assembler level analyzing debugger for Microsoft Windows. Emphasis on binary code analysis makes it particularly useful in cases where source is unavailable. OllyDbg features an intuitive user interface, advanced code analysis capable of recognizing procedures, loops, API calls, switches, tables, constants and strings, an ability to attach to a running program, and good multithread support. OllyDbg is shareware, free to download and use, but no source code is provided. More information can be obtained at http://www.ollydbg.de.

- IDA Pro: IDA Pro is deemed to be the de facto standard for host code analysis and vulnerability research. It is a commercial, interactive Windows and Linux multiprocessor disassembler and debugger that can also be programmed. It can also be used for COTS product validation and privacy protection analysis. More information can be obtained at http://www.hex-rays.com/idapro.

- .Net Reflector: A tool that enables you easily to view, navigate, and search through the class hierarchies of .NET assemblies, even if you do not have the code for them. With it, you can decompile and analyze .NET assemblies in C#, Visual Basic, and MSIL. This is useful for understanding the internal working of a .Net assembly and can be used for security research and vulnerability assessment. It supports add-ins that can be configured, which makes .Net Reflector a powerful tool in the arsenal of tools needed for security testing .Net applications. More information can be obtained at http://www.red-gate.com/products/reflector.

E.9 Source Code Analyzers

- IBM Ounce 6: IBM's acquisition of Ouncelabs added to their security product suite Ounce 6, which is a source code analyzing solution for vulnerabilities and threat exposures in software. By integrating into the SDLC, Ounce 6 helps to ensure data privacy, document compliance efforts, and security of outsourced code. More information can be obtained at http://www.ouncelabs.com/products.

- Fortify Software: Both a static and dynamic source code analyzer. The source code analyzer component examines the applications source code for exploitable vulnerabilities and can be used during the development phase of the SDLC to catch security issues early. The program trace analyzer component identifies vulnerabilities that can be found when the application is running and can be used during the software testing or QA phase. The real-time analyzer monitors deployed applications, identifying how and when the application is being attacked. It provides detailed information about the internals of the application that identifies the vulnerabilities that are being exploited. This can be used while the application is in production to determine security weaknesses that were missed during development. The company also has an on-demand SaaS offering. More information can be obtained at http://www.fortify.com/products.

E.10 Vulnerability Exploitation Tools

■ Metasploit Framework: A de facto tool in the hands of any security researcher or penetration tester. It provides useful information and tools for penetration testers, security researchers, and IDS signature developers. This project was created to provide information on exploit techniques and to create a functional knowledge base for exploit developers and security professionals. The tools and information on this site are provided for legal security research and testing purposes only. More information can be obtained at http://www.metasploit.com.

■ CANVAS: Developed by Immunity, CANVAS is a comprehensive commercial exploitation framework that makes available hundreds of exploits, including Zero day exploits, along with its exploitation system. It also provides a development framework for penetration testers and security researchers. More information can be obtained at http://www.immunitysec.com.

■ CORE IMPACT: The security testing software solutions from CORE IMPACT provide a comprehensive approach to assessing organizational readiness when facing real-world security threats. They can be used to expose vulnerabilities proactively, measure operational risk, and assure security effectiveness across various information systems. They can be used for penetration testing, and they come with a plethora of professional exploits. More information can be obtained at http://www.coresecurity.com.

■ Browser Exploitation Framework: BeEF provides a modular framework that can be easily integrated with the browser. It can be used to demonstrate the impact of browser and cross-site scripting (XSS) issues in real time. Current modules include Metasploit, port scanning, keylogging, The Onion Routing (Tor) detection, and more. More information can be obtained at http://www.bindshell.net/tools/beef.

■ Netcat and Socat: Deemed the Swiss Army Knife for network security, Netcat is a simple utility that reads and writes data across TCP and UDP network connections. It has a built-in port scanner and is a feature-rich debugging and exploration tool that can create almost any kind of connection, including port binding to accept incoming connections. A similar tool to Netcat is Socat, which extends Netcat to support other socket types, SSL encryption, SOCKS proxies, and more. More information can be obtained at http://netcat.sourceforge.net.

E.11 Security-Oriented Operating Systems

■ BackTrack: A Linux-based penetration testing OS that aids security professionals and penetration testers in performing security assessments. It can be installed on the hard drive as the primary OS or can be booted from a LiveDVD or even a USB key fob (or thumb drive). BackTrack has been customized down to every package, kernel configuration, script, and patch solely for the purpose of the penetration tester. It has a variety of security and forensic tools that are preinstalled, and it is very popular among renowned penetration testers. More information can be obtained at http://www.backtrack-linux.org.

■ Knoppix-NSM: Dedicated to providing a framework for individuals wanting to learn about network security monitoring (NSM) or who want quickly and reliably to deploy NSM in their network. It is now succeeded by Securix-NSM. More information can be obtained at http://www.securixlive.com/knoppix-nsm.

■ Helix: A customized distribution of the Knoppix Live Linux CD. Helix is more than just a bootable live CD. You can still boot into a customized Linux environment that includes customized Linux kernels, excellent hardware detection, and many applications dedicated to incident response and forensics. More information can be obtained at http://www.e-fense.com/helix.

■ OpenBSD: A free multiplatform Berkeley Software Distribution (BSD) based UNIX-like OS that emphasizes portability, standardization, correctness, proactive security, and integrated cryptography. With a track record of minimal security bugs in the default install, it is said to be one of the most proactive, secure OSes. One of their greatest accomplishment is developing OpenSSH and the packet-filtering firewall tool (PF). More information can be obtained from http://www.openbsd.org.

■ Bastille: Bastille is not actually an OS, but a security hardening script for "locking down" an operating system, proactively configuring the system for increased security and decreasing its susceptibility to compromise. Bastille can also assess a system's current state of hardening, granularly reporting on each of the security settings with which it works. Bastille currently supports the Red Hat (Fedora Core, Enterprise, and Numbered/Classic), SUSE, Debian, Gentoo, and Mandrake distributions, along with HP-UX and Mac OS X. Bastille's focus is on letting the system's user/administrator choose exactly how to harden the operating system. In its default hardening mode, it interactively asks the user questions, explains the topics of those questions, and builds a policy based on the user's answers. It then applies the policy to the system. In its assessment mode, it builds a report intended to teach the user about available security settings as well as inform the user as to which settings have been tightened. More information can be obtained at http://bastille-linux.sourceforge.net.

E.12 Privacy Testing Tools

■ The Onion Router (Tor): Tor is a system for using the Internet anonymously. It is free software and a network of virtual tunnels that allows people and groups to defend against network surveillance and provides anonymity online. It helps by anonymizing Web browsing and publishing, instant messaging, remote login, and other applications that use the TCP protocol. Tor provides protection by bouncing communications around a distributed network of relays all around the world, which prevents anyone watching the Internet connection from learning the site you visit or your physical location. Using Tor, one can build new applications with built-in anonymity and safety and privacy features and gain the assurance of privacy and anonymity in their applications that run over TCP. More information can be obtained at http://www.torproject.org.

■ Stunnel – Universal SSL wrapper: Stunnel is a program that allows you to encrypt arbitrary TCP connections inside SSL and is available on both Unix and Windows. Stunnel can allow you to secure non-SSL aware daemons and protocols (e.g., POP, IMAP, LDAP) by having Stunnel provide the encryption, requiring no changes to the daemon's code. It can be used for verification of confidentiality assurance when sensitive data are transmitted in the network. More information can be obtained at http://www.stunnel.org.

Index

Page numbers followed by f and t indicate figures and tables, respectively.